# Stern's Guide to the
# Cruise Vacation

# REVIEWER COMMENTS

*Stern's Guide to the Cruise Vacation is an excellent resource for novice and experienced cruisers alike. It offers sound information on the ships as well as the places they anchor . . . Stern exhibits experience in the complex world of cruises with an ability to combine careful reporting with reasoned opinion.*

SHEILA F. BUCKMASTER, SENIOR EDITOR
*NATIONAL GEOGRAPHIC TRAVELER*

*This is the book with which to gain a full and thorough understanding of the wonderful world of cruising. Repeat cruisers and novices alike will gain enormously from the huge volume of features—menus, daily schedules, photos, as well as the details on every cruise ship and port of call throughout the world. This should be the encyclopedia for any cruise aficionado.*

SIMON VENESS, EDITOR
*WORLD OF CRUISING MAGAZINE*

*Stern's Guide to the Cruise Vacation is one of the most comprehensive authorities and a must-have for both the novice and the seasoned cruiser.*

*PORTHOLE MAGAZINE*

*Travelers adrift in a sea of luxury voyage options can get their sea legs with the new edition of Stern's Guide to the Cruise Vacation, which boasts detailed descriptions of every major cruise ship and port of call around the globe.*

*NEW YORK DAILY NEWS*

*To say this book is thorough is rather like saying your local telephone book provides information . . . Stern's Guide to the Cruise Vacation is required reading.*

*STATESMAN JOURNAL*
SALEM, OREGON

*Covers virtually everything you need to know about cruise vacations.*

CYNTHIA BOAL JANSSENS
*CHICAGO TRIBUNE*

*The extent of detail given . . . is good not only for the novice cruiser finding their way around the hundreds of opportunities that now exist, but also for the veteran cruiser who wants to know the latest about the newest ships.*

MARK TRÉ
CYBERCRUISES.COM

*A softbound review of everything (and I mean everything) you'd ever want to know about taking a seafaring vacation anywhere in the world . . . Nothing has ever given us the depth of information available in Stern's offering . . . it would be good insurance of getting exactly what you want from any world cruise long before stepping on the ship.*

PETER WAGNER
*NORTHWEST IOWA REVIEW*

*A clever system of awarded stars makes overall judgments easy to make.*

*INTERNATIONAL TRAVEL NEWS*

2014 EDITION

# Stern's Guide to the
# Cruise Vacation

## STEVEN B. STERN

| Library of Congress Control Number: | 2013914767 | |
|---|---|---|
| ISBN: | Softcover | 978-1-4836-8417-8 |
| | eBook | 978-1-4836-8419-2 |

Information in this guidebook is based on authoritative data available at the time of printing. Prices listed are subject to change without notice. Readers are asked to take this into account when consulting this guide.

This book was printed in the United States of America.

Rev. date: 10/18/2013

**To order additional copies of this book, contact:**
Xlibris Corporation
1-888-795-4274
www.Xlibris.com
Orders@Xlibris.com
135704

# Contents

## AUTHOR'S RECOMMENDATION

When selecting a cruise, the following steps are those that I personally follow: First, I decide upon the date I wish to sail. Next, I decide in what part of the world to cruise and what ports of call I wish to visit. Then I consult the *Official Steamship Guide*, which lists every cruise ship sailing in every location around the world as well as their ports of call throughout the year. This allows me to narrow down my search to those ships that are realistic possibilities. For more information, go to www.officialsteamshipguide.com.

# Preface

Over the past forty-one years, I have had the pleasure of experiencing some marvelous vacations and unforgettable moments aboard cruise ships. I have seen the cruise industry grow from a formal haven for the very rich to a fun-filled, exciting, bargain holiday for a broad cross section of our population. Every year, greater numbers of travelers are wisely spending their vacation dollars on a cruise. It has been estimated that the cruise-passenger market has increased 1,800 percent since 1970, when half a million people took a cruise. In 2013, over fourteen million North Americans are expected to enjoy a cruise vacation. Since 2000, nearly 115 new ships have joined the cruise market, and plans to build numerous additional vessels over the next few years have been announced by various cruise lines. Seventy percent of today's cruisers are between the ages of twenty-five and fifty-nine and include singles, couples of all ages, families with children, honeymooners, and groups. Undoubtedly, cruising is the most popular and fastest-growing segment of the travel industry.

Cruise ships built in the 1960s, '70s, and '80s are quite different from those built today. Today's vessels are generally larger and provide more public areas, larger staterooms (with more facilities and amenities), and better-trained crews. They offer greater dining options; more menu selections, including healthy cuisine; enlarged buffet-style dining areas on lido decks; upscale, reservation-only specialty restaurants; larger state-of-the-art fitness centers; sophisticated spas with a bevy of treatment options; computer, Internet, Wi-Fi, and high-tech facilities; more upscale entertainment, including Vegas-quality productions; increased children and teen programs and facilities; and more exotic ports of call.

This guide has been written to familiarize those who have never encountered the delights of the open sea with what they can expect from a cruise vacation as well as to assist seasoned sailors in making intelligent selections for their next ship and cruise grounds. Chapter 9 offers a detailed description of each major cruise line and the vessels of its fleet. Included are overall ratings for each ship (Star Awards) as well as a description of medical facilities, photographs, sample menus, and daily programs for each cruise line. Chapter 10 provides similar coverage for every major riverboat and barge company. Chapter 11 summarizes the overall ratings (Star Awards) and goes on to rate ships from each major cruise line in eleven specific categories. Riverboats and barges are not rated in this book, and for a more detailed coverage and ratings of these vessels, go to *Stern's Guide to European Riverboats and Hotel Barges*.

The book also includes a description of the various cruise grounds and ports of call, setting forth points of interest, restaurants, beaches, sports facilities, and what you can cover with only limited time ashore.

## NOTE

Due to the turmoil throughout various areas of the world (including wars, terrorist attacks, revolutions, and outbreaks of disease as well as government warnings not to travel to these areas), many cruise lines have found it necessary to change the deployment of their vessels from time to time. Inasmuch as these decisions are made frequently, it is impossible to be completely up to date when describing itineraries for the various ships. The itineraries we list are based upon the information given to us by the cruise lines prior to publication. Therefore, we strongly suggest that you verify itineraries with the cruise line prior to making your own cruising plans. For more up-to-date itineraries, visit www.officialsteamshipguide.com.

## New Ships Coming on Line

With the ever-increasing growth of the cruise industry, major cruise lines are continuously building new vessels both to expand their fleets and to replace older ships. During the period extending from mid-2014 to the end of 2016, the following new vessels are scheduled to enter service:

Aida Cruises:
unnamed 125,000 tons; 3,250 pax. March 2015
unnamed 125,000 tons; 3,250 pax. March 2016
unnamed 125,000 tons; 3,250 pax. March 2016

AmaWaterways:
*AmaSonata* N/A; 164 pax. Spring 2014

Avalon Waterways:
*Avalon Poetry II* N/A; 128 pax. March 2014
*Avalon Impression* N/A; 166 pax. March 2014
*Avalon Illumination* N/A; 166 pax. May 2014

Carnival Cruise Lines:
*Carnival Sunrise* 135,000 tons; 4,000 pax. December 2016

Costa Cruises:
*Costa Diadema* 132,500 tons; 3,700-4,928 pax. Fall 2014

Holland America:
unnamed 99,000 tons; 2,660 pax. Fall 2016

Norwegian Cruise Line:
*Breakaway* + I 163,000 tons; 4,200 pax. 2015

P&O Cruises:
unnamed 141,000 tons; 3,611 pax. March 2015

Princess Cruises:
*Regal Princess* 141,000 tons: 3,600 pax. Spring 2014

Royal Caribbean:
    *Quantum of the Seas*    158,000 tons; 4,100 pax. Fall 2014
    *Anthem of the Seas*    158,000 tons; 4,100 pax. Spring 2015
    *Oasis*-class vessel    225,282 tons; 5,400 pax. Mid-2016

Tauck River Cruises:
    MS *Inspire*    N/A; N/A March 2014
    MS *Savor*    N/A; N/A June 2014

TUI Cruises:
    *Mein Schiff 3*    99,000 tons; 2,500 pax. Spring 2014
    *Mein Schiff 4*    99,000 tons; 2,500 pax. Spring 2015

Uniworld River Cruises:
    SS *Catherine* N/A;    159 pax. Spring 2014

Viking Ocean Cruises:
    unnamed    47,000 tons; 888 pax. Spring 2014
    unnamed    47,000 tons; 888 pax. Spring 2015

With the ever-increasing growth of the cruise industry, major cruise lines are continuously building.

# Chapter One

# The Cruise:
# A Complete Vacation

## An Introduction to Cruising
## (With Four Case Studies)

Lively and exciting, yet serene and relaxing; romantic and glamorous, yet interesting and broadening; elegant and luxurious, yet casual and economical; gregarious and convivial, yet intimate and private. All of these descriptions, although antithetical at first glance, in fact apply to the cruise vacation. A cruise is a truly unique travel experience, the ultimate escape from reality that does not lend itself to a simple definition.

Taking a cruise vacation is partaking in varied programs of exciting activities with interesting and congenial fellow passengers from diverse walks of life. It may be indulging in the finest gourmet cuisine prepared by Continental chefs and impeccably served by an experienced crew who cater to your every whim. It is unwinding and relaxing in comfortable, posh surroundings with an impressive variety of facilities and modern conveniences. It is traveling to exotic ports of call, viewing breathtaking scenery, and exploring historic points of interest. It is a cool dip in the pool, breakfast in bed, a relaxing sauna and massage, moonlit walks on deck, costume balls, movies, bridge tournaments, games, entertainment, cocktail parties, shopping, sunning, dancing, romance, companionship, enlightenment, and, best of all, this can be yours for less than you would spend on any comparable land-based vacation.

Although the price of any cruise will vary on the basis of your accommodations, economy-conscious travelers who book minimum cabins can obtain the best possible buy for their vacation dollar. If you reside in the Southeast, for example, you can take a seven-day cruise from Miami stopping at four or five Caribbean ports for as little as $700 to $950. If you live in the Midwest, you can purchase an "air-sea package" (offered by numerous cruise lines), fly to Puerto Rico, and cruise to South America plus five additional Caribbean islands in a seven-day period for as little as $1,200, including your room, all meals and entertainment, round-trip airfare, and transfers to and from the airport and ship. Of course, the majority of accommodations aboard ships will cost two to three times more depending on the market category of the vessel. To duplicate these trips flying from place to place by plane and frequenting restaurants and hotels with food and accommodations comparable to those found on the ship would easily cost a great deal more.

On a land vacation, you will have a greater opportunity for in-depth sightseeing and pursuing more time-consuming activities, such as golf and fishing. However, to visit as many varied places and to engage in activities similar to those offered on a cruise would require you to be constantly on the move. One of the most unique characteristics of a cruise vacation is that everything is conveniently located aboard ship. You need not run around seeking out restaurants, nightclubs, hairdressers, laundries, or companionship. It is all right there. Additionally, you are afforded the opportunity to visit many glamorous and diverse foreign countries without the necessity of lugging around heavy baggage, waiting in line at several airports, and constantly changing hotels. After you have spent a busy day in port sightseeing, swimming, and shopping, you can return to your friendly, familiar floating hotel to dine, drink, dance, and be entertained before you finally retire to awake the following morning already delivered to your next exciting port of call.

Cruising has grown impressively in popularity over the past few decades. New modern luxury liners are being built, and older vessels are being remodeled to meet the ever-increasing lure of travelers to the high seas. This demand can be attributed, perhaps, to the fact that today's cruise offers something for just about everyone—young and old, singles and couples, adults and children, gourmets and gourmands, the gregarious and the inhibited, sun worshippers and those who prefer indoor relaxation. The rich can reserve the most expensive suite aboard and ensconce themselves in the lap of luxury, and the not so rich often can enjoy the same food, entertainment, and public facilities while booking a less expensive cabin. Those who desire recreation can participate in a diverse range of events and activities around the clock, while those who wish to relax can sit back and let the experienced staff and crew serve and entertain them. The athletic types can join the exercise class, work out in the gym, jog around the deck, and on shore can swim, play tennis, or catch a fast eighteen holes of golf, while the spectator types can watch a movie, attend a lecture, or view the nightly entertainment. The working person can find a cruise that coincides with his or her one-, two-, or three-week vacation, while retired persons can opt to cruise for three to four months around the world.

During the past twenty years, major cruise lines have introduced numerous state-of-the-art vessels with features not found on ships built in the 1980s and 1990s. These features include an abundance of veranda cabins; specialty, reservation-only fine-dining restaurants; elaborate spas with large fully equipped gyms; lounges and bars dedicated to wines and champagne, cigar smokers, martini drinkers, sport enthusiasts, etc.; computer cafés; and more extravagant décors. Many of the older vessels pale by comparison. Therefore, if you haven't cruised in several years, you may be pleasantly surprised with the new generation of ships.

For the cruiser who feels he has seen it all and does not wish to return to ports previously visited, consider an interesting riverboat adventure through the waterways of Europe, China, or Southeast Asia, or a relaxing barge sojourn along the lovely waterways of France. These forms of cruising have become very popular over the past few years. Like the oceangoing cruise lines, the riverboat and barge companies have been building more luxurious vessels with accommodations as large and comfortable as those found on cruise ships. For a comprehensive description of every aspect of this type of cruising, I suggest *Stern's Guide to European Riverboats and Hotel Barges*.

## Four Case Studies

### John and Martha

John, a bookkeeper from Omaha, Nebraska, and his wife, Martha, who have just seen the last of their three children graduate from college, are looking forward to letting loose and having the time of their lives on a very special cruise. They get up early the first morning at sea to watch the sunrise while enjoying some coffee, juice, and rolls on deck. After a few deep knee bends and stretches at the exercise class, they are ready for a hearty breakfast in the dining room with fresh pineapple and melon, smoked salmon, a cheese omelet, sausages, fried potatoes, toast, and pastries.

Following breakfast, they participate in a Ping-Pong tournament and deck games at the pool, followed by a free salsa lesson. After a cool dip in the pool, they are ready for an elegant lunch in the dining room with an opportunity to try some exotic foreign dishes. Sunning and swimming fill up the early hours of the afternoon, still leaving time for the duplicate bridge tournament. A little workout on the elliptical and treadmill at the gym, followed by a sauna and massage, helps John work off a few of those piña coladas he was sipping all afternoon. He then showers and shaves while Martha is having her hair set at the beauty salon.

John and Martha don their fancy clothes in time to attend the captain's cocktail party and practice the new dance steps they learned earlier. Then comes the "welcome aboard" dinner in the dining room, complete from caviar to crêpes Suzette. Martha wants to play a few games of bingo before the evening variety show, and John tries his luck at blackjack and roulette in the casino.

After the evening's entertainment in the main lounge, a few cold cuts, cheeses, and desserts at the midnight buffet just hit the spot; and then it is time to go up to the discotheque to swing with the night owls into the wee hours. Following a leisurely stroll around the deck, our active couple is ready for bed. It was never like this in Omaha!

### Michael and Vivian

Michael, an overworked New York attorney, and his wife, Vivian, a harassed primary-school teacher, never had a chance to take a trip when they got married last June. This cruise represents a long-overdue honeymoon. They start their first day at sea by enjoying a leisurely breakfast in bed, followed by some quiet hours soaking up the sun on deck. One shuffleboard game, a short swim in the pool, and a stroll up to the bridge are just enough excitement to help them work up an appetite for a delicious buffet lunch served on deck by the pool.

A little more sun, a few chapters of a good book, a first-run movie in the theater, some tea and cakes on the promenade deck, and our honeymooners are ready for rest and relaxation in their cabin before dressing for the evening. They elect to drink the bottle of champagne their travel agent sent them, while enjoying some hot hors d'oeuvres in the lounge; then it's off to the dining room for an eight-course gourmet meal. After the evening entertainment, Michael and Vivian have the first opportunity since their wedding to dance to a romantic orchestra. A chance to gaze at the stars on deck caps off the night. What new marriage couldn't use a day like this?

## Joan and Ron

Joan, who works in a Miami insurance office, wants to make the most out of her one remaining week of vacation time. She wants to relax and visit some new places, and she wouldn't object to meeting a handsome tall dark stranger if he came along. On the first day at sea, she misses breakfast in the dining room but enjoys some juice, croissants, and coffee served on the deck for the late sleepers. Off comes the cover-up, revealing her new bikini. She takes a stroll around the pool to let all those who are interested know she is aboard.

The eleven o'clock dance class is a must, since it affords her a controlled atmosphere for meeting other passengers. At the class, she meets two women from California, and they decide to sit at the same table for lunch. The understanding maître d' arranges a large table for singles, where Joan and her two new friends are joined by another woman traveling alone and four eligible bachelors. The group decides to spend the afternoon at the pool, swimming and playing backgammon. Several of the other singles come over to watch, and by the afternoon "singles only" cocktail party, Joan has already met most of the other single passengers aboard ship.

Ron, one of the eligible bachelors at Joan's table, is an advertising executive from Boston who is recently divorced and in search of some feminine companionship. He initially decides that he and Joan are basically looking for different things; however, her popularity with other single female passengers indicates that she is a good mixer and a potential source of introductions. By participating in the deck games and making frequent trips to the numerous bars, Ron manages to meet a few more women, and those he missed show up at the "singles only" cocktail party. By dinnertime, he has three or four interesting prospects for the evening. He decides to have a drink with Joan and her friends before dinner; however, he passes up the planned evening entertainment and goes straight to the discotheque where he can dance with all of the other young women he has met.

After dinner, Joan prefers to see the variety show, browse through the shops, and try the one-arm bandits before joining the other singles at the discotheque at midnight. By the time she arrives, Ron has already run through half a dozen possibilities and decided that he really can't relate to any of them. Ron asks Joan to dance, and both feel a strange new chemistry that wasn't evident earlier that evening. Joan and Ron won't give permission to print the rest of the story; therefore, you can select your own ending.

## Scotty and Jamie

Scotty, age eight, and his big sister Jamie, age fourteen, could hardly sleep the night before their mom and dad took them on their first seven-day Caribbean cruise. By sharing a four-berth cabin with their parents, it only cost an extra $375 apiece to bring them along.

The first afternoon aboard ship was exciting. The band was playing, passengers were partying and throwing colorful streamers overboard, and crew members were passing out drinks and sandwiches. Upon arriving at their cabin, Scotty was delighted to find that he had been assigned an upper berth, but Jamie pouted when her dad told her that the other top bunk was hers.

After the ship set sail, Scotty migrated to the electronic game room, where he met numerous other youngsters around his age. After a while, he and a new friend went up on deck to play Ping-Pong and shuffleboard by the pool. At five o'clock, there was a get-together at the disco for teens, which Jamie anxiously attended. A member of the ship's social staff outlined the special events and programs that would be offered throughout the cruise for the teenage set. At the same time, there was a similar meeting for the preteens at the ice-cream emporium. Here Scotty learned about the daily movies, bingo, deck sports, pool games, scavenger hunts, masquerade balls, talent shows, and "Coke-tail" parties that would dominate his days aboard ship.

After dinner, Scotty and his new friend went to the movies, followed by pizza and a soda in the special pizzeria. Jamie attended the first-night-aboard party in the show lounge, where she was introduced to the cruise staff and took part in the audience-participation games. After the party, she went to the teen disco, which was already packed to the rafters with enthusiastic young passengers getting to know each other.

Days ashore were especially enjoyable. The varied ports of call offered pristine white-sand beaches, water sports, horseback riding, tennis, historic sites, cute souvenir shops, and scenic drives. Mealtimes were also great fun. Each evening, the dining room was decorated in a different ethnic theme, and the attentive waiters were dressed to blend in. Scotty was able to order hamburgers and hot dogs for lunch and a big, fat steak and fries for dinner. Jamie, an aspiring gourmet, elected to sample the more esoteric offerings.

On the last evening aboard, the lights were turned down, and all the waiters paraded around the dining room carrying baked Alaskas with sparklers while the passengers sang "Auld Lang Syne." The seven days had passed too quickly, and our two young sailors were very sad the morning the ship sailed back into its home port. They had visited exciting and different islands, made many new friends, and participated in numerous good times. As for Mom and Dad . . . they showed up at dinner, bedtime, and when the youngsters needed quarters for the game machines. When Scotty and Jamie were asked how they liked the cruise, their joint answer was, "Awesome!"

The remaining chapters of this book are designed to familiarize you with the different aspects of the cruise vacation. Chapter 2, titled "Getting Ready for the Cruise," starts by detailing how to go about planning and booking a cruise and proceeds to set forth objective standards for selecting a ship. The chapter goes on to delineate the factors that will determine the cost of your cabin and list the items you will want to be certain to bring along. Chapter 3 describes your day at sea, depicting the customary facilities found aboard ship as well as the typical program of round-the-clock activities. The dining experience is then portrayed with descriptions of the numerous meals and varieties of cuisine as well as some suggestions relating to multiple sittings and tipping. Chapter 4 analyzes the pros and cons of cruising for singles. The desirability and cost of bringing along your children are explored in chapter 5, together with a description of the events and facilities aboard ships that are designed specifically for their interests as well as the best ships for traveling families. In chapter 6, you will find a summary of the various cruise areas and highlights of the most popular cruise stops, with suggestions on what you can see and do during your day in port. Chapter 7 describes where to go in each port to swim.

Chapter 8 describes what to expect when cruising on riverboats and barges in Europe and how they differ from oceangoing vessels. Chapter 9 includes a description of every major cruise line and cruise ship, including my overall ratings (in the form of Star Awards), photographs, sample menus, and daily programs. Chapter 10 provides similar details for riverboats and hotel barges. Chapter 11 summarizes my Star Awards and goes on to evaluate the individual ships of each major line in eleven specific categories.

The growing concern of prospective cruisers as to available medical facilities on the various ships is covered in this edition. An analysis of medical care at sea is discussed in chapter 2, and the facilities, equipment, and personnel available aboard each ship (as represented by the cruise lines) are included in chapter 9.

# Chapter Two

# Getting Ready for the Cruise

## Planning and Booking a Cruise

When planning a cruise, you must consider a number of factors. First of all, you must decide at what time of year you will be taking your cruise vacation. If you choose to travel in the late fall or winter, you may prefer cruising in the warmer climate and calmer waters of the Caribbean, South Pacific, Indian Ocean, or the Far East. Transatlantic crossings at this time of year can be a bit rough for all but the hardiest sea dogs.

On the other hand, a late spring, summer, or early-fall cruise in the Eastern Mediterranean to the Greek Islands, Turkish Coast, and Middle East; in the Western Mediterranean to ports of call in Italy, France, and Spain; or in the Baltics, North Sea, and Norwegian fjords to cities in England, Holland, Sweden, Norway, Denmark, Germany, and Russia can afford you a very interesting opportunity to mingle with passengers from other countries. Transatlantic crossings at these times of year are not necessarily rough, but they are not recommended for your first exploration of the sea. Be aware that ships crossing the Atlantic by the southern route will encounter better weather, permitting more days on deck than those ships taking the northern route.

After you have decided upon the time of the year to go and the general geographic area to see, the next step is to find out which ships will be cruising in that area on the dates you have available. If you are set on cruising on a specific ship, then to determine where you will be sailing at any given time to any given place, I recommend that you consult a copy of the *Official Steamship Guide International*. This magazine is subscribed to by most travel agencies, is updated seasonally, and contains a complete list of prospective cruises for all ships for the upcoming twelve-month period as soon as the line makes the dates public. *Ocean Cruise News, Portholes, Cruise Business News, World of Cruising,* and *Cruise Travel* magazines are periodicals that list prospective cruises and include articles describing ships, ports of call, and updates on what is going on in the cruise industry. *World of Cruising Magazine*, the leading cruise magazine in Great Britain, is especially informative, well written, and can be subscribed to in the United States. Their fax number is 011-44-(0)8704292683, and their Web site is www.woconline.com. Also several Web sites provide information about cruise ships and the latest developments in cruising. Alan Wilson's *Cruise News Daily* sends its subscribers daily information by e-mail. Of course, each of the cruise lines has a Web site where you can obtain specific information about their ships and itineraries.

Over the past few years, numerous travel agencies that specialize in cruising have sprung up. Frequently they can offer deep-discount tickets due to prior arrangements with some of the cruise lines. You will want to check the cruise/discount-fare advertisements in the travel section of your Sunday newspaper as well as the various cruise periodicals and Web sites. Once you have cruised on a particular line, you will be placed on its mailing list and be provided from time to time with brochures offering special discounted sailings.

When consulting the available guides, you will also have to consider the length of time you have for your vacation. If you have only a week or ten days, seek out a ship with a correspondingly shorter itinerary. However, if you have two weeks or more, you can also consider the longer cruises.

Now that you have traced the ships that are sailing in the geographic area of your choice during the period you have scheduled for your vacation, you will want to study the credentials and offerings of each of these vessels. Do you prefer French food, Italian service, Scandinavian joie de vivre, Dutch hospitality, or British efficiency? Do you wish to storm seven ports in seven days, or do you prefer spending three or four relaxing days at sea? Do you desire the intimacy of a small ship, or is a large superliner your cup of tea? These are the questions that you must ask, and the following section of this chapter, as well as chapters 9 through 11, are devoted to helping you arrive at your decision.

After you have finally selected a vessel, it is desirable to include a second and even a third choice, for now you must determine whether space on the ship you desire is still available. A later section of this chapter on "Costs and Your Cabin" will point out the factors to be considered in choosing accommodations.

When booking reservations for a cabin, you can go either to your travel agent or directly to the cruise line office in your locality or to its Web site. Booking through a travel agent generally has the advantage of having someone else obtain your tickets, make all arrangements, provide you with necessary instructions, and maybe even throw in a bottle of the bubbly when you arrive on ship. However, if your agent tells you that the space you desire is not available, do not give up. Either call another agent, search Web sites, or contact the line directly, request that you be wait-listed, and explain how you are dying to cruise on their ships but can go only at a certain time and for a certain price. Call them up every week or so to check on whether there has been a cancellation. Persistence may pay off because vacationers often change their minds, and there are usually a great number of last-minute cancellations.

To play it safe, you can accept a more expensive room, for example, and ask to be wait-listed for the first cheaper one that becomes available. I do not know for a fact what procedures the various lines follow; however, it is possible that some cruise lines will sell a room that becomes available to a new customer rather than to one who has already accepted another room and has been wait-listed. Therefore, if you are set on obtaining specific accommodations, you may have a better chance if you do not accept a substitute. On the other hand, if you don't, you may be left behind. Here, again, it will pay off to contact the numerous travel agencies that specialize in cruising since they may have an inventory of prepurchased accommodations or a little extra clout with the cruise line.

As you would expect, it is more difficult to book cruises for holidays such as Christmas, New Year's, Easter, Thanksgiving, Memorial Day, the Fourth of July, and Labor Day. Everyone wants to go away at these times, and you must book far in advance (as much as six months to a year for a Christmas or New Year's cruise on some ships).

For those who choose to book their cruise through the Internet, cruise lines and travel agencies have established Web sites that provide information on sailings and rates. If you are comfortable with booking travel in this manner, you may find some excellent last-minute bargains.

I always recommend that cruisers arrive at the port of embarkation at least one day in advance in order to avoid airplane delays and the possibility of "missing the boat." There is nothing more frustrating than trying to catch up with a ship at its next port of call or having to turn around and go home. Although you may have purchased insurance to cover this possibility, it will certainly be a disappointment.

It is generally possible to purchase air travel through the cruise line, which will have negotiated rates with the airlines. Although the rates can be higher than those on the Internet or those available for advanced purchases through the airlines, the fact remains that the cruise line will have the responsibility of attending to you until they can get you on the ship.

Most major cruise lines now encourage passengers to print out their boarding passes and select their dining and excursion options via e-mail. Some require these preparations to be done in this fashion because it greatly simplifies the boarding process.

## Selecting a Ship

What kind of ship you select will depend upon your feelings about people, food, relaxation, activity, aesthetics, and so on. Whereas one reader may be delighted by a ship that offers a diverse Continental menu of gourmet delights, another may feel dissatisfied because the kitchen staff cannot prepare a thick juicy sirloin steak. One couple may fall in love with a cruise ship because of the super time they had dancing to good music every evening and taking part in a masquerade ball, but another couple may feel that the same ship was not a good buy because it offered no "big name" entertainment. The fact that any particular ship may appeal to one does not mean it will appeal to another. Also, the food and service on any given ship can vary from time to time, just as it does in a restaurant or hotel. A change in chefs, for example, can make a big difference.

How, then, can you compare ships and make a selection? To a certain extent, you will rely on the opinions of others. You are encouraged to discuss this with your travel agent as well as with friends (holding similar interests and tastes) who have cruised on the ships you are considering. Acquire all the brochures and other promotional matter printed by the cruise lines. These pamphlets usually contain pictures of the public rooms and cabins, prices, enumeration of facilities, description of ports of call, and a deck plan. If your travel agent does not have the relevant brochure for the ship in which you are interested, you can write directly to the line or go to its Web site. Almost all cruise lines have Web sites providing detailed information for each of their ships, as well as for all itineraries and fares. Do not hesitate to contact the line about any specific bit of information you may wish to obtain.

To assist you further with your selection, detailed descriptions, per diem fares, and ratings for most cruise ships, as well as photos, sample menus, and activity programs, appear in chapters 9 through 11 of this book.

The following is an analysis of many of the factors that I recommend you consider in comparing potential cruises.

## Ports of Call and Shore Excursions

Check to see at which ports the ship will be calling and then review what each of those ports has to offer (see analysis of ports in chapter 6). Do you prefer spending your days ashore shopping, sunning at a beautiful beach, exploring archeological ruins, hiking through natural scenery, or visiting historic museums? Be certain that the ship stops at a port that will afford you an opportunity to pursue the activities you enjoy.

When sailing the Caribbean, the islands of St. Thomas, St. Croix, and Curaçao are considered to have the most diversified shopping, with the best bargains in French perfume being found in Martinique, Guadeloupe, and St. Martin. The finest beaches for swimming and sunning are found in the Grand Caymans, Bermuda, St. Thomas, St. Croix, St. John, Virgin Gorda, Aruba, Barbados, Antigua, Anguilla, Jamaica, St. Martin, Grenada, the Bahamas, and Cozumel. Archeology buffs will want to visit Cancun, Costa Maya, Guatemala, and the ports of the Yucatán.

Although the beaches of the Mediterranean, Baltics, and North Sea don't compare with those of the Caribbean, the offering of historic points of interest, art, museums, and shopping is far superior in the Mediterranean and Northern European ports. Today it is possible to cruise almost anywhere in the world, including such faraway areas as the South Seas, the Far East, Australia, Africa, the Indian Ocean, and even Antarctica.

As mentioned earlier, you will want to determine how many ports are on the itinerary of the cruises you may be considering. For example, some ships visit as many as six ports on a seven-day cruise, whereas others stop at only one or two. Do you prefer a busy itinerary, where you are in port almost every day, or do you prefer spending the majority of your days on the open sea?

Next, you should check out the period of time the ship is docked at each port. Too often, a ship may be in port for so short a period that there is not time to visit the places you have mapped out. For example, several ships stop in Montego Bay for only five hours, not leaving sufficient time to drive to Dunn's Falls or take the jungle river raft ride down the Martha Brae. Other ships dock at San Juan only in the later afternoon and evening to permit passengers to gamble, while leaving insufficient time to explore the island. There are still other ships that include in their brochures "ports of call" where the vessels dock for merely an hour to pick up passengers. Certain Mediterranean cruises drop anchor at Gibraltar, Cannes, Genoa, and Naples to receive embarking passengers but don't stop long enough to permit any exploration. You should carefully analyze the itinerary of each ship you are considering.

All ships have a "shore excursion" department, where various tours are offered for each port of call. These excursions range from inactive to very active and include bus orientation tours, snorkeling and/or scuba outings, beach parties, glass-bottom boat and submarine explorations, four-wheel drive tours, zip line rides through jungles, shark feeding, swimming with stingrays, helicopter and float-plane rides, and visits to places of interest in the port. Unfortunately, most of these excursions incur a stiff charge and greatly increase the cost of the cruise. On many lines, a schedule of the available tours can be obtained in advance online and prebooked.

## Dining

As pointed out in detail in the next chapter, the dining experience aboard ship is one of the highlights of the cruise. Therefore, a good deal of consideration should be given to the fare offered by the different lines. Although many ships rate far above the average restaurant in this department, the types and varieties of victuals do vary from ship to ship.

Most of the lunch and dinner menus offer an interesting assortment of food, with an emphasis on ethnic dishes that are representative of the nationality of the dining room staff and chef. If you require kosher food, baby food, or have any special dietary restrictions, you should check with the ship line in advance to determine whether the required foods will be available. A very popular concept is the inclusion of alternative specialty restaurants in addition to the main dining room, which affords passengers an opportunity to break up the nightly routine and opt for a more intimate dining experience. These venues generally feature steak house, Italian, French, or Asian cuisine. Casual, alternative-dining restaurants are available on almost all of the major vessels. Wine, caviar, and espresso bars along with pizza parlors are rapidly being added to many of the ships that have come on line during the past few years.

In chapter 9, you will find sample menus from ships representing the various lines. Because the menus tend to be similar for ships of the same line, these samples should give you some idea of what to expect. (Caution: You will see steak and lobster offered on almost all of the menus, but the quality may vary radically. Beef shipped from the United States and lobster caught off the coast of Maine may be quite a bit more tender than beef picked up in Mexico or lobsters caught in the Caribbean.) In addition, food and dining room service often will be superior on the flagship of each line. Generally, the chefs and waiters earn the privilege of serving on the flagship by working their way up the ladder on the other vessels. The ratings for dining quality found in chapter 11 may assist you in comparing the ships of the various cruise lines.

Many ships now allow passengers to make dining arrangements and reservations for specialty restaurants online prior to the cruise.

## Service

The quality of service rendered by the dining room staff, the cabin stewards, and social staff can significantly affect your enjoyment of the cruise. A pleasant, efficient waiter can perk up a mediocre meal; an understanding and helpful cabin steward can minimize the inconvenience of a small or otherwise inadequate cabin; and a tactful, perceptive social director can bring together people of common interests and add an additional dimension to your vacation.

Naturally, the quality of service varies from line to line and even among ships of the same line. I have found that ships with European dining room and cabin staffs offer the best all-around service. These waiters and stewards seem to have received the best training, maintain the best attitudes, and are the most anxious to please. I found the mixed European crew on Crystal, Hapag-Lloyd, Oceania, Regent Seven Seas, Seabourn, SeaDream, and Silversea to be superior in these areas. The Greek ships tend to economize and overwork their crews, with the obvious results. Those ships using mixed service crews from the Caribbean islands, South America, India, Indonesia, Philippines, Asia, and Mexico do so as an economy factor. Unfortunately, these people do not have the training or "know-how" of most of the European crews. Many of the cruise lines' predominant use of Indonesian and/or Filipino waiters and room stewards has proved to be somewhat of a mixed bag: some cruisers find them charming and attentive, while others have found the service mediocre because of the serious language problem and lack of experience. The all-American crews on several of the U.S. cruise lines are often inexperienced. The nationality of the dining room and cabin crews is indicated in chapter 9. Service may vary from one year to the next on the same ship, especially when a line is striving to improve this area. Therefore, obtain knowledgeable opinions on the standard of service for any ships you are considering.

## Medical Care at Sea

Considering the millions of people of all ages and levels of health who cruise each year to exotic and remote areas where access to state-of-the-art hospitals and well-trained physicians may be limited, one must conclude that the availability and quality of medical facilities and personnel aboard ship should be a major consideration when selecting a particular vessel.

Certainly, a significant segment of the cruising population that opts for longer cruises to more out-of-the-way destinations is retired and getting on in years. When encountering an emergency at home, these senior citizens can call 911 and be rushed to a modern hospital, but when they find themselves in the middle of the Pacific or docked at a primitive port in New Guinea, the best they can hope for is a decent medical facility and physician aboard ship. Many younger passengers have infirmities that could require special medical attention, while others may suffer accidental injuries either on the ship or during port explorations. Here again, the only available emergency equipment and supplies may be at the ship's medical facility.

Therefore, the experience and specialties of a ship's physician and nurses, the technological equipment and pharmaceuticals available, as well as the X-ray, operating, and emergency facilities should receive as much consideration by older cruisers and those with preexisting medical problems as the level of dining, activities, and shore excursions.

Generally, the larger vessels carry more medical staff and are equipped with expanded facilities in anticipation of a greater demand by both passengers and crew members. Many smaller ships have also made ample provision for medical emergencies. However, over the years, I have found that ships unwisely economize in this department. Ships sometimes carry too small a medical staff to cope with the passenger or crew load, hire physicians for short durations or who are not trained to deal with multiple emergencies, have limited equipment and supplies available, and tend to downplay their responsibility for passenger health needs.

The American College of Emergency Physicians has published *Guidelines of Care for Cruise Ship Medical Facilities*. Among the numerous recommendations are the following:

1. A medical staff, available around the clock, board-certified in emergency medicine, family practice, and internal medicine, with two to three years of clinical experience, emergency/critical care experience, advanced trauma and cardiac life-support skills, minor surgical skills, and fluency in the major language of the passengers and crew.

2. Emergency medical equipment and medications, including primary and backup cardiac monitors, primary and backup portable defibrillators, electrocardiograph, wheelchairs, refrigerator/freezer, extrication device, C-collar immobilization capability, trauma-cart supplies, airway equipment, volume pumps, ventilators, pulse oximeter, external pacer capability, portable oxygen sufficient until patient can disembark ship, and medications comparable to those required to run two emergency department-code carts, including advanced cardiac support drugs.

3. Basic laboratory capabilities—including an X-ray unit; capability to perform hemoglobin, urinalysis, pregnancy, and glucose tolerance tests; a microscope; and a universal crew-blood-donor list.

4. A passenger information program regarding onboard health and safety, a preassessment of passengers' medical needs, and a program to meet Physical Disabilities Act standards.

5. A crew screening program covering all communicable diseases and certain other conditions as well as a crew safety program.

6. Examination and treatment areas and an inpatient holding unit adequate for the size of the ship.

Heads of hospital staff on various cruise lines have suggested that ship doctors be trained in advanced trauma and life support, have broad experience in family and emergency medicine, and be backed up by sufficient registered nurses with similar practical experience to formulate an efficient emergency-response team to deal with cardiac arrest and other serious medical traumas. They advise that when the combined passenger/crew population exceeds one thousand, a second physician is advisable, as well as an expanded nursing staff. Facilities should include a well-stocked, computer-controlled pharmacy; a satisfactory range of X-ray facilities; a fully equipped operating theater; biochemistry and full blood count equipment; at least one or two intensive-care wards that include a cardiac monitor, EKG machine, and pulse oximetry; and, if possible, a telemedical facility, enabling the shipboard doctor to consult with and obtain advice from hospitals and specialists ashore while giving advice or performing procedures with which he may not be familiar, at sea.

We have attempted to elicit information as to the experience of the medical personnel and the extent of the medical facilities, equipment, and systems aboard each cruise ship. However, it would be naive to believe that one could obtain totally honest responses when surveying the various cruise lines as to the quality of the facilities, equipment, and staff aboard their ships. No cruise line would admit to be remiss in any of these areas, although my personal observation leads me to suspect some are inadequately staffed or equipped to handle the passenger and crew load they carry.

Any potential cruiser with a medical problem, in a high-risk group, or with general concerns as to medical facilities aboard a particular ship would be well advised to contact the medical director of the cruise line in advance of booking the trip to determine if the caliber of medical support and facilities he or she may require will be available. Probably, it would be prudent to make a written inquiry and request a written reply so that the party responding is careful to research the matter before making any representations. Similar investigation can be made into the ship's ability to satisfy special dietary needs, as well as possible inoculations that may be advisable. When in doubt, an ounce of prevention is worth a pound of cure, or some such euphemism.

*Note: After the short summaries of each ship listed in chapter 9, we have added a code designating the medical personnel, facilities, and equipment that the cruise line has represented is available aboard the vessel. Where the cruise line has not responded to our inquiries, the failure to respond is indicated. I must emphasize that this information was given by an employee of the cruise line, has not been verified by the author or publisher, and may have changed by the time you read this information. A written inquiry made directly to the medical director of the cruise line is your most prudent course.*

Code Designating Medical Personnel, Facilities, and Equipment

| | |
|---|---|
| C | Number of wheelchair-accessible cabins |
| P | Number of physicians |
| EM | Certified in emergency medicine |
| CLS | Certified in advanced trauma and cardiac life support |
| MS | Ability to perform minor surgical procedures |
| N | Number of nurses experienced in emergency medicine or critical care |

Emergency Medical Equipment, Lab Equipment, and Facilities

CM      Primary and backup cardiac monitors
PD      Primary and backup portable defibrillators
BC      Equipment for biochemistry, full blood count, and urinalysis
EKG     Electrocardiograph machine
TC      Trauma-cart supplies
PO      Pulse oximeter
EPC     External pacer capability
OX      Portable oxygen
WC      At least one wheelchair for three hundred passengers and crew
OR      Operating room sufficient for minor surgery (If this is important, you need to obtain details from the cruise line.)
ICU     Intensive care unit
X       X-ray unit
M       Microscope
CCP     Computer-controlled pharmacy
D       Dialysis equipment
TM      Telemedical capability
LJ      Life jackets located at muster stations (as well as in cabins) sufficient for all passengers

This is not required by SOLA; some cruise lines have a limited number at the muster stations. Where "LJ" is included, it indicates that the cruise line has represented to me that it has life jackets sufficient to accommodate all passengers at muster stations, in addition to those in the cabins.

## Facilities for the Physically Challenged

Cruising is possibly the most convenient way for the physically challenged to visit places of interest around the world. Today, most new ships have increased the number of wheelchair-accessible cabins and have improved public facilities to make them more user-friendly for those with physical impairments. A cruise experience is available today for the visually or hearing impaired, diabetics, dialysis patients, pulmonary sufferers, and wheelchair users.

The cruise lines and ships that have provided the most facilities and accommodations for the physically challenged are Celebrity, Regent Seven Seas, Norwegian, Crystal, Disney, Princess, Royal Caribbean, Carnival's 100,000-plus-ton ships, Holland America's newest ships, Genting Hong Kong's new builds, Hapag-Lloyd's *Europa*, and P&O's newer ships. Although there are various sites you can go to online, the most prudent procedure would be to contact the cruise line you are interested in and obtain timely details about the facilities on their ships.

## Other Facilities

The facilities will vary from ship to ship, with the most facilities being found on the larger crafts. The megaships (more than 70,000 gross register tons) of Royal Caribbean, Princess, P&O, Cunard, Celebrity, Disney, Genting Hong Kong, Holland America, Costa, MSC, Norwegian, and Carnival cruise lines, for example, have just about every facility found in a large resort hotel and then some. However, even the midsize and smaller vessels make clever use of the area they have, offering passengers almost the same facilities as the larger ships but on a smaller scale. The age of the ship may be a factor here, and if you are considering an older ship, it is important to find out if it has been recently remodeled. Currently, Royal Caribbean's *Oasis*-class, *Voyager*-class, and *Freedom*-class ships boast the most impressive facilities at sea, with Princess's *Grand*-class ships, Norwegian's and Carnival's larger ships, and the *Queen Mary 2* running close behind.

Consider and compare the public rooms, swimming pools (number and size), deck areas, restaurant facilities, gymnasium, sauna, deck sports, library, elevators, movie theater, chapel, dance bands, bars, game rooms, hospital, cabins, bathrooms, and so on. Some of the more common facilities are included in the descriptions of the various ships in chapter 11. A better description and pictures of these facilities can be found in the ship's promotional brochures. Be careful! These brochures are like most advertising material; they have a tendency to portray the ship as larger and more beautiful than it may appear on actual inspection.

## Activities

Although almost all ships offer a wide range of varied activities, not all ships subscribe to the same program. Golf addicts will want to consider those ships that offer golf clinics and feature excursions to golf courses ashore, joggers should check out which ships afford jogging decks, and amateur chefs may wish to select a ship with gourmet-cooking lessons. The vast range of daily activities is more thoroughly described in the next chapter, and chapter 9 contains sample daily programs from ships of most of the major cruise lines.

In general, I have found that the ships offering regular cruises from Florida, California, San Juan, New York, and other U.S. ports have the most activities per day at sea, with the Royal Caribbean, Holland America, Celebrity, Norwegian, Carnival, Crystal, Costa, and Princess lines leading in this department. Ships sailing the Mediterranean and Northern Europe seem to offer the least activities (probably because they spend the majority of days in port). Several of the lines offer "once-a-year, special activity" cruises featuring classical or jazz music festivals, gourmet-cooking classes, wine seminars, or Broadway theater.

Today most of the major cruise lines offer "learning at sea" agendas, which may include computer lessons; language lessons; photography and computer technology; lectures on wine, archeology, history, and marine biology; hands-on cooking classes by well-known chefs; musical lessons; painting, weaving, pottery, and other crafts; and numerous other useful courses. We found the Crystal and Princess lines' enrichment programs two of the best.

If you are cruising with children, be sure to note those vessels that offer a special children's program. I was particularly impressed with the children's programs on Carnival, Disney, Princess, Norwegian, and Royal Caribbean cruise lines, which include special counselors, age-appropriate children's activities, special discos, electronic game rooms, and ice-cream and pizza parlors. Most of the other larger ships also have good facilities and programs for children.

Many of the vessels built after 1990 have special areas and facilities for business meetings and seminars, as well as public computer rooms with instructional classes.

## Computers/Internet/E-Mail/Cell Phones

With the growing demand of passengers wishing to send e-mails and check their favorite Web sites, cruise lines have rapidly caught on and are now competing to furnish the most comprehensive computer facilities. Most of the new ships that have come on line during the past few years have quite impressive Internet cafés and computer facilities.

Some cruise lines provide facilities permitting passengers to connect their own personal laptops, while others require you to use the equipment available aboard ship. Most of the major cruise lines have recently expanded their computer facilities and instructional programs. Many of the ships provide wireless access, or Wi-Fi, at various spots throughout the ship, including cabins, so that those who bring their own laptops can access the Internet remotely. One significant benefit is the lower cost of communicating back home by e-mail as opposed to the expensive telephone and fax procedures aboard ships. Since there will be variances among the cruise lines and from ship to ship of the same line as to facilities and charges for Internet access, it would be prudent to check out what is available before sailing.

SeaMobile, which enables passengers to use their cell phones on the ship to both place outgoing and receive incoming calls, is being installed on many ships. You are simply billed a roaming rate by your cell provider. Where this service is available, you will also be able to connect your laptop computer to the Internet.

## Accommodations

As previously explained, each ship prints an attractive brochure that includes a deck plan describing the size of each room, number of closets, dresser space, bathroom facilities, type of beds (single, double, queen, king, or bunk), and general layouts. Thus, it is possible for you to review these facts before booking your cabin. Generally, you will pay more for added space, with the deluxe suites going for two to three times the price of the average cabin. There is often a difference between similarly priced accommodations on different ships. If living quarters are one of your major concerns, then this comparison of rooms will be an important factor in your selection of vessels.

I have been especially impressed with the accommodations in the average room on the vessels of Carnival, Celebrity, Crystal, Cunard, Disney, Hapag-Lloyd, Holland America, Regent Seven Seas, Seabourn, and Silversea, as well as the newer ships of Princess Cruises.

Ships built during the past ten years have put a greater emphasis on providing verandas for those who enjoy sitting out on their own private balcony overlooking the sea. Prime examples are the Princess and Silversea cruise lines, the newest ships of Celebrity Cruises, Disney, Holland America, Norwegian Cruise Line, Oceania, and the Regent Seven Seas cruise lines. The *Seven Seas Mariner* and *Voyager* are the first ships offering verandas in every accommodation throughout the ship. Although cabins with balconies fetch a higher price, many cruisers, after experiencing the joys of a "veranda at sea," find this luxury well worth the extra tariff. Verandas attached to suites tend to be larger and more utilitarian than those adjoining standard cabins, and on a few ships, they include an outdoor Jacuzzi tub.

Other features becoming more prevalent on cruise lines include flat-screen TVs, upgraded mattresses and bedding, custom pillows, refrigerators, robes, slippers, and Wi-Fi.

Most fine hotels around the world provide at least one presidential or ultragrand suite or villa where visiting dignitaries, wealthy clientele, or special VIPs can be accommodated with facilities that can house a small entourage, entertain guests, and provide extra services and amenities. In my research for *Stern's Guide to the Greatest Resorts of the World*, I have encountered many awesome accommodations, some measuring up to five thousand square feet and with price tags as high as $6,000 per night.

Therefore, it is not surprising that "fine hotels at sea" would offer similar luxury accommodations. Historically, the existence of ultragrand suites on ships has undergone a metamorphosis. During the era of the legendary superliners such as the *Titanic*, *Normandie*, and *Queen Mary*, offering extremely large ultradeluxe accommodations was *de rigueur*. However, from 1970 to 1990, when cruising gained popularity with the mass market of vacationers, expensive suites were not a priority, and cruise lines considered a four-hundred- to six-hundred-square-foot stateroom more than sufficient for important clientele.

The final decade of the twentieth century and the first thirteen years of the twenty-first century have been periods of unprecedented growth for the cruise industry, during which small companies were gobbled up by the major leaguers who raised funds to acquire and/or build new ships by selling shares of stock to the public. Millions of dollars were spent annually on advertising and publicity in an attempt to stay afloat with the competition and to create the image of having the most prestigious vessels. Savvy cruise operators—seeking top ratings among ship reviewers as well as wishing to appeal to high-profile personalities and a wealthy clientele who could afford and demand the very best—wisely included at least one or two special ultradeluxe suites in the 800- to 1,600-square-foot range on their new vessels, at fares ranging from $750 to $2,000 per person per night (for those who pay the published rate).

It is not uncommon for these grand suites at sea to include a master bath with a separate glassed-in shower stall; a large Jacuzzi tub; double vanities; toilet and bidet compartments; a second guest bathroom; an entryway; a large elegantly furnished living room with a dining area; several giant TVs with DVD, and CD attachments; a full-facility, fully stocked pantry where a chef can prepare meals; and one or more large verandas for alfresco entertaining or relaxing. Butler service, nightly gourmet hors d'oeuvres, champagne, an open bar, priority treatment throughout the ship, dinner with the captain, and many other perks are often included. Of course, rooms at the top vary from ship to ship, and some are neither "at the top" (of the ship) nor much more inviting than the deluxe category of suites otherwise available on the ship. However, for those that can pay the tariff, it's the only way to go.

## Price

What do you get for your money? The answer may depend upon whether you are looking for quality or quantity, although it is not necessary to sacrifice either. If you divide the price of the cruise by the number of nights afloat, you will arrive at the average cost per day, which can serve as one standard of comparison. Do not use days afloat because this may be deceptive. A ship that leaves at 7:00 p.m. on a Sunday and returns at 8:00 a.m. on a Saturday may be advertised as a "seven-day cruise," when in fact you are spending only six nights and five days aboard.

After you arrive at your average daily cost, determine what kind of cabin this amount of money will purchase on comparable ships. Also compare the miles traveled and the number of ports of call. The existence of the "air-sea package," mentioned earlier and described later, will significantly affect your calculations. If you are comparing two ships and one offers an air-sea package, you must add in the cost of air transportation before making your comparison.

The price of cruising has escalated over the past decade, reflecting the increased demand by travelers as well as the increased cost of food, fuel, and labor. A number of the great "luxury" vessels of the 1960s—such as the *France, Michaelangelo,* and *Raffaello*—were retired because the French and Italian lines could not afford to keep up the high standard of food and service without losing millions of dollars each year. However, the cruise vacation still represents one of the best bargains around for travelers.

You will find that cruises on the Crystal, Cunard, Seabourn, Silversea, and Regent Seven Seas cruise lines are the most expensive. However, these vessels offer a certain elegance and such a high standard of service that many travelers are willing to pay a little extra. The tariff for the choice suites on the ships of the Celebrity, Disney, Holland America, Norwegian, Princess, Royal Caribbean, and Windstar lines will run almost as high, and often higher. A luxury suite on almost any fine cruise ship will cost the most.

Beware of some of the "superlow" rates. When a ship offers a cruise for 50 percent less than another, something has to go (and it usually isn't the ship owner's profits). This does not mean that they will not offer many of the same amenities of the more expensive cruises; however, the food, service, and accommodations will not be of the same quality. One exception would be "loss leaders," offered by lines attempting to open up a new cruise market or attempting to fill their ships to capacity during the off season or during a poor economy. These can be real bargains.

More often than not, brochure tariffs have little or no bearing on the prices passengers actually end up paying. People like to think they are getting a bargain, and by marking up the brochure price and then offering various discounted fares, the cruise lines give the impression that they are providing the customer a good buy. Various discounting vehicles have been employed: lower fares for last-minute bookings; early-purchase discounts (often as high as 50 percent); two-for-one deals, where the first passenger pays brochure fare and the second sails free (which is really a 50 percent discount); air-sea fares, where airfare to the port of embarkation is offered gratis or at a reduced rate; and special group rates. In addition, numerous travel agencies purchase blocks of space on ships and offer them to their customers at discounted rates. These discount agencies generally advertise in travel sections of newspapers and cruise periodicals. In general, discounted rates and other price-saving deals are greatest well in advance of the sailing and diminish proportionately as the ship fills up.

This practice of charging varying rates at different times can be disturbing because you do not know whether you have received the best reduction until you are aboard ship comparing prices with fellow passengers. However, for better or worse, the practice exists, and those of you wishing to obtain the best bargain have to do your homework.

An emerging trend among the economy, mass-market, and premium cruise lines is to keep the cruise fares competitive while recouping revenues by nickel-and-diming passengers during the cruise for beverages, shore excursions, and expected gratuities. Some observers have predicted that during the next few years, many of the cruise lines will be charging extra for activities and entertainment. Onboard revenue is the key to the profitable operation of a ship for the cruise line. Although you may be paying as low as $100 or $150 a day for your cruise, your onboard charges will often equal or exceed this amount. The largest source of onboard revenue is from the sale of beverages. Whether you are ordering an expensive bottle of wine, a martini at the bar, a bottle of beer or a coke, the markup is substantial (as well as the 15 percent gratuity), and opportunities to purchase beverages aboard ship are substantial. The second-largest source of revenues is from the markup for shore excursions. Some of the more exotic offerings can run from $200 to $1,000 per person, whereas an average shore excursion is generally from $60 to $100. I have seen some ships charge bus passengers $40 or $50 going to a public beach. Other onboard sources of revenue include purchases of photos from the ship's photographer (these can run from $7 to $30 each), gambling at the casinos and other games of chance such as bingo and horse racing, shops on board as well as rake-offs from shops ashore that are allowed to promote their establishment on the ship, spa and beauty treatments, telephone and Internet charges, and last, but not least, the automatic gratuity that is added on to your shipboard account.

## Age of Ship

Unlike fine wine, ships do not necessarily improve with age. Unless a ship is well maintained and frequently refurbished, it will soon show signs of wear. Fortunately, most lines frequently rebuild and refurbish their crafts so as to prevent deterioration. Chapter 9 indicates the age of the ships as well as the last date they were significantly refurbished. These dates will be of interest to you in comparing the various vessels.

The most exquisite public areas with bright modern décor can be found on the new Carnival, Celebrity, Crystal, Cunard, Holland America, Norwegian, Princess, Royal Caribbean, Regent Seven Seas, Seabourn, and Silversea ships. For a more traditional décor and elegance, you may prefer the public areas of some of the vintage ships; however, do not expect to find the quaint, stately elegance of the old *Queen Mary*, *Queen Elizabeth*, or *Ile de France*. Sadly, it no longer exists.

By October 1, 1997, all ships were required to meet the standards of the International Convention for the International Convention for the Safety of Life at Sea (SOLAS), an international treaty that addresses the safe operation of ships and has been signed by all seafaring nations who are members of the International Maritime Organization. Most of the standards deal with fire safety and involve refitting cabins with sprinkler systems and smoke detectors. For economic reasons, many of the cruise lines have taken their older ships out of service because of the potential cost to meet these standards. Many of the ships built by the major cruise lines in the 1960s, 1970s, and early 1980s have been sold to smaller and/or emerging cruise lines servicing the economy and foreign markets, renamed, and recycled.

## People

People who like people will love cruising. There is no other vacation that affords you as great an opportunity to meet people from all over the world and from all walks of life. This does not mean that you will like everyone you meet any more than you like all of your neighbors or relatives. However, the camaraderie of a cruise offers an ideal climate to make new friends and strike up conversations with people from many different places.

What kind of people will be your fellow passengers? Although there is always a cross section of varied backgrounds, many of the passengers will be indigenous to the area surrounding the port of embarkation. Passengers from New York and the East Coast will predominate on a cruise emanating from New York. If the cruise departs from California, you can expect a majority of travelers to be from the West Coast and states of the Southwest. Midwesterners tend to leave from Miami, Fort Lauderdale, and the Caribbean; however, today you will find many Easterners and Californians on these cruises. The development of the air-sea package has changed this lineup somewhat, and cruise lines are flying passengers from all over the country to meet their ships.

Cruises commencing in the Mediterranean or Northern European ports often will have numerous European passengers, with the majority being of the same nationality as the vessel. P&O and Cunard's ships tend to attract more British, Germans, and Northern Europeans. Peter Deilmann Cruises, Hapag-Lloyd, and Aida Cruises cater almost exclusively to a German clientele. MSC and Costa's ships, when cruising the Mediterranean, are booked mostly by Italians, and when cruising South America, mostly by South Americans.

Commencing in 2002, many of the major cruise lines repositioned ships to the European market, and many are building new ships to service the expanding cruising interests developing throughout the European population. Carnival Inc. and RCI, the two largest publicly held cruise companies, have purchased or established various European subsidiaries to attract specific European markets.

## Entertainment

As mentioned previously, the opportunity to witness big-name performers is important to many travelers, while others are just as content to dance to good music and make their own fun. The quality of entertainment has vastly improved over the past few years, and many stars and talented artists are now performing on ships. When ships offer big-name entertainers, they will advertise the event. Generally, the cruises on the larger ships leaving from New York or Florida offer the best talent because many of these performers actually rotate ships, staying on the Caribbean circuit. I have found less in the way of talent during European and Pacific cruises.

Some of the best entertainment on ships is of a more informal variety, with emphasis on audience-participation events—such as adult games for prizes, dancing, costume balls, gambling, talent shows, and so on. Most ships also offer a wide selection of first-run movies. Several of the Princess, Disney, and newest Carnival, Costa, and MSC ships feature outdoor movies around the pool, accompanied by free snacks and drinks. Many vessels offer closed-circuit television movies or videos in your cabin. The newest high-tech ships feature interactive televisions on which you can select your own videos. If the caliber of entertainment and entertainers is an important consideration, be certain to check out what will be offered on the cruise you are investigating.

## Size of Ship

In chapter 9 I have set forth the size of the major cruise ships, including tonnage, length, width, passenger capacity, and number of cabins. Thus, you will be able to easily compare the relative sizes of each vessel. The larger ships of the Carnival, Celebrity, Costa, Cunard, Holland America, MSC, Norwegian, Princess, and Royal Caribbean lines tend to offer more facilities, entertainment, dining options, and activities for all age-groups, while the smaller vessels are more intimate, friendlier, easier to negotiate, less congested, and can dock at a greater number of ports. Most ships built during the 1970s ranged in size from 16,000 to 23,000 tons. However, during the 1980s and 1990s, the cruise lines introduced many new ships in the 45,000- to 85,000-ton-and-up range, as well as an assortment of small yacht-like vessels. During the late 1990s and into this century, vessels weighing in over 100,000 GRT have become the fad. Although these behemoths may offer endless options not available on other vessels, passengers must be willing to accept long lines, long waits, and long walks. The largest ships built to date, the 220,000-ton, 5,400-passenger *Oasis of the Seas* and *Allure of the Seas,* entered service for Royal Caribbean in late 2009 and 2010.

Young children and teens will be better accommodated on the larger ships, where there are more activities and special programs designed to entertain them. This is especially the situation on all of the ships built during the past decade that weigh in over 80,000 tons (Carnival, Disney, Norwegian, Princess, and Royal Caribbean being the leaders in this area).

## Nationality of Crew

Chapter 9 also covers the nationality of the service crew for each ship. The nationality of the crew often sets the tone for the cruise, and on European and Mediterranean cruises, it may determine the official language spoken. The difference in the nationality of the crew, and what it may mean, is discussed in this chapter under "Service."

Few ships offer a totally American crew. Chances are that you will take a ship with a foreign crew, and it will be quite like spending time in the country the ship represents. You may find that this makes cruising all the more interesting and educational. You will most likely want to try ships of different nationalities each time you take a cruise vacation. Unfortunately, almost all of the lines have switched to crews of mixed nationalities for economic reasons. Only the top officers reflect the advertised nationality of the ship. This move has destroyed much of the old-country charm and flavor and has created some language barriers.

## Shore Excursions

Traditionally, all ships offer a selection of shore excursions that range from less active land and sea sightseeing tours to more active events—such as snorkeling, diving, river rafting, horseback riding, and helicopter rides. Over the past few years, the cruise lines have expanded the variety of tours, and the offerings have become increasingly more adventurous. Some of the newer tours include interacting with dolphins; feeding sharks; swimming with stingrays; "canopy tours," where cables are strung from tree to tree and passengers traverse on cable cars from platform to platform above rain forests and jungles (available in Costa Rica; Colon, Panama; and Montego Bay, Jamaica); helicopter rides landing on glaciers and float-plane excursions; kayaking, biking, jeep, and dune buggy tours; snuba (a cross between scuba and snorkeling) and power snorkeling; and a host of other offerings geared to appeal to passengers in all age-groups. Unfortunately, many of these tours can be very pricey, especially for families who must pay on a "per person" basis. This is one of the methods cruise lines use to increase their revenue to compensate for lower fares. On several of the luxury class ships, excursions are included in the fare. Shore excursions are also included on riverboat cruises.

## Outstanding Dining, Service, and Luxury

For those who can afford the steep tariffs, the highest standard of food and service and the most comfortable accommodations will be found on the following ships: *Large vessels* (over 50,000 GRT): all of the Crystal ships, *Seven Seas Mariner* and *Voyager*, Oceania's *Mariner* and *Riviera*, and "Grill Class" on the Cunard ships. *Medium-size vessels* (20,000 to 50,000 GRT): *Seabourn Odyssey, Seabourn Sojourn,* and *Quest*; Hapag-Lloyd's *Europa* and *Europa II*; *Seven Seas Navigator*; Peter Deilmann's *Deutschland*; *Silver Shadow, Silver Whisper,* and *Silver Spirit* of Silversea Cruises; and *Regatta, Insignia,* and *Nautica* of Oceania Cruises; *Azamara Journey* and *Quest*. *Small vessels* (under 20,000 GRT): *Seabourn Pride, Legend,* and *Spirit* (to be transferred to Windstar); Silversea's *Silver Cloud* and *Silver Wind*; and the two *SeaDream* ships. On the larger vessels, you must opt for a suite or deluxe cabin to enjoy the best experiences.

# Costs and Your Cabin_____

Given a comparable cabin on a comparable deck during the same season for cruises of similar duration, your tariff on most ships in the same market category (see chapter 11) should not vary more than 10 to 20 percent.

The rates will be higher for single rooms than for rooms shared by two people. Adding a third or fourth person to the room will bring the tariff down even more. Children under twelve sharing a cabin with two full-fare adults will generally pay only half of the minimum fare (the price charged for the least expensive accommodations on the ship).

The more expensive rooms are usually located on a higher deck and are often a little larger. Outside staterooms with verandas, windows, or portholes go for a higher price than inside ones without a view to the sea. This price differential may range from $200 to $2,000 per person on a seven-day cruise. The trend today is to provide balconies in a greater percentage of staterooms. Many cruisers who have experienced this perk now refuse to cruise without one.

Cabins with a double or two lower beds will go for more than those with a lower and an upper bunk. The same room on the same ship will cost more "in season" (mid-December to mid-April in the Caribbean and Pacific; June through September in Europe, with variations) than it will off-season. On transatlantic crossings, you will want to carefully investigate the varying prices for "peak season," "intermediate season," and "low season." You may be able to save as much as 50 percent by sailing eastward in late May rather than mid-June, or by returning westward in early June rather than late July. If your travel agent cannot obtain a discounted rate, he or she may still be able to obtain a cabin upgrade for you if he or she is persistent.

Of course, the longer the duration of the cruise, the more you will pay. This is possibly the only variation that makes real sense. Your per-person cost for a "minimum" room on an average seven-day cruise may range from $850 to $1,750. For ten-day cruises, your average minimum cost may vary from $1,100 to $2,100, and for fourteen-day cruises, from $1,750 to $3,500. Do not be misled by newspaper advertisements publicizing rooms starting at $100 per day per person. Often there are only a handful of rooms at this modest cost, and they are only available to those who book many months in advance or at the last moment. The average-priced room will be at least 50 percent higher than the minimum-priced one. If your decision as to whether or not to take a cruise is dependent upon the minimum offering, you should start making plans nine months to a year in advance. Several of the luxury-category cruise lines offer free cruises and other perks for loyal customers who have spent the required days at sea with that particular cruise line.

The higher the deck, the more you will pay. Possibly the greatest differential on any given cruise is based upon which deck your cabin is located. Contrary to popular belief, the least motion will be felt in the interior of the lower decks, as long as you are not located over the engines. You do not have to be a student of science to comprehend this principle if you can just imagine a tree blowing in the wind.

The difference in cost between the most expensive and the least expensive cabin on the same ship can vary from 100 percent to 250 percent on the average ship, and up to 500 percent on the super-luxury liners. Although there will exist a difference in area, closet, and dresser space, and general accommodations between rooms, all passengers on a cruise enjoy the use of all public facilities, participate in the same activities, and eat the same food. Only your immediate neighbors will know which cabin you occupy, and only snobs will care, so if economy is a major consideration, book the most inexpensive cabin available. However, if you tend toward claustrophobia or feel that lounging around a comfortable room is a prerequisite to enjoying your vacation, then you will have to pay for more expensive quarters. On many of the smaller luxury vessels, all accommodations are junior suites, and all go for about the same fare, with a small variance based on which deck you are located.

The price structure on the *Queen Victoria*, *Queen Elizabeth*, and *QM2* of Cunard Line is somewhat different from other cruises. Passengers booking the more expensive suites and cabins will eat better food served by more experienced waiters and will enjoy a great deal more pampering.

Before leaving the subject of cost, a final word on port charges, tipping, and the air-sea package is in order. A universally practiced deception is the tacking on of port charges after quoting the cruise fare. These can run from $60 up to several hundred dollars on longer cruises. Since the cruise line brochures generally quote cabin prices with an asterisk (*) to the effect that port charges will be added, potential customers are often misled as to the total fare. Today, most of the major cruise lines that require tipping will add the gratuity to your onboard account. It can range from 11 to 15 percent per person per day. Although you have the option to have the amount adjusted up or down, few cruisers bother, wishing to avoid the potential embarrassment. On a more positive note, many of the cruise lines have made arrangements with the private and regularly scheduled air carriers to obtain special package rates for parties who are flying directly to the port of embarkation on the day of the cruise and flying home the day the ship returns to its home port. It works like this: you check in your luggage upon arriving at your home airport; upon landing, you are transported by bus to the dock and your luggage is taken separately from the airport and brought right to your cabin. The airfare is sometimes lower than the normal economy rate. However, often you can do better on your own. In addition, you do save on taxi fares and tips to porters, and you are assured that the ship will not leave without you if your plane is delayed. The value of the air-sea package may vary from season to season on the same ship, and on some cruise lines, it is only available to passengers purchasing medium- and higher-priced cabins. Therefore, when considering different cruises, you may wish to see the extent to which the air-sea package is available to you for the particular sailing you contemplate taking.

In recent years, the pricing policy of many of the cruise lines has become confusing at best, and possibly deceptive. Many of the companies will offer a few minimum cabins several hundred dollars lower than the other less-expensive cabins. This is done in order to advertise the cruise as starting at a price lower than their competitors are. When you call to reserve one of these cabins, you are often told that these cabins are all booked, and you are quoted cabins at a higher price bracket. In addition, air-sea packages have become complicated in that some lines offer free air or air with a slight add-on (under $100), whereas others merely offer airfares that are only slightly reduced from normal coach fares.

To make matters worse, many of the lines offer an assortment of discounts for early and last-minute bookings. Others discount cabins to tour operators and travel agents guaranteeing to sell a number of cruises. (See the section on "Prices" above.) Therefore, you will often find that the couple in the adjoining stateroom with identical accommodations is paying a much different price from what you are paying. For those wishing to obtain discounted rates, it would be desirable to check with your travel agent or an agency that specializes in cruises as to which lines are offering early-booking discounts as well as last-minute discounts. You may be able to save 25 to 50 percent by booking six months in advance or just a few days before a cruise. Generally, a cruise line with available cabins a few days prior to sailing will offer substantial cabin upgrades at minimum fares in order to fill up its berths.

Because pricing has become so illusory, my division of ships into four price/market categories (in chapters 9 and 11) is not based upon published fares alone. I also take into consideration the cost of items while on the ship (drinks, tours, tipping, etc.) as well as the passenger market the cruise line seeks to attract and actually does attract. Therefore, you may find certain ships placed in categories that do not always correlate with the prices advertised in periodicals and brochures.

## What to Bring Along

Due to recent laws, a valid U.S. passport is required for U.S. citizens traveling outside the United States. To obtain this document, you must apply in person to the Passport Division or passport agencies of the State Department. In some cities, this function is handled by the clerk of the federal court or by the federal post office. When making an application, you must present a birth certificate or proof that you either were born in the United States or became a naturalized citizen, as well as two identical photographs that you've signed, together with another identification. Your passport will be good for ten years from the date issued.

This is an indispensable document abroad and should be diligently guarded. Should you lose it or have it stolen, head for the nearest U.S. embassy or consulate to report the loss. For this reason, you would be wise to keep a separate record of your passport number, date, and place of issuance. A passport is your best means of identification in any foreign land when cashing traveler's checks or otherwise establishing credit. It is also wise to bring along your driver's license and a charge card as additional identification.

Certain foreign countries also require visas and/or vaccination certificates. It is best to check with your travel agent or with the cruise line before each trip to determine which, if any, of these documents you may need.

You will want to bring along charge cards and money, of course, and the best way to carry money when traveling is in traveler's checks. Do not forget to keep a record of the check numbers in a separate place from the checks so that you are in a position to report a loss. Personal checks might help in an emergency, but do not count on many places honoring them. Most ships will not cash personal checks, much to the dismay and displeasure of the unwary traveler. You will receive information on ship as to how to change your dollars to local currency upon arriving in a foreign port.

The amount of money you should bring along depends upon the length of the cruise as well as your personal spending habits. Generally, on ship, you will need money for tobacco, cocktails, wine, miscellaneous medicines and sundry items, photographs, stamps, laundry, cleaning, games of chance, and tips. On very few ships you pay as you go, while on almost all there is a compulsory "charge it" system in which you are presented with an itemized invoice of your shipboard charges at the close of the cruise. When in port, you will need money for cab fares, restaurants, shopping, and any other activity you plan to pursue. It would be wise to sit down before you leave and analyze how much the foregoing expenditures may run—then add 30 to 40 percent to be safe.

While on the subject of money and shopping, remember that as a U.S. citizen, you will be permitted to bring back duty-free up to $400 of goods purchased abroad ($600 to $800 from most Caribbean islands), including up to one quart of liquor or wine. Should your ship stop in any of the U.S. Virgin Islands (most Caribbean cruises do), Guam, or American Samoa, you can increase your purchase limit to $1,200 per person and include five liters of wine or spirits (provided your purchases in excess of $400 and one quart of liquor or wine are made on one of these islands). Meats, fruits, vegetables, plants, and plant products will be impounded by U.S. Customs unless they are accompanied by an import license from a U.S. government agency. Americans abroad can also mail home gifts of no more than $10 in value ($20 from the U.S. possessions in the Caribbean and Pacific) to friends and family that are free of duty or tax if the recipient does not receive more than one package a day. These gifts do not have to be declared by the sender. Liquor and tobacco products may not be mailed, however.

When getting ready to pack, be certain that you have sturdy, substantial luggage. Should you rise early on the morning your ship pulls into the port of final disembarkation, you may be shocked to see your favorite Gucci bag being tossed from man to man like a football as it makes its way to the dock. Luggage is frequently damaged while being transported onto and off of the ship, so valuable or fragile pieces should probably be left at home. Be sure to bring along a small traveling bag (about one foot by two feet). These are handy for carrying bathing suits, towels, a change of clothes, suntan lotion, and so on when spending a day ashore.

Your selection of clothes depends to a great extent upon the climate, length of the cruise, and your personal habits. Some travelers prefer to travel light with a few drip-dry garments, while others are not content to wear the same outfit twice. However, on a cruise you are not bothered with having to frequently pack and unpack, and in view of this you may wish to take advantage of the opportunity to display many of your fineries that do not normally make it on your vacations.

On a short cruise (seven days, for example), there are usually only two formal nights, while there are more on the longer cruises. You will find a greater percentage of men wearing a tuxedo on the ships of the Celebrity, Crystal, Cunard, Hapag-Lloyd, Holland America, Princess, Seabourn, and Silversea cruise lines, because these ships tend to attract a wealthier, older, and more formal clientele. Many of the ships now provide tuxedo rentals aboard ship. Although there are always a respectable number of male passengers in plain business suits, this can vary among ships. For the nonformal evenings, the men will wear suits and sport jackets, and for the casual evenings, no jacket or tie is required. Most cruise lines have dispensed with the "nonformal" evenings, which were intended to be somewhere between formal and casual. Most evenings are designated country-club casual or business casual, which means anything other than shorts and T-shirts. Most cruisers still choose to dress smartly, but men do not need to wear jackets. Azamara, Hapag-Lloyd, Oceania, Regent Seven Seas, SeaDream Yacht Club, and Star Clippers are prime examples. To be safe, check with the line before leaving.

A robe for the shower, sauna, and pool is advisable, although robes are provided on most of the luxury—and several of the premium-market cruise ships. A comfortable pair of deck shoes will get you through the day, and at night, you will need dress shoes to coordinate with your suits and jackets. It is generally helpful to stay with one color when possible so you will not need as many different accessories. And don't forget socks, underwear, pajamas, bathing suits, sports shirts, dress shirts, ties, shorts, slacks, a sweater, and a raincoat. The same items you need aboard ship will generally work out for your shore excursions, so a separate wardrobe is unnecessary.

For the women, several of the chic numbers you have been reluctant to wear at home will be right in order. The number of dresses you pack will depend upon how often you wish to change. Again, it will be helpful to coordinate your choices with the same purse, dress shoes, and other accessories so as to cut down on the bulk of items that must be included in your wardrobe. As a rule of thumb, for every seven nights afloat, you can count on needing a dress outfit for two nights, a casual outfit for two nights, and something in between for the other evenings.

During the day, you will need swimming attire, a cover-up, sandals, shorts, skirts, blouses, slacks, a sweater, raincoat, and undergarments. Round this off with your favorite negligee, and you are ready to sail.

Most ships have laundry and cleaning services, which vary from moderately expensive to very expensive. Many vessels have self-service Laundromats, so you can feel like you have never left home. Frequently, the lines waiting to use these machines are quite long.

Whether to bring along expensive jewelry is a difficult question. Opportunities for theft exist on a ship, and all jewelry and valuables should be kept locked up when not in use. Almost all vessels provide a personal electronic wall safe in your cabin.

You may wish to personally carry aboard your jewelry, cosmetics, and medicines and the clothes you plan to wear the first evening at sea. All too often, your luggage will not find its way to your room until several hours after the ship sails. You may feel more comfortable and less panicky if you follow this suggestion.

Some of the miscellaneous items you will not want to forget are sunglasses, suntan lotion, prescription drugs (as well as your prescription for an emergency), a traveling alarm clock, a cell phone (with international access where applicable), and last, but not least, your camera (don't worry about film—all but the most uncommon brands are obtainable). Although most of the ships have their own photographer, who will be happy to record your every movement, these pictures can become expensive ($6 each and up), and they often do not capture you at your best angle. On a cruise, you will experience many beautiful and memorable moments, and you will meet many interesting and often unforgettable people. Don't miss recording them for posterity.

## Documents

A valid passport is now required for all travel to or from the United States by air, sea, or land. It is possible to purchase a passport card, which is somewhat less expensive than a passport, to facilitate entry into the United States by land and at seaports when arriving from Canada, Mexico, the Caribbean, and Bermuda. These cards cannot be used for travel by air. Both documents are valid for ten years for adults. A new passport costs $100, and a new passport card, $45. For more information, go to www.travel. state.gov/passport.

# Chapter Three

# Your Day at Sea

Although your selection of a cabin will help determine cost and although the ports of call will elicit "oohs" and "aahs" from your neighbors back home when you exhibit your photos, your daily activities aboard ship as well as your dining experiences will be the decisive factor in forming your overall opinion of the ship.

Most cruise ships make only brief stops in port, permitting just a superficial exploration of the environs—a preview, if you will, for later in-depth visits. Therefore, it is your day at sea that must be given top priority in selecting a cruise.

## Facilities and Activities

The facilities and public rooms found on different ships will vary somewhat with the size of the craft and the duration of the cruise. All of the major cruise lines print elaborate color brochures, which you can obtain from travel agents or by contacting the line directly. These brochures will describe and often illustrate the numerous facilities found aboard.

Almost every cruise ship afloat today is fully air-conditioned and equipped with the necessary stabilizers to keep the roll and pitch at a minimum. Most ships have radio rooms, providing the opportunity to place calls and fax messages home. Most of the new ships, or those recently renovated, have direct-dial telephones in the private cabins and e-mail facilities somewhere in the public areas. A well-stocked library and cardroom are standard, and you will usually find a ship's hospital and pharmacy with at least one qualified doctor. Hair salons are also available, but make your beauty shop appointments early on formal nights. Most women aboard who have their hair done will want an appointment the day of the captain's dinner.

You will find at least one and as many as six swimming pools. Because of the limited space, however, most pools offer an opportunity, at best, for only a dunk and five or six good strokes. Most ships of the major cruise lines have gymnasiums, and attached to the gym you will often find Jacuzzis, saunas, and massage rooms. In fact, on most of the larger new ships, there are fully equipped health spas offering a variety of treatments. The ships that devote the most area and provide the best fitness and spa facilities are of Carnival, Celebrity, Costa, Crystal, Cunard, Disney, Princess, MSC, Norwegian, Regent Seven Seas, and Royal Caribbean.

The shops aboard ship will offer clothes, jewelry, and trinkets from numerous foreign ports at bargain prices. The larger ships generally have a variety of shops, while the smaller vessels only have one or two. Liquor, cigarettes, and perfume are generally the best buys. However, if your ship is stopping at a "free port," such as St. Thomas, you may wish to wait and compare prices ashore. Almost all ships provide laundry and cleaning facilities, and many have self-service Laundromats. Many of the large ships now have facilities for tuxedo rental as well.

For those inclined to try their hand at Lady Luck, most cruise ships have slot machines aboard as well as fully stocked casinos, complete with craps tables, roulette, poker, and blackjack. Again, the larger vessels tend to have the more complete casinos—some of the smaller ships only offer slot machines and one or two blackjack tables.

The usual public rooms consist of two or more grand ballrooms, one or more dining rooms, several smaller lounges, show lounges, cardrooms, a library, a game room, numerous bars, a movie theater, a discotheque, and a buffet restaurant near the pool with an outdoor grill area. With the popularity of the Internet and e-mail, most ships now have computer facilities available as well as Internet cafés, some serving coffee, drinks, and snacks. Regular computer classes may also be offered while at sea. Many of the ships built after 1990 have included conference facilities; wine, specialty coffee, and caviar and champagne bars; elaborate Broadway-caliber show lounges; alternate specialty restaurants; inventive children and teen areas; and a bevy of high-tech accouterments.

Upon rising each morning, you will find a schedule of the day's activities pushed under the door of your cabin. This very important document will indicate what is going on every minute of the day, which movies will be shown in the theater and on your TV, and the dress required for dinner. You will most certainly want to study this publication carefully so you will not miss any activity or happening in which you may wish to participate (see sample programs in chapter 9).

Your ship will have a cruise director and a social staff, who are there to organize activities, bring the passengers together (especially the singles), give orientation lectures on ports of call, sell shore excursion tickets, and generally act as mentors to the passengers. Some are excellent and can contribute to making your trip a delight. Others vary from indifferent to detrimental, giving wrong information about places of interest in ports or even directing visitors to tourist traps (where they may have a little something going on the side). Be careful to check out the recommendations they may offer on shops and restaurants. It may be advisable to consult your guidebook or one of the tourist magazines that are printed by the tourist boards of the various ports and distributed on ship.

The adventures of John, Martha, Michael, Vivian, Joan, Ron, Scotty, and Jamie described in chapter 1 are just a few examples of the various ways you may elect to spend your days at sea. For those who do not wish just to relax, a cruise also offers a vast range of activities around the clock designed to appeal to every taste. There is probably no resort on earth that offers as much as often.

For the early risers, there are the morning exercise and aerobics classes, walking, jogging, shuffleboard, Ping-Pong, and deck tennis. Many of the larger ships carry a full-time golf pro and offer a morning golf clinic. In addition to the group lessons aboard ship, the golf pro will arrange tours to the local golf courses when ashore. Several lines have occasionally offered a tennis clinic program on some of their cruises, which includes daily lessons on the ship and organized games in port. You may wish to attend morning lectures on forthcoming ports of call, especially if you have not been to that port previously. Foreign-language classes in the native tongue of the crew—such as French, Italian, or Greek—are common, as are lessons in bridge, backgammon, blackjack, and chess. A number of the ships offer investment and estate planning seminars, while others offer cooking and needlepoint lessons, wine tastings, musical concerts, trapshooting, bingo, and deck horse races. Many cruise ships carry a professional dance team that gives complimentary dance lessons each morning.

After lunch, there are duplicate bridge, backgammon, and gin-rummy tournaments, as well as first-run movies and bingo. For the children and ambitious adults, there are swimming games at the pool and deck-sport tournaments. In addition to the usual deck sports, a few ships have miniature golf courses and/or golf simulators, and many vessels of the Carnival, Celebrity, Costa, Disney, Princess, Norwegian, and Royal Caribbean lines have basketball courts. At some point in each cruise, you are given an opportunity to visit the bridge or tour the kitchen. Late in the afternoon, many passengers squeeze in the hairdresser or a sauna and massage. Many of you will find that just lying out in the deck chair by the pool and soaking up the sun can be one of the nicest experiences during the day. Add music from the ship's calypso band and a rum punch, and it is just like being at a pool on one of the Caribbean islands.

Evenings are usually the most exciting part of the cruise. Even on cruises that hit numerous ports, the majority of evenings are spent at sea. You will probably start out in the cocktail lounges before dinner, where you can sample some hors d'oeuvres, music, and exotic drinks. The captain's welcome-aboard cocktail party is held before dinner, usually on the second night at sea. On this occasion, each passenger is introduced personally to the captain, treated to free drinks, and has an opportunity to meet the other passengers aboard. After dinner each evening, there are several popular quiz show and parlor games—such as bingo, Liar's Club, and the Newlywed Game, as well as karaoke. The casinos also are active at this time.

During the majority of evenings at sea, most ships offer a variety or cabaret show. Several of the lines have a policy of offering two completely different shows each evening, one in the main lounge and one later at night in the cabaret or discotheque. These shows feature singers, comedians, magicians, dancers, puppeteers, and more singers. As pointed out in an earlier chapter, the quality of the entertainment has improved in recent years.

One night during each cruise, some ships hold a passenger talent show, and on another night, a passenger costume party. These affairs often afford more laughs than many of the second-rate comedians, magicians, and singers who get paid to perform. Once you get into the spirit of things, you may find that the audience-participation events will leave you with more memorable experiences than the average, run-of-the-mill variety show. For those who prefer something different, most ships offer a first-run movie each evening in the theater. The movies are varied throughout the cruise and generally repeated at least once, so you can choose which afternoon or evening you wish to give up some other activity. Outdoor movies by the pool are featured on some of the Carnival, Disney, MSC, Princess, Royal Caribbean, and Seabourn ships and on the new builds of several other lines. Closed-circuit television movies or DVDs in your cabin have been introduced on many of the newer vessels. On most ships, these have replaced the movie theater.

Around midnight, ships traditionally offered the midnight buffet; however, in recent years many ships have replaced the buffet with around-the-clock alternate dining facilities or waiters who serve the public rooms with late-night snacks. Also, later in the evening, things start to swing in the late-night spots, where couples and singles can indulge in some romantic dancing before the traditional stroll on deck. No matter how involved you become in activities, and no matter how tired you may be, you should save a few minutes each night to walk out on deck under the stars and watch the black sea splash against the hull of the ship. Looking out across the sea at such a moment offers a unique opportunity for reflection. (This can also be enjoyed from your veranda).

From the foregoing description, it is obvious that there is something for everyone aboard a cruise ship. After a day or two, you should be able to adapt to your own pace and intensity and alternate between playing and relaxing with your usual agility. Chapter 9 includes a sample of daily program schedules for many of the ships.

## Dining

Some of your most memorable experiences aboard ships will be your adventures in dining. Over the years, many of the great ships offered some of the finest restaurants to be found anywhere in the world. Dining on many of the vessels, with both European kitchen and dining room staff, is comparable to feasting at the best establishments on the Continent. During the past few years, the quality of the dining experience aboard ship has greatly improved.

Can you imagine starting your evening repast with gobs of beluga caviar, imported gravlax, a dozen escargots, or perhaps a slice of quiche lorraine, followed by lobster bisque or some onion soup with freshly grated Gruyère and Parmesan cheeses too thick to cut with a knife? Next comes your fish course of poached salmon or turbot with hollandaise sauce, Dover sole amandine, lobster thermidor, or possibly some trout stuffed with crabmeat. For your entree, you may decide upon roast duckling à l'orange, steak au poivre, rack of lamb, or Chateaubriand with béarnaise sauce. The entree may be complemented with some sautéed champignons or truffles. For dessert, why not try a napoleon slice or another French pastry? Many of the ships have the headwaiters going from table to table each evening, preparing bananas flambé, cherries jubilee, or crêpes Suzette. To round things off, you may try an assortment of cheeses from Switzerland, Holland, France, and Italy, followed by some after-dinner mints. Naturally, each course should be accompanied by the proper wine, unless you prefer a shot of vodka with your caviar and Cognac with your coffee.

Although this meal could easily cost $100 to $200 per person in a good French restaurant in Paris or New York, most of these goodies are featured for dinner aboard the vessels of many of the cruise lines at least once or twice during each sailing and nightly on the deluxe vessels. However, many of the ships have been cutting back on the more expensive offerings in recent years.

There are several ships with Italian kitchens and dining room staff that offer a wide selection of Italian dishes, including a different variety of pasta with each lunch and dinner. Before the cruise comes to an end, you will have been exposed to spaghetti, macaroni, mostaccioli, rigatoni, cannelloni, lasagna, manicotti, pizza, gnocchi, and a dozen other lesser-known varieties. Among the more popular ships with Italian kitchens sailing from U.S. ports are the vessels of Costa Cruise Lines and MSC Cruises. There are exceptional Italian specialty restaurants on the Crystal, Disney, Hapag-Lloyd, Oceania, Princess, Silversea, and Regent Seven Seas vessels (see chapter 13). The most ambitious and gastronomic specialty restaurants at sea today can be found on Celebrity's *Millennium*-class and *Solstice*-class ships, featuring Continental French-style cuisine. Signatures on *Seven Seas Mariner* and *Seven Seas Voyager* and Le Champagne on *Silver Spirit* are three outstanding French restaurants, possibly the best at sea.

Many recent cruisers have expressed the opinion that today the vessels of the Azamara, Crystal, Hapag-Lloyd, Oceania, Regent Seven Seas, Seabourn, SeaDream, and Silversea cruise lines have the finest kitchens afloat. The food on these ships is Continental, with the European chefs creating an amazingly diverse range of culinary delights. The dining room staffs are mixed European. I have found the overall dining experience on these ships to be superior to most ships currently sailing. Among the more elegant dining rooms afloat with the most lavish gourmet cuisine are the Queens and Princess Grills of the *QM2*, *Queen Victoria*, and *Queen Elizabeth*. Unfortunately, these dining rooms are open only to those passengers booking the most expensive suites and staterooms.

A variety of Continental, ethnic, and American dishes are offered on the ships of most cruise lines. Although the quantity and quality of the food on ships is generally satisfactory, service often suffers from the use of mixed crews, including less-experienced waiters and stewards from the Caribbean, Central and South America, the Philippines, and Southeast Asia. Some of the less widely publicized ships and some of the bargain cruises do not offer the same high quality and vast quantity of food that has come to be associated with cruising. However, most of the major cruise lines now provide an alternate menu available every evening that includes such universally desired items as steak, chicken, fish, and pasta, as well as vegetarian fare.

If you wish to have special dishes that do not appear on the menu, you must make arrangements with the maître d' at least a day in advance. Generally, he will be anxious to accommodate you, and, of course, you are expected to reciprocate at the end of the cruise with a suitable gratuity. Don't hesitate to ask for any dish that may tickle your palate. A cruise is an excellent opportunity to sample all those special preparations for which you never wanted to splurge in an expensive restaurant. Unfortunately, most ships today are discouraging this practice, and the opportunity to order special gourmet dishes has been completely eliminated on most cruise lines. The corporate policy of most lines to make larger and larger profits has ruled out much of the elegance and special pampering that has long been associated with cruising.

The wine selection aboard many of the ships is perhaps too limited for the tastes of a discerning connoisseur. The prices of wines have escalated, and the cost of wine on ships is almost as expensive today as the cost in restaurants. On the majority of ships, some of the sommeliers have had too little training, lack the necessary familiarity with and knowledge of wine, and are too harassed to serve it properly; but with the ever-growing popularity of wine drinking, this department has greatly improved in recent years. It should be noted that the ships of Azamara, Crystal, Regent Seven Seas, SeaDream, Seabourn, and Silversea, cruise lines, many riverboats, and all barges give their passengers free wine with lunch and dinner each day.

Because dining is such an important part of the cruise, you should book your table and choose your sitting carefully. The experienced cruiser will go to the dining steward immediately upon boarding ship to make these arrangements.

Many cruises have both a first and second sitting, which results in two entirely different daily schedules. Should you be traveling with friends, be sure that you all take the same sitting. If your friends take the first sitting and you the second, you may never see them. While you are enjoying cocktails, they may be eating dinner, and while you are having dinner, they may be seeing the first show. While you are watching the second show, they may be dancing, and so on. Ships that provide two sittings also provide two schedules for activities, so all passengers have an opportunity to take part in the various events offered.

When deciding upon whether to take the first or second seating, you must consider your usual eating habits as well as your dining preferences while on a vacation. If you are an early riser, prefer dinner around six-thirty or seven-thirty, and wish to conclude your evening's entertainment to be in bed by eleven or twelve o'clock, you will prefer the first seating. If, however, you wish to sleep late, partake in cocktail hour, and not eat until eight-thirty or nine o'clock, then the second sitting is for you. Several of the cruise lines now offer seatings at four different times.

Almost all ships have tables for parties of two, four, six, eight, and ten. If you are honeymooners or second honeymooners and want to be alone, you will prefer a table for two. However, if you have a fight, you're out of luck because it may be difficult to switch tables later. If you feel you will prefer other company, ask the dining room maître d' to make the arrangements. The larger the table, the more people you will get to know, and should one or two at your table not be congenial, there certainly will be others who are.

Upscale vessels such as the ships of SeaDream, Silversea, Regent Seven Seas, Seabourn, and Crystal have adopted an open-seating policy with no prearranged dining assignments. Several of the premium- and mass-market cruise ships have adopted an open-seating "dine when you please and with whom you please" policy, including Azamara, Carnival, Crystal Cruises, Holland America, Norwegian Cruise Line, Oceania, Paul Gauguin, Princess, Royal Caribbean, and Windstar. However, Carnival, Holland America, Princess, and Royal Caribbean also give passengers the option of traditional fixed-table seating. Other cruise lines can be expected to follow suit, at least in some of their dining areas. Thus, passengers can change table companions as often as they wish.

Most of the newer ships that have come on line over the past fifteen years offer one or more special gourmet dining rooms where a limited number of passengers can enjoy a more intimate upscale dinner on certain evenings. For example, the ships of Crystal Cruises have Asian and Italian restaurants in addition to the main dining rooms; the Celebrity *Millennium*- and *Solstice*-class ships, Regent Seven Seas, Holland America, Cunard, Oceania's *Marina* and *Riviera*, and *Disney Dream* and *Disney Fantasy* feature a French Continental dining room; and Hapag-Lloyd's *Europa* and *Europa II*, as well as the Azamara, Costa, Disney, Oceania Cruise Lines, Princess, and Royal Caribbean ships also have special (advanced reservation) Italian restaurants. Most cruise lines offer pizza parlors or pizza stations. Exceptional steak and chophouses are also emerging on many of the cruise lines, including Azamara, Carnival, Oceania, Princess, and Royal Caribbean. Carrying this concept further, the *Seven Seas Mariner* and V*oyager, Europa 2,* and the newer ships of Norwegian, Royal Caribbean, and Genting Hong Kong feature numerous alternative restaurants. Norwegian's recent new builds not only offer French, Italian, and Asian restaurants but also a Japanese sushi bar, teppanyaki rooms, a fusion restaurant, a Tex-Mex restaurant, a tapas bar, and several more eclectic options in addition to the two main dining rooms. The giant *Oasis of the Seas, Allure of the Seas,* and Norwegian's *Norwegian Epic* boast over ten different dining venues. Many of these specialty restaurants feature menus designed by famous chefs.

As mentioned earlier, on the *QM2, Queen Victoria,* and *Queen Elizabeth* the dining rooms are divided into classifications. And there is a difference in food and service between the grillrooms, for those booking the most expensive cabins and suites; and the other dining rooms, for those who book the less luxurious accommodations. On other cruise lines everyone is considered to be in one class; therefore, whether you pay $750 per week or $10,000 per week for your room, you will eat the same food in the same dining room.

All of the cruise ships have adopted the custom of offering numerous feedings in order to give you the impression that you are getting a lot for your money. As a matter of fact, you are, but quite candidly, few of you will be able to attend each gastronomical offering and do it justice.

The first culinary event is the "early-bird breakfast," which consists of coffee, tea, rolls, and juice, starting at 6:00 or 6:30 a.m. Regular breakfast in the dining room commences sometime between 7:30 a.m. and 8:30 a.m. and, on many ships, is available in your cabin at any time. Breakfast will generally consist of the usual offerings, such as various fruits, juices, cereals, eggs, breakfast meats, rolls, pancakes, and so on. However, on ships where non-U.S. passengers prevail, the food is usually typical of the nationality of the crew.

Traditionally, you could ring for a cabin steward who would bring you a hot breakfast from the regular kitchen or a Continental breakfast from his service kitchen. Many of the ships have eliminated this possibility or varied the routine, requiring passengers who wish breakfast in their cabins to fill out and turn in an order form before going to bed. This has the obvious disadvantage of forcing you to decide in advance what time you want to get up and have breakfast. However, most ships offer a room-service menu available around the clock. Several of the cruise lines even feature multicourse meals from the dining room's evening menu served in your staterooms (at an additional charge on some ships). Cunard, MSC, and Norwegian, the new Princess and HAL ships, and some other cruise lines are now offering breakfast in private dining room venues for suite passengers. Many ships with large spas offer spa breakfasts with spa cuisine for spa suite passengers.

Almost all ships have an alternative indoor/outdoor breakfast buffet for the late risers. Having your morning coffee while sitting out in the fresh salt-sea air during a morning at sea is especially delightful.

For those who cannot hold out until lunch, there is a late-morning tea, bullion, cookies, and cakes at about eleven o'clock. Of course, by this time many of your fellow passengers may already be working on their second Bloody Mary or screwdriver. Lunch is generally served in the dining room from twelve to two, depending on your sitting. An indoor/outdoor buffet for those passengers who do not wish to dress to go to the dining room for lunch is generally offered. Buffets on ships are usually quite elaborate and include exotic assortments of cold meats (roast beef, duck, ham, chicken, and venison) attractively displayed with numerous salads, cheeses, pastas, several hot dishes, and yummy desserts. Usually, adjacent to the buffet is an outdoor grill offering hamburgers, hot dogs, and other grilled items. When in port, you may find it inconvenient to return to the ship at noon. Some of the ships will furnish you with a box lunch to take with you; otherwise, you may wish to utilize the opportunity to sample some of the local restaurants.

About four or four-thirty in the afternoon, tea, snacks, and sweets are served. You then can partake of cocktails and hors d'oeuvres from six-thirty to eight-thirty. After cocktails comes the pièce de résistance of your gastronomical day-dinner. The variety of ethnic cuisine was discussed earlier. To break up the monotony, many ships adopt a different theme for each dinner meal. There may be Italian night, French night, or Caribbean night, where the cuisine will be indigenous to the country or area that is being featured. Most ships offer numerous courses, and you are encouraged to sample as many dishes as you wish. The appetizers usually include juices, a fruit cup, some form of seafood cocktail, relishes, smoked salmon, and perhaps caviar on special evenings. The next course is soups and pastas. As a rule of thumb, you are best advised to choose a dish from the same country of origin as the chef—that is, the pastas are better on Italian ships, moussaka is best on Greek vessels, and quiche should be prepared by a French chef. The rolls and breads on the Italian and French ships are usually superb and irresistible.

The entrees are generally divided between fish and seafood offerings and meat and fowl preparations. Even if you cannot consume all of this food, you may wish to order a course and share it just to have an opportunity to sample something unusual. Most of the better ships offer a standby—such as steak, roast beef, chicken, salmon, and a vegetarian dish every evening for those who are not so adventurous. For those who enjoy wine with the meal, you are best advised to make a selection at lunch or during the prior evening. This will enable the wine steward to have the bottle waiting for you and properly aired. Otherwise, if he is very busy, your wine may not arrive until your dessert. If you do not finish the entire bottle, request that the wine steward store it for you until the following evening.

The desserts are varied, ranging from assorted ice creams and ices to fancy cakes, pastries, and cheeses. As mentioned earlier, many ships have their headwaiters wandering around each night making crêpes Suzette and cherries jubilee so that each table receives these desserts at least once during the cruise. Traditionally, flaming baked Alaska is served on almost every ship on the night of the captain's dinner. This affair generally takes place toward the end of the cruise. Staff and crew alike make every human effort to surpass and outdo all that has preceded the event. The food is the best; the service is even better; there are special decorations; and generally a jovial, festive atmosphere prevails.

Last, but not least, is the midnight buffet. This is the gourmand's delight, where everything that has not been consumed previously on the cruise is refurbished and attractively displayed on a buffet table that often covers the width of the dining room. Many ships go further and prepare some special dishes and fancy desserts for the occasion. However, as mentioned above, most ships have eliminated this feeding and replaced it with items served in the late evening in the buffet restaurant.

On the ships of most major cruise lines, there are pizza stations open in the afternoon and evening; and on Disney, Carnival, and Norwegian's latest ships, they are open around the clock. Many other ships offer special ice-cream shops, caviar-champagne bars, and wine and coffee bistros.

Recognizing many cruisers' preference for not dressing up each evening, many of the ships are offering a casual dining policy under which all meals are alternatively offered in the buffet restaurant for passengers not wishing to eat in the dining rooms. This seems to have become fairly standard today.

The dress for dinner varies from evening to evening, from casual (no tie or coat required) for evenings in port, to formal attire, which is suggested for the captain's cocktail party, the captain's dinner, and other special occasions. It is, of course, permissible for men to wear a plain business suit and tie on formal evenings; and on the less expensive ships and shorter cruises, most of the male passengers do not bother to bring along a tux. The women, however, generally dress to the hilt, as there is no better place to show off a wardrobe. This does not mean that you will have to run out and spend hundreds or thousands of dollars on clothes in order to enjoy a cruise. Few people do. However, you will want to bring along a variety of your special fineries, depending upon the length of the cruise. An increasing number of cruise lines are opting for country club casual dress throughout the cruise and do not even require men to wear jackets. These cruise lines include Azamara, Disney, Hapag-Lloyd, SeaDream Yacht Club, Oceania, Regent Seven Seas, Star Clippers, and Windstar.

The waiters in the dining room will be especially determined to satisfy your every whim because they are hoping to receive a token of your gratitude by way of a tip. You do not tip them at every meal but wait until the end of the cruise and then place your gratuity in an envelope with a little thank-you note. Most of the ships will indicate the recommended tipping procedures in a bulletin to passengers; on others, you are left on your own. On the Seabourn, SeaDream, Silversea, and Regent Seven Seas lines, tipping is not required. Where there is open seating, the cruise lines add a gratuity to your shipboard account with the option to adjust them upward or downward before disembarking. This is rapidly becoming the normal custom throughout the industry and is the policy on Carnival, Costa, Cunard, Holland America, Norwegian, Oceania, and Princess cruise lines. The amount charged ranges from $11 to $15 per person, per day. Celebrity, Crystal, Disney, Hapag-Lloyd, and Royal Caribbean still distribute envelopes for passengers to personally disseminate the tips (this can change); however, passengers are allowed to charge gratuities to their personal, onboard accounts.

If in doubt, the chief purser is a reliable source from whom to obtain an explanation of the usual procedures. Although many people adhere to the usual 10 to 15 percent of the passage divided between waiters, cabin stewards, and others who have performed a special service on their behalf, this is not always suitable. Whether your ticket costs $850 or $2,000, you require the same service, and there is a big difference between spreading around $85 and spreading around $200. You will probably be about average if you tip $3.50 to $4.50 per day per person to your waiter and a similar amount to your cabin steward. (Some ships recommend that the busboy be tipped a specified amount in addition to the tip you give the waiter. On others, the waiter shares his tip with the busboy.)

If you are particularly pleased with the service, you may want to tip more, and if the service is unsatisfactory, you should notify the maître d' or the hotel manager early in the voyage so that your trip is not ruined. Don't forget to tip the wine steward, the maître d', the waiters in the bar, and anyone else whom you may call upon for a special service. Their tips will be about the same as you would normally give at home. However, on many ships, a 15 percent service charge already has been added to drinks and wine orders.

## Specialty Restaurants at Sea

Passengers on cruise ships generally do not have the option of leaving the ship for dinner as they do when vacationing ashore at a hotel or resort. Therefore, the challenge for cruise operators has been keeping the dining experience sufficiently interesting and diverse to prevent guests from becoming bored or dissatisfied.

The various lines attempt to vary the menus each day of the cruise and to provide theme nights in an effort to make each dinner seem special. However, experienced cruisers soon realize that the environs, the style of preparation, and one's table companions (except on open-seating vessels) are the same, and they often feel that a change would be welcome.

The existence of an alternate dining venue with a new decor, separate kitchen, different style of cuisine, and an option to dine with a dining companion or companions of your choice becomes a welcome plus, enhancing the cruise experience.

In recent years, a competition has developed among cruise lines to boast the very finest alternative, reservation-only, gourmet, specialty restaurant at sea. During the 1990s, pizza venues, casual evening dinners at the poolside buffet restaurant, ice-cream parlors, and hamburger/hot dog grills near the pool became *de rigueur*, available on most major cruise lines. However, discerning cruisers, tired of the ennui of dining night after night in the main dining room, quickly became enamored with alternative specialty restaurants offering more upscale cuisine and service as well as the opportunity to dine when you want and with whom you want.

The first ships to introduce fine-dining specialty restaurants as an alternative to the main dining room were the Crystal Cruise Line ships, offering both elegant Italian and atmospheric Asian restaurants. Not to be outdone, the other cruise lines followed suit. Today, Azamara, Carnival, Celebrity, Costa, Cunard, Peter Deilmann, Disney, Hapag-Lloyd, Holland America, MSC, Norwegian, Oceania, P&O, Princess, Regent Seven Seas, Royal Caribbean, Seabourn, Silversea, Genting Hong Kong, Victoria, and Windstar all offer guests one or more alternative dining possibilities.

Initially, alternative Italian restaurants sprung up since Italian cuisine was considered the most universally popular ethnic fare. This was followed by steak houses and chophouses, Asian-style restaurants (including sushi and teppanyaki specialty areas), and more formal French and Continental-style dining rooms.

The different cruise lines have varying policies on exacting a surcharge for these restaurants. On some, there is no additional charge; on others, there is a minimal charge of $5 to $10 largely to cover tips for the waiters; and on the more upscale French-Continental dining rooms, the tariff can reach from $22 to $35 per person. However, the multicourse repast (with impeccable service) in these dining rooms is well worth the price and could easily run two to four times as much in a comparable restaurant in Europe or the United States. Some of the more upscale ships offer special, ultragourmet, wine-pairing dinners during each cruise where the charges run anywhere from $75 per person to $1,000 and up.

Since more and more cruise lines are experimenting with alternative specialty restaurants as well as keeping their buffet restaurants open for dinner, those readers who find these features important would be well advised to check with the cruise line at the time of booking.

Dining is most certainly one of the biggest highlights of the cruise and must therefore be given its due importance when selecting a ship. You will find sample menus from many of the cruise ships and riverboats in chapters 9 and 10. Because the quality of food and service varies from year to year on ships as it does in restaurants, you will want to solicit the opinion of your travel agent and anyone you may find who has recently cruised on the ship that you are considering. My ratings for food and service can be found in chapter 11. These are based upon my most recent cruise on each ship and may vary from year to year, depending upon the kitchen and dining room staffs.

# Chapter Four

# Cruising for Singles

With the growing popularity of the cruise vacation and the onslaught of vigorous advertising, more and more singles are being attracted to the high seas. The image of the elderly passenger propped up in a deck chair, covered with blankets, and sipping tea has given way to the sophisticated younger single of the modern era.

There is no question that the thought of a cruise should conjure up some romantic visions in the mind of the average single. Imagine watching the sun set over the mountains on a balmy tropical evening as your ship slowly pulls out of port, or dancing to the melodious tunes of a romantic Italian band until the early hours of the morning, followed by a hand-in-hand stroll on deck to view the moon and stars on a clear Caribbean evening.

Of course, cruising has a great deal more than romance to offer the single. In addition to the numerous activities, exciting ports, and fine cuisine (discussed earlier), the cruise offers the single traveler a planned, organized vacation where most major arrangements have already been taken care of. Who could fail to appreciate not having to constantly tote heavy luggage, tip porters, wave down taxis, arrange itineraries, determine a respectable nightspot, or suffer the empty feeling of being alone in a strange land?

What kind of companionship can a single person traveling alone expect to find aboard ship? Generally, it takes a day or so to become familiar with the new surroundings and lose your normal inhibitions. By the second evening at sea, all but the most pretentious bores will have warmed up and gotten into the swing of things. Your fellow passengers may smile and nod as you pass them in corridors, the passengers in the adjoining deck chairs may initiate a conversation, and the couple sitting at the next table in the lounge may invite you to join them. The intimate, often-cozy atmosphere of the ship, together with the realization that you are all at the mercy of the high seas and that no one is getting off, stimulates a feeling of togetherness and cordiality.

However, the cruise staff of the ship will not leave you to your own devices to find companionship. The entertainment director and social hostess will stimulate comingling through singles' cocktail parties, group games, dancing classes, bridge tournaments, and similar get-together functions. Of course, no pressure is ever placed upon anyone to attend these activities, and you are free to just relax, cuddle up with a good book, and do your own thing.

Many of the married couples on ship will be very friendly. The unescorted single may find it quite advantageous to strike up a social relationship with several amenable couples so as not to limit his or her companionship just to the other singles aboard. A well-traveled couple may prove to be far more interesting company on a shore excursion than some other single who may not share your tastes or interests. In addition, it is often desirable to have an assortment of other people to join in the ship's public rooms when you are avoiding some other single or do not wish to sit alone.

Often your married companions will insist upon buying you a drink; however, you will want to reciprocate at the earliest possible opportunity so as not to give the impression that you are tagging along for a free ride. When sharing taxis or eating at a restaurant in port, etiquette and common sense dictate that you insist upon paying your own share. Your newfound friends will soon abandon you if it turns out that you have become an expense they didn't include in their vacation budget. The women will be well advised to follow the same principle with regard to any male escort who becomes a semiregular. He may have bargained on paying for a few drinks and an occasional meal, but he probably did not bring along enough cash to take you on as a dependent.

Having touched upon the existence of the feeling of general camaraderie on the cruise and the desirability of not neglecting married couples as potential shipboard pals, we will now explore the question of what kind of companionship the single can expect from singles of the opposite sex. First of all, it is no secret that singles will be in the minority, as they are at most vacation spots. Most newspaper advertisements for "singles' cruises" are misleading. A travel agency or tour operator will prebook a number of cabins on a regular cruise and attempt to attract a number of single customers through advertising. Second, single females will generally outnumber single males by two to one.

The greatest number of younger singles will be found on the three- and four-day cruises, on the ships of the Royal Caribbean, Norwegian, and Carnival lines, or on less expensive cruises. Most younger singles on more expensive cruises are traveling with their families.

Longer cruises (fifteen to ninety days or more) would not be advisable for the single who feels he or she needs good and exciting companionship to make the trip fulfilling. You may be fortunate enough to find "Mr. Right" or "Ms. Right" and have the most heavenly time of your life, but if you don't, you are going to be unhappy for an awfully long time.

Several of the cruise lines feature "gentlemen hosts," who generally are mature gentlemen (ages fifty-five to seventy) who receive a free cruise in return for acting as dance and bridge partners for women traveling solo. For many years, this program has been available on the Cunard, Holland America, Seabourn, Crystal, Regent Seven Seas, and Silversea cruise lines. The program was best satirized in the Jack Lemon-Walter Matthau movie *Out to Sea*.

What, then, is the best cruise for the single? Obviously, you should first select a ship by utilizing the same standards that a couple would consider—that is, food, service, program, ports of call, and so forth. You are still spending your vacation time and hard-earned money, and there is no reason why you should not make your decision with objectivity and discrimination.

However, assuming all else to be equal, the larger the ship, the greater number of singles to choose from as prospective acquaintances and companions. On the other hand, on a very large ship you will find it difficult to become exposed to all of the other passengers early in the trip. It is entirely possible to spend seven days on such a ship without once crossing the path of a fellow passenger who has been on the same ship with you all week. A smaller ship is more intimate, and people warm up more rapidly, but there are fewer people to choose from. You may wish to compare this situation to a small and a large hotel. If you were going to a Caribbean island, would you prefer to stay at a large resort or a smaller, more intimate hotel, assuming similar quality and facilities?

When traveling alone, the cabin price is usually higher, and there will be significant savings if you are able to travel with a friend or share a cabin for two. Some of the lines will pair up singles (of the same sex), and others will not. You will have to check with each line in order to determine their current policy. Cabin space in an economy room is limited, and sharing small closets, dressers, and a washroom with even a close friend is often difficult and with a stranger almost impossible. However, if economy is a prime consideration, privacy and comfort may have to be sacrificed. Fortunately, some of the newer ships are being built with a greater number of single-occupancy staterooms at rates closer to those charged for each person sharing a double room. The *Norwegian Epic* has numerous cabins designed for single passengers, with a special lounge for those passengers.

Let me again emphasize that your enjoyment of the cruise vacation does not depend necessarily upon your making friends, finding escorts, or experiencing eternal romance. However, those of you who may be interested in any of these pursuits should consider the following tips:

Let your hair down immediately and freely respond to a fellow passenger's friendly nod or glance. If you insist upon being coy, proper, or aloof, valuable days of the cruise will flee by before you get into the swing of things.

While waiting in the terminal to board ship, survey the prospective group and do not hesitate to introduce yourself to someone who interests you. Inasmuch as you will have to select a table in the dining room as soon as you come on board, this may be as good a time as any to start looking for interesting prospects. (*Note:* Everyone looks a bit dull and seedy when waiting in line to come aboard. Don't worry. They will all look better by tomorrow in different surroundings.)

Upon boarding ships with assigned dinner sittings, go right to the dining room steward and sign up for the late-dinner seating at as large a table as possible. The late seating gives you time to attend cocktail hour each night, and a large table affords you a greater opportunity to meet a variety of other passengers. Even if some of the people at the table turn out to be bores, you should find at least a few that you can relate to. Seating arrangements may be difficult to change after the cruise starts; therefore, it is best to stack your table with as many desirable companions as possible in the very beginning. As mentioned earlier, the trend among ships today is to get away from assigned seating and to allow passengers to dine when they want and with whomever they want. Here again, the maître d' can be helpful in placing you at a table of other singles.

Force yourself (if necessary) to make friends with whomever you meet when you first board ship. This can best be accomplished in the bars, in the public rooms, or just walking around the decks—everyone is touring the ship at this point. Each person you meet will introduce you to someone else whom he or she has met, all of which has a pyramid effect, exposing you to the greatest number of people possible in the shortest period of time. Once you have been introduced to the eligible singles on the ship, you can start to become selective. However, if you start out being selective, you may never meet enough other singles to permit you to make a selection.

Make friends with married couples because they often are the best matchmakers around.

During the cruise, singles tend to gravitate to the many bars, lounges, and discotheques, and therefore these are often the best locations to meet other singles (who are looking to meet other singles).

Don't miss the singles' get-together cocktail party, which is usually held the first or second day at sea. No matter how corny it may seem to attend this event, the singles' party offers a good opportunity to meet the other singles and to make introductions. Having said this, I must admit that more often than not, very few passengers show up for these parties.

During the first few days, try to attend the card tournaments, dancing classes, deck games, religious services, and other organized events. These social gatherings tend to help break the ice and serve to get the passengers together on a more personal basis.

Stay up for the late, late dancing after midnight. By this time, those not so staunch of heart or steadfast of foot will have retired, the field will be narrowed, and whatever is left is all yours!

Avoid pairing off with one person during the first few days unless you have found a good one. If you panic and grab the first available, the others will think you are taken, and you may blow an opportunity to meet all the other singles. On the other hand, if you really have found a good one, hold tight, because you are going to have some stiff competition.

Ladies should not depend too heavily on the crew for companionship. Many are married, some are gay, and 99 percent of the balance aren't very sincere and are interested only in lassoing you and bedding you for the duration of the cruise. This obviously won't do much for your opportunity to meet other interesting passengers.

Fellows, move faster than the crew. Your toughest competition will be the ship's officers and waiters. Although they may not beat out the town idiot ashore, while on ship they appear to be Greek gods. Because they are away from their families for long periods of time, they have become quite adroit at the "quick romance." In fact, acquiring the affections of the more select ladies for the duration of the cruise has become the biggest game in town among the younger officers and members of the crew. However, in recent years this has been forbidden on almost all ships. All is not lost. You have the advantage. You will have the first opportunity to romance the ladies because the crews are usually busy working until the second evening at sea. Stake your claims early. In addition, the ladies will soon realize that the members of the crew are only available at limited times and generally are only interested in one thing. On the other hand, you are available all day and can offer them a little more well-rounded experience.

Pace yourself. Don't wait too long to make your move, or the cruise will be over. On the other hand, the object of your affection may get turned off by someone who is obviously a jerk. On a seven- to ten-day cruise, you can count on the majority of shipboard romances dying midway through the journey. This is because the couples were not well matched and would have broken up after a few dates no matter where they met. Therefore, an attractive candidate who appears to be taken the first day may become very available a little later on.

Don't burn yourself out. Too much sun, food, drink, late hours, and whatever can make you ill and spoil the cruise. You will often stay up until two or three o'clock and still want to get up early because the ship is scheduled to arrive in port later that morning. You will find that a few hours' nap late in the afternoon is revitalizing under such combat conditions.

Those who do find the ultimate mate aboard ship may be interested to know that many of the major cruise lines can arrange weddings when the ship is docked in certain ports, and most of the lines offer special honeymoon packages.

Although the cruising single might not find the same variety of available mates as he or she would at the local singles bar and although the chance for a lasting romance may be slim, the cruise vacation does offer the single an opportunity to spend a fun and even relaxing vacation with plenty of companionship while visiting several interesting and exciting foreign ports. (See chapter 11 for how well each ship rates for singles.)

# Chapter Five

# Cruising with Children

Prior to considering the pros and cons of cruising with children, you must decide whether to take them along on the vacation in the first place. For those of you who embrace the philosophy that a vacation is an opportunity for a second honeymoon—an escape from dishes, housecleaning, commuter trains, and alarm clocks—there exists no argument that could persuade you to embark upon a family sojourn. Certainly, there is no doubt that travel with children requires a degree of sacrifice on the part of the parent.

However, for those of you who feel that vacation time is family time and an opportunity to share some pleasant experiences with your children, consideration of a family cruise should be given top priority on your list of possible holidays.

Although children's requirements and interests vary with age, by and large the preteen crowd is happy swimming, playing, eating hamburgers, and staying up late. Your first reaction may be to take them for a dip in the neighborhood pool, followed by dinner at McDonald's and the late-night horror show. Upon longer reflection, you may conclude that the purpose of traveling with children is not only to show them a good time but also for you to have a good time with them while broadening their intellectual and cultural horizons. Disney World or a family camping trip may prove to be an excellent first endeavor, but the frequent and seasoned traveler will certainly want to move on to more worldly pursuits.

My personal experience would indicate that there is nothing more perfect for a family vacation than a cruise. Where but on a cruise can you find a sufficient variety of delectable foods, entertainment, activities, and events to meet the personal preferences of parent and child alike? Where but on a cruise can your children be royally entertained from morning until night while you just relax?

One of the truly rewarding pluses for a parent is unpacking the luggage only on one occasion while still being able to see a variety of exotic places. Many an adventurous family has been discouraged from taking in several European countries or Caribbean islands because of the hassle of dragging children and baggage from airport to airport and from hotel to hotel. On a cruise, you and the children have the unique opportunity of exploring as many different ports as your time may allow while your hotel floats along with you. On those cruises that offer an air-sea package, you part with your bags upon entering your hometown airport, then do not see them again until they are brought to your private cabin on the ship.

During the day, a cruise offers a great variety of activities for children. In addition to the standard swimming pools, shuffleboard, deck tennis, Ping-Pong, electronic game room, and gymnasium, which are open continuously, many cruise ships provide counselors and a special program for younger children, including scavenger hunts, arts and crafts, disco parties, supervised shore excursions, costume balls, ice cream and pizza socials, and access to high-tech educational games. In fact, several of the lines have programs in which the children are picked up after breakfast, entertained and fed all day, and not returned until after they have had their evening meal. In addition to the specially designed activities, the children will usually wish to participate in many of the adult-oriented events. During a typical day at sea, most cruises offer such activities as first-run movies, games around the pool, dancing classes, exercise groups, golf instruction, bingo, horse racing, and other parlor games. Don't be surprised if your children have a great deal of difficulty making their selections from the bulletin of the next day's activities that is pushed under your door every morning.

Dining on a ship with children is infinitely simpler and vastly more enjoyable than dragging them around from one restaurant to another in hopes of finding a mutually acceptable establishment. Since on many ships you have an assigned table with the same waiter for most of your meals, the waiter will soon learn your children's special needs and be able to efficiently accommodate them. Whether it is a booster chair, chocolate milk, or catsup for the pommes frites, you need only ask once, and it should be there the remainder of the trip. The waiters are there to please you, and they have been trained to service your entire family in grand style. Although your children will certainly want to sample the numerous international and gourmet offerings, it is possible to arrange for them to have hamburgers, steaks, French fries, or similar "American pie" items at every meal. However, you may be in store for a big surprise when your finicky offspring, who at home insists on having his orange juice strained and the last drop of gravy removed from his meat, orders eggplant Parmesan, tournedos Rossini, or crêpes Suzette.

Although most of the major cruise lines now offer open seating and unrestricted dining times in their main dining rooms as an option, when traveling with children, it may be better to opt for the traditional fixed-table seating if it is available. This way you retain the same waiter as well as a set time for dining, as opposed to moving the children from table to table with different passengers each evening. Several cruise lines have special times for family dining, and others provide options for the children to dine with counselors on formal or other special evenings. Most ships also offer casual evening dining in the buffet restaurant. Thus, parents can feed their offspring early if they wish to dine alone later.

There is usually no babysitting problem on a ship. During the day and early evening, most ships provide counselors and/or a children's program. Late in the evening, you may be able to hire one of the cabin attendants to sit with your children for a reasonable price. Some ships provide group babysitting facilities. If your children are not of too tender an age, you may elect to leave them alone in the room. On a ship, you are only moments away from your cabin, and it is convenient to check up on the youngsters frequently without detracting from your own evening. To be safe, it is always advisable to check out the babysitting situation with the cruise line prior to booking your cruise.

In case of an emergency, it is comforting to know that most ships have a hospital, pharmacy, and sailing physician. Contrary to some popularly expressed opinions, ships are as safe a place for children as almost anywhere else. Young children must be cautioned and watched so they do not lean over an open rail or run down wet steps. However, this is certainly no different from preventing them from leaning over an open balcony in a hotel or running around a slippery pool.

It is unlikely that children will be bored. Even before they have an opportunity to search out the many corners of the ship, they will find themselves in port. On most cruises, you will be visiting a different place during a majority of the days afloat. This affords the children an opportunity to stretch their legs and partake in the same activities they would have pursued had you flown to the port rather than sailed. Most ships give lectures and provide you with magazines describing the places of interest in each port prior to your arrival. Thus, there exists ample time and facility to carefully plan your tour of the port so as to include items of interest to the children.

This should not suggest that you must give up your own sightseeing or shopping plans. It is entirely possible in the popular port of St. Thomas to divide your day between shopping for bargains in the wide selection of international stores and then having a leisurely lunch and swim at one of the seaside hotels or magnificent white-sand beaches. Should your ship dock at Montego Bay, your family could raft down an authentic tropical jungle river; climb from the sea up a natural waterfall; ride donkeys through a lush plantation; swim at a clear, palm-laden beach; and take in a native limbo show, all within six to eight hours.

Although almost every cruise will offer most of the activities and programs described above, the best ships for children are probably the larger vessels (over 50,000 tons), because they usually have more facilities, more extensive programs, and more space to move around. The Carnival, Celebrity, Cunard, Disney, Norwegian, Princess, and Royal Caribbean cruise lines have excellent facilities for preschool children. The two 83,000-ton, 2,400-passenger Disney ships that debuted in 1998 and 1999, the *Disney Magic* and *Disney Wonder*, are totally geared and designed for families cruising with youngsters. The 140,000-plus-ton ships of Royal Caribbean, the *Grand Princess*-class ships of Princess, the post-2000 ships of Norwegian, and the 100-plus-ton ships of Carnival offer an amazing assortment of activities and facilities that will appeal to teens and preteens alike. Ships of most of the lines have special programs for children during the summer and on holiday cruises. Most of the larger ships also offer special events for teenagers. When selecting an itinerary, you may be well advised to concentrate on the shorter cruises (three to seven days) that travel in calm sunny climes and avoid cruises where the waters could be choppy and the weather inclement. Those Caribbean cruises embarking from U.S. ports and Caribbean islands may be an ideal first venture.

If your children are seven years or older, I would especially recommend taking them on a Mediterranean cruise that visits such historic civilizations as Italy, Turkey, Greece, Spain, France, Egypt, or Israel, or on a Northern European cruise that may dock at such cities as Southampton (Port of London), Le Havre (Port of Paris), Amsterdam, Hamburg, Copenhagen, Oslo, Stockholm, Helsinki, and St. Petersburg. Such Mediterranean and Northern European cruises are marvelous, painless ways to expand your children's education and exposure to foreign lands and cultures. An adult might prefer visiting a different country each year in order to slowly assimilate the culture rather than barnstorming many countries at one time. However, for a child, it is easier to comprehend, remember, and compare the differences when viewed in close proximity—an experience more akin to reading about different countries in a textbook at school.

Probably the greatest argument for cruising with children is the moderate cost. Almost every ship's schedule of fares provides that a child under a certain age (generally twelve) sharing a room with two adults need pay only half or less of the minimum fare (the fare charged for the least expensive accommodations aboard). Thus, on a cruise where the fares range from $1,000 to $2,000 per person, it is possible to book a minimum quad (a room accommodating four persons) and pay $1,000 for each adult and $500 for each child. Travelers who desire more sumptuous accommodations can take a room at the more expensive rate and still only pay $500 for any child who may share that room. Should the ship not be completely filled, you may be able to obtain two adjoining double rooms for the same price as sharing a minimum quad. In any event, it never hurts to check with the chief purser or hotel manager upon getting on the ship to see if such an arrangement is available.

The following cruise lines advertise special programs for young children, preteens, and teens: Carnival Cruise Lines, Celebrity Cruises, Costa Cruise Lines, Crystal Cruises, Cunard Line, Disney Cruise Line, Holland America Line, Norwegian Cruise Line, Princess Cruises (on most ships), and Royal Caribbean International. All of these lines have special children's facilities, children's menus, reduced rates in a shared cabin, cribs for the cabins, and children's counselors with special programs. Some of them provide private babysitters in the evenings.

I recently compared the programs for tots and teens on the industry's largest vessels. I found that Disney was the most oriented to programs and events for children under twelve years of age, including live Disney musicals, highly supervised programs, and numerous visits and photo ops with the major Disney characters. The 142,000-plus-GRT ships of Royal Caribbean, the *Grand*-class ships of Princess, and the ships of Carnival boast the most expanded and impressive facilities for young children, teens, and adults alike. Their organized children's programs easily rival those of Disney, and their facilities may be preferred by teens, especially older teens. The ships of these three cruise lines have equal appeal to adults traveling without children, offering them a more varied cruise experience. The newest ships of Norwegian also have very impressive facilities for children and teens.

Of course, every parent knows his or her own children and whether or not they would adjust to the cruise vacation. However, many a parent has been pleasantly surprised at how well behaved and well adjusted his or her children have been on a cruise as compared to their normal behavior at home. Parents often fail to give their children sufficient credit for acquiring maturity. On a cruise, a child for the first time may experience such hedonistic delights as being pampered and waited upon by foreign strangers, tasting the finest culinary creations offered anywhere in the world, witnessing the breathtaking beauty of exotic ports, being lavishly entertained from morning 'til night, and last, but not least, being treated like an adult. Children will more often than not rise to the occasion. Who wouldn't? (See the charts below and chapter 11 for how well each ship rates for children.)

The following chart summarizes the special facilities, activities, and other features you will want to consider when comparing "children-friendly ships." Only the larger cruise lines that promote family cruising are included.

### CODE TO CHART

Overall rating of ship for cruising families:
5—Excellent
4—Very Good
3—Good
2—Fair
1—Poor

A. Youth counselors and supervised activities
B. Supervised playrooms with age-appropriate equipment and facilities
C. Designated teen facilities and programs
D. Children's menus in dining rooms
E. Special lower fares for children sharing a stateroom with two adults
F. Evenings when children can dine with youth counselors
G. Group babysitting facilities in the evenings
H. Private babysitting available in cabins
I. Special children's pool or wading pool
J. Children's outside playground
K. Video arcade
L. Basketball court
M. Miniature golf
N. Hamburger, hot dog, and pizza facilities
O. Special program and/or facilities for children on cruise line's private island visits

## CRUISE LINES

Carnival Cruise Line: 5+
   A, B, C, D, E (special rates for third and fourth guest in a room), F, G, I, J, K, L (on larger ships), M (on some ships), N, O

Celebrity Cruises: 4
   A, B (five age-groups), C, D, F, G, H, I, K, L, N

Costa Cruise Lines: 4
   A, B, C, D, E (sometimes), F, G (ages three and up), I, J, K, N

Crystal Cruises: 4
   A (10:00 a.m. to noon, 2:00 p.m. to 5:00 p.m., and 7:00 p.m. to 9:00 p.m.), B (three age-groups), C, D, F (on selected evenings), H (rates range from $7.50 to $12.50 per hour based on number of children), I, K, N

Cunard Line: 4+
   A (9:00 a.m. to midnight, except between noon and 2:00 p.m. and 5:00 p.m. and 6:00 p.m.), B (ages one through seven), D, E (special fares for third and fourth person in cabin), F, G, I, J, N

Disney Cruise Line: 5+
   A (9:00 a.m. to midnight), B (six different age-groups), C, D, E, F, G (infant to three years), I, K, L, N, O

Holland America Line: 4+ (all ships except *Prinsendam*)
   A (8:00 a.m. to noon, 1:00 p.m. to 5:00 p.m., and 8:00 p.m. to 10:00 p.m.), B, C, D, E, G (ages three and older from 10:00 p.m. to midnight at $5 per hour), H, I (on *Statendam*-class ships only), K, L, N, O

MSC Cruises: 4 (post-2000 ships only: *Armonia*, *Sinfonia*, *Musica*, *Opera*, and *Lirica*)
   A, B, D, E (in Caribbean), H, I, J, and L (except on *Opera*), K, M, N

Norwegian Cruise Line: 5 (post-2000 ships)
   A (sea days 9:00 a.m. to noon, 2:00 p.m. to 5:00 p.m., and 7:00 p.m. to 10:00 p.m.), B, C, D, E (special fares for third and fourth person in cabin), F (one time per cruise), G, I, K, L, N

P&O Cruises: 4 (*Oceana*, *Aurora*, and *Oriana*)
   A, B, D (special children's sitting at 5:15 p.m.), E, F, G (six months to five years), I, J, K, L, N

Princess Cruises: 5+ (all ships except *Pacific Princess* and *Tahitian Princess*)

A, B (three age-groups), C, D, E (reduced fares for third and fourth person in cabin), F, G (for children ages three to twelve from 10:00 p.m. to 1:00 a.m. at $5 per hour), I, J, K, L, M (on *Grand*-class ships), N, O

Royal Caribbean International: 5+

A, B (five age-groups), C, D, E (special rates for third and fourth person in cabin), F (several nights during cruise), G (10:00 p.m. to 1:00 a.m. for $5 an hour for those over three and toilet trained), H (for $8 per hour), I, J, L, M (on most ships), K, N

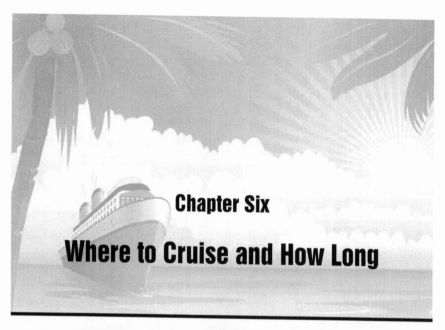

# Chapter Six

# Where to Cruise and How Long

## Cruise Grounds, Ports of Call, Points of Interest, and What to Do with Limited Hours in Port

### Cruise Grounds

The possibilities for places to cruise are as infinite as the coastal cities found on a map of the world. Today it is feasible to sail about almost anywhere in the seven seas, provided you are endowed with the time, finances, and inclination.

You can board ship at Fort Lauderdale or Miami and sail to Bermuda, the Bahamas, or to any of the tropical islands in the Caribbean. A growing number of vessels provide embarkations for such Caribbean cruises from Palm Beach, Tampa, Port Canaveral, New Orleans, Texas, New York, Baltimore, Philadelphia, Galveston, cities along the eastern seaboard, and even Puerto Rico, while others include stops in Central and South America.

Should you live near the West Coast, there are numerous cruises leaving from Los Angeles, San Diego, and San Francisco sailing to Mexico, Central America, South America, Hawaii, Alaska, the South Sea Islands, Australia, and the Orient.

If you are traveling in Europe, you can board ship in England, France, Holland, Copenhagen, Sweden, or Germany for cruises traversing the fjords of Norway or visiting ports in the Baltics, Northern Europe, and even Russia. Perhaps you would prefer a ship leaving Cannes, Monte Carlo, Athens, Venice, Naples, or Genoa, visiting Southern Spain, Northern Africa, Sicily, the Greek islands, the Turkish Coast, or the Middle East. Dozens of ships based in Piraeus (Port of Athens) offer regular cruises to the myriad of lovely Greek islands as well as to ports in Turkey, Israel, Egypt, and on the Black Sea, and to other Middle Eastern coastal cities. During the spring and summer months, numerous riverboats and barges cruise down the rivers and waterways of France, as well as down the Elbe, Havel, Main, Rhine, and Moselle rivers in Germany, the Danube in Austria and Hungary, the Nile in Egypt, and the waterways of England and Holland.

Several vessels offer "around the world" cruises extending from forty to ninety days and calling at sample ports in Europe, Africa, Asia, Australia, South America, and various islands along the way. If you do not have time for such a long vacation, it is possible on some of these ships to board and disembark at certain points midway into the cruise. It would be somewhat beyond the scope of this book to cover every conceivable port and every possible itinerary. However, the following sections on "Ports of Call" describe almost all of the popular stops in the more widely traversed cruise areas. The description of each port is not intended to be exhaustive but is designed to suggest points of interest, scenic places to visit, shopping, beaches, and restaurants for passengers of cruise ships who have from six to twelve hours to spend in port. Current itineraries for the various ships can be found in *Official Steamship Guide International.*

## Ports of Call

*The United States, Bermuda, the Bahamas, and the Caribbean*
*South America*
*The Mediterranean, Greek Islands, Middle East, and Environs*
*Northern Europe, the Baltics, the North Sea, the Fjords, and the Rivers of Europe*
*Cruises from the United States' West Coast, Mexico, the South Seas, Hawaii, and the Far East*
*East Africa and the Indian Ocean*
*Transatlantic Crossings*

*Note*: In the following descriptions of ports of call, there are numerous references to specific restaurants and hotels. It is best to make advance reservations before visiting any of these establishments since some do not welcome cruise-ship passengers, and others may have changed ownership or ceased to operate subsequent to this printing.

# The United States, Bermuda, the Bahamas, and the Caribbean

*The Caribbean*

*Caribbean beach, courtesy Little Dix Bay*

The lush blue Caribbean is one of the most desirable areas for the cruise vacation because the waters are calm and the variety of islands is endless. Until the 1970s, the major cruise ships embarked from New York, resulting in several days at the beginning and end of each cruise being spent in the rougher waters of the Atlantic. During the late fall, winter, and early spring, the weather in the Atlantic is often inclement and the ocean is choppy, making it impossible for you to sit out on deck until your ship is well past Cape Hatteras.

Today, most ships positioned in the United States depart from Port Everglades (Port of Fort Lauderdale), Dodge Island (Port of Miami), Tampa, Port Canaveral (Port of Orlando), New Orleans, Palm Beach, or Puerto Rico. However, several of the larger cruise lines are now initiating cruises from numerous other U.S. cities accessible by waterways to the ocean, including Baltimore, Philadelphia, New York, Galveston, Jacksonville, and other ports along the eastern seaboard. Cruises embarking from the southern U.S. ports offer the traveler instant sun and the time to visit a greater number of islands because the traveling distance has been reduced. Some of the seven-day cruises from these southern ports make as many as six stops, and the fourteen-day cruises may call on five to twelve different ports.

The islands in the Caribbean area are varied, each with its own individual flavor. The natives of Bermuda, Barbados, Grenada, Jamaica, and the Bahamas still speak with a British accent. French is the official language of Haiti, Martinique, Guadeloupe, St. Barts, and part of St. Martin. The little towns and brightly painted buildings in Aruba, Bonaire, Curaçao, and the other part of Saint Maarten (St. Martin) are reminiscent of Holland, as are the language and restaurants. Spanish is the native tongue in Puerto Rico, Santo Domingo, and Caracas. Although the United States bought St. Thomas, St. John, and St. Croix (the U.S. Virgin Islands) from Denmark in 1917, the Danes left their mark. Some of the streets still bear names similar to the streets of Copenhagen, and Danish *smörbrod* and beer can still be purchased in a few local restaurants.

Which islands you will enjoy most depends upon your personal tastes and interests. Many of the ships make a point of stopping at least at one island where there is gambling, one island where there is shopping, and one where there is swimming. Most of the islands offer duty-free shopping bargains of one kind or another, and most have beautiful beaches. Rather than running off to a public beach with limited facilities, consider going to a large hotel or resort where you can make a quick change and enjoy the comforts of the hotel's beach, pool, restaurants, and other facilities.

Several of the major cruise lines that deploy numerous ships in the Caribbean own or lease private islands (or parts of islands), offering passengers a one-day beach party. A typical private island will have beach chairs and umbrellas, bathroom facilities, several bars, a dining area or pavilion, a straw market, a boutique, a calypso band, various land and water sport facilities, and hiking paths. Costa Cruises' island, Serena Cay, is located in the Dominican Republic. Disney Cruises' one-thousand-acre island, Castaway Cay, lies in the Abaco chain of the Bahamas. Holland America Line's 2,400-acre Half Moon Cay rests southeast of Nassau in the Bahamas. Norwegian's Great Stirrup Cay sits in the Bahama-Berry Islands chain. Princess Cruises' Princess Cay is a forty-acre peninsula on the southern tip of Eleuthera in the Bahamas. MSC's Cayo Levantado is located in the Dominican Public. Royal Caribbean International boasts two private island beaches: Labadee, a 260-acre peninsula on the northern coast of Haiti, and Coco Cay, a 140-acre island in the Bahamas.

The following are the highlights of some of the more popular ports in this area:

## ANGUILLA

The most northerly of the Leeward Islands in the eastern Caribbean lies five miles north of St. Martin. Once a part of a federation with St. Kitts and Nevis, Anguilla gained its independence from that association in 1980 and has since been a self-governed British possession. Only sixteen miles in length, the island is easily traversed by rental car or taxi.

Anguilla boasts some of the finest resorts in the Caribbean. Malliouhana at Meads Bay is perhaps the most perfect property in the Caribbean, and a marvelous place to spend your day. The beach is among the best on the island. The children's aquatic playground and the state-of-the-art spa/fitness center are extremely impressive. The incredibly charming indoor/outdoor restaurant perched on a cliff overlooking the sea is not only romantic but features the imaginative French cuisine of the Rostang family. Whether you opt for lunch or dinner, it is one of those uniquely perfect dining experiences that we constantly seek but rarely find.

Cap Juluca at Maundays Bay is a unique Moorish-style retreat spread along a lovely strand of white-sand beach, featuring Pimms (an outstanding restaurant) and a new fitness/spa facility. CuisinArt, with its Mediterranean-influenced architecture, is yet another outstanding beachfront resort. If time permits, you will want to visit at least one of these fabulous properties.

The best public beaches are at Shoal Bay and Sandy Ground, where there are some colorful restaurants and small shops. A top choice for a day trip would be a snorkeling expedition to either Sandy Island or Little Cay Bay. Sandy Island, accessible by ferry or motorboat from Sandy Ground, is a tiny islet with a few palm trees, surrounded by powder-fine sand and good reefs for snorkeling. The open-air restaurant features barbecued ribs, chicken, and lobster, accompanied by cold beer or rum punch. Little Cay Bay is a picturesque secluded cove accessible only by boat. Island Harbour Restaurant at Scilly Cay is a good choice on the beach. Here you will find a tiny white-sand beach with turquoise, azure, and verdant green waters—a romantic spot for a private picnic, with good snorkeling possibilities.

## ANTIGUA

Antigua is a 108-square-mile Caribbean island located about midway between Martinique and St. Thomas and noted most for its numerous white-sand beaches. The travel brochures tout this "Island Paradise" as having 365 beaches—one for each day of the year. The climate is mild, with temperatures varying between the midseventies and mideighties.

Your ship will dock at Heritage Quay or at Deep Water Harbor near **St. Johns**, the capital. A small shopping center is located near both piers, with several shops featuring local handicrafts, souvenirs, T-shirts, and a few imported items. Points of interest include English Harbour and Nelson's Dockyard (an eighteenth-century naval base), St. John's Cathedral, Clarence House, Fig Tree Hill Drive, Devil's Bridge, and Fort Berkeley. There is an eighteen-hole golf course at Cedar Valley, and nine-hole courses at Antigua Beach Hotel and Half Moon Bay. Casinos are located at the St. James's Club, the Royal Antigua Hotel in Dickenson Bay, Halcyon Cove Beach Resort at Dickenson Bay, King's Casino in St. John, and at the Heritage Quay. The most upscale resorts are Curtain Bluff, Jumby Bay, and Galley Bay. The most popular restaurants on the island include Admiral's Inn (seafood), Chez Pascal (French), Coconut Grove at Dickenson Bay, Le Bistro (French and seafood), Lobster Pot (Caribbean dishes and seafood), and Alberto's (Italian).

With only six to ten hours in port, I would recommend spending your day at the St. James's Club, Hawksbill Beach Hotel, or at the Rex Halcyon Cove Beach Resort. To visit Curtain Bluff or Jumby Bay, you would need to make advance arrangements. These resorts are located on lovely strands of white-sand beach with warm, clear waters.

They feature adequate swimming pools, numerous shops, water sports (water-skiing, snorkeling, scuba, and sailing), decent tennis courts, a casino, and picturesque restaurants. The best public beaches are at Pigeon Point, Dickenson Bay, Carlisle Bay, Hawksbill, and Half Moon Bay.

## THE BAHAMAS

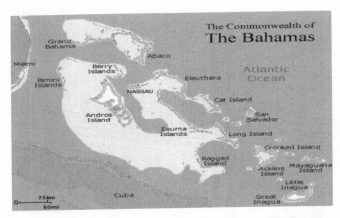

*Atlantis, Paradise Island, Nassau*

The Bahamas consist of a stretch of hundreds of islands extending off the coast of Florida down to Haiti. Cruise ships generally stop at **Nassau** or **Freeport**, **Grand Bahama**, which are the most populous and developed of the Bahamian islands.

Several of the cruise lines have purchased and developed pristine "out-islands" in the Bahamas, where their ships stop for a beach party and snorkeling.

Although the Bahamas have gained complete independence from the motherland, you are constantly reminded of the British influence. In Nassau, you can shop in the native straw market adjacent to the docks at Rawson Square, sample some Bahamian conch chowder at a quaint seaside restaurant, take a horse-and-buggy ride through the streets of town, play tennis at any of the large hotels, swim in the absolutely still, clear waters of the beautiful beaches of **Paradise Island,** or visit the casino and elegant restaurants.

A short excursion to Coral World on Coral Island is worthwhile. Here you can view sea life and fish indigenous to this part of the world, including sharks, stingrays, and giant turtles. Also located here are an open-air restaurant and a snorkeling trail.

Many passengers enjoy spending their day exploring Paradise Island, which is accessible for a $3 charge by motor launches that depart right at the pier between the cruise ships and town. **Until the '90s,** this was a beautiful, pristine island where visitors could walk along miles of white-sand beach and paths running through pine forests past azure lagoons. Unfortunately, the group owning the Atlantis Hotel Complex purchased the majority of the island, knocked down most of the forests, eliminated the lagoons, and constructed glitzy megahotels. The Atlantis is an awesome resort with a myriad of pools, beaches, shops, restaurants, bars, a humongous casino, aquariums, sea-life ponds, and just about everything else you could imagine. It is truly an adult Disney World. The golf course remains on the far side of the island, near the Ocean Club, a more intimate and upscale property. The beaches at Cable Beach Hotel and the Radisson on Nassau are also excellent for sunning, swimming, and water sports and are accessible by a ten-minute bus ride.

When shopping at Grand Bahama, you will not want to miss the variety of imported merchandise in the colorful international bazaar, where you can stroll down cobbled streets into shops with imports from Scandinavia, Great Britain, Hong Kong, Japan, India, Spain, and France. You also will want to taste some delectable conch fritters and sausages with ale at one of the atmospheric British pubs, try your luck at El Casino adjoining the bazaar, or swim at one of the white-sand beaches in the fashionable Lucaya area.

## BARBADOS

Barbados is twenty-one miles long and fourteen miles wide, with 260,000 inhabitants who are independent members of the British Commonwealth. They enjoy a dry, sunny climate with temperatures varying from seventy to eighty degrees. The island's British heritage is most evident in the capital, **Bridgetown**, with its quaint houses and its statue of Lord Nelson in Trafalgar Square. Taste the local rum that is reputed to be the best in the world; shop at the Terminal at Bridgeport Harbor or in the Broad Street area for duty-free British woolens, Irish linens, English bone china, French perfumes, Japanese cameras, local black-coral jewelry, and Swiss watches; browse through the local arts and crafts offered for sale at Pelican Village off the Princess Alice Highway; see sugar refined at a local factory; or play tennis, sunbathe, and swim in crystal clear waters on one of the long stretches of fine-sand beach or at one of the large luxury hotels— such as the Sandy Lane, Glitter Bay, Royal Pavilion, the House, and the Coral Reef Club, all of which are located on the west coast, where the waters are extremely calm. There are tennis courts, a golf course, and a beautiful beach at the recently renovated Sandy Lane, one of the Caribbean's most luxurious properties, with a world-class spa; however, the hotel is not hospitable to cruise passengers, and arrangements have to be made in advance to enter this and most other hotels. Hotels on the Atlantic east coast enjoy panoramic vistas; however, the sea is frequently not safe for swimming. Public beaches frequented by cruise passengers include Carlisle Bay Beach, which has changing facilities, and the beach adjacent to Sandy Beach Island Resort. Several cruise lines offer pre- and postcruise options at Accra Beach Hotel, which is located on a nice beach and has good facilities. All of the resorts offer a variety of dining opportunities. The most popular local restaurants outside the resorts include Bagutelle Great House (Continental), Carambola (Thai and Continental), Sandy Bay (Continental), Ile de France (French), Pisces (seafood), Josef's (Scandinavian), Daphne's at the House (hotel), and Fish Pot (seafood). One of the best restaurants on the island, Luna Café, is located atop the Little Arches Hotel. Dining under the stars on the Castilian-style terrace is an extremely romantic experience. Food and service are right up there with the atmosphere.

Other points of interests include the Barbados Museum; the Flower Forest, an eight-acre floral park; Harrison's Cave, which you tour by electric tram; Barbados Wildlife Reserve; and the oldest synagogue in the Western Hemisphere, dating back to 1654.

## BERMUDA

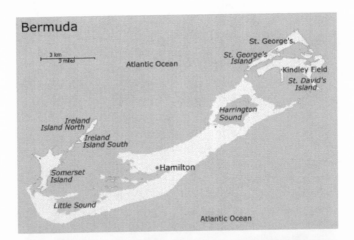

*Bermuda beach*

Bermuda is a self-governing member of the British Commonwealth. It covers twenty-one square miles and has an English-speaking population of fifty-five thousand. The people are very British, and the island boasts a mild climate, with lovely scenery, pastel houses, and coral-pink beaches. Temperatures vary from fifty-eight to seventy-six degrees from November through April and from sixty-five to eighty-six degrees from May through October. If your ship docks at Hamilton Harbor, you can look for bargains in friendly shops along Front Street, which feature English bone china and woolens, French perfumes, Danish silver, and Swiss watches. You can also visit the botanical gardens, government house, historical society museum, and the completely restored nineteenth-century fortification at Fort St. Catherine; explore the Crystal Cave, a natural cavern that ranks as Bermuda's most beautiful attraction; visit Fort Hamilton, a nineteenth-century fortress with great views of the city and harbor, and the nearby Bermuda Underwater Exploration Institute; play tennis or golf at one of the island's luxury hotels; rent a motorcycle and take a ride across the island; or just swim in the calm blue waters of a quiet cove along a soft, pink-sand beach. There are some excellent tennis courts at the Southampton Princess and the Sonesta Beach hotels. To the left of the Southampton Princess Hotel is one of the most beautiful stretches of pink-sand beach, inlets, and coves to be found anywhere in the world. You may wish to have your waiter on the ship pack a box lunch with a bottle of wine so you can picnic on this lovely public beach. The Southampton Princess also offers numerous gourmet restaurants, as well as those specializing in seafood and steaks.

Many of the larger ships dock at the Royal Naval Dockyard. This is a sprawling compound of stone fortifications offering restaurants, shops, attractions, the Bermuda Maritime Museum, and the Dolphin Quest Experience for in-the-water encounters with dolphins.

If your ship docks at **St. George,** an old English village with pastel cottages, you can visit St. Peter's Church, the Western Hemisphere's first Anglican place of worship. You will find numerous souvenir shops and boutiques right at the harbor. The most interesting and accessible beach is at Tobacco Bay. The mile-and-a-half path that runs along the harbor and ocean between the dock and Tobacco Bay past Fort St. Catherine is scenic and worth exploring.

## THE CAYMAN ISLANDS

The Cayman Islands, peaceful little islands lying a hundred miles northwest of Jamaica, have a colorful history dating to their discovery by Columbus on his fourth voyage to the West Indies. They are now a crown colony of the United Kingdom, and their favorable tax policy makes these islands one of the world's most attractive tax havens. Several cruise ships tender to **Georgetown** on Grand Cayman to permit their passengers to enjoy a day exploring one of the most beautiful stretches of white-sand beach in the Caribbean. Although **Grand Cayman** is only twenty-two miles long and eight miles across, it boasts a seven-mile strand of beach lined with pines, palms, and small cottage-like hotel complexes. You can spend your day swimming and snorkeling in the crystal clear waters; visiting a turtle farm, where turtles are bred and raised; playing with stingrays at Stingray City (available by motor launch); golfing at the Britannia or Safe Haven courses; or browsing through the duty-free shops in Georgetown in search of bargains in china and crystal imported from all over Europe, Swiss watches, black-coral jewelry, and French perfumes.

Should you be docking in the evening, you can dine at Chef Tell's Grand Old House on a broad veranda and watch the sun set over the beautiful blue waters of the Caribbean while enjoying some of the best food on the island. Hemingway's at the Hyatt Regency; Lantanas at the Caribbean Club; Pappagallo, an Italian and seafood restaurant set in a bird sanctuary overlooking a lagoon; and Ottmars are also excellent. The Ritz-Carlton, Hyatt, Westin, and Radisson are the largest hotels on the island, and each offers tennis courts, a swimming pool, and beaches with full facilities. Those who wish to scuba or snorkel can make arrangements in Georgetown or at any of the larger hotels.

## COSTA RICA

Cruise ships traversing the Panama Canal often stop at Central America's most developed democratic republic, which is bordered by Nicaragua to the north and Panama to the south. The beauty of the country is its varied scenery, which includes lush green mountains and valleys, volcanoes, ranches, farmland, rolling hills, lovely streams and waterfalls, jungles, and beaches.

In the center of the country, surrounded by mountains, sits **San Jose**, the capital, where tourists may wish to visit the many parks, the lavish Teatro National (an architectural jewel built in the nineteenth century that presently offers concerts, ballet, opera, and theater), the National Museum with its archeological and historical artifacts, the Museum of Contemporary Art, the Museo de Oro with its displays of all kinds of gold, the Jade Museum, and the president's home.

Ships call at either the Atlantic port of Limon or the nearby Pacific ports of Caldera and Puntarenas. On the Atlantic side, the best beaches are at the National Park of Cahuita; on the Pacific, they are on Nicaya Peninsula. From Puntarenas, ferries traverse the gulf of Nicaya to Tambor and Paquera; however, timetables for returns can be unreliable, and anyone wishing to visit this area is advised to be certain about the timing of their return. From Tambor or Paquera, you can take a taxi to the beaches and hotels at Playa Tambor, Playa Montezuma, and Cabo Blanco.

Cruise ships generally offer excursions to San Jose, Sarachi (the handicraft town where you can purchase the famous Costa Rican hand-painted oxcarts as well as wineglasses and decanters), and the rain forest at Carrara Biological Reserve, and the opportunity to enjoy horseback rides through tropical valleys and forests, river rafting, aerial tram rides, canopy tours, ecojungle cruises, and visits to an orchid farm, a macaw sanctuary, the Britt Coffee Plantation, and Poas Volcano National Park. Those venturing out on their own can hire a taxi at the port (maximum four passengers) and for about $150 for three to five hours see the beautiful countryside, visit the Carrara Rain Forest, and explore Jaco, where there is a long stretch of black-sand beach, horseback riding, souvenir shops, and several local restaurants. Unfortunately, some of the more popular resort communities cannot be accessed during a one-day visit.

## DEVIL'S ISLAND

Lying nine miles off the coast of Guyana are three small islands that were known as the Devil's Islands until 1753, when they were renamed the Salut Islands (islands of salvation).

The largest is L'ile Royale. St. Joseph to the east is the most beautiful, and Devil's Island to the north is the wildest. These islands were the site of the notorious French penal colony.

Cruise ships send tenders to **L'ile Royale**, where there is a small rustic inn offering limited shopping and cold drinks. Around the island are some of the vestiges of the prison colony, including the prison cells, a chapel, death row cells, warden's accommodations, a hospital, a morgue, and a children's cemetery.

L'ile Royale receives a lot of rain and as a result is very lush and verdant. There are numerous paths around the island, rewarding visitors with magnificent views of palms, rocky ocean coastlines, and the two neighboring islands. It is possible to walk or jog around the island. A protected sea area known as the Prisoner's Pool is located directly across the island from the dock. However, the waters in the vicinity are infested with sharks, and I do not know how safe it would be to swim here.

## DOMINICA

Dominica is a 291-square-mile mountainous island with lush vegetation, dense rain forests, and over 350 waterfalls. Ships dock at the capital city of Roseau, where there are souvenir shops, a local market, and small restaurants and hotels. It is one of the least-developed islands in the Caribbean, and there are no good beaches. Swimming is possible in rivers under waterfalls. Hiking and mountain climbing are the most popular pastimes. A favorite excursion offered by all cruise ships is a panoramic ride in the rain forest aerial gondolas, along with a short hike through the forest over a suspension bridge. Tour guides narrate the excursion, pointing out hundreds of varieties of exotic vegetation. Within twenty minutes from town is Trafalgar Falls. Even closer is the Botanic Gardens, with a trail up Morne Bruce, affording a panoramic view of the island. Kayak and snorkel tours are often available.

## THE DOMINICAN REPUBLIC

The Dominican Republic shares the island of Hispaniola with Haiti. Although this Spanish-speaking island boasts some majestic mountains and jungle rivers, your ship will probably not dock for a sufficient time to permit you to explore the island. If the ship docks at **Santo Domingo**, you may wish to visit such historical landmarks as Alcazar de Colon (the restored sixteenth-century palace built for Columbus's son Diego) and the four-hundred-year-old Cathedral Santa Maria La Menor. The National Museum of the Dominican Republic offers some interesting Indian artifacts, while the National Museum of Fine Arts features the work of more recent painters and sculptors. The 445-acre Botanical Gardens at Arroyo Hondo are the largest in all of Latin America and can be toured on foot, by horse carriage, or by boat. The best buys are in amber, which is mined and crafted on the island. You can swim at the pool, play tennis, and gamble at El Embajador Hotel, Jaragua Renaissance, Intercontinental, or the Sheraton. If time permits, drive out to the Caribbean's largest full-facility resort, Casa De Campo at La Romana, where there are three challenging golf courses, thirteen tennis courts, a riding stable, water sports, a picturesque Romanesque-designed artist's village with shops and restaurants, a shooting range, numerous restaurants, and a beautiful beach. Ships of Costa Cruises currently offer beach parties on a private island, with optional excursions to Casa De Campo.

Some ships anchor near Samana and Cayo Levantado Island on the northeast shores of the Dominican Republic. At Samana City and the town of Terrenas, there are small shops and restaurants. Whale watching and scuba diving are the main attractions. Visits to El Limon Waterfall and the rain forest at Los Haitises National Park are also worthwhile. There are nice beaches for swimming at Las Terrenas, El Portillo, and Playa Popy. However, most cruise ships tender passengers to the picturesque island of Cayo Levantado in Samana Bay. Here there is a large beach with white powdery sand lapped by turquoise waters. Many lounging chairs are spread out on the beach, and surrounding the beach are small bars, outdoor barbeque restaurants, and native shops. One can spend an ideal beach day here.

In **Puerto Plata** there is little to do other than shop for amber in the local market, but if you feel adventurous, rent a horse at the dock and ride through the countryside to the beach. Several new hotels have been built at Playa Dorado, the site of a Robert Trent Jones-designed golf course. Properties with the most facilities include Jack Tar Village, Caribbean Village Club on the Green, and Plaza Dorado Hotel and Casino. The best beach is located fifteen miles east of town at Sosua.

## THE DUTCH ISLANDS (ABC ISLANDS)

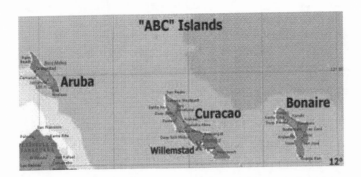

The Dutch Islands of Aruba, Bonaire, and Curaçao (also referred to as the ABC Islands) represent the Netherlands in miniature, with gabled, pastel-colored buildings along picturesque streets. Dutch is the official language, although employees in the shops, hotels, and restaurants all speak English. The climate is sunny and dry, cooled by pleasant trade winds with temperatures ranging from a mean of eighty degrees in the winter to eighty-four degrees in the summer.

In **Curaçao**, you will find a fair selection of merchandise in a number of shops offering bargains in jewelry, watches, china, perfumes, and antiques. T-shirts and souvenir items are particularly attractive and inexpensive. Willemstad is no longer the shopping haven it used to be. You can see the world-famous floating pontoon bridge in Willemstad swing open to allow ships into the harbor. Or from atop the thirty-three-foot-thick fortress walls, you can watch the ships sail into the harbor. However, most cruise ships now dock at the new terminal and no longer pass through the bridge. One of the oldest synagogues in the Western world still in use, the Mikve Israel Emanuel Synagogue, is right in town; and on the outskirts of town you can visit the Jewish cemetery, which is one of the oldest Caucasian burial places in the New World. You can sample Curaçao liqueur at the distillery where it is made in Chobolobo; eat *rijsttafel* (rice with forty or more exotic complements) at Doeloe or the Rijsttafel Indonesia Restaurant (located outside of town); or you can try *kapucijners* (meat, chick peas, beans, bacon, onions, and sauces) at the historic Fort Nassau Restaurant, a renovated military fort on a hill overlooking the city. Try the French and Swiss cuisine at Bistro le Clochard, a quaint indoor/outdoor restaurant located in the small shopping center between the pier terminal and the pontoon bridge. Astrolab at the Kura Hulanda Hotel is the place for seafood. For tennis or swimming, your best bets are Marriott Beach Hotel and Casino, Hilton Beach Hotel and Casino, or Avila Beach Hotel. The Hyatt Regency Curacao opened in 2008, and a giant Renaissance Complex is under construction in town. Baoase is a hip resort with Balinese-style rooms and a Zen spa. Other attractions include the Christoffel National Park, Curaçao Seaquarium, Curaçao's Ostrich Farm, Curaçao Underwater Marine Park, and Hato Caves. The best public beaches are Kon Tiki (near the Seaquarium), Blue Bay, and Barbara Beach.

**Bonaire** boasts eighteen miles of reef that surround the island, offering some of the most spectacular scuba diving, spearfishing, and underwater photography in the Caribbean. At many of the larger hotels, arrangements can be made for these activities, as well as for swimming, water-skiing, sailing, and glass-bottom boat rides. Harbour Village Beach club has a nice beach. The beaches here are not particularly attractive, and cruise passengers may be better off opting for one of the snorkeling, diving, or sailing excursions offered by the cruise lines. This is also the island of the flamingos, and in the late afternoon, bird watchers can see these graceful birds as well as thousands of herons, snipe, pelicans, parrots, parakeets, and others making their way across the blue Caribbean skies. Mona Lisa Bar and Restaurant offers French and local cuisine.

**Aruba's** capital is Oranjestad, where you can see many traditional multicolored Dutch houses with red-tile roofs, as well as a charming deep-water harbor. Don't miss the strange Divi-Divi tree and the huge monolithic boulder formations at Casibari. Swim at the beautiful wide Palm Beach, which services the Aruba Marriott, Hyatt, Radisson, Westin, Holiday Inn, Bucuti Beach Resort, and numerous other large full-facility hotels, all of which contain casinos and restaurants. For dining, Madame Janette (French and international) is considered the best on the island. Other popular restaurants include Chez Mathilde near the Renaissance Hotel (Continental), Papiamento (Caribbean and seafood), La Dome (French), Flying Fishbone (seafood on the beach), and Chalet Suisse (international, seafood, and steaks). The town is near the harbor and contains numerous shops offering international bargains.

Across from the dock area in the heart of downtown is the Renaissance Hotel, with several restaurants, a large casino, a well-equipped gym, a pool, a shopping arcade, and a picturesque white-sand beach located on a private island with tropical foliage, a bird sanctuary, and a restaurant, accessible by private launch from the hotel lobby.

There are golf courses at the Tierra del Sol Resort and Country Club and at the Aruba Golf Club.

## GRENADA

Grenada, which became an independent nation in 1974, is known as the Spice Island because it is here that cloves, mace, cinnamon, ginger, and nutmeg are produced and shipped throughout the world. The 133-square-mile island has a population of 105,000 and an average year-round temperature of eighty degrees. The capital, **St. George**, is often referred to as the most picturesque harbor in the Caribbean, and you will want to climb up one of its quaint cobblestone streets to get a panoramic view of the magnificent waterfront. You may wish to swim at one of the hotels located on the beautiful Grand Anse Beach, such as Spice Island Inn, Coyaba Beach Resort, and Grenada Renaissance. Or you may prefer to drive to Annandale Falls, the most accessible of the island's waterfalls; Seven Sisters Falls, at a nutmeg plantation; or Concorde Falls to picnic and swim in tropical pools beneath cascading waterfalls. You can visit the nutmeg factories at Gouyave and Grenville and purchase samples of the island's spices at the factory or almost anywhere in town. Although the island and the beaches are lovely, you will be harassed constantly by vendors and beggars to the point of distraction. The highest-touted restaurants are La Dolce Vita, Coconut Beach (on Grand Anse Beach), La Belle Creole, Canboulay, and Spice Island Inn. LaBelle Creole and Canboulay both serve West Indian cuisine, with hillside panoramic views. Spice Island Inn overlooks the beach and sea.

## GUADELOUPE

Guadeloupe is a French department made up of two islands separated by a narrow channel—giving the appearance from the air of being a butterfly. Pointe-à-Pitre is in **Grande-Terre**, which is a flat, developed island with fine beaches. **Basse-Terre** is mountainous, with volcanic peaks, tropical green forests, lush vegetation, mountain streams, and waterfalls. The 327,800 inhabitants speak French and live in a basically warm climate that has a great deal of rain from July to November. You may wish to sample some French or Creole cooking at one of the hotel restaurants or in town, or shop for some of the excellent bargains in French perfumes, linens, and wines.

Good beaches include Anse de la Gourde between St. Francois and Pointe des Chateaux, Caravelle Beach near St. Anne, the beachfront at Gosier, and Le Grand Anse north of Deshaies on Basse-Terre; there are nudist beaches at Place Crawen, Pointe Tarare, Illet du Gosier, and Pointe des Chateaux. However, you will find the most facilities at the beautiful tree-lined, white-sand beach of the Club Med Caravelle Hotel, where you can water-ski, play tennis, and have lunch. You may have to pay to get on the premises. Other large hotels with facilities include La Plantation

Ste-Marthe and Le Meridien at St. Francois and La Creole Beach Hotel, Novotel Bas Du Fort, and Auberge de la Vieille Tour, located on the five-mile beach at Gosier. The highest-rated restaurants on Grand Terre include Auberge de la Vieille Tour, Rosini, La Bananier, La Canne a Sucre, La Louisiane, Les Oiseaux, and Le Chateau de Feuilles. In Pointe-a-Pitre, try Café Jardin and Sacre-Sale.

If you have enough time, you can drive forty miles from Pointe-à-Pitre to Basse-Terre and pass through sugarcane plantations, tropical forests at Guadeloupe's National Park, banana trees, beautiful hibiscus, and the high volcanic peaks of La Soufriére with its waterfalls, lakes, and streams. Crayfish Falls at the National Park is one of the most popular sites on the island.

## HAITI

*Note:* Due to the horrific earthquake in 2010, few cruise ships other than those of Royal Caribbean, whose destination is the private beach at Labadee, are visiting this island. The information below is pre-earthquake.

Haiti is a tropical country occupying the western portion of the island of Hispaniola. French is the official language, but the majority of the inhabitants speak a Creole tongue that is difficult to distinguish.

**Port-au-Prince** is an unusual town with a blend of African and French cultures exhibited in the exquisite native paintings and crafts. You may wish to visit one of the luxury hotels located in the cooler heights of Petionville. Here again, the most facilities will be found at the Club Med; however, you must make advance arrangements to be admitted. You will enjoy tasting some of the French-Creole delicacies as well as the local Barbancourt rum and liqueur. If you have time, you can take a taxi up into the mountains and visit the Barbancourt factory to sample their many different beverages. At night, you can dance at a local club, witness a fairly authentic voodoo ceremony, or gamble at the International Casino on the waterfront.

Several ships dock at **Cap Haitien**, two hundred miles from Port-au-Prince. This picturesque but poor little city once was the richest colonial city in the French empire. Here you can explore the ruins of the Sans Souci Palace and Christophe's Citadelle atop a donkey, or you can browse through the native market. Whether you are in Port-au-Prince or Cap Haitien, the things to buy are native paintings and sculpture. Much of the arts and crafts sold throughout the other Caribbean islands are produced in Haiti.

## ISLES DES SAINTES

Isles des Saintes is composed of a cluster of eight islands off the southern coast of Guadeloupe. Most visitors and cruise ships will stop at Terre-de-Haute, a very scenic island with a panoramic harbor. A short walk across the island from the port will bring you to Plage de Pompierre, a half-moon strand of white sand bordering aqua waters with a backdrop of palms and verdant hills. Anse Crawen is a nudist beach, and Plage du Figuier is the best spot for snorkeling. The best hotel is Les Petits Saints. There are numerous small cafés and boutiques near the disembarkation pier in town.

## JAMAICA

Jamaica is one of the lushest and most beautiful of the Caribbean islands. It is a land of white-sand beaches, still emerald-blue waters, green forests, jungle rivers, and the Blue Mountains. The climate is warm and sunny throughout the year, with little seasonal variation in temperature. Montego Bay, Negril, and Ocho Rios are fashionable resort areas with numerous fine hotels on long stretches of white-sand beach. Unfortunately, because the attitude and aggressive behavior of some of the citizens have turned off prospective visitors, fewer cruise ships have chosen Jamaica as a port of call.

If your ship docks at **Montego Bay**, you can take a short taxi ride to town and browse through the shops displaying the local crafts, jewelry, watches, and foreign imports. You may wish to tour Rosehall or Greenwood Great Houses, visit Croydin Plantation, take a donkey ride, or go for a swim at Doctor's Cave Beach, Walter Fletcher Beach, or Cornwall Beach, where there is an underwater marine park. You may also wish to take the drive to raft down the tropical Martha Brae River or at Mountain Valley from the Lethe Plantation ten miles south of town. Perennially, the best resort hotels here have been Round Hill; Tryall Golf, Tennis, and Beach Club; Half Moon Golf, Tennis, and Beach Club; Ritz-Carlton; and Sandals.

Many cruise ships dock at **Ocho Rios**. Within walking distance of the dock are numerous shops, a public beach, and two semi-high-rise hotels that have changed ownership numerous times over the years and are presently operated as the Grande Renaissance Resort. If you wish to spend the day at one of the better hotels or resorts—such as San Souci Lido, Plantation Inn, Jamaica Inn, Ciboney, Sandals Dunn's River, Boscobel Beach, or Couples—you must make arrangements in advance because you will have difficulty getting past the front gates.

Probably the most unusual tourist attraction here is Dunn's River Falls, about a five- to ten-minute taxi ride from the port. You can take photos and wander around the park that surrounds these incredible multilevel falls that descend to the sea, or you can experience climbing them with the assistance of a trained guide. Climbing the falls is a sensational experience; however, it is rather dangerous and not advisable for preteenage children. Wear a bathing suit and either waterproof athletic shoes or sandals that will not fall off.

From Ocho Rios, you could drive to Kingston via beautiful Fern Gully and the breathtaking Blue Mountains. This is a beautiful but somewhat dangerous drive that should be attempted only if you are not in a hurry. You would need at least ten hours in port at Montego Bay to have sufficient time to raft down the Martha Brae, visit Dunn's River Falls and Fern Gully at Ocho Rios, and have lunch and a swim at a hotel. If time allows, you may wish to drive in the opposite direction to explore the beautiful beaches at **Negril,** also the location of numerous full-facility resorts. The most facilities will be found at Negril's all-inclusive resorts—such as Grand Hotel Lido, Couples, Beaches, Hedonism II, and Sandals, or the more upscale Poinciana Beach Hotel. Since it may be difficult to camp out at one of these properties, a good choice would be Margaritaville, where you can have a comfortable beach chair and enjoy drinks, lunch, and water sports. You will enjoy walking along Negril's seven-mile beach.

Should you be in Jamaica during the evening, don't miss taking in a native calypso or limbo show at the local clubs or hotels. There are no outstanding restaurants around the island, and you are best off dining at one of the better hotels. Best items to purchase are Tia Maria liqueur and the local rums.

## KEY WEST, FLORIDA

Key West is not in the Bahamas or the Caribbean, but it is becoming a popular stop for many cruise ships. Technically the southernmost point in the continental United States, Key West is about eight miles farther south than the southernmost point in Texas. Lying between the Gulf of Mexico and the Atlantic Ocean, this final vestige of the Florida Keys will remind visitors of the Bahamas, New Orleans, and South Florida rolled into one. Only two miles by four miles in size, the island is easy to navigate on foot or bicycle.

Adjacent to the harbor, visitors can pick up the Old Town Trolley or the Conch Tour Train, both of which provide an excellent overview of the island. Points of interest include Mel Fisher's Maritime Heritage Society Museum; the Ernest Hemingway House, where the famous author wrote many of his novels; the Audubon House, a museum displaying many works of art by the famous artist and naturalist; and the Curry Museum, a turn-of-the-century National Historic Register museum with three stories of period furnishings. If you elect to walk from the harbor into town (about a mile and a half), you will pass through a lovely residential area.

Arrangements can be made for deep-sea fishing charters (at Mallory Square), glass-bottom boat rides to a living coral reef, snorkeling and scuba tours, and sailboat racing. Golf is available at the eighteen-hole Key West Golf Club north of town.

Most tourists enjoy browsing through the hundreds of souvenir shops and colorful bars that line Duval and neighboring streets—Sloppy Joe's (Hemingway's favorite bar) and Jimmy Buffet's Margaritaville are the best-known drinking establishments. A two-hour pub tour that visits five pubs and includes four drinks departs daily at 2:30 p.m. There are numerous small restaurants featuring fresh fish and seafood. The most highly touted restaurants are Café des Artistes (French Caribbean), Louie's Backyard (fresh seafood), Bagatelle (eclectic), Mangoes (Florida Caribbean and pizza), and Blue Heaven and Pepe's (where the locals go to "see and be seen"). The largest hotels are the Hilton, Hyatt, and the Ritz-Carlton.

## MARTINIQUE

Martinique, like Guadeloupe, is a department of France, and its 340,000 inhabitants speak French and a Creole dialect. The weather is generally very warm throughout the year, with considerable rain from July through November. Here, you can see the black-sand beaches that inspired the paintings of Gauguin, visit the birthplace of Empress Josephine at Trois-Ilets, walk through a petrified forest, drive out to the Mont Pelée Volcano and see the lava-drowned town of St. Pierre (sometimes referred to as the Caribbean Pompeii), swim at the hotel beaches on Trois-Ilets or at Anse Mitan, or just stroll around the old, quaint harbor town of Fort de France.

You will want to save time to visit the shops along Rue Victor Hugo, where you can pick up some excellent bargains in French perfume, Lalique and Baccarat crystal, Limoges china, gloves, and other French imports. However, the town has become quite run-down and seedy over the past few years. You can sample French-Creole cooking in town or take a motorboat across the bay to Trois-Ilets/Pointe Du Boute. If time permits, you may prefer to take the fifty-kilometer ride to the Club Mediterranean's vacation village at Buccaneer's Creek. Here you will find the island's best beach and water sports. However, you may have great difficulty getting on the premises, so it is best to call before you undertake the long drive. Noteworthy restaurants include Leyritz Plantation at Basse-Pointe (Creole), La Grande Voile in Fort de France (Creole), Le Planteur in Fort de France (French and Creole), Le Verger at La Mentin (French), and La Villa Creole at Trois-Ilets.

## MEXICO (EAST COAST)

**Cancún** is a man-made resort area on the northeast tip of Mexico's Yucatán Peninsula. Ships generally dock at Playa del Carmen, from which it is a thirty-minute ride to Cancún, or at the recently built port of Calica, which is fifteen minutes farther away. Here you will find fourteen miles of white-sand beaches, crystal clear waters, and an average year-round temperature of eighty degrees. You can spend your day swimming, sunning, snorkeling, or playing tennis at one of the posh resort hotels—such as the Ritz-Carlton, Meridien, Fiesta Americana, Hyatt, or Marriott. You can enjoy eighteen holes of championship golf at Pok-Ta-Pok, water sports at Aqua Bay Marina, snorkeling at Xel-Ha River near Tulum, a day of horseback riding through the jungle and beach trails at Rancho Bonita, or the incredible experience of swimming for thirty minutes down an underground river through prehistoric caverns and grottoes at the picturesque Xcaret Archeological Park adjacent to Calica. Xcaret is a unique attraction. In addition to two exotic underground rivers, visitors can swim with dolphins; snorkel and relax at a picturesque beach; browse through an indoor-outdoor aquarium; visit a wildlife refuge, a bird sanctuary populated with exotic local birds, a butterfly pavilion, an orchard and mushroom nursery, a botanical garden, and many archeological treasures; go horseback riding through jungle trails; and enjoy lunch at one of several restaurants spread around the property.

Most cruises that stop at this area offer optional side trips to **Tulum** or **Chichen Itza** to explore the ruins of these ancient Mayan civilizations.

A newly developed port, a good distance to the south, is Mahahual in the area sometimes referred to as **Costa Maya**. Cruise lines offer tours from here to the archeological ruins at Chacchoben and Kohunlich and to the beach at Uvero. Where once there was little other than a shopping area at the end of the pier and two small beaches, the port was rebuilt following a hurricane in 2007. Now there is a plethora of excursions offered: a zip-line tour, a sea-trek tour enabling participants to explore the ocean in helmets piped with oxygen, beach and catamaran snorkeling, airboat rides through the mangroves, mountain biking, kayaking, horseback riding, fishing, speedboat adventures, and dune-buggy and ATV safaris.

**Cozumel** is a small island off the southeastern coast of the Yucatán, with fine beaches for swimming, snorkeling, and scuba. The best beach to swim and enjoy a snack or drink is Mia Playa, formerly Playa del Sol, about ten miles from town; however, there is an $8 entrance fee. Mr. Sancho, a beach club half a mile down the road (the original location of Playa del Sol), is more appealing and has no entry fee. For snorkeling, Chankanaab Lagoon Park is only about five miles from town. You can spend the day at Stouffer's Presidente Hotel or Fiesta Americana's Sol Carib, both only a short distance from town, with nice pools and restaurants but no outstanding beaches. In town, there are many typical restaurants and art, crafts, souvenir, and jewelry shops. Lunch or drinks at Carlos 'n' Charlie's or Senor Frog's is always wild and fun. Many of the cruise lines offer excursions to out-of-the-way beaches via kayaks, small motorboats, or jeeps.

## NEW ORLEANS

New Orleans is the home port for various cruise ships of major cruise lines, such as Carnival and American Canadian Caribbean. Passengers frequently opt to spend a few days before or after their sailing in this colorful, historic city. Located at the junction of 19,000 miles of inland waterways created by the Mississippi River, its tributaries, and the Gulf Intracoastal Waterways with access to the Gulf of Mexico, New Orleans has developed into one of the United States' major international seaports.

Tourists most frequently gravitate to the French Quarter, drawn to its centuries-old buildings, with unique ironwork and courtyards and its concentration of fine restaurants, nightclubs, bars, shops, and cafés. When touring this area by foot, you may wish to visit historic Jackson Square to see Clark Mill's equestrian statue of Andrew Jackson; eighteenth-century St. Louis Cathedral and the Cabildo, which now houses part of the Louisiana State Museum; the Pontalba Apartments, which include the 1850 House and the Le Pétit Théâtre du Vieux Carré; the Manheim Gallery in the old Bank of Louisiana building; Casa Faurie (which houses the famous Brennan's Restaurant); the 1792 Merieult House, location of the Historic New Orleans Collection; the picturesque

Brulator Court and the Court of the Two Lions; Preservation Hall; Pirates Alley; Père Antoine Alley; Cathedral Garden; Gallier House; and the Haunted House—all of which are located on or just off Royal Street; Soniat House, Beauregard-Keyes House, Old Ursuline Convent, the Pharmacy Museum, and Napoleon House on Chartres Street; as well as the French Market on Barracks Street, where you can sample freshly prepared beignets and chicory coffee, a Louisiana culinary tradition. It would be best to purchase a map of the French Quarter to assist you in your exploration.

Other areas of interest located throughout the city include the Faubourg Marigny Historic District, just east of the French Quarter, with its varied collection of eighteenth- and nineteenth-century Creole-style structures built on narrow lots; the elegant Garden District; the Audubon Aquarium of the Americas with its underwater walkway; Audubon Zoo; the New Orleans Museum of Art in City Park; the National World War II Museum; and the shops and restaurants along the Riverwalk and connecting Ernest N. Morial Convention Center, proximate to the cruise ship terminal.

If you wish to stay overnight in the French Quarter, the most highly rated hotels include the Omni Royal Orleans, Royal Sonesta, Hotel Maison de Ville, Holiday Inn French Quarter, and Marriott. Best choices nearer to the Central Business District and convention center include the Harrah's New Orleans Casino, Ritz-Carlton, Fairmont, Hyatt Regency, Hilton, Sheraton, Westin, Radisson, and Windsor Court.

Extraordinary dining is New Orleans' tour de force. Although new restaurants surface from time to time, the traditional establishments are the most reliable and world-renowned. Commander's Palace, set in an 1880s restored building with lush green patios and gardens and a jazz band on Saturdays and Sundays, is a must for visitors seeking typical Creole dishes. Other perennial favorites include Brennan's, Broussard's, Antoine's, Galatoire's, Nola's, Peristyle, Dickie Brennan's Steakhouse, Bacco, Mr. B's Bistro, Emeril's, and Pascal's Manale Restaurant. K-Paul's Louisiana Kitchen, in the French Quarter, is an unpretentious establishment where New Orleans' most famous chef, Paul Prudhomme, dispenses his special interpretations of Creole, Cajun, French, and New Orleans cuisine. For more elegant Continental and French dining, you may wish to try Rib Room at Omni Royal Orleans, Sazerac at the Fairmont, and the Grill Room at the Windsor Court. Of course, any respectable tourist would not miss the compulsory pilgrimage to Café du Monde in the French Market for café au lait and beignets.

For nightlife, you will want to stroll through the streets of the French Quarter (especially Bourbon Street) to barhop, listen to jazz bands, browse through souvenir shops, and experience the after-dark sounds, smells, and exuberant vitality most associated with this city. Many of the larger hotels have quiet piano lounges, as well as music for listening and dancing. Another nighttime possibility would be to take in the riverfront attractions along the Moonwalk and Riverwalk.

New Orleans is also a shopper's paradise where you can search out bargains in antiques or peruse designer shops. The best shopping areas for tourists include Canal Street, the French Quarter, Magazine Street, and the complexes at One Canal Place and Riverwalk.

## PUERTO RICO

Puerto Rico is a commonwealth voluntarily associated with the United States. Spanish is the native tongue of the 2,690,000 inhabitants, although many also speak English. The climate is reliably sunny and warm throughout the year. Cruise ships dock at the harbor in **San Juan**, the colorful cosmopolitan capital of the island. During the day, you can explore the quaint, authentically Spanish section of town known as "Old San Juan." Here you walk through cobbled streets surrounded by pretty plazas, Spanish-style buildings, shops, art galleries, restaurants, and museums. Outlet stores with designer discounted merchandise can be found on Cristo Street. You can visit the El Morro Fortress and the San José Church and try some arróz con pollo, paella, asopao, or black bean soup at one of the Spanish restaurants.

In New San Juan, you can visit the sea museum and botanical gardens or just relax, swim, play tennis, or sip a piña colada at one of the large oceanfront hotels. Perhaps you will have time to drive out to the tropical El Yunqué rain forest and witness the beautiful lush vegetation and impressive variety of birds.

The spectacular El Conquistador Resort is located thirty-one miles east of San Juan. This megaresort descends down a cliff and offers an eighteen-hole golf course, seven tennis courts, several pools, a fabulous water park for families, and its own private beach on Palomino Island, a twenty-minute motor-launch ride from the hotel marina.

In the evening, you can stroll through Old San Juan, take in top-name entertainment, dance at the many nightclubs, or try your luck at the elegant hotel casinos. In San Juan, there are casinos and nightclubs at the Caribe Hilton, El San Juan, the Ritz-Carlton, the Holiday Inn, the Condado Beach, the Sands, and the Radisson.

## ST. BARTHELEMY

Located fifteen miles southeast of St. Martin and 140 miles north of Guadeloupe, St. Barts, a political dependency of Guadeloupe, is the most unique of the French West Indian islands. Its predominantly white population is of French and Swedish descent, and the atmosphere is more akin to a small French village on the Côte d'Azur than an island in the heart of the Caribbean.

Most visitors rent jeeps, mokes, or small cars and enjoy visiting the numerous white-sand beaches, small hotels, guesthouses, atmospheric open-air restaurants, and cafés spread around this eight-square-mile island. **Gustavia,** the capital, is a quaint town with numerous cafés, restaurants, souvenir shops, and boutiques featuring a wide selection of imported goods.

Of the fourteen white-sand beaches spread around the island, Baie De St. Jean is the most popular and a colorful strand on which to people-watch or take a stroll. Grand Cul-de-Sac on the northern shore is another local favorite. The most scenic beaches are Anse du Gouverneur, Anse de Grand Saline, and Anse de Colombier. Shell Beach, which is not very attractive, is within walking distance of town.

The two hotels boasting the most facilities on St. Barts are Guanahani at Anse de Grand Cul-de-Sac and Manapany at Anse des Cayes—both offering pools, good beaches, tennis, gourmet restaurants, and expensive exclusivity. In Gustavia, the most highly touted restaurants are Carl Gustav, Sapotillier, La Cremaillère, La Banane, On the Rocks, and Aux Trois Gourmands. Other restaurants of note outside of town include Francois Plantation, Adam, Maya's, La Playa on Plage St. Jean, and Le Tamarin.

## ST. KITTS AND NEVIS

This two-island nation was an associated state of Great Britain until it chose independence in 1983. St. Kitts covers sixty-five square miles and has a population of forty thousand, while Nevis is only thirty-six square miles with nine thousand inhabitants. Jets can fly into St. Kitts, but Nevis is only accessible by smaller craft or by a forty-minute ferry ride from its sister island. The islands were first settled by the English and French in the early seventeenth century and became important producers of tobacco, ginger, cotton, and sugar as well as a major hub for slave trading.

Today the islands offer an ideal climate with warm Caribbean sunshine cooled by trade winds. There is sufficient rain to keep the interiors lush, verdant, and tropical.

St. Kitts is dominated by Mount Misery with its crater lake that rises four thousand feet amid rolling hills of sugarcane and palm trees. Cruise ships can dock at Deep Water Harbor, which is only a five-dollar taxi ride or a thirty-minute walk from the main town of **Basse-Terre**, with its shops specializing in batiks. About three miles from the harbor is Frigate Bay, where there are shops, restaurants, "so-so" Atlantic and Caribbean beaches, and a giant full-facility Marriott resort with three meandering, free-form pools—one with a swim-up bar, several restaurants, tennis courts, an eighteen-hole golf course, and a lovely beach. Attached to the resort is the large Royal Beach Casino. Good beaches for swimming on the southern portion of the island include South Friar's Bay, Sand Bank Bay, Turtle Beach, and Cockleshell Bay. A typical, casual place for a seafood lunch or dinner would be Fisherman's Wharf. For West Indian and Continental dishes, try the restaurants at the Golden Lemon, Ottley's Plantation, the restaurants at the Marriott, and at the Rawlins Plantation hotels.

Points of interest include Brimstone Hill, an imposing fort situated seven hundred feet above the sea affording views of Statia, Saba, St. Martin, and St. Barts; Romney Manor, a seventeenth-century plantation producing batik handicrafts; and an impressive tropical rain forest. The best beaches are at Banana Bay, Cockleshell Bay, and the Caribbean side of Friar's Bay.

The main town in Nevis, **Charlestown**, is a small unusually clean Caribbean town with a few guesthouses, small inns and hotels, restaurants, and shops. There is a nice strand of beach about three miles from town that is used by some cruise ships for beach parties.

Nesbit Plantation on the north of the island also has a good beach, a restaurant, tennis courts, horseback riding, and water sports. In the early 1990s, the Four Seasons Hotel chain opened Four Seasons Resort Nevis (one of the most luxurious resorts in the Caribbean), which features an eighteen-hole Robert Trent Jones II golf course, ten illuminated tennis courts, long stretches of sand on Pinney's Beach, water sports, horseback riding, and several restaurants. From St. Kitts, visitors must take the resort's private shuttle boat from its dock in Basseterre. Three plantation-house hotels, pleasant places for lunch, are Golden Rock Estate, Hermitage Beach Club, and Nesbit Plantation Beach Club.

## ST. LUCIA

St. Lucia, an independent member of the British Commonwealth, twenty-one miles south of Martinique, has a population of 101,000. The climate is dry and sunny in the winter, but a bit warmer and a great deal wetter during the summer months. The capital, **Castries**, is a picturesque town with a beautiful landlocked harbor where you can shop for duty-free bargains in crystal, jewelry, cameras, watches, perfume, and liquor or sample the island's famous lobsters at a local restaurant. You can drive to Morne Fortuné, one of the two hills behind the town, and at the top explore the remains of Fort Charlotte, a typical eighteenth-century stronghold. You can take a two-hour voyage by launch to the fishing village of Soufrière, which is located at the base of St. Lucia's famous twin mountains, the Pitons. Here you can drive up Mount Soufrière, the only "drive-in" volcano in the world. You can actually drive right up to the lip of the smoldering crater and look in. Nearby, you can take a dip in sulphur springs, which are said to be therapeutic for sufferers of arthritis and rheumatism.

There is excellent swimming at all the public beaches; however, I would recommend spending the day on one of the hotel beaches at Jalousie Plantation, Sandals St. Lucia and Sandals Halcyon, Anse Chastanet (black sand), or at nearby Rodney Bay, the location of Le Sport, the Royal St. Lucien, and the Rex St. Lucien. The restaurants touted to be the best on the island are Green Parrot (seafood), San Antoine (Continental), Piton Restaurant and Bar (Caribbean), Dasheene Restaurant and Bar (Caribbean), Capone's (Italian), and Great House (French-Creole).

## ST. MARTIN

St. Martin (Saint Maarten) is a thirty-seven-square-mile island that was divided by the Dutch and French in 1648. **Philipsburg** is the capital of the Dutch section (Saint Maarten), and **Marigot** is the capital of the French (St. Martin). In addition to Dutch and French, the fourteen thousand inhabitants also speak English. The climate is dry and pleasant, with temperatures varying from seventy-one to eighty-six degrees. In Philipsburg, you can try numerous Continental and ethnic restaurants and shop for duty-free bargains in delft and Royal Dutch pewter. In Marigot, you can sample French cuisine and purchase duty-free bargains in French wines, perfume, and gloves. Other than the scenery, there are not many attractions of significant interest to tourists. There are casinos in some of the hotels. Orient is a very colorful beach, a fifteen-minute drive from Philipsburg. It is reminiscent of Tahiti Beach in St. Tropez, France, and offers topless and nude bathing, as well as numerous small beachfront restaurants and boutiques. Spartico is an excellent Italian restaurant located on the road between the airport and Marigot. Other good restaurants include LeBec Fin (Continental), Oyster Pond Beach Hotel (Continental), Le Perroquet (French), Chez Martine (French), Rainbow (Continental and West Indian), La Vie en Rose (French), Alizea (French), and L'Auberge Gourmande (French). LaSamanna is the most exclusive resort on the island and is located on Baie Longue, one of the best beaches. If you make arrangements to have lunch at its highly acclaimed restaurant, chances are you can have access to the beach.

## ST. VINCENT AND THE GRENADINES

Lying south of St. Lucia, north of Grenada, and west of Barbados in the southern part of Caribbean's Windward Islands is the nation of St. Vincent, which is composed of thirty-two islands and cays. The largest island is named St. Vincent and is the site of the Caribbean's most active volcano, La Soufrière, which last erupted in 1979.

South of the island of St. Vincent are the islands of Bequia, Mustique, Canouan, Mayreau, Palm Island, Union Island, and Petit St. Vincent, all low-key tourist destinations occasionally visited by cruise ships.

If your ship stops at the island of St. Vincent, two mediocre public beaches for swimming are Villa Beach and Buccament Bay, a black-sand beach on the west coast. A favorite excursion is the boat trip to Baleine Falls, where you can swim in a freshwater pool, climb under the sixty-three-foot falls, and enjoy scenic views of the island. Hotels with the most facilities include Grand View Beach Hotel and Young Island. Young Island boasts the best beach and best resort restaurant and is accessible by a five-minute ride on the hotel's launch from Villa Beach. Arrangements must be made in advance with the hotel.

Nine miles south of the island of St. Vincent is Bequia, the largest island, known for its long stretches of nearly deserted beaches, snorkeling, and diving. The best beaches are at Friendship Bay, Industry Bay, Lower Bay, and Princess Margaret. The picturesque beach and hotel restaurant and bar at Friendship Bay Hotel is a comfortable spot to spend a beach day. Frangipani, overlooking the yacht harbor, is one of the best restaurants on the island.

On Canouan, your best bets are the Tamarind Beach Hotel and Yacht Club or Raffles Resort; on Mayreau, Salt Whistle Bay Club and Salt Whistle Bay Beach; on Mustique, Cotton House; and on Palm Island, Palm Island Resort. Petit St. Vincent is a 113-acre private island, the location of one of the Caribbean's highest-rated resorts.

On **Mayreau**, a tiny one-and-a-half-square-mile cay, there is a steep, mountainous path that runs from the dock and beach at Saline Bay to Salt Whistle Bay, where there is a small rustic hotel and a pristine beach. Both beaches are panoramic and excellent for swimming. A land taxi or water taxi will provide optional transportation. An occasional ship tenders passengers to a long stretch of so-so beach on Union Island.

## SAN FRANCISCO

San Francisco is frequently described by some as the United States' most cultural, European-style city; by others as its most romantic and charming, with picture-perfect backdrops of famous bridges, bay vistas, cable cars, and colorful residents; and by still others as its most liberal and hip community. Take your choice, but the fact remains that the San Francisco Bay area is one of the most popular tourist destinations in the world, steeped in history, diversity, and natural beauty.

Possibly the best way to explore the city is on foot. Walking excursions around the various neighborhoods will enable you to absorb the unique flavor of each while visiting the major places of interest. Some of the sites and experiences that are most popular with visitors include

- Golden Gate Park: San Francisco's answer to New York's Central Park and London's Hyde Park covers one thousand acres stretching inland from the Pacific Coast at Ocean Beach up to Stanyun Street. On a sunny day, the numerous gardens and wooded paths are particularly attractive. Recreational facilities include tennis courts, a golf course, riding stables, fly-casting pools, boat rentals, and baseball, soccer, and polo fields. Within the grounds are the Steinhart Aquarium, the Morrison Planetarium, the Strybing Arboretum and Botanical Gardens, the Natural History Museum, and the Japanese Tea Garden.
- Union Square: This is the center of the city's commercial area with luxury hotels, fine restaurants, galleries, department stores, and upscale boutiques. Chinatown is directly to the north, the Financial District to the east, SoMa to the south, and Nob Hill to the west.
- Fisherman's Wharf: A perennial favorite for tourists are the shopping malls with their overpriced restaurants and shops in this area which include the Wharf, Ghiradelli Square, Pier 39, the Cannery, and the Anchorage.
- Chinatown: A stroll through Chinatown with its colorful markets, shops, and restaurants is a must for every visitor. Pass through the Gateway Arch at Bush Street and Grant Avenue and stroll along Stockton or Grant to Portsmouth Square, which is filled with locals enjoying themselves.
- Other worthwhile and popular sites include the Golden Gate Bridge, Alcatraz Island, Coit Tower atop Telegraph Hill, a cable-car ride from Nob Hill to Fisherman's Wharf on the Powell-Hyde line, and a walk through Castro and Haight Ashbury (two of the city's most colorful gay and hippie neighborhoods). Museums include the Aquarium of the Bay at Fisherman's Wharf, the Asian Art Museum at the Civic Center, the Cable Car Museum at Mason and Washington Streets, the Exploratorium (a science museum in the Marina District), Maritime National Historical Park, Wells Fargo History Museum, the Yerba Buena Center for the Arts and Yerba Buena Gardens (the city's cultural facility similar to New York's Lincoln Center), the Berkeley Art Museum in Berkeley, and the San Francisco Museum of Modern Art near Union Square.

Along with New York, New Orleans, and Chicago, San Francisco is considered one of the great dining areas of the United States, boasting some of the country's best restaurants, bistros, and pubs, with a cornucopia of cuisine running the gamut from French, Italian, Japanese, and Chinese to Afghan, Moroccan, Vietnamese, Cambodian, and almost every other country around the world. It would be impossible to list all of the dining possibilities.

Only an hour's drive to the north lies the wine country of the Napa and Sonoma Valleys, the location of the United States' most famous wineries. Amid the mountains dipping into grapevine-trellised valleys, you will experience an entirely different environment and climate replete with some of the world's finest wineries and best restaurants. It is possible to book a hot-air-balloon ride over the entire area.

Napa Valley, with its neighboring towns and villages, is the largest and the most commercial of the two towns and has the greater number of wineries, hotels, and restaurants; Sonoma is more laid back. In Napa Valley, you will find such world-class properties as Opus One, Robert Mondavi, and Domaine Chandon. The most luxurious retreat, Auberge du Soleil, is set high above a thirty-seven-acre vine grove and boasts a world-class spa and marvelous restaurant. Sonoma's more than thirty-five wineries include Buena Vista, Glen Ellen, Kenwood, and Sebastiani.

## SOUTHEAST U.S. CRUISE PORTS AND BARRIER ISLANDS IN THE ATLANTIC

The scene of major Revolutionary War naval battles, legendary pirate tales, and Civil War sieges, **Charleston, South Carolina,** is brimming with history and culture.

It is possible to take tours to many of the more important points of interest. You can tour Magnolia Plantation and Gardens, Boone Hall Plantation, Charleston's Tea Plantation, Drayton Hall, Edmonston-Alston House, a Bulldog walking tour to Charleston's infamous and haunted sites, a tour to Charleston County Water Parks, a SpiritLine cruise or a Schooner Pride cruise around the harbor, and a visit to historic Fort Sumter National Monument

Shopping opportunities abound with countless retail stores, art galleries, and antique shops. Primary shopping areas include the Old City Market, King Street, Broad Street, the Historic French Quarter, and Mount Pleasant Town Center. Opera, ballet, and symphonies are performed at the historic Dock Street Theater.

Charleston is well-known for its low-country cuisine and many excellent restaurants. Husk Restaurant and Bar is located in a structure dating back to 1893 and evokes the grandeur of old Charleston. The casual Anson Street Fish House and Raw Bar and the Charleston Crab House emphasize local fresh fish and seafood. Blu Restaurant set alongside Tides Folly Beach offers both indoor and outdoor dining with fresh local seafood and contemporary coastal cuisine. For fine dining, Peninsula Grill and McCrady's features award-winning cuisine and extensive wine lists.

The city is rich in accommodations ranging from exclusive resorts and most hotel chains to charming old homes, inns, and B&Bs. Resorts and hotels of note are Kiawah Island Golf Resort, Sanctuary at Keawah Island, Charleston Harbor Resort, Charleston Place, French Quarter Inn, Wentworth Mansion, and Woodlands Resort and Inn.

Located on Port Royal Island in the heart of the Sea Islands, **Beaufort, South Carolina,** is the second oldest city in South Carolina behind Charleston. It is best known for its scenic location and for maintaining its historic character through its impressive antebellum architecture. The city's history includes Spanish and French explorers, Native American inhabitants, British settlements, and significant Civil War battles. Today horse-drawn carriages bring visitors through narrow streets of the historic district past eighteenth and nineteenth century homes famous for their unique Beaufort-style architecture.

Major attractions include Hunting Island State Park, located on a large secluded barrier reef with wildlife, a beach, a lighthouse, hiding trails, and camp sites; Henry C. Chambers Waterfront Park with activities for both young and older children; Pigeon Point Park with its children's playground and picnic tables; the Point historic neighborhood with its interesting architecture; the shops and art galleries along Bay Street; and the Downtown Marina.

Some of the more popular tours include a carriage tour through the historic district, the Beaufort Kayak Tour, the Beaufort Walking Tour, Captain Dick's Beaufort River Tour and Dolphin Watch, John Sharp's Walking History Tour, and the River Safari.

Seafood, especially the crabs are the cuisine most notable in Beaufort. Popular restaurants include Breakwater Restaurant and Bar, Emily's Restaurant & Tapas Bar for shrimp and grits, Wrens, and Plum's Bistro.

Hotels include City Loft Hotel, the Beaufort Inn, the Rhett House Inn, and Best Western Plus Sea Island Inn.

**Hilton Head, South Carolina,** is the second largest barrier island along the Southeast Atlantic Coast with twelve miles of sandy beachfront. The island has a long and rich history of Native American settlements, European explorations and Civil War operations. Hilton Head is a first class resort known for its championship golf courses and natural beauty. A boat tour of the pristine lakes of the Sea Pines Forest Preserve gives you a close-up view of the islands indigenous plant and animal life.

From chic boutiques to exclusive outlet shops, Hilton Head Island offers fashionable, fine-quality products in a pleasant shopping atmosphere. Island shops are located in intimate plazas, quaint marinas, elegant harbors and full-service shopping centers. On the Island, you will find the Mall at Shelter Cove, the only mall and indoor, air-conditioned shopping destination, as well as a wide range of outlets just over the bridge in Bluffton at the Tanger Outlets.

The island boasts numerous upscale hotels and resorts including the Sea Pines Resort, the Westin Hilton Head Island Resort and Spa, the Inn at Harbor Town, the Crowne Plaza, and the Marriott.

Notable restaurants include Marley's Island Grill, Alexander's, Old Oyster Factory, Frosty Frog Café, the Crazy Crab, and Crane's Tavern.

**Jekyll Island, Georgia,** is part of Georgia's Sea Isles and boasts Millionaire's Village, 240 acres of extravagant homes and winter cottages recognized as a National Historic Landmark. At the end of the nineteenth century, some of the wealthiest men in America, including J.P. Morgan, Joseph Pulitzer, William Rockefeller and Cornelius Vanderbilt, purchased the entire island as a hunting resort.

Jekyll Island is one of only four Georgia barrier islands that feature a paved causeway to access the island by car. It features 5,700 acres of land, including a 200-acre Jekyll Island Club Historic District. The island measures about seven miles long by 1.5 miles wide, has eight miles of wide, flat beaches on its east shore with sand packed hard enough for easy walking or biking, and boasts twenty miles of hiking trails.

Attractions and tours include the Georgia Sea Turtle Center, bird watching tours, dolphin tours, shrimping expeditions, kayak tours, canoe rentals, nature walks, and Segway tours.

**St. Simons Island, Georgia,** has an enthralling past of momentous eighteenth-century battles and sprawling antebellum plantations. The St. Simons Lighthouse houses a fantastic museum devoted to the history of the Georgia Coast. Its natural beauty is enhanced by a diverse range of wildlife.

St. Simons Island is the largest of the Golden Isles along Georgia's southern Atlantic coast. Eighteen square miles in size, its history is rich with skirmishes between the French, Spanish, and English all vying for settlements along the southeast coast. Fort

Frederica is the product of the English buffering themselves for the Spanish incursions from Florida. The town of St. Simons is not very interesting. There are numerous T-shirt/souvenir-type shops, small boutiques, and a few casual bars and restaurants.

St. Simons has a wide array of lodging choices ranging from stately hotels to comfy B&Bs, golf resorts, and vacation homes. Nearby, Sea Island boasts two of the country's top resorts, the Cloister and the Lodge, which is surrounded by three championship golf courses.

**Sapelo Island**, the fourth largest of Georgia's islands, is a state-protected island located in McIntosh County Georgia. The island is reachable only by airplane or boat, with the primary ferry coming from the Sapelo Island Visitors Center in McIntosh County, Georgia, a seven-mile (eleven kilometers), twenty-minute trip.

Approximately 97 percent of the island is owned by the State of Georgia and is managed by the Georgia Department of Natural Resources; the remaining is under private ownership. The western perimeter of Sapelo is the Sapelo Island National Estuarine Research Reserve, which is part of the National Estuarine Research Reserve system. The University of Georgia Marine Institute, which is devoted to research and education, is located on 1,500 acres on the south end of the island. The Reynold's Mansion, a Georgia State Park, also lies on the south end of the island. Visitors to the island must be a part of an organized tour or guests of residents on the island. The island also has a small private airport run by the State of Georgia.

The community of Hog Hammock includes a general store, a bar, and other small businesses. There are two active churches in the town. The residents of the town are African Americans part of the Gullah or *Geechee* community, and have been living on the island for generations. The current population in the community is estimated to be forty seven. The residents must bring over all supplies from the mainland or purchase them in the small store on the island.

Other attractions include Fofwyl-Broadfield Plantation and the Colonial Coast Birding Trail.

**Savanna, Georgia,** is a bustling seaport with renowned historic districts that preserve its phenomenal nineteenth-century wealth and opulence. With historic city squares, beautiful flowering parks and classic southern grace, Savannah has earned its nickname as "Hostess City of the South."

Savannah's Historic District is home to dozens of hotels, inns, and B&Bs, some of modern design and others restored to yesterday's grandeur. Compact enough to explore on your own, the Historic District also offers an array of guided tours to help you understand the essence of Savannah. Not to be missed is the Southern Cuisine that helps shape the identity of Savannah. You may wish to join a narrated tour of its "Historic and Victorian Districts," brave an evening Ghost Walk, or explore the magnificent streets alive with music, southern delicacies, and exotic shops.

Savannah restaurants have earned a reputation as some of the best dining options in the South. Georgia's First City embraces contemporary cuisine while staying true to its culinary traditions. Each of the city's unique dining establishments offers distinctive flavor in both cuisine and décor. Dine at a quaint outdoor café under the stars one night, feast at a fabulous five-star restaurant another. Dining Savannah-style combines a fun, chic ambiance with flavors from every corner of the world, along with distinctive low-country cuisine and fresh seafood. The three most upscale restaurants are the Pink House, Bistro 45, and the Mansion at Forsyth Park. There are numerous casual eateries along River Street including Huey's, Shrimp Factory, and the Oyster Bar.

## SOUTH FLORIDA

The vast majority of cruise ships leaving for the Caribbean and Bahamas embark from either Miami or Fort Lauderdale. Numerous hotels and resorts in these areas can accommodate pre- and postcruise extensions for almost any pocketbook. In Fort Lauderdale, the three best hotels, all located less than ten minutes from Port Everglades, are Hyatt Pier 66, Marriott's Harbor Beach Resort, and Bahia Mar. The latter two are located on the beach and the Hyatt on the intercoastal, surrounded by luxury yachts.

In Miami Beach, there are literally hundreds of hotels. Some visitors prefer the art-deco, hip area of South Beach with its stream of cafés, restaurants, discos, and quaint renovated hotels, of which the Delano is the most European and most famous. Joe's Stone Crab, a South Beach icon, is the most famous eatery. Those seeking a golf resort and/or a spa will prefer the Doral Golf Resort and Spa, which is inland in Miami not far from Carnival Cruise Line's headquarters.

There are numerous shopping malls, the largest being Sawgrass Mills (a twenty- to thirty-minute drive), the Galleria in Fort Lauderdale, and Aventura Mall, just to the north of Miami and not far from the luxurious Diplomat Hotel in Hollywood. Visitors will enjoy strolling along Las Olas in Fort Lauderdale or Lincoln Road in Miami Beach and visiting the numerous boutiques and restaurants.

An interesting drive would be along AIA, the coastal road from Miami up to Palm Beach, past luxury residential communities. Excursions may include an airboat ride through the Florida Everglades, Miami Seaquarium, Miami's Parrot Jungle, and Butterfly World in Coconut Creek.

## TORTOLA, PETER ISLAND, AND VIRGIN GORDA
## (THE BRITISH VIRGIN ISLANDS)

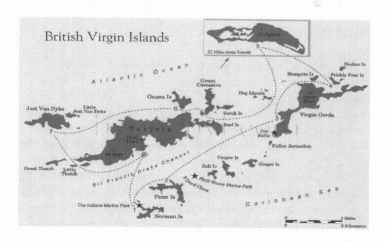

Several of the cruise ships traversing the Virgin Islands spend a day at **Tortola**. From Tortola, passengers can take a ferry to St. John and to most of the British Virgin Islands. Unspoiled Peter Island Resort and Yacht Harbor is only a twenty-minute ride away. There you can sunbathe and swim at one of the resort's lovely pristine beaches, have lunch, play tennis, and participate in numerous water sports.

Your ship will tender you into **Road Town**, the main city of Tortola and capital of the British Virgin Islands. Road Town is not a duty-free port; however, there are bargains on imported British goods and local handicrafts. You can take a taxi ride west to Mount Sage, the island's highest peak, where you will be rewarded with a view of Peter, Salt, Cooper, and Ginger islands. Another excellent view is at Skyworld, a mountaintop restaurant and Tortola's most popular luncheon spot.

There are good beaches with white sand and clear warm water at Smuggler's Cove, Long Bay, Apple Bay (where there is good surfing), and Cane Garden Bay. The last one is the most pristine, and if you spend the day there, you can lunch at the colorful Rhymer's Restaurant. Also recommended is 1748 at Long Bay Beach.

Scuba diving and snorkeling are popular here. The wreck of the *Rhone* is one of the most famous dive sites in the Caribbean and the location for the filming of *The Deep*. The *Rhone* was a British mail steamer that sank in 1867. Snorkelers and divers will want to visit the many reefs that follow the coastal beaches on the north side of the island, Smuggler's Cove being most snorkelers' favorite.

Those not opting to take the ferry to Peter Island can enjoy a day at one of the resorts on Tortola, which include Long Bay Hotel on the north shore and Prospect Reef Resort and Frenchman's Cay Hotel and Yacht Club on Frenchman's Cay, which is connected to Tortola by a bridge.

**Virgin Gorda** is one of the more picturesque and quaint of the British Virgins. Visitors will enjoy meandering through the shops and pubs in the small town near the harbor, visiting the unique "baths" where they can explore caves and natural pools formed by large boulders while snorkeling in aqua-blue waters, or spending the day at world-famous Little Dix Bay Resort with its magnificent beach and lovely grounds. Some ships drop anchor at the opposite end of the island, so passengers can spend the day at Bitter End Resort or nearby Biras Creek.

## TRINIDAD AND TOBAGO

Trinidad and Tobago compose a two-island republic nine miles off the coast of Venezuela that became an independent member of the British Commonwealth in 1976. Trinidad is the largest island in the southern part of the Caribbean, having an area of 1,980 square miles and a pleasant sunny climate. Its more than one million residents are a mixture of African, East Indian, Middle Eastern, and Asian cultures. Trinidad is said to be the birthplace of the calypso, steel band, and limbo, and should your ship be in port during the evening, don't miss an exciting and colorful native show. In **Port-of-Spain**, the capital, there is "inbound" shopping for numerous duty-free bargains that are sent by the storekeeper directly to your ship. Tobago, which lies twenty miles northeast of Trinidad and is twenty-seven miles long by seven and a half miles wide, offers sandy beaches, unspoiled rain forests, and coral reefs.

Trinidad boasts beautiful mountains, tropical jungles, lush plantations, and sweeping white-sand beaches. You can drive to Pitch Lake near La Brea, where tons of asphalt are excavated and shipped throughout the world, or you may wish to take the Skyline Highway to the beautiful white-sand Maracas Beach, which is surrounded by palm trees and mountains. (The major hotels are not located near the beaches.) Additionally, you can visit a sugar or coconut plantation, the Caroni Bird Sanctuary, and the Royal Botanic Gardens.

If you wish to dine in Trinidad, you may enjoy the Italian food at Lucianos and Topo Caro, the East Indian food at Gaylords or Mangals, Chinese cuisine at Tiki Village, or French-Continental food in the restaurants at the Trinidad Hilton and the Normandie hotels.

In Tobago, a nice beach, golf, and tennis are available at Mount Irvine Bay Hotel and Golf Club. Golf is also available at Tobago Plantation Golf & Country Club. The most highly rated resorts are Hilton Tobago, located on a five-thousand-foot beach surrounded by mangrove forests; Le Grand Courlan near Black Rock, set on a sandy beach with a good restaurant; and Coco Reef near Pigeon Point on Coconut Bay. The best restaurants include Dillon's (international near Crown Point), Tamara's (international in the Coco Reef Resort), the Blue Crab (Caribbean/international in Scarborough), Jemmas (local at Speyside), and La Belle Creole (Cajun in the Half-Moon Blue Hotel). The best beach is at Pigeon Point, which is surrounded by Royal Palms and offers food kiosks, craft shops, paddleboat rides, and a diving concession. The best snorkeling is at Back Bay and at Buccoo Reef off Pigeon Point. There are numerous dive operations all over the island. In the event your ship anchors off of Charlotteville, the only beach less than a two-hour drive is at Blue Water Inn near Speyside.

## TURKS AND CAICOS

Although these islands lie at the extreme southeast of the Bahamian archipelago, they have a separate government and are rarely considered a part of the Bahamas. The five hundred miles of coral reefs and incredible array of beaches here attract snorkelers and divers; however, there is little tourism apart from the hotels on the Providenciales, commonly referred to as "Provo."

On **Provo,** white-sand beaches abutting crystal clear waters stretch for twelve miles along the northeast coast. Most of the hotels and restaurants are located on or near Grace Bay Beach between Long Point and Thomas Stubbs Point. Hotels on the beach with good facilities include Beaches Resort & Spa, Grace Bay Club, Point Grace, Club Med Turkoise, Ocean Club, and Royal West Indies Resort. Anacaon at the Grace Bay Club is one of the better restaurants, featuring grilled lobster, fresh fish, and conch chowder. Aqua at Long Point, the trendiest spot, has a terrace overlooking the marina and also specializes in fresh fish and seafood. For a Mediterranean environment with Italian cuisine, Baci near Long Point is also a good choice, as is Coy-abe for Continental/Caribbean fare in a tropical garden. Visitors can enjoy eighteen holes of golf at the Provo Golf Club. Fishing excursions can be booked through Silver Deep and sailing, kayaking, and parasailing are offered by B&B Tours at the Leeward Marina.

For diving equipment, go to Art Pickering's Provo Turtle Divers, located in front of the Miramar resort, where tennis courts are also available.

Prior to 2006, few ships stopped at **Grand Turk,** where there was almost nothing of interest save some pristine beaches with few facilities. The best strand was at Governor's Beach in front of the governor's residence. Some of the finest diving in the archipelagos is around Grand Turk and cruise ships that anchor here generally organize diving and snorkeling excursions. In 2005-2006, Carnival Cruise Line constructed a deepwater dock and a cruise center, with a shopping area, a white-sand beach with umbrellas and sheltered cabanas, and an enormous pool, which is adjacent to a Jimmy Buffet Margaritaville restaurant and watering hole. Many passengers opt to spend the day at this expansive facility. Taxis, buses, and car rentals are available for those wishing to tour the island.

## U.S. VIRGIN ISLANDS

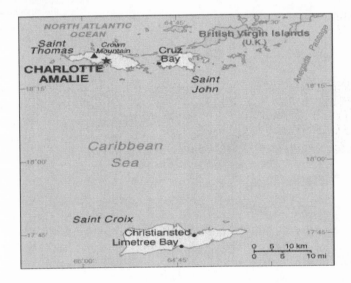

The U.S. Virgin Islands were purchased from Denmark in 1917, and they offer the finest shopping and possibly the most beautiful beaches and most desirable climate in the Caribbean. Cruise ships dock at the islands of St. Thomas and St. Croix, and those wishing to explore St. John catch a ferry from the center of town or Red Hook Beach in St. Thomas. (Watch your time here so you don't miss the ship.) In both St. Thomas and St. Croix, you will want to leave ample time for duty-free shopping at the hundreds of attractive stores that line the main streets. Remember that when purchasing merchandise in the U.S. Virgin Islands, your duty-free allowance increases to $1,400 and your liquor quota increases to five liters.

In **St. Thomas,** you can swim in crystal clear waters at one of the truly beautiful beaches such as Magens Bay, Coki Point, Sapphire Bay, Red Hook, Morningstar Beach, and Limetree Beach. You may wish to visit Fort Christian, Bluebeard's Tower, and take a glass-bottom boat ride. At night, go to one of the hotels and see a local limbo show. For those who wish to play tennis and swim at one of the outstanding beaches, I would recommend spending the afternoon at the Virgin Grand Resort, which has a pool, private beach, restaurants, and tennis courts and is across the road from the fantastic Coki Beach and Coral World. Marriott recently took over and renovated Frenchmen's Reef, which also has tennis courts and is only a few minutes from where you dock; however, it is located on Morningstar Beach, which is fine for swimming but is not quite as beautiful or unspoiled as the others. The most luxurious resort is the Ritz-Carlton, which has a nice pool and small beach. There are numerous restaurants in town and in the hotels. Many cruisers have indicated that L'Escargot on the waterfront is the best.

Shoppers will enjoy exploring the hundreds of stores lined up for a mile along the main drag in town. I have found the best selections at Continental (for crystal, jewelry, imported woolens, and European goods), A. H. Riise (for perfume, china, crystal, watches, jewelry, and liquors), Sparky's (for liquor), and Little Switzerland (for watches and jewelry). Branches of these shops and many others are located in the shopping mall adjacent to where your ship docks. Therefore, it is not necessary to go into town if time is limited.

From **St. Croix,** you can sail out to **Buck Island** for some of the best underwater snorkeling in the Caribbean, or you can swim at one of the excellent beaches at the various hotels. The Buccaneer Hotel has a fair beach, a golf course, and excellent tennis courts. Westin Carambola Resort has a lovely beach and good restaurants, and its golf course—four miles from the resort—is considered one of the best and most picturesque in the Caribbean. Don't miss walking through the charming town of **Christiansted,** where Danish architecture is evident in the little pastel-colored homes and stores. Unfortunately, most ships dock at **Fredericksted,** and you must take a long bus or taxi ride to get to Christiansted, which is on the other side of the island.

For those travelers who have already been to St. Thomas and first-time cruisers seeking "heavenly perfection," I recommend spending the day at Caneel Bay Resort or the Westin on the island of **St. John.** To get there, you must take a thirty-minute taxi ride from your cruise ship to Red Hook Bay, where you catch a ferry for a pleasant thirty-minute boat ride to the island of St. John, followed by another ten-minute taxi or bus ride to the hotels. A few times each day, boats leave from the center of town and go directly to St. John. This may sound like a long trip, but it is well worth it. At Caneel Bay, you can explore six horseshoe-shaped virgin, private white-sand beaches studded with palm trees; lie out on a secluded hammock overlooking the sea; swim in clear, warm waters with beautiful tropical fish weaving between your legs; play tennis on one of seven excellent courts; and have a drink and buffet or à la carte lunch in the main building or at Turtle Beach. Joggers will want to scurry down the miles of paths connecting the various beaches, facilities, and cottages; and snorkel enthusiasts will wish to head out for the nearby Trunk Bay, where appropriate equipment can be rented to explore an underwater trail of flora and coral formations. Few resorts in the Caribbean surpass the beautiful grounds of Caneel Bay.

Several smaller vessels now offer regular cruises to St. John as well as some of the more remote British Virgin Islands.

## SOUTH AMERICA

Cruising to foreign lands offers you an opportunity to sample numerous ports to determine whether or not you would wish to return for a longer, in-depth vacation. Just as you can cruise to several Caribbean islands, different countries in the Far East, or various ports in the Mediterranean, so can you cruise to many of the major cities of South America. Because air travel to South America is so expensive, cruising represents an economical yet pleasurable alternative.

Most of the major cities in South America are close enough to the equator to afford year-round sunshine and mild climates. Inasmuch as the seasons are reversed in the Southern Hemisphere, even Buenos Aires has warm weather between December and April.

In recent years, several cruise lines have been tapping the wealthy South American market, promoting trips to many of the major cities, including Rio de Janeiro, Montevideo, and Buenos Aires as well as cruises up the Amazon River. Each year, vessels of the Celebrity, Costa, Crystal, Cunard, Holland America, Seabourn, and Silversea lines stop at a number of South American ports. It is also possible to explore the Galapagos and the west coast of South America on ships of the Celebrity Cruise Line and Metropolitan Touring. Several cruise lines offer cruises that circumnavigate the continent, while others offer exploration cruises south of Argentina into Antarctica.

## AMAZON RIVER CRUISES

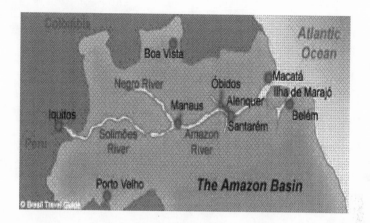

The Amazon River, the largest river in the world and estimated to contain one-fifth of all the fresh water on earth, stretches 4,000 miles from its source in the Andes to the Atlantic Ocean. Although oceangoing ships can navigate inland for some 2,300 miles, many of the regular cruises offering Amazon itineraries enter at Belem, the 200-mile-wide mouth of the river, traverse the Narrows of Breves, stop at Santarem, and conclude their exploration at Manaus. The river is so wide at spots that you will be unable to see the other side; however, when passing through the Narrows of Breves you are treated to miles of beautiful green flora and tributaries located on both sides of your ship. The Amazon hosts 1,500 species of fish, 14,000 species of mammals, 15,000 species of insects, and 3,500 species of birds, although few of these will be visible on your cruise.

Many cruisers opting for an Amazon River itinerary expect to experience a ride up a picturesque jungle river right out of the Tarzan movies. Unfortunately, most cruises do not afford an opportunity to explore the more primitive areas, and most of your time will be spent sailing up a brown-colored river with ever-changing scenery and some unusual, but not fascinating, ports of call.

**Belem** is situated on Guajara Bay at the gateway to the Amazon and is often the first or last stop for cruise ships exploring the river. The town thrived during the rubber boom of the early 1900s and is still the great trading center of the Amazon.

Your ship will either dock adjacent to the downtown area, where everything is within walking distance, or anchor at Scoraci and tender passengers ashore.

The Hilton Hotel is located in the center of the town and is a good focal point for your explorations. Points of interest include the Jungle Park, a zoo filled with local animals in their natural habitat; the Goeldi Museum, with its extensive collection of Indian artifacts; the neoclassical Teatro de Paz, built in 1874; the Basilica de Nossa Senhora de Nazere, built in 1909 as a replica of St. Peter's; the cathedral in the old colonial section of town, built in the eighteenth century and restored in 1887; Fort de Castelo; and Ver-o-Peso market on the waterfront.

Numerous little shops offering handicrafts and souvenir items are spread along President Vargas Street between the Hilton and the waterfront.

Many ships also commence or conclude their Amazon River cruises at **Manaus** because its airport can service large planes, affording passengers access to the middle of the Amazon by air. Although it was a thriving commercial metropolis in the late 1800s during the rubber boom, today one might refer to Manaus as the armpit of South America. However, that reference may be unfair to numerous other South American cities that deservedly have received the same accolade yet by comparison look like Beverly Hills. Rarely can one find a city where every building, street, and sidewalk is in total disrepair and cluttered with garbage.

The city bus tour visits São Sebastião Square, the nineteenth-century Palacio Rio Negro, the Opera House that dates back to 1896, the Indian Museum, and the military zoo. Branches of the two largest South American jewelry chains, H. Stern and Amsterdam Sauer, offer transportation from your ship to their shops.

A more interesting option would be the riverboat ride down the Rio Negro to Lake January. Here are the boat docks, and you can take a walk on a wooden bridge into a jungle swamp to a pond filled with giant lily pads and an occasional alligator. The night tour to Lake January is dedicated to seeking out alligators by flashlight. Our guide was supposed to wrestle one; however, the match never took place. Although not as picture-perfect as the all-inclusive jungle ride at Disney World, these tours are through an authentic jungle and provide an opportunity to take some unique photographs to show the fans back home. If you are more adventurous, you can attempt to hire your own boat and guide and possibly get deeper into the jungle.

Halfway between Belem at the mouth of the Amazon and Manaus lies the third-largest town in the Brazilian Amazon-Santarem. The population grew to fifty thousand during the years of the gold rush in the 1920s.

Buses meet ships at the harbor to transport passengers to either the marketplace (*imercado*), which lies about a mile and a half downstream, or inland about a mile to the Hotel Tropical, where you can relax by the swimming pool and enjoy a local beer or a *caipirinha,* the traditional drink of the region consisting of smashed lime, sugar, and rum. Santarem is less crowded and in better repair than Manaus and is therefore a more comfortable place to shop for local crafts, many of which can be purchased from the artisans right at the gangway to your ship.

**Alter do Chão** is a sandy beach fifteen miles from Santarem on the Tapajos River. Some ships offer beach parties here.

## ARGENTINA—BUENOS AIRES

Most ships that call at **Buenos Aires** only remain from eight to twenty-four hours, not permitting sufficient time to explore this cosmopolitan metropolis that is the only place in South America reminiscent of European cities in France, Spain, and Italy. Because your time will be limited, you will want to take an organized morning tour of the city, where you can visit the principal square, Plaza de Mayo; La Catedral, where you can see the tomb of General José de San Martin, the obelisk which is the symbol of the city; the Teatro Colón, an important opera house; La Boca, an Italian district near the old port area; Museo de Art; Jardin Zoologico; the botanical gardens; the Recoleta, a vast-walled complex and site of Evita's tomb; and the residence of the president.

During the afternoon, you will want to stroll down Florida and Lavalle, the major shopping streets, as well as Galerias Pacifico, where you will find excellent bargains on leather shoes and purses in addition to a good selection of European-style boutiques. The quality of the merchandise and inexpensive prices make Buenos Aires the best shopping city in South America. Visitors often enjoy having a steak with all the trimmings and a bottle of local beer or wine at a typical Argentine restaurant. Popular spots include Casa Cruz, Bar Uriarte, La Cabana, La Cabrera, and Bar Sur or El Viejo Almacea for dinner and a tango show. The best hotels include the Four Seasons, Alvear Palace, and Faena.

## BRAZIL

When taking a cruise from **Rio de Janeiro**, you'll want to arrange to stay over in this unique city for a few days at the beginning or end of the cruise. Rio's beauty is due to its natural environs in which green-clad mountains border a city of high-rise apartments and hotels situated across from a string of beaches on the Atlantic Ocean. The hotel-beach-restaurant area starts in the north at the District of Leme and continues south through the districts of Copacabana, Ipanema, Leblon, and Gavea. The best hotels in Copacabana are the Rio Palace, the Rio Othon Palace, the Copacabana Palace, and the Sofitel. In Ipanema, it's the Caesar Park. The Sheraton lies at the intersection of Leblon and Gavea, and the Intercontinental Resort Hotel is still farther away in Gavea. All of these hotels are across the road from the beach and feature private pools, numerous restaurants, shops, and bars. If you desire a resort atmosphere, you will prefer either the Sheraton or the Intercontinental, which are farther away from the main part of the city.

You can eat quite inexpensively at one of the numerous pizzerias that line the beach area, or you can sample local Brazilian and Continental dishes at most of the hotel restaurants.

Tennis buffs can rent a court at either the Sheraton or Intercontinental hotels, and joggers can wear out their "New Balance specials" along the walk that stretches for six miles from Leme Beach to the end of Ipanema. Don't miss the samba show at Oba Oba or Plataforma I nor the picturesque cable-car ride to the top of Sugar Loaf Mountain, where you have a panoramic view of the entire city. A train ride to the top of Corcovada Mountain, where the statue of Christ towers over the entire city, is also a must for all visitors. If time permits, there are organized tours to Tijuca Forest, Paradise, and the Paqueta Islands.

There are many shops and boutiques on Copacabana Avenue, two blocks up from the beach, as well as in the Ipanema area, offering leather goods, jewelry, sportswear, and local handicrafts; however, I found few bargains. Gemstones and jewelry are reputed to be the best buys. H. Stern, the world's leading retail jewelry enterprise, has shops in all the major hotels.

One of the most enjoyable stops is Salvador (Bahia), where you can sun on one of the two beautiful beaches at Piata and Itapoa; visit numerous cathedrals and museums throughout the city; shop for silver, jewelry, and hand-carved rosewood at Mercado Modelo, silver at Gerson shops, and arts and crafts at Instituto (Mauá); play tennis at the

Hotel Méridien, which has a restaurant at the top that offers the best view of the city; or take an excursion to the island of Itaparica to swim and stroll through a charming small town filled with parks. You will want to sample the unique Bahian cuisine (combining African and European cooking styles) at Chica da Silva, Yemanja, Lampiao, and Moenda. For French and Continental cuisine, the best in town are St. Honore (at the Hotel Méridien) and Chez Bernard. With limited time, you can spend your day at either Hotel Méridien Bahia or Bahia Othon Palace, which offer good pools, shops, and restaurants.

## COLOMBIA—CARTAGENA

Located on the Caribbean Coast of Colombia, this 450-year-old city of Spanish heritage has become a popular stop for ships traversing the Panama Canal.

Visitors will want to visit the seventeenth-century fortress of San Felipe, with its impressive walls, tunnels, and cannons; the old walled city composed of colonial-style buildings with wood balconies and red tile roofs, parks, monasteries, and monuments; La Popa Hill, five hundred feet high, for a spectacular view of the city; and the new city area of resort hotels, beaches, shops, and restaurants.

The best shopping is at Prerino Gallo Plaza, near the Hilton, where there are several emerald shops, leather stores, craft shops, a disco, and a casino.

The beaches are crowded and dirty, and those wishing to sun and swim are best off going to the Cartagena Hilton, where there is a nice pool area, tennis courts, a health club, shops, and restaurants.

Walkers and joggers may enjoy the path along the sea, which starts at the old city and extends into the new city for three miles or so to the Hilton. Walking or jogging from the port to the old fortress or into the middle of town also is possible because both are only a mile or two from the harbor.

## URUGUAY—MONTEVIDEO

In Montevideo, you will have the best view of the city from the top of the town hall, where you can also eat lunch at Panormacico Municipal, one of Montevideo's better restaurants. Below town hall is the shopping district, where you can buy leather goods and woolens.

With only one day in port, you can take the city tour and see the obelisk, the La Carreta statue, the flea market, the natural history museum, the cathedral, and the mausoleum of José Artigas; or you can take a taxi out to the resort area of Carrasco, where you will find beautiful homes, restaurants, hotels, and beaches. Those traveling with children may wish to visit the zoological gardens and Rodo Park, an amusement park with rides, ponies, and theaters.

In the evening, there is a tango show and Uruguayan folk music at Tangueria del 40 in the Columbia Palace Hotel, dinner and dancing at El Mirador in the Hotel Oceania, and several discos—including Zum Zum, Lancelot, and Ton Ton Metek.

If time allows, **Punte del Este** is a charming resort town with numerous excellent beaches. L'Auberge and La Posta del Cangrejo are the two best hotels on the beach with good restaurants.

## VENEZUELA—CARACAS

The South American port most frequently visited by cruise ships is **La Guaira** (Caracas), Venezuela. This is the richest nation in South America because of its large oil production; however, the economic good fortune of the country has not passed down to the average man in the street, who appears to be living in relative poverty. The shacks of the poor offer a contrast to the opulent residences of the rich. Caracas is a city in a valley surrounded by mountains. The best view is from Mount Avila at its 6,500-foot summit. Check whether the cable car to the top is working—it is almost always out of order. You can also get a good view of the city from atop the Hilton Hotel.

A city tour will visit La Cathedral, with its artistically decorated interior; Santa Teresa Basilica, housing the oldest image of Christ in Venezuela; the capitol building, featuring the paintings of Tovar; Bólivar's birthplace, an outstanding example of colonial architecture; Los Caobos Park; Los Proceres Park; and the Museum of Natural Science, with its collection of stuffed animals.

There is little shopping that is worthwhile. The shops offer a variety of gold jewelry, but there are no bargains. Should you be in Caracas on Sunday, you can attend a bullfight at Plaza de Toros. For tennis or swimming, try the Macuto Hotel in La Guaira. The beach is not terrific, but the hotel has a large pool, shops, restaurants, a disco, theater, nightclub, and many facilities. Many cruisers not wishing to take the hectic tour of Caracas spend the day at the hotel.

Caracas also boasts many good restaurants offering French, Italian, and Venezuelan cuisines.

## THE MEDITERRANEAN, GREEK ISLANDS, MIDDLE EAST, AND ENVIRONS

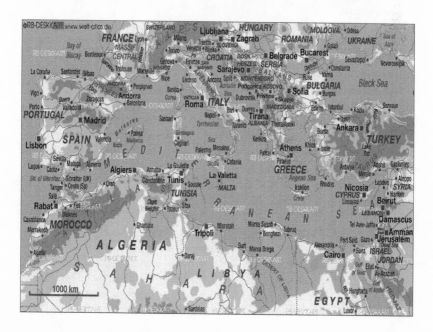

Like the Caribbean, the Mediterranean, Adriatic, Aegean, and Black seas are calm, and the weather in the area is generally pleasant, except for certain winter months.

There are probably no cruise grounds that offer as representative a sampling of history, as great a diversity in cultures, or as many varied and exciting places of interest as the Mediterranean. Imagine climbing up to the ancient Acropolis in Athens, standing before the Wailing Wall of Jerusalem, strolling through the famous shopping bazaar of Istanbul, gambling at the posh casinos in Monte Carlo, sunning at the jet-set beaches of the Côte d'Azur or Greek islands, all in seven to fourteen days.

For a number of years, various smaller Greek cruise lines have been running regularly scheduled cruises from Piraeus to the Greek islands and to the coastal cities of Turkey. Many of the vessels have seven-day itineraries, calling at such ancient and legendary islands as Rhodes, Mykonos, Delos, Santorini, Crete, Corfu, and Patmos, as well as such unusual Turkish ports as Istanbul, Marmaris, and Kusadasi. Some of these ships return to Piraeus between the third and fourth day, permitting passengers with tight schedules to take only half of the itinerary.

Regular cruises to other parts of the Mediterranean and adjoining seas leaving from Genoa, Venice, Naples, Nice, Cannes, Monte Carlo, Athens, or Istanbul have recently been offered by the Celebrity, Club Med, Costa, Crystal, Cunard, MSC, Oceania, Orient, Princess, Regent Seven Seas, Seabourn, Silversea, and Windstar cruise lines. In addition to the aforementioned Greek islands and Middle Eastern ports, these cruises may call in the Western Mediterranean at Capri, Sorrento, Palma de Mallorca, Barcelona, Sicily, Malta, Sardinia, Elba, Corsica, or Algeciras; in Africa or off the African coast at Casablanca, Tunis, Dakar, Tangier, Tenerife, Las Palmas, or Funchal; in the Adriatic at Split, Bari, or Dubrovnik; in the Black Sea at Odessa, Yalta, or Sochi; and in the Middle East at Haifa, Israel, Alexandria, Egypt, Beirut, or Cyprus, Dubai and Oman.

Although the majority of these ports have harbors that can accommodate only the smaller vessels, the large ships can drop anchor outside the harbor and transport the passengers ashore in small tenders. Today, a growing number of large luxury liners from the above-mentioned lines are scheduling numerous cruises each summer in the Mediterranean area. These cruises appeal to Europeans as well as to Americans, and have resulted in the development of a highly competitive Mediterranean cruise program paralleling that found in the Caribbean. Unfortunately, terrorism, local wars, and general unrest have caused ships to cancel their itineraries from time to time.

The following are the highlights of some of the more popular cruise stops in this area:

## ALGERIA

**Algiers,** with its population of nine hundred thousand, is Algeria's capital. It is a Mediterranean seaport standing on a hillside overlooking the bay. At the bottom of the hill is the modern city, and farther up is the old Moorish section called the Casbah, named for the citadel that stands on the top of the hill. The unique Casbah is an interesting section of crowded, narrow alleys, courtyards, and shops. The climate is varied, with temperatures falling to the twenties in the winter and up over a hundred during the summer months. The best season to visit Algiers' "turquoise coast" is between April and November. Worth visiting are several distinguished mosques dating from the Ottoman era, the National Museum of Moslem and Classic Antiquities, the Essai Gardens, and the university. You can take a bus ride, which provides superb views of the city, to the chic residential suburb of El Biar past the palace of the president. Algiers is flanked by several fine beaches on the Mediterranean, where you can swim and snorkel from March through October. The nightlife is limited largely to hotel bars and cabarets catering to foreigners.

## CROATIA

**Dubrovnik** is a small Croatian port with a population of twenty-six thousand located on the Adriatic Sea across from Italy. Its mild climate and medieval architecture have made it a favorite tourist attraction. As you sail into the harbor, you will note its fjord-like coastline. From the harbor, you can take a boat across to the island of Lokrum, which is a botanical preserve with interesting foliage, gardens, and a natural history museum. You can drive up Zarkovica Hill for a magnificent view of the city and swim at the beaches at Lapad and Sumratin. The area called the "old town" is completely encircled by a wall built during the fourteenth century. There are no motor vehicles allowed in the old town, and you will enjoy walking through the main street, Placa, and visiting St. Blaise's Church, Sponza Palace, the colorful market in Gundulic Square, the Rector's Palace, the cathedral, the Trade Union House, the tiny shops on the nearby street called Ulica od Puca, and the Fortress Minceta, where you can view the city from atop a circular tower at the highest point on the wall.

At the Dubrovnik President Hotel, a five-minute ride from the harbor, there are numerous bars, a glass-enclosed indoor pool, an outdoor lounge area, both a regular and a nude gravel beach, and an excellent shopping center a block away. Visitors can opt to take a scenic walk or jog back to the harbor from here—it is about two miles, all downhill.

At night, you can go to one of the fine local restaurants and taste such native dishes as *borec*, a kind of flaky pastry containing cheese, meat, or fruit; djuvech, thin slivers of pork grilled with rice, vegetables, and pepper; raznici, a lamb kebab; and kruskovac, a pear brandy. After dinner, there are numerous nightclubs, including the outdoor Labyrinth Club at the gate of the old town that offers music, dancing, and a striptease. You can try your luck at the gambling casino, dance at a discotheque, or attend Dubrovnik's summer festival, which features ballets, concerts, and various European artists.

## CYPRUS

Cyprus is an island republic in the northeast corner of the Mediterranean, south of Turkey and west of Syria. The island covers 3,500 square miles, and its 650,000 inhabitants are of Greek and Turkish origin. Cyprus has lofty mountain resorts that offer skiing during the winter, some interesting hilltop monasteries and castles, and beautiful forests filled with the regal cedar of Lebanon trees. Cruise ships generally dock at the ports of **Limassol**. Limassol is a resort town bordering the sea with many fine hotels. Le Meridien, Four Seasons, Hawaii Beach, and Amathus Beach hotels offer the most facilities, large pool areas, not-so-nice beaches, water sports, tennis, and restaurants. The entire ten-mile stretch between the harbor and Le Meridien lends itself to walking expeditions with visits to luxury hotels, restaurants, shops, and tavernas. Apart from the resort hotels and sea front, there is little of interest for tourists in this city. The old city of **Famagusta** is surrounded by an impressive wall and fortification containing such sights of historical and architectural interest as the Venetian Palace, Othello's Tower, the Church of St. Peter and St. Paul, and the Cathedral of St. Nicholas. Modern Famagusta, called Varoska, lies a mile to the south of the walled city and is a prosperous Greek community with sandy beaches, shops, tavernas, discos, and bars.

Fifty miles from Famagusta is **Nicosia**, which is part Greek and part Turkish. Within the walls of the Old City, you can visit St. John's Church (built in 1662) and the Folk Art Museum (formerly a Gothic monastery of the fifteenth century). There is also the Cyprus Museum, with well-preserved artifacts from archeological excavations. If you drive on the southern coast to the monastery of Stavrovouni, located on the crest of a mountain 2,260 feet above the sea, you can enjoy a breathtaking view of Cyprus, watch the monks at their work, and perhaps break bread with them at lunchtime. Other popular excursions include exploring the Greco-Roman theater at Curium and the wine-producing village of Omodus.

## EGYPT

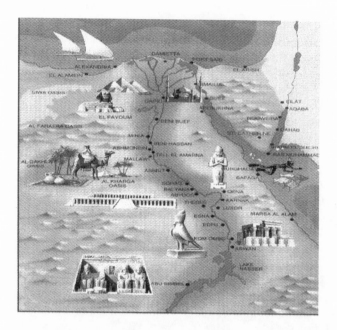

Ships generally dock at either **Port Said** or **Alexandria**, both of which are rather dirty, polluted port cities. Alexandria is the chief port and second-largest city in Egypt, lying on the northeastern end of the Nile River Delta on a strip of land between the Mediterranean Sea and Lake Mareotis. The temperatures climb from the fifties and sixties in winter to the nineties in summer. The city, which was founded by Alexander the Great in 332 BC, was a center of Greek culture and learning, but it has lost much of its former importance under the Egyptians. You may enjoy chartering a small boat to take you on a tour of the harbor, or you may prefer to relax on the twenty miles of sandy (so-so) beaches at Montaza, Maamura, or Agami. You can visit the Catacombs of Komel Shuquafa constructed in AD 2, the Roman Amphitheater, the Mosque of Aboual-Abaas Mursi, and the Montaza Palace with its beautiful grounds and gardens, which was a former residence of King Farouk and today has been converted to a guesthouse for government officials. The main shopping areas are Mansheya Square, Ramle Tram Station, and the Gold Souk. However, the main reason for your visit to either port is to permit a tour to **Cairo**, Egypt's capital, where you can explore the Egyptian Museum, which houses the most important collection of Egyptian antiquities, including the Tutankhamen treasures; Coptic Museum; Abdin Palace; the Ibn Tulun Mosque; the Sultan Hasan Mosque; the El Ashar Mosque; the "Old Cairo" area (site of numerous ancient Christian churches); or the shops at Kahn al Kahlil and the Musky Bazaar.

Certainly the highlight of any visit to Cairo is the site of the Pyramids of Giza and the legendary Sphinx, located in the Sahara Desert right outside the city. You can tour these magnificent antiquities on foot, on horseback, or by camel. Those not subject to claustrophobia may enjoy walking through the steep, low passages of the interior chambers of one of the pyramids. The Pyramid of Cheops is one of the remaining Seven Wonders of the Ancient World. Built in 2650 BC, it is still the largest and most massive stone structure in the modern world. A convenient oasis for lunch would be the historic Mena House, a deluxe hotel that was formerly a palatial hunting lodge and is located only minutes from the pyramids. You may prefer one of the river-cruising restaurants along the Nile operated by the Oberoi Hotels group.

Those wishing to visit the antiquities of ancient Egypt will want to consider one of the Nile River cruises from **Luxor** offered by ships of Sheraton Nile Cruises, Sonesta Hotels and Nile Cruises, and Abercrombie & Kent cruise lines. At Luxor, you will want to visit the awesome ruins of Karnak, the largest temple in the world, as well as the temple of Luxor. Across the river on the western bank lies the "city of the dead," with its ornate tombs and artifacts. The ships generally conclude their cruises in *Aswân*, where you can visit the Aswan Dam.

## FRANCE (INCLUDING CÔTE D'AZUR AND MONTE CARLO)

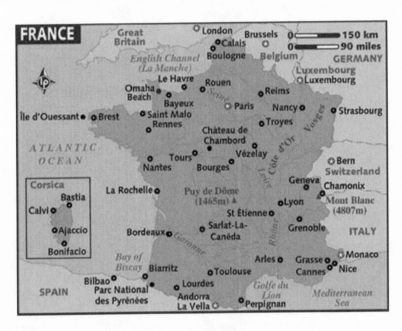

**Calvi,** on the island of Corsica, has recently become a port for some of the smaller cruise ships. For many years an Italian island, Corsica was sold to France in 1786. However, you may find the island more reminiscent of Greece or Italy than France. The small streets that wind around the harbor offer numerous small restaurants, cafés, souvenir shops, boutiques, and food stores. Above the harbor (a five-minute walk) sits the Citadel of Calvi, which dominates the landscape when you approach the town by boat. Walking left from the town will bring you to a long strand of beach surrounded by a pine forest. There are lounges and umbrellas for rent and numerous small bars and snack shops here. Although not well-known, Calvi is a charming cruise stop where you can spend a relaxed day at the beach and browsing around the quaint little village.

**Cannes** and **Nice** on the Côte d'Azur (French Riviera) are the most popular cruise ports in southern France. The climate is warm and sunny throughout the year, except for the winter months, when temperatures at night and in the morning can be quite chilly. You will enjoy walking down the world's most chic promenade, "The Croissette," stopping to browse in smart boutiques or to rest at an outdoor café where you can nibble on cheese and crisp bread while you watch the beautiful French women parade by in their bikinis. The beaches in Cannes and Nice are quite colorful, although not ideal for swimming. You can drive west to **St. Tropez** and sun and swim at Tahiti Beach, which has sand and numerous rental lounges, small restaurants, bars, and facilities, but is not all that much more desirable for swimming. On all the beaches, the majority of the women go topless. If your ship stops at St. Tropez, in addition to the beaches, you may enjoy exploring the numerous small boutiques and bistros in town spread along the streets and alleys around the harbor. Some of the cruise lines offer excursions from St. Tropez inland through Provence to visit the wine vineyards.

An interesting side trip would be to the old walled town of **St. Paul-de-Vence**, which rests on a hill terraced with vineyards. This charming little walled city consists of narrow, winding, cobblestone streets lined with quaint shops and villas. You can enjoy lunch and dinner at Chateau du Domaine St. Martin or Le Mas d'Artigny—two of my favorite French inns—or the Colombe d'Or, all of which are located near the city. In the evening in both Cannes and Nice, you may wish to dine at one of the many fine French restaurants, dance at a discotheque, or gamble at the elegant casinos.

The largest hotels in Cannes with the most facilities are the Majestic, the Carlton, the Martinez, and the Grand. My favorite French restaurants on the Riviera are L'Oasis, Moulins de Mougins, the Chanteclair at the Negresco, Eden Rock at Hotel du Cap, and the main dining room at Chateau du Domaine St. Martin, all of which are highly rated and très cher.

**Monte Carlo**, in the principality of Monaco, has become a popular port for smaller cruise ships that can pull right up to the docks in town. The harbor area is colorful with bars and cafés. The main tourist attraction, however, is the main square that is surrounded by the world-famous Casino of Monte Carlo, Hotel de Paris, and Café de Paris. Here you can browse through designer shops, dine at elegant restaurants in Hotel de Paris and the Hermitage, or at the more casual Café de Paris, or try your luck at the Casino, and soak up the ultraposh environment. Those preferring American-style gambling can be accommodated at the casino across the square from Hotel de Paris or at the former Loew's Hotel, now the Le Monte Carlo Grand Hotel. The Palace, its gardens, and an aquatic museum sit on a hill overlooking the harbor, accessible by taxi, bus, car, or a picturesque stroll. Passengers on ships stopping at Monte Carlo or Ville France may wish to take the short drive to the ancient Village of Eze, where they will be rewarded with panoramic views, a quaint, small French town, and various dining options including the acclaimed restaurant at Chateau Chevre d'Or.

## GIBRALTAR

**Gibraltar** is a British territory on the southern tip of the Iberian Peninsula with 29,300 English-speaking residents. At the Gibraltar Museum, visitors can experience an audio-visual presentation of the country's fascinating history.

From the cruise terminal it is a fifteen-minute walk (or a £2.5 shuttle ride) to the center of town. A pedestrian shopping street runs for over a mile and terminates near the entrance to where a cable car will transport you to the top of the Rock of Gibraltar, stopping at the middle station to visit the famous Barbary Apes, more properly called the Barbary Macaques. At the top, you can enjoy impressive views of the Andalusian and Moroccan coastlines. An option would be to take a sightseeing taxi ride up the Rock for £25 per person. Other places of interest include the Crystal Factory and the eighth-century Moorish Castle. Best buys are duty-free liquors, brandies, and crystal.

## GREECE AND THE GREEK ISLANDS

**Piraeus** is the port of Athens and the busiest cruise port in the Mediterranean area. You will enjoy dining at one of the smaller outdoor restaurants along the waterfront, where you can select your own fish or lobster and watch it cooked to order.

It is approximately a five-mile drive into **Athens,** where you can visit the ancient Acropolis, the symbol of the glory of ancient Greece. Here you can climb its marble steps reaching the entrance, the Propylaea, a masterpiece of classical architecture. Then view the Parthenon, the most perfect example of classical architecture in the world. Looking down from the Acropolis, you can see the two ancient theaters, the Greek Theater of Dionysus and the grand Roman Theater of Herod Atticus, restored and used for concerts and classical plays. At the foot of the hill beneath the Acropolis are numerous charming garden restaurants where you can enjoy lunch or a cold drink. Daphne is my favorite.

Other important sites include Athens Olympic Stadium; the National Archaeological Museum; Syntagma Square and the former royal palace, now Parliament; Hadrian's Arch, Mount Lycabettus; and the National Garden, filled with paths winding through botanical gardens, ancient statuary, ponds, a zoo, and cafés.

After a day of sightseeing, you may enjoy shopping for local jewelry, handicrafts, antiques, designer fashions, and furs at the Ermon Pedestrian Zone right off Syntagma Square or taking a short drive to Vouliagmeni Beach, which is a mediocre public beach with decent facilities. In the evening, don't miss the impressive sound and light program across from the Acropolis, where the story of ancient Greece is recounted with music, lights, and sound effects. Later in the evening, you will want to visit the charming "plaka" area, where hundreds of tavernas offer authentic *bouzouki* music, Greek dancing, ouzo, and local wines. Most of the tavernas are on or near Mnisikleos Street. On a warm evening, one of the more scenic and romantic experiences in Athens is dining at Orizontas Restaurant at the top of Mount Lycabettus (accessible by cable car) while watching the sun set over the Acropolis (very expensive).

If you are spending a day before or after the cruise in Athens, the best hotels are the Grand Bretagne on Syntagma Square and the Hilton, Intercontinental, Leda Marriott, and St. George Lycabettus. These hotels feature numerous restaurants and other amenities. The Electra Palace enjoys a convenient location in the Plaka and offers a roof garden with a small pool and enviable view. If time permits, your best bet is the extensive resort complex that comprises the Astir Palace in Vouliagmeni, about a half-hour drive from Athens.

When taking a taxi, be certain to obtain some idea of the correct fare before embarking. Often the meters are not working, or when they are, the driver may frequently adjust the meter up as the trip progresses.

**Corfu** is the northernmost Greek island, located in the Ionian Sea, and has a population of a little more than one hundred thousand. The best weather is in late spring and early fall, with the summers being quite hot. Its 229 square miles are covered with green mountains, beautiful flowers, and millions of gnarled olive trees. Don't miss swimming in the warm, calm Ionian Sea at one of the hotels or taking a horse-and-buggy ride through the quaint little town with its winding streets and interesting people. Places of interest include the Achilleion Palace Museum, the Archeological Museum, the fourteenth-century Palaio Frourio (literally "old fortress"), the royal palace museum complex, and the Esplanade.

You may wish to spend your day at the Corfu Holiday Palace (formerly the Corfu Hilton) overlooking "Mouse Island," two and a half miles from town, or the Corfu Imperial Resort complex on Komeno Bay, six miles out of the city. These hotels feature lovely pools, beaches, water sports, and good restaurants. The Corfu Holiday Palace boasts a very picturesque setting. You can spend a part of the day by the pool then have lunch, followed by a climb down the olive tree-clad hill leading to the azure-blue sea and the bridge over to Mouse Island.

One of the more picturesque areas in Corfu is the beach at Paleokastritsa. It has little grottos, restaurants, and an incomparably beautiful setting. Other nice beaches more suitable for swimming can be found at Glifada and Pelekas on the west coast, Sidari on the north coast, Dassia and Ipsos on the east coast, and Kavos at the southern tip of the island. Those wishing to take a scenic drive, reminiscent of the Amalfi Drive in southern Italy, should start at the beach at Dassia and proceed north to the charming village of Kassiopi, passing through Ipsos, Nissaki, Kalami, and Kouloura.

**Crete (Heraklion)** is located eighty-one miles south of mainland Greece between the Aegean and Mediterranean seas. It is the largest and most important of the Greek islands, covering 3,200 square miles and having a population of 483,000. A chain of high mountains divides the island into four distinct regions, each having a different scenery combining to form the impressive beauty of the Cretan landscape. The people are friendly and hospitable and often can be seen in local costumes observing their age-old traditions. The Archaeological Museum of Heraklion has twenty-three halls that house the remains of the highly developed Minoan civilization, which flourished for more than two thousand years. If you drive out to Knossos, you can see a maze of ruins, including the remarkable excavation of the partially restored palace of King Minos. You can also drive out to a fishing village in the south and spend a quiet day swimming and sunbathing.

**Delos,** an uninhabited island one and a half miles southwest of Mykonos in the center of the Aegean Sea, was the legendary birthplace of Zeus's children, Apollo and Artemis, and the most sacred of the Greek islands during Hellenistic times. Under Roman rule, the island grew in stature and wealth, only to be ravaged later by wars and pirate raids. Today, cruise ships dock for a few hours to enable passengers to walk through the ancient ruins, visit the island's small museum, and see the most impressive remains—the lions made of Naxos marble. Delos is considered to be one of the greatest open-air archeological museums in the world.

**Katakolan** lies 193 miles due west of Athens in the northwest Peloponnese. Cruise ships stop here on the way to Athens to permit passengers to explore the ancient city of Olympia, where the first Olympic races were held in 776 BC. Set between the Alphios and Kladeos rivers in a pine-shaded valley is the site of some important archaeological treasures. Places to visit include the Temple of Zeus (456 BC); the Temple of Hera (600 BC); the Archeological Museum, which houses numerous ancient Greek sculptures; Praxiteles's statue of Hermes; the Head of Hera; Paionios's Winged Victory; and athletic paraphernalia from the ancient games. For visitors wishing to spend a relaxing day by the sea, it is only a twenty-minute taxi drive to Aldemar Hotel's Olympic Village complex, which is a large first-class property situated on several miles of brown-sand beach with two inviting free-form swimming pools, tennis courts, a few shops, and a good restaurant to sample Greek specialties for lunch. Also there are several souvenir shops, boutiques, and tavernas in the town adjacent to the harbor where ships dock.

Situated in the Aegean Sea not far from the coast of Turkey lies **Kos,** a 170-square-mile island with twenty thousand inhabitants. It is rich in history, but is best known as the birthplace of Hippocrates, the "father of medicine." Most of the important sites are within walking distance of the harbor; however, many visitors opt to rent bicycles, which of course permit greater mobility for exploring the island. Surrounding the harbor are hundreds of small souvenir shops offering T-shirts, beach attire, leather goods, gold, and pottery as well as small taverns and restaurants. There are a number of beaches near the town of Kos, including Psalidi, Lambi, and Aghios Fokas. Seven miles west of town is a somewhat better beach at Tigaki, and two miles farther are nice sandy beaches at Marmari, Kardamen, and Kafalos. From the harbor, charter boats offer trips to neighboring islands.

Ancient Kos has two sections. Immediately adjacent to the harbor is the famous Castle of the Knights of St. John, which is a fortress with two enclosures dating back to the fourteenth and fifteenth centuries. It is surrounded by a deep moat, and it was originally built as a medical center. Nearby are several Turkish mosques and the famous Hippocrates Tree, reputed to be the oldest tree in Europe and the site where Hippocrates treated the sick.

Southwest of the harbor in the other section of ancient Kos, you can visit impressive ruins, including a vast Roman bath, the Casa Romana, with its well-preserved mosaic floor from the third century AD depicting the abduction of Europa by Zeus, the fourteen-tier Odeon from the Roman period, and the remains of the old Roman Way.

Two miles south of the town of Kos is the sacred shrine of Asklepion, the god of healing. Considered the first medical school in the world, it dates back to the fifth century BC, when Hippocrates opened the school to encourage the study of medicine. The island was the center of medical practice in ancient times.

**Mykonos** is the favorite island of the young, bargain travelers as well as the jet-set. Here you can stroll through little whitewashed towns with windmills, churches and winding streets, shop for bargains in handmade woolens and jewelry in its small boutiques, buy a designer dress from Galatis at his shop right off the main square, or swim and sun at one of its many excellent sandy beaches on the crystal clear, blue Aegean Sea. The three best beaches, which can only be reached by taxi or a short boat ride, are the Paradise, the Super Paradise, and the Elia. All three feature nude bathing. Elia is the most beautiful of the three. There is also a nice beach two miles from town, Ayios Stephanos. The town is known for its windmills on the site of the ancient city, its hundreds of small churches and its mascot, Petros the Pelican, who can be found strolling near the harbor. In the evening, you will want to visit the tavernas and cafés bursting with the sounds of bouzouki music and fragrant with the aroma of ouzo, coffee, and baklava.

**Nafplion,** Greece's first capital after the Greek War of Independence of the 1820s, is located four miles across the Argolic Gulf from Argos, in the Peloponnese area of Greece. The town is known for its three fortresses: the 1714 citadel of Palamidi, which served as a prison until 1980; the Akronalphia fortress, which served as a prison until 1956; and Bourtze, a tiny island fortress six hundred yards offshore, which dates back to 1472. This is a big tourist destination for Greeks and other Europeans, with numerous walking streets lined with a mélange of shops, wine stores, and small restaurants. Many of the seaside eateries offer fish and typical Greek fare. The town boasts some of the creamiest gelati in the country, as well as the eighteenth-century Venetian arsenal that dominates the Plateia Syntagma. Hellas Restaurant in the Syntagma and Karamanlis on the waterfront are recommended. The town is a base for tours to the ancient ruins in Mycenae (site of Europe's oldest monumental structure, the famous Lion's Gate), the ruins at Epidaurus, and ancient Corinth with its archeological wonders of the kingdom of Pelops.

**Patmos** is in the northern section of the Greek islands, lying close to Asia Minor in the Aegean Sea. This tiny island of only thirteen square miles with 2,500 inhabitants is the most sacred of the Greek islands today. It was here that John the Apostle wrote the Apocalypse (the Book of Revelation). The site where St. John saw his prophetic visions is marked by a Byzantine-style church. You can also visit the grotto where he lived or the eleventh-century monastery nearby that houses priceless manuscripts and religious works of art. You can walk or ride up to the monastery, which offers some of the most spectacular and beautiful views you may ever experience, or you can swim at one of the colorful sandy beaches—Griko Beach and Dikofti Beach being the most popular.

**Rhodes,** with its area of 540 square miles and population of sixty-four thousand, is located twelve miles off the coast of Turkey in the Aegean Sea. The island's long and eventful history is represented by pre-Hellenic temples, Byzantine churches, mosques and minarets, classical monuments, medieval walled towns, fortresses, and picturesque little villages. This large fertile island was called "Bride of the Sun" by Homer and "Island of Roses" by more recent poets. In ancient times, it was a prosperous island, and the medieval Knights of St. John of Jerusalem settled here and built a walled, fortified city that is now the best-preserved such town in the Mediterranean area. Rhodes divides into the new and the old town. The new town consists of hotels, boutiques, restaurants, and public beaches; the old town, situated near the harbor behind the walls of the Castle of the Knights, is a maze of narrow cobbled streets, arched facades, and antiquities. Here you will find hundreds of small tourist shops, tavernas, and restaurants as you work your way up to the historic sites. Sightseeing in the old town of Rhodes should include the fourteenth-century Palace of the Grand Master, the remarkable Street of the Knights, the mosques built during the Turkish occupation, and the quaint Jewish synagogue.

This is possibly the most developed resort area in the Greek islands, with hundreds of hotels, the most fashionable being the Rodos Palace and Rodos Park Suites. All the large hotels feature desirable shops, restaurants, and swimming pools and are situated on beaches. Most of the beaches are dirty, pebbly, and hot; however, the water is clear, warm, and delightful for swimming. There are numerous good indoor/outdoor restaurants near the Grand Hotel in the center of town, and several of the outdoor garden restaurants in the old town area appear inviting.

In the evening, you may enjoy the sound and light performance in the Palace of the Knights or the wine festival at Rodini Park, where you can consume all the wine you can drink for a few drachmas.

Beach enthusiasts will prefer to take the scenic thirty-two-mile drive across the east coast of the island past charming villages set among orchards and olive trees to the town of **Lindos**, where there are sandy beaches that offer excellent swimming. Here you also can ride a donkey up to the ancient acropolis situated on top of a scenic hill, browse through souvenir shops, and have a beer at a local taverna.

**Santorini,** the site of Greece's active volcano, is located on the Aegean Sea, north of Crete and south of Mykonos. The bay on the west coast was once part of the island that sank after a violent eruption of the volcano. Your ship will anchor in the harbor, and you can take either a donkey ride or a cable car to the whitewashed town of Thira, with its narrow streets perched on the edge of a steep cliff rising from the sea and offering a superb panorama. An important site is the ancient ruins of Akortiri. The excavations date back to 2000 BC, when the town was destroyed by earthquakes and volcanic eruptions. Akortiri was once one of the best-preserved ruins of an ancient Greek town in existence, but today there is little to see. You can visit the Boutari Winery, located midway between Thira and Akortiki, where you can tour the winery and taste a selection of Boutari wines. Oenophiles will also enjoy a wine tasting at the Koutsogiannopoulos Winery, found in an extraordinary natural cave. Strolling through the winding streets of Thira, with its small shops, rooftop restaurants, small hotels, and outside cafés overlooking the sea is a delightful experience. Kastro and Zafora, near the cable-car station, and Koukoumavlos, below the Hotel Atlantis, offer a nice selection of Greek dishes and beverages and afford an excellent panorama of the town and harbor. Sphinx, across the walk from Atlantis Hotel, features a Continental menu and also overlooks the harbor. The two most highly regarded upscale restaurants, Selene and Aris, are only open for dinner. Palia Kameni, to the right of Sphinx, is a pleasant small alfresco bar, a good choice for a drink with a view. You can hike to the crater of an active volcano on the island of Nea Kameni or visit the quaint village of Oia at the northern tip of the island, where cobbled streets are lined with tiny shops.

**Skiathos** is an incredibly charming, pine-studded island that has not yet suffered the effects of the hordes of European tourists that inundate Mykonos, Rhodes, and Corfu. This beautifully pristine haven in the Northern Aegean boasts colorful shops and cafés that line the waterfront's cobblestone streets and sandy strands that beckon beachgoers to enjoy the warm waters of the azure sea. The best beach is at Koukounaries, situated at the foot of the Skiathos Palace Hotel, a twenty-minute bus or taxi ride from the harbor. Unusual rock formations and a secluded beach can be found at Lalaria, which is accessible by boat. In addition to the beaches, tourists will enjoy strolling through the streets that emanate from the harbor, browsing through the small shops, and having a drink or light meal at one of the numerous outdoor cafés.

## ISRAEL

**Israel** is the small nation on the eastern shore of the Mediterranean founded in 1948 as a homeland for Jews from all parts of the world. The weather is most pleasant in the spring and fall, when the days are warm and the evenings cool. Your ship may dock at **Haifa**, where lovely Mount Carmel descends to the sea. An underground metro can transport you from a station behind the port to the top of Mount Carmel in a commercial area near the Dan Panorama Hotel. If you only have a short time in port and cannot drive to Jerusalem, you can spend a delightful day in the vicinity of Haifa, where you can visit the Bahai Temple, Elijah's cave, the artist colonies at Ein Hod and Safad, the Druze villages, and a nearby kibbutz (a communal farm where the residents grow the food they eat and lead an industrious, self-sufficient life, seldom leaving their own community). You may wish to relax and have lunch or dinner at the Rondo Grill in the beautiful Dan Carmel Hotel, which offers a spectacular view of the city and harbor, or at the nearby Dan Panorama Hotel. If you have time, take in a local folkloric show with Israeli dancing and singing, then try Israel's delicious answer to the hot dog—a falafel sandwich, hummus (mashed chick peas and olive oil), vegetables, and spicy yogurt sauces stuffed into pita bread.

If your ship docks at **Ashod** or anchors overnight in Haifa, you will have time to drive down the coast to Tel Aviv, a modern, industrious Israeli city. There are lovely beaches here and in the nearby suburb of **Herzliya**. In the evening, you will enjoy walking through the quaint streets and shops in the old town of **Jaffa,** where there are good Continental and Israeli restaurants and nightclubs. The most highly acclaimed French-Continental-Israeli restaurants in Tel Aviv are Twelve Tribes at the Sheraton and Mesa; and for typical Middle Eastern specialties, your best bet is Shaul's Inn near the Carmel market. If time allows, you may want to stay overnight at one of the deluxe seashore hotels, such as the Hilton, Dan Panorama, Sheraton, Carlton, Hyatt, Intercontinental, or Holiday Inn.

You can drive or take a bus or taxi to **Jerusalem** in about one hour from Tel Aviv or an hour and a half from Ashdod. Within the walls of the old city are contained some of the holiest sanctuaries of Christianity, Judaism, and Islam. After entering one of the historic gates, you will walk through narrow winding streets lined with shops and intriguing passageways to the Western Wall or "Wailing Wall," the holiest of Jewish sites and the only remnant of the walls surrounding the temple of biblical times. You can walk down the Via Dolorosa, with its fourteen Stations of the Cross, to the Church of the Holy Sepulchre, which stands on Golgotha, the traditional site of the crucifixion of Jesus. The Dome of the Rock nearby marks the spot where Mohammed is said to have ascended to heaven. While in Jerusalem, you may also wish to see the Chagall windows at the Hadassah Hospital, the Kennedy Memorial, Yad Vashem, the memorial to the Holocaust, the Dead Sea Scrolls at the Shrine of the Book, the Knesset building, and the views of the city from the Mount of Olives and Mount Scopus. If you wish to sample typical Middle Eastern dishes in a comfortable atmosphere, you will enjoy Minaret Restaurant, a few blocks from King David Citadel Hotel, where four generations of Abo Salah's family have entertained locals, tourists, and dignitaries since 1960. Start off with a tasting of mixed salads including hummus, tahina, baba ganush, and several other varieties followed by a sampling of grilled meats and poultries on skewers. Currently popular French-Continental restaurants include Arcadia, Mishkenot Sha'anim, Katy's, Darna (Moroccan/French/kosher), and Ocean (seafood); however, in Israel many upscale restaurants frequently come and go. The best hotel facilities are at the King David Hotel, which is a centrally located hotel with a great deal of old-world charm; the Hilton; King David Citadel; Laromma; the Sheraton; and the Hyatt, which sits on Mount Scopus near Hadassah Hospital overlooking the old city.

**Bethlehem** is only a short drive from Jerusalem, and you can continue on to the famous Dead Sea. Here you can float in hot water so dense with salt that it is impossible to sink. If time allows, you will want to visit historic Masada, the recently uncovered ruins of the mountaintop fortress where an entire city of Jews made a last stand against the Romans in AD 70, all preferring to take their lives rather than surrender. Continuing back to Haifa, you can take a lovely drive past the Sea of Galilee, Tiberius, and the Golan Heights.

## ITALY

**Civitavecchia Port of Rome**: The crowded port at Civitavecchia has become a popular choice among cruise lines for embarking and disembarking passengers because of its proximity to Rome's international airport. Just as Rome wasn't built in a day, it is probably impossible to adequately explore this expansive metropolitan city in a day. Therefore, many cruise lines offer pre- and postcruise land options in the eternal city. Should this only be a one-day stopover, and you have never visited Rome, you probably are best off taking one of the ship's organized tours. However, for those who have been there before or who have opted for the pre- or postcruise stay over, there is a plethora of possibilities to discover.

Although one would have to spend a week here to thoroughly explore the environs, given limited time, the following would be the most important, "don't miss" points of interest: St. Peter's Square and the Vatican, home of the Pieta by Michelangelo, as well as the Vatican Museum and the Sistine Chapel with the paintings of Michelangelo; the Roman Forum and the nearby Colosseum; the Pantheon, the most intact building from ancient Rome located near the Piazza Navona; the Catacombs of the Appian Way; the Piazza di Spagna (Spanish Steps) leading up to the Borghese Gardens and the famous Galleria Borghese with its numerous Italian masterpieces; the cafés and shops along the Via Veneto; Trevi Fountain; Galleria Nazionale d'Arte Antica, which is located in the Palazzo Barberini, with paintings from the thirteenth to sixteenth century; Michelangelo's statue of Moses located in the Church of San Pietro in Vincoli; and the old Jewish Ghetto near Campo de' Fiori and the Theater of Marcellus.

Serious shoppers will prefer the designer boutiques that line the streets that are across from the Piazza di Spagna, including Via Borgognona and Via Condotti. Other major shopping streets would include Via del Corso, Via Francesco Crispi, Via Frattina, Via Sistina, Via Vittorio Veneto, and Via Barberini. Although it would be difficult to picture the following suggestion without a map, a walking tour that would cover most of this would start at the Spanish Steps, visiting the shops on the streets across from the bottom of the steps, then ascending to the top and following Via Sistina to Piazza Barberini and continuing on to Via Vittorio Veneto, and ending at the Via Veneto, where you can stop for a beverage or lunch at an outdoor café. After this pause, you can continue on to the Borghese Gardens. After exploring Galleria Borghese, you can proceed through this colorful park and end up back at the Spanish Steps. With a map, this will not be as difficult as it sounds.

There are hundreds of hotels and restaurants in Rome, as in any large city. Your best bet for lunch is to opt for one near where you're touring that looks appealing and has a menu in your price range. There are a concentration of restaurants on the Piazza Navona, on the Via Veneto, and in the Trastevere area. The most expensive hotels, including Hassler, Lord Byron, Eden, and Excelsior, all boast excellent restaurants. However, there are many fine moderately priced restaurants as well.

**Elba** is a small Italian island with ninety-one miles of coastline lying in the Mediterranean between Corsica and mainland Italy, and is best known as Napoleon's place of exile in 1814. His residence in Portoferraio and country home in San Martino are still open today as museums for visitors. Ships dock at the capital, **Portoferraio**, a not-so-beautiful busy port town with a few shops, restaurants, a fortress, and a decent public beach (with pebbles and no sand). For those not venturing out from town, La Ferrigna is touted to be the place for lunch to try Elban cooking with emphasis on fresh fish and seafood.

After taking a tour around the island, which should include Napoleon's country home in San Martino, the port town of **Porto Azzurro**, and the fishing village at Marciana Marina, you may wish to have lunch and spend the afternoon at the beach areas at Procchio, Marina di Campo, or the Bay of Biodola. The Bay of Biodola is only a ten-minute drive from port and has a long strand of brown-sand beach, a lovely setting, and numerous upscale hotels with private beach areas, pools, and restaurants. The Heritage is probably your best bet.

**Genoa**, **Portofino**, **Cinque Terre**, and environs: **Genoa** is Italy's largest port and ranks second in size only to Marseilles among Mediterranean ports. Few ships stop at Genoa as a port of call unless they are embarking from that city. Most ships anchor off of Portofino and tender into its charming, picturesque harbor.

It has been said that Genoa is a city of layers or levels: the lowest level is the noisy and dirty harbor area, with its ships, dance halls, and bars; the middle level contains large hotels, shops, good restaurants, cinemas, the opera house, and the Via Garibaldi, with its chain of late Renaissance palaces; and the upper level is a series of hills, winding streets, and funiculars. Genoa lies in the middle of Italy's two Rivieras, and you can drive to such seaside resort towns as San Remo, Rapallo, Santa Margarita Ligure, Portofino, La Spezia, and Viareggio.

With only limited time, your best bet is to drive to **Portofino**, fifty miles southeast of Genoa. As previously mentioned, the vast majority of ships visiting this area of Italy tender passengers directly into the horseshoe-shaped harbor of Portofino. Here you can explore small boutiques, souvenir shops, and small outdoor cafés. Since the entire town is so small, your exploration will take only a few hours. You may wish to take the uphill climb to the fashionable Splendido Hotel, a yachtsmen's rendezvous perched on the side of a mountain overlooking the harbor. Here you can enjoy lunch or a drink with a panoramic vista. The hotel recently built an annex right on the harbor where the tender leaves you off, appropriately named Splendido Mare. An alfresco lunch here is also excellent and memorable. Another possibility would be to take the ten-minute bus ride or fifty-minute walk from Portofino to the neighboring town of Santa Margarita Ligure. This is also a colorful village with more hotels, shops, and restaurants than you will find in Portofino.

The coastline towns commonly referred to as the **Cinque Terre** lie five miles east of Genoa and are set among olive and chestnut groves on a steep, rocky terrain overlooking the sea. They include the communities of Monterosso, Vernazza, Corniglia, Manarola, and Riomaggiore. Most cruise ships anchor off the coast of Portovenere, which is adjacent to these communities. The best way to explore the area and enjoy the landscape is by excursion boat. For the more hearty (Olympic types), fourteen walking trails are available for wandering from town to town. The easiest, shortest, and most popular scenic walk is between Riomaggiore and Manarola. The only sandy beach is a crowded strand in Monterosso. Typical restaurants for Lingurian seafood abound in each of the communities.

**Livorno Port for Florence**: Since **Florence** is not located on the sea, ships call at Livorno to enable passengers to take overland trips to Florence, Pisa, and Siena. Usually the ships will offer expensive bus tours to Florence; however, it is possible to take an hour-and-a-half train ride from Livorno for as little as $11 round trip. Although Florence is one of Italy's largest cities, it is possible to get around by foot while covering all the major points of interest. The distance from the train station to the famous Ponte Vecchio (old bridge) is only a bit over a mile.

Your sightseeing should include visits to the Galleria dell'Accademia, home of Michelangelo's famous statue of David (be prepared for a very long wait to get in); Galleria degli Uffizi, one of the world's outstanding museums and Italy's finest collection of art; the Cathedral of Santa Maria del Fiore (Duomo), with its unique bell tower designed by Giotto; Santa Croce, a Franciscan Gothic church with frescoes by Giotto, as well as the tombs of Michelangelo, Machiavelli, Rossini, and Galileo; the thirteenth-century Palazzo Vecchio with its 308-foot tower, once home to the Medici; and the colorful area surrounding the Ponte Vecchio, spanning the Arno River, surrounded by shops and small trattorias. The shops on the bridge carry exquisite jewelry by some of Italy's great designers.

Florence also offers numerous designer boutiques, the best of which are located on Via dè Tornabuoni, Via Vigna Nuova, and Via Porta Rossa. Some of the city's most excellent restaurants include Enoteca, I Quattro Amici, Alle Murate, and Sabatini's. For a less expensive meal, try Cavallino, Buca dell'Orafo, or Le Fonticine. Many tourists enjoy sipping a cappuccino or other beverage on Piazza della Signoria, one of the country's most dramatic squares. For a splendid panorama of the city, you can cross the Arno and climb up a small hill to Piazzale Michelangelo, where a bronze copy of Michelangelo's David dominates the square.

**Naples, Sorrento, Capri, Amalfi, and Positano**: Many ships visit Naples or Sorrento on their way to and from Rome. Accessible from both ports are the ruins of Pompei, the island of Capri, and the romantic villages of Positano and Amalfi that sit along the picturesque Amalfi Drive.

If your ship stops in **Naples**, it is quite easy to take the one-hour hydrofoil ride to the island of Capri or to take the fifteen-mile drive to Pompei. If you wish to visit the towns along the Amalfi Drive, you must first take a thirty- to sixty-minute drive to either Sorrento or Salerno, where you gain access to this fantastically beautiful and breathtaking coastal road that winds around cliffs and passes through quaint little seaside towns. Recently, ships more frequently tender into Sorrento because it is more accessible for exploration of the Amalfi coast, and it only takes twenty minutes to travel by hydrofoil from here to Capri.

Tours to Pompei include an explanation of the well-preserved ruins of this ancient city destroyed by the eruption of Mount Vesuvius in AD 79. The crater of Mount Vesuvius can be ascended by chairlift. In the city of Naples, you can visit the National Museum to see its valuable art collections and relics from Pompei. Also worthwhile are the Aquarium of Naples, the San Carlo Opera House, and many of the beautiful churches and castles.

If you do not take an organized tour along the Amalfi Drive, it is possible to rent a car or hire a taxi for the day. You will want to explore the quaint seaside towns of **Amalfi** and **Positano** and drive up to **Ravello** for an exquisite view of this entire area. **Positano**, with its pedestrian path lined with shops and boutiques that winds down the cliff from the main road to the sea, is the most frequented town for tourists. Two outstanding and romantic resorts in Positano are San Pietro and Le Sirenuse, both excellent places to stop for lunch or dinner. Next 2 is also a highly touted restaurant. In **Amalfi,** another charmer is the Santa Catarina. Those wishing to stop here for lunch will take an elevator from the main hotel through the cliff to an outdoor terrace surrounded by citrus trees, overlooking the sea and the pool. In **Ravello,** the best place for lunch with an awesome view of the other towns and sea is the terrace of the Hotel Palumbo, where the proprietor will serve you wine from the hotel's own vineyards.

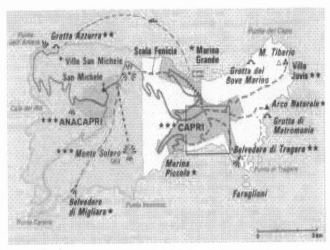

*Capri Island*

From either Naples or Sorrento, you can take the hydrofoil (*aliscafi*) to the beautiful floral Isle of **Capri**, where you will be dropped off in a pretty little harbor. You must then purchase a ticket to take the short ride up the funicular railway to the main square, where you can sit at an outdoor café and watch one of the world's most colorful assortment of tourists pass by. There is a pebbled beach at Marina Piccolo, but it is probably not worth the effort if your time ashore is limited. The best hotel in Capri is the Grand Hotel Quisisana, which sits at one end of the path that leads from the town square. Lunch by the pool here or dinner at Restaurant Quisi in the hotel is truly a rewarding experiences. There are many designer shops that line the path from the main square to Grand Hotel Quisisana, as well as on the path that leads from the hotel toward the point where tourists go to take photos of the Faraglioni Rocks. Other options include a short bus ride up to Anacapri, another town that sits at the top of the mountain, where there are additional hotels, restaurants and shops, and panoramic views down to Capri Town and the sea, as well as a boat ride from the main harbor to the famous Blue Grotto or around the island.

This area south of Naples (Amalfi, Positano, Sorrento, Ravello, and the Isle of Capri) is possibly the most beautiful part of Southern Europe and should not be missed.

## Sardinia

If your ship visits **Port Cervo** on the Costa Smeralda area of this Mediterranean island, you will tender into a harbor with a large concentration of luxury yachts. You can browse through boutiques and shops that surround the harbor and are located in the nearby Hotel Cervo, play eighteen holes of golf at the Robert Trent Jones-designed Pevero Golf Club, or spend the day at a beach. Since all the beaches are public, you may wish to visit the beach adjoining the luxury resort Cala di Volpe (about a ten-minute taxi ride from the harbor). If you are willing to pay the price, you can join the resort's affluent clientele for an extremely lavish lunch buffet. Other luxury resorts located nearby include Romazzino and Pitriccia.

## SICILY

Sicily is an Italian island off the coast of Italy with an area of 9,900 square miles, making it the largest island in the Mediterranean. Its 4,800,000 inhabitants live in a mild climate, with the average temperature ranging from forty-five degrees Fahrenheit in the winter to eighty degrees Fahrenheit in the summer. Cruise ships stop either at Palermo or at the port cities of Naxos, Messina, or Catania for visits to Taormina.

In **Palermo**, you can browse through the fine shops on the Via Liberta, Via Roma, and Via Ruggero Settimo and visit the old Royal Palace, which contains a lovely chapel well known for its mosaics and marble floors. You can take a taxi to the sanctuary on Monte Pellegrino at two thousand feet above sea level, offering a striking view of the island. From Palermo, you can drive to Syracuse to see a classical production at the ancient Roman amphitheater. You can drive to Mondello, where there are pleasant beaches and fine seafood restaurants, or you may prefer spending the day at Citta Del Mare in Terrasini, twenty miles away, which is a Club Med-style resort village complete with eleven tennis courts, a miniature golf course, an Olympic-size pool, a series of water slides leading down to the sea, a cinema, a discotheque, and several restaurants and bars.

If your ship docks at a port on the east coast of the island, you can take a tour, a taxi, or public bus to the resort town of **Taormina.** This picturesque village winds in and out of hills, then drops to the sea. Any stop at Taormina should include a visit to the Greek-Roman Theater, an illustrious monument built by the ancient Greeks and rebuilt by the Romans. The shops and better restaurants are located in the center of the city, which lies high up in the hills. If time permits, a nice place to visit and have lunch is the San Domenico Palace. This is an old monastery converted to an elegant hotel, replete with hundreds of original antiques and Renaissance paintings. The gardens here are beautiful and afford a breathtaking panorama of the coast and sea below. The craggy coastline is dotted with European-style beaches (not particularly attractive), where you can rent chairs and purchase snacks and drinks. There is little shopping on the beaches, and the restaurants that line the streets, by and large, are mediocre.

Above Taormina is the world-famous volcano Mount Etna. Rising 10,784 feet from the sea, it is the highest volcano in Europe. You can take a tour to the six-thousand-foot level and have lunch, then continue up to the observatory at nine thousand feet.

**Venice**: This most unusual and fabled city on the Adriatic, lying on a cluster of small islands divided by canals, has been the subject matter of many novels and the photogenic centerfold for countless cruise and travel brochures. Most of the larger cruise ships dock at the maritime terminal near the railroad station, a ten-minute Vapori (motorboat bus) ride, or an hour's walk from the city's main plaza, Piazza San Marco. However, some smaller vessels and riverboats pull up on the Grand Canal, about a fifteen-minute stroll in a westerly direction to San Marco.

In this famous piazza (square), surrounded by shops and restaurants with outdoor cafés, inundated with swarms of pigeons, is the Palace of the Doges, with its Italian Gothic-style architecture and priceless collection of paintings, linked by the Bridge of Sighs to an infamous prison; the Basilica di San Marco, a fine example of Byzantine architecture; and the Campanile, an old bell tower that dominates the city's skyline, with an elevator to the top for a bird's-eye view of the city. From late afternoon throughout the evening, tourists swarm to the numerous outdoor cafés that line the square for an espresso or other beverage while listening to romantic Italian bands. The two most famous and most pricey cafés are Quadri and Florian. You may remember this as the site where Rossano Brazzi picked up Katherine Hepburn in the 1950s movie *Summertime*.

In front of the Piazza, you can charter a private gondola for a ride through the winding canals that compose the streets of Venice. Directly behind the Piazza, you can embark on your journey through the narrow streets lined with shops and restaurants that meander across picturesque stone bridges to the famous sixteenth-century Rialto Bridge. Spanning the bridge and in this general area, you will find outdoor shopping stalls with inexpensive souvenirs and "knockoff items." The better shops are located in the streets between San Marco and the Rialto Bridge. Items indigenous to Venice are the decorative papier-mâché masks and, of course, the world-famous Venetian glass, which is manufactured on the nearby island of Murano. There are tours to Murano to visit the factory and watch the artisans blow the glass into varied designs.

Those wishing to dine ashore can wander into countless small trattorias, not all of which are that rewarding, in spite of their appealing appearance. The best restaurant within easy walking distance of San Marco is Do Leone in the Londra Palace Hotel. Other excellent choices are the rooftop restaurant at the Royal Danieli and the restaurants on the Canal at the Gritti Palace and Bauer Grunwald. These are also the best hotels for a pre- or postcruise overnight, the Londra Palace being the less expensive, more intimate gem. Many tourists (of which I am not one) feel it is a must to visit the famous Harry's Bar, immediately to the west of San Marco. For a special treat, have lunch by the pool or dinner overlooking the Canal at the Hotel Cipriani on Giudecca Island, a five-minute ride by the hotel's private water taxi from the dock, also immediately to the west of San Marco. This is the best full-facility resort in Venice and one of the most luxurious in Italy.

The most famous art museums are Accademia, featuring Italian masters spanning the fourteenth to the eighteenth century, and Collezione Peggy Guggenheim at Venier dei Leoni, with its comprehensive modern-art collections, including works of Picasso, Chagall, Pollock, and Dali.

For those who have already explored Venice, I suggest an optional excursion to the island of Lido, a twenty-minute Vapori ride from San Marco or a thirty-minute Vapori ride from the maritime station. This is a clean, floral island with a nice assortment of restaurants, shops, and hotels, as well as a casino. The largest hotels with piers and sand beaches are the Grand Hotel des Bain and the Excelsior Palace.

## MALTA

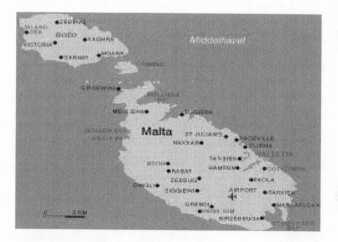

Malta, an island located in the Mediterranean between Italy and Africa, previously part of the British Commonwealth, is today a self-governing constitutional monarchy. The climate is mild during the winter and dry and hot in the summer. After your ship pulls into the port city of **Valletta**, you can charter a horse-and-buggy and ride into the main section of town. You will find some fine examples of baroque and Renaissance art and architecture if you visit the Palace of the Grand Masters, the Royal Malta Library, or the Cathedral of St. John. Other attractions include the view from the Upper Barrakka Gardens, the fortified peninsulas of Vittoriosa and Seneglea, the town of Cospicua and the Mediterranean Conference Center's audiovisual production about Maltese history. You may enjoy stopping for lunch at the venerable Phoenecia Hotel (now a Meridien), adjacent to town. You can take a twenty-minute drive to the Malta Hilton or the Westin Hotels. These hotels are located on the ocean and have magnificent pools and beach clubs rivaling anything you may find in France or Italy. Lace, homespun cotton clothes, and wool rugs are the best buys; however, shopping is not particularly attractive here. In the evening, you may wish to stroll through the area referred to as "The Gut," with its dives, honky-tonks, beer parlors, and cabarets.

## MOROCCO

**Casablanca** is a major port in North Africa, with more than a million inhabitants enjoying a mild, warm climate. Some of the more popular tourist attractions include the tiny old Medina near the harbor, which is a historical relic and site of the earliest settlement; the new Medina on the eastern side of town, where you can watch cases being tried at the local courts; and the United Nations Square, which is surrounded by tropical gardens grouped around government buildings. At United Nations Square, you can walk through the local shops and find bargains in ancient and modern carpets, leather, jewelry, and local crafts. You can stop in a Moroccan restaurant and try kabobs *harira* (a type of chicken soup), *pastia* (layers of filo leaves stuffed with chicken, eggs, cinnamon, and exotic spices), *tajin* (a type of stew), and some local wine. If you wish to relax at a beach or pool, you will prefer to take a leisurely ride along the corniche to Anfa and Ain Diab. If time permits, you will want to travel to the ancient city of **Marrakesh**, driving through this colorful town in an open, horse-drawn carriage. The best restaurants in Marrakesh are Casa Lalla and Palar's Jed Mahal.

## PORTUGAL

Overlooking a broad bay, **Lisbon** lies on Portugal's west coast, about seven miles from the Atlantic Ocean. The city's 820,000 inhabitants enjoy an ideal climate where temperatures average in the fifties in January and in the seventies in July. Although once considered one of Europe's most picturesque cities, today it appears a bit worn and dirty. Of greatest interest are the numerous monuments, churches, and museums. You will want to walk through the Baixa, the colorful, downtown section of the city, with its pavements of black and white mosaics in checked patterns or forming scenes that recall outstanding events from Lisbon's history. The narrow streets are lined with so-so shops and cafés. Start at Placa do Comercio and proceed up Rue Agusto to Rossio Square. Shoppers will wish to consider the handmade shoes, decorative glazed tiles, beautiful pottery, copperware, and leather goods. Colombie, located in the Benefice district, is a large shopping mall, the largest in Portugal. You may wish to stroll through the historic Alfama area, with its maze of cobblestone streets, lanes, Moorish and medieval buildings, and old castle enclosed by moats with reedy waters filled with ducks, fish, and flamingos. Nearby, you can visit the twelfth-century Romanesque Sé Cathedral and the King's Fountain.

The top hotels include the Ritz, Avenida Palace, Sheraton, and Alpha Lisboa. Recommended restaurants include Gabrinius (fish and seafood), Veranda at the Ritz (international), Casa do Leao (Portuguese cuisine with a view), Oterraco (gourmet with a view), Casa de Comida (Continental and Portuguese), and Al Fana Grill at the Sheraton (Portuguese and international). A pleasant alternative way to spend your day would be to take the twenty-minute train ride to Estoril and Cascais, the resort area north of the city. In **Estoril**, there are numerous hotels, a casino, several sandy beaches, boutiques, and restaurants. **Cascais** is a most charming village with cobbled streets, a medieval fortress, shops, and an abundance of cafés, seafood restaurants, and pizzerias. My favorite is the romantic courtyard at Pizzeria Lucullus, where you may wish to try the gazpacho, sangria, and delicious crusty pizza. This excursion is definitely the best choice for repeat visitors.

**Funchal** is the port of the Portuguese Madeira Islands, which lie in the Atlantic five hundred miles off the coast of Lisbon. These volcanic islands enjoy a mild, sunny climate, with temperatures ranging from the sixties in winter to the seventies in summer. As you approach port, you will notice the rocky coastline studded with quaint lighthouses, fishing ports, and whaling villages. As you disembark, you will be greeted by the natives in rowboats filled with fruit, baskets, and embroideries welcoming you to this island covered with flowers, bushes, trees, and other vegetation.

Funchal is a resort town with a lazy holiday atmosphere, and you will enjoy walking through the main square, stopping to visit the Jesuit church, town hall, and the bishop's palace. You can browse through quaint shops for antiques as well as for beautiful embroideries on Irish linens and French silks, or you can stroll through the open-air market. You can sip some famous Madeira wine and relax at one of the hotel pools overlooking the cliffs, since the beaches have volcanic black pebbles and are not desirable for swimming. If time allows, you can drive to Cabo Girao to visit the vineyards, to Curral las Freiras to visit a village monastery hidden from view by rocks, or to Comacha to see the house where Madeira baskets are made. You can enjoy a great view from Cabao Girao, Europe's second-highest cliff, 1,800 feet above the ocean. Reid's Hotel is a famous, elegant hotel that dates back to 1891 and is presently managed by Orient-Express. Both the Royal and Savoy Hotels offer restaurants, bars, swimming pools, tennis courts, spas, and gardens.

**Oporto**, Portugal's second-largest city, is set along the Douro River and surrounded by the vineyards of the Douro Valley. A major attraction is touring the wine caves along the Cais de Gaia, including Sandeman and Taylor, two major producers of port wine. Be prepared to walk up and down steep hills to get from one side of the river to the other.

You can explore the shops and cafés in the Baixa (the old district), many of which offer wine samplings. Rue de Santa Catarina is the major shopping street and Centro Comercial Via Catarina is an elegant shopping mall. The Cais da Ribeira is an interesting district made up of medieval streets and alleyways with traditional boats floating quayside. Here you can visit Palacio da Bolsa, a municipal showplace; Sao Francisco, a Gothic church built between 1383 and 1410; the Romanesque-style Sé Catedral; and the Ethnography Museum. Another place of interest is the Torre dos Clerigos, a baroque tower designed in 1754 that rises 249 feet, one of the tallest in northern Portugal. Recommended restaurants include Dona Filipa for local fare, Tronho for regional cuisine, and the small historical Café Pinguim.

## SENEGAL

**Dakar** is an Atlantic port and the capital of Senegal in Western Africa; it has a hot climate and much rain during the summer. The city itself reflects a great deal of European style and French influence, but the people have a definite African character. Some of the more interesting sights include the graceful Presidential Palace; the elegant new Parliament Building; the university; the teeming Sandaga Market; the Ifan Museum, with its magnificent collection of West African carvings, pottery, cloth, and musical instruments; and the medina, with its colorful, cluttered market. There are nice beaches for swimming at N'Gor and Bernard Inlet. If possible, try to attend a native *mechoui,* which is a colorful feast including the barbecue of a sheep or goat. At the Craftsman's Village at Soumbedioune, you will find bargains on native jewelry, leatherwork, pottery, filigree, and woven goods.

## SPAIN

**Algeciras** is a port in southeastern Spain across the bay from Gibraltar. From this town, you can take an overnight boat train to Madrid, a two-and-a-half-hour ferry ride to Tangier in North Africa, or a several hours' drive to the Costa del Sol area and visit the picturesque towns of Marbella, Malaga, Torremolinos, and Porto Banus. On the Costa del Sol, you will find numerous resort hotels, beaches, boutiques, shops, good restaurants, nightspots, and tourists from all over Europe. The best resorts with the most facilities are Marbella Club and Puente Romano, both located in Marbella. The most colorful harbor area is at Puerto Banus, a ten-minute ride from Marbella. Here you can stroll along the waterfront filled with giant yachts and visit some of the best shops and small ethnic restaurants to be found in Spain.

The famous Rock of Gibraltar, at the western entrance to the Mediterranean, is located in the British colony of **Gibraltar**. If your ship stops here, you can ascend the Rock by cable car, visit St. Michael's Cave (a natural grotto), Apes' Den (inhabited by wild Barbary apes), and meander through duty-free shops and pubs on Main Street.

If your ship docks in the harbor of **Malaga**, you will be able to take the tour to **Granada** and visit the famous Alhambra Castle and charming surrounding parks and attractions. On your way, you may wish to stop for lunch or a drink at the magnificent La Bobadilla Resort, which is built on a hillside in the style of a Moorish village. If you prefer, about an hour's drive along the coast to the west will permit visits to **Torremolinos**, **Marbella**, and **Porto Banus**.

**Barcelona** is located on the Mediterranean coast of northern Spain not far from France. This busy city with more than two million inhabitants is the largest Spanish-speaking port in the world after Buenos Aires. You will be able to capture the Spanish flavor by taking in the traditional bullfight, enjoying a flamenco show, or having some gazpacho and paella at a typical Spanish restaurant. You can visit the historic cathedral known as "La Seu" in the old town as well as the interesting building nearby; drive or take the cable car up to the top of the hill of Tibidabo, from the heights of which you can see the Pyrenees; visit the National Museum, the museum of Catalan Art in the Palacio Nacional, the Miro Foundation in Montjuïc Park, and the Picasso Museum; stop by Gaudi's famous Cathedral of the Holy Family; or walk down the Paseo de Gracia or the tree-lined Ramblas Avenue with its colorful flower stalls and shop for leather goods, linens, and souvenirs. The best restaurants in town are La Dama (gourmet French Catalan), Talaia Mar (Spanish and French food and a good view of the city), Jaume de Provenca (Spanish and Continental food in a lovely setting at reasonable prices), Botafumiero (seafood), and Via Veneto (Continental menu in a grand environment—expensive).

The forty-four-story, full-facility Hotel Arts managed by the Ritz-Carlton chain is Barcelona's most prestigious residence, located in Marina City next to a long strand of sandy beach and a small-craft marina. This is an excellent pre- and postcruise option.

Ships call at the port city of **Cadiz** (Europe's oldest city) to enable passengers to visit the historical city of **Seville**, the capital of the region of Andalusia. About five to ten minutes from the marina in Cadiz is Plaza de San Juan Dias and Plaza de la Cathedral. Most of the shops and restaurants are located on small streets emanating from these plazas. About an hour away is Jerez de la Frontera, the center of Spain's sherry industry. Here you can visit the vineyards and tour the wine-producing facilities, as well as visit the surrounding estates and opulent churches.

The bus ride to Seville takes about an hour and a half. Steeped in history, Seville is one of the loveliest cities in Spain with a wealth of fascinating styles of architecture spanning various centuries. Entering the city, you will enjoy driving down Avenue de la Palmeras to view the dozens of international pavilions constructed for the 1929 Latin American Exposition. Stop at Plaza Espagne and Plaza America, two photo-friendly squares with impressive early twentieth-century Andalusian architecture. At Plaza America is an archeological museum.

Walking tours would be the best way to enjoy the city's most important sites. Commence at the Gardens of Murilla, site of the monument to Columbus, and proceed through the Santa Cruz area, which was the posh, residential sector originally inhabited by Seville's Jewish population during the twelfth and thirteenth centuries prior to the Spanish Inquisition. Soon you will find your way to the impressive Cathedral of Seville and its Giralda Tower. The third largest cathedral in the world, it was built as a mosque during the twelfth century and expanded in the sixteenth century when it became a Catholic church. Directly to the south is the famous Alcazar Palace and gardens, the oldest operational palace in Europe, a fine example of Mudejar architecture. Numerous souvenir shops and small restaurants line the streets and alleys surrounding the church and palace. A short distance away is Plaza Nueva with its banks, hotels, and designer shops. Other interesting sites on the banks of the river that runs through the town are the thirteenth-century Tower of Gold, now a maritime museum, and the baroque Maestranza Bullring.

The **Canary Islands** are a group of seven Spanish islands in the Atlantic Ocean sixty miles off the coast of northwest Africa. The islands are mountainous and have a mild climate with temperatures ranging from the sixties in winter to the seventies in summer. Most cruise ships stop at either **Las Palmas** on the Grand Canary Island or **Santa Cruz** on the island of Tenerife. The islands are volcanic, resulting in several black-sand beaches. Although there are no famous restaurants, you will want to try the fish and seafood as well as some of the local rice dishes. At Las Palmas, you can shop at a number of attractive duty-free stores; explore the narrow streets and plazas of the old part of the city by horse and carriage; watch the sunset at an open-air café; swim at the beaches of Las Canteras, Alcaravaneras, or La Laja; or witness a cockfight.

**Santa Cruz** is a lively town that may seem to be more beautiful than Las Palmas. Here you can visit the archeological and anthropological museum, the seventeenth-century Carta Palace, and the historical relics of the Church of the Concepción. There are beaches at Las Tereitas and Las Gaviotas. Tourists often take an excursion from Santa Cruz through the town of La Laguna, followed by a beautiful drive to Orotava and Porto de la Cruz, passing by beautiful coastlines, tropical flowers, and foliage. From Orotava, you ascend the Teide Mountain, which includes a funicular railroad ride to the volcano's cone, where you can witness a panoramic view of all the Canary Islands. On the way back to Santa Cruz, you may wish to swim in the warm waters and lounge on the fine sand of El Medano Beach. Another attraction is Siam Park, a water park with a restaurant, a beach club, and several amusement park rides and attractions. There are good dining possibilities around Plaza de las Americas, Los Cristianos, and Arona. At Costa Adeje there is a twenty-seven-hole golf course and driving range.

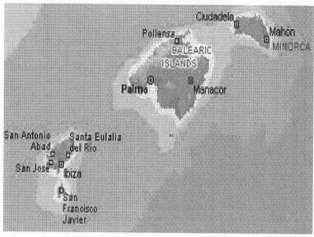

*Balearic Islands*

**Palma** is the main resort area and port of Majorca, one of the Spanish **Balearic Islands** lying in the Mediterranean 120 miles south of Barcelona. Tourists from all over the world pour into Palma each year to enjoy its mild winters and beautiful summers. In town, there are numerous Spanish-style restaurants (El Patio is among the best) and excellent shops where you can obtain bargains in pearls and leather goods. The best shopping area is along Jaime III, General Mola, and Paseo de Borne streets. The larger hotels in Palma are not on the ocean, and you will have to travel away from the city to bathe in the sea. A worthwhile trip that will take an entire day would include a visit to the Drach caves at Porto Cristo, followed by a trip to **Formentor.** The Drach caves are the largest in the world, with magnificent stalagmites and stalactites and a natural underground lake and auditorium where you can witness a truly unique concert. The drive up a mountain and down to the hotel at Formentor is breathtaking. Here you can enjoy a delicious lunch complete with sangria; swim at a sheltered, pine-studded bathing beach; play tennis on modern courts; and go horseback riding in the mountains. The best resorts near the town of Palma are the Son Vida, a delightful choice for an outdoor lunch by the pool, and Arabella Golf Hotel, a sister hotel on a scenic golf course.

Some cruise ships call at ports on other Balearic Islands. Most ships visiting the island of **Menorca**, anchor or tender to the port of **Mahon** (Mao). Here there is little of interest other than taking a picturesque walk along the harbor where you will find small cafés and a few souvenir shops, or walking up the stairs near the main harbor to the town where you can explore charming little streets and visit additional shops and restaurants. There are beaches located around the island accessible by taxi. Ibiza is a more interesting cruise stop and a major vacation destination for the British and Germans. Right off the harbor are narrow streets lined with restaurants and souvenir and leather shops. You will want to visit the fortress and castle that sit above the harbor and one of the colorful beaches (some of which include nude bathing). Salines is the most popular beach and only a short bus ride from the town.

## TUNISIA

Your ship will dock at LaGoulette or Bizerte, the ports for **Tunis** and Carthage. Your best choice will be to take an organized tour that transports you to Tunis and visits the ruins of ancient Carthage dating back to 814 BC. You will probably stop at the National Archeological Museum; the pretty suburb of Sidi Abon Said, with its white buildings and cobbled streets; and the interesting Casbah, with its mosques and numerous *souks* (shopping streets) featuring Oriental rugs, brass trays, gold jewelry, linens, and souvenirs.

## TURKEY

Turkey has become a very popular stop and even a home base for Greek-island and Mediterranean cruises. Traditionally, the two ports most often visited were Istanbul and Kusadasi. Today, many ships offer stops at the more scenic coastal resort towns of Bodrum, Marmaris, and Antalya. During the summer months, the average daily temperatures range from the midseventies to the midnineties.

**Istanbul**, formerly Constantinople, is the city of legend and history where East and West meet. This great commercial seaport is the largest city in Turkey, stretching along both the European and Asiatic sides of the Bosporus, which connects the Sea of Marmara with the Black Sea. You will not want to miss the Grand Bazaar in the heart of the old city, which is one of the most unique shopping areas in the world. Here you can browse through thousands of tiny shops spread along ninety-two winding streets and see bargains in gold, copper, ceramics, jewelry, rugs, leather, suede, handicrafts, and just about anything else you can imagine. There are a number of stores both in the bazaar and nearby where you can have leather and suede outfits made to order while you wait. Another don't-miss attraction is the famous Topkapi Museum, formerly the Palace of the Sultans, where today you can view some of the world's most valuable and beautiful works of art, rare stones, jewels, ancient weapons, furnishings, antiquities, and the harems of the sultans.

One of the most unique sights when sailing into Istanbul is the skyline filled with beautiful mosques with their domes, semidomes, and minarets. The most famous is the Blue Mosque, or Sultan Ahmed Mosque, located near the Topkapi Museum. You will also want to visit St. Sophia, which was commissioned by Emperor Justinian in the sixth century as a Christian church, altered to a mosque, and later turned into a museum with its magnificent architecture, important mosaics, and unusual chandeliers. Aghia Sophia (as it is now called) is said to be the world's finest example of Byzantine architecture. If time allows, other outstanding attractions include the city walls, castle, and other old Byzantine fortifications at Yedikule Hisari; the Alexander the Great Sarcophagus, with carvings depicting the famous leader, and other antiquities at the Archeological Museum; the world's most precious Byzantine mosaics and frescos at the lovely fourteenth-century church of St. Savior of Chora, now a museum; Cicek Pasaji, a nineteenth-century shopping arcade with numerous cafés and restaurants; and the spice market. For the children, visit the amusement park at Miniaturk with its miniature reproductions of over a hundred Turkish buildings, palaces, mosques, and shopping malls and the Rahmi M Koç Museum of transportation with exhibits of vintage trains, cars, boats, planes, and a submarine.

After all of this sightseeing, you can relax at a hamam for a Turkish bath. Cemberlitas Hamami is one of the most famous; however, you may prefer to take advantage of Turkish baths located in your hotel.

You can stop at a restaurant where the locals eat in the Cicek Pasaji or atop the fourteenth-century Galeta Tower, not far from the pier, for simple versions of Turkish appetizers and salads, fish, seafood, shish kebab, baklava, and coffee. For fresh fish and seafood, your best bet is at one of the waterfront restaurants at Kumkapi. You may wish to have a drink or dine at one of the magnificent Istanbul hotels such as the Ciragan Palace, Ritz-Carlton, Hilton, Four Seasons, Intercontinental, or Conrad. All of these make excellent pre- or postcruise headquarters with central locations, panoramic views, numerous restaurants, large health clubs, and pools. We found that the hotel restaurants offered all the indigenous Turkish dishes with a better presentation and higher quality than many of the touted local restaurants.

Some ships stop at the small port town of **Dikili** to enable passengers to take the fourteen-mile drive through rolling hills, pine trees, and vineyards to the modern town of Bergama and the ancient ruins of Pergamon. The Greek city of Pergamon in Asia Minor dates to the third century BC. It lies on the acropolis on the north side of the Kaikos River. Places of interest here include the Archeological Museum and the Red Court, a second-century temple dedicated to Egyptian gods and goddesses and later converted to a basilica. There is nothing of interest or beauty in the town of Dikili; however, attractions near Dikili include the ancient caverns in Demirtas and Delitas villages, the crater lake in Mordiventi village, the nearby thermal springs, and the Merkez Mosque, a rare example of wooden construction without the use of nails dating from 1789.

**Izmir** and **Kusadasi** are ports in Turkey where cruise ships frequently stop. Izmir is an important, colorful port and the headquarters for the NATO Command guarding the eastern Mediterranean. **Kusadasi** is a summer resort town where you can swim at small beaches, ride a camel on the sand, or shop for gold, jewelry, rugs, leather, suede, and antiques at one of its many stores. Bargains on leather are probably among the best in the world. Kusadasi has several excellent resort hotels with lovely pool areas, including the Fantasia, Onur, and Koru-Mar. The Koru-Mar is only a mile away from the harbor and affords picturesque views of the city and sea. There are numerous restaurants spread throughout the town, most specializing in fresh fish and seafood. **Ephesus** is inland from Izmir and Kusadasi. This ancient city, uncovered by Austrian archeologists, has some of the most impressive archeological ruins in the world, including a mile-long marble road, restored buildings, the Arcadian Way, Temple of Hadrian, the Library, the Odeon, public toilets, the ruins of the Temple of Diana, the site of the Temple of Artemis (considered one of the Seven Wonders of the World), and the Last Abode of Mary. Cruise ships frequently offer concerts and cocktail parties in the ancient amphitheater. It is also possible to visit the ruins of the Basilica of St. John in the town of Seljuk and Mount Pagus, reputedly the home of the Virgin Mary.

Once a tiny sleeping village leveled by a devastating earthquake in 1057, **Marmaris** has been resurrected as Turkey's most beautiful, upscale resort area and yacht haven. Fringing a protected bay surrounded by rugged pine-forested mountains, the town has a floral beach walk that meanders along the harbor and bay past numerous hotels, posh resorts, restaurants, tavernas, and shops. The harbor where the cruise ships generally dock is dotted with private yachts and sailing vessels and is only a ten-minute walk from the town center, where you will find dozens of restaurants, bars, and tavernas reminiscent of St. Tropez and Puerto Banus. In the town center, there is also a covered bazaar that offers many of the same bargains in gold, jewelry, leather goods, carpets, and other merchandise found in the Grand Bazaar of Istanbul or in the shops of Kusadasi, except in a less crowded, more pleasant surroundings. You will want to visit the Armutalan Hamam and the sixteenth-century Marmaris Castle, which houses the Marmaris Museum. Extending for about five miles from the town center is the beach walk mentioned above. The most beautiful resort is the Marmaris Palace, which has private bungalows and hotel rooms with pools, restaurants, and lush grounds that run down pine-clad hills to the beach area. The clientele is mostly German. Other nice beach resorts in the area include Mares Marmaris and Elegance Hotel. Side trips can be taken to the typical Turkish seaside villages of Icmeler, Tarunc, and Kumlubuk where there are nice beaches, and tours are also offered to the graves of Likya and the ruins of Caunos.

**Antalya**, set on a majestic coastline of beaches and rocky caves, is a very attractive resort city with shady, palm-lined boulevards, a picturesque marina, and an old quarter called Kaleici with narrow, winding streets and quaint, old wood houses next to the city walls. Places of interest include the Archeology Museum, the clock tower, Hadrian's Gate, Hidirlik Tower, Kesik Minaret complex, and the Turban Kaleici Marina. There are several full-facility resort hotels, the Sheraton Voyager being the most upscale. Other choices overlooking the sea include Talya, Falez, and Cender. The beaches, although picturesque, are pebbly and uninviting. Excursions away from the city may include the upper and lower Dudden waterfalls, the restored archeological ruins at Perge or the archeological sites and beaches at Patara. Golfers may wish to opt for the twenty-four-mile drive to the National Golf Club in Belek, where they will find both a nine-hole and a championship eighteen-hole course situated amongst shady pine forests near pretty beach areas.

Situated on a beautiful peninsula, **Bodrum** is a popular Aegean holiday resort and picturesque yacht harbor filled with sailboats, yachts, outdoor cafés, and streets bustling with small shops selling carpets, leatherwear, jewelry, natural sponges, and local artwork. The town's charm is well-known, attracting a diverse population of vacationers who stroll along its long palm-lined waterfront. Bodrum has been referred to as the "hot spot" of the Aegean coast. From the marina, you can take a tour in a Turkish *gulet* (a craft built of pinewood), sailing the magnificent coves of the Bodrum peninsula to explore isolated bays, inlets, and small villages; swim, sunbathe, and partake in water sports on miles of sandy beaches; and take a Turkish bath at the hamam. The major places of interest include Bodrum Castle. Built by the Knights of Rhodes, it is a fine example of fifteenth-century crusader architecture and houses the Bodrum Museum of Underwater Archaeology. You may also visit the Mausoleum of Halicarnassus, the site of King Mausolus's tomb, considered one of the Seven Wonders of the World and the origin of the word "mausoleum"; the Golturkbuku Bay area on the other side of the peninsula, considered the St. Tropez of Turkey with bars, discos, restaurants, and small boutique hotels; and eight miles out of the city, accessible by way of a panoramic drive, is the Kempinski Hotel Barbaros, set on a cliff top overlooking a private bay, offering swimming pools, restaurants, a private beach, and the famous Six Senses Spa.

There are several beaches only minutes from town where you can swim in clear, warm seas. Scuba divers, especially, will want to explore the numerous reefs, caves, and majestic rock formations offering an immense variety of aquatic life. Horseback riding and river rafting are available a short distance from the city, and there are two aqua parks, one next to the TMT Hotel.

The evenings in Bodrum are for sitting idly in one of the city's many restaurants, dining on fresh seafood and other Aegean specialties. Afterward, nightclubs and discos swing until dawn. Popular restaurants serving Turkish specialties include La Jolla Bistro, Epsilon, Marina Yacht Club, New Season at Bitez, Tuti in the Marmara Bodrum Hotel, Antique Theater Hotel Restaurant, Bodrum Bodrum, and all of the restaurants at the seaside resort town of Turbuku with their tables set on pontoons.

## UKRAINE, RUSSIA, BULGARIA, AND BLACK SEA PORTS

A number of ships cruise the Black Sea, stopping at such Ukrainian ports as Odessa, Sevastapol, and Yalta; the port of Sochi; and the Bulgarian port of Nessebar.

**Odessa**, located in the south central Ukraine, is called "the pearl of the Black Sea," with its picturesque seascape, streets, and marketplaces. To the landlocked Russian, this is a town of sun, golden-sand beaches, and green parks. However, to the Western visitor it is a town in total disrepair. You can stroll from one end of the seafront to the other, visiting the Potempkin steps, Pushkin Statue, the Opera House, the Vorontsov Palace, the Square of the Commune, and the archeological museum. The main shopping is along Deribasovskaya Street. You may wish to visit one of the city's beaches at Arcadia, Luzanovska, and Chernomorka. Other points of interest accessible by taxi are Shomrei Shabbos Synagogue, the old main Synagogue on Yevreyskaya Street, Gargarin Palace, Tolstoy Palace, the Russian Byzantine-style Uspensky Cathedral, and the Museum of Fine Arts.

**Sochi**, Russia, is the largest seaside resort in the former USSR, protected from cold winds and sudden temperature changes by the Caucasus Mountains. There is a large central pebble bathing beach as well as many smaller beaches with adjoining *sanatoria* (nonluxurious Russian health resorts with clinics, solarium pools, beaches, public rooms, and sports facilities). You may wish to visit the famous Dendrarium Botanical Gardens, containing fountains, statues, subtropical flora, and trees and shrubs from all over the world. A visit to Stalin's Dacha is interesting, as are the mineral springs and spa at Matsesta and the Dagomy Tea Plantation.

**Yalta**, Ukraine, is a Black Sea port on the southern coast of the Crimean Peninsula at the southern foothills of the Yaila Mountains. The city is also sheltered by mountains and enjoys a temperate climate. This seaside resort town that ascends up the mountain slopes is surrounded by evergreen forests and parks, vineyards, and fruit farms where pear, almond, peach, apple, and apricot trees are grown. It is the most beautiful of the Black Sea cities and is reminiscent of Greek islands and Mediterranean ports. There are three main beaches and numerous sanatoria. You can walk along the Lenin Quay, where you will find the main shops, hotels, cafés, and restaurants. Places and points of interest include the Ethnographic Museum (devoted to Eastern art), the Tchekhov Museum (which was once the author's house), Yuri Gagarin Park, Livadia Palace, the summer residence of the Tsar Nicholas II and site of the Yalta Conference in 1945, Alupka Palace and art museum, Massandra Palace, Park and Combine (famous for its wines), the Alexander Nevsky Cathedral with its onion-shaped domes, and the Nikitsky Botanical Gardens.

The principal shopping area extends along the Roosevelt and Lenin Quays; however, items of interest would be limited to Matryoshka dolls, lacquer boxes, traditional embroideries, amber jewelry, caviar, and vodka. Swallow's Nest, precariously perched on a rock overlooking the sea, was built in 1911 to resemble a medieval castle and offers a lovely panorama. This is a major tourist attraction and some ship tours utilize the location for a typical Crimean-style lunch.

**Sevastapol**, Ukraine, sits on a group of hills forming a natural amphitheater overlooking Bakhtiarsky Bay on the Crimean Peninsula. The city offers charming gardens, attractive squares and boulevards, numerous monuments, and museums. From the port you can take a ten-minute walk through a park to a local beach (concrete) to see the locals at leisure. Points of interest would include Vladimir Cathedral; the archeological site of Chersonesus, where the last Greek colony existed on the Northern Black Sea; the adjoining museum; the sixteenth-century Khan's Palace, the eighth-century Uspensky Monastery, and the Sevastopol Aquarium.

**Nessebar**, Bulgaria, is also located on the Black Sea. Your ship will dock only minutes away from the picturesque, charming old quarter of town situated on the Nessebar Peninsula, an architectural/archeological reserve, dating back to the tenth and eleventh centuries. North and South of the peninsula are small strips of beach. The town is composed of colorful, winding streets lined with stone and timber houses, restaurants, and shops.

Also in town, you can visit the Archeological Museum, several medieval churches, and the walls and towers of Hellenistic and Byzantine fortresses (fifth to fifteenth century).

You may wish to shop for bargains on "knockoff" designer sunglasses, perfumes, and other items (not close to the quality of the real thing), local souvenirs, local art, and embroidered linens. An especially desirable crystal shop is located at 20 Mitropolitska Street. It specializes in unique hand-painted and individually blown table crystal. Tours also visit the vineyards at Promerie wine center.

## Northern Europe, the Baltics, the North Sea, the Fjords, and the Rivers of Europe

During the late spring and summer, a number of ships offer cruises to Northern European ports in the Baltic and North Sea, as well as up to the picturesque fjords of Norway and down the rivers of Germany, Austria, Hungary, and France. Although the climate may not be as ideal as in the Caribbean or Mediterranean, the weather is generally mild enough at these times of year to permit you to sit out on deck and take in the magnificent sights and scenery.

The cruises are generally longer (at least ten to fourteen days) and more expensive than those found in the Mediterranean; however, they afford you an opportunity to visit a large number of interesting ports while sampling a variety of cultures all in one trip without the inconvenience of flying from place to place.

These cruises usually initiate from Southampton, Dover, Tilbury, Stockholm, Amsterdam, Hamburg, or Copenhagen, and the ships either sail up the coast of Norway to the fjords and "Land of the Midnight Sun," circumnavigate the British Isles, or stop at such interesting Northern European ports as Amsterdam, Oslo, Helsinki, Stockholm, Copenhagen, Hamburg, Gdynia, Tallinn, Visby, and St. Petersburg.

The ships of most major cruise lines cruise these areas.

For a totally different experience, seasoned cruisers will enjoy a leisurely riverboat trip on the Rhine, Mosel, Danube, Elbe, Seine, Saône, or Rhône rivers with visits to historic cities and charming villages.

The following are the highlights of some of the more popular northern ports:

## BELGIUM

Cruise ships visiting Belgium dock at **Zeebrugge**, a seaside resort and fishing port linked to the historic metropolis of Brugge by a 7.5-mile canal. Train service is available to Brugge (fifteen minutes), Ghent (one hour), and Brussels (two hours). Flemish is spoken in the northern part of Belgium and French in the southern.

**Brugge** is one of the most charming cities in Europe with its ten-mile network of canals filled with swans and ducks, flowing under small bridges surrounded by parks and attractive buildings built over the centuries in Romanesque, Gothic, neo-Gothic, Baroque, and Renaissance styles. The market square, located in the center of town, is dominated by the fourteenth-century Belfry, a 275-foot medieval tower where forty-seven bells chime every fifteen minutes. The square is surrounded by Flemish buildings and numerous restaurants, bistros, and shops. Nearby is the Burg, a medieval square and site of the fourteenth-century Town Hall and the Basilica of the Holy Blood. Other points of interest include the cathedral with a Michelangelo statue of Mary and child, Groeninge Museum with its fine collection of Flemish primitive painters, the Chocolate Museum, and the Diamond Museum.

Alternative ways to explore the city would be by motorboat tours on the canals or by horse and buggy. Brugge is famous for its chocolates, mussels, and beer. The major shopping streets are Steenstraat and Katelynestraat, where you can shop for Belgian lace, chocolates, ceramics, crystal, linen, and pewter.

# DANUBE RIVER

The Danube River emanates in the southeast portion of Germany and passes through eight European countries before it connects with the Black Sea. Most riverboats embark passengers in **Passau,** a quaint town with a romantic setting located at the confluence of three rivers: the Danube, Inn, and Ilz. Quite close to the point where the rivers converge is the old town area, where you can walk through narrow cobblestone streets and alleys. Visit St. Stephan's Cathedral, with its baroque stuccoed ceiling, Gothic architecture, and frescoes. During the summer, you can hear a classical concert at noon on the world's largest church organ. Make sure you see the town hall and the thirteenth-century Castle Oberhaus—the location of a museum, art gallery, and observatory. You can rest along the way at an outdoor café overlooking the river and sample a local beer, ice cream, or pastry. Blauer Bock, set in a fourteenth-century building with a riverside terrace, would be a good choice. The main shopping streets off Ludwigsplatz are quite colorful, with numerous shops and small cafés.

The stretch of the river extending between Passau and Vienna is the most picturesque, meandering through verdant hills and symmetrical forests. Each evening, passengers are mesmerized by the sunset over the smooth waters of the Danube, creating the appearance of a bright orange ball melting into the river.

After Passau, your boat will pass through the **Wachau** region, a wine-producing area with vine-clad rolling slopes. The round towers of fortified churches and the battlement turrets of ancient castles frequently emerge as the river winds its way through Austria.

Prior to reaching Vienna, most boats visit **Dürnstein,** a charming Austrian village dominated by the beautiful baroque tower of an early eighteenth-century convent. You can visit the cathedral, stroll the narrow streets of the town as they wind up a hill, taste wine at a local vintner, have a coffee and pastry on an outdoor terrace overlooking the river, or walk along the paths bordered by vineyards that follow the river. You can even enjoy the panoramic view from the twelfth-century castle that sits on a steep hill, 520 feet above the town, and is connected by an ancient wall. This castle is where King Richard the Lion-Hearted was said to have been incarcerated. Between Passau and Durnstein lies the Village of **Melk,** where you can visit the Melk Abbey, one of the finest baroque buildings in the world.

The next major stop is one of the highlights of any cruise on the Danube, Austria's famous capital, **Vienna.** From the river, you will want to take a taxi or the metro (train No. 1) to Stephansplatz, which is in the middle of the historic and commercial core of the city, as well as the site of the soaring St. Stephan's, an impressive Gothic cathedral with a steeple that rises 450 feet. In this area are numerous traditional Viennese coffeehouses, outside cafés, and pedestrian-only shopping streets, the Kartnerstrasse being the liveliest. Within easy walking distance are the seven-hundred-year-old, 2,600-room Hofburg Palace (about two dozen rooms are open to the public, as is the crown jewel collection); the Museum of Fine Arts; the State Opera House; the 1,441-room early-seventeenth-century Schonbrunn Palace; and the city park with its statue of Johann Strauss.

There are highly rated, more formal restaurants in the deluxe hotels such as the Bristol, Sacher, Hilton, and Imperial. Less expensive typical Viennese restaurants are spread throughout this area. I especially enjoyed lunch on the protected patio of the Sacher Hotel dining room, where Viennese specialties reach top gourmet level, embellished by the excellent service staff. If you do not have time for a meal, a must is sampling a coffee and pastry, or at least an Austrian beer, in a coffeehouse. Although a version of Sacher Torte is available throughout the city, purists can enjoy a slice of the rich chocolate delight in the café connected to the Sacher Hotel.

On your way back to the river in the evening, you can visit the amusement park at the Prater, where a Ferris wheel with large enclosed gondolas offers a scenic ten-minute ride affording the best views of the city. Another spot to enjoy the view of the city while having a coffee is the café that revolves 590 feet above ground on the Danube Tower.

Another port of call on most itineraries, **Bratislava**, Slovakia, is of interest to tourists mostly due to its political history and the evolution of its varied governments. The Bratislava Hrad (castle) houses a historical museum and sits on a hill overlooking the city above the old town. Other scenic views of the town and river are possible from S.N.P. Bridge and Tower. The Danube is a fairly new, modern hotel on the river; however, the best luxury hotel is the Carlton, now managed by Radisson and located across from the Opera House and Philharmonic Concert Hall at the top of the Promenade, one of the colorful main thoroughfares in the city center. Emanating north from the Promenade are several other streets lined with shops, restaurants, and cafés. Follow the streets, and you will find yourself at the town square, locale of a historical museum and Café Mayer and Café Roland, two of the best indoor/outdoor people-watching cafés in which to enjoy a drink or meal.

The shorter cruises that do not extend to the Black Sea generally turn around at **Budapest**, one of the most picturesque and interesting cities along the Danube. The capital of Hungary with a population of three million is actually composed of two cities, Buda and Pest, which are connected by a series of bridges that span the river.

The most popular tourist areas on the Buda side are Castle Hill and Gellert Hill. Castle Hill was the center of Buda during the Middle Ages; today it is composed of small souvenir shops, cafés, restaurants, the Hilton Hotel and Casino, the thirteenth-century Matthias Church, and the Royal palace, which houses a historical museum and national art gallery and numerous statues and structures of historical interest.

Although Castle Hill is an excellent location from which to look across to the Pest side of the city and the Houses of Parliament, the panoramic vista of the Danube from 770 feet above on Gellert Hill is the most awesome. The Citadel on Gellert Hill was built in 1849 as a prison and is now a tourist attraction with restaurants, shops, and nightclubs. Also located here is Liberty Statue. Visible throughout the city, it was built as a tribute to the Soviet liberators.

On the Pest side are many of the larger hotels, restaurants, and pedestrian shopping streets as well as the Houses of Parliament, St. Stephan's Basilica, the statues and monuments at Hero's Square (constructed in 1896), the oldest synagogue in Europe, and several museums. The Four Seasons, the Atrium Sofitel Intercontinental and the Marriott enjoy excellent locations and provide many facilities, making them excellent choices for pre- or postcruise overnight stays. Other top hotels include the Kempinski, Meridien and Forum.

Margaret Island, which is connected by a bridge to both Buda and Pest, is an attractive large park with tennis courts, soccer fields, children's playgrounds, small restaurants, a public swimming pool, a garden theater, and the Grand Hotel, another good choice to overnight. The park is a very popular recreational area for the citizens of the city.

Gundel's, which occupies a palatial mansion in City Park, is the home of "pancakes Gundel," offers one of the finer (and most expensive) dining experiences in Budapest and is the place to see and be seen. Onxy, more centrally located, is a *Michelin*-starred restaurant—*tres cher*. On the Buda side, I recommend lunch at 21 for a reasonable spot with typical Hungarian cuisine, and Alabardos for a gourmet Hungarian dinner in a charming atmosphere.

Some of the more popular English-speaking riverboat lines cruising on the Danube include AMA Waterways, Avalon Waterways, Grand Circle, Scenic River Cruises, Tauck River Cruises, Uniworld Luxury River Boats, Vantage River Cruises, and Viking River Cruises. There are many other companies with riverboats cruising this area; however, most are sold as a charter or exclusively to the German-speaking market.

If you are heading in the opposite direction from Passau, your riverboat may make two additional stops on the upper Danube at Regensburg and Nurenburg.

**Regensburg,** one of Germany's best-preserved cities, dates back to AD 77 as a Celtic settlement. The Romans took over in AD 179 and remnants of the Roman occupation can be seen in the ancient Porta Praetoria behind the cathedral, with its huge stones piled in front of an arched gateway and the sixteen-arch Steinerne Brucke (the oldest bridge in Germany). Regensburg flourished in the twelfth and thirteenth centuries as Germany's wealthiest town and a major center of trade and commerce. The best example of Gothic architecture in Bavaria is the cathedral located in the heart of the Old Town area where the famous boys choir performs on Sunday mornings. Visitors will also enjoy touring the magnificent palace and monastery of the family Thurn and Taxis. Those wishing to experience a taste of Bavaria may enjoy coffee and pastry at the historic Princess Konditorei, wurst and sauerkraut at the Salzstadt building below the Steinerne bridge, or a full meal at the Ratskeller or Rosenpalais Restaurant and Bistro.

Almost all major attractions, hotels, and restaurants in **Nurenberg** lie in a one-mile area stretching between the main railway station to the south and the medieval Kaiserberg Castle atop a hill at the northern edge of the Altstadt (the Old City). Within this area you may wish to visit the Hauptmarkt, the central market square; the Town Hall; Handwerkerhof, near the railway station, a craft mall in a medieval castle setting; Justizgebaude, where the Nurenberg trials were held; the Albrecht Durer House, the only completely Gothic house in the city devoted to the life and works of the fifteenth/sixteenth-century artist Albrecht Durer; Germanisches Nationalmuseum, the largest museum of German art and culture, covering the entire historical spectrum of German craftsmanship and fine arts; Kaiserburg Castle, residence of kings and emperors with portions built in the twelfth, fourteenth, and fifteenth centuries; Spielzeug Museum, with exhibits of toys dating back over the centuries; St. Lorenz Church, built between the thirteenth and fifteenth centuries; and St. Sebaldus Church, an example of transition from Romanesque to German Gothic styles. You can shop for children's toys at Obletter, at Kistner for antique books, prints, and engravings from the masters, and at the aforementioned Handwerkerhof for local handicrafts, glassware, pewter, woodcarvings, and toys.

The top hotels are Le Meridien Grand, Maritim, Atrium, and Durer. Essigbratlein, in a house dating back to 1550, serving French-Continental cuisine is touted as the best restaurant in town along with Goldenes Posthorn, featuring a Franconian menu along with wines dating as far back as 1889. Heilig-Geist-Spital is the city's largest historical wine house. It is over 650 years old, featuring one hundred vintages of wine along with Franconian cuisine. For an inexpensive bratwurst, kraut, and beer, try Bratwurst-Hausle, Historische Bratwurst-Glocklien, or Herrenbrau at the Hauptmarkt.

## DENMARK

**Copenhagen**, the capital and chief port of Denmark, is a friendly, charming, cosmopolitan city with some of the finest restaurants and shops in Europe. From the Raadhuspladsen, the main square with its towering town hall, you can walk (or ride a rented bicycle) down the winding Strøget street toward Kongens Nytorv and the harbor area of Nyhavn. On the Strøget, you can browse through such famous shops as Illums Bolighus (modern design center), Georg Jensen (silver), Royal Copenhagen (china), and Birger Christensen (furs). From Nyhavn, you are only a short distance from Langelinie Pavillion, where you can have an outdoor lunch or dinner in a park overlooking the Little Mermaid, a statue inspired by Hans Christian Andersen's fairy tale that gracefully sits on a rock overlooking the harbor.

If you head in the opposite direction from the main square (Raadhuspladsen), you can visit the Glyptothek Museum, with its excellent collection of French paintings and Egyptian sculpture, and the fantastic Tivoli Gardens, with its flowers, open-air theater, concert hall, amusement rides, restaurants, nightclubs, and nightly fireworks. You may also enjoy visiting the lovely Copenhagen Zoo, Rosenborg Palace with its crown jewels, the National Art Museum, or the Carlsberg Beer factory. You will want to try one of the delicious open-face sandwiches called *smörbrod,* as well as the great Tuborg and Carlsberg beers.

Inside the Tivoli Gardens are numerous excellent restaurants in which to sample *smörbrod.* Ida Davidson's (formerly Oscar Davidson's) at Store Kongensgade 70 has been the most famous establishment for *smörbrod* since 1888. For fish and seafood, you will want to try Krogs, Fiskekaelderen, and DenGlydne Fortun. Gourmets will enjoy Kommandanten; Noma, Kong Hans Kaelder, Lenore Christine, Hermans, Les Etoiles, or one of the exceptional restaurants in the Nimb, Royal, Plaza, D'Angleterre, Scandinavia, and several other hotels. Actually, it would be difficult to have anything but a good meal in Copenhagen, wherever you might stop.

Possible excursions would include visits to Frilandsmuseet, an open-air museum set in the pastoral countryside to the north, where there is a display of Danish farmhouses from various regions set in their natural environs; a visit to Kronborg Castle at Helsingor, famous as the setting of Shakespeare's Hamlet and forty-five minutes north of Copenhagen; or Denmark's National History Museum, housed in Frederiksborg Castle in Hillerod, where you can boat on the castle's lake.

## ESTONIA

**Tallinn** is the major port city with a population of five hundred thousand. Dating back nine centuries, almost every building in the Old Town has some historic or architectural interest. Cruise ships on their way to Helsinki and St. Petersburg have found this a convenient stop where passengers can stroll through cobblestone streets while viewing Gothic architecture, a variety of churches and museums, numerous historic sites, and lovely parks.

It is recommended that visitors tour Tallinn by foot in order to take full advantage of the many places of interest. You may wish to start your tour at Toompea, the upper town, which is situated on a hill that affords a panoramic view of the city and harbor. Here you can visit the sixteenth-century Cannon Tower, Toompea Palace, St. Alexander Nevski's Cathedral, the thirteenth-century Dome Church, and take a walk through narrow Kohter Street to the observation platform, where you will enjoy the best view of the lower Old Town. There are several souvenir shops here and refreshments can be purchased at the café adjacent to the Virgin's Tower.

In the lower town you can visit the Town Hall constructed at the beginning of the fifteenth century; the homes and guildhalls along Pikk Street; the thirteenth-century spire of St. Olan's Church, which dominates the Tallinn skyline; and the Maritime Museum housed in the sixteenth-century Cannon Tower known as Fat Margaret.

Tours are generally offered to farms in the countryside. The largest hotel in town is the Viru Hotel, which is located near numerous restaurants and shops. Shuttle buses from your ship will generally leave you off in front of this hotel.

A major attraction is Kadriorg Palace and Gardens housing the Western and Russian Art Museum and the president's residence.

## FINLAND

**Helsinki** is the capital, largest city, and chief port of Finland, and it lies on the southern coast on the Gulf of Finland. Tourists will find this a refreshing, clean city with its new buildings, lovely parks, and spacious walks and streets. You will enjoy shopping for Finnish-designed household items, reindeer slippers, boots, clothing, Marimekko, ceramics, and furs, either at Stockmann's (Helsinki's largest department store) or at one of the many friendly shops at the Forum Shopping Center, the Senate Center, or along the Esplanade. In the morning, there is an open-air market right at the harbor, with numerous stalls featuring flowers, vegetables, fish, wearing apparel, and handicrafts. Behind the market is the Esplanade that not only is lined with shops and boutiques but also is the location of numerous restaurants and outdoor cafés. Places of interest include the Finnish Design Center, the cathedral, the State Council Building, and the university library in Senate Square, the monument to Sibelius, the Temppeliaukio Church built into solid rock, the town hall, the Empress Stone Obelisk, and the Fountain of Havis Amanda in the Market Square. Other excellent places to visit are the parliament house, the national museum, the National Art Gallery, the magnificent new Finlandia Concert Hall, the botanical gardens and their water tower, Linnanmäki (Helsinki's permanent amusement park), and the open-air Museum of Seurasaari (which contains specimens of various types of wooden houses built by the Finns over the centuries). You will want to try a Finnish sauna as well as a Finnish smörgasbord, which will include many native Finnish dishes in addition to the usual fare. A list of the best restaurants in Helsinki will include Motti, Karl König, Havis Amanda Fish Restaurant, Savoy, and Esplanadikappeli.

## FINLAND-STOCKHOLM CAR FERRY CRUISES

Several large cruise ships with capacity to carry automobiles offer overnight cruise experiences between Stockholm, Sweden, and either Helsinki or Turku, Finland. The largest and most upscale ships with this itinerary include *Silja Europa* (Silja Line, 3,000 passengers, entered service 1993), *Silja Symphony* (Silja Line, 2,700 passengers, entered service 1991), *Cinderella* (Viking Line, 2,500 passengers, entered service 1989), *Mariella* (Viking Line, 2,500 passengers, entered service 1985), *Amorella* (Viking Line, 2,480 passengers), *Gabriella* (Viking Line, 2,420 passengers), and *Isabella* (Viking Line, 2,214 passengers). Most passengers utilize these ships as a means of transportation from one country to the other, and many take their families and automobiles. These ships offer numerous alternative restaurants, and dining is generally not included in the cruise fare. There are theaters, live entertainment, casinos, and an array of facilities on these ships where passengers party into the wee hours. Departures are generally in the late afternoon and arrivals early the following morning. Do not expect the quality of comfort, food, service, or entertainment found on most cruise ships.

# FRANCE

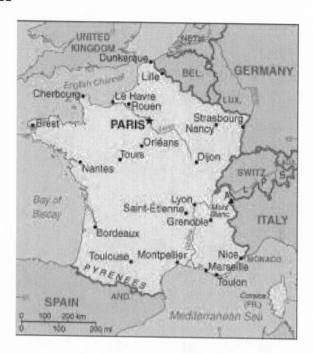

Your ship may dock at **Le Havre**, an important French harbor at the mouth of the Seine River on the English Channel. From here, you can take a train to **Paris**, where you will want to visit as many of the following sites as time allows: the colossal Arc de Triomphe; the famous Eiffel Tower, standing a thousand feet high; the magnificent Théâtre de l'Opéra; the fashionable Champs-Elysées; the beautiful Place de la Concorde; the Tuileries; Notre-Dame de Paris; the world-famous Louvre, home of the *Mona Lisa, Winged Victory*, and the *Venus de Milo*; l'Orangerie Art Museum; the Left Bank area with its small cafés, artists, and colorful crowds; the basilica of Sacre Coeur on the top of Montmartre; the palace at Versailles; and a boat tour down the Seine on the *bateaux mouches.* You can shop for crystal at Lalique and Baccarat; jewelry at Cartier and Boucheron; menswear at Pierre Cardin, Givenchy's, and Laroche's; handbags at Morabito and Gucci; gloves at Hermes; and French perfumes at most department stores, shops, and *parfumeries.* You can also visit one of the couture houses such as Balenciaga, Yves Saint Laurent, Givenchy, Pierre Cardin, Balmain, Carven, Courreges, Guy Laroche, Jean Patou, Lanvin, Madeleine de Rauch, and Nina Ricci.

You will not want to miss having a meal at a French restaurant in Paris. The most famous and most expensive gastronomic palaces are the Tour d'Argent, Lucas Carton, Jamin, Rostang, Taillevant, Le Pré Catelan, Laurent, Amboissie, Apicius, Jacques Cagne, Jules Verne (on the Eiffel Tower), Maxim's, and Lasserre; however, there are many excellent, less expensive establishments where you can obtain a meal in the true French fashion. Later in the evening, you may wish to take in the Folies Bergère, the lavish production at the Lido, the Moulin Rouge, one of the many other nightspots in the Montmartre area, or one of the many discotheques, jazz spots, or cabarets along the Saint-Germain-des-Pres.

If time allows, an overnight or several-day trip to the Burgundy country between Paris and Lyon or the Château country in the Loire Valley could prove to be a most charming and rewarding experience. I would recommend staying at one of the charming French inns that are owned and run by today's great chefs of France. My favorite is George Blanc's in Vonnas. Other superior choices would be Château d'Esclimont (only a short drive from Paris), Auberge des Templiers (Les Bèzards), Les Crayères (Reims), Château d'Artigny (Tours), La Côte Saint-Jacque (Joigny), and Domaine des Hauts de Loire (Onzain).

## RHÔNE AND SAÔNE RIVERS

Numerous riverboats offer cruises up and down the Rhône and Saône rivers and visit some of the more interesting and historic cities and villages along the way. These cruises afford excellent opportunities to visit the famous vineyards of the Rhône and Burgundy regions as well as some of the most famous restaurants in France. (See chapter 10.)

**Arles** is a charming town, originally inhabited by the Greeks and Romans. It boasts numerous imposing ancient ruins, including a Roman amphitheater that seats twenty-one thousand spectators and the Theater Antique, both of which were constructed in the late first century. The quaint "Old Town" area includes art museums and Romanesque cathedrals, as well as bars, bistros, restaurants, and shops. Arles was the site for many Van Gogh works, including his masterpiece, *Pont de Trinquetaille* (The Bridge). The ancient Roman cemetery at Alyscamps was the subject matter of paintings by both Van Gogh and Gauguin. There are numerous small shops specializing in colorful linens, place mats, and souvenirs in the colors and designs of Provence.

**Avignon** is another quaint city surrounded by three miles of totally preserved ancient ramparts with their original seven entrances and thirty-nine protective towers. Inside these walls are shops, restaurants, hotels, apartments, and such famous historic monuments as the fourteenth-century Pope's Palace, one of the largest medieval palaces in the world and residence of numerous popes during the Renaissance period, when the papal seat was moved here from Rome. In the evening, your boat or barge may pass by the remains of the St. Beneget Bridge, made famous by the song "Sur le Pont d'Avignon" and a marvelous vantage point from which to view the Pope's Palace and ancient walls. You may wish to visit the vineyards of Chateauneuf-du-Pape, which are only a short drive from the city. The most famous restaurants here are Hiely and Christian Etienne, both located in the center of town. The most famous hotels are Hotel d'Europe and La Mirande, an eighteenth-century mansion.

**Viviers** is a small medieval village rich in history, typical of many French towns in the countryside. Visitors can walk narrow cobblestone paths past restored buildings and ancient gates to the interesting Cathedral of Viviers, which was built in the twelfth to fifteenth centuries in a combination of Romanesque, classical, and Gothic styles. From the top of the hill behind the cathedral, you have a panoramic view of the region. You can take a tour that drives through the rolling hills, green valleys, and vineyards of the Ardéche countryside with a visit to the nearby vineyards of Côte Vivarais for a wine tasting.

**Tournon** is a small village that sits across the Rhône from the famous vineyards of the Hermitage. Here you can explore such wine houses as Chapoutier and Jaboulet. Your boat will dock across the road from the historic fourteenth-century castle, and you can stroll or cycle along the river Doux, a tributary of the Rhône. You can visit the Romanesque former Abbey of Saint-Philibert. Also from Tournon, you can take a two-hour train ride on a turn-of-the-century steam train along the Doux and Ardéche valleys.

**Vienne** is yet another historic city founded by the Roman legions in AD 50. Of interest are the Gothic Cathedral of St. Maurier, dating back to 1200; the excavations at St. Romain en Galle; the old Amphitheater; the Pyramid; and the Temple of Augustus. Nearby are the vineyards of Côte Rotie, considered the very finest wine of the Rhône region. In town, across from the Pyramid, is the famous restaurant of Ferdinand Pointe, who was the teacher for many of the best chefs in France. Pointe died many years ago, and although the restaurant is excellent, it no longer receives the same acclaim as in the past.

**Lyon**, the second-largest city in France, is set along the Rhône and Saône rivers and has much to offer its visitors. Stroll through one of the lovely parks or through the cobbled streets of old Lyon on the right bank of the Saône, with its numerous shops, boutiques, restaurants, and bistros.

Musée des Beaux-Arts is France's second-largest fine arts museum with an outstanding collection of nineteenth- and twentieth-century paintings. Musée de la Civilisation Gallo-Romaine, which is built into the Fourvière Hill, has ancient Roman relics and is located next to the old Roman Theater—the oldest in France—built in AD 19. Another Roman amphitheater is located at Croix Rousse.

The region of Lyon is a gastronomic paradise and gourmet heaven, being the location of many of the very best restaurants in France. In the city, you can dine at the famous Leon de Lyon and Orsi (both *Michelin* two-star establishments). Only minutes from the city is the world-famous restaurant of Chef Paul Bocuse in Collange Mount d'Or (*Michelin* three-star). Within an hour's drive are George Blanc in Vonnas, Troisgros in Roanne, and Alain Chappel in Mionney.

Some of the cruises go up to **Macon**, in the heart of the Burgundy region, where a short drive will bring you to all of the famous vineyards of the Côte de Nuit, Côte d'Or, Beaujolais, Maconnais, and Chablis wine regions.

**St. Malo** is set on the English Channel in the middle of Brittany, on the northwest coast of France. This is a convenient port of call for ships cruising between Great Britain and Spain. The major attraction is the charming walled town known as Intra-Muras, filled with seventeenth- and eighteenth-century buildings, winding cobblestone streets, shops, bistros, restaurants, museums, and cathedrals. You can walk the ramparts around the entire city, which afford spectacular views of the Brittany coastline. Among the numerous excellent restaurants, several of note include La Duchesse Anne, Le Chalut, Le Chasse Maree, Abordage, and Etrave. The specialty in all restaurants is fresh fish and seafood, especially mussels. The most popular tour from St. Malo is the drive to the picturesque island fortress of Mont St. Michel with its Benedictine abbey and gothic buildings.

Normandy is the area in the northwestern portion of France, a portion of which abuts the English Channel. Cruise ships most often visit the charming seaside fishing village of **Honfleur**, located at the mouth of the Seine River, connected to Le Havre by a recently constructed span bridge. The town, with its narrow cobbled streets lined with timbered buildings dating back to the fifteenth and sixteenth centuries, is best explored on foot. You can stroll along "Vieux Bassin," the horseshoe-shaped seventeenth-century harbor, with its numerous restaurants, cafés, shops, art galleries, and museums. Points of interest include Musée Eugene Boudin housing paintings by Boudin and other impressionists, Musée du Vieux Honfleur, and the timbered Saint Catherine's Church and bell tower, with its vaulted roof reminiscent of a ship's hull.

Honfleur is the place to sample Calvados liqueur, such great cheeses of Normandy as pont l'eveque, camembert, and liverot, mussels, and fresh fish and seafood. There are numerous small restaurants that surround the old harbor, the most highly rated being Terrace et L'Assiette (one-star *Michelin*), L'Absinthe, and Entre Terre el Mer.

A twelve-mile drive from Honfleur through the French countryside will bring you to **Deauville**, site of the annual American Film Festival. The environs surrounding the casino and Hotel Normandie, with its designer shops, is one of the most sophisticated, elegant areas in France. Avenue du Lucien Barrier, leading from the casino to the promenade bordering the beach, is the place to see and be seen. On the expansive beach, you can rent an umbrella or cabana named after a famous American movie star, and you can linger over a coffee or drink served in an outdoor café. Nearby, the Pleasure Harbor filled with sailboats and yachts is surrounded by restaurants, bistros, and small boutiques.

## GERMANY

**Bremerhaven**, located on the North Sea between Denmark and Holland, is the outer port of Bremen, which is one of Germany's largest ports, with excellent harbor facilities. In Bremen, you may wish to visit the Old Town, which lies on the right bank of the Weser, with its historic old Gothic buildings, the Roland Monument, St. Peter's Cathedral, and the Rathaus. You can try a German meal at the Rathskeller, Essighause, St. Petrus Weinstuben und Flett, and the Atles Bremer Brauhaus.

You can drive to **Travemünde**, a Baltic beach resort with sandy dune beaches, surrounded by thick pine forests. There you can visit its casino, nightclub, and restaurant. You can also take the short trip to **Hamburg** and visit the Renaissance Rathaus with its tall clock tower, the Kunsthalle, the Stadtpark, the Musikhalle, the Historical Museum, the Schnapps Museum, the Bismarck Monument, and St. Michael's Church. Here you may wish to browse through the shops along Jungfernsteig, Grosse Bleichen, Neuer Wall, and Ballindamm; take an hour-long boat ride on the beautiful Lake Alster; eat in one of its many excellent restaurants; or partake in the city's roaring nightlife along the Reeperbahn (undoubtedly the naughtiest street in the world). Some ships travel down the Elbe River and dock at Hamburg. During the evening, the two-hour twilight boat ride around Lake Alster and its tributaries is especially enjoyable. Afterward, a typical Hamburg dinner at Friesenkeller (opposite the Lake Alster dock) is a good bet, or one of the outdoor restaurants along the Colonnaden. For fine dining, the best-known restaurants include Landhaus Sherrer, Landhaus Dill, the dining rooms at Vier Jahreszeiten and Louis Jacob Hotels, Le Canard, and Fischereihafen.

Some ships stop at **Lübeck,** which has been an important port and city of trade since the twelfth century. If you do not opt to take the one-hour drive to Hamburg, you may wish to browse through this somewhat quaint town. Places of interest include St. Mary's Church, the third largest in Germany, housing the world's largest mechanical organ; the Town Hall, featuring Gothic and Renaissance styles; and St. Anne's Museum, an old monastery that displays local handicrafts. Schiffergesellschaft is a very atmospheric, typical German restaurant housed in a sixteenth-century sailor's guild house, an excellent choice for lunch ashore.

## RHINE AND MOSELLE RIVERS

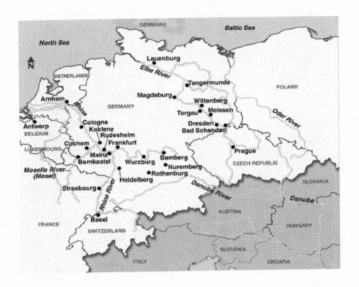

Numerous riverboat cruise lines offer cruises down the Rhine or Moselle rivers, passing castles and vineyards and stopping at little villages and cities along the way. These riverboats are considerably smaller than most cruise ships, and they offer fewer activities and amenities. However, on the first-class vessels, the food and service are Continental and impeccable. On all the ships, each public room and cabin is designed to permit a panoramic view of the scenery as your boat lazily sails along the river. (See chapter 10 for a description of riverboat cruise lines.)

The Rhine River is one of the longest in Europe, flowing from its source in the Swiss Alps to the North Sea at Rotterdam. The Moselle has its source in the Vosges Mountains in France and flows through Luxembourg into Germany until it converges with the Rhine at Koblenz. Most of the Rhine cruises travel between Amsterdam or Rotterdam in the Netherlands and Basel, Switzerland, stopping at Düsseldorf, Cologne, Speyer, Braubach, Rüdesheim, and Heidelberg in Germany and Strasbourg in France. The most scenic area of the Rhine is the portion extending between Rüdesheim and Koblenz, which offers the greatest concentration of historic castles and fortresses, as well as the legendary Loreley cliff. Moselle River itineraries run between Koblenz at the mouth of the Moselle and the ancient village of Trier, with stops at such villages as

Alken, Cochem, Beilstein, Zell, and Bernkastle-Kues. Some riverboats also continue on to Luxembourg. Overall, the Moselle itinerary is the more scenic and romantic.

**Basel** is a moderately large cosmopolitan city in northern Switzerland, a short distance from both the French and German borders. You will want to visit the Kunstmuseum of art, Münster (cathedral), Tinguely Museum, zoo, university, and shops and restaurants in the old town area. Although the Drei Könige is the best hostelry in town, if you are only staying overnight waiting to board your boat, you may prefer the Hilton, which is modern, very comfortable, has a pool and sauna, and is right near the harbor and railroad station. Hans Stucki's Bruderholz Restaurant vies for top honors in Switzerland and is a good choice for excellent haute cuisine.

**Strasbourg** is a charming French town on the Rhine that is definitely affected by the German influence of its neighbor. Its Gothic cathedral is one of the most impressive in existence, and the area around the cathedral is perfect for having a drink in an outdoor café, people watching, and browsing through shops. There is an impressive collection of Picasso, Dali, and Kandinsky at the Museum of Modern and Contemporary Art. One of the best ways to see Strasbourg is from a canal cruise. For a special treat, you can have lunch or dinner at the world-famous Beuerehiesel Restaurant, which sits in the middle of the lovely Orangerie Park and commands three stars from *Michelin*. Another *Michelin*-starred favorite here is Au Crocodile. These are a must for every aficionado of fine dining. Joggers and hikers will want to run or walk along the quay of the river (to the right as you disembark from the ship) for about a mile to Orangerie and run along the paths of the park past a children's zoo, pretty lake, and outdoor musical performances.

**Heidelberg** is a picturesque university town with lovely old homes and buildings built on hills along the banks of the River Neckar. The old town area consists of shops, hotels, and restaurants surrounding the university. It is quite atmospheric and dates back to the Roman era. Have lunch or a drink at the historic Ritter Hotel, which exemplifies Heidelberg in the days of *The Student Prince*. Performances of this operetta in English as well as concerts are performed on the grounds of the famous fourteenth-century Heidelberg Castle, which is located directly above the town overlooking the Neckar. This is also the site of the largest wine cask in existence. Riverboats offerings tours to Heidelberg generally dock at Speyer. When exploring Speyer, the major attractions include the Kaiserdom, one of the finest Romanesque cathedrals in the world; the Historical Museum of the Palatinate; the old Jewish synagogue with its well-preserved *mikva*, or ritual baths; and the Technik Museum with its large collections of locomotives, aircraft, vintage automobiles, and automatic musical instruments, as well as a historical 420-ton U-boat. Two atmospheric restaurants are the Ratskeller in the city hall and Wirtshaft zum Alten Engel.

**Rüdesheim** is in the middle of the Rheingau wine area. You will want to visit the gardens and impressive monastery at Eberbach that date back to 1136. Here you can enjoy a tasting of wines from the Rheingau and explore the ancient Gothic chapel, cloisters, and wine cellars. The most interesting attraction in the city is the Siegfried's Music Museum with its fascinating display and demonstrations of mechanical musical instruments from the past hundred years. In the evening, you can wander through the numerous typical restaurants, inns, wine and beer halls, and shops located up and down the streets along the river. The most activity will be found along Drosselgasse. A good choice to dine or have a drink along with music would be Breuer's Rudesheimer Schloss. This is one of the best towns in Germany to partake of the colorful nightlife. Many of the wine gardens have orchestras specializing in folk dancing. This is the spot to watch (and join) the people having fun. Next to where the boat docks are tennis courts, a park, and a giant swimming pool. You will also enjoy the scenic ten-minute cable-car ride to Niederwald Monument.

**Cologne** is a lovely historic city with a picturesque vista of the Rhine. Dominating the center of town stands the beautifully preserved cathedral, which is the largest Gothic building in the world. If you are able to negotiate the 360-step climb up a spiral staircase to the top of the cathedral, you will be rewarded with a splendid view of the city. The Museum Ludwig contains a large collection of Picassos as well as works by Dali, Lichtenstein, and Warhol. Among the top-rated restaurants are Die Bastei, located in an elevated, glassed-in, three-quarter-circle building jutting out over the waters of the Rhine; the elegant Stüben House at the Excelsior Ernst Hotel; Le Moissonnieer (French), the Schweizer Stübe, a Swiss eatery near the cathedral; and the Alt Köln and Sion, which feature typical German fare. The most interesting area in which to take a walk or stop for a drink is located between the three bridges on the west bank of the river. Immediately behind the river walk are several streets filled with shops and outdoor shopping stalls. Located nine miles from Cologne is the Grandhotel Schloss Bensberg, a restored baroque castle that houses excellent French and Italian restaurants.

You can take an organized bus tour around Düsseldorf, a large modern metropolis with tall buildings, elegant shops, and a good mass-transportation system. You will enjoy roaming around the colorful old town section, where you will find hundreds of little bars, shops, restaurants, and discotheques. Riverboats generally stop here only in the evening to permit passengers to partake of the nightlife in the old town area. The most highly rated restaurant in Düsseldorf is Im Schiffchen (French). For German cooking, try Aalschokker and Victorian.

**Koblenz**, a charming city at the confluence of the Rhine and Moselle rivers, dates back to the Roman era and contains numerous historic landmarks. You will want to visit the Deutsches Eck monument (nineteenth century) at the point where the rivers meet; the pillars, towers, balconies, and dormer windows of the Balduin Bridge (fourteenth century); the Elector's Palace (eighteenth century), a neoclassical building; the "Plan," a square with shops and restaurants surrounded by old mansions; the Florinsmarket in the old town with its old buildings, alleyways, and wine taverns; Stolzenfels Castle (nineteenth century); the Church of Our Lady, a combination of Romanesque, Gothic, and baroque architectural styles; St. Castor's Church (twelfth century); and of course, the little restaurants and taverns along the riverfront.

**Cochem** enjoys an enviable position in the heart of the Moselle wine country and is the most inundated with tourists. Many of the day boats stop here, and it is an excellent place to bed down for the night for those exploring the area by car. You can try Hotel Alte/Thorschenke (a historic inn from the fourteenth century),

Lochspeicher, or the Landenberg. Cruise boats stop here to allow passengers to explore Reichsburg Castle and the many shops, restaurants, wine stores, bars, and guesthouses along the river. Excursions to the famous Eltz castle emanate from here also.

**Bernkastel-Kues** is undoubtedly the most charming, picturesque village on any of the rivers. When you step off the boat and take in the river filled with ducks and swans beneath the old bridge and the gingerbread-timbered houses and colorful dormers and steeples with a backdrop of green forests and steep vineyards as far as the eye can see, you will believe that you have just entered the world of *Hansel and Gretel*. This is also the site of the famous Bernkasteler-Doktor vineyards, and bottles of what is possibly the best of the Moselle wines can be purchased in shops here for far less than they are offered throughout the rest of the world. You will enjoy visiting the Moselle wine museum, Castle of Landshut ruins, market square; strolling down the cobblestone streets and through the shops; sampling the wine; and dining in one of the old inns or taverns.

**Trier**, a two-thousand-year-old Roman town, sits near the end of the Moselle River, right after the junction of the Ruwer and before the Moselle splits into the Saar and tapers off. This is an important center of the Moselle wine industry and is surrounded by vineyards. You will want to visit the Roman amphitheater, the Basilica, Imperial thermal baths, Porta Nigra, the ancient black gate, the birth home of Karl Marx, and the Landesmuseum (wine artifacts) and take a stroll down one of the wine-paths (*weinlehrpfad*) that pass by numerous vineyards. Moselle River cruises either embark or terminate in Trier, and there are several restaurants immediately above the dock, including Pfeffermuhle, one of the best in the city. Two conveniently located restaurants in the middle of town are Zum Christophel and Romisher Kaiser. Overnight accommodations are available at the Europa Park Hotel, Holiday Inn, or Hotel Petrisberg.

## GREAT BRITAIN

Your ship may dock at Southampton, where you will board a train to **London**, the capital and great historical city of Britain. Some ships dock at Tilbury or Dover. Smaller ships can negotiate the Thames and dock right near the Tower Bridge. Since there are hundreds of points of interest here, you will have to budget your short time in port carefully. Places of interest, history, and importance include Westminster Abbey, where kings and queens are crowned and important personages buried; the Houses of Parliament, Big Ben, and the Palace of Westminster; Piccadilly, which is the Times Square of London; the fine shops on Bond Street, Oxford Street, and Regent Street; Trafalgar Square, with its statue of Nelson and the National Gallery; St. Paul's Cathedral, built by Sir Christopher Wren; the historic Tower of London, which now houses the crown jewels; Grosvenor Square, which is the site of the American embassy and Roosevelt Memorial; the fashionable Mayfair area, with its fine homes, hotels, and shepherd's market; beautiful Hyde Park; the law courts and Inns of Court; the British Museum; the Wax Museum; the restaurants and clubs in the Soho district; Kensington Palace; the artists' area of Chelsea; and Buckingham Palace, with its changing of the guard.

There are many well-known, excellent restaurants in London, including La Gavroche, Tante Claire, Chez Nico, the Chelsea Room and Rib Room at the Hyatt, Connaught Grill, Gordon Ramsey at Hotel Claridge, and the Savoy Grill. At lunchtime, you may enjoy trying one of the atmospheric local pubs or perhaps the historic Cheshire Cheese, built in 1667. In the evening, you may wish to take in a play or a musical at one of London's many theaters, dine and dance at one of the fine nightclubs, or gamble at a gaming club (you must arrange in advance for membership). London also offers several world-famous department stores, including Harrod's in Knightsbridge, Selfridge's on Oxford Street, and Fortnum and Mason in Piccadilly.

A short distance from **Southampton**, ninety miles south of London, near **New Milton**, is England's most charming and luxurious resort, Chewton Glen. You will enjoy dining at this uniquely beautiful and elegant country manor house and taking a stroll around its magnificent parks, nearby forests, and seaside. Another rewarding deviation, a thirty-minute drive from London, is Michel Roux's Waterside Inn at **Bray**, which sits on one of the more picturesque section of the Thames. This is considered by many to be Great Britain's finest dining establishment. This is definitely a "do not miss" experience.

## HOLLAND

**Amsterdam** is the capital and largest city in the Netherlands and one of the chief commercial ports of Europe. This city is made up of numerous islands surrounded by circular canals with bridges that connect the islands. You can obtain a good overall picture of the city by taking one of the glass-roofed boat tours of the canals. This is a charming, colorful city with friendly people, and you will enjoy exploring many of the areas on foot. You can visit the Royal Palace, the Tower of Tears, Rembrandt's House, the tropical museum, the Van Gogh Museum, the Amsterdam Historical Museum, the Jewish Historical Museum, Anne Frank House, and the world-famous Rijksmuseum, which houses many Dutch and European masterpieces, including Rembrandt's *The Night Watch*. You will want to shop for fine porcelains, pewter, delft, jewelry, and the antiques on Kalverstraat, Rokin, and the Leidsestraat.

There are several good cabarets and nightclubs and numerous fine Dutch and cosmopolitan restaurants. On the various narrow streets that emanate from the Leidseplein and Leidestraat, you will find hundreds of excellent ethnic restaurants including French, Italian, Greek, Argentinean, Indian, Indonesian, and even a Hard Rock Café. For something different, try *rijsttafel* at one of the Indonesian restaurants such as Sahid Jaya, Djawa, Samba Sebo, Speciaal, or Tempo Doeloe. Other venerable Dutch/Continental eateries around town include the Silver Spoon (De Silveren Spiegel), the Five Flies (D'Vijff Vlieghen), De Roode Leeuw, and the Black Sheep (Swarte Schaep). La Rive is a *Michelin*-rated French restaurant. After dinner, you may enjoy the numerous jazz clubs or the discos in the hotels. Or you may wish to explore Amsterdam's notorious red-light district near the Ouderkerksplein, where ladies of the evening of all nationalities are perched in windows luring customers. The city is also well-known for its coffee houses that specialize in offering marijuana to their patrons.

## NORWAY

Norway is a long, narrow country on the northwestern edge of the European continent whose coastline is marked by long, narrow inlets called "fjords." The northern part of the country lies above the Arctic Circle and is called the "Land of the Midnight Sun" because it has long periods every summer when the sun shines twenty-four hours a day. Many cruise ships traverse the rocky western coast of Norway, where there is surprisingly mild weather due to the warm North Atlantic current of the Gulf Stream.

**Bergen** sits on the natural harbor of a sheltered fjord where mountains rise majestically around a valley. This is Norway's second-largest city, where you will want to visit the colorful fish, flower, and fruit markets along the quay, Rosencrantz Tower, Bryggen (a group of wooden medieval-style warehouses along the wharf), the Hanseatic Museum, the new aquarium, Lungegardsvann (a lake surrounded by trees and flowers), Trollhaugen (the home of composer Edvard Grieg), and the Bergenhus Fortress and Haakon's Hall. A must for every visitor (when weather permits) is the funicular railway ride up one thousand feet to the top of Mount Floyen where you can enjoy a spectacular panorama, have a snack, and hike on mountain trails. You can shop and have lunch at Bryggen or the Galleriet shopping center. The best buys are Norwegian-style sweaters. The best restaurants are the Bellevue, which has excellent views, service, and cuisine; Enfjorinen, a wharfhouse specializing in fish and seafood; To Kokker, next door; Fiskeroyen; Augustin; and Bryggestuen. For a traditional Norwegian evening, you will enjoy Fana Folklore for dining, dancing, and singing.

**Stavanger** is an interesting town where the major industries are sardine exporting and shipbuilding. Its marketplace is a colorful spot where peasants come from miles around to shop for fish, vegetables, and fruits. Nearby is the famous Lysefjord, thought to be one of the most spectacular fjords in the country, with its towering mountains, farms, and Pulpit Rock, which hangs 1,800 feet above the fjord. Two good restaurants are Restaurationen and Prinsen.

**Trondheim** is a delightful colonial city where you may want to visit the famous Nidaros Cathedral, which is one of Europe's finest Gothic buildings; the Stiftsgarden, which is a royal residence dating from the eighteenth century and made of wood; the Bishop's Palace; and the Museum of Music at Ringve, with its remarkable collection of musical instruments. Try the restaurant at the Britannia Hotel.

**Hammerfest** is one of the most northerly cities in the world, lying north of the Arctic Circle in the Land of the Midnight Sun. Here the sun does not set from May through July. From Hammerfest, your ship will proceed to Skarsvog, the North Cape, and Honningsvaag.

**Oslo**, located in the southern part of the country, is the capital and the largest city in Norway. Here you will want to walk down the charming main street, Karl Johansgate, to the Royal Palace, past the National Theater, the University of Oslo, the statues of Ibsen and Björnson, the cathedral, and the National Art Museum. This street is also home to the principal shopping district. You may also wish to visit the town hall, Akershus Castle (dating back to AD 1300, rebuilt in the seventeenth century), Frogner Park (scene of 150 groups of bronze and granite sculptures by Gustav Vigeland),

Edvard Munch Museum, the Viking Ship Museum, and the Kon Tiki Museum at Bygdøy. At lunchtime, you will want to stop at a Norwegian restaurant and partake of the *koldtbord* (cold table), featuring fish, seafood, cheeses, meats, and salads. The Norwegians also serve *smörbrod* (open-face sandwiches) in many varieties. You may wish to shop for local handicrafts in ceramics, woven textiles, and carved woods, as well as in silver, pewter, and glass. You can see a permanent exhibition of Norwegian arts, crafts, and furniture at the Forum and at the Norwegian Design Store. The restaurants in the Grand, Scandinavia, and Intercontinental hotels are all excellent, or you can try one of the outdoor cafés or restaurants along the waterfront at Aker Brygge.

## PASSENGER AND CAR FERRY SERVICE BETWEEN EUROPE AND NORWAY

Since 1990, the cruise ships of Color Line have provided transportation between Europe and Norway on comfortable vessels that accommodate both passengers and automobiles. Cabins vary greatly in size, price, and creature comforts. The least expensive are generally located below the car deck, can accommodate up to four persons in upper and lower berths, and have washbasins but no shower or toilet. The most expensive luxury suites include small lounge areas, desks, minibars, televisions, radios, telephones, full bathrooms with robes, and hair dryers.

Public areas on all ships include vast duty-free shops, several bars, show lounges, indoor pools, saunas, movie theaters, children's playrooms, Internet cafés, and a variety of restaurants ranging from cafeterias and coffee shops to Norwegian buffets and Continental à la carte restaurants. Meals are not included in the cruise fare.

Service between Hirtshals, Denmark, and Kristiansand, Norway, which takes four and a half hours, and to Oslo, Norway, which takes eight and a half hours, is offered on either the *Color Festival* (entered service 1985; 34,314 GRT; carrying 2,000 passengers in 588 cabins, 340 cars), the *Skagen* (entered service 1975; 12,333 GRT; carrying 1,238 passengers, 430 cars), or the *Christian IV* (entered service 1981; 15,064 GRT; carrying 2,000 passengers, 530 cars).

Service between Kiel, Germany, and Oslo, Norway, which takes nineteen hours, is offered daily on the *Prinsesse Ragnhild* (entered service 1981 and renovated in 1992; 38,500 GRT; carrying 1,875 passengers, 770 cars).

Service between Newcastle, Great Britain, and Bergen, Haugesund, and Stavanger in Norway, which takes about twenty-three hours, is available three times each week on the *Color Viking* (entered service 1975 and was stretched and renovated in 1989; 20,581 GRT; carrying 1,250 passengers in 420 cabins, 320 cars). Cost-conscious passengers can spend the night in a reclining airplane-style chair instead of a cabin (not recommended).

The 75,000-ton, 2,750-passenger *Color Fantasy* entered service in 2004, operating between Oslo and Kiel. It is the largest and most expensive ferry every built. A similar ship, *Color Magic,* entered service in 2007. Both vessels have a passenger capacity of 2,700 in 1,016 cabins and can carry 550 cars on the car decks. These two ships have large show-lounges with cabaret shows, Internet cafés, casinos, boutiques, playrooms and water parks for children, discos, conference centers, spas and fitness centers, numerous bars, and restaurants.

During the summer season, these ships can be quite crowded with families. The primary purpose of the line is to provide transportation for tourists, families, and those on automobile vacations with numerous diversions during the crossings. You cannot compare the level of comfort with cruise ships where passengers come to relax and luxuriate.

The general agents in the United States are Bergen Line at 405 Fifth Avenue, New York, NY 10022, telephone: (800) 323-7436.

Bergen Line Inc. also markets Norwegian Coastal Voyages, a company that has been operating for more than one hundred years and calls at thirty-four Norwegian ports daily. The line presently has eleven ships, most of which were built since 1993, with passenger capacities between 169 and 674. Each ship has lounges, dining rooms, twenty-four-hour cafeterias, and souvenir and sundry shops. The newer vessels have children's playrooms, conference facilities, elevators, and cabins for disabled passengers. Fares for outside cabins range from $120 to $230 per person per day, with suites costing more and inside cabins less.

The ships offer cruises six days southbound, seven days northbound, and twelve days round-trip. Itineraries include the cultural cities of Bergen and Trondheim; small arctic towns such as Tromso, Oksfjord, and Hammerfest; and passages through narrow straits and past magnificent fjords.

The newest ships of the line, the 16,053-ton *Trollfjord* and *Midnatsol* entered service in 2002 and 2003, respectively. The ships have 290 cabins and nineteen suites and can accommodate 822 passengers. Public areas include numerous dining venues, a conference area, a children's area and arcade, a library, and several lounges. The ships cruise round trip from Bergen, Norway, to Kirkenes in eleven days.

## POLAND

**Gdynia** is the Polish port where most cruise ships stop, and it is only a few miles from the popular seaside resort of Sopot, with its beautiful beaches and festivals. Here you can sun, swim, and dance. The weather is generally moderate, with temperatures ranging from the thirties in the winter to the seventies in the summer. You are also only a short distance from **Gdansk** (Danzig), the hub of the Polish shipping industry. Here you can see a rebuilt city that was nearly destroyed during World War II, and you can try one of the several good restaurants where you can consume sausages, cabbage, *czarzy chleb* (coarse rye bread), *bigos* (sauerkraut and smoked meats), *barszcz* soup, and some delicious pastries and wash it all down with one of the domestic beers.

## SCOTLAND

The smaller cruise ships can dock at **Leith,** which is a couple of miles from the center of Edinburgh. Larger ships anchor off shore and passengers must take an hour bus ride into town. Places of interest include Edinburgh Castle, Palace of Holyroodhouse, National Gallery of Scotland, Scottish National Gallery of Modern Art, Princess Street Gardens, and the shops along Princess Street, George Street, and Royal Mile. The Witchery by the Castle is one of Edinburgh's most well-known restaurants.

## SWEDEN

**Stockholm** is the beautiful capital of Sweden, built on more than fourteen islands connected by bridges. You can walk through the cobbled, winding streets of the old town, with its ancient buildings crowded together in medieval fashion and the site of the Royal Palace and Museum. Here you can also visit antique shops, fashionable boutiques, cellar bars, and nightclubs. You will want to shop in the modern department stores such as Nordiska Kompaniet, Paul U. Bergström, and Ahlen, where you will find quality furs, Orrefors and Kosta Swedish crystal, and beautiful silver and stainless steel. You will also want to visit the town hall, one of the major architectural works of our time; Drottningholm Castle; the home of Swedish sculptor Carl Milles, filled with his own works of art; the National Museum, with its huge collection of Swedish and foreign art; and the Opera House.

You may enjoy a short trip to Skansen, with its zoological and botanical gardens, its charming old homes, concerts, restaurants, nightclubs, discotheques, and open-air dancing on warm summer evenings. There are opera and ballet performances at the Royal Opera and concerts at the Stockholm Concert Hall. Some of the local restaurants offer Swedish *smörgasbord*, with its large variety of fish, meat, and cheese courses. This is most often accompanied by Swedish, Danish, or German beer. Operakällaren has been considered the outstanding restaurant in Stockholm for decades. Other distinguished establishments include Restaurant Riche, the restaurants at the Grand Hotel, and the Stalmästaregarden, Diana, Kallaren Aurora, Fem Sma Hus (for atmosphere), and Stortorgskallaren. The Sheraton and the Grand Hotel are both good locations for exploration of the city and the Old Town. The Grand Hotel has a wonderful smörgasbord at both lunch and dinner time.

## FERRY SERVICE FROM SWEDEN

Birka Lines, headquartered in Mariehamn, Aland Islands, offers cruises from Stockholm to Helsinki-Turku-Talinn and other Baltic countries. The 34,728-ton, 1,800-passenger *Birka Paradise* entered service in 2004. The *Birka Paradise* has many amenities similar to large cruise ships. Most of the 734 accommodations have four beds and there are some suites, including duplex suites. Public areas include a Caribbean-themed lido area, known as Paradise Beach, with a sliding glass roof, a swimming pool, two Jacuzzis, artificial palms, and artificial sunlight solar fixtures. At night, the pool is covered with an automatic sliding dance floor, and the area converts to a nightclub with Latin rhythms. In addition, there are three saunas, a spa with five treatment rooms, numerous lounges, bars, and dance venues, duty-free shops, two main buffet restaurants, and an upscale á la carte restaurant.

## RUSSIA

Most of the ships that cruise to the Northern European capitals stop for several days at **St. Petersburg**, formerly Leningrad, offering Western tourists an opportunity to look at the lifestyle of the Russians. St. Petersburg is the second-largest city in Russia, lying on the Baltic Sea at the eastern end of the Gulf of Finland, four hundred miles northwest of Moscow. This city was built by Peter the Great in the eighteenth century and originally called St. Petersburg, then renamed in 1924 after V. I. Lenin, the founder of the Communist party, and then returned to its original name after the breakup of the USSR. Most of the city is on the southern bank of the Neva River, but it also covers many islands spanned by more than one hundred bridges. St. Petersburg is a city noted for its splendid palaces, fountains, parks, monuments, and eighteenth- and nineteenth-century baroque and neoclassical architecture.

The main part of the city is divided by three long avenues that meet at the Admiralty Building, which stands in the center of the city and dominates the skyline. Close to the Admiralty stands the Winter Palace, which was built in the baroque style during the eighteenth century and served as a winter residence for the czars until 1917. Today, it is part of the Hermitage Museum and houses many famous masterpieces from the ancient Greeks, the Italian Renaissance, and the French moderns. Nearby you can also see the Alexandrovskaya column, commemorating the Russian victory over Napoleon; the massive St. Isaac's Cathedral, with its 112 monolithic columns and three-hundred-foot gilt cupola; and the monument to Peter the Great known as the Bronze Horseman.

In addition to the many stores, restaurants, and cafés that line the principal thoroughfare, Nevsky Prospekt, you will also want to see the Smolny Monastery and Institute, built in the ninteenth century, the Kazansky Cathedral (which now houses a museum), the Pioneer Palace (a children's recreational center), the Russian Museum, the public library, and the Kirov Theater. You may also wish to visit the Park of Culture and Rest, the Leningrad Mosque, Peter-Paul Cathedral, and Kirov Stadium. Or you can take a short drive to **Petrodvorets**, the summer residence of Peter the Great, where there are a number of beautiful palaces, parks, pavilions, fountains, and statues created during the eighteenth and nineteenth centuries.

On Nevsky Prospekt is the Grand Hotel Europa, a very clean, elegant European-style hotel with numerous restaurants. This is a desirable place to stop and break up your tour.

Seventeen miles south of St. Petersburg is an area formerly known as the Czar's Village and the site of the Catherine Palace, named in honor of Peter the Great's wife, Catherine I. Nearby is the town of Pushkin, where the noted poet Alexandra Pushkin studied in the early nineteenth century. On your return, you could visit Pavlovsk, one of Russia's most beautifully restored palaces.

Although Russian restaurants are a far cry from those of Western Europe, you may wish to stop in and soak up some local atmosphere while drinking vodka and sampling some caviar, borscht, *kasha*, or *zakouski* (highly seasoned hot hors d'oeuvres). Don't drink the water and be prepared for very slow service. Recommended Russian restaurants include Astoria, St. Petersburg, and the restaurants in the Grand Hotel Europa. If your time is limited, you may be wise to book a tour through St. Petersburg's "Intourist" travel service. They will supply you with a car and an English-speaking guide who will escort you through all of the above sites while offering some local history along the way. With the massive changes taking place in East-West relations, you can expect vast improvements in this part of the world as a tour destination.

## Cruises from the United States' West Coast, Mexico, the South Seas, Hawaii, and the Far East

To accommodate potential cruisers living on the West Coast and in the southwestern states, a number of cruise lines have based their ships in Los Angeles. Vessels of most of the major cruise lines offer a variety of cruise vacations departing from Los Angeles or San Francisco.

A number of the cruises follow the southwestern coast, calling at such Mexican ports as Cabo San Lucas, Mazatlan, Manzanillo, Puerto Vallarta, Zihuatanejo-Ixtapa, and Acapulco. Many of the ships extend their itineraries through Central America, crossing through the Panama Canal, cruising in the Caribbean, and terminating at either San Juan, Puerto Rico, or Port Everglades, Florida. During the spring and summer months, most of these same ships shift their itineraries, sailing to Canada and Alaska.

Several ships of Norwegian Cruise Line provide regular weekly cruises around the Hawaiian Islands, stopping at the islands of Oahu, Hawaii, Maui, and Kauai.

Several of the lines have scheduled longer cruises from California that stop at such exotic South Sea islands as Tahiti, Bora Bora, Moorea, Tonga, Samoa, New Caledonia, Vanuatu, and Fiji. Many of these ships go on to New Zealand, the Great Barrier Reef, and Australia, and even as far as Japan, Hong Kong, the Philippines, Indonesia, and Malaysia. The Celebrity, Crystal, Cunard, Oceania, Princess, Regent Seven Seas,

Renaissance, Royal Caribbean, and Silversea cruise lines offer several cruises each year in the Far East. Star Cruises, based in Singapore, is a relative newcomer to the cruise business, specializing in diverse Asian itineraries geared for an Asian clientele. Several cruise lines offer regular cruises in French Polynesia. P&O Australia and Princess have itineraries emanating from Australia.

The following are the highlights of some of the more popular Alaskan, Mexican, Hawaiian, South Pacific, and Far Eastern ports:

## ALASKA

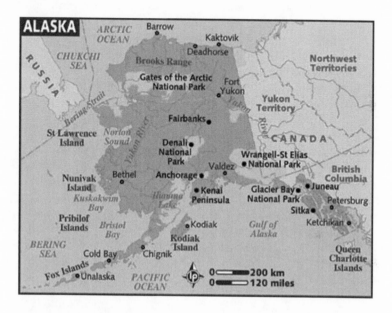

Alaska and British Columbia have become cruise grounds for a number of ships departing from the West Coast.

**Juneau**, the capital of Alaska, is also the third-largest and one of the most colorful cities in the state, with a history dating back to the discovery of gold in 1879. You will enjoy cruising the myriad of fjords, straits, sounds, and passages of the Tongass National Forest, with its unsurpassed scenery and abundant wildlife. Other points of interest include the aerial tram ride that takes visitors from the cruise terminal to the top of Mount Roberts, the incomparable Glacier Bay National Park, the Mendenhall Glacier, the Alaska State Museum, and the Golden Creek Mine Town. Most ships offer a variety of tours to Mendenhall Glacier, to the Golden Creek Mine Town, and to an Alaska salmon bake to sample the area's most famous delicacy. Other shore excursions offered by many of the cruise ships include a rafting trip down the Mendenhall River, a helicopter flight over the Mendenhall Glacier and other glaciers with a landing on an ice field, and a float-plane ride to Taku Lodge through the glaciers to a wilderness habitat where visitors can gorge themselves with barbecued salmon and take a nature walk. Most ships cruising this area meander into Glacier Bay. This affords passengers an opportunity to photograph both the mirror-like blue waters with bobbing ice formations, all surrounded by jagged wilderness, mountain peaks, and fjords interlaced with gleaming white glaciers.

**Ketchikan** is known as Alaska's first city because it is the first major community travelers see as they journey north. The city is located on a large island at the foot of Deer Mountain with fishing, timber, and tourism comprising the major industries. The city is known for its outstanding collection of native totem poles located at Totem Heritage Center, Totem Bight Historical Park, and Saxman Village. Excursions include tours of the town and totem poles; a visit to Saxman Village to explore a native community and to view totem carvers at work and folkloric performances; a float plane ride to Misty Fjord National Monument, a 2.2-million-acre wilderness area, home to brown and black bears, mountain goats, moose, and bald eagles; a hike up the three-mile trail from town to the top of Deer Mountain to enjoy a spectacular panorama of the harbor and wilderness; a mountain-bike tour along the shore of the Inside Passage; canoe and kayak tours; a float plane ride over the Misty Fjord; rain forest zip line adventures; and sport fishing for salmon.

**Sitka** is a picturesque little city reflecting the early Russian influence of its first European settlers. You will see harbors filled with little fishing boats, roofs lined with gulls, and a backdrop of snow-peaked mountains. In the summer, you can take a three-hour jet boat cruise past little islands to view bald eagles, sea otters, and humpback whales. You may wish to visit the Sitka National Monument to see its museum, totem poles, craft shops, and spruce forest paths; the Alaska museum; and St. Michael's Cathedral; or see the scenic Harbor Mountain or Mount Verstovia and the Mount Edgecumbe Crater. The helicopter tour, weather permitting, is a good way to see many of these sites. Possible options include a catamaran tour of Sitka's islands combined with motorized raft rides to a wildlife sanctuary, the scenic Silver Bay Cruise, or a fishing charter.

**Skagway,** dating back to the Gold Rush days of Alaska, is presently a tribute to that era. From the pier where your cruise ship docks, you can walk to downtown Skagway, or you can take a horse-drawn carriage or antique bus on a tour. Options for tourists include a spectacular helicopter ride landing on a glacier or a glider ride over ice fields and Glacier Bay, with a float trip through a bald eagle preserve, a city and historical tour on a streetcar, a tour to an 1898 gold miners' camp, a cruise on the *Glacier Queen* to Smuggler's Avenue and the old Gold Rush town of Dyea, a bicycle or horseback ride on the Dyea Plains, a railroad tour to White Pass Summit, or a hike from town to Upper Dewey Lake.

## AUSTRALIA

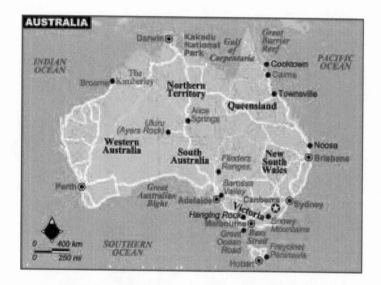

Australia is a young, growing country. Its location south of the equator results in the seasons being reversed, with the best weather coming in September through April. Many cruise ships dock at **Sydney**, where you will pull into a magnificent harbor and see the Sydney Harbor Bridge, the largest arch bridge in the world. You may want to browse through the shops at Centrepoint Shopping Center and look for woolens, Australian opals, jewelry, and kangaroo furs, followed by lunch or dinner at its revolving tower restaurant, which affords a spectacular view of the city and surrounding area.

Perhaps you would prefer to test your skills at surfing and skin-diving at one of the many beautiful beaches. There are numerous small sheltered, romantic coves hemmed in by high rocky cliffs, as well as wide strands of white-sand beaches with magnificent surf. Bondi Beach, five miles south of town, offers good surf, restaurants, a pavilion, and swimming pool; Manly Beach is a resort with a lovely park, pool, and numerous restaurants reached via a twenty-minute ferry ride; and Palm Beach, the most beautiful of all, is an hour-and-a-half drive north from the city. You can see the koala and the duckbill platypus at the famous Taronga Park Zoo or visit Parliament House, the botanic gardens, Hyde Park, Randwick Racecourse, and the unusually designed Sydney Opera House.

If you have time, you can take a trip through the Blue Mountains to the limestone caverns and wildlife sanctuaries at Jenolan Caves. You can go down to Circular Quay in the harbor and take a boat trip, or visit "The Rocks," an atmospheric, old-town area with pubs, restaurants, souvenir shops, and art galleries. In the evening, you may want to see the theaters, bars, and nightlife in the King's Cross area, or take in a concert, opera, play, or ballet at the Sydney Opera House.

Several ships traverse the **Whitsunday Islands** area near **Cairns** and the Great Barrier Reef. Generally, passengers participate in organized tours on smaller crafts to see the reef. If time allows, you would enjoy visiting Hayman Island Resort, located on its own private island and considered one of the most exclusive properties in this part of the world. Visitors fly into Hamilton Island Airport and are transported to Hayman Island by one of the resort's private launches.

## British Columbia

**Vancouver**, with a population of more than one million, is Canada's third-largest and most scenic city, as well as her busiest and most famous seaport. Located just twenty-five miles from the U.S. border, Vancouver is the center of Canada's fishing, mining, and lumber industries. The mild climate is due to the protective mountains and warm winds from the Pacific. Places of interest to the tourist include spectacular Stanley Park, the one-thousand-acre-wilderness woodland set on a peninsula with its famous zoo, aquarium, totem poles, children's amusements, and Evergreens, a half-mile seawall path ideal for long walks, jogging, cycling, and in-line skating, and the half-mile walking/jogging path around lovely Lost Lagoon; Chinatown along Pender Street; the historic gaslight district known as Gastown; shops, restaurants, and cafés on Robson Street; the botanical gardens and arboretum in Queen Elizabeth Park; the fountain display in front of the City Courthouse, with its changing patterns of water and lights; and the skyride up to the top of Grouse Mountain, where there is a restaurant with a beautiful view of the environs. Shop for English woolens, china, and imports. The best shopping center is the Pacific Center Mall and boutiques on the adjoining streets.

The best hotels are Four Seasons, Pan Pacific, Sutton Place, and Hyatt for luxury and proximity to the business district where the cruise ship docks at Canada Place. However, those opting for a pre- or postcruise stay may prefer Westin Bayshore at the entrance to Stanley Park, where the tower rooms enjoy spectacular views of the park, harbor, and snowcapped mountains. Although there are numerous restaurants featuring cuisine from around the world, for a very special gastronomic dinner, Chartwell's at the Four Seasons is a don't-miss. Here preparation, presentation, ambiance, and service blend to offer a world-class experience.

**Victoria**, the capital of British Columbia, is the largest city on Vancouver Island. It can be reached only by ferryboat from Vancouver. Vancouver Island is the largest island on the Pacific Coast of North America, lying directly west of Vancouver and the state of Washington. Victoria is often referred to as Canada's most British city, with its flower gardens, narrow winding streets, Parliament buildings, Provincial Museum, and Empress Hotel (an excellent choice for an Indian buffet lunch). Lumbering is the city's chief industry, and you will see beautiful forests of fir, cedar, and hemlock on mountain slopes. You may wish to see the thirty-five-acre Butchart Gardens; one of the tallest totem poles in the world at Beacon Hill Park; numerous other totem poles at Thunderbird Park; Oak Bary Marina and Sealand; Dunsmuir Castle; the Pacific Undersea Gardens, a natural aquarium with an undersea theater; the Royal London Wax Museum; or Chaucer Lane, with its replicas of Shakespeare's and Ann Hathaway's English cottages.

## BORNEO

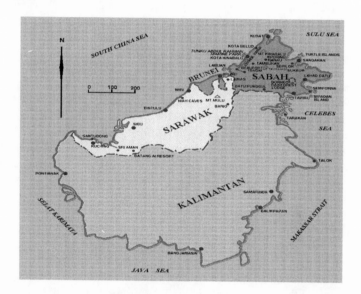

**Borneo** is the name of the large island located south of the Philippines and northeast of Indonesia that is surrounded by the South China, Sulu, and Java Seas. The southeast portion of the island, known as Kalimantan, is a province of Indonesia. The northwest section is made up of the tiny Sultanate of Brunei, which is bordered by the Malaysian states of Sabah to its north and Sarawak to its south.

Cruise ships most commonly visit **Kota Kinabalu**, the capital city of Sabah, or **Brunei**. Known as Jesseltown prior to 1968, **Kota Kinabalu** has a population of approximately 150,000 people of Chinese, Malay, Filipino, and Indonesian origins. Your tour of the city should include the State Mosque with its 216-foot-high minarets and lavish furnishings, the Sabah Museum, the outdoor market at Kampong Ayer Square, the thirty-story cylindrical tower of the Sabah Foundation, the view of the town and offshore islands from Signal Hill, and the resort area at the Tanjung Aru Beach Hotel.

Excursions outside the city may include a visit to a tribal community at Mengkabong water village, where thatch-roofed homes built on stilts over the sea are inhabited by the Bajous. Penampang Village is where the Kadagan tribe lives today in modern stilt houses furnished with electricity, water, and hi-fi's. Here you will also see skulls wrapped in palm leaves hung from living room ceilings like wine bottles as heirlooms of the families' head-hunting ancestors. A popular all-day tour will take you to the National Park to view hundreds of varieties of wild orchids and other flora, as well as birds, monkeys, deer, a rain forest, and the famous Mount Kinabalu, which towers 13,455 feet above the sea and is the tallest mountain in Southeast Asia.

Beach people will enjoy spending a perfect day at the lovely Tanjung Aru Beach Resort, ten minutes from town. At the hotel, visitors can sunbathe and swim in the sea or in a picturesque large pool, play tennis and golf, sample excellently prepared Malaysian and Chinese cuisine, and visit one of the unspoiled pristine islands that sit in the bay. For approximately $8 per person, the hotel's motor launch will transport you to Sulug, Memutik, Gaya, Manukan, or Sapi. These islands, reminiscent of the Yasawa Group off Fiji, boast white-sand beaches, lush tropical forests, rare varieties of sea shells, clear waters, good swimming and snorkeling, and few, if any, other visitors.

**Brunei** gained its independence from Great Britain in 1983 and today is an independent Islamic sultanate covering only 2,230 square miles. Most of its Malay and Chinese population enjoy a somewhat higher standard of living than their neighbors due to the large production of oil and gasoline in this country.

From the port of Muara at the mouth of the Brunei River, you can take the seventeen-mile drive to the capital city of Bandar Seri Begawan (BSB), or you can take a boat up the river past mangrove swamps and tie up at a wharf in the city. Across from the center of the city, connected by water taxis, is Kampang Ayer, the water village of stilt houses that encircles the Omar Ali Saifuddin Mosque, one of the largest mosques in Asia. The golden dome of the mosque dominates the view of BSB.

You will want to include a visit to the Churchill Memorial and museum; the billion-dollar Sultan's Palace, with its minarets, extensive grounds, two thousand rooms, and one thousand servants; and the ruins of the Stone Fort at Kota Batu, once the palace of the sultans. The Sheraton is the deluxe hotel in BSB, and you will find numerous good Malay, Chinese, and Indonesian restaurants around town. An interesting forty-five-minute boat ride will take you to visit a communal long house in the Temburong district, where Iban tribal people will greet you with dancing, and where you can see shrunken heads hanging from roofs.

## THE FIJI ISLANDS

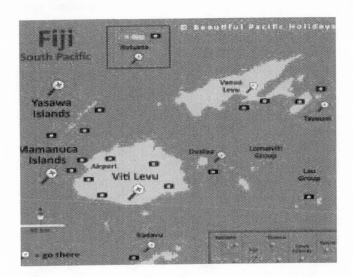

The Fiji Islands consist of more than five hundred scattered islands northeast of Australia in the South Pacific, with temperatures ranging from the mideighties during the day down to the low seventies at night, and with much rain from June through October. Fiji was a British Crown Colony until 1970, when it became independent. The population of approximately 550,000 is 40 percent native Fijians (originally from Africa), 10 percent miscellaneous, and 50 percent descendants of laborers brought to the island from India. Most of the islands were formed by volcanoes and have high volcanic peaks, rolling hills, rivers, tropical rain forests, and coral reefs.

Your ship will dock at the largest island, **Viti Levu**, at either **Suva** or **Lautoka**, the port nearest to **Nandi**. The towns themselves are of little interest, and the real beauty is in the scenery and beaches. Depending upon your time limitations, you may wish to take a boat ride to one of the lovely, unspoiled outer islands in the Mamanuca group that lies off the coast of Lautoka. One-day trips can be arranged to Plantation, Mana, Beachcomber, Castaway, or Treasure islands, all of which offer water sports and small resorts with facilities.

If your time is more limited, you will want to spend your day at either the Fijian, Westin Denarau Island, or Sheraton Fiji Resorts. The Fijian offers a lovely beach, tennis, horseback riding, golf, numerous shops, restaurants, and other facilities. The two Sheratons are newer, more lavish, have nice pool areas, and are closer to Nandi; however, the beaches are not as desirable, and they have fewer facilities. In the evening, you may enjoy attending a Fijian *mangiti*, where meats, vegetables, and seafood are wrapped in banana leaves and steamed in an oven of hot stones in the ground. After dinner, you will be entertained by native dancers in a *meke* performance (all of which is similar to the Hawaiian luau).

The most picturesque and pristine outer islands are in the **Yasawa** group, which includes Turtle Island and Sawa-I-Lau cave, where the movie *Blue Lagoon* was filmed. Presently, Blue Lagoon Cruises and Seafarer Cruises Ltd. offer three- and four-night cruises to the Yasawas from the dock at Lautoka; and Captain Cook cruises from the marina at the Westin Denarau Resorts. These are very small boats on which the accommodations, food, and service were historically a far cry from your usual cruise ship; however, newer more upscale vessels were built in the 1990s and offer more comfortable surroundings.

For a very special, tropical-island experience before or after your cruise, the Wakaya Club, Turtle Island Resort, and Vatulele Island Resort, each located on its own private island, offer the ultimate in casual luxury.

## THE HAWAIIAN ISLANDS

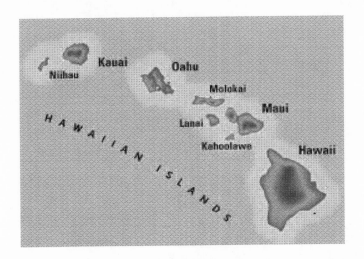

Hawaii, composed of more than twenty islands and atolls 2,300 miles southwest of California, has a total population of approximately eight hundred thousand and a year-round average temperature of seventy-five degrees. Cruise ships dock at the harbors of Honolulu in Oahu, Hilo, and Kona, on the big island of Hawaii, Nawiliwili in Kauai, and Lahaina in Maui.

In **Honolulu**, on the island of Oahu, you will want to walk along the famous Waikiki Beach, lined with giant hotels and crowds of sunbathers, swimmers, and surfers. You can shop for your *muumuu* and other items in the mall at the Ala Moana Shopping Center, and later sail out to the *Arizona Memorial* at Pearl Harbor. If you drive past Diamond Head to the posh Kahala section, you can see beautiful homes and landscaping and finally stop at the lovely Kahala Hotel & Resort for a cool drink, a dip in the ocean, or just to watch the feeding of the dolphins and tropical fish in the hotel lagoon. If time allows, attend a luau at one of the large hotels or drive around the island to the Polynesian Cultural Center, where you can see exhibits, clothes, dances, and crafts as well as sample foods from six different Polynesian islands. There are many exceptional restaurants on Oahu, including Hoku's at the Kahala, La Mer at Halekulani, Micheles at the Colony Surf, and Nicholas Nicholas. The most upscale resorts on Oahu are the Kahala, Halekulani, and Ihilani, the latter located in the Ko Olina development. All are only twenty-minute drives from the airport.

When your ship pulls into the town of **Hilo** on the big island of Hawaii, you can rent a car at the airport only ten minutes' drive from town and purchase a map of the Hilo area. If you take Hawaii Highway 19 north for a fifteen-minute drive, you will reach Akaka Falls, where you can take a half-hour walk through banyan trees, ti plants, ginger plants, and other tropical vegetation to view two different waterfalls. On your drive back toward Hilo, look for the "Hawaiian Warrior Marker" on Waianunue Avenue, which will direct you to the lookout above the Rainbow Falls that flow into the Wailuku River gorge. Early in the morning, you can see a rainbow on the mist of the falls.

At the north end of Banyan Drive, you can visit the thirty-acre replica of Japanese gardens. If you drive for thirty miles on Hawaii Highway 11, you will arrive at Hawaii Volcanoes National Park, where you can have lunch overlooking the crater of Kilauea, an active volcano that periodically pours out molten lava. Head back by way of Chain of Craters Road to Hawaii Highway 130, following the Kalapana coastline to Kaimue black-sand beach (near where Hawaii Highway 130 intersects Hawaii Highway 137). Here, there is a small cove dramatically lined with a dense grove of tall coconut trees. On the way back to Hilo on Hawaii Highway 11, you can visit the macadamia nut factory.

If you are in the area of **Kona**, on the west side of the island, you can visit coffee plantations and the Parker Ranch (second largest in the United States) or partake of the famous buffet lunch at the Mauna Kea Beach Hotel near Kamuela (a forty-five-mile drive north of Kona) or at its sister property, Hapuna Beach Hotel. At these hotels, you can play tennis on championship Lay-Kold courts, golf at the Robert Trent Jones-designed championship course, or sun and swim in the crystal waters of the two best beaches on the island. Nearby is the equally excellent Mauna Lani Resort, which also boasts a lovely beach, pool, tennis courts, golf courses, a diversity of good restaurants, and lovely grounds. The Hilton Waikoloa features one of the most exotic swimming-pool complexes in the world, as well as vast facilities and excellent restaurants. Four Seasons Hualalai is perhaps the most elegant resort in the Kona area and offers golf, tennis, a health spa and fine dining. All over the island, you will be able to see the towering peaks of the Mauna Kea and Mauna Loa mountains. There is shopping in Kona at the Kona Inn Shopping Village and Akona Kai Mall. There are a number of short cruises offered that explore the Kona coast, such as Capt. Bean's sunset cruise or moonlight cruise, the *Capt. Cook VII* glass-bottom boat cruise, and the Fairwind Tours' fifty-foot trimaran (snorkeling) cruise. There is a beach at Kahaluu Beach Park, four miles south of Kona.

**Kauai** is the lushest and greenest of the islands. Here you will want to drive up to the top of Waimea Canyon, which is reminiscent of the Grand Canyon in Arizona; body surf at Poipu Beach; take a boat down the Wailua River to visit the famous Fern Grotto; and swim at Lumahai Beach, possibly one of the more picturesque golden-sand beaches in the world. The finest resort on the island is the Hyatt Regency Kauai near Poipu Beach. The pool complex and health spa are awesome, as are the setting and decor. Another good choice is at Princeville on Hanalai Bay.

On the island of **Maui** you can visit the Halekala Crater, which is the largest dormant volcanic crater in the world; see the two-thousand-foot Iao Needle, which rises from the beautiful Iao Valley; walk through the historic and charming whaling village of **Lahaina**, with its shops, pubs, and restaurants; swim, golf, play tennis, and shop at the hotels in the posh **Kaanapali** area, such as the Hyatt, Sheraton, Westin, and Royal Lahaina; or take the picturesque, winding drive to heavenly **Hana**, stopping to explore the Waianapanapa Cave and black-sand beach, the unique Hana Ranch Hotel, Hamoa Beach, and the Seven Sacred Pools. Excellent resorts with full facilities include the Hyatt Regency Maui in Kaanapali, the Four Seasons and Grand Wailea in **Wailea,** and Kapalua Bay Resort and the Ritz-Carlton in the **Kapalua** area.

Although ships do not presently visit **Lanai,** this small island, proximate to Maui, is the home of two of Hawaii's finest resorts and golf courses. The Lodge at Koele and Manele Bay are two upscale properties with reciprocal privileges that offer the ultimate vacation experience for the well-heeled traveler.

## INDIA

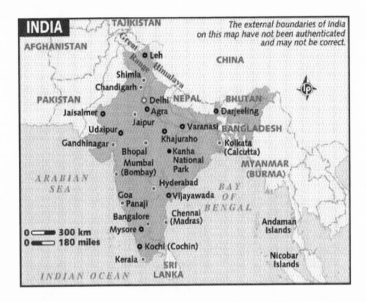

**Mumbai** (formerly known as **Bombay**) India's major harbor city and one of the largest ports in the world, sprawls over seven islands linked by causeways and bridges. The city is an industrial and commercial center and the country's film capital. Your ship will dock in the Fort District near Victoria Terminus train station, the Gateway of India arch, and the famous Taj Mahal Intercontinental Hotel. This is an extremely crowded and dirty city and most streets and walks are in bad condition, which results in very slow traffic. Allow yourself plenty of time when venturing out on your own.

Major tourist attractions include the Prince of Wales Museum, with its fine display of Asian art, archeology, porcelain, and jade; the Jahangir Art Gallery; Rajabai Clock Tower, a semi-Gothic monument rising 260 feet; Crawford Market, erected in 1867, where cloth, meat, fish, and vegetables are sold; Javeri Bazaar; the Jewelers Market; and Chor Bazaar, the flea market; Victoria Museum and Victoria Gardens, where elephant, camel, and pony rides are available. The Aquarium, the elegant residences, Hanging Gardens, and Kamala Nehru Park are all on Malabar Hill, an excellent locale to observe a panorama of the city, especially at sunset.

Excursions from Mumbai could include Elephanta Island, six miles across Bombay Harbor. There you can view caves with impressive displays of early Hindu religious art, including the eighteen-foot-high panel of Siva Trimurti (a three-headed statue depicting the triple aspect of Hindu divinity); the Kanheri Caves, located in a national park twenty-eight miles from the city, where more than one thousand caves were carved between the second and fifteenth centuries. Or you can take a two-hour flight to **Agra** for a visit to the world-renowned Taj Mahal, built in the seventeenth century by the Mogul emperor Shah Jahan in tribute to his wife.

When dining in Mumbai, you will want to sample authentic Indian curries (spicy stews), prawn patia (a combination of prawns, tomato, and dried spices), Dahi Maach (fish in a yogurt-ginger sauce), Biriani (saffron rice with chicken or lamb), tandoori (clay-oven prepared chicken marinated in yogurt and seasonings), and tandoori naan bread (leavened bread cooked in a clay oven). All of the better hotels, such as the Oberoi and Taj Mahal Intercontinental, have excellent Indian-style and Continental restaurants. My favorite for tandoori Indian cuisine with a great view is the Kondahar on the second floor of the Oberoi.

You may enjoy bargaining in the shops for gold and silver jewelry, precious stones, marble from Agra, embroidered silks, leather goods, pottery from Jaipur, Tibetan-style carpets, and Mogul paintings reproduced on silk. The shopping arcade at the Oberoi Hotel offers several floors of shops in a clean environment away from the clamor of the streets and markets. Bargains abound and prices are as cheap as can be found anywhere in the world for this type of merchandise.

**Chennai** (formerly known as Madras) is India's fourth-largest city, featuring an abundance of squalor, pollution, dense street traffic, and aggressive, annoying vendors and taxi drivers. Although this is a most disappointing port of call, many ships still visit Chennai on extended world cruises because it is one of the only options en route to break up the journey from Bangkok or Singapore to the Middle East and Africa.

The city's maze of streets is easy to get lost in. You are best advised either to take an organized tour or hire your own taxi. There are three upscale hotels in the city in which to have lunch or to use as your headquarters: the Taj Cormandal, Park Sheraton, and Chola Sheraton. Although there are shopping emporiums, you will not find the selection that exists in Bombay and Delhi. If you wish to take a walk, the least-polluted area is along Marina and Elliot's Beach, which are located about a mile to the left (south) of the harbor. You will pass by the War Memorial, Madras University, Senate House, the Moorish-style Cepauk Palace, Presidentia College, the Auna Memorial, and the Marina Swimming Pool and Aquarium.

Tours outside of Chennai should include the ruins at Mahabalipuram, which date back to the seventh century AD and include the "Rathas" carved out of rocks in the form of temple chariots decorated with pillars, stone elephants, and guardian animals. If you prefer to spend your day at a beach resort, Taj Fisherman's Cove on Covelong Beach and V.G.P. Golden Beach Resort can be accessed south of the city on the road to Mahabalipuram.

## INDONESIA

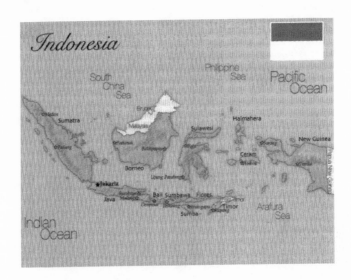

Indonesia is the world's largest archipelago, consisting of 13,677 volcanic verdant islands straddling the equator, 900 of which are settled.

Beautiful **Bali**, one of Indonesia's islands, is a tropical land with lush vegetation, rice paddies, soaring volcanic peaks, sandy seacoasts, and dense jungles of palms, bamboo, rattan, and banyan trees. The best time to visit Bali is during the dry summer season or in very early fall before the monsoons. On your tour of the island, you will want to include a visit to the most sacred Balinese temple, Pura Besakih, on the slopes of Mount Agung; the village of Ubud for paintings and the Museum of Modern Balinese Art; the village of Mas for woodcarvings; the village of Celuk for gold and silver work; the village of Klungkung for wood and bone carvings; and the Nusa Dua Beach area, with its shops and resort hotels (the Bali Grand Hyatt, Sheraton, Bali Hilton, and Nusa Dua Beach being the largest).

If your time is limited, you may wish to use one of these hotels as the focal point of your visit. Each is a lovely hotel capturing the Balinese atmosphere, offering an interesting pool area, tennis courts, a sandy beach, beautiful grounds, representative shops, and an outdoor dining area where in the evening you can watch Balinese dancers and sample such Indonesian cuisine as *rijsttafel* (numerous dishes of meats, vegetables, and condiments with rice), *satay* (meat or chicken barbecued on skewers with peanut-coconut sauce), *babi guling* (baked pig), and *nasi goreng* (Indonesian fried rice). From here, you can take side tours to the various villages to shop for native crafts.

You will want to witness a performance of the Balinese dances. The "Kejak-monkey dance," where groups of nearly two hundred men sit in concentric circles and act out a Balinese mythological story, is performed most evenings in several villages. There are also the "Legong," performed by three girls; the "Djoged Bumbung"; and the colorful

"Barong," with its costumed characters portraying the fight between good and evil. I found the Barong dance to be the most interesting. If you prefer to spend your day at a uniquely picturesque luxury resort, there are six exquisite choices: the Four Seasons and Ayana at Jimbaran Bay, Amandari or Four Seasons-Sayan near Ubud, Amanusa above Nusa Dua Beach, and Amankila on the east side of the island. These are possibly the most unique romantic luxury properties in the world.

## JAPAN

Off the coast of Asia, Japan consists of a group of islands with a population of more than one hundred million people in an area about the size of the state of California. The weather is similar to the central United States, with cold winters, rainy springs, hot summers, and lovely autumns. Ships dock at **Yokohama**, the port of **Tokyo**, where you will disembark and then proceed to Tokyo, a modern, busy, crowded, energetic city. The best values are Japanese cameras, binoculars, transistor radios, watches, jewelry, and pearls. Be sure to bring along your passport to take advantage of the fact that many items are sold tax free to tourists, although there are few real bargains today, and most of the Japanese goods can be purchased for less in Hong Kong. The best shopping can be found in the department stores located along the Ginza area or in the arcades of the large hotels.

You will want to try such traditional Japanese dishes as *sukiyaki* (meat and vegetables sautéed in soy sauce and *sake*), **teriyaki** (slices of beef marinated in soy sauce), *tempura* (seafood or vegetables dipped in batter and deep-fried), *yakitori* (bits of chicken barbecued on a skewer), *oil-yaki* (steak broiled in oil), *shabu-shabu* (beef and vegetables cooked in a hot broth), and, of course, *sushi* and *sashimi*. All of these can be washed down with *sake* (rice wine) or Japanese beer. If you prefer, there are also excellent Italian, German, Chinese, and French restaurants in Tokyo. All food, especially beef, is outrageously expensive in restaurants. Plastic models of the food served in the restaurants are displayed outside the window of each establishment.

You may wish to attend a geisha party, where local geisha girls in kimonos serve dinner and drinks, play guitars, sing, and entertain; or you may enjoy a Noh performance, which is a historical Japanese play with music and dancing where the actors wear masks; or perhaps you will want to try a Japanese bath, where a pretty Japanese girl guides you through the ritual of steam bath, water bath, and massage, the best being at the Tokyo Onsen.

Getting around in Tokyo is difficult because many of the streets have no names or street numbers. Therefore, it is best to take a tour or have a local draw you a map with landmarks. Places of interest to visit in Tokyo include the Imperial Palace, Yasukuni Shrine, the Tokyo Tower, Shinjuku Gyoen Gardens, Zojoji Temple, Sengakuju Temple, and National Museum; or drive out thirty miles to Kamakura and visit the Hachiman Shrine and the site of the great seven-hundred-year-old bronze Buddha, which stands forty-two feet high and is considered one of the world's great sculptural masterpieces. If time permits, you may wish to take a train to the Fuji Lake area and see Mount Fujiyama and one of Japan's summer resort districts offering good fishing and hunting, or you may wish to proceed on to Kyoto and visit its beautiful gardens, parks, palaces, and shrines.

Cruise ships often stop at **Kagoshima**. Located on the southernmost of Japan's four major islands, Kagoshima was the first city to introduce Western civilization to Japan, serving as the gateway for trade and exchange between Japan and the world. The city looks out across Kinko Bay to the silhouette of Sakurajima, an active volcano. Visitors often take tours to Senganen, a serene Japanese-style landscape garden constructed in 1660, the Shuko Shuseikan Museum, and the car ferry over to Sakurajima Island to view the lunar-like landscape and lava fields created by past eruptions. The Arimura Lava Observatory, located on a small hill, is an excellent vantage point from which to observe the volcano. Excursions from Kagoshima may include the castle town of **Chiran**, best known for its well-preserved samurai street, and the Satsuma Peninsula with its hot springs, subtropical flora, beaches, and rocky coastlines. Here you will have views of Mount Kaimon, a three-thousand-foot-high volcano, and you can visit the famous hot springs resort of Ibusuki.

**Nagasaki** is another city frequently visited by cruise ships. Points of interest include the Nagasaki Peace Park and the Peace Memorial Statue, the Atomic Bomb Museum, Glover Garden, an open-air museum, and the town of Narita, the birthplace of Japanese ceramics, where you can view master works from various Japanese historical periods and make purchases to take back home.

## MALAYSIA

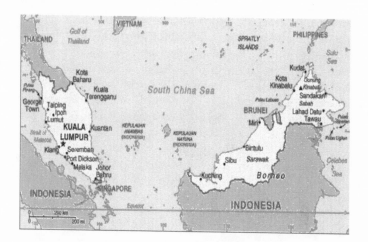

The country of Malaysia as we know it today was formed in 1963. Its eleven million inhabitants, living in eleven states that constitute the Federation of Malaya, Sabah, and Sarawak, are made up of Malays, Chinese, and Indians. It is a country with a warm, tropical climate, much rain, and lush forests where palms, rubber trees, orchids, and hibiscus abound.

Many ships stop at the lovely topical island of **Penang**, which offers wide expanses of golden-sand beaches with calm, warm waters, dense forests, excellent tourist resort hotels, and a relatively high standard of living for its residents. This is one of the major resort areas in Asia. Tourist attractions include the Buddhist Temple, the Snake Temple, Botanic Gardens, a visit to a batik factory, and a ride on the funicular railway up Penang Hill. You may enjoy spending the day at the Rasa Sayang Hotel, which contains most of the facilities and amenities of luxury-class Caribbean resort hotels, including a beautiful beach with all water sports; two pools; four tennis courts; a putting range; a disco; Japanese, Malay, and Continental restaurants; shops; and lovely grounds. Similar facilities can be found nearby at the Golden Sands Hotel or at the Matiara.

Some ships also dock at **Port Kelang**, twenty-eight miles from **Kuala Lumpur**, the capital of Malaysia, where you can drive to the outskirts and visit rubber estates, palm plantations, and tin mines. Seven miles north of the city are the Bata Caves, where you take a funicular cable car to see some excellent limestone caverns with illuminated stalagmites. On your drive into the city, you can visit the beautiful Blue Mosque and gardens. In and around the city, you can visit the National Museum, with displays relating to Malaysian history, arts, crafts, and commerce; the Sri Mahamariamman, a large ornate Hindu temple; the National mosque; the Lake Gardens; Chinatown; the gambling casino at Genting Highlands; the Selangor pewter factory (the largest in the world); the Petronas Twin Towers, one of the tallest buildings in the world and largest shopping malls in Southeast Asia; and the Selayang batik factory. You will want to sample the many different types of Chinese cuisine as well as native Malay food, especially the delicious Malaysian *satay*. *Satay* is beef or chicken grilled on bamboo skewers with a hot sauce made from peanuts, coconut milk, and hot peppers. There are excellent Continental, Chinese, and Malay restaurants in the Hilton, Shangri-La, Marriott, Mandarin Oriental, and Regent hotels. When shopping for Malaysian handicrafts, silks, batik, and pewter, you will find the best selections (but no bargains) at the TDC Bukit Nanas Handicraft Center at Jalan Raja Chulan, the Sundie Wang Shopping Complex across from the Regent Hotel, and the Sunday Market in the heart of Kumpung Bharu.

The cluster of 104 unspoiled islands that comprise the archipelago of **Langkawi** lies off the northwestern tip of Malaysia. Many cruise ships spend a day at the largest island, **Pulau Langkawi**, with its mountainous interior, long sandy beaches, wildlife, marine national parks, lush vegetation, and duty-free shopping. You will enjoy spending a portion of your visit at one of the large hotels or resorts, most of which are located on lovely beaches and afford opportunities to taste Malaysian dishes at their seaside restaurants. A good choice would be the Pelangi Beach Resort, only a ten-minute drive from the port with acres of grounds, beach, and exotic pools, the Tanjung Rhu, located on a vast expanse of white-sand beach overlooking interesting caves and rock formations, as well as, the Four Seasons. The Datai, located on the northwest tip, is a most unique property, with large bungalows set in a tropical forest that leads down to a beach, and the island's largest golf course is nearby. However, the attitude at Datai is very snobbish, and they do not permit nonguests to roam around the property.

(For a discussion of the Malaysian region of Sabah and Kota Kinabalu, see Borneo above.)

## MEXICO (WEST COAST)

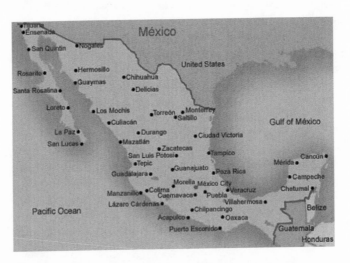

Mexico is as historically interesting and as culturally different as any country in Europe or Asia. The Spanish-speaking inhabitants can trace their origins to the ancient Aztec Indians, who were conquered by Spain in the sixteenth century. Today you can see this blend of culture against a background of breathtaking landscapes, picturesque little villages, and a sophisticated range of entertainment. The most popular cruise stops on the west coast are Cabo San Lucas, Acapulco, Mazatlan, Puerto Vallarta, Manzanillo, and Zihuatanejo-Ixtapa, which are all seacoast towns with warm winters and hot summers. Although you will be able to sample such Mexican dishes as nachos, carne asada, tacos, enchiladas, and flautas at most places, the majority of the better restaurants and hotels specialize in Continental, French, and Italian cuisine.

For many years **Acapulco** has been a favorite tourist attraction of both the jet set and the average tourist because of its guaranteed good climate; large selection of hotels, restaurants, and nightclubs; and informal atmosphere. You can eat, drink, dance, sun, swim, play tennis, and golf at a number of the super-deluxe hotels. The Fairmont Acapulco Princess, built in the design of an Aztec pyramid, offers four imaginative, picturesque swimming pools, an eighteen-hole golf course, outdoor and indoor air-conditioned tennis courts, parasailing, water-skiing, horseback riding, seven restaurants, a state-of-the-art fitness center and luxury spa, and a discotheque. For romantics, you cannot beat the villas with private pools overlooking Acapulco Bay at Las Brisas. Other deluxe hotels with good facilities are the Mayan Palace, Camino Real, Villa Vera, Acapulco Hyatt Regency, and the Fairmont Pierre Marques. You can shop in town for native crafts in leather, pottery, wood, and silver. You can ride a parachute high in the sky behind a speedboat (parasailing), and on Sundays during the winter months, you can watch a bullfight.

A late-afternoon lunch at the open-air Paradise Restaurant on the beach (near the El Presidente Hotel) is a must. Here you can snack on grilled snapper and shrimp, sip exotic tropical drinks, dance to a lively band, haggle with vendors, and watch the locals pass by. For dinner, Acapulco boasts numerous fine restaurants, including Baikel (Continental), Carlos'n Charlie's (eclectic), Hacienda (Mexican) at the Fairmont Princess, Tabachins (gourmet) at the Fairmont Pierre Marques, Bella Vista (Continental) at Las Brisas Hotel, Madieras (Continental), located about a half-mile from Las Brisas, Kookaburra (seafood), Casanova (Italian), Coyuca 22 (steak and seafood), and Le Jardin Des Artistes (French). At eight-fifteen, nine-fifteen, ten-thirty, and eleven-thirty each evening from the nearby El Mirador Hotel, you can watch the divers at La Quebrada leap 150 feet off a cliff past jagged rocks to the sea. The Flying Pole Dancers of Papantla perform nightly at 10:30 p.m. in a huge garden next to the Hyatt Regency Hotel. Still later in the evening, disco is in full swing at Baby O's, Carlos's Chili'n Dance Hall, Hard Rock Café, Madara, Siboney, Palladium, and Salon Q. There are variety shows at most of the larger hotels and at Acapulco Centro Entertainment Complex.

**Cabo San Lucas** is a small village in Las Cabos at the tip of Baja California. Ships generally stop here for only a few hours. Tenders will drop you off in front of open-air shopping stalls that offer T-shirts, serapes, Mexican-style dresses, jewelry, and most of the same items you saw in the other Mexican ports. There are several hotels within a mile of the harbor: the Melia and the Hacienda, which have the best swimming beach and tennis courts; the Finistera, which sits atop a steep hill; and the Solar, which is fronted by a dramatic beach on the Atlantic that is not safe for swimming. Many visitors take the boat ride around "Los Arcos" to obtain a better view of these picturesque rock formations, the pelicans, and seals. There are also small boats that will transport you to and from the pristine beach that abuts the rocks and offers an ideal place to snorkel, picnic, and get away from it all. Recommended restaurants include Macambo (seafood), Mi Casa (Mexican), Ruth's Chris (steak house), and Giggling Marlin (wild and eclectic). If time permits, the best resort complex with golf, tennis, restaurants, pools, and a beach is Las Ventanas, a twenty- to thirty-minute drive from Cabo San Lucas; however, you need to make arrangements well in advance to gain admittance. Other full-facility up-scale resorts include Pamilla, Four Seasons, Esperanza, Sheraton, and Westin.

**Manzanillo** is a busy Mexican port with fine beaches. If your ship docks here for a day, you may wish to take a ten-minute drive to Las Hadas. This ultraposh resort was built in 1974 for $60 million by Bolivian tin magnate Antenor Patino. Here you will find 204 charming villas and rooms built in Moorish, Mediterranean, and Mexican styles, with minarets and domes on top of all-white buildings, set off by colorful tropical plants and bougainvillea. The resort complex includes a king-size, lagoon-like pool with its own island, suspension bridge, waterfall, and swim-up bar, ten tennis courts, an eighteen-hole golf course, four restaurants, six bars, and a long strand of beach. This is where the movie *10* was filmed. Another excellent luxury resort also a short drive from where you dock is the luxurious Grand Bay Resort.

**Mazatlan** is the world's sport fishing capital, where you can charter a boat and fish for marlin and sailfish. You can take a horse-drawn *araña* along the shoreline drive or to the historic plaza and cathedral. As your ship pulls into the harbor, you can see the 515-foot El Faro lighthouse, which is the second-highest lighthouse in the world. You can shop for silver, jewelry, leather, Mexican pottery, and crafts at the numerous shops along the Golden Zone and at Mazatlan Arts and Crafts Center. In the Golden Zone is the stadium where you can watch the open-air performance by folkloric dancers followed by the aerial acrobatics of the famed Papantla Flyers, who twirl around a seventy-five-foot pole. If you wish to spend the day using hotel facilities, you may wish to try El Cid or Camino Real. El Cid is the largest hotel, offering a picturesque large pool, fifteen clay tennis courts, an eighteen-hole golf course, water-skiing, parasailing, and numerous restaurants. If you proceed south from El Cid, you will pass by numerous shops and restaurants. For lunch, try the Shrimp Bucket, Casa Loma, or Señor Frog's, a very happening place to chill out on margaritas.

**Puerto Vallarta** has been described as a sleepy little village, ruggedly beautiful, and romantically placed on a superb beach. The Gringo Gulch area consists of houses inhabited by wealthy foreigners. The heart of the shopping area is Juarez Street, where you will find bargains in sandals, silver, jewelry, embroidered works, colorful skirts, and dresses. You may want to swim at the beaches at the hotels, which are located a few minutes' walk from where your ship docks, and utilize their other facilities. You can try some excellent Mexican specialties while lunching at the outdoor restaurants at these hotels, or you may enjoy Las Palmas, Señor Frog's, Blue Shrimp, Café des Artistes, Thierry Blouet, and Carlos O'Brian's in the middle of town. Mismaloya, a more protected beach with a backdrop of verdant hills, is located six miles south of downtown. La Jolla de Mismaloya, an upscale hotel, is located here, as well as several secluded beaches only accessible by boat from Mismaloya Beach. Marina Vallarta, north of the harbor, in the direction of the airport, is a recently developed 445-acre resort condominium complex consisting of numerous shops, restaurants, a 400-berth marina, a 6,500-yard golf course, and numerous new hotels including the Marriott,

Melia, and Villas Quinta Real. The most luxurious resort with all facilities is the Four Seasons, Punta Mita; however, it is over an hour's drive from the cruise dock.

Many of the cruise lines offer mountain bike excursions, horseback riding, kayaking, and jungle canopy adventures, as well as sailing, snorkeling, diving, and dolphin encounters.

**Zihuatanejo-Ixtapa** is a picturesque, pristine, unspoiled fishing village surrounded by mountains on a sparkling, protected bay. The clear waters, perfect for scuba diving and snorkeling, reveal pink coral and interesting underwater life. The brilliant flowers scent the air with a delightful fragrance, and coconut palms line the shore, where peaceful fishermen sit making their daily catch. You can spend the day at one of the numerous resorts with lovely beaches in Ixtapa, or you can take a trip by boat to the uninhabited Ixtapa Island, where you can swim, sun, and snack on a sheltered beach facing the mainland. The hotels with the most facilities are the Camino Real, Krystal, Omni, and Sheraton. There are numerous shops across from the strip of hotels in Ixtapa and there are craft shops and boutiques near the dock in Zihuatanejo. If you are in port for dinner, in addition to the hotel restaurants, you may wish to try Bogart's or the local branch of Carlos 'n' Charlie's.

## MYANMAR (FORMERLY BURMA)

Situated at the crossroads of Asia with India and Bangladesh on its western border and China, Thailand, and Laos to the east, this 261,000-square-mile country is a conglomeration of people and traditions. Eighty percent are Buddhists, and visitors will view Buddhist monks in yellow-orange-colored robes walking around the country.

The capital city, **Yangon (formerly Rangoon)**, is connected to the sea by a twenty-mile stretch of the Yangon River, which can be navigated by smaller cruise ships, while others transport passengers by ferryboat. The most famous site is the golden-domed, jewel-studded Shwedagon Pagoda, one of the most dynamic and important Buddhist shrines in Southeast Asia, situated on Singuttara Hill near Royal Lake and Gardens about two miles north of the city center. This is an awesome conglomeration of temples, shrines, statuary, and Buddhist architecture that you must explore barefoot. You may also enjoy visiting Sule Pagoda, a shrine believed to be built in the third century BC and said to contain a single hair from Buddha; the National Museum; Peoples Park; and the shopping center in town. Yangon is noted for lacquerware, fine gemstones, and jewelry including blood rubies, sapphires, and jade. Beware of fakes, and although prices are higher and less flexible in government-controlled tourist stores, they may be the safest.

The Strand is the traditional, colonial hotel reminiscent of Raffles, and the Inya Lake and Thamada are two additional first-class hostelries. Visitors often opt for lunch at either the Royal Garden or Karaweik restaurants, both colorful structures that give the appearance of native boats floating on Royal Lake overlooking Shwedagon Pagoda.

## NEW CALEDONIA

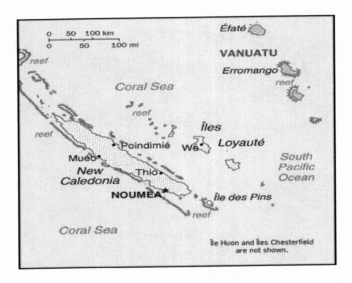

**New Caledonia** is an archipelago in Melanesia, southeast of New Guinea and northeast of Australia. Captain Cook discovered these islands in 1774 when the people still practiced cannibalism. France took possession in 1853 and created a penal colony where convicts were sent to mine nickel deposits. In 1956, New Caledonia became a French Overseas Territory, and in 1998, there was a referendum for self-determination. Possessing 44 percent of the world's reserves of nickel together with an abundance of other minerals, these islands are among the most prosperous in the South Pacific and are the last stronghold of white colonialism in Melanesia.

**Nouméa** is the capital of the main island of Grande Terre, which is 250 miles long, thirty miles wide, and protected by reefs with picturesque coastal beaches and many ridges of craggy mountains in the interior. The town is near the harbor where you may wish to visit the public market, Place des Cocotiers with its flaming royal poincianas, New Caledonian Museum for native art, St. Joseph Cathedral, and the old town hall. A more scenic itinerary would include a walk commencing at Le Meridien Hotel along the waterfront at Anse Vata, past the small aquarium to the beach at Baie de Citron.

Those wishing to spend a day at a resort can choose among Kuendu Beach Resort to the south or Le Meridien, Club Med, and Park Royal, all on Anse Vata. Two upscale (and expensive) French seafood restaurants on Anse Vata are Miratti Gascon behind the Park Royal and LaCoupole near the aquarium.

**Ile des Pins**, lying to the south of Grande Terre, is a lovely pine-studded island with chalk-white beaches popular with divers and sun-worshippers. You can arrange an outrigger canoe trip to the secluded beaches and warm shallow waters of Baie d'Upi and Baie d'Oro on the east coast or many of the little surrounding sandy atolls. Most cruise ships tender into Baie de Kuto, where there is an exceptional, long strand of beach lapped by aqua-blue waters. Immediately behind is Baie de Kanumera, which is more isolated and even more picturesque. Nearby are wooded forests, nature villages, camping grounds, and Hotel Kou-Bugny, a small but impressive conclave of roundevals with a pool and a restaurant a few yards off the beach at Kuto. This is one of the finest beach islands in the South Pacific.

## NEW ZEALAND

New Zealand is an unusual country with green fields, tropical foliage, fjords, and snowcapped mountains. Your ship will pull into beautiful Waitemata Harbor at **Auckland**, the country's chief port, which is as far south of the equator as San Francisco is north, with similar weather, but reverse seasons. In Auckland, you can visit the crater of an extinct volcano at the top of Mount Eden, see the rare flightless kiwi bird at the zoo, look out at the city from the Intercontinental Hotel's rooftop restaurant, or take a sightseeing tour along the city's picturesque Waterfront Drive, up through the residential suburb of Tamaki Heights, and then on to Ellerslie Race Course. The best beach is Takapuna, four miles north of the city. Shoppers can purchase natural lamb's wool products at the duty-free shop near the harbor.

If you drive up to the fishing village of **Russel**, you can take a cruise through the Bay of Islands, passing through beautiful little islands, inlets, remote farms, beaches, and game-fishing waters. You will not want to miss taking the trip to Waitomo Caves to see the unique Glowworm Grotto, which is a huge cavern illuminated solely by the bluish glow of millions of tiny glowworms affixed to the rocky ceilings. If you fly or take a bus to **Rotorua,** you can see spectacular, steaming geysers such as Pohutu Geyser at Whakarewarewa, the hot waterfalls, colored pools, and deeply gashed craters at Waiotapu, the geysers at Wairakei near a resort complex adjoining Geyser Valley, or take the one-hour tour to Waiora Valley. Here you may wish to visit the Agrodome to watch a sheep-shearing demonstration, learn how sheep are raised, and purchase lamb's wool products.

If your ship stops at **Christchurch**, you can fly, drive, or take a bus tour of the Southern Alps, visiting **Mount Cook**, Franz Joseph Glacier, and Milford Sound, with its waterfalls and fjords. At Queenstown near the southern tip of New Zealand, you can take a cable car up a mountain to view Whakatipu Glacier Lake and the Southern Alps or you can take a "jet boat" ride down the rivers past waterfalls and picturesque countryside.

## PEOPLE'S REPUBLIC OF CHINA

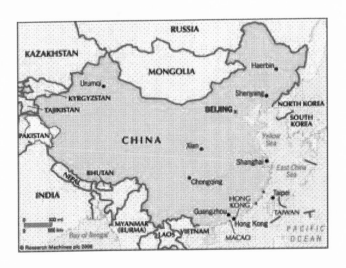

**Beijing**, the grand capital of the People's Republic of China, occupies a vast, sprawling area of several thousand miles. Located in the center of the city is Tiananmen Square, the world's largest public square and the site of the Mao Zedong Memorial Hall and tomb. Across the road from the square is the entrance to the Forbidden City of the Ming Dynasty, 175 acres of elegant palaces, pavilions, courtyards, and gardens, the largest palace complex in the world.

Other important places to see and things of interest to do within the city include a visit to the Beijing Zoo, which boasts more than five thousand animals including its most famous residents, the pandas; a rickshaw ride through Hutong's ancient city alleys bordering courtyards where local families reside in contrast to the more modern high-rise apartments; and a performance of the unique Beijing Opera. Outside the city, you will want to visit the Sacred Way and Ming Tombs, the Badaling Hills, the best-preserved sector of the fabled Great Wall of China, and the magnificent Summer Palace, a seven-hundred-acre garden and complex of lakes, ponds, and pavilions.

Composed of 236 islands and home to five million inhabitants, **Hong Kong**, a former British crown colony and now a part of the People's Republic of China, is possibly the most exciting and fun cruise stop in this part of the world. Most of the population, industry, and commerce are concentrated in the city of Kowloon and on neighboring Hong Kong Island. These teeming metropolises are separated by lovely Victoria Harbor, which can be crossed in seven minutes on the local *Star Ferry* at a cost of approximately fifteen cents. You can capture the magnificence of the harbor with its imposing skyline of high-rise buildings while crossing on this ferry or from the top of Victoria Peak, which is accessible by an eight-minute ride up the "Peak Train" (located on Hong Kong Island a mile from the ferry station). The weather is best during the dry season from July to March. In the summer, temperatures vary from the midseventies to the high eighties, but winter temperatures are usually in the fifties and sixties.

You can arrange for various sightseeing tours that visit the floating city of Aberdeen (where the floating "Jumbo" restaurants of Hong Kong are located), where people live on junks and sampans; panoramic Victoria Peak and Peak Tower amusement and shopping complex (there, the best places to eat are Café Disco Bar and Grill and Zens); the Zoological and Botanical Gardens; a so-so beach and semiresort area at Repulse Bay; Ocean Park (a good family destination); and the New Territories, with their industrial complexes, farming villages, and skyscraper towns. Within a five-minute walk from Ocean Terminal in Kowloon where your ship docks are the Hong Kong Center for the Performing Arts, the Space Museum, which is a large planetarium, Kowloon Park, the *Star Ferry* terminal, and a giant indoor shopping mall. For an interesting view across to Hong Kong Island, as well as an opportunity to sample the flavor of Kowloon, take the walk along the promenade that borders the harbor and extends from where your ship docks at Ocean Terminal, past the Clock Tower, Space Museum, and luxury waterfront hotels, and ends at the post office.

With most visitors, however, sightseeing generally plays a subordinate role to the main order of the day: shopping and bargaining. Nowhere in the world can one find as vast an array of shops and quality merchandise at such competitive prices (sometimes one-third to one-half of the prices in the United States). No matter where you are, you will find shopping centers with an assortment of shops that make the major shopping malls in the United States seem like dime stores. The shops in the side streets that intersect Nathan Road (Kowloon) are touted to offer the best bargains, although you may find it easier to maneuver in the shopping centers that are found in the large office buildings and hotels, adjacent to the *Star Ferry* (Kowloon side), or those connected to the New World Hotel. On Hong Kong Island, the Admiralty Complex comprises four shopping centers connected by elevated walkways including the popular Pacific Place. The best bargains are in gold, jewelry, European designer clothes, ivory, oriental furniture and antiques, cameras, optical goods, linens, watches, pearls, jade, and leather. If you have a few days, many tailor shops will provide you with a tailor-made suit or shirts at a reasonable price (the fabrics are quality but the tailoring is not).

If all of this shopping drains your energy, you can rejuvenate at one of Hong Kong's thousands of fine restaurants, which offer cuisine from every country of the world and every region of China. Western-style steak houses, fast-food franchises, and gourmet Continental establishments also abound here. It would be impossible to list all of the good restaurants; however, if I had to pick the two best (and most expensive) with imposing panoramas, I would recommend Petrus on top the Island Shangri-La as the best French restaurant in Hong Kong, and perhaps all of Asia, where you will be treated to exquisite French cuisine accompanied by an impressive variety of international wines, and Man Wah's at the top of the Mandarin Oriental. It has an established tradition for gourmet northern Chinese dishes with a view. Other restaurants of note include in Kowloon—Yu (seafood) and Spoon (French) at the Intercontinental; Gaddis (French), Felix (Continental), and Spring Moon (Cantonese) at the Peninsula; Margaux (French) and Shang Palace (Chinese) at the Kowloon Shangri-La. On Hong Kong Island—Café Too (international) at the Island Shangri-La; Toscana (Italian) at the Ritz Carlton; Isola at the International Finance Center (Italian with a view); and Grissini (Italian) at the Grand Hyatt.

There are many excellent luxury hotels, the largest and best being the Mandarin Oriental, Ritz-Carlton, Four Seasons, Island Shangri-La, Grand Hyatt, Conrad, and Marriott on Hong Kong Island and the Intercontinental, Peninsula, Shangri-La, Hyatt Regency, and Nikko on Kowloon. We found the Island Shangri-La outstanding in all areas including decor, room comfort, service, dining, and amenities.

If time allows, you may wish to arrange a one- or two-day side tour to the Portuguese territory of Macau or to other border cities of the People's Republic of China.

**Kuangchow (formerly Canton)** lies on the Pearl River 113 miles from Hong Kong (accessible by a three-hour train ride or hoverferry). Autumn is the best time of year to visit, with the least rain and temperatures in the seventies. Summers are somewhat hotter, and in the winter the temperatures vary from the high forties to the low sixties.

Few of the six million inhabitants of Kuangchow and its environs speak English well enough to answer your questions. Therefore, getting from place to place is very difficult, and you will see more on an organized tour. Do not depend on the taxi drivers, hotel attendants, or service people in the restaurants to understand English. If you go off by yourself, have the name of the place you are visiting as well as the name of the place to which you plan to return written out in Chinese letters. Taxis are the best means of transportation, and they are relatively inexpensive.

Although Kuangchow is reputed to be one of the gastronomic capitals of Chinese cuisine, you will find the food in all the restaurants a far cry from the Cantonese food you have eaten at home, in Hong Kong, or in other Asian cities. You can shop for Chinese arts and handicrafts in the Friendship Stores or the People's Department Store.

In Kuangchow proper, you will want to visit the "Temple of the Six Banyan Trees" and the neighboring nine-story-high "Flowering Pagoda," the Canton Zoo, which is the home of the Chinese panda, the Guangzhou museum in Yuexiu Park, Guangxiao Temple, Dr. Sun Yat-Sen Memorial Hall, the Cultural Park, the South China Botanical Gardens, and the Orchid Garden. If you are in Kuangchow in the fall or spring, you can visit the Kuangchow Export Trade Fair.

Scenic spots to be found outside the city are Seven-Star Crags, seventy miles west, with cliffs, caves, lakes, and Chinese pavilions; Conghua Hot Springs, fifty miles northeast, a tourist health resort; Xiqiao Hill scenic area, forty miles west, with seventy-two peaks, stone caves, waterfalls, and springs; and Foshan City, seventeen miles southwest, famous for its artistic porcelain, pottery works, art, crafts, and its nine-hundred-year-old Ancestral Temple.

During the past several decades, **Shanghai** has established itself as one of the major ports of call in mainland China. The shopping and dining options here are every bit as attractive as Hong Kong, as are the numerous districts of the city, each with its own unique characteristics. Any exploration of the city should include the Bund, a broad waterfront boulevard lined with stately European-influenced buildings and upscale restaurants and shops; the Pudong New District, site of the futuristic Oriental Pearl TV Tower and the incredible Jin Mao Building (the fourth-tallest in the world), which houses offices, shops, and the Grand Hyatt Hotel; the Old Town, a vibrant marketplace surrounding the unique, beautiful YuYuan Garden with its exquisite rockeries, dragon walls, pavilions, and towers. Be sure to also visit the shops along Nanjing Lu Street; People's Square and People's Park; the Shanghai Museum with the country's premier collection of art and artifacts; and the Jade Buddha, a six-and-a-half-foot high, 455-pound seated Buddha constructed of white jade. Shanghai boasts some of Southeast Asia's most modern and magnificent hotels, as well as a plethora of fine-dining possibilities with cuisines from the various regions of China as well as from countries around the world.

Many visitors include the historical city of **Xian** on their way to a Yangtze River cruise. Encircled by a complete ancient city wall with deep moats and drawbridges, the wall stretches for nine miles. Within the city, points of interest include the Bell Tower, Drum Tower, and China's greatest archeological treasure, the Qin Mausoleum, housing one of the eight wonders of the ancient world, the Terra Cotta Army. Here more than seven thousand life-size terra cotta warriors in full battle gear standing in formation were buried along with Emperor Qin Shi Huang over two hundred years before the common era. A great place to overnight would be the Sofitel in Xian, one of the more modern and posh hotels in China. In the evening, the exceptional dinner and the Vegas-style song and dance performance at the Tang Dynasty Restaurant is a must.

## YANGTZE RIVER

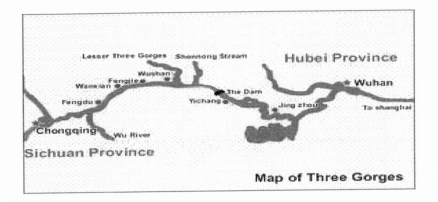

Many visitors to China opt for a Yangtze River cruise since the river is surrounded by some of the world's most spectacular landscapes: mist mountains, breathtaking gorges, and serene lagoons. Key ports along the way include Chongqing, the gateway for downstream Yangtze River cruises and a large bustling city; Fengdu, a forty-minute drive from the one-mile-long Snow Jade Cave with its limestone formations; the Shibaozai Temple, a twelve-story red pagoda perched on a sheer cliff built in the seventeenth century; the renowned Three Gorges with the misty green mountains of Wu (Witches) Gorge and the Twelve Peaks; the remarkable canyons of the Lesser Three Gorges on the Daning River, where sheer cliffs and steep mountains rise on either side and clear water flows between towering peaks covered with lush greenery; Sandouping, the site of the five-state locks of the Three Gorges Dam, the world's largest; and Wuhan, the gateway from upstream Yangtze cruises and the location of the Hubei Provincial Museum. Since most of the riverboats only have Chinese doctors and Chinese medicines, travelers on these cruises would be well-advised to bring along their own antibiotics, cold medicines, and any other drugs they may need should they become ill.

## PHILIPPINES

The Philippines is a mountainous country with fertile plains, tropical vegetation, and dense forests. After 350 years of Spanish rule, it became a U.S. possession and was given its independence in 1946. The official languages are English, Filipino, and Spanish. Most of the people speak a dialect of English that is very difficult to understand.

The country is composed of more than seven thousand islands, the principal city of **Manila** being located on the island of Luzon. Your tour of the city should include the Ayala Historical Museum; the Cultural Center; the National Museum; the Nayong Filipino, a showcase of the country's six major regions, exhibiting typical living quarters and handicrafts; the wealthy residential area of Forbes Park; and the walled city at Intramuros, the site of the first Spanish settlement.

Although shopping in Manila does not compare with shopping in Hong Kong, Singapore, or Bangkok, there are bargains to be found in handicrafts, rattan, sarongs, embroideries, ladies' bags, and rings. The best shopping areas are in the Ermita district, along Roxas Boulevard, and the Makati Commercial Center. Those wishing to try their luck at craps, roulette, blackjack, baccarat, and fan-tan can be accommodated twenty-four hours a day at a large casino in the Philippine Village Hotel. Most of the major luxury hotels and restaurants are located in the Ermita and "reclaimed area" districts along Manila Bay. The Philippines Plaza Hotel and Shangri-La are large hotels that command impressive views of the bay and offer a wide range of amenities.

Typical Philippine food includes *lechon* (pig on a spit), chicken and pork *adobo* (a spicy dish), *lumpia* (a crêpe-like food combining coconut, pork, shrimp, and vegetables in a tissue-thin wrapping), various fresh local fish, and delicious pineapple, bananas, mango, and papaya. Although the food is not as tasty, colorful, or well-prepared as Chinese food, the local San Miguel beer is one of the richest, most tasty brews I have come across. Western-style foods (Continental, French, Italian, steaks, and so on) and token Filipino fare can be found at restaurants and in all the major hotels, where you will also find nightclubs and discos for dancing.

If your time is not too limited, the real beauty of the islands is to be found outside of the densely populated, dirty cities. A two-hour drive to Pagsanjan Falls will take you past native villages, green-clad mountains, and beautiful palm forests to an interesting river and waterfall. Here you can rent a canoe with two skilled paddlers and "shoot the rapids." The trip up and down the river takes about one and a half to two hours, during which you wind through tall hills covered with giant palms. Parts of the river are calm, with water buffalo lazily bathing in the sun, while other portions contain strong currents and rapids.

The half-day trip to Hidden Valley is one of the most rewarding excursions I have ever experienced in my travels. Here you can hike down a one-mile trail through a forest of countless varieties of tropical trees, past natural pools, and then to a picturesque waterfall. The first pool you encounter provides one of the most satisfying treats for the senses you could imagine. The setting is that of two blue-green pools separated by a tiny waterfall surrounded by hills laden with tropical trees and vegetation. The water is clear and warm, and the area smells of fragrant flowers. Swimming in that pool is an occasion you will never forget and never equal. The price of about $7.50 per person to enter Hidden Valley includes lunch, soft drinks, and full use of the facilities.

The excursion to Hidden Valley can be combined with a trip to Pagsanjan and can be completed in about nine hours.

## SAMOA

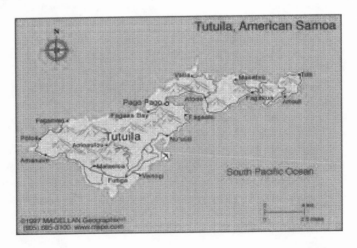

Samoa consists of sixteen islands in the South Pacific, the six most easterly ones being owned by the United States. The 192,000 people are mostly Polynesian. The temperature is hot and humid, getting up to the nineties during the day. There is a great deal of heavy rain in the winter months. Most of the restaurants serve American-style food. You can attend a tribal feast that is called *fia-fia* and is similar to the Hawaiian *luau*, the Tahitian *itamaaroa*, and the Fijian *mangiti*, featuring pig, chicken, or fish steamed over a hot stone oven. American Samoa's main island, Tutilla, consists of volcanic formations surrounded by coral reefs, with green tropical forests and small villages.

The main village, **Pago Pago** (pronounced "Pango Pango"), is adjacent to the harbor, contains a few craft shops, grocery stores, and K-mart-style department stores. The only hotel, the Rainmaker, is a five-minute walk from where your ship docks, and contains two hundred rooms. It is located on a peninsula jutting out into the bay and includes a small pool, an area to swim in the bay, a restaurant, and a souvenir shop. If you take a drive along the South Coast, you will pass a few small villages, the airport, numerous small churches, native huts called *fares,* and eventually arrive at Amanave Beach, which is somewhat picturesque but has no changing facilities and too many rocks to permit serious swimming. The organized tours afford an opportunity to sample typical island food and folklore shows. You may wish you had passed up the food. Golfers can play the nine-hole course near the airport.

## SINGAPORE

The island of Singapore is situated at the southern extremity of the Malay Peninsula, only eighty-five miles north of the equator, with a hot and humid climate varying from seventy-five degrees at night up to ninety degrees during the day. The country is only twenty-six miles long by fourteen miles wide and was a British colony for 140 years. In 1963, it became part of the Federation of Malaysia, but tensions between Malays and ethnic Chinese led to Singapore becoming a separate nation two years later. Its population of 2.5 million is 76 percent Chinese, 15 percent Malay, and 9 percent mixed English, Indian, and Pakistani. You will find it to be the cleanest, most modern country in Eastern Asia.

Your sightseeing tour of Singapore should include the lush botanic gardens, an excellent venue for walking or jogging, the golden Hindu temple of Sri Mariamman, China Town, the Arab District, Asian Civilizations Museum, Singapore History Museum, Marina Square, Zoological Gardens and Night Safari Park, the food stalls in the street markets, the Jarong Bird Park, Raffles City, and the panoramic cable-car ride from Mount Faber to Sentosa Island.

**Sentosa Island** lies directly across from the World Trade Center, and those not opting for the cable-car ride can take a five-minute ferryboat or a bus. The best way to obtain a feel for the island is to take the free monorail excursion. The beaches here are beautiful, and a good destination is the Rasa Sentosa Resort, which lies on a palm-lined, white-sand protected beach across from the Underwater World Oceanarium and monorail stop. Other attractions here include Volcanoland Theme Park; Fountain Gardens; the Coralarium; Asian Village; a wax museum, Fort Siloso; and several historical museums.

Although prices are somewhat higher than in Hong Kong, Singapore offers good free port shopping. You will find large varieties of cameras, watches, radios, antiques, leather goods, jewelry, ivory, and carpets. The major shopping areas are Change Alley, Raffles City and Raffles Hotel Arcade, the numerous large shopping centers along and near Orchard Road, Singapore Handicraft Center, Tanglin Shopping Center, Far East Plaza, Shaw Center, Lucky Plaza, Tangs, Scotts, Tong Building, and Wisma Atria.

Singapore boasts numerous restaurants with excellent Western, Chinese, Thai, Malaysian, and Indian cuisine. Many of the hotels offer elaborate international buffets enabling guests to sample all of these varied cuisines at one sitting. Mezza Nine at the Grand Hyatt features menus from nine different countries and may be a good choice for lunch. Some of the more highly recommended Chinese restaurants include Jiang Nan-Chun at the Four Seasons, Chang Palace at the Shangri-La, Li Bai at the Sheraton Towers, and Chang Jiang at the Goodwood Park. Other popular restaurants, featuring a variety of international cuisine, include Les Ami in the Botanical Gardens, Blu on top of the Shangri-La, Oscars at the Conrad, L'Aigle d'Or at the Duxton, Tandoor at the Holiday Inn Park View, Nadaman at the Shangri-La, Compass Rose at the Westin, Michaelangelo, and Indochine. The famous Raffles Hotel has been restored and is the "in place" for high tea. Although less appealing, you can inexpensively sample a variety of all the foods of Eastern Asia in the food stalls at Newton Circus and at Rasa Singapura behind the Handicraft Center and on Sentosa Island.

There are Asian cultural shows offered with dinner at many of the larger hotels, as well as at nightclubs, discos, and supper clubs. The luxury hotels offering the most facilities, restaurants, and entertainment are the Shangri-La, Ritz-Carlton Millenium, Four Seasons, Westin, Oriental, Marina Mandarin, Pan Pacific, Conrad, and Grand Hyatt.

# Society Islands—French Polynesia (Bora Bora, Huahine, Moorea, Raiatea/Tahaa, and Tahiti)

French Polynesia, or the Society Islands, is a group of fourteen inhabited islands in the South Pacific, 4,200 miles southwest of San Francisco that enjoys an ideal climate and trade winds with temperatures ranging from a low of around seventy to the upper eighties. December through April can be humid and rainy.

The islands are administered as an overseas territory of France, and French is the official language. Life is quite informal, and jackets and ties are seldom seen.

I found the Tahitian people working in the hotels, restaurants, and shops to be unhelpful, impatient, and generally rude. This gives one a feeling of annoyance when visiting these otherwise lovely islands.

Although there are numerous French-style restaurants in the hotels and in Papeete (Tahiti), none approach the quality of French restaurants in Europe or in the United States, and service is generally disappointing considering the high prices. Shopping is limited to souvenirs, T-shirts, *pareos* (native skirts), and a few French imports. If possible, you will enjoy attending a *tamaaroa*, a native feast similar to a *luau*, at one of the hotels, where a pig or chicken will be roasted over hot stones and served with vegetables, fruits, and coconut.

The largest of the islands, but—contrary to popular belief—not the prettiest, is **Tahiti**, with its main town of **Papeete**. Here you can stroll down a picturesque waterfront looking out at the island of Moorea, shop for a few French imports, dine at several so-so French restaurants, or take a drive around the island and visit the Gauguin Museum, the blowhole at Arahoko, the Cascade of Vaipahi, the water grotto of Maraa, and the waterfalls and rapid streams that cut into the steep mountains. There are no great beaches on the island of Tahiti; however, there are three "first-class" (not deluxe) hotels that have pools and beaches, and will arrange deep-sea fishing, water-skiing, or a tour of the lagoon. The Intercontinental (formerly the Tahiti Beachcomber Parkroyal) is about four miles from Papeete (your best bet). Other possibilities include Le Meridien, about nine miles from Papeete, and the Outrigger, only a few minutes from town. You can try the restaurants in the hotels, or La Chaumiere or Belvedere up in the mountains (a short taxi ride away), which offer a good view of the island.

The Lotus, situated on the lagoon at Tahiti Beachcomber Parkroyal, offers the most picturesque setting, along with an impressive French menu. L'eau a la Bouche, in town, is reputed to serve up some of the best cuisine, and Coco's is currently the place to see and be seen.

**Bora Bora** is a small unspoiled dream island with haunting mountains and some of the most beautiful palm tree-lined, snow-white beaches in the world. The waters surrounding the main island (which is only twenty miles in circumference) are protected by a coral reef that creates miles of a beautiful aqua-colored lagoon containing tiny pristine islets where you can sun on virgin beaches and swim in crystal clear waters.

The main town of **Vaitape** is composed of small grocery stores, a hospital, and a few souvenir shops. In the lagoon, set on their own private islands are the Four Seasons Bora Bora, St. Regis Bora Bora, Intercontinental Resort and Thalasso Bora Bora, Le Meridien Bora Bora, and Pearl Beach Resorts, where you may wish to make arrangements to have lunch and spend the day. These properties are as close to paradise in the South Seas as you will find. Other possibilities to spend your day in port include Hotel Bora Bora, three miles from town (if it has reopened after being hit by a hurricane), and the Intercontinental Le Moana Bora Bora (formerly Moana Beach Parkroyal Hotel), a mile farther down the road. All of these hotels are quite posh by Polynesian standards, with excellent restaurants and lovely white-sand beaches. There is snorkeling in the waters in front of all the hotels.

There is only one road that circles seventeen miles around the island. You can navigate around this road and explore the island by renting a Jeep "funcar," moped, or bicycle.

Probably the most spectacular experience to be had in Bora Bora is watching the sun set slowly over the lagoon and mountains, followed by the illumination of the sky and sea to a bright orange and purple.

**Huahine** is located approximately 110 miles from Tahiti. The islands' population of 5,400 is spread along two separate islands measuring twenty-eight square miles. Huahine Nui (Big Huahine) to the north and Huahine Iti (Little Huahine) to the south are connected by a small bridge. The island's rugged landscape and blue bays provide a colorful setting for the myriad of archeological and historical sites.

Places of interest include the small museum and cultural center at the sixteenth-century Fare Pote'e; a restored ancient temple, Matairea-Rahi, on Matairea Hill; Marae Manunu, a Polynesian religious temple that rises up between the sea and lagoon on Oavarei Motu; the blue- and green-eyed sacred eels, measuring sixteen to twenty-three feet, at the village of Faie; and the typical south sea village of Fare with its so-so boutiques, snack bars, and copra warehouses. From Fare you can take the Te Tiare Beach Resort's motor launch to this lovely, secluded resort with a small white-sand beach, pool, restaurant, bar, and forty-one gardens, beaches, and overwater bungalows. This is the most enjoyable way to spend your day. Another possiblity is the Hotel Sofitel, which also is situated on a beach.

**Moorea** is another incredibly lovely, lush, tropical island somewhat larger than Bora Bora, only twelve miles from the island of Tahiti, accessible by launch or air taxi. Here there are numerous needle mountain spires (including the fabled Bali Hai), green valleys, and white-sand beaches bordering a protected lagoon. You can take the thirty-seven-mile drive around the island by car or motor scooter. The most picturesque spot is Belvedere, about a fifteen-minute drive west of the airport. Here you proceed up a road through pineapple fields, coconut palms, and numerous varieties of tropical vegetation to a lookout point where you have a magnificent view of Cook's Bay, Papetoai Bay, and Moorea's jagged mountain peaks. You can swim, snorkel, water-ski, take a sailboat ride, play tennis, and have lunch at any of the **larger** hotels on the island: Sofitel Moorea la Ora Beach, Hilton Moorea Lagoon, and Moorea Pearl Resort. The most upscale resort on the island is the Intercontinental (formerly Moorea Beachcomber Parkroyal), an excellent place to spend a few days before or after your cruise. A branch of Dolphin Quest is located at the resort.

There is no special shopping center, only an occasional boutique offering native dresses, *pareos*, T-shirts, and wicker baskets. On the road behind the property that was Club Med are shops and small restaurants. The Plantation and L'Aventura located here are excellent choices for a French dinner in charming island settings.

**Rangiora** in the Tuamotu Archipelago in French Polynesia, located two hundred miles northwest of Papeete, is composed of a series of islands and motus surrounding a blue lagoon. The one major hotel, Kia Ora, is composed of beachfront and over-water bungalows, a restaurant, and a so-so beach. Unless you opt for snorkeling, diving, or a glass-bottom-boat excursion, the only other choice is a scenic walk along the lagoon on the Pacific side of the island.

**Raiatea and Tahaa**—these two mountainous islands, located immediately to the south of Bora Bora, 125 miles northwest from Tahiti, share a common coral foundation and a protected lagoon filled with small white-sand motus. Mount Tefateaiti, rising 3,333 feet, dominates Raiatea, and Mount Ohiri at 1,935 feet is the highest point on Tahaa.

There are no respectable beaches on either island, but snorkeling, scuba diving, and swimming opportunities are offered on sailing excursions to the motus. Paul Gauguin Cruises has an idyllic motu off of Tahaa where they hold beach parties. A popular way to explore Raiatea is a tour that commences in a motorized outrigger canoe along the perimeter of the island and up the jungle Faaroa River, followed by a Jeep ride back along the single road that stops along the way to explore small coconut and vanilla plantations, waterfalls, and the base of verdant mountains. A boat shuttle operates between Raiatea and Tahaa. The few small hotels have no beaches and are not worth visiting. Points of interest include the vanilla plantations, Polynesian petroghes carved in basaltic stone in the Mitimitiaute and Haapapaara Valleys, the Taputapuatea archeological site, and the tiarelipetechi, a rare white flower found on Temehani Mountain.

**Raratonga** is one of the Cook Islands. The center of the island is the eroded remains of a once mighty volcano whose crags now form saw-tooth peaks and razor-backed ridges covered with tropical jungle. These are separated by streams running down steep valleys. The twenty-mile circumference of the island is surrounded by a lagoon that extends several hundred miles out to a reef, which then slopes steeply to deep water.

It is possible to rent motor scooters to explore the island; and, the round-the-island buses follow the road that encircles the island in both directions. This is inexpensive and passengers can disembark at different stops and then reboard the next time the bus comes around. The main attraction is Muri Beach, a long stretch of white sand with crystal clear waters. Since the water is never deeper than chest high, it is possible to walk out to one of the motus that dot the lagoon. Both the small Pacific Resort and the Beach Club Hotel are places on the beach to stop for a drink or lunch.

## SOUTH KOREA

Cruise ships visiting South Korea dock in the port city of **Incheon**. Sites in Incheon include the Incheon Landing Hall, the Yeonan Pier Fish Market, and the Jayu Freedom Park. From this port city it is necessary to take a three-quarter to one-hour drive to the capital city of Seoul. Peeking out from megamodern high-rises and scattered among the twelve-lane highways and the Han River are traces of the city's five-thousand-year history: temples, city gates, palaces, and gardens. Visits to this city should include the new national Museum of Korea, the world's sixth-largest museum and the premier institution of Korean National Culture exhibits; the Namdaemun Market, a traditional market for shopping and bargaining; a few of the well-preserved palaces located within the city; Namsan Park; a Zen meditation service and tea ceremony at the Jogyejong Buddhist Temple; the Korean Folk Village; the DMZ (Demilitarized Zone) and the Third Tunnel. Deluxe hotels scattered around Seoul include the Grand Hyatt, Ritz-Carlton, Swiss Grand, Westin Chosun, Hilton, and Grand Intercontinental.

## TAIWAN (REPUBLIC OF CHINA)

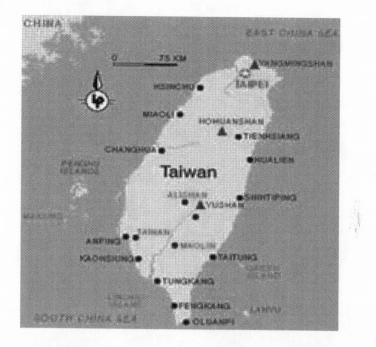

Surrounded by mountains and crisscrossed by rivers, **Taipei**, the center of government for the Republic of China, is a modern, cosmopolitan city infused with ancient culture and tradition. From the port city of Chilung where ships dock, it is a thirty- to forty-minute drive to Taipei. The most important sites include the National Palace Museum, which houses an important art collection of seven hundred thousand items of jade, bronze, porcelain, lacquers, and ancient Chinese paintings and prints; Martyrs' Shrine, a memorial to those who sacrificed their lives in founding the Republic of China, with plaques detailing the past 150 years of the country's history; the Chiang Kai-shek Memorial set in sixty-three acres of parks and landscaped gardens; Sun Yat-sen's Memorial; Taipei 101, formerly the world's tallest building; and Yangmingshan National Park with its butterfly corridor, bird-watching trail, hot springs, volcanic hollows, mountains, and cherry blossoms.

## THAILAND

**Bangkok**, the capital of Thailand (known as Siam until 1939), with its six million inhabitants, 94 percent of whom are Buddhists, is a city of contrasts. At first glance, it appears to be a noisy, polluted city with hundreds of hotels, massage parlors, shops, poverty, and horrendous traffic jams. Further exploration reveals a fascinating, well-preserved Asian culture represented by its beautiful temples, palaces, and the more primitive way of life to which many of its people still cling.

Any visit to Bangkok must start with an early-morning cruise down the Chao Phraya River (River of the Kings) to the "floating markets." The trip will start at the dock next to the Oriental and Shangri-La hotels and will take you past the huts and junks of the "river people," past numerous Buddhist temples (called "wats"), and past the marketplace where the river people come in their dugout canoes to buy and sell their wares. Before you return, your boat will visit one of the most famous and colorful wats, the Temple of the Dawn. You can also take an afternoon tour into the adjoining countryside on the "Rice Barge Cruise" to view rural family life along the canals.

In the city, you will want to tour the magnificent Grand Palace and the adjacent Wat Phra Keo housing the chapel of the Emerald Buddha, which is thirty-one inches high, carved out of emerald-colored jasper, and adorned with gold and jewels. You will also want to visit Wat Traimitr, the temple of the famous Golden Buddha, which is 5.5 tons of solid gold, Wat Pho, the Temple of the Reclining Buddha, the National Art Gallery, and the National Museum.

An interesting afternoon tour outside the city goes to the Rose Garden, where energetic young Thais entertain you with an excellent cultural show that includes Thai boxing, sword fighting, classical and folk dancing, and elephants at work.

The six most posh hotels with pools, restaurants, entertainment, and other facilities are the Oriental (which is considered by many to be the "best hotel in the world"), Shangri-La, Regent, Peninsula, Ritz-Carlton, and Dusit Thani. The best French-style restaurant is the Normandie, which sits on top of the Oriental Hotel, overlooking the River of the Kings. This ultraposh, romantic, and expensive dining room features gourmet French cuisine with menus created by acclaimed French chefs. Angelini, the Italian restaurant at the Shangri-La, is also excellent, as is Mezzaluna.

You can try authentic, spicy, Thai food at numerous restaurants throughout the city. It is best to get a recommendation from a local resident. Several tourist-oriented Thai restaurants provide a fixed menu of toned-down Thai dishes, together with Thai dancing. These include the Thai restaurants located on the river at the Oriental and Shangri-La Hotels, as well as the Spice Market at the Regent. Sala Rim Naam at the Oriental is exceptional and its lunch buffet provides an opportunity to sample a large variety of Thai dishes. Dinner cruises up and down the River of the Kings are also widely available. In the evening, many visitors enjoy exploring the notorious Patpong Road (a few blocks from the Dusit Thani Hotel) with its massage parlors and live sex shows.

The stores offering the best variety of Thai silks, handicrafts, paintings, and jewelry are located in the shopping centers adjacent to many of the hotels; however the best bargains are found in the stalls along the streets.

Some ships dock near the resort town of **Pattaya**, eighty-five miles from Bangkok. This is a rather crowded strip of resort hotels, souvenir shops, restaurants, massage parlors, and mediocre beaches. The largest and most secluded hotel with the best beach, pool, tennis courts, and restaurants is the Royal Cliff, which occupies some impressive acreage on a cliff overlooking the Bay of Thailand.

**Ko Sumui** is one of the most scenic islands in Thailand's eighty small-island archipelago. Places to visit include Wat Phra Yai, a temple housing the giant golden "Big Buddha," Safari Elephant Camp for an elephant show, Namuang Waterfall, as well as a rice field to watch a buffalo show or coconut and rubber plantations. Other choices may include elephant trekking through tropical jungles or relaxing on one of the numerous white-sand beaches. Chaweng Beach is lined with numerous hotels and is the most populated stretch of the island. Central Samui Beach Resort offers the most facilities in this area. Royal Meridien is a luxury resort with a pristine beach near the port area; however, prior arrangements must be made to gain entrance.

**Phuket** is a small island south of the mainland in the Andaman Sea. The beaches here are among the best in the world. Amanpuri Resort is situated on a coconut plantation on Pansea Beach and is one of the most romantic and exotically beautiful resorts in the world—as well as an excellent choice for lunch and a refreshing swim in warm, crystal clear waters. The Dusit Laguna, Sheraton Grand Laguna, Allemanda, and the luxurious Banyon Tree resorts are located at the Laguna Phuket Resort complex on Bang Tao Beach. This is the best place to experience an elephant ride. At Banyon Tree there is a full-scale spa facility with an eighteen-hole golf course and the most lavish pool villas in the world. A cruise around Phang Nga Bay is a must. Here you will find a labyrinth of forested limestone pillars rearing out of the Andaman Sea. You can explore caves, caverns, mangrove-lined tropical rivers, and the island where the James Bond movie *Man with the Golden Gun* was filmed. Half-day cruises to numerous pristine islands and excellent diving and snorkeling locations are also available, including excursions to the Surin Islands, Similan Islands, Rok Nok, Khai Nok, Krabi and Phi Phi Islands. Other sights of interest include the Nan Tok Tone Sai Waterfall in Khao Phra Taew Park, a national forest and wildlife preserve; the Marine Station, with its display of more than one hundred species of fish; the temple of Wat Chalong; Phuket Fantasea theme park on Kamala Bay, Thai Cultural Village for a performance of Thai dancing, sword fighting, boxing and elephants at work, and Phuket Town. Shopping for Thai silk and batik fabrics, precious stones and silver, gold, copies of designer watches, souvenirs, and lacquerware items is best along Patong Beach, a colorful area lined with hotels, restaurants, and shops, which is located across from Phuket's most populated public beach.

## VANUATU

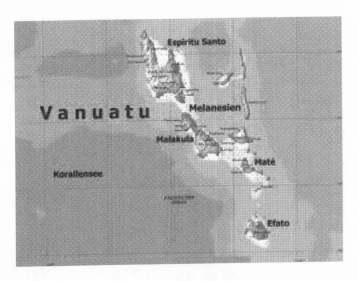

This Y-shaped archipelago of eighty-two islands covering four hundred miles in the Melanesia area of the South Pacific, northwest of Fiji, north of New Zealand, and east of Australia, gained its independence from a combined French and English rule in 1980 when it was known as New Hebrides. There are two main islands, Espiritu Santo and Efate.

**Luganville**, or Santo, as it is locally called, is the only large town on Espiritu Santo, where one hundred thousand U.S. servicemen were stationed during World War II. Today there is little of interest in town save the open-air farmers' market by the river or a stroll along the paths separating the native homes. Possible tours include snorkeling at Million Dollar Point, an outrigger canoe ride on the Sarakata River, or a tour around the island to see some historic points from World War II.

**Port Vila** on Efate Island is the administrative, commercial, and tourist center lying on a sleepy lagoon bordered by vibrant tropical jungles. Here you can take a glass-bottom boat ride circumnavigating Port Vila's harbor, snorkel and swim in a secluded bay, spend the day at two of the island's larger resorts—Le Meridien or Le Lagon Parkroyal (which are only five minutes from town)—or take a helicopter ride and view dense, impenetrable jungles, breathtaking waterfalls, clear rivers, and blue lagoons. The fifteen-minute drive to Mele Maat is a must. Here you can climb up a jungle mountain path over a succession of charming pools fed by cascading waterfalls.

## VIETNAM

Wedged between China, Laos, Cambodia, and the South China Sea, this historic, war-ravaged country, about the size of Norway but with a vastly larger population, has become a favorite visit for cruise ships traversing Southeast Asia.

**Ho Chi Minh City** (formerly Saigon), with a population of more than five million, is the largest, most dynamic of the Vietnamese cities and the center of culture and commerce. In the middle of the commercial section, not far from the harbor, are Saigon Square and Dong Khoi Street, an area with numerous hotels, shops, art galleries, and restaurants. The Rex Hotel gained public notice during the Vietnam War; however, several more modern hotels have recently been built, including the Sofitel, Hyatt, Marriott, Intercontinental, and Caravelle. Nam Kah is the best seafood restaurant in the city. Points of interest include Reunification Hall (formerly the

Presidential Palace), the Museum of Vietnamese History, the view from the top of the new modern trade center, and Choulan, the bustling Chinese quarter. A don't-miss attraction is the superb water-puppet show, a unique Vietnamese art form. Another enjoyable experience is the performance of traditional Vietnamese musical instruments offered throughout the day at Reunification Hall.

**Da Nang**, located in the center of the country, is another favorite port of call. Sightseeing should include visits to the former trade center of the country in Hoi-An, where today you can visit art galleries and silk factories; a climb to the top of Marble Mountain, the sight of many battles during the Vietnam War, and which today offers an excellent panorama of the surroundings; and the modern, five-star Furama Hotel that sits in the middle of famous China Beach. Tours are generally offered to the imperial city of Hue, to the Ho Chi Minh Trail, and the Cham Museum, which houses the world's best collection of art from the Cham civilization. Lunch by the pool at the Furama Hotel is a delightful experience and affords an opportunity to sample a variety of Asian cuisine.

**Hanoi**, the capital of Vietnam, a two- to three-hour drive from the port of Haiphong (or a one-hour helicopter ride), is less cosmopolitan and less colorful than Ho Chi Minh City. The hordes of bicycles and motorcycles that do not stop at intersections, or for pedestrians, make it a real challenge to cross streets. (This is also true throughout the country.) The main tourist attractions include the grandiose, Stalinist-style mausoleum of Ho Chi Minh, the country's most revered leader; his former homes with their surrounding gardens and ponds; the Ho Chi Minh Museum; the One Pillar Pagoda; the Temple of Literature, a well-preserved example of Vietnamese architecture housing eighty-two stone tablet artifacts; and the thirty-six streets in the old quarter of town, where each street is named after the merchandise offered, i.e., "Fish Street," "Meat Street," "Vegetable Street," "Basket Street," etc.

## East Africa and the Indian Ocean

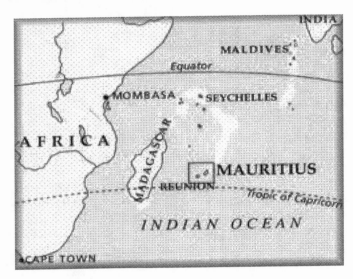

Well-traveled cruisers looking for new and exotic cruise areas are beginning to explore the eastern coast of Africa and the unusual islands in the Indian Ocean that stretch from the southern tip of Africa to India.

For decades, most of the superliners offering world cruises visited the ports of Durban, Madagascar, Mombasa, Zanzibar, Mauritius, Reunion, and the Seychelle and Maldive group of islands. Recently, several of the more upscale vessels have begun offering a series of seven- to fourteen-day cruises in this area and provide passengers a pre- or postcruise option to enjoy a safari experience at game preserves in Kenya and Tanzania.

## COMORES ISLANDS

Anjouan, Grande Comore, Mayotte, and Moheli—the four islands in the Comores—are located between Madagascar and Mozambique, Africa, in the Indian Ocean. The islands have a long history. During the nineteenth century, they were ruled by sultanates, and the major industries were the export of spices and slaves. Slavery was abolished in 1904, and in 1912 the four islands became French colonies. In 1975, all of the islands except Mayotte became independent. Having wisely voted to retain the French influence, Mayotte is the only island in the Comores with a decent standard of living and not suffering from overpopulation and poverty. The people of the Comores speak French, Arabic, and a native dialect. They are mostly Moslems, and many practice polygamy.

Most cruise ships stop at **Anjouan** because it is the most scenic of the four islands with verdant hills, mountains, and valleys covered with towering palms, banana trees, and tropical forests dotted with waterfalls and streams—all looking down to the blue waters of the Indian Ocean. The port town of Mutsamudu is dirty, crowded, and of little interest. You will want to drive out into the country to the scenic point at Mount Ntingui to a factory that processes oil from the ylang-ylang flower used in French perfumes or to one of the picturesque beaches. The best beach is at Moya Plage, where there is a nice hotel; however, it takes ninety minutes to drive there. One mile from town is a small scenic white-sand beach connected to Comotel Al-Amal, where there is also a small pool, bar, and restaurant.

The largest of the Comores is **Grande Comore**. In town, you can stroll through a clutter of homes and narrow alleys reminiscent of Greek island villages (but much dirtier). You can drive out to see the Karthala Volcano, which has the largest crater in the world. The best beach is at Maloudja, also the location of the best hotel. Other choices may include Novotel Ylang-Ylang and Istranda Palace.

**Mayotte**, the least impoverished of the four islands and still a French colony, is surrounded by a coral reef. Many private yachts anchor at the beach at Soulou to shower and picnic at the waterfall located there. The best beach for swimming and snorkeling is at N'Goudja, where there is also a decent hotel. Moheli has little development; however, there are good beaches at Miremani, Sambadjon, Sambia, and Itsamia.

## KENYA

Kenya, an independent republic within the British Commonwealth, intersected by the equator, is possibly the destination that offers the greatest variety of attractions for visitors to Africa. You can visit **Nairobi**, East Africa's most cosmopolitan city, then go on safari through some of the best game reserves in the world, or relax at a beach resort along the clear, blue waters of the Indian Ocean.

One day to explore this country is not nearly sufficient. Therefore, many cruise ships, when calling at **Mombasa**, the port city of Kenya, generally arrange overnight or two- to four-day pre- and postcruise excursions. Because you will want to make the most of your time, I suggest that you make arrangements with a reliable tour organization to plan and conduct your tour. Abercrombie & Kent (A&K) and Micato Safaris are deservingly the favorites of the major cruise lines. Micato has been owned and operated for more than forty years by the Pinto family. Their itineraries include a warm, personalized orientation dinner at the home of Felix and Jane Pinto, high atop Lavington Hill, overlooking the twinkling lights of Nairobi; excellent professional English-speaking tour guides in modern, air-conditioned safari vehicles; and guaranteed reservations at Kenya's best hotels, lodges, and tent camps. A&K is well-known around the world and offers a comparable safari experience. United Touring is another large operator in the area.

If your cruise commences or ends in Kenya, you will fly in or out of Nairobi's international airport. The best hotels in Nairobi include the venerable Norfolk, Nairobi Safari Club, Hilton, Serena, and Intercontinental. Windsor Hotel and Country Club is situated thirty minutes from Nairobi and twenty minutes from the airport in a suburb surrounded by parks, woodlands, and coffee plantations. This is the most comfortable choice for a few days of rest, relaxation, and possibly a few rounds of golf.

For dining in Nairobi, your best bets are the Grill Room at the Norfolk (Continental), Tamarind (seafood), and Carnivore (unique game). You will want to visit the National Museum and Aviary to view its collection of tribal ornaments, native wildlife, and Dr. Louis Leakey's exhibit on prehistoric man; Karen Estates, former home of Baroness Karen von Blixen, who wrote *Out of Africa* and other literary works under the pseudonym of Isak Dinesen; Giraffe Manor, where you can hand-feed giraffes; and Nairobi National Park with its lion population and animal orphanage.

Of course, the greatest attraction in Kenya is a camera safari to one of the country's game reserves. If you only have time for one such reserve, the largest concentration of game to be observed is at the Masai Mara Park, which borders the Serengeti in Tanzania. Game that abound here include giraffes, elephants, lions, baboons, zebra, gazelles, impalas, and wildebeests. Masai Mara Sopa Lodge, located near a native Masai village, enjoys an enviable elevated location with breathtaking views of Olooliumutia Valley and the Mara plains. Other lodges in the Masai include Mara Serena Safari Lodge and Kakrok. For those wishing to "rough it" at a modernly equipped tented camp, the best of the lot are Mara Intrepids Camp, Gouvenor's Camp, Sarova Mara, Siana Springs, and Kichwa Tempo.

Other top safari destinations include mountain lodge Treetop Hotel in Mount Kenya National Park, where you can view a multitude of animals when they come to drink at a waterhole around which the lodge is built. While in this area, you may want to spend a day or two relaxing at the world-famous Mount Kenya Safari Club, set in a lovely park in the foothills of snow-capped Mount Kenya and surrounded by the world's most famous game conservation park. The resort was once owned by the late William Holden, but is now owned by Lonrho Hotels. The private game reserve and animal orphanage adjacent to the resort are owned by actress Stephanie Powers and the renowned conservationists Don and Iris Hunt.

Still other excellent national parks in which to view game include Samburu, Amboseli, Tsavo, and Aberderes. At Amboseli National Park, preferred camps are Tortilis Camp and Amboseli Serena Safari Lodge.

The port city of **Mombasa**, an old town rich in history, is located largely on an island that connects to the mainland by causeway. The airport is on the mainland, but the port and city are on the island. Of interest is Fort Jesus, built by the Portuguese at the turn of the sixteenth century, which dominates the harbor and the old town itself. The two best hotels are the Castle in the middle of town and the Outrigger Hotel at Ras Liwatoni on the beach. Numerous beach hotels stretch out to the south and north of mainland Mombasa, and there is a national marine park and scuba diving at Malindi. Traditional African dance can be observed at Giriami Villages.

**Lamu Island**, a small Kenyan island that sits off the coast with an exclusively Muslim population, is a place that appeals to some tourists for an "away-from-it-all" holiday. Several cruise ships make a short visit here after Mombasa. Lamu is often referred to as the Katmandu of Africa and was popular with the hippies in the 1960s and early 1970s. It is a rather dirty town with not much of interest other than the museum with its display of a traditional Swahili house and models of various types of *dhow*, the unique wood boat that is the major method of transportation (other than donkey) around the island. If you have a few hours, the best bet is to take the forty-five-minute walk along the coast, or a short dhow ride to Shela Village, using Peponi Hotel as your home base. The beach extending for several miles past Peponi is a magnificent stretch of light sand, dunes, and small palms lapped by the warm waters of the Indian Ocean. Here you can also wander around the small Islamic Village and have a cold beer or snack at Peponi.

## MADAGASCAR

Madagascar, the fourth-largest island in the world, is thought to have geologically split off from Africa. It was not inhabited until AD 500, when it was settled by Indonesians and Malaysians. In 1500, the Portuguese came to settle and colonize, and they were followed by the Dutch, British, and French. The country was a French colony from 1896 until it gained its independence in 1960. The population of eleven million is Malagasy, a mixture of black Africans, Indonesians, and Arabs. The language is French; however, France and most of the Western world lost interest in Madagascar after its independence, and today it is a poor, overpopulated country that experiences very little tourism.

Most cruise ships visit **Nose Be** and **Nose Komba**, two small tropical islands that lie off the northwest coast of the main island. This is a very picturesque area, one where the sea is generally calm and picture-postcard little islands peek out of the water with green peaks surrounded by blue sky and low-hanging, puffy cumulus clouds.

From the dock at Nose Be, you can either walk about a half-mile or take the shuttle bus into town. If you walk, you will pass by the large colonial-style homes built by the French in the early 1900s, which are now dilapidated. In town, there is an open marketplace and a few craft and souvenir shops. You can take a forty-five-minute drive across this verdant island of rolling hills, rivers, towering palms, sugar cane, coffee, and banana and ylang-ylang trees to Audilana Beach. On this beautiful tan-sand beach covered with tall palm trees, you can bathe in the very warm, clear waters of the Indian Ocean. This is also the location of a Club Med.

**Nose Komba** is a tiny island best known for its rare lemur sanctuary. Your tender will leave you off on a picturesque brown-sand beach with coral reefs for snorkeling, surrounded by hills covered with deep-green tropical flora. You can walk through a secluded, self-sustaining native village to an area that is the rare lemur's habitat. If you bring bananas, the friendly primates will jump on your shoulder and consume the bananas out of your hand. It's messy, but fun. The natives of the village are very friendly, the children are darling, and if you wish, you can purchase seashells, primitive handicrafts, or linens.

The beach is excellent for snorkeling, but you need to wear plastic sandals if you are venturing out in the water for a swim.

The port town of **Antsiranara** (formerly Diego Suarez) is set on the northeastern tip of Madagascar. The town, with its fifty thousand inhabitants, is about three-fourths of a mile from the dock area, both of which are quite dirty, in total disrepair and not of much interest. Ramena Beach, the best and most popular beach in this area, lies eighteen miles from the city. It would be a sixty-minute drive to the southward to visit Ambre National Park, with its volcanic mountains and beautiful crater lakes. In the same direction is Roussettes Waterfalls and Rainforest.

## MALDIVE ISLANDS

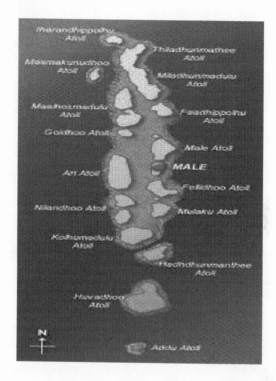

Referred to by Marco Polo as "the flower of the Indies," the Maldives lie 450 miles southwest of Sri Lanka and consist of 1,190 tiny, palm-decked coral islands in twenty-six atoll clusters that trail down the Indian Ocean and overlap the equator. Only 220 are inhabited by a population totaling 270,000, which consists of a mixture of Sri Lankans, Indians, Indonesians, Malayans, Arabs, Africans, and Europeans. The Maldives broke away from Great Britain in 1965 as an independent Islamic republic. Twenty-five percent live in Male, the capital, where most of the inhabitants fish for a living. More than eighty islands have opened small hideaway resorts, the nearer ones in the north and south Male atolls being accessible by motorboats or water taxis called *dhoni*. The others can be reached by helicopter and seaplane from the airport that sits on a small island near Male.

There is not much of interest in Male other than the Sultan's Park, the National Museum, and a few souvenir shops. The real reason for visiting the Maldives is to witness the beauty of the hundreds of pristine islands and underwater life. The waters are crystal clear—ideal for swimming, snorkeling, and diving.

Most of the resorts offer extensive diving programs and are frequented by scuba-diving enthusiasts. However, in recent years several luxury resorts have opened that feature not only great diving programs, water sports, and incredible fine-white-sand, palm-studded beaches and lagoons, but also sumptuous beachfront and overwater bungalows, good dining, and upscale service. Four Seasons on Kuda

Huraa Island and Banyon Tree on Vabbinfaru Island are both in the north Male atoll, only a twenty-five-minute motorboat ride from Male or the airport. Another popular resort accessible by motorboat is the Island Hideaway at Dhonakulhi.

Some ships visit the Maldives because they are directly on the route between Africa and India, as well as to other Asian countries. Be certain that the ship intends to provide a tour of the islands, assist you with your own arrangements to book transportation to an island, or at least hold a beach party on one of the islands; otherwise, stopping here is not very rewarding.

## MAURITIUS

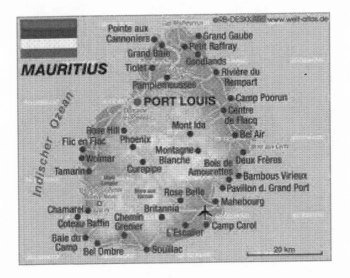

Lying 480 miles east of Madagascar and 3,600 miles to the west of Australia, in the Indian Ocean, lies the Republic of Mauritius, a volcanic island best known for its picturesque beaches, water activities, and colorful melange of cultures. Its 1.1 million population is half Hindu (the descendants of indentured Indian laborers), and the other half a mixture of African, Chinese, French, and British. At various times a possession of the Dutch, French, and British, this tiny island gained its independence from Britain in 1968 and became a republic in 1992. The hottest months are during the rainy season from January through April, and the coolest extending from early July through September. Sugar cane is a major export and tourism an important source of revenue.

**Port Louis**, on the northwest coast, is the major commercial center. Here you can visit the Natural History Museum, Jummah Mosque, the city market, Pere Laval's Shrine, Fort Adelaide, the Casela Bird Park, and take the fifteen-minute drive to view exotic plants and palm trees in the botanical gardens at Pamplemousses. The best hotel here is Labourdonnais on the waterfront, and nearby are numerous restaurants, bars, a casino, and cinemas.

Beach resort areas include Trou aux Biches, Choisy and Grand Baie to the north of Port Louis, Flic en Flac to the south of Port Louis, and Pointe de Flac, Trou d'Eau Douche, Ile Aux Cerfs, Belle Mare, and Blue Bay all on the eastern coast. All forms of boating and water sports are available at the myriad of luxury resorts. Numerous companies offer deep-sea fishing and diving. Walking and trekking are popular in the mountains and valleys of the island's interior. Other places of interest include Black River Gorge National Park, Chamarel Falls, and the crater at Trou Aux Cerfs.

Mauritius boasts many exotic luxury resorts, each with extremely comfortable accommodations, a diverse range of restaurants, beautiful beaches, every imaginable water sport, and lovely landscapes. The most popular on the east coast are St. Geran at Pointe de Flacq, Touessrok at Trou d'Eau Douche, and the more exotic Le Prince Maurice at Poste de Flac. On the west coast, the Oberoi at Baie aux Tortues, Royal Palm at Grand Baie, and the Sugar Beach Resort are your best choices. If you do not elect to utilize one of these hotels, a pleasant beach day can be spent at Ile aux Cerfs, a public beach-park with a blue lagoon, a white sandy beach, restaurants, bars, souvenir shops, and water sports.

## OMAN

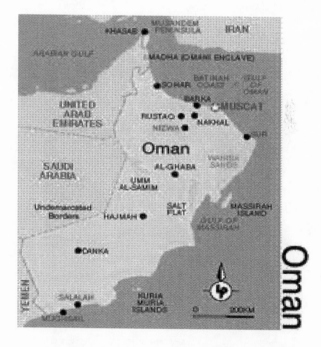

Oman is the oldest of all of the established Arab countries. Muscat, known as the "capital region," is made up of three distinct cities, separated geographically by hills and ridges, each with its own particular identity. **Muscat** is the old port area and the location of most of the places of interest; **Matrah**, to the northwest, is the main trading district and the country's most important harbor; **Ruwi**, a few miles inland, is a modern commercial and administrative center. The coastline is dynamic, with jagged rocky cliffs rising above picturesque, whitewashed towns with mosques and minarets.

Visitors will want to tour the old city of Muscat to view the spectacularly beautiful Al-Alam Palace and gardens flanked by two sixteenth-century Portuguese forts, Jalali to the east and Mirani to the west. Another impressive Portuguese sixteenth-century fort sits atop a cliff near the harbor in Matrah and affords a good panorama of the city.

Sightseeing in Oman should also include a visit to the Natural History Museum as well as the Oman Museum, which houses old manuscripts, local arts and crafts, and displays of Omani architecture and design. Bargaining at the souks in Muscat and Matrah are popular tourist priorities. Here you will find antique jewelry, souvenirs, sandals, colorful textiles, gold, silver, spices, and incense.

Dining is best and safest at one of the better hotels such as Al-Bustan Palace Intercontinental, a five-minute drive past Muscat, where you will find a long strand of beach, a pool, tennis courts, numerous restaurants, and a good example of Arabian opulence.

Those wishing to take a long walk or jog will especially appreciate the corniche, the road and path along the gulf extending from the harbor in Matrah to the town of Muscat, a distance of about two miles.

## REUNION

Lying 480 miles east of Madagascar, southeast of Mauritius in the Indian Ocean, this overseas department of France boasts breathtaking landscapes, volcanic peaks and verdant gorges. Originally settled by the French during the seventeenth century, today its population of approximately seven hundred thousand is 40 percent Creole, 20 percent Indian, and a 40 percent mixture of French, other Europeans, and Chinese. French is the national language, although most residents speak Creole. The French franc is the official currency. Few residents speak English.

The prime attraction for visitors is trekking the volcanic peaks and valleys. Beach resorts with an abundance of water sports are available; however, nearby Mauritius is far more popular with the sun-worshiping crowd. The island, dominated by two major mountain ranges, is 120 miles in circumference with hot, rainy summers, extending from October through March, and cool, dry winters from April through September. Cyclone activity is possible in February and March.

Ships generally drop anchor near Le Port, which is midway between the capital city of St. Denis, and the most popular beach area of St. Gilles-Les Bains; both are accessible by a thirty-minute taxi or bus ride. (Taxis are outrageously expensive).

**St. Denis** is the lively capital city with a population of 130,000. The most interesting area is Le Barachois, located at the western end of the waterfront. It is composed of bars, sidewalk cafés, shops, and the city's largest hotel, Le St. Denis. Attractions include the Musee Leon Dierx, an art museum; Jardin l'Etat, a botanical garden; the Hindu Temple; the Grande Mosque; and the handicraft market. The better shops and boutiques can be found on Rue du Marechal and Rue le Clerc.

St. Giles-Les Bains is the most popular beach resort area, easily accessible by an hour bus or taxi ride from St. Denis and a half-hour from Le Port. The most upscale hotel is St. Alexis, located near the locals' favorite beach at Bocan Canot. You can have lunch at one of the seafood restaurants or pizzerias located at the harbor-beach area at St. Gilles. I especially enjoyed the pizza, pastas, and salads on the second level of Quai de la Pasta, a delightful spot overlooking the harbor and beach. Surfing, scuba, deep-sea fishing and numerous water sports are available; however, shark incidents have occurred here. Golf and horseback riding can also be arranged.

## SEYCHELLE ISLANDS

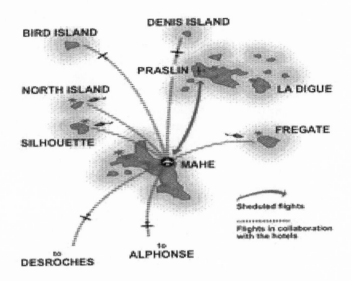

These unique, dynamically beautiful tropical islands that encompass a seventy-five-square-mile archipelago are located in the Indian Ocean near the equator, a thousand miles east of Kenya and a thousand miles away from any other land mass. The islands were uninhabited until the mideighteenth century, when France took possession. Over the years, the 115 islands (eighty of which are still deserted) were settled by Europeans, Africans, and Asians, and today the seventy thousand inhabitants speak Creole, French, and English.

These islands are geologically unique in that they are of solid-granite origin rather than volcanic rock, with dramatic cliffs that rise from the sea, carpeted with lush vegetation and interesting boulder formations that are the debris of gigantic movements of the earth's crust thousands of years ago. The Seychelle beaches are the very best in the world, and the warm seas surrounding the islands offer countless opportunities for swimming, water sports, scuba, and snorkeling. Several of the islands are home for rare species of sea birds and plant life found nowhere else in the world. The weather is hot, humid, and sometimes windy during the monsoon seasons. December and January are the worst months, and May through October are the best.

There are several international airplane flights each week into **Mahé**—the largest of the islands. The harbor at Mahé's largest city, Victoria, is the port of call for many cruise ships. Ninety-five percent of the population of the Seychelles lives on Mahé. It is here that you will find the major hotels, the best restaurants, and the best shopping, as well as sixty-eight beautiful beaches. The most pristine and picturesque beaches are Anse Royale on the southeast coast and Anse Intendence on the southwest coast; the most popular, but not the most beautiful, is at Baie Beau Vallon, where numerous hotels are located.

The capital town of **Victoria,** which sits near the harbor, is very clean but not terribly interesting. There are a number of shops and boutiques, as well as several restaurants. The better hotels, resorts, and restaurants are located around the island and not in Victoria.

Presently, the three first-class resorts on the island are Banyon Tree, Four Seasons at Baie Lazare, and Maia at Anse Boileau, all of which offers lovely grounds, very comfortable accommodations, and many amenities. A number of luxury hotel chains are in the process of developing resorts on this island. Other hotels with facilities are Le Meridian at Barbarons, Le Meridian Fisherman's Cove, Berjaya Beau Vallon Bay Beach Resort, Hilton Seychelles at Notholme. All of these hotels have beaches, pools, tennis courts, shops, and good restaurants. The best restaurants are Chez Plume at Anse Boileau, La Perle Noire at Beau Vallon, and Le Corsaire and LaScala at Bel Ombre.

To really appreciate this incredibly lush island, you should rent a car or minimoke or hire a taxi to drive you around Mahé. Nowhere in the world can you witness such incredible beauty.

Praslin lies to the northwest of Mahé and is a two-and-a-half-hour ferryboat ride or fifteen-minute propeller flight. Here you can enjoy the one-mile walk through the 450-acre Valley-De-Mai, a lovely forest and the home of the botanical rarity, the coco-de-mer palm, as well as such rare birds as the black parrot, blue pigeon, and bulbul. This seven-mile-long island is surrounded by a coral reef and boasts numerous silver-white-sand beaches. Cote d'Or and Anse Volbert make up a two-and-a-half-mile stretch of white-sand beach lined with palm trees only five or six miles from the pier where your tender docks. Here you can swim, snorkel, and have lunch or a snack at one of the small hotels or restaurants located along the beach, including Berjaya Praslin Beach Hotel, Paradise Hotel, and Acajou.

A few miles farther down the road, you will experience one of the most idyllic beaches in the world, the incomparable Anse Lazio. The setting of palms, pines, seagrapes, and flowers is breathtaking; the powder-white sand is firm and excellent for strolling and jogging; and the absolutely crystal clear warm waters are the very finest for swimming. Adjacent to this extraordinary beach is an equally extraordinary semi-open-air restaurant, Richelieu Verlaque's Bon Bon Plume, which features exceptional fresh fish, seafoods, Creole dishes, French wines, and other beverages and overlooks the panorama of Anse Lazio. Those opting to spend their day ashore at Anse Lazio and Bon Bon Plume will be rewarded with one of the most exquisite island experiences they may ever encounter.

The best resorts on the island are the ultradeluxe, Lemurea at Anse Kerlan near the airport, Le Duc de Praslin, Chateau de Feuilles, La Reserve and Acajou, all located on the east coast. At Lemurea there is an eighteen-hole golf course. If you are in Praslin in the evening, the two best restaurants, other than those at Lemurea, are the charming semi-open-air restaurant sitting on an over-water jetty at La Reserve and the elegant Tante Mimi, situated in a colonial-style building above the casino and serving Continental cuisine.

**La Digue**, a thirty-minute boat ride from Praslin or three hours from Mahé, is the most beautiful, pristine, and photographed of the Seychelle Islands. The breathtakingly scenic Anse Source D'Argent, in my opinion, is the most picturesque beach setting in the world. Here, warm turquoise waters with the mildest of currents lap silver-white-sand beaches and tiny private coves interspersed with geometric gray boulder formations, palm trees, and other tropical flora and green hills in the background. This is the scene that appears most often on postcards and brochures depicting the Seychelles. The island is surrounded by a coral reef, and opportunities to snorkel and swim are abundant.

From La Passe, where your boat or tender docks, you can walk or rent a bicycle or oxcart for the two-mile trek through town, past La Digue Lodge (a small hotel) and L'Union Estate, to Anse Source D'Argent. Select any of the private coves to leave your towel and snorkel gear. After you have strolled along the mile or so of sandy paths, rock formations, and coves, and taken some of the most scenic photos imaginable, you will want to settle down and enjoy the sun, soothing warm waters, and picturesque surroundings. This is the perfect romantic hideaway. If you have no one with whom to share romance, it is a great place to sit and reflect.

There are many other spectacular beaches on the island, including Grand Anse and Petite Anse (two magnificent half-mile-long expanses of white sand beach with crystal clear waters and heavy waves and current), as well as Anse CoCo, Anse Fourmis, Anse Banane, Anse Patates, and Anse Gaulettes. If time permits, you can ride a bicycle around the island, although there are some places where you will have to proceed by foot. The winds and currents can be rather strong from May through October, and generally the safest place to swim is at Anse Source D'Argent. Places to visit include Black Paradise Flycatcher Reserve, a thirty-seven-acre shaded woodland where these rare birds make their home; and L'Union Estate, an old coconut plantation with a traditional colonial house, shipyard, colony of giant tortoises, and horseback riding.

**Aride**, a nature reserve, is two hours by boat from Mahé. Wardens, who live on the island, will take you on a tour of nature paths to view the beautiful Wright's gardenia, other flora indigenous to the island, and the largest collection of sea birds in the world, including the roseate sooty and bridled tern, the lesser and common noddy, and the white-tailed tropic bird. The pure white-sand beach in front of the wooded area is very beautiful, but swimming and snorkeling can be a bit dangerous when the waves are high.

**Curieuse** is a small island two miles long that is a half-mile from the north coast of Praslin. Here you can take a rather rugged nature walk across a steep hill to a swamp to view a colony of one hundred giant Aldalra tortoises. The long stretch of white-sand beach is picturesque and borders clean, warm waters ideal for swimming and some of the best snorkeling in the Seychelles. Several cruise ships offer barbecues or picnics here.

**Cousins** is a seventy-acre island bird reserve sanctuary for the rare Seychelle ground doves, weaver birds, toc toc, and thousands of other species. There is a half-mile expanse of beach, but the water is generally pretty rough and snorkeling is only fair. Bird Island, Desroches, and Poivre are three islands offering good game fishing.

## UNITED ARAB EMIRATES

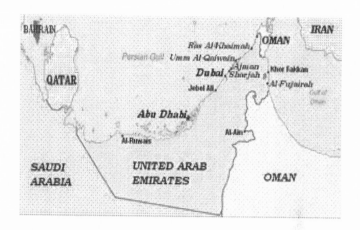

**Dubai**, which lies one hundred miles down the coastal road from Abu Dhabi, is really two cities divided by an inlet from the Persian Gulf known as "The Creek." On the north side of the Creek is the village of Deira and on the south, Dubai. Your ship will dock at Port Rashid on the Dubai side, two miles from the center of town. With a half-million inhabitants, it is the second largest of the seven emirates, offering the visitor a distinctive blend of modern city and timeless desert.

There are many deluxe hotels, including Burj Al Arab, Jumeirah Beach Hotel, Madinat Jumeirah, Grand Hyatt, Hyatt Regency, and JW Marriott. At these establishments you will be rewarded with fine dining, shops, panoramic views, and a good home base for your exploration. You will want to sample Arabian specialties such as hummus (a chickpea and sesame seed puree), *taboule* (cracked wheat salad with tomatoes, mint, and parsley), and the variety of spicy lamb dishes, fish, and seafood indigenous to the region. In the small restaurants, the traditional repast is *shawarma*, grilled slivers of lamb or chicken mixed with salad and stuffed inside pita-bread pockets. Several hotels and tour organizations feature "desert safari dinners," where guests enjoy a barbecue dinner under the stars while seated on a carpet under a canopy.

You will want to browse the traditional souks and tiny shops of the old town core and test your skills at bargaining. The famous Gold Souk in Dubai has hundreds of shops and gold is sold by its weight. Persian carpets here are considered the best buys outside of Iran. Also, there are modern multilevel shopping malls at Al Rega Road, Karama, Al Dhiyafa Road, and Bani Yas Square.

Dubai is home to the annual PGA Desert Golf Classic and the only eighteen-hole golf course in the emirates with real greens. Swimming and water sports are available at Jumeirah Beach Park and Al Mimzer Park, south of the port.

A fun way to cross the Creek is on a shared water taxi called abras. The Creek offers a picturesque glimpse of the city's trading heritage.

Places of interest include Al Fahide Fort, renovated in 1970 to house an archaeological museum; the view from the top of the World Trade Center; Dubai

Zoo; Dubai World Amusement Park; the camel racetrack; the shops and restaurants at Holiday Center; the Textile Souk on Al Fahidi Street; the Spice Souk; the Gold Souk; Majlis Gallery; and Juneira Mosque, a spectacular example of modern Islamic architecture.

## ZANZIBAR ISLAND, TANZANIA

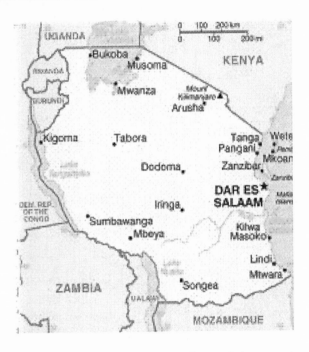

Known as the "Spice Island," Zanzibar has been ruled at one time or another by Egyptians, Indians, Chinese, Portuguese, Persians, Dutch, Arabs, and English. The island reached prominence during the nineteenth century as the hub of the slave-trading industry and as a major grower and exporter of spices—especially cloves, which are grown on plantations around the island. Ninety percent of the island's inhabitants are Muslims, and Arab influence is present in the architecture, numerous ruins, and customs.

If you do not opt to take an organized tour, you can readily hire an English-speaking taxi driver for about seven to ten dollars an hour. You may wish to explore the labyrinth of narrow winding streets with whitewashed coral houses, shops, restaurants, and public buildings in the "Old Stone Town" area. Attractions here include two former sultans' palaces, a Portuguese fort built in 1700, a mosque, several cathedrals, a museum, the old slave market, and the indoor/outdoor public market, where produce, fish, and meats are sold. The favored restaurant amongst tourists in the Old Stone Town is Fisherman's Restaurant, which features fresh fish, lobster, and other seafood.

To appreciate the tropical splendor of Zanzibar, you must drive out to the beaches, native villages, and spice plantations. Zanzibar is a major producer of cloves. A lovely spot to spend a few hours is Mawimbine Club Village, on the west side of the island where you dock, about a fifteen-minute drive from town. This is a charming tropical resort with sixty-four thatched bungalows set in lush gardens with a pool, bar, restaurant, and a nice strand of white-sand beach. Water sports and deep-sea fishing can be arranged here. Down the road is a small native village and spice plantation that can be visited in combination with the drive to Mawimbine.

There are a number of fine beaches on the opposite (east) side of the island at Jambiani and Bwejuu, but you probably will not have enough time to get there.

## Transatlantic Crossings

When planning your European vacation, why not plan to sail at least one way? Prior to the jet age, cruising to and from Europe was considered by many as "the only way to go." Today, however, the relaxed luxury of sailing abroad has given way to the desires of the typical traveler who wishes to take in as much as he can in as short a time as possible. Those of you who find it difficult to immediately unwind at the beginning of a vacation may find that a five-day ocean crossing is just what the doctor ordered. Others who have been exhausted from the hustle and bustle of a whirlwind European tour may prefer to take a relaxing cruise home to rest up before going back to the demands of everyday life.

As the cruise lines are scheduling a greater number of cruises in the Caribbean and Mediterranean, their ships are making fewer transatlantic crossings. Whereas thirty years ago a traveler leaving for Europe had numerous vessels to choose from, today only a few ships make regularly scheduled trips. However, it is possible to cruise on numerous lines when they are repositioning their vessels between the United States and Europe in late spring and early fall.

Some ships make a few crossings by the southern route. This route takes from five to fifteen days, depending on your point of embarkation and ports of call. Typically, the ships stop at a few of the following ports: Lisbon, Algeciras, Barcelona, Cannes, Genoa, Naples, and Piraeus.

The *QM2* and other ships of Cunard Line offer a number of regularly scheduled crossings by the northern route between New York and Southampton, which take from five to seven days.

As pointed out earlier in the book, when sailing transatlantic, you will find that the seas are rougher than in the Caribbean or Mediterranean, and that the southern route will allow more sunny days on deck than the northern route.

However, don't let these factors discourage you. Sailing on a modern luxury liner is an unforgettable experience. If your vacation plans will not permit a longer cruise and Europe is on your agenda, treat yourself to a transatlantic crossing for at least one leg of your trip.

## Length of Cruise

How long a cruise should you take? The answer, of course, depends upon how much time you have available as well as what length vacation you may prefer. If you are the type that becomes fidgety after having spent a week at a vacation spot, you also probably will become restless should you spend longer than a week at sea. On the other hand, if it takes you a week just to unwind and longer vacations are your preference, a longer cruise will appeal to you.

The duration of a cruise can vary from a one- or two-day journey to "nowhere" to an around-the-world cruise that may take from 90 to 120 days. If you have only a short time to spend afloat, you may wish to consider cruises to "nowhere" from New York, Miami, Fort Lauderdale, Orlando, or Los Angeles, which are offered by a number of the cruise lines. On these outings, the ships merely sail out into the ocean for one or two days, giving the passengers a sample of life aboard a cruise ship at sea. One or two ships of Carnival, Celebrity, Royal Caribbean, Disney, and Norwegian offer short-duration cruises (three or four days) from Florida to the Bahamas. Several ships offer three- and four-day cruises from Piraeus to the Greek islands and Turkish Coast. In addition, there are a few short cruises running from time to time from Los Angeles and between islands in the Caribbean.

If you can spend a week, there are numerous seven-day cruises offered by the major cruise lines. Cruises to Bermuda and the Bahamas are run on a regular basis out of New York. Years ago, the Norwegian Caribbean Line (renamed Norwegian Cruise Line in 1988) pioneered the concept of regular seven-day cruises from Florida to the Caribbean, and today every major cruise line offers regular seven-day Caribbean cruises from Florida. If you prefer a seven-day cruise from a California port to ports in Mexico, you can be obliged by ships of the Carnival, Celebrity, Royal Caribbean, Princess, and other cruise lines. Several ships that offer three- and four-day cruises to the Greek islands and Turkish Coast also have seven-day itineraries. Most lines offer regular spring, summer, and early fall cruises in the Eastern and Western Mediterranean. Many of the lines offering cruises from Florida also make weekly trips from Puerto Rico to a variety of Caribbean islands. Almost all other major cruise lines offer a number of seven-day cruises from time to time in various seas of the world, but not on a regular basis. Thus, the traveler with only seven days to spend has a great variety of ships and cruise areas from which to choose.

These seven-day cruises are of three basic types. There are the barnstorming cruises that make as many as six or seven stops in seven days, giving you maximum exposure to a number of different ports for your dollar but affording little time to catch your breath. Then there are certain cruises that hit only a few ports and let you spend most of your time playing and relaxing on ship. The third type of seven-day cruise makes short trips, such as from New York to Bermuda and Nassau. These ships dock in one port several days, acting as your hotel and leaving you plenty of time to explore the island.

There are a number of cruises with eight- to thirteen-day durations, but the ten-day to fourteen-day cruise has become extremely popular because it coincides with many travelers' two-week vacations and offers plenty of time to call on a large number of ports while still leaving several relaxing days at sea. Many of the previously mentioned lines offer regular ten- or fourteen-day itineraries traversing the Panama Canal, or leaving from Florida to the Caribbean, from Los Angeles to Mexico or Alaska, as well as from various Mediterranean ports to other ports on the Mediterranean.

If you wish to cruise to the Hawaiian Islands, the South Pacific, the Far East, South America, or the Northlands, your cruise, by necessity, will be of a longer duration, unless you can arrange to fly part of the way and take only a portion of the itinerary. Ships of the Cunard, Regent Seven Seas, Silversea, Crystal, Holland America, and Seabourn lines specialize in long cruises that call on ports in several continents and sometimes circumnavigate the globe. Some of the superliners (such as the *QM2*) and the Crystal and the Holland America ships make one or more of these "longer" or around-the-world journeys each year. Princess, Regent Seven Seas, Seabourn, Silversea, Holland America, Crystal, and a number of other cruise lines feature fascinating itineraries for some of their vessels in the Far East, visiting such exotic ports of call as Bali, Singapore, Bangkok, Phuket, Vietnam, Bombay, and Hong Kong. Many of the other cruise lines have indicated they will be entering this market in the near future.

Although it is always dangerous to generalize, one can say that the majority of passengers on the longer cruises are usually over fifty-five, retired, semiretired, or of independent means, since the everyday working man seldom can afford to take so much time off for a vacation. The first-time sailors tend to gravitate toward the seven- to fourteen-day cruises that offer the larger sampling of ports. It would be difficult to make any additional generalizations. Most other categories of cruise vacationers will select cruises with durations and itineraries matching their personal tastes. However, there is often a geographical proximity between the cruiser's hometown and the ports of embarkation.

If you are contemplating a longer cruise, you may wish to avoid too small a vessel, since you will want more space to move around. Although it may be intimate and even cozy to frequent the same public rooms of a small ship on a seven- or even fourteen-day cruise, after a month or so you could be climbing the walls. The larger vessels offer more space, facilities, and public rooms, as well as a greater variety of people to meet.

In conclusion, I feel that however long your vacation, however extensive or limited your budget, wherever it is you prefer to cruise, and whatever your preference in ships, there exists a cruise vacation meeting your requirements—and a cruise vacation is one experience in life that should not be missed.

# Chapter Seven

# "Beaching It" When in Port

Since childhood, I have retained fond memories of romping about on a beautiful beach. I recall the total experience—the smell of the saltwater, the tingling of spray from the waves, the hot sand on the bottom of my feet, the warm sun on my shoulders, and the exhilaration of a cool dip. Those who share this nostalgic identity with the sea may feel that a vacation is not complete unless it includes staying at a beach resort. However, it is possible to combine "cruising" and "beaching."

Most every ship cruising the Caribbean, Mexico, and Hawaii spends the majority of days in ports where beach aficionados can dawdle away lazy hours on a variety of lovely beaches. Just pack a small bag with a beach towel, change of clothes, and suntan lotion and head out to your favorite watering hole.

Several of the major cruise lines that deploy numerous ships in the Caribbean own or lease private islands (or parts of islands), offering passengers a one-day beach party. A typical private island will have beach chairs and umbrellas, bathroom facilities, several bars, a dining area or pavilion, a straw market, a boutique, a calypso band, various land and water-sport facilities, and hiking paths. Costa Cruises' island, Serena Cay, is located in the Dominican Republic. Disney Cruises' 1,000-acre island, Castaway Cay, lies in the Abaco chain of the Bahamas. Holland America Line's 2,400-acre Half Moon Cay rests southeast of Nassau in the Bahamas. Norwegian Lines' Great Stirrup Cay sits in the Bahama-Berry Islands chain. Princess Cruises' Princess Cay is a forty-acre peninsula on the southern tip of Eleuthera in the Bahamas. MSC's Cayo Levantado is located in the Dominican Republic. Royal Caribbean International boasts two private island beaches: Labadee, a 260-acre peninsula on the northern coast of Haiti, and Coco Cay, a 140-acre island in the Bahamas.

Although there are countless beautiful virgin strands, many are unsafe for swimming and offer no facilities for changing clothes or purchasing a cold drink. Therefore, I generally prefer selecting a beach with facilities adjoining a resort hotel. Often, these are among the most beautiful on the island. The following is an alphabetical list of my favorites:

## Africa and Indian Ocean

### KENYA

Along Kenya's shoreline, there are long strands of beach with numerous hotels that stretch both to the north and south of Mombasa. In addition, there is also a good sand-dune beach on Lamu Island at Shela Village past Peponi Hotel.

### NOSE BE (MADAGASCAR)

The best beach is at the Audilava Beach Hotel, where there is also a pool, tennis court, and other facilities.

### SEYCHELLES

*Anse Source D'Argent on La Digue*

The islands of the Seychelles boast the finest beaches in the world. On Mahé, the best beaches are at Anse Royale, Anse Intendence, and Grand Anse, on Praslin at Anse Lazio and Anse Volbert, and on La Digue at Anse Source D'Argent, Grand Anse, and Petite Anse. Actually, every beach in these islands is incredible. The beaches offer the most idyllic settings and warmest water. They are incomparable.

### TANZANIA

If your ship stops at Zanzibar Island, a fifteen-minute drive from port will take you to Mawimbine Club Village, where there is a good beach for swimming in the warm Indian Ocean.

## AUSTRALIA

*Bondi Beach near Sydney Australia*

There are numerous large sandy beaches in the suburbs of Sydney, described earlier in chapter 6. All of the islands around the Great Barrier Reef boast lovely beaches for swimming, including Lizard Island and Hayman Island.

# The Caribbean and Atlantic

### ANGUILLA

The beach at Malliouhana is the best and least windy on the island. The beaches at Cap Juluca, Shoal Bay, and Sandy Island are also very picturesque and enjoyable.

*Courtesy Malliouhana Resort, Anguilla*

## ANTIGUA

You can't go wrong at any of the alleged 365 beaches. My preference is to spend the day at the beaches at St. James's Club, Dickenson Cove, or Halcyon Cove, because of the additional facilities.

## ARUBA

*Palm Beach, Aruba*

Your best bet is Palm Beach, the long stretch of white-sand beach fronting the strip of deluxe hotels that includes the Marriott, Westin, Radisson, Holiday Inn, and Hyatt. All of these hotels have swimming pools, tennis courts, and informal poolside dining. The water is usually quiet and warm and without waves or surf. The hotels are located less than ten minutes from the harbor.

For a special beach experience, visit the private tropical island with its protected white-sand beach accessible by motor launch from the lobby of the Aruba Renaissance Hotel in town. Some cruise ships offer excursions here; otherwise, arrangements have to be made at the hotel.

## BAHAMAS

**Abacos**—Here you will find miles of virgin beach on Treasure Cay or Guana Cay. These are among the most beautiful unspoiled beaches in the Caribbean.

**Grand Bahama (Freeport/Lucaya)**—The beach in front of the Holiday Inn Hotel in Lucaya is unquestionably the best on the island; however, it involves an expensive twenty- to thirty-minute taxi ride from the harbor. Most cruisers utilize the beach across from the former Xanadu Princess. The beach is crowded and the sea often too shallow for serious swimming.

**Nassau**—The best beaches are at Cable Beach and on Paradise Island. The most pristine, unspoiled strand is lined with pine trees and fronts the posh Ocean Club. To get there, cross over the toll bridge to Paradise Island, go straight to the sea, turn right, and walk about three blocks. If you turned left, you would be at a very nice beach in front of what formerly were the Paradise Island and Britannia Beach hotels and now is the Atlantis Hotel complex. All of these hotels have large pools, tennis courts, changing facilities, and informal outdoor restaurants.

*Atlantis beach on Paradise Island, Nassau*

## BARBADOS

The best beaches can be found on the Caribbean side at Sandy Lane, Glitter Bay, Royal Pavilion, and Paradise Beach Club. All of these hotels are less than an hour's ride from the harbor. The beach at Sandy Lane is one of the best in the Caribbean; however, you would have to sneak on, unless you can make prior arrangements with the hotel.

## BERMUDA

*Horseshoe Beach Bermuda*

One of my personal favorites is Horseshoe Beach, the several miles of pink-sand beach directly to the left of the Southampton Princess Hotel. Here you will find little coves, shady hills, and warm, clear water. The Southampton Princess is only a fifteen- to twenty-minute ride from the harbor.

## CARACAS (VENEZUELA)

The only beach is at the former Macuto Sheraton, now the Macuto Hotel, in La Guaira. It is not very beautiful and not worth the special trip unless you are going to the hotel for other reasons. The pool at the Macuto is much nicer than the beach.

## CARTAGENA

Your best bet is the public beach in front of the Hilton. At the Hilton, there are tennis courts, an outdoor bar, and several restaurants.

## CAYMAN ISLANDS

*Seven Mile Beach, Grand Cayman Island*

Many consider the seven-mile stretch of beach on Grand Cayman Island to be one of the most beautiful in the Caribbean. This is the favorite of scuba divers and snorkelers. A five-minute taxi ride from town will take you to the Ritz-Carlton, **Westin**, or the Hyatt Regency Grand Cayman, the largest and best hotels on the island. Go down to the beach, turn left (or right), and walk for miles on an unspoiled, white-sand beach lined with pines and palms. The Hyatt, Treasure Island, Westin, and Ritz-Carlton are the only hotels here offering a pool, tennis, a restaurant, snorkeling gear, and a large private beach area.

## CURAÇAO

There are nice beaches at the Grand Hyatt and Renaissance, Hilton, and Avila Beach hotels.

## DOMINICAN REPUBLIC

If your ship stops at Santo Domingo, the nearest beach is at Boca Chica. There are hotel pools in town in El Embajador, the Ramada, and the Sheraton. If time allows, go to the beach at Casa de Campo in La Romana. This is one of the best beaches on the island, and Casa de Campo is possibly the most complete resort in the Caribbean. Costa ships stop at their private beach at Serena Cay.

## FORTALEZA (BRAZIL)

Within seven miles of town, there are lovely beaches at Iracema, Meirelles, Mucuripe, de Futuro, and Caca e Pesca.

## GRENADA

Grand Anse Beach in front of the Grenada Beach Hotel and Spice Island Inn is convenient because it is only a short taxi ride from town and offers the most facilities. This is a long, fine, white-sand beach with warm, deep-blue waters. However, the constant stream of hawkers and peddlers that aggressively approach you with beads and spices is so annoying that it is difficult to relax. Most of the other hotels with beaches are a great deal farther away, and the taxi rides can be prohibitively expensive.

## GUADELOUPE

My favorite is the picturesque beach at the Club Med Caravelle. You will have to make advance arrangements and pay a fee to get through the gates. Sneaking onto the property also is possible if this doesn't make you uncomfortable. There are also nice beaches, pools, and tennis courts at the Frantel, La Creole Beach, and Meridien-Guadeloupe.

## JAMAICA

*Dunns River Falls, Ocho Rios*

**Ocho Rios**—If your time is limited, you may wish to settle for a beach at the foot of Dunn's Falls after climbing the most important scenic attraction in Jamaica. If you prefer a private beach, pools, tennis courts, and other amenities, you can try any of the larger hotels, such as San Souci and Ciboney. So-so beaches and pools can be found at the Renaissance Hotel, which is located near where your ship docks.

**Montego Bay**—Most cruisers end up at the public strip known as Doctor's Cave Beach or Cornwall Beach, where there is an underwater marine park. Those wishing a private beach with tennis, pools, restaurants, and other facilities should try Round Hill, Tryall, the Half Moon, or the Holiday Inn. Midway between Montego Bay and Ocho Rios, the Ritz-Carlton has the best facilities.

**Negril**—The best beaches in Jamaica are at Negril; however, it takes several hours to reach this area from Montego Bay, and this would prevent you from exploring any other part of the island.

## MARTINIQUE

The best beach is at Club Med-Buccaneer's Creek. However, this is a several-hour drive from Fort-de-France, and advance arrangements would have to be made here as in Guadeloupe. You may prefer to take a twenty-minute motor-launch ride from Fort-de-France to Pointe du Bout, where the former Meridien and Bakoua Hotels are located adjacent to each other. Both hotels offer mediocre, "partially topless" beaches, tennis courts, a swimming pool, and French-Creole restaurants.

## PUERTO RICO

The beaches in Puerto Rico contain darker sand and lack the pristine beauty of the beaches on many of the other islands. If your time is limited, the closest beach with facilities would be at the Caribe Hilton Hotel, which is only five minutes by taxi from the harbor. The beaches at the Sheraton, Ritz-Carlton, and El San Juan are also nice. The full-facility El Conquistador Hotel, a one- to one-and-a-half-hour drive from San Juan, has its own private island beach, with numerous water-sport facilities, a shop, and a restaurant.

### RECIFE (BRAZIL)

You can choose from Pina or Boa Viagem beaches in the city, with its five-mile ocean promenade lined with coconut palms, or from the more pristine beaches at Piedade, Venda Grande, Candeias, or Borra de Jangadar—all a ten- to twenty-mile drive away.

### RIO DE JANEIRO (BRAZIL)

*Copacabana Beach Rio de Janeiro with Sugar Loaf in background*

The city is lined with a long stretch of beach that is most noted for its local color. The most populated beach is Copacabana. Ipanema runs a close second. The only hotel directly on a beach is the Sheraton, which is at the juncture of Ipanema and Gavea.

### ST. BARTS

The best beaches are at Grand Cul-de-Sac and St. Jean.

### ST. LUCIA

Renuit Beach is very nice, easily accessible, and fronts several nice hotels. There is a white-sand beach at the Hilton Jalousie Plantation and another scenic beach at Anse Chastanet.

## ST. MAARTEN

The beach at La Samana is magnificent; however, you would have to make special arrangements with the hotel. Orient Beach, about a fifteen-minute ride from Philipsburg, is reminiscent of Tahiti Beach in St. Tropez, France, with topless and nude bathing and numerous small beach restaurants and boutiques.

## TOBAGO

The best beach is at Pigeon Point.

## TRINIDAD

The nearest beach is fourteen miles from the capital at Maracas Bay. There are no facilities here. You may be better off settling for the pool at the Trinidad Hilton.

## TURKS AND CAICOS

The best beach on Provo is Grace Bay Beach and on Grand Turk, Governor's Beach (though it has no facilities) and at the new port facility, with a nice beach, gigantic pool, a restaurant, and shops. There are many hotels on Grace Bay Beach.

## VIRGIN ISLANDS

**St. Croix**—There are nice beaches, tennis courts, and informal restaurants at the Carambola and the Buccaneer Beach Hotel. Buck Island would be the best choice.

**St. John**—The several horseshoe-shaped, private beaches at Caneel Bay Resort are possibly the loveliest in the Caribbean. A day in port at this resort is a must whenever possible. The tennis courts are excellent and usually empty, and the paths running through the acres of vegetation are a jogger's dream. The Westin is also exquisite; however, the beach is not as desirable as those at Caneel. Trunk Bay is the best choice for snorkelers or those seeking a public beach.

**St. Thomas**—Magen's Bay is deservingly reputed to be one of the top beaches in the world. I personally prefer spending the day at the Virgin Grand Resort and taking my dip at "nearby" Coki Beach. There is also good swimming at Marriott's Frenchman's Reef on Morningstar Beach, only a five-minute taxi ride from the harbor. The beach at the Ritz-Carlton has too many stones and pebbles.

**Tortola**—There are several fine beaches, but the best bet is Sugar Cane Bay, which is a long strand with facilities and a colorful restaurant. Snorkelers should head out to Smuggler's Cove.

**Virgin Gorda**—The Baths is an attraction with unique boulder formations that visitors can climb and explore, all adjacent to a nice strand of white-sand beach. Many cruise ships offer excursions here. Possibly one of the very best beaches in the Caribbean is at Little Dix Bay Resort; however, visitors must make arrangements with the hotel.

*The Baths at Virgin Gorda, BWI*

## Europe

Because there are not many "great beaches" in Europe, I will mention just a few that make up in local color what they lack in pristine beauty. Some of the best strands can be found on the island of Ibiza and at Hotel Formentor on the Spanish island of Majorca. Other sandy beaches include Lido Beach near Venice, the numerous beaches in Mykonos and Skiathos, Tahiti Beach in St. Tropez, the beach resorts in Kusadasi and Marmaris (Turkey), and the main beach in Tel Aviv. Some colorful beach resort areas with little sand include the beaches of Capri, Cannes, Nice, Corfu, Rhodes, Costa del Sol, and the Italian Riviera.

On the island of Calvi, there is a long strand of beach surrounded by a pine forest to the left of the main part of town. In Cannes, the best place to spend the day is at one of the various beach clubs and restaurants with beach facilities that line the sea in front of the major thoroughfare. Here you can walk in all directions to take advantage of the exotic human scenery. The beaches in Marbella are widely frequented, but you will probably prefer the pools at the various hotels.

*Tahiti Beach, San Tropez, France*

## Far East

There are a number of great beaches in the Far East. The best "resort beach" areas can be found at Phuket, Ko Samui, the various islands in the Andaman Sea, and Pataya in Thailand; Penang, Langawi, and Sabah in Malaysia; and Bali in Indonesia. Repulse Bay in Hong Kong is just so-so. The small uninhabited islets are a short boat ride from the Tanjung Aru Beach Resort in Sabah, and those in Phuket and its neighboring islands offer some of the most beautiful beaches and best swimming in the world.

*Beach at Amanpuri Resort, Phuket, Thailand*

# Mexico

## ACAPULCO

Although none of the beaches in Acapulco compare with those in the Caribbean or Cancún, the best of the lot is in front of the Princess and Pierre Marques hotels. The myriad of pools at the Princess is interesting and exciting. For local color, try Caleta Beach.

*Beach in Acapulco, Mexico*

## CABO SAN LUCAS

The best beach for swimming is in front of the Hacienda Hotel, five minutes from where you disembark from your tender. The beach fronting the Solmar and Finistera hotels is more picturesque, but too dangerous for swimming. Lover's Beach, accessible only by boat, is the most picturesque.

## CANCÚN

There are ten miles of beautiful white-sand beach stretching in front of the all of the hotels in the hotel area. Here the water is clear but the waves can be too strong for safe swimming. If your ship docks at Calica, don't miss the beaches and underground-river swimming at Xcaret.

*Beach in Cancun, Mexico*

### COZUMEL

Playa del Sol and Mr. Sanchos, about a twenty-minute drive from town, offer the best sand, swimming, and facilities.

### MANZANILLO

The beaches at Las Hadas and Grand Bay Resorts are very nice, as are the picturesque pools.

### PUERTO VALLARTA

The beaches in Puerto Vallarta, as in Acapulco, are not exceptional. The hotels with beaches closest to the harbor are the Posada Vallarta, Fiesta Americana, and the Holiday Inn. For local color go to Los Muertos.

### ZIHUATANEHO-IXTAPA

The beach that runs along the stretch of high-rise hotels in Ixtapa and the more private beach at the Camino Real are the best. In Zihuatanejo, go to Playa la Ropa.

## Middle East

Sandy beaches can be found in Herzelia, Eilat, and Tel Aviv in Israel; Kusadasi and Marmaris in Turkey; and in Cyprus; however, they are nothing to write home about. For those cruising the Greek islands, the beaches are best at Mykonos and Skiathos. The beaches at Lindos in Rhodes, Corfu, Kos, and Crete are decent.

*Beach at Tel Aviv, Israel*

# Pacific

## FIJI

The best beach on the big island of Viti Levu is found at the Fijian Resort. There are lovely, pristine beaches in the Yasawa Islands group and on Mana Island, Beachcomber Island, Plantation Island, Treasure Island, and Turtle Island. These also are among the best in the world.

*Beach in Fiji*

## HAWAII

For those cruising the Hawaiian islands, you will want to consider the following beaches:

**Oahu**—The best strand is in front of the Kahala Resort, fifteen minutes from Waikiki, and at Ihilani. The beaches in Waikiki are too crowded with tourists; however, the beach in front of the Hilton Hawaiian Village is the best of the lot.

**Maui**—The beach in Kaanapali fronting all the hotels, the beaches at Wailea, or the beach at Kapalua Bay resort are your best bets.

**Kauai**—One of my favorite beaches in the world is Lumahai Beach, where *South Pacific* was filmed. Although this involves an hour-and-a-half drive, you will be rewarded with witnessing as much as Mother Nature can provide. There are no facilities here, and swimming is dangerous in the winter months. If you do not have time to visit Lumaha, then bodysurfers will want to go to Poipu, between the Sheraton and Hyatt resorts, and nonsurfers will prefer the facilities at the beach fronting the Kauai Marriott at Kauai Lagoons. The Hyatt Regency Kauai, with its pool complex and protected beach, is your most exotic locale.

*Lunahai Beach, Kauai, Hawaii*

**Hawaii**—If your ship docks at Hilo, you will enjoy the scenic black-sand beach at Kaimu. This may be too dangerous for swimming. At Kona, the best beaches can be found at the Mauna Kea Beach, Hapuna, and Mauna Lani Hotels. Nearby at Hilton Waikoloa is one of the most extensive and imaginative pool complexes in the world.

**Lanai**—The best beach is at the Manele Bay resort.

## NEW CALEDONIA

Ile des Pins is a lovely pine-studded island with numerous chalk-white beaches ideal for swimmers, divers, and sun worshipers.

## TAHITI

**Bora Bora**—In Bora Bora, there are numerous little islets with nothing but palms, sandy beaches, and crystal clear waters sitting in a very large protected lagoon. The half-mile of crescent-shaped beach at the Hotel Bora Bora and Intercontinental Le Moana Resort on the mainland offer some good snorkeling close to the shore. Romantics may prefer the setting at Pearl Beach Resort, Four Seasons, St. Regis, Hilton, Intercontinental Thalasso, or Le Meridien Bora Bora, all of which can be reached by the resorts' private launches.

*Beach in Bora Bora*

**Moorea**—In Moorea, the best beach with water sport facilities at the Intercontinental Moorea Beachcomber

**Tahiti**—On the big island of Tahiti, your best bets are the unique sand-bottom pools and lagoons at the Intercontinental Tahiti Beachcomber Parkroyal and the Meridien. These are by far the best places to swim and sun.

# Chapter Eight

# European Riverboats, Hotel Barges, and Expedition Cruises

For those who appreciate a cruise vacation but for diversion would enjoy a more intimate, low-key experience sailing down scenic inland waterways and visiting noncoastal European cities, a riverboat or barge may be the perfect solution.

Numerous riverboat companies operate in Europe, traversing the Rhine, Main, Moselle, Elbe, Havel, Danube, Seine, Saône, Rhône, and Volga rivers, as well as waterways in Russia, Holland, China, and other countries. These companies are marketed in North America, Europe, and other countries around the world. A few are only marketed in Europe. The companies that own their own riverboats and seek to interest passengers outside of Europe include AMA Waterways, Avalon Waterways, Grand Circle Cruises, Luftner River Cruises, Sea Cloud River Cruises, Scenic Tours, Tauck River Cruising, Uniworld, Vantage Cruise Tours, and Viking River Cruises. (See full descriptions in chapter 10.)

Many of the riverboats are also promoted through package-tour operators.

Although there are many differences from one riverboat to another, typically they are long and narrow, with two or three passenger decks, plus a sundeck atop the vessel. The boats are designed to accommodate rivers with low bridges and numerous locks, the limitations of which dictate the dimensions of the vessels. During the past few years, the major riverboat companies have built more elegant vessels, many with French balconies and/or full balconies, as well as larger cabins and suites and alternative dining venues.

Historically, passenger cabins generally emulate small- to average-size cabins on cruise ships, although on nonluxury boats they tend to be a bit smaller. Recently built vessels generally provide two twin beds convertible to a double bed arrangement, whereas those boats built prior to 2000 tend to have twin beds on opposite sides of the cabin where one or both beds fold up and convert to a couch during the daytime. Most have large picture windows, wardrobes, dressers, televisions, telephones, air conditioning, and small bathrooms with a toilet, vanity, and shower. The more upscale riverboats provide hair dryers, writing desks, glassed-in shower stalls, robes, refrigerators, and private safes in the cabins, and generally offer some junior and/or full suites. As mentioned above, many of the newer boats sport French windows that open to small balconies. Some have actual outdoor balconies. Generally, the cabins on the lowest deck are the smallest and least desirable. (See descriptions of the various riverboat companies in chapter 10 for more information about each.)

Public areas on all riverboats include a large main dining room, a lounge with a bar and section for a musical entertainer, a reception area sometimes adjoining a small shop, library and/or hairdresser and a sundeck with lounge chairs. Other facilities that can be found on some (but not all) riverboats include a gym, sauna, small pool or whirlpool, additional bars and restaurants atop ship, laundry, and outdoor dining areas.

In the past, little entertainment has been offered on riverboats other than piano music in the evenings, port lectures, and local musicians, entertainers, or dance groups that are occasionally brought aboard ship while in port. This may be changing as the riverboat companies seek to attract a more diverse and younger clientele. A recent entry into the market, the four A-Rosa vessels (now a Carnival brand) provide a more active Club Med-style environment with expanded facilities and indoor and alfresco, buffet dining. However, these ships are sold largely in the German market (except when under charter to English-speaking cruise lines).

The main thrust of riverboat travel is watching the passing scenery and the shore excursion options. Itineraries on all rivers feature the major cities and villages that would be of interest to tourists. The boats visit one or more different destinations daily and offer tours to major attractions and points of interest. Most of the cruise lines do not charge for the majority of these tours.

The trend is toward offering all-inclusive cruises where the fare includes all spirits, wine, soft drinks, specialty coffees, gratuities, shore excursions, airport transfers, and pre- and/or postcruise hotel stays. Scenic Tours and Tauck have offered all-inclusive for many years. Uniworld is adopting all-inclusive in 2014, and other Riverboat lines offer a scaled-down version.

A typical itinerary on a Danube/Main Canal cruise would include such cities as Nuremberg, Regensberg, and Passau in Germany; Melk, Durnstein, and Vienna in Austria; Bratislava in Slovakia; and Budapest in Hungary. Rhine cruises generally stop at Basel, Switzerland; Strasbourg, France; Heidelberg, Rudesheim, Koblenz, and Cologne in Germany; and Amsterdam, Netherlands. Some may extend into the Moselle to visit Alken, Cochem, Zell, Bernkastler-Kues, and Trier. Cruises in France either run up the Seine from Paris to Honfleur or on the Rhône and Saône rivers between Arles or Avignon and Lyon or Beaune. Elbe River cruises often emanate from Hamburg or Berlin down to Dresden or Bad Schandau with optional excursions to Prague. Riverboats also ply the waterways between St. Petersburg and Moscow in Russia, from Budapest to the Black Sea and between Amsterdam and Brussels.

While cruising, passengers enjoy the scenic sites along the rivers such as castles, vineyards, small villages, and ancient cathedrals.

Usually breakfast is laid out buffet style with an array of Continental offerings such as salmon, herring, pâtés, cold cuts, and cheeses in addition to the more traditional eggs, breakfast meats, fruits, juices, cereals, and pastries. Lunch is often a combination of salads, cold meats, and cheeses from the buffet complemented by warm offerings from the kitchen. Multicourse dinners are common; however, on most ships there is either a fixed menu or one offering two choices for the appetizer and main course. Do not expect the variety of selections found on oceangoing cruise ships.

On-deck barbeques and Bavarian-style buffets are featured at least once during each cruise on many of the lines; and alternative dining venues are appearing on the newer vessels.

The riverboats of Viking and Victoria offer river cruises on the Yangtze. The ships are quite upscale and comfortable.

Commencing in 2012, two authentic steam-powered riverboats commenced offering cruises on the Mississippi River and its tributaries—American Cruise Line's *Mississippi Queen* and Great American Steamboat Company's *Grand American Queen*. These are quite different from the narrow riverboats that traverse the European rivers, and more akin to oceangoing cruise ships. Another similar vessel of American Cruise Line, *Queen of the West*, sails on the Columbia and Snake rivers.

All of these riverboats are covered in chapter 10.

Barges, on the other hand, traverse smaller rivers, canals, and waterways not accessible to riverboats due to the low water levels and numerous locks. They operate throughout France and Holland as well as in parts of Great Britain. European Waterways, French Country Waterways, and Orient-Express are the major companies offering either charters and/or individual accommodations on barges. There are several independent travel agencies that specialize in selling barge cruises on individually owned barges, as well as those owned by the major companies. They include Abercrombie & Kent, the Barge Connection, the Barge Lady, Barges in France, Canal Barge Cruises, and France Cruises.

In general, barges contain two- to eight-passenger cabins, each with a small private bathroom. They are not lavishly furnished but are utilitarian and provide adequate storage space for the journey. The condition of the plumbing and air conditioning can be a problem on some of the older vessels if they have not been well maintained. Public areas consist of a main, all-purpose lounge with a well-stocked complimentary bar, a dining area adjacent to the lounge, and a small outside deck for sunning, dining, enjoying a coffee or drink, or just watching the scenery.

Some barges, such as *Renaissance* of European Waterways, are quite lavish with large staterooms and bathrooms akin to a first-class hotel and beautifully decorated public areas. The barges of French Country Waterways, though not quite as lavish, are also very nice, as are those of many of the European Waterways and Orient-Express fleet. (See chapter 10.)

Barges are generally sold in six-night segments or are chartered to families or groups for other time periods. Many barges require a charter of the entire boat and will not accept individual passengers. Prices tend to be quite steep and can run from $2,000 up to $6,000 per person for a six-night sojourn.

Dining is generally superb on the vessels of the companies mentioned above. Since there are only a few passengers, a barge provides a private, yacht-like experience where the individual passengers can be catered to. The barge carries an experienced chef who prepares gourmet meals using fresh products purchased daily. When cruising in France, wines and cheeses indigenous to the region will be described and offered at each meal. Special requests are often honored and wines, soft drinks, and alcoholic beverages are included in the fare.

During the day, the barge sails slowly down picturesque waterways, allowing passengers to enjoy the passing scenery. Bicycles are provided, enabling passengers to exit the barge at a port or lock for a leisurely ride and meet their boat at its next stop. Shore excursions to vineyards, wineries, farms, castles, churches, and other points of interest are offered daily. Passengers are transported to these destinations by a minivan that accompanies the barge along its journey. Barges travel only during the daylight hours and hunker down each evening at some village. Some of the barge companies offer a dinner ashore at least once during the cruise. French Country Waterways and some of the ships of European Waterways include dining at a one-, two-, or three-star *Michelin*-rated restaurant.

There are many other barge companies that will charter small barges without a crew. The cost may be somewhat less, but this experience will be best enjoyed by those experienced in handling some other form of watercraft and who do not mind assisting in the opening and closing of locks along the way.

The foregoing descriptions may not entice those cruisers who enjoy expansive facilities, large suites, nightly entertainment, gambling, and diverse dining options. However, for seasoned cruisers who prefer a more intimate, laid-back experience with fine dining, and the opportunity to visit cities, villages, and scenic areas not available to oceangoing vessels, a riverboat or barge experience will prove most rewarding. The three major barge companies and their vessels are described in chapter 10. For definitive coverage of the barge experience, where they sail, and a description of the privately owned barges, I recommend *Stern's Guide to European Riverboats and Hotel Barges*, available in both paperback and a color e-book version.

A number of cruise lines offer adventure travel where passengers explore wildlife, jungles, polar regions, animal and bird habitats, and other off-the-beaten-path environments. Linblad Expeditions, Orion Expedition Cruises, Aqua Expeditions, Aurora Expeditions, Hurtigruten, Viking River Cruises and Victoria Cruises on the Yangtze River in China, Hapag-Lloyd Cruise Line's *Hanseatic*, Celebrity Cruise Line's *Xpedition*, Silversea Cruises' *Silver Adventure*, Captain Cook Cruises, Blue Lagoon Cruises, just to name a few, offer passengers cruises designed for exploration of the regions visited. Passengers opting for these cruises are most interested in the adventure, the lectures and cultural aspects, and are not as interested in the shipboard activities and entertainment. However, cruise ships competing for these passengers have found it necessary to offer creature comforts to stay on top of this niche market. For many of these expeditions, one must be fit and able to navigate difficult terrain. Some of these ships are more comfortable than others, and it is prudent to look into what each has to offer.

*Note*: The major riverboat, barge, and expedition cruise lines are covered in chapter 10, while ports of call along the Danube, Rhine, Rhone, Saone, and Moselle rivers are described in chapter 6. For more definitive descriptions of riverboats, barges, and their ports of call, see *Stern's Guide to European Riverboats and Hotel Barges*.

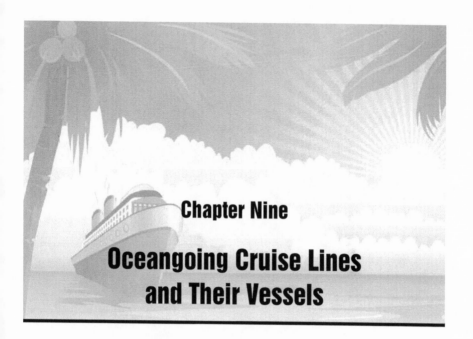

# Chapter Nine

# Oceangoing Cruise Lines and Their Vessels

In this chapter, you will find a section describing every major oceangoing cruise line, including photographs for those we were able to obtain them from, a dinner menu, and a daily program for most of the ships of each line. The synopsis at the beginning of each section lists the vessels currently sailing, their former names, the date they entered service, the date they were refurbished, the gross tonnage, the length and width, the maximum passenger capacity, the number of cabins, the nationality of officers and crew, the usual itineraries, and my overall ratings, that is, "Star Awards." (An explanation of the significance of the Star Awards is given in chapter 11.) Briefly, the ships are divided into four market categories based on the per diem prices for average cabins, the onboard costs, and the economic class of passengers the cruise line seeks to attract:

Category A    (black stars) the most expensive—Deluxe
Category B    (crisscrossed stars) the next most expensive—Premium
Category C    (diagonal stars) the middle-priced market—Standard
Category D    (white stars) the least expensive—Economy

The ships are then rated on a six-point system, six+ stars being the highest. Only oceangoing cruise ships are rated. Barges and riverboats are covered in chapter 10 but not rated in this book. (See *Stern's Guide to European Riverboats and Hotel Barges* for ratings.)

In the text of each section, you will find a brief history of the cruise line and a description of the physical makeup of each ship, including cabins, inside and outside public areas, dining, service, pricing, usual itineraries, and my opinion of the strongest points.

The intent of this chapter is to provide readers with as much information as possible in a succinct, organized fashion so as to enable them to make their own intelligent selections for their cruise vacation. For a summary of ship statistics, ratings, and current itineraries, visit www.stevensterntravel.com.

## THE CRUISE LINES AND THEIR VESSELS

Aida Cruises
American Cruise Lines
Aqua Expeditions
Azamara Club Cruises
Blount Small Ship Adventures
Carnival Cruise Lines
Celebration Cruise Line
Celebrity Cruises Inc.
Club Med Cruises
Compagnie du Ponant
Costa Cruise Lines
Crystal Cruises
Cunard Line Ltd.
Peter Deilmann Cruises
Disney Cruise Line
Fred. Olsen Cruise Line
Genting Hong Kong Ltd.
Hapag-Lloyd

Holland America Line
Hurtigruten
MSC Cruises
Norwegian Cruise Line
Oceania Cruises
P O Cruises
P O Cruises Australia
Paul Gauguin Cruises
Princess Cruises
Regent Seven Seas Cruises
ResidenSea Management Ltd.
Royal Caribbean International
Seabourn Cruise Line
Sea Cloud Cruises
SeaDream Yacht Club
Silversea Cruises Ltd.
Star Clippers Inc.
Windstar Cruises

## MISCELLANEOUS ADDITIONAL CRUISE LINES

Blue Lagoon Cruises
Captain Cook Cruises
CDF Croisieres De France
Classic International Cruises
Cruceros Australis
Hebridean Island Cruises
HNA Cruises
Ibero Cruceros
Linblad Expeditions
Louis Cruise Line
Page and Moy

Pullmantur Cruises
Quark Expeditions
Saga Cruises
Silja Line
Swan Hellenic
Thompson Cruises
TUI Cruises
Un-Cruise Adventures
Voyages to Antiquity
Voyages of Discovery

# AIDA CRUISES

**Am Strande 3d L 18055**
**Rostock, Germany**
**Tel.: +49(0) 381 444 8026**
**Fax: +49(0) 381 444 8025**
**www.aida.de**

*AIDAAura*: entered service in 2003; 42,289 GRT; 665.5 × 92.2 feet; 1,582-passenger capacity (1,266 lower berths); 633 cabins; German and international officers and crew (Category C—not rated)

*AIDABella*, *AIDADiva*, and *AIDALunaj*: entered service in 2008, 2007, and 2009, respectively; 69,203 GRT; 817 × 106 feet; 2,500-passenger capacity (2,050 lower berths); 1,025 cabins; German and international officers and crew (Category C—not rated)

*AIDABlu*: entered service in 2010; 71,100 GRT; 2,580-passenger capacity (2,192 lower berths); 1,096 cabins; German and international officers and crew (Category C—not rated)

*AIDACara* (formerly *AIDA*): entered service in 1996; 38,557 GRT; 634.2 × 90.6 feet; 1,339-passenger capacity (1,180 lower berths); 590 cabins; German and international officers and crew (Category C—not rated)

*AIDASol* and *AIDAMar*: entered service in 2011 and 2012, respectively; 71,100 GRT; 2,580-passenger capacity (2,194 lower berths); 1,097 cabins; German and international officers and crew (Category C—not rated)

*AIDAStella*: entered service in 2013; 71,304 GRT; 2,050-passenger capacity; 1,025 cabins; German and international officers and crew (Category C—not rated)

*AIDAVita*: entered service in 2002; 42,289 GRT; 665.5 × 92.2 feet; 1,582-passenger capacity (1,266 lower berths); 633 cabins; German and international officers and crew (Category C—not rated)

*Note*: The ships operate in the Mediterranean, Northern Europe, the Caribbean, Dubai, around the Canary Islands, North and South America, and Asia.

Originally owned by Deutsche Seereederei and Seetours, the company was acquired by P O/Princess Cruises in 2000. P O/Princess Cruises was then acquired by Carnival Corporation in 2003.

The cruise line describes itself as a club product especially tailored for the German-speaking market. Actually, its target groups are families and the younger German market (younger than fifty years)—possibly described as the German version of Club Med at Sea. Certainly, it is a contrast to such other German-market vessels as the *Deutschland* or *Europa*, which appeal mostly to an older, more sophisticated demographic. The trademark of the ships is the red lips and blue eyes painted on the bow. The accent is on a casual environment, many activities on board, and active shore excursions. Few passengers come from nations other than Germany, Austria, and Switzerland.

Emphasis is on self-service, and all self-service restaurants are included in the cruise fare along with soft drinks, beer, and wine served at lunch and dinner.

The original *AIDABlu*, the former *Crown Princess*, which sailed for the AIDA Cruises brand from 2005 until 2006, was transferred to Ocean Village.

*AIDACara*, the former *AIDA*, has 391 ocean-view cabins (including thirty-two with balconies, twelve junior suites, and four full suites). There are 200 inside cabins and 8 cabins that are wheelchair accessible. The smallest measures 145 square feet, and the four suites increase to 377 square feet, share a common balcony, and include a bathtub and stocked minibar. In the remaining accommodations, storage space is limited, but there are hair dryers in the living area, TVs, and a refrigerator. For dining, guests have a choice of two self-service buffet restaurants with large selections or a more intimate à la carte, reservation-only dining room. The ship features an extensive fitness, wellness, and sports program, including a large full-facility spa.

The 42,289-ton, 1,266-passenger *AIDAAura* and *AIDAVita* (1,582-passenger capacity with every berth occupied) offer 422 outside cabins and 211 inside, 4 wheelchair-accessible cabins, and 60 cabins and suites with balconies. Accommodations range in size from 145- to 344-square-foot suites. They are similar in facilities to the *AIDACara*. Similarly, there are two self-service buffet restaurants as well as a reservation-only à la carte dining room; extensive fitness, wellness, and sports programs; and spas offering many treatments. Typical of many German ships, they have a nude sunbathing deck and bicycles for shore excursions, but no casino.

The 69,203-ton, 2,050-passenger *AIDADiva* entered service in 2007, followed by its sister ship, *AIDABella*, in 2008. Of the 1,025 accommodations, 666 face the sea and 439 have balconies. There are eighteen suites. Public rooms are atop ship, and staterooms are on the lower decks. All accommodations have TVs, Internet access, safes, and hair dryers. There are seven restaurants, four of which are self-service. Diners at Rossini, Buffalo, and Sushi Bar pay an extra charge. The central common area, the Theatrium, is a combination atrium and show lounge spanning three decks. Other public areas include a disco, a spa, a gym, a two-deck-high pool with a sliding glass roof, and a relaxation area with water beds, hammocks, and a large Jacuzzi. Additional facilities include two more pools, three more Jacuzzis, a golf driving range, a volley ball court, a squash court, a climbing wall, a jogging track, and several lounges. There are dedicated play areas, facilities, and programs for children ages four to seven years and eight to thirteen years.

In 2009, 2010, 2011, 2012, and 2013, five additional 71,100-ton, 2,174-passenger ships joined the fleet. *AIDALuna* debuted in 2009, *AIDABlu* in 2010, *AIDASol* in 2011, *AIDAMar* in 2012, and *AIDAStella* in 2013. The inside staterooms on *AidaStella* have forty-two-inch wall monitor flat-panel TVs displaying views of the sea, giving the feeling of having a window. Sixty-five percent of the accommodations are outside, and most have balconies. Two 128,000-ton, 3,250-passenger ships will debut in March of 2015 and 2016.

## Strong Points

These ships are ideal for families and younger German-speaking cruisers looking for a casual atmosphere and many activities.

*Courtesy AIDA Cruises*

*Courtesy AIDA Cruises*

*Courtesy AIDA Cruises*

*Courtesy AIDA Cruises*

## AMERICAN CRUISE LINES

**741 Boston Post Road, Suite 200**
**Guilford, CT 06437**
**(800) 814-6880**
**Fax: (203) 453-0417**
**www.americancruiselines.com**

*MV American Glory:* entered service in 2002; 180 × 42 feet; four decks; 31 staterooms; 49-passenger capacity; American officers and crew; six-, seven-, ten-, and fourteen-night cruises along the East Coast of the United States from Maine to Florida (Category B/C—not rated)

*MV American Spirit:* entered service in 2005; 2,000 GRT; 225 × 45 feet; four decks; 51 staterooms; 100-passenger capacity; American officers and crew; seven-night cruises of the Puget Sound and San Juan Islands; seven—and eleven-night cruises in Southeast Alaska and Alaska's Inside Passage (Category B/C—not rated)

*MV American Star:* entered service in 2007; 2,000 GRT; 225 × 45 feet; four decks; 51 staterooms; 100-passenger capacity; American officers and crew; six-, seven-, ten-, and fourteen night cruises along the East Coast of the United States from Maine to Florida (Category B/C—not rated)

*MV Independence:* entered service in 2010; 3,000 GRT; 238 × 50 feet; 54 staterooms; 100-passenger capacity; American officers and crew; six-, seven-, ten-, and fourteen-night cruises from Maine to Florida (Category B/C—3+ stars)

*Queen of the West:* entered service in 1995 (stern wheeler), renovated in 2011; 230 × 50 feet; 65 staterooms; 120-passenger capacity; American officers and crew; seven-night cruises from Portland, Oregon, and Clarkston, Washington, on the Columbia and Snake rivers (Category B/C—not rated)

*Queen of the Mississippi:* entered service in 2012; 3,500 GRT; 260 × 53 feet; 78 staterooms; 150-passenger capacity; American officers and crew; six-, seven-, and ten-night cruises along the Mississippi River and Ohio River systems (Category B/C—not rated)

(Medical facilities: each ship has two to three wheelchair-accessible staterooms; P-0; N-0; EM-1; CM; PD; TC; PO; EPC; OX; WC; TM; LJ)

American Cruise Lines was founded in 1974. In the years since its inception, the company has operated several vessels, including the original *MV Eagle, MV*

*Independence, MV America, MV Charleston, MV New Orleans,* and *MV Savannah.* Today, it operates five later-date vessels: introducing a new *MV Independence* in 2010 as well as *Queen of the West,* which it acquired the same year. In 2012, the *Queen of the Mississippi* commenced operations for the cruise line.

Each vessel is specifically designed to allow travel in unique rivers, inland waterways, secluded coves, and hidden harbors where larger vessels cannot go. Itineraries include six-, seven-, ten-, and fourteen-night cruises emanating from Providence, Rhode Island; New York, New York; Baltimore, Maryland; Bangor, Maine; Charleston, South Carolina; Jacksonville, St. Augustine, and Sanford, Florida; Portland, Oregon; Clarkston, Washington; New Orleans, Louisiana; Memphis and Nashville, Tennessee; St. Louis, Missouri; St. Paul, Minnesota; Cincinnati, Ohio; Seattle, Washington; and Juneau, Alaska. Prices on a seven-night cruise range from $3,750 per person (double occupancy) to $6,385 for suites with balconies. Single cabins start at $4,540. Early-booking discounts are available.

All staterooms on these ships face outside with large opening windows or balconies (sliding glass doors to balconies offered on *Queen of the Mississippi*). Fourteen on the *Glory,* twenty-five on the *Spirit,* twenty-six on the *Star,* forty on the *Independence,* forty-five on the *Queen of the West,* and sixty-five on the *Queen of the Mississippi* have private balconies.

Most of the staterooms on the *Independence* measure 265 square feet, and the suites measure 315 square feet. Forty accommodations have relatively large private balconies, and all include twin- or king-size beds, private bathroom facilities, hair dryers, satellite TVs, DVD players, and private climate control. Gourmet coffee brewers are available on *Queen of the Mississippi.* There are no telephones (except on *Queen of the Mississippi*), private safes, refrigerators, robes, slippers, or headboards on the beds. All accommodations in every category are quite large (200-300+ square feet) with abundant drawer and closet space and a simple yet elegant décor.

Public areas include a sundeck atop ship with lounge chairs and tables, various exercise equipment, and a putting green; a three-meals-a-day, single-seating dining room with panoramic views; an elevator servicing all decks; one main lounge, the venue for lectures, cocktail hour, and nightly entertainment; various smaller lounges, including a library, computers and Internet access, literature, and board games. There is no sundry shop, no spa facilities, no information desk, and no physician or nurse.

The dress aboard is resort casual. Special features include complimentary cocktails and hors d'oeuvres before dinner, complimentary wines with lunch and dinner, complimentary coffees, espresso, and snacks throughout the day and onboard lecturers by historians and naturalists. Room service is available on *Queen of the Mississippi.* There are no phones (except on *Queen of the Mississippi*); however, cell phones will work throughout the ship while cruising as well as in port or ashore. Cabin service is available only in the morning. Several nights each cruise, musical entertainment is brought aboard. The emphasis on these ships is the daily excursions covering the history, culture and points of interest for the ports visited.

The demographics of the passengers tend to be sixty-five years in age or older, and often retired. The average age of the service staff is in the early twenties.

*Queen of the West* is an authentic stern-wheeled overnight passenger vessel. She was originally owned by the now defunct American West Steamboat Co. After the acquisition, the number of staterooms and passengers was reduced and twenty new balconies were added (for a total of forty-five). The dining room, cuisine, and service were upgraded to coincide with the high standard of the other American Cruise Lines vessels.

*Queen of the Mississippi* is also an authentic stern-wheeled overnight passenger vessel. Staterooms on the *Queen of the Mississippi* measure from 244 to 480 square feet and include sixty twin staterooms, six twin suites, and twelve single staterooms. Sixty-five of these have balconies, and all include large opening picture windows, twin- or king-sized beds, private bathrooms with vanity and hair dryers, flat-screen satellite TVs, high-speed Internet access, and oversized closets. The ship's six lounges include an Internet lounge, a cardroom, a sky lounge, a fully stocked library, a paddlewheel lounge, and a chart room. In addition, there is a room for shows and productions, a grand dining salon, an upper deck with a recreational area and a calliope, a putting green, and an exercise area.

## Strong Points

Intimate small ships with a homogenous older clientele providing an opportunity to explore cities, villages, and waterways along the East Coast of the United States, the Mississippi River and its tributaries, the Colorado and Snake rivers, and the inland waterways of Alaska. *Queen of the West* and *Queen of the Mississippi* are currently two of three authentic stern-wheeled steamboats offering passengers cruise vacations.

*Balcony stateroom on Queen of Mississippi, courtesy American Cruise Line*

*Queen of Mississippi, courtesy American Cruise Line*

*Paddle Wheel Lounge on Queen of Mississippi, courtesy American Cruise Line*

*Lounge on Independence, courtesy American Cruise Line*

*Indendence, courtesy American Cruise Line*

Dining onboard the *Queen of the Mississippi* will be an experience unto itself. You can expect the best classic American cuisine from savory soups, to delicate seafood and choice cut meats, all prepared to perfection and using only the freshest ingredients.

## QUEEN OF THE MISSISSIPPI
### Sample Dinner Menu

*First Course*

Bayou Style Seafood Gumbo
Creole Spiced Gulf Shrimp Cocktail
Marinated Black Eyed Pea Salad &
Zesty Remoulade

Warm Baby Spinach Salad
Ripe Cherry Tomatoes,
Roasted Cippolini Onions,
Blue Cheese Crumbles,
& Warm Bacon Vinaigrette

*Entrée*

Pecan Crusted Grouper Filet
Hominy Grits, Smothered Creole Vegetables,
& Lemon Herb Butter

Dixie Lager Braised Chicken
Crisp Andouille Sausage
& Slow Cooked Red Beans & Rice

Pan Seared Beef Tenderloin
Herb Crusted Baby Potatoes, Stewed Okra,
& Red Wine Reduction Sauce

*Dessert*

Bananas Foster Crème Brulee
Praline Scented Whipped Cream

Peach Melba
Candied Peach Slices, Vanilla Ice Cream,
Raspberry Sauce, & Chopped
Toasted Almonds

Bourbon Pecan Pie
Rich Caramel Sauce

Assorted Ice Creams
Chocolate, Vanilla,
Sugar Free Vanilla, Strawberry

AMERICAN
CRUISE LINES

*Dinner Menu for Queen of the Mississippi*

## Welcome Aboard—Queen of the Mississippi

**10:00 A.M.**      Warm cookies will be served in the Magnolia Lounge as Beale Street Stutters perform

**12:00 P.M.**      Join us for a Safety briefing in the Magnolia Lounge

**12:30 P.M.**      Welcome Aboard Luncheon service in the Dining Salon located on the First Deck

**2:30 P.M.**      Join us in the Magnolia Lounge for a tour briefing & introduction to your onboard guest speakers *Bill Wiemuth & Laura Sable*

**3:30 P.M.**      Join *Bill Wiemuth* in the Magnolia Lounge for an introduction to the week

**5:30 P.M.**      Cocktails and hors d'oeuvres will be served in the Magnolia Lounge.

**6:30-7:30 P.M.**      Open seating for dinner service in the Dining Salon


## Port day (Savannah)—Independence

**6:30 A.M.**      Early Risers' coffee, tea, juice, and muffins in the Chesapeake Lounge

**7:30-9:00 A.M.**      Breakfast service in the Dining Salon

**9:15 A.M.**      Join us for a narrated trolley tour of Savannah, GA with a stop made at the Juliet Gordon Low Birthplace

**10:00 A.M.**      Warm cookies will be served in the Chesapeake Lounge

**12:30 P.M.**      Luncheon service in the Dining Salon

**1:30P.M.**      Join us for a tour to the Mighty Eighth Air Force Museum dedicated to the Air Force during WWII

**2:00 P.M.**      Join Rachel Perkins for a walking tour of historic Savannah. The walk will cover approximately 2 miles

**5:30 P.M.**      Cocktails and hors d'oeuvres will be served in the Chesapeake Lounge

**6:30-7:30 P.M.**      Open seating for dinner service in the Dining Salon

*Daily Program Mississippi Queen, courtesy American Cruise Line*

# AQUA EXPEDITIONS

**Operational Headquarters:**
**Calle Iquitos 1167**
**Punchana**
**Maynas**
**Loreto, Perú**
**Tel: (51 65) 60 1053**
**Fax: (51 65) 25 5082**
**Sales & Marketing:**
**Tel: (51 1) 434 5544**
**Fax: (51 1) 434 1364**
**Toll free number: 1 (866) 603 3687 (US & Canada)**

MV *AQUA*: entered service in 2008; 130 × 24 feet; twenty-four-passenger capacity; twelve staterooms; three- and four- and seven-night cruises from Iquitos, Peru

MV *ARIA*: entered service in 2011; 147 × 29.5 feet: thirty-two-passenger capacity; sixteen staterooms

(These ships have not been rated.)

Aqua Expeditions is a Peru luxury tour operator and the first adventure travel company to introduce five-star luxury cruises on the Amazon River in Peru.

All twelve staterooms on the *Aqua* and sixteen on the *Aria* face outside are located on two decks, have large panoramic windows, are air-conditioned, have with twin beds that can be converted to a king, and a sitting area. On the *Aqua*, four master suites measure 240 square feet and eight measure 230 square feet. Four suites interconnect for families. On the *Aria*, all sixteen suites measure 250 square feet and four interconnect.

Common areas on both vessels include an indoor bar-lounge, a dining room, an outside lounge, a boutique and an outside, partially protected observations deck above the two passenger decks. On the *Aria* there is also an outdoor Jacuzzi and an exercise room.

The vessels sail on the Amazon, Maranon, Puinahua, Ucayali, Choroyacu, Pacaya, and Tacsha rivers. Activities include Piranha fishing, dolphin watching, birds and monkey expeditions, jungle walks to meet the natives, rain forest walks, fishing trips, and visits to Pacaya Samiria Reserve, Puerto Miguel Village and a visit to Manatee RescueCenter.

Included in the fare are all meals, all excursions, nonalcoholic beverages, wine and beer, and Pacaya Samiria entrance fees. Three nights per person (double occupancy) rates range from $2,685 to $2,985; four nights, from $3,580 to $3,980; and seven nights, from $6,265 to $6,965.

*Aria, courtesy Aqua Expedtions*

*Cabin on Aria, courtesy Aqua Expeditions*

# SATURDAY

## DINNER

## TASTING MENU

### APPETIZER

Fresh hearts of palm tofu with armored catfish caviar
Tiger catfish tiradito with cashew fruit-lime juice

### MAIN COURSE

Fresh water shrimp warm salad with poached egg and wild greens
Pork tenderloin with sapote fruit and local pumpkin

### DESSERT

Granite: Mandarin
Deep fried yucas with spiced syrup and aguaje ice cream

### PETTIT FOURS

Charapita chili pepper marshmallows

*Dinner Menu, courtesy Aqua Expeditions*

 AQUA

# DAILY PROGRAM

**(courtesy, Aqua Expeditions)**

**Day 3:**     **Sunday**

**UCAYALI/YANALLPA/DORADO RIVERS/PACAYA SAMIRIA NATIONAL RESERVE**

7:00 a.m.     Breakfast

8:30 a.m.     Visit to the seasonally-flooded forests of Yanallpa

This morning you will explore with our guides the Yanallpa Stream looking for wildlife such as the bald uakari monkey, squirrel monkeys, saddleback tamarin monkeys, sloths and many other species. We will observe the trees which grow in these seasonally-flooded areas and our guides will explain the natural mechanisms through which the vegetation withstands the water during these months.

11:30 a.m.     Return to the M/V Aria

12:30 p.m.     Lunch, followed by a siesta

4:00 p.m.     Excursion to watch Monkeys and Dolphins

On this trip, you will be able to appreciate the different types of freshwater dolphin, including the rare pink dolphins found along the Ucayali River. We recommend that you bring your binoculars as there will also be opportunities to observe some species of birds, among which the macaws stand out, as well as a spectacular sundown. Depending on how the evening progresses, you will be able to watch nocturnal wildlife on the Dorado River, especially the caimans. Sometimes, our guides attempt to capture some of these ancient reptiles and you will have the opportunity to take photos.

7:30 p.m.     Return to the M/V Aria

8:30 p.m.     Dinner

# AZAMARA CLUB CRUISES

**1050 Caribbean Way
Miami, FL 33132
(877) 222-2526
www.azamaraclubcruises.com**

*Azamara Journey* and *Azamara Quest* (formerly *R-6* and *R-7* of Renaissance Cruises): entered service in 2000; renovated in 2007; 30,277 GRT; 592 × 84 feet; 694-passenger capacity (double occupancy); 347 staterooms; international officers and crew; ships sail to Asia, Mediterranean and Black Sea, Western and Northern Europe, West Indies, Panama Canal, and Central America, Sea of Cortés, and Californian Coast (Category A/B—six stars)

(Medical Facilities: C-0; P-1, CLS, MS; N-1; CM; PD; BC; EKG; OX; TC; PO; EPC; WC; ICU; X; CP; TM)

These ships are rated in eleven separate categories in the second half of chapter 14.

In 2007, Celebrity Cruises acquired two former Renaissance Cruise Lines ships from Pullmantur. Originally, the ships were named *Celebrity Journey* and *Celebrity Quest*, and they were to be operated under the Celebrity Xpeditions brand, specializing in cruises to less frequented cruise destinations. In 2007, however, the cruise line decided to establish the new Azamara brand and rename the ships *Azamara Journey* and *Azamara Quest*. Under the stewardship of CEO Larry Pimentel (former CEO of Cunard, Seabourn, and SeaDream Yacht Club) since 2009, these two ships offer up-market travelers more amenities, longer visits and more overnights in port to provide guests the opportunity for night touring on exotic itineraries, and a higher degree of pampering in a smaller, more intimate environment. In April 2010, the cruise line was renamed Azamara Club Cruises.

In November 2012, the *Azamara Quest* underwent refurbishments while in dry dock, as did the *Azamara Journey* in January, 2013. Highlights of the refurbishments include new dark-blue-painted hulls; resurfaced pool with new sun loungers and pool towels; captains' quarters were refurbished to allow for small intimate cocktail gatherings; new mattresses in all suites and staterooms; newly refurbished balconies with upgraded furniture; new caviar and champagne bar in Aqualina; new Chef's Table concept with three wine degustation menus—Italian, French and Californian; new contemporary color palette in Mosaic Café, Discoveries Restaurant and Lounge; new furniture and an expanded and new bar area in the Casino Bar; upgraded steam room and showers; and new state-of-the-art Life Fitness cardio equipment.

There are seventeen categories of accommodations on the Azamara vessels, including 6 Club Owner suites at 560 square feet plus 233 sq. ft. veranda, 4 Club Ocean suites at 440 to 501 square feet plus 233 sq. ft. veranda, 32 Club Continent suites at 266 square feet plus 60 sq. ft. veranda, 10 Club Deluxe veranda staterooms at 175 square feet plus 46 to 64 sq. ft. veranda, 189 Club Veranda staterooms at 175 square feet with 40 sq. ft. veranda, 88 Club Ocean-View staterooms at 143 to 170 square feet, and 26 Club Interior staterooms at 158 square feet. Six accommodations are accessible staterooms and can accommodate the physically challenged.

All accommodations offer European bedding with Egyptian cotton bed linen with duvet, terry bathrobes and slippers, twenty-four-hour room service, welcome fruit basket at embarkation, fresh-cut flowers, a tote bag, complimentary use of umbrellas and binoculars, complimentary shoe-shine service, a daily news bulletin, twin beds convertible to queen size, plasma flat-screen TVs, refrigerators with minibars with select beverages, in-room safes, hand-held hair dryers, and in-room movies through pay-per-view.

Club suites also include English butler service, priority check-in and departure, complimentary garment pressing for two items, welcome sparkling wine, in-suite afternoon tea service and in-suite dining from restaurant menus, priority tender service in anchor ports, complimentary seating throughout the voyage in specialty-dining restaurants, and one bottle each of vodka, rum and Scotch whiskey.

Dining options include an open-seating with a menu of Continental favorites; Windows' Café, which offers a buffet-style breakfast and lunch with casual dining at dinner; Prime C specialty steak house restaurant; Aqualina restaurant, which features a gourmet menu with Mediterranean overtones; Mosaic Café, surrounded by tables overlooking the lobby atrium, serving specialty coffees, pastries, wine, champagne, martinis, snacks, and other beverages; the pool grill; and twenty-four-hour room service. There are no formal nights, and resort-casual wear is acceptable in all restaurants. A house selection of complimentary boutique wines from around the world and international beers and spirits is served with lunch and dinner in all restaurants, as well as in bars and lounges when open. There is a charge of $25 per person in Prime C and Aqualina restaurants for nonsuite passengers.

Other public areas include a show lounge offering nightly cabaret and production shows, several additional bars and lounges with musical entertainment, a supervised Internet café, a casino, a photo shop, boutiques offering expensive and faux jewelry, souvenir and sundry items, a spa, a well-equipped gym, Pilates, spinning, and body sculpting classes, a comfortable outdoor pool/lido area, guest relations and excursion desks, and a medical facility. There are no formal children's programs or youth staff. A no-smoking policy prevails throughout the ship, except in one designated area. The ships offer a good variety of talented entertainers.

In 2014, the ships will visit 240 ports in sixty-six countries and feature overnights and late-evening stays on every voyage to allow guests to have more time to explore the ports. Guests also enjoy an authentic, exclusive, and AzAmazing Evenings event on every voyage, an inclusive night touring event that cannot be bought off the shelf from any operator and showcases the true and sometimes unexpected colors and flavors of a destination. Gratuities for housekeeping, dining, and bar staff are included in the cruise fare. Also included are specialty coffees, teas, sodas, and bottled water throughout the ship, self-service laundry, and shuttle bus service in port when offered.

## Strong Points

An intimate cruise experience with key focus on destination immersion, meaning longer stays, and more overnights in ports than any other cruise line, allowing guests to experience the destinations by day and night. The ships are smaller and can visit destinations larger ships cannot reach. The ships offer courteous and caring service as well as a variety of entertainments, fine-dining options, and attentive service throughout the ship.

*Prime Steakhouse, Azamara Journey, courtesy Azamara Cruises*

*Azamara Quest, courtesy Azamara Cruises*

*Bar and Lounge Azamara Quest. courtesy Azamara Cruises*

*Balcony Stateroom, courtesy Azamara Cruises*

# Azamara Dinner Menu

## Classic Dinner Favorites

Azamara Fruitini

Cold-Poached Shrimp with Traditional Cocktail Sauce

Chicken Consommé with Chives and Sherry

Caesar Salad with Parmesan Flakes and Garlic Croutons

Available with Grilled Chicken or Shrimp

Sautéed Filet of Salmon with Herb Butter and Provençal-Grilled Vegetables*

Lemon-Marinated Grilled Chicken Breast

Broiled New York Strip Steak with Café de Paris Butter or Sauce Béarnaise

Steamed Vegetables, Creamed Spinach, Baked Potato or Rice Pilaf *

Selection of International Cheeses with Artisan Breads, Fruits and Crackers

Tahitian Vanilla Crème Brûlée

New York Cheese Cake

Selection of Ice Creams, Sherbets and Low-Fat Frozen Yogurts

Choice of Chocolate Fudge Sauce, Vanilla Sauce, Butterscotch Sauce

Raspberry Sauce, Chantilly Whipped Cream

## Azamara Cellars

Our Sommeliers have selected the following wines by the bottle to complement tonight's menu:

*White*: Albarino, Paco & Lola, Rias Baxias, Spain $52

A fun wine loaded with fruit and floral notes. Great aromatics which makes it a perfect match for our Grilled Lemon and Herb-Flavored Grouper

*White*: Greco Di Tufo, Campania, Italy $38

A clean refreshing wine accompanied best with food. An almond like quality and some background notes of pears. Although historically a sweet wine now served quite dry and a great paring with our Healthy Choice Rare Seared Yellow fin Tuna.

*Red*: Pinot Noir, Benton Lane Estates, Willamette Valley $68
Tastes like strawberries, raspberries, cherries and plums. With age, it develops
mushroom and earthy characters. It's the wine that can blend to any meal so it's the
perfect choice

for our Surf & Turf.

*Red*: Chianti Classico, Tenuta Nozzole Riserva, Italy  $40
Rich & spicy, this remarkable wine is primarily
Sangiovese with a high acid content begging for red meat and rich pasta. Try it with
our Sautéed Duck Breast with Orange-Flavored Honey and Pink Pepper

## Boutique Wines:
Please ask your wait staff for the featured wines of the day

## Appetizers

Baked Brie with Pinot Noir-Poached Pear and Hot Plum Jam (v)

Fresh Lime-Scented Prawns and Avocado with Thousand Island Dressing

Thai-Inspired Beef Tenderloin Salad, Belgian Endive, Watercress,
Cilantro & Lime Dressing*

## Soups and Salads

Pacific Oyster and Spinach Soup with Coconut Milk

French Cream of Celery with Crispy Bacon Bits

Gazpacho with Sour Cream Quenelle and Fried Basil (v)

Witlof, Escarole, Red Oak, Green Asparagus and Spanish Onions (v)

Dressings of the Day:
Ranch, Italian, Shallot Vinaigrette
Always Available: Traditional and Fat-Free Dressings

# Salad Entrée

Tomato and Blue Cheese Salad with Red Onion and Chives (v)

# Special Pasta Entrée

Fried Pork Dumplings on Baby Bok Choy, Sweet & Sour Glaze

# Healthy Choice

Rare Seared Yellowfin Tuna, Stir-Fried Scallion and Ginger Jasmine Rice,
Edamame and Shoyu Glaze*

# Main Courses

Grilled Lemon and Herb-Flavored Grouper, Haricots Verts, Baked Zucchini,
Gratinated Eggplant with Sauce Provençale

Pan-Seared Chicken Breast stuffed with Ricotta and Leek,
Parmesan Crusted Potatoes and Green Beans

Sautéed Duck Breast with Orange-Flavored Honey and Pink Pepper,
Braised Carrots, Potato Blinis

Surf and Turf
Grilled Filet Mignon and Half Lobster Tail, Potatoes Boulangères,
Green Asparagus, Basil & Lemon Hollandaise*

Marinated, Grilled and Baked Eggplant with Yellow Squash,
Crouton and Onion-Stuffed Tomato Provençale (v)

Vegetarian Selection-(v)

* Consuming raw or undercooked meats, seafood, shellfish, eggs, milk,
or poultry may increase your risk of food borne illness,
especially if you have certain medical conditions.

*Dinner Menu, main dining room, courrtesy Azamara Club Cruises*

# Tips of the Day

## Astral Spa

Sign up today for your Thalassotherapy Pool and open deck cruise pass, and have access from 8:00am to 8:00pm daily.

## Photo Gallery

**Digital Cameras Onboard**
The latest Digital Cameras & accessories are available onboard at Tax & Duty Free prices from the Photo Gallery on Deck 5.

## Journey Shop

Toothpaste, Sundries and your every day basic essentials are available in the Journey Shop.

## Connoisseur Dinner

On the 18th & 23rd October, we'll be offering a special Connoisseur Dinner, where great wines are expertly paired with outstanding cuisine. Please sign up at the Guest Relations Desk, cover charge $70.00 per person.

## Interactive Television
Azamara Journey's Interactive Television System (I-TV) gives you access to a wealth of information and services, in the comfort of your own stateroom.
Through I-TV, you have access to many features, including:

- Pay-Per-View Movies
- Ordering Food & Wine from Room Service
- Free Videos
- Reviewing your KeyCard Account
- Booking Azamara Shore Excursions

## Climate Control
Your stateroom, like the rest of the ship, is fully air-conditioned. The temperature can be controlled by an individual thermostat. We kindly ask that you refrain from leaving veranda doors open, as this reduces air conditioning efficiency and causes excess humidity. It will also help prevent flies and other insects from entering the ship while we are in port.

## Complimentary Shuttle Service (where applicable)
Please note that shuttle buses are operated on a first come, first served basis. Scheduled timelines are guidelines only, and departure times may change depending on unforeseen delays such as traffic, and if the shuttle buses are filled to capacity. As this is a locally operated shuttle bus service, Azamara Club Cruises is not responsible for any change or delay to the shuttle schedule. Taxis are an alternative form of transportation, but no refund is due for non-use of the complimentary shuttle bus service.

## KeyCard
In addition to functioning as your boarding pass and stateroom key, your KeyCard can also be used throughout the ship for any purchases or services you may desire. In case of Emergency while in port, call collect 01-305-982-2700. At the end of the cruise you will receive an itemized account statement that can be settled in cash or travelers checks. Accepted credit cards are: MasterCard, Visa, Discover Card and American Express.

## Le Club Voyage
We would like to extend a warm welcome to all Azamara repeat guests, whether you have sailed with us on the Journey or our sister ship the Quest. As loyal returning guests, you are eligible for all the benefits of our Loyalty Program: Le Club Voyage. If you are already a Captain's Club member, after this cruise you will be automatically enrolled in Le Club Voyage. In the near future you will receive your membership number. If you are not a member yet, you are earnestly encouraged and invited to enroll in this program, details of which may be obtained from our Le Club Voyage Hostess, Dina, in the Reception Lobby, Deck 4. All eligible guests for these benefits (including Classic, Select & Elite Captain's Club members & Platinum, Emerald, Diamond, Diamond Plus & Pinnacle Club Crown & Anchor Society members) should have their tier level identified on their Azamara KeyCard. If, for any reason, this is missing from your KeyCard, then please see Dina during desk hours or leave a message at the Guest Relations Desk.

## Needle & Medical Waste Disposal
Please do not dispose of medical waste, new or used needles or syringes in your stateroom trash container. Contact your Stateroom Attendant or the Medical Center for an appropriate (Sharps) disposal container and further instructions.

## Public Health Advisory
Guests are strongly encouraged to frequently wash their hands thoroughly with soap and hot water after using the restroom and before eating or handling food. Medical experts say this is one of the best ways to prevent illnesses from starting or spreading.

## Safety First
Emergency instructions are posted on the inside of your stateroom door. Please read these instructions carefully and familiarize yourself with them. All guests are requested to please make sure you have the proper amount of life jackets (one per adult) in your stateroom; the life-jackets are located in your closet. Please ask your Stateroom Attendant for children/infant life-jackets, or additional adult life-jackets if necessary. Please note: life-jackets are not to be removed from staterooms except in the event of an real emergency.

## Ship's Dress Codes
Appropriate attire on Azamara is always resort casual. While there are no formal nights, guests are welcome to wear formal attire if they desire. Please note: No bare feet, tank tops, ball caps, bathing suits, shorts or jeans are allowed in Discoveries dining room, Aqualina or Prime C. Although the proximity of Windows Café to the pool is close, guests are asked to cover up and wear shirts & footwear at all times in Windows Café.

## Smoking Area
Azamara Journey has one designated smoking area. The area is located on the starboard section of the Pool Deck. The smoking area has a sign indicating that smoking is permitted there. All other areas of the ship are non-smoking.

11:30am  Welcome Aboard Azamara Journey.
We invite you to enjoy the public areas until your stateroom is prepared. An announcement will be made throughout the ship informing all guests when your staterooms are available for occupancy (Approximately 2:00pm).

11:30am  Azamara Journey Safety Video ..................... TV Channel 17

11:30am  Welcome Onboard Luncheon is served
(until 3:00pm) ............................................. Windows Café, 9

1:00pm  Meet the Fitness Instructor, Chris & the Spa Team for a full tour of our facilities (until 4:00pm).... Fitness Center, 9

3:15pm  All guests onboard the Azamara Journey.

3:15pm  Emergency Lifeboat Drill for all Guests and Crew.
(This drill is mandatory).

3:45pm  Bingo Suite Preview: meet at ....... Guest Relations Lobby, 4

4:00pm  Azamara Journey sails for Haifa, Israel

4:00pm  Ship Tour: We invite you to explore the Journey
(Public areas only) ............................. Mosaic Café, 5

4:00pm  Suite Upgrade Bingo Cards go on sale .................. Cabaret, 5

4:30pm  Suite Upgrade Bingo Game Begins ...................... Cabaret, 5

5:00pm  Cruise Critic Social ........................... Looking Glass, 10

5:30pm  Champagne Cocktail Tasting (until 8:30pm)
(fee applies) .................................... Looking Glass, 10

5:30pm  Spa Raffle (Treatments to be won) ........... Fitness Center, 9

5:30pm  Welcome Aboard Dinner Buffet
with Seafood Live Station ......................... Windows Café, 9

5:45pm  Wellness Seminar:
Eat More to Weigh Less ............................... Astral Spa, 9

6:00pm  Destination Enrichment with Warren Wiltsie
Topic: Masada, the Last Fortress ......................... Cabaret, 5

6:30pm  Free Gaming Lessons ............................... Casino Luxe, 5

7:30pm  Martini Melodies with Virtuosic Harpist,
Jacqueline Dolan ........................... Discoveries Lounge, 5

9:30pm  Azamara Proudly Presents: Bon Voyage Introductions
& Cruise Director's Welcome Aboard.
A Sneak Preview of Entertainment to Come! .... Cabaret, 5

9:45pm  Azamara Proudly Presents: "Play Stop & Rewind"
with our Journey Singers & Dancers ................... Cabaret, 5

10:30pm  Jet Laggers Dance Party with Great Escape Duo,
DJ Marcio ................................... Looking Glass, 10

10:30pm  Welcome Aboard with Cabaret Entertainer,
Paulo De Sousa ........................... Mosaic @ Night, 5

10:45pm  Texas Hold'em Cash Game ........................... Casino Luxe, 5

11:00pm  Paradise Lotto Draw ........................... Casino Luxe, 5

*Daily Program, courtesy Azamara Cruises*

---

Astral Spa, 9 .................................. 11:00am –10:00pm
Dial ext. 2800 to book your appointment
  Acupuncture, 9 ............................ 11:00am –10:00pm
  Beauty Shop, 9 ............................ 11:00am –10:00pm
  Thalassotherapy Pool, 9 ...................... 11:00am – 9:00pm
  Fitness Center, 9 ............................ 11:00am –11:00pm

Concierge Desk, 4 ............................ 4:00pm – 8:00pm

Casino Luxe, 5
  Slot Machines ............................ 4:30pm – Late
  Tables ............................ 4:30pm – Late
  (Guests 18 years & above are welcome in the Casino.)

eConnections Computer Center, 9 ............................ 24 hours
  IT Assistant ............. 2:00pm – 5:00pm & 6:00pm – 8:00pm

Guest Relations Desk, 4 ............................ 24 hours

Laundry (Self Service, opposite stateroom # 7076) Deck 7
  ............................ 1:00pm – 10:00pm

Le Club Voyage Hostess & Cruise Sales Manager, 4
  ............................ 2:00pm - 5:00pm

Library (The Drawing Room), 10 ............................ 24 Hours

Medical Center, 4 ............................ 6:00pm – 7:00pm

Photo Gallery, 5 in the Casino.. 7:00pm – 8:00pm & 9:00pm – 11:00pm

Shore Excursions Desk, 4 ............................ 1:00pm – 7:00pm
  (Closed during the Guest Lifeboat Drill)

The Journey Shop, 5 Upper Hall .................... 4:00pm - 11:00pm
  La Boutique, Deck 4 ........................... 4:00pm - 11:00pm
  Indulgences, 5 Upper Hall ........................ 4:00pm - 11:00pm

# BLOUNT SMALL SHIP ADVENTURES

461 Water Street
PO Box 368
Warren, RI 02885
(800) 556-7450
Fax: (401) 247-2350
www.blountsmallshipadventures.com

*Grande Caribe*: entered service in 1997, refurbished in 2009; 98 GRT; 184 × 40 feet; 96-passenger capacity; forty-four cabins; American officers and crew; cruises through Chesapeake Bay, Erie Canal, Saguenay River, Gulf Coast, Intracoastal Waterway, Maine, New England Islands, Great Lakes, Mississippi River, Canada, and Central and South America (Category C/D—not rated)

*Grande Mariner*: entered service in 1998, refurbished in 2010; 98 GRT; 184 × 40 feet; 96-passenger capacity; forty-four cabins; American officers and crew; cruises to Chesapeake Bay, Erie Canal, Saguenay River, Gulf Coast, Intracoastal Waterway, Maine, New England Islands, Great Lakes, Mississippi River, Canada, and Central and South America (Category C/D—not rated)

(Medical facilities: There are no health care or handicap facilities aboard these vessels. There are stair lifts.)

Luther H. Blount, the owner and designer of the ships of Blount Small Ship Adventures, founded the cruise line in 1966. It is now managed by his daughter, the president of the line, Nancy Blount. These uniquely designed smaller ships specialize in destination cruises to out-of-the-way ports of call that larger vessels cannot navigate through. Cruise itineraries include Central and South America, the Caribbean, New England, the Great Lakes, Erie Canal, Mississippi River, Chesapeake Bay, U.S. Intracoastal Waterway, and Canadian east coast rivers and canals.

Public areas include one dining room that accommodates all passengers in a single seating and one lounge used for receptions and lectures. Historical and cultural programs are conducted by naturalists, historians, scientists, and local guides. Some staterooms have upper and lower berths, whereas others have two lower berths and some can be made into a double bed. All have small private facilities and limited storage.

*Grande Caribe* and *Grand Mariner* were refitted in 2009 and 2010 with a nautical theme and updated lounges and dining areas. Some cabins now have a separate shower. The *Grande Mariner* was similarly retrofitted in 2010.

The line advertises itself as "the original small ship cruise line . . . no-frills, informal, unpretentious, casual and friendly . . . with an emphasis on the destination, not the ship . . . no room service, no glitz and 'bring-your-own-bottle bar policy' . . . we offer unpretentious adventure for the mature, experienced traveler. Our ships go where the others cannot and are designed to allow access to canals or deserted beaches." Prices start at $340 per person per night, with most itineraries ranging from six to sixteen days.

*Stateroom, courtesy Blount Small Ship Adventures*

*Dining room, courtesy Blount Small Ship Adventures*

*Bar and Lounge, courtesy Blount Small Ship Adventures*

*Grande Caribe, courtesy Blount Small Ship Adventures*

# CARNIVAL CRUISE LINES

3655 N.W. 87th Avenue
Miami, FL 33178
(800) CARNIVAL
www.carnival.com

*Carnival Conquest, Carnival Glory, Carnival Valor, Carnival Liberty,* and *Carnival Freedom*: entered service in 2002, 2003, 2004, 2005, and 2007, respectively; *Carnival Liberty* was renovated in 2011, while *Carnival Conquest, Carnival Dream,* and *Carnival Glory* were renovated in 2012; 110,000 GRT; 952 × 116 feet; 3,700-passenger capacity (2,974 double occupancy); 1,487 cabins; Italian officers and international crew; seven-day Caribbean itineraries from Galveston/Miami for *Conquest*; from Miami/ New York/Boston for *Glory*; and from San Juan for *Valor*; *Carnival Liberty* operates seven-day cruises from Miami; *Carnival Freedom* operates six- and eight-day Caribbean cruises from Fort Lauderdale (Category C—five stars)

(Medical facilities: C-27; P-1, EM, CLS, MS; N-4; PD; BC; EKG; TC; PO; EPC; OX; WC; OR; ICU; X; M; LJ)

*Carnival Sunshine*: entered service in 2013 (following $155 million refit, was formerly the *Carnival Destiny* which entered service in 1996); 101,353 GRT (will increase in 2013); 893 × 116 feet; 2,642-passenger capacity (3,006 after April 2013); 1,321 cabins (1,503 after April 2013); Italian officers and international crew; European voyages in the summer of 2013 and then seven-day cruise to the Caribbean from New Orleans (Category C—five stars)

*Carnival Dream, Carnival Magic,* and *Carnival Breeze*: entered service in 2009, 2011, and 2012, respectively; 130,000 GRT; 1,004 × 158 feet; 3,646-passenger capacity (4,631 with every berth filled); 1,823 cabins on *Carnival Dream* and 1,845 on *Carnival Magic* and *Carnival Breeze*; Italian officers and international crew; *Carnival Dream* offers seven-night eastern and western Caribbean itineraries from Port Canaveral, Florida; *Carnival Magic* offers seven-night Caribbean cruises from Galveston, Texas; and *Carnival Breeze* offers six- and eight-day Caribbean voyages from Miami, Florida (Category C—five stars)

*Carnival Splendor*: entered service in 2008; 113,300 GRT; 3,006-passenger capacity (double occupancy); 1,503 cabins; Italian officers and international crew; thirteen- to eighteen-day South America sailings in spring 2013 and eight-day Caribbean cruises from New York thereafter (Category C—five stars)

(Medical facilities: C-27; P-1, EM, CLS, MS; N-4; PD; BC; EKG; TC; PO; EPC; OX; WC; OR; ICU; X; M; LJ)

*Carnival Spirit, Carnival Pride, Carnival Legend,* and *Carnival Miracle*: entered service in 2001, 2001, 2002, and 2004, respectively; renovations to *Carnival Legend* and *Pride* in 2013; 88,500 GRT; 960 × 105.7 feet; 2,124-passenger capacity; 1,062 cabins; Italian officers and international crew; *Carnival Spirit* offers eight- to thirteen-day voyages to the Pacific Islands from Sydney, Australia; *Carnival Pride's* seven-day sailings commence from Baltimore, Maryland, and cruise the Bahamas and Florida; *Carnival Miracle* offers seven- and eight-day sailings from Long Beach to Mexican Riviera and Seattle to Alaska; *Carnival Legend* offers seven-day cruises from Tampa and twelve-day European Europe with departures from Dover, Barcelona, and Venice from the spring to the fall 2013 (Category C—five stars)

(Medical facilities: C-16; P-1, EM, CLS, MS; N-3; CM; PD; BC; EKG; TC; PO; EPC; OX; WC; OR; ICU; X; M; TM; LJ)

*Carnival Triumph* and *Carnival Victory*: entered service in 1999 and 2000, respectively; renovations to *Carnival Victory* in 2013; 102,000 GRT; 893 × 116 feet; 2,758-passenger capacity; 1,379 cabins; Italian officers and international crew; *Carnival Triumph* offers four- and five-day cruises in western Caribbean from Galveston, Texas; *Carnival Victory* offers four- and five-day sailings from Miami to the Caribbean (Category C—five stars)

(Medical facilities: C-27; P-1; EM, CLS, MS; N-4; CM; PD; BC; EKG; TC; PO; EPC; OX; WC; OR; ICU; X; M; LJ)

*Carnival Ecstasy* and *Carnival Fantasy*: entered service in 1991 and 1990, respectively; *Carnival Fantasy* was renovated in 2005; 70,367 GRT; 855 × 103 feet; 2,052- and 2,056-passenger capacity; 1,026 and 1,028 cabins; Italian officers and international crew; *Carnival Fantasy* operates seven-day Bahamas cruises from Charleston, South Carolina; *Carnival Ecstasy* operates four- and five-day Bahamas cruises from Port Canaveral, Florida and will reposition to Miami in January 2014 for three- and four-day cruises (Category C—four stars)

(Medical facilities: C-20; P-1; EM, CLS, MS; N-3; CM; PD; BC; EKG; TC; PO; EPC; OX; WC; OR; X; ICU; M; LJ)

*Carnival Sensation, Carnival Fascination, Carnival Imagination, Carnival Inspiration, Carnival Elation,* and *Carnival Paradise*: entered service in 1993, 1994, 1995, 1996, 1998, and 1998, respectively; various renovations took place to these ships between 2006 and 2010; *Carnival Fascination* and *Carnival Sensation* were renovated in 2006 and 2009, respectively; 70,367 GRT; 855 × 103 feet; 2,052-passenger capacity; 1,026 cabins; Italian officers and international crew; *Carnival Sensation* operates three- and four-day cruises from Port Canaveral, Florida, to the Bahamas; *Carnival Fascination* operates four- and five-day Key West/Bahamas sailings from Jacksonville, Florida; *Carnival Imagination* offers three- and four-day Bahamas/western Caribbean cruises from Miami, Florida and will reposition to Long Beach to offer three- and four-day Baja cruises beginning in January 2014; *Carnival Inspiration* operates three- and four-day Baja cruises from Long Beach, California; *Carnival Elation* operates three- and four-day cruises from New Orleans to the western Caribbean; *Carnival Paradise* operates four- and five-day cruises from Tampa to the western Caribbean (Category C—four+ stars)

(Medical facilities: C-20; P-1; EM; CLS, MS; N-3; CM; PD; BC; EKG; TC; PO; EPC; OX; OR; WC; ICU; X; M; LJ)

Note: Passenger capacities listed are based on double occupancy.

These ships are rated in eleven separate categories in the second half of chapter 14.

Carnival's founder, Ted Arison, started the company in 1972 with the purchase of the *Empress of Canada* from the Canadian Pacific Line. After a refurbishing, it entered the Caribbean market as the *Mardi Gras*. This was followed by the purchase and refurbishing of the sister ship, *Empress of Britain*, which commenced service in 1976 as the *Carnivale*. The former *S.A. Vaal* of the Union Castle Line, refurbished for more than $30 million and renamed the *Festivale*, was added in 1978. Major advertising and promotion of these vessels as the "Fun Ships," together with attractive air-sea packaging, quickly made Carnival one of the most financially successful cruise lines in the industry.

This led to the construction of the *Tropicale* for more than $100 million, designed to be the forerunner of the cruise line's updated, full-capacity "Fun Ships" of the 1980s. It entered service in 1982 with Mexican Riviera cruises from Los Angeles. In February 2001, the ship was transferred to Carnival's sister company, Costa Cruises.

Continued financial success and belief in the future of the American cruise market led to the construction of three new vessels in the 46,000- to 48,000-ton category. *Holiday* entered Caribbean service in 1985, followed by *Jubilee* in 1986 and *Celebration* in 1987. With the addition of these newer ships with expanded passenger capacity on seven-day Caribbean itineraries, the aging *Mardi Gras* and *Carnivale* were relegated to three- and four-day runs from Florida to the Bahamas. Subsequently, *Mardi Gras* and *Carnivale* were sold to the now-defunct Epirotiki Lines, and *Festivale* was sold to the now-defunct Dolphin Cruise Line. *Jubilee* was transferred to Carnival's P&O Cruises Australia in 2004. *Celebration* and *Holiday* were transferred to one of Carnival's sister companies, Ibero Cruceros, in 2008 and 2009, respectively.

Today, Carnival is one of the leading cruise lines in the middle-cruise market, with ships that have the capacity to put more than fifty thousand passengers afloat each week in lower berths. (If you include sailings for less than a week's duration, this figure is somewhat higher.) By summer 2012, the Carnival fleet will number twenty-four. The casual, amusement-park environment, the plethora of activities and entertainment, the round-the-clock activities, and the attractive packaging have interested a new generation of younger cruisers—singles, couples, and families. This is one of the few major cruise lines where 70 percent of passengers are younger than fifty-five years old, with 30 percent younger than thirty-five years. During the summer and the holidays, a large percentage of passengers are families traveling with children.

Carnival contracted to build eight 70,000+-ton sister cruise ships with more than $225 million price tags in the 1990s: the *Carnival Fantasy* commenced service in March 1990, the *Carnival Ecstasy* in June 1991, the *Carnival Sensation* in November 1993, the *Carnival Fascination* in 1994, the *Carnival Imagination* in 1995, the *Carnival Inspiration* in 1996, and the *Carnival Elation* and *Carnival Paradise* in 1998. The 101,353-ton *Carnival Destiny*, with more than 1,300 cabins, entered service in 1996. Sister ships to the *Carnival Destiny*, the 102,000-ton *Carnival Triumph* and *Carnival Victory*, entered service in 1999 and 2000, respectively. Five additional 110,000-ton ships named *Carnival Conquest*, *Carnival Glory*, *Carnival Valor*, *Carnival Liberty*, and *Carnival Freedom* entered service in 2002, 2003, 2004, 2005, and 2007, respectively. The 88,500-ton *Carnival Spirit* entered service in the spring of 2001, the *Carnival Pride* in December 2001, the *Carnival Legend* in August 2002, and the *Carnival Miracle* in 2004. Eighty percent of the staterooms on these four ships offer a sitting area and ocean views, and approximately two-thirds have balconies.

The *Fantasy*, *Ecstasy*, *Sensation*, *Fascination*, *Imagination*, *Inspiration*, *Elation*, and *Paradise* are very similar in layout and design; however, they differ in decor, and with each new ship, there have been innovations and improvements. The later entries have less dazzle, are a bit more traditional in decor, and, in my opinion, are more tasteful.

Each of these ships measures a little more than 70,000+ tons, extends approximately 855 feet in length, has 1,026 cabins that accommodate 2,052 double occupancy, and 2,606 if all of the upper berths are filled. Standard cabins measure 183 to 190 square feet, featuring twin beds that convert to double beds, closed-circuit color TVs, private safes, telephones, moderate closet and drawer space, and bathrooms with large showers but limited storage space. Forty percent of the cabins are inside; however, they are very similar to the outside accommodations, except that they have no windows or portholes and are 10 to 20 percent smaller. Some have upper and lower berths. The twenty-eight most expensive suites have verandas, refrigerators, a small sitting area, a small walk-in closet, and a combination Jacuzzi tub and shower. The twenty-six demi-suites are a bit larger than the standard cabins and include a very small sitting area and a narrow veranda. The full suites measure 350 square feet, with 71-square-foot balconies. During the past few years, balconies have been added to ninety-eight staterooms on the *Carnival Sensation, Carnival Ecstasy*, and *Carnival Fascination*, responding to the tremendous demand for these accommodations.

The focal point of each ship is a spectacular grand atrium rising seven decks to an immense skylight, with two glass birdcage elevators traversing between top and bottom. Most the cabins except the veranda suites are located on the four lower decks, with the public rooms and two dining rooms on the upper levels of the ship.

Public rooms include a multilevel, state-of-the-art show lounge with a turntable stage and several more intimate lounges that feature a variety of nightly entertainment, ranging from discos with neon arcs and copper lightning bolts to variety acts, comedians, and other entertainers. Extending into the wee hours, there is something nightly for everyone.

The casinos offer numerous blackjack, roulette, craps, and Caribbean poker tables as well as dozens of slots. The libraries are more traditional and offer a quiet respite. The boutiques feature jewelry, logo items, T-shirts, men and women's cruise and formal wear, liquor, and sundries.

Sports and health enthusiasts will appreciate the padded jogging tracks, the pool-deck areas, and the spa/health clubs that include an aerobics room, gymnasium with weights, cardiovascular and exercise equipment looking out to sea, men and women's locker rooms with sauna, steam and multinozzled showers, hairdressing salon, and an area featuring numerous beauty and massage treatments normally found only at fancy spas.

Beginning in 2006, the *Fantasy*-class ships were refurbished and received various additions, including new comfort bedding and flat-screen TVs in the staterooms, remodeled bathrooms, a new atrium bar and Internet café, expanded children's facilities, a new teen center, a nine-hole miniature golf course, and a patisserie/coffee bar. During the next few years, the *Fantasy*-class ships received additional innovations, such as part of the line's $350 million "Evolutions of Fun" refurbishment program, new Caribbean-resort-style pool and lido areas and Carnival Water Works, sporting the longest, most elaborate waterslides at sea (four-deck-high, three-hundred-foot-long cascading waterslide and an eighty-two-foot-long dual racing waterslide). Also new is the Serenity adults-only deck area, with outdoor deck space furnished with plush chaise lounges, chairs, and oversized umbrellas. These areas include a large sheltered area, two whirlpools, and bar service. In addition, the spa facilities were renovated and enhanced. In early 2009, ninety-eight balcony staterooms were added to the *Carnival Sensation*.

*Carnival Destiny* was the first cruise ship to exceed 100,000 tons (the ship was completely renovated and was renamed *Carnival Sunshine* in spring 2013). She carried a crew of 1,050 that can service 1,321 staterooms, with a potential passenger capacity of 3,400; however, double occupancy capacity is 2,642. For cruisers who enjoy the extra facilities and options found on megaships, the *Carnival Destiny* will surely fill the bill. The *Carnival Triumph* and *Carnival Victory* are sister ships with similar facilities.

In 2005, the *Carnival Destiny* received a multimillion-dollar renovation that included a new teen club, a renovated lido restaurant, children's pool, casino, and updated suite accommodations. In 2008, the ship was equipped with a 270-square-foot outdoor LED movie screen on lido deck. However, in 2013, the ship was taken out of service from February to April and received a $155 million makeover. One partial deck was added and two others were expanded; 182 new staterooms were added, 92 of which are spa staterooms; passenger capacity double occupancy was increased to 3,006; several new specialty restaurants and theme bars (the entire "Fun Ship 2.0" enhancements) were added. A three-level adults-only serenity retreat with a pool, whirlpool, waterfall, dining area, and plush chaise lounges and chairs was added. The ship was renamed *Carnival Sunshine* and operated a series of nine- to twelve-day European voyages before being deployed to New Orleans on year-round seven-day Caribbean cruises.

The 110,000-ton, 2,974-passenger capacity *Carnival Conquest, Carnival Glory, Carnival Valor, Carnival Liberty,* and *Carnival Freedom* entered service in 2002, 2003, 2004, 2005, and 2007, respectively. Similar in design and facilities to the *Destiny*-class ships, they are sixty feet longer and have expanded children and teen facilities and programs as well as elegant supper clubs. Sixty-one percent of the staterooms face the sea, and 37 percent have balconies. When every berth is filled, they can accommodate 3,700 passengers.

*Carnival Liberty* was the first ship in the fleet to receive many of the new dining and bar concepts that are part of the "Fun Ship 2.0," a multiship $500 million renovation program. *Carnival Breeze, Dream, Conquest,* and *Glory* have many of the features as well in 2012. Among the additions are RedFrog Rum Bar, BlueIguana Tequila Bar, Guy's Burger Joint, Blue Iguana Cantina, DJ IRIE, Alchemy Bar, EA Sports Bar Punchliners Comedy Club Brunch presented by George Lopez, and Hasbro, the Game Show. (Not all of these were added to each of the ships.)

*Carnival Valor* was the first ship in the fleet (and world) to feature 100 percent, bow-to-stern wireless Internet access in all staterooms and public areas. This new Wi-Fi system complements the ship's Internet café. If you do not wish to bring your own laptop, you can rent one while aboard. The program was subsequently extended to *Carnival Liberty* and *Carnival Freedom* with the remainder of the fleet offering Wi-Fi Internet access in virtually all public rooms and areas.

*Carnival Liberty* and *Carnival Freedom* were the first ships in the cruise line to introduce the Carnival Seaside Theater, a 12-foot-high, 220-foot-wide LED outdoor movie screen located on lido deck. The theater features movies, sporting events, concerts, and various programs while guests relax in lounge chairs and enjoy drinks, popcorn, and other typical movie fare. This technology has been extended to other ships in the fleet.

During 2008, *Carnival Destiny, Carnival Triumph,* and *Carnival Liberty* spent time in dry dock, and forty-eight 230-square-foot staterooms were reconfigured to balcony staterooms. *Carnival Liberty* received two new 750-square-foot deluxe staterooms.

The 113,300-ton *Carnival Splendor* entered service in July 2008. Sixty percent of the 1,503 staterooms have sea views and 60 percent of these sport balconies. The spa facilities were expanded to 21,000 square feet, spanning two decks, with a thalasso pool, thermal suites, and sixty-eight spa staterooms. For the younger set, there are 5,500 square feet of children's playroom space across two levels as well as extensive water park facilities.

The 130,000-ton, 3,646-passenger capacity *Carnival Dream* entered service in September 2009 as the largest and most innovative ship in the Carnival fleet. A sister ship, *Carnival Magic*, entered service in May 2011, followed by *Carnival Breeze* in 2012. In addition to the facilities and amenities described previously for the 110,000- and 113,000-ton ships, these new generation ships have numerous additional features.

The accommodations include twelve penthouse suites, which measure 430 square feet including balconies; a new category of balcony stateroom called "cove" staterooms located close to the water; new five-berth family staterooms, which include a second bathroom with a junior tub, shower, and sink; and sixty-five spa cabins and suites located adjacent to the 23,750 square feet of spa/health club facilities. The latter rooms enjoy exclusive amenities, priority treatment times, and unlimited spa access. For a daily or weekly fee, other guests can use the thermal suite and thalassotherapy pool.

Dining venues, in addition to the two elegant two-level main dining rooms that offer a choice between traditional fixed seating and "dine as you please," include a reservation-only steak house ($35 surcharge); a two-level buffet restaurant with offerings from Italy, Mexico, India, China, and Southeast Asia as well as a New York-style deli, a multi-item salad bar, yogurt bar, pizza station, and hamburger/hot dog grill; a sushi bar; and the unique Ocean Plaza, an indoor/outdoor café where guests can enjoy pastries, specialty coffees, and alcoholic beverages while watching a variety of live entertainment, enjoying Wi-Fi access, or participating in various contests and activities.

Outside on deck in addition to the swimming pools, numerous whirlpools (several cantilevering over the sides of the ship), giant LED movie screen, basketball court, and jogging track, the *Carnival Dream* has added Water Works. This area is composed of several unusual water slides, including a 303-foot-long twister water slide, a splash zone, and spray toys. Also found on deck are the new 11,250-square-foot serenity area accommodating two hundred adult guests with special comfortable lounges, two whirlpools, and a shaded beverage bar; an eighteen-hole miniature golf course; and a fifteen-minute choreographed laser show accompanied by rock music. *Carnival Magic* and *Carnival Breeze* have an outdoor fitness center called SportSquare. This includes an innovative rope course called "sky course," which is suspended above the top deck, offering views 150 feet above the water line. Here, guests zigzag across twenty different rope bridge options. Also at SportSquare, there are exercise equipment; an 800-foot jogging track; a six-station exercise course; a space for basketball, volleyball, foosball, and soccer; and a two-level mini golf course. *Carnival Magic* and *Carnival Breeze* also include both RedFrog Pub, a Caribbean-inspired watering hole featuring its own private label beer, and Cucina del Capitano (the Captain's Kitchen), a family-style Italian restaurant that pays homage to the line's Italian captains (all Carnival ships have Italian captains).

The *Carnival Dream*-class ships offer production shows; piano bars; a karaoke lounge as well as numerous other lounges; a large casino; a comprehensive, age-appropriate children and teen program, one of the best at sea; and all of the other activities and facilities found on other Carnival ships. In addition, it features a comedy club offering twenty-four performances each cruise and the Fun Hub, a comprehensive multistation intranet portal allowing social networking as well as access to a wide range of information covering ship services, activities, menus, tours, and other items.

Dining standards on the Carnival ships have significantly improved over the years. The line now offers a variety of dining possibilities with varied menus. The two main dining rooms serve all three meals. Five-course dinners are featured, which include a variety of appetizers, soups, salads, pasta entrees, and desserts, with steak, chicken, and health-conscious options always available. The large indoor/outdoor lido restaurants offer a mediocre breakfast buffet, but on the larger ships, exceptional lunch and dinner buffets include salad bars, freshly made pasta, hamburgers, jumbo hot dogs, pizza hot from the oven, self-serve frozen yogurt and ice cream available twenty-four hours a day, New York-style delis, Asian-cuisine stations, specialty seafood venues, and a rotating variety of ethnic favorites from around the world. New gourmet-style Spa Carnival fare (healthy cuisine) was first introduced on *Carnival Freedom* and thereafter was extended fleetwide. In 2009, Carnival inaugurated "Your Choice Dining," in which passengers select between early and late seating, or "Your Time" seating, which allows diners to eat wherever they choose at any time between 5:45 and 9:30 p.m. When approaching the dining room for a reservation, passengers are given a pager, which beeps when the table is available. This procedure was adopted throughout the fleet by the summer of 2010.

In addition, a larger percentage of passengers are availing themselves of the casual alternative dinner service in the Seaview Bistro/lido restaurants. The more recent Carnival ships (including all the *Spirit-* and *Conquest*-class ships) and the *Carnival Splendor, Carnival Dream, Carnival Magic,* and *Carnival Breeze* include an elegant, reservations-only supper club offering prime steaks, lobster tails, escargot, caviar, and other upscale cuisine with all the trimmings as well as dynamic desserts. Each course is imaginatively presented and impeccably served. There is a $35-per-person surcharge to eat here. I found these restaurants among the best specialty restaurants at sea. A new dining venue, the Chef's Table, has been added to all ships. Here, up to twelve passengers enjoy a private dinner and reception with the chef at a cost of $75 each. Other dining options include patisseries, sushi bars, and twenty-four-hour cabin service. On the *Carnival Magic* and *Carnival Breeze*, additional dining venues include RedFrog Pub, an indoor/outdoor casual spot for beer, drinks, and regional snacks; and Cucina del Capitano, a self-service lunch and waiter-service dinner Italian restaurant where the dinner servers talk and sing in Italian. Expanded sport facilities include more water slides and the first ropes course at sea.

The line features three different children's programs—Camp Carnival for two- to eleven-year-olds, Circle "C" for twelve- to fourteen-year-olds, and Club O2 for fifteen- to seventeen-year-olds—on all the ships. In addition, the ships offer children's menus, youth counselors, and video-game rooms. Children can also have dinner with the youth staff on lido deck, allowing parents to have a free evening.

In 2005, Carnival upgraded stateroom amenities with a new Carnival Comfort Bed, which includes custom pillows, fine quality duvet covers, pillow cases, and a spring mattress set. All Carnival ships now offer cell phone service and wireless Internet access.

Although Carnival Cruise Lines is certainly comfortable with its dominant position in the mass-market category of cruise lines, the spacious outside cabins and quality cuisine in the various restaurants rival the parent corporation's premium-cruise category brands. Carnival Cruise Lines is the flagship company of Carnival Corporation, a multiline cruise conglomerate (traded on the New York and London Stock Exchanges). In addition to Carnival Cruise Lines, the corporation owns AIDA Cruises, Costa Cruises, Cunard Line, Holland America Line, Ibero Cruceros, P&O Cruises, P&O Cruises Australia, Princess Cruises, and Seabourn, all of which are operated and promoted as separate products.

In 2007, Carnival entered into a joint venture with Iberojet Tours of Spain, wherein Carnival acquired 75 percent of Iberojet Cruises, which owned two ships, the 47,000-ton *Grand Mistral* and the 25,000-ton *Grand Voyager*. The new venture was named Ibero Cruceros. Carnival Corporation transferred the 1,486-passenger-capacity *Celebration* and the 1,452-passenger-capacity *Holiday* from its Carnival Cruise Lines brand to the new venture, and it is anticipated that Carnival may transfer additional ships in the future.

Carnival frequently changes the deployment of its vessels, so it is best to consult the cruise line and not rely on any but the most recent brochures.

## Strong Points

Glamorous, newer ships, a variety of daytime and evening activities and entertainment, a casual lively atmosphere, fine dining, and plenty of fellow passengers from twenty to fifty-five years old. An excellent choice for active families and good value for money. Truly the "Fun Ships" as advertised.

*Carnival Breeze, courtesy Carnival Cruise Line*

*Carnival Breeze Atrium, courtesy Carnival Cruise Line*

*Stateroom, Carnival Breeze, courtesy Carnival Cruise Line*

*Dining Room, courtesy Carnival Cruise Line*

*Carnival Breeze pool/water works/lido area, courtesy Carnival Cruise Line*

# today

**starter**  baked stuffed white mushrooms
spinach, romano cheese and fine herbs

♥ greek farmer salad
iceberg lettuce, cucumbers, bell peppers, tomatoes, onions
black olives and feta cheese, tossed with vinaigrette

black tiger shrimp cocktail
served with american cocktail sauce

minestrone milanese
italian vegetable soup with plum tomatoes, beans and pasta

west indian roasted pumpkin soup
gently roasted in the oven, blended with chicken stock and a touch of cream

strawberry bisque
chilled creamy strawberry soup with fresh mint

## didja (as in did you ever ...)
food you always wanted to try, but did not dare

spicy alligator fritters
served on tropical tomato salsa

**main**  spaghetti carbonara
tossed with a creamy bacon, cheese and garlic sauce; also available as starter

♥ grilled fillet of corvina
roasted broccoli, lemon caper dressing

broiled maine lobster tail and jumbo black tiger shrimp
potato mash, roasted broccoli florets

\* tender roasted prime rib of american beef au jus
cooked to perfection, baked potato with traditional toppings

chili rellenos
tomato and broccoli stuffed pepper
baked with aged cheddar and manchego cheese

**from our
comfort kitchen**  barbecued st. louis style pork spare ribs
grilled corn on the cob, spring onion, fries and creamy coleslaw

♥ denotes healthy options which are low in fat, cholesterol and sodium

# every day

starter ♥ fresh fruit cocktail

chilled shrimp cocktail
served with american cocktail sauce

fried vegetable spring rolls
tomato, oregano and olive oil sauce

caesar salad
hearts of romaine lettuce tossed with our caesar
dressing freshly grated parmesan cheese, anchovies and herb croutons

main ♥ broiled fillet of atlantic salmon
served with steamed vegetables of the day

* grilled flat iron steak from USDA choice beef
served with steamed vegetables of the day

♥ grilled chicken breast
served with steamed vegetables of the day

indian vegetarian
two fresh vegetables, lentils and basmati rice

southern fried chicken
served with mashed potatoes and gravy, steamed vegetables of the day

* gourmet burger
freshly grilled 8-oz hamburger on toasted Kaiser roll
sautéed mushrooms and onions, bacon, or guacamole
choice of cheese: swiss, cheddar, monterey jack (american too!)
served with french fries, tomato, pickle, onion ring and lettuce

side
all main dishes are served with appropriate sides
these listed below are optional

baked idaho potatoes with sour cream and chives
steamed white rice
french fries
assorted steamed vegetable

* public health advisory: consuming raw or undercooked meats, poultry, seafood, shellfish, or eggs may increase your risk for foodborne illness, especially
if you have certain medical conditions.

# after dinner

## desserts

vanilla crème brûlée
baked vanilla cream, garnished with assorted berries

black forest gateau
chocolate cake filled with bing cherries, heavy cream and kirschwasser

♥ diet orange cake
diet sponge cake filled with low calorie orange cream
dessert is prepared with a sugar substitute

warm chocolate melting cake
served with vanilla ice cream

♥ fresh tropical fruit plate

vanilla • chocolate • strawberry • butter pecan ice cream
sugar-free ice cream is available upon request

orange • pineapple • lime sherbet

port salut • brie • gouda • imported swiss • danish bleu cheese

♥ denotes that these desserts are prepared without sugar, or a sugar substitute

## beverages

freshly brewed coffee, regular or decaffeinated
milk • skimmed milk • hot chocolate • iced, hot and herbal teas
espresso • cappuccino

\* liqueurs
sambuca • kahlúa • grand marnier • amaretto di saronno

\* cognacs and brandies
hardy v.s.o.p. • rémy martin v.s.o.p. • courvoisier v.s.

\* dessert wines and ports
croft distinction • graham's six grapes
quady electra, california

\* regular bar prices apply

*Courtesy Carnival Cruise Lines*

# Carnival®

**FUNTIMES**

Sunrise: 6:05am • Sunset: 6:18pm

**TUESDAY, MARCH 26, 2013**

**SEA DAY**

*courtesy Carnival Cruise Lines*

## CELEBRATION CRUISE LINE

**2419 East Commercial Blvd. Suite 302**
**Fort Lauderdale, FL 33308**
(800) 957-7408
www.bahamascelebration.com

*Bahamas Celebration* (formerly *Princess Ragnhild*): entered service in 1981; renovated and refurbished in 1992 and 2009; 35,855 GRT; 673 × 87 feet; 500 cabins; 1,200-passenger capacity (1,000 double occupancy); international officers and crew; two-night cruises from Palm Beach to the Bahamas (Category D—four+ stars)

In 2009, the *Bahamas Celebration* made its American debut under new ownership, sailing out of Port Everglades in Fort Lauderdale to Nassau, Bahamas. In 2010, it switched its home port to Palm Beach. The vessel began life as a passenger and car ferry, and despite its numerous renovations, experienced cruisers will find the layout, condition, and facilities unlike most ships in the South Florida cruise market. However, cruise rates are among the least expensive available, and the cruise line provides excellent dining as well as a full cruise experience: numerous dining options, a fully stocked casino, a variety of entertainment, and around-the-clock activities. Most passengers will consider this a two-night opportunity to party and/or introduce their children to cruising. The cruise line also offers the unique vacation option of sailing two nights on the ship and spending two or four nights in a Bahamas resort.

Most cabins are quite small at 144 square feet; however, there are also many 86-square-foot "coach" cabins that are primarily sold to passengers traveling alone or on a tight budget. Most cabins have double beds with an option for an upper bunk and bathrooms with shower, sink, and toilet. Many have TVs but no refrigerators, private safes, or hair dryers. Storage is very limited, so don't bring too many clothes. The cruise is very casual and therefore dressy garments are not necessary. The twelve deluxe suites at 269 square feet and thirty additional staterooms labeled suites at 253 square feet are larger, have sitting areas, minibar/refrigerators, flat-screen TVs, and additional storage.

Dining options include the Crystal Restaurant, offering five-course lunches and dinners as well as wine service, all on par with more expensive, mass-market ships; Rios, a buffet-style venue with roving Brazilian gaucho carvers at dinner; Trattoria Di Gerry, a small help-yourself Italian buffet featuring pasta, pizzas, salads, and sweets; an outdoor buffet and grill facility atop ship, open for breakfast and lunch; and the Cove, the fine-dining, reservation-only option for those wishing for more upscale fare, at a $25 per person surcharge. Our dinner at the Cove was exceptional. New specialty dining options include the Rock, with Asian-inspired cooking at the table at a $25 per person surcharge, and the Bull, serving gourmet burgers and sandwiches at menu pricing.

Many families elect a short cruise on this line, affording an introduction to cruising for their children. There are supervised age-appropriate programs throughout the day and early evening. On top deck, there is a 180-foot slide as well as a children's splash pool.

The View is the location for live entertainment, after-dinner shows, and all-night dance parties. Music and dancing are also offered in several lounges and atop deck. The old-fashioned, English-style pub is another popular venue for imbibing. The fully stocked casino on board and the gambling possibilities in Grand Bahama Island are also attractive to numbers of passengers.

Although there is a full-service spa, there are no changing rooms, sauna, steam room, or showers. The small exercise room has no treadmills and the ship has no jogging/walking track. Atop ship is a convoluted deck with many lounge chairs for sunning, a bar, the outdoor buffet restaurant with numerous tables, a bandstand, a small pool, and two Jacuzzis.

The physical ship is not as new or glamorous as others leaving from South Florida, but those wishing to enjoy a full cruise experience with enjoyable dining and plenty of activities at a bargain price will appreciate the value offered by a *Bahamas Celebration* cruise.

*Lounge Bahamas Celebration,*
*courtesy Celebration Cruise Line*

*The Cove Dining Room, Bahamas Celebration,*
*courtesy Celebration Cruise Line*

*Suite, Bahamas Celebration, courtesy Celebration Cruise Line*

*Bahamas Celebration, courtesy Celebration Cruise Line*

# Bahamas Celebration Welcomes You To The

# Crystal Restaurant

## Appetizers

**Spicy Shrimp Chipotle Sauce and Fuji Apple**
With Onion Zucchini Pakora

◇**Vegetarian Burrito Curried Lentil**
Served with Cilantro-Scallion Yogurt Dressing

## Soups

**Caribbean Style Onion Soup**
◇**Butternut Squash Soup**

## Salads

◇**Iceberg and Romaine Lettuce Tossed with Vinaigrette and Topped
With Garden Vegetables**

◇**Sweet and Spicy Pineapple and Frisee Salad**

## This Evenings Entrées

◇**Pan Seared Pacific Salmon Filet**
Caribbean Mango Salsa, Served with Coconut Flavored Jasmine Rice

**Pork Rack Marinated Asian Style**
Served with Over Gingered Sweet Potatoes, Five Spice Apples and Fresh Green Beans

**Beef Wellington\***
Fillet of Beef Tenderloin with Potatoes and Mushrooms Gratin, Served With Winter Root
Vegetable

◇ **Healthy Choice-If you have any type of food allergy, please advise your server**

\* Consuming raw or undercooked meats, seafood, shellfish, eggs, milk or poultry may increase your risk of food borne
illness, especially if you have certain medical conditions

# The Chef's Signature Entrees

**Spicy Rotisserie Chicken**
Served Over Chickpea Curry

# Vegetarian Entrees

◇**Tempura Vegetable Tofu Roll**
Miso Marinated Served Over Scented Jasmine Rice, Wakami Salad In Mirin Jus

◇**Bryani With Raita**

# Bahamas Celebration Simplicity Entrees

**Grilled Chicken Caesar Salad**
**Sirloin Steak Ciabata bread Sandwich served with Potato Chips**
**Spaghetti with Alfredo Sauce**
**Mushroom Ravioli**

# ▬ Sweet Endings ▬

**Celebration Mini Indulgence**
Un4gettable Individual Serving of Classic Desserts
◇**No Sugar Added Roasted Plum Strudel, Sake- Ginger Pudding**

# Sommelier Wine Pairing Suggestion

**Riesling Arbor Crest, Columbia Valley, Washington, $29**
**Chateauneuf Du Pape, Ch. Mont Redon, Rhone Valley, France $49**

# After Dinner Drinks

Exotic Coffees, Ports, Brandy And Cognac Are Available At Current Bar Pricing.
Please Ask Your Server

---

◇ **Healthy Choice- If you have any type of food allergy, please advise your server**
\* Consuming raw or undercooked meats, seafood, shellfish, eggs, milk or poultry may increase your risk of food borne illness, especially if you have certain medical conditions

# CELEBRITY CRUISES INC.

**1050 Caribbean Way
Miami, FL 33132
(305) 539-6000; (800) 437-3111
Fax: (800) 437-9111
www.celebritycruises.com**

*Celebrity Century*: entered service in 1995; renovated in 2006; 71,545 GRT; 815 × 105 feet; 1,814-passenger capacity; 907 cabins; Greek officers and international crew; offers sailings to Hawaii and the Pacific Islands, Alaska, and the Panama Canal (Category B—five stars)

*Celebrity Constellation*: entered service in 2002; renovated in 2010; 91,000 GRT; 964.6 × 105.6 feet; 2,038-passenger capacity; 1019 cabins; Greek officers and international crew; cruises from Miami and Fort Lauderdale to the Caribbean, in Northern Europe and transatlantic crossings (Category B—five+ stars)

*Celebrity Infinity*: entered service in 2001; renovated in 2011; 91,000 GRT; 964.6 × 105.6 feet; 2,170-passenger capacity; 1,085 cabins; Greek officers and international crew; Panama Canal cruises, South American cruises, Europe cruises, and cruises from Seattle and transatlantic crossings (Category B—five+ stars)

*Celebrity Millennium*: entered service in 2000; renovated in 2012; 91,000 GRT; 964.6 × 105.6 feet; 2,034-passenger capacity; 1,079 cabins; Greek officers and international crew; cruises to the Caribbean, cruises in Asia, Australia, New Zealand, Hawaii and the Pacific Islands, Alaska, Panama Canal, and transpacific crossings (Category B—five+ stars)

*Celebrity Solstice, Celebrity Equinox, Celebrity Eclipse, Celebrity Silhouette,* and *Celebrity Reflection*: entered service in 2008, 2009, 2010, 2011, and 2012, respectively; *Solstice, Equinox,* and *Eclipse* are 122,000 GRT; *Silhouette* is 122,400 GRT; and *Reflection* is 126,000 GRT; 1,033 × 121 feet; 1,426 cabins and 2,850-passenger capacity for *Solstice, Equinox,* and *Eclipse*; *Silhouette* has 2,886-passenger capacity and 1,443 cabins, and *Reflection* has 3,030-passenger capacity and 1,523 cabins. Greek officers and international crew; cruise various regions, including the Caribbean, Bahamas, Alaska,

Australia, New Zealand, Hawaii and the Pacific Islands, Europe, Mediterranean, and transatlantic crossings (Category B—five++ stars)

*Celebrity Summit*: entered service in 2001; renovated in 2012; 91,000 GRT; 964.6 × 105.6 feet; 2,158-passenger capacity; 1,079 cabins; Greek officers and international crew; Caribbean and Bermuda cruises from San Juan and Cape Liberty; Canada and New England cruises from Cape Liberty (Category B—five+ stars)

*Celebrity Xpedition*: entered service in 2004; 2,329 GRT; 296 × 43 feet; 96-passenger capacity; forty-five cabins; Ecuadorian officers and crew; seven-, ten-, eleven-, and thirteen-night Galapagos experiences (Category B—not rated)

(Medical facilities: C-8 on *Century*; C-26 on *Millennium*, *Infinity*, *Constellation*, and *Summit*; C-30 on *Solstice*, *Eclipse*, and *Equinox*; P-2, EM, CLS, MS on *Silhouette* and *Reflection*; N-3; CM; PD; BC; EKG; TC; PO; EPC; OX; WC; ICU; X; M; LJ)

These ships are rated in eleven separate categories in the second half of chapter 11.

In 1990, Chandris created a new Celebrity Cruises division to compete in the premium-cruise market while continuing its Fantasy Cruises division at the budget end of the market. For its new Celebrity Cruises division, Chandris rebuilt, lengthened, redesigned, and refurbished the former *Galileo* in 1989, renaming her *Meridian*, and built *Horizon*, which entered service in 1990, and *Zenith*, which entered service in 1992. The two divisions promoted their ships like separate companies and did not advertise the Chandris name. In 1994, the name of the U.S. company was changed to Celebrity Cruises Inc. In 1995, 1996, and 1997, Celebrity introduced three 70,000+-ton innovative high-tech vessels, *Century*, *Galaxy*, and *Mercury*. In 1997, *Meridian* was sold. During the summer of 1997, Royal Caribbean Cruises Ltd. acquired Celebrity and now operates Celebrity Cruises as a separate brand.

In 1999, Celebrity announced plans to construct four 91,000-ton ships to enter service during a three-year period. The first of the new class, appropriately named *Celebrity Millennium*, entered service in the spring of 2000, offering varied itineraries. The second vessel, *Celebrity Infinity*, entered service in the spring of 2001. The third vessel, *Celebrity Summit*, entered service in the fall of 2001. And the fourth vessel, *Celebrity Constellation*, entered service in the spring of 2002. In the fall of 2008, the 122,000-ton, 2,850-passenger capacity *Celebrity Solstice* came on line. Four additional *Solstice*-class ships, *Celebrity Equinox*, *Celebrity Eclipse*, *Celebrity Silhouette*, and *Celebrity Reflection*, followed in 2009, 2010, 2011, and 2012, respectively.

The *Horizon* and *Zenith* were cleverly conceived ships for the 1990s and later updated for the new millennium. In October 2005, the *Horizon* was transferred to Island Cruises, a joint venture between Royal Caribbean and British-based package operator First Choice Holidays. In 2007, *Zenith* was transferred to Pullmantur, a subsidiary of Royal Caribbean. At the same time, the former *R-6* of Renaissance Cruises was transferred to Celebrity and renamed *Celebrity Journey*. In 2007, the former *R-7* of Renaissance Cruises and the *Blue Moon* of Pullmantur also was transferred to Celebrity and renamed *Celebrity Quest*. Subsequently, in 2007, the Azamara brand was created and the ships were rebranded and renamed *Azamara Journey* and *Azamara Quest*. In 2010, the brand name was changed to Azamara Club Cruises. These ships offer longer cruises to destinations around the world, calling at ports not often visited by other Celebrity ships.

There is a high ratio of service staff to passengers (1:2) on all Celebrity ships. Service in the dining rooms, staterooms, and various lounges is among the best in the premium market, and the ships carry a large number of social and entertainment staff. The diversity and the presentation of food offerings in the dining rooms have been exceptional for ships in the premium-class category.

In December 1995, Celebrity introduced the 70,000+-ton, 815-foot, 1,814-passenger capacity *Celebrity Century*, followed by the 77,713-ton, 866-foot, 1,870-passenger capacity *Celebrity Galaxy* in December 1996 and its sister ship, *Celebrity Mercury*, in November 1997. The vessels were equipped with a sophisticated array of entertainment options and interactive audio, video, and in-cabin entertainment systems. These high-tech amenities include a fully equipped, state-of-the art conference center with electronic voting chair pads and broadcast capabilities; a 921-seat, multilevel, amphitheater-style show lounge designed to accommodate Broadway-scale productions with its revolving stage, hydraulic orchestra pit, and sophisticated special-effects capability; a revolutionary high-tech-equipped lounge and disco; and in-cabin interactive TVs featuring the Celebrity Network, an innovation that permits guests to order room service, select their dinner wine, purchase shore excursions, gamble at casino games charged to their personal accounts, review their shipboard account, and purchase pay-per-view movies. *Celebrity Galaxy* was transferred in 2010 to a new venture between RCL and TUI of Germany. *Celebrity Mercury* followed in 2011.

All of the 907 staterooms on *Celebrity Century* include ample closet and drawer space, convertible twin beds, dressing table and mirror, direct-dial telephones, minibar/refrigerators, electronic safes, hair dryers, waffle robes, interactive TV systems, and nice-size bathrooms with showers, sinks, and storage more generous than on most ships. The eight spacious 537-square-foot Royal Suites (with 94-square-foot verandas) and the fifty-four Sky Suites (with even larger verandas) include video systems, marble baths with whirlpool jets, champagne, personalized stationery and business cards, afternoon tea and snacks, nightly hors d'oeuvres, and twenty-four-hour butler service. Additional deluxe cabins also have verandas. The two penthouse suites, which are 1,219 square feet, include a master bedroom with its own bathroom, living room, dining room, kitchen pantry, powder room, large balcony with an outdoor Jacuzzi, a sophisticated security system, and can be combined with the adjoining suite to accommodate two additional guests. Comfort and service in the suites emulate that found on more expensive ships that compete in the deluxe-category cruise market. Cruisers who demand luxurious suites, personalized butler service, and gourmet cuisine but who also require ships offering an abundance of activities and entertainment will find the "suite life" on all

Celebrity vessels viable alternatives to many of the more expensive deluxe cruise ships. There are also several wheelchair-accessible staterooms, and the design of the vessel is especially well adapted for the handicapped. The *Century* also offers Concierge Class staterooms with the amenities described earlier.

The ship is attractively furbished in contemporary/art deco designs with outstanding, multimillion-dollar art collections originally assembled by Christina Chandris. The two-tiered Grand Restaurant features majestic staircases, a piano balcony where soft dinner music is played by a quartet, two-story picture windows looking out to the sea, and Continental menus and wine lists. Complimentary room service is available around the clock in all staterooms, and suites also feature service such as full breakfasts served in the suite. Casual buffet-style breakfasts and lunches, which feature four separate buffet areas and a sushi café, are offered atop ship in the lido cafés. Celebrity has created the atmosphere of a European bistro in the lido, a backdrop for casual dinners served most evenings. For additional variety, there are hamburger/hot dog grills and pizza ovens by the pool, martini, wine, and espresso bars, and caviar and champagne bars.

Also offered is AquaSpa by Elemis, one of the more complete health spas at sea, operated by Elemis Ltd. In addition to a large fully equipped exercise and aerobics room with dozens of cardiovascular machines, a hair salon, his and hers dressing rooms with showers, steam rooms, and saunas, there is also a marvelous thalassotherapy pool and a bevy of beauty, health, relaxation, and massage treatments available. AquaSpa packages may be booked in advance. Treatments and services range in price from $15 to $325. The thalassotherapy pool was removed from the *Celebrity Century* during its renovation in 2006 and replaced with a Persian Garden offering steam, sauna, and a variety of showers.

Other public facilities on this ship include a 7,500-foot casino; an impressive observation lounge that converts to disco at night; a cabaret-style nightclub; an advanced-technology, supervised children's playroom; numerous electronic game facilities; a three-story "Grand" foyer that rises from the marble main lobby and features extensive shopping galleries; a lido deck with two attached swimming pools, four whirlpools, designated sport areas, small jogging tracks, and several bars; and a library, an Internet café, and a cardroom.

During the spring of 2006, the *Century* went into dry dock and received $55 million in renovations, which included 14 new Sky Suites; 10 new staterooms; 314 new verandas; new bedding; flat-screen TVs and wireless Internet access in the staterooms; a 66-seat specialty restaurant, Murano (similar to those on the *Millennium*-class ships); a sushi bar; the Ocean Grill, a casual limited-menu restaurant atop ship open in the evenings as an alternative to the dining room; a Cova Café; expansion of the AquaSpa; addition of the Acupuncture at Sea program; a new spa café; a new martini bar; a teen lounge with a jukebox, dance floor, and video arcade; expanded Internet facilities and computer classes; and an updated and expanded fitness center.

The 2,158-passenger capacity, 91,000-ton *Millennium* entered service in the late spring of 2000, boasting numerous innovations and facilities not available on the other vessels as well as providing 80 percent ocean-view accommodations with verandas in 57 percent of those staterooms and suites. Two almost identical sister ships, *Infinity* and *Summit*, came on line during 2001 with an additional sibling, *Constellation*, during the spring of 2002. The smallest inside cabin measures a generous 170 square feet and includes a sitting area with a sofa and an entertainment tower with a private safe, a minibar, an interactive TV, and a DVD player, a radio, a direct-dial telephone, a hair dryer, and robes. Premium ocean-view staterooms (including verandas) are 232 to 513 square feet, and the suites (including verandas) range in size from 308 square feet for the Sky Suites, 467 square feet for the eight Celebrity Suites, 733 square feet for the very spacious and desirable Royal Suites, and 1,432 feet for two ultradeluxe penthouse suites (with additional 1,100-square-foot wraparound verandas). These two charmers, two of the largest suites afloat, include all the features of the penthouse suites described previously on the *Century*, plus a baby grand piano, exercise equipment, fax machine, enlarged master bathroom with a deep-soaking whirlpool tub surrounded by bay windows looking out to sea and a separate jet-spray shower, two state-of-the-art audiovisual entertainment systems with large TVs, flat-screen PC with Internet access and printer, expansive veranda with an outdoor whirlpool, wet bar and lounge seating area, and lavish decorations such as a foyer with mosaic floors.

Another innovation on *Celebrity Millennium* is the first specialty restaurant in the Celebrity fleet, named the Olympic, after the RMS Olympic, sister ship to the Titanic, which was launched in 1911. The decor, which includes the original walnut paneling from the Olympic, expresses the elegance and romance of the turn-of-the-century transatlantic liners. A 300+-label wine cellar as well as suggested wines by the glass and bottle to accompany each course enhance this gourmet experience. The other three *Millennium*-class ships also include artifacts and themes from classic ocean liners. The name of the specialty restaurant on the *Celebrity Infinity* is United States; on the *Celebrity Summit*, Normandie; and on the *Celebrity Constellation*, Ocean Liners. These are four of the finest gourmet specialty restaurants at sea. A similar specialty restaurant, Murano, was added to *Celebrity Century* during her renovation, and comparable restaurants were added to the *Solstice*-class vessels.

The 25,000-square foot AquaSpa facility is considerably expanded (twice the size as on the *Celebrity Century*-class vessels), boasting some of the largest and most extensive spa facilities afloat, including a spacious outdoor (but glassed-in and heat-controlled) Solarium pool surrounded by day-use cabanas on *Celebrity Infinity*, *Summit*, and *Constellation*. The 14,467-foot shopping mall, the Emporium, with its interesting diversity of shops, all indoor and outdoor public areas, and facilities for the physically challenged have also been greatly enlarged and expanded. *Millennium* was the first cruise ship to incorporate gas-turbine technology, which reduces exhaust emissions up to 90 percent and curtails noise and vibration.

Other facilities available include the following: the AquaSpa Café, offering heart-healthy spa cuisine alfresco; a martini bar and a champagne bar serving caviar; Michael's Club, the comfortable English-Georgian-style piano bar and fine liqueurs lounge as well as over thirty different craft beers; Café al Bacio & Gelateria, an Italian-inspired eatery offering freshly baked pastries, signature coffees and teas, and Italian ices; the three-deck, 901-seat Celebrity Theater, venue for production shows; and Celebrity iLounge, the first Authorized Apple Reseller at sea with Internet access (for a fee) and entertainment on the latest audio and video products, including engaging courses.

Passengers have Internet access in all staterooms aboard the *Celebrity Infinity, Constellation,* and *Summit*; music and traditional book libraries; a three-hundred-seat cinema/conference center; five additional meeting/function rooms; a conservatory with botanical gardens; a resort/pool deck with two pools, four whirlpools, expansive lounge areas, and an adjacent fitness center, and the AquaSpa by Elemis, offering a variety of exotic and rejuvenating treatments as well as a choice of several facial treatments, a beauty salon as well as the Persian Garden and sport facilities, including basketball, paddle tennis, volleyball, quoits, a running/jogging track; a Fun Factory and video-game arcade for children and the X Club venue, dedicated to teen entertainment; a giant casino; a glass-enclosed observation lounge atop ship with nightly entertainment for dancing; and numerous other lounges, bars, and areas designed for guests to socialize and enjoy a variety of amusements. The ships also offer massages and fashion shows by the pool and an "Acupuncture at Sea" as part of their new "wellness program." The four *Millennium*-class vessels are virtually similar except for variations in decor.

Celebrity has added several new premium stateroom categories on select ships, including Concierge Class, AquaClass staterooms and suites, and the jaw-dropping Reflection and Signature Suites. Concierge Class staterooms include a complimentary bottle of champagne, fresh flowers, a selection of fruit, upscale bedding and pillows, afternoon canapés, luggage service, personalized stationery, additional room amenities, a special room service breakfast menu, priority shore-excursion bookings, and early embarkation and debarkation as well as special concierge services.

In 2011 and 2010, respectively, the *Celebrity Infinity* and the *Celebrity Constellation* were "Solsticized" by adding select *Solstice*-class features, such as Tuscan Grille, an Italian steak house; Café al Bacio & Gelateria; Bistro on Five crêperie; the new ice-top Martini Bar and Crush; the uniquely unordinary specialty restaurant Qsine (not on *Constellation*); Celebrity iLounge; AquaClass accommodations offering exclusive access to the stylish health-themed, Mediterranean specialty restaurant Blu; flat-screen TVs in all accommodations and new upholstery and bedding; and a gelateria. The *Summit* and *Millennium* received similar upgrades in 2012.

In the summer of 2004, Celebrity entered the small-ship/expedition market with the introduction of its 2,842-ton, ninety-six-passenger *Celebrity Xpedition*. The ship offers seven-, ten-, eleven-, and thirteen-night itineraries in the Galapagos with pre- and postcruise stopovers in Quito, Ecuador, and Peru. Both *Celebrity Journey* and *Celebrity Quest* were to be operated under the Celebrity Xpeditions brand, specializing in cruises to less frequented cruise destinations; however, in 2007, the cruise line decided to establish the new Azamara Club Cruises brand and rename the ships *Azamara Journey* and *Azamara Quest*.

Captains can now marry couples legally at sea. In 2006, the cruise line entered into an arrangement with Leap Frog School House to provide multisensory, educational learning tools for its youth programs.

With the introduction of the 122,000-ton, 2,850-passenger (double occupancy) *Solstice*-class ships in 2008, 2009, and 2010, Celebrity increased the size of its ships and passenger capacity by one-third from that of the *Millennium*-class vessels. Celebrity aficionados have expressed mixed opinions whether they prefer these larger ships. Some feel the *Millennium*-class ships were the optimum size for a large cruise ship and that the trade-off for additional facilities, activities, and options is more crowds, longer lines, and less ambiance.

Ninety percent of the staterooms face the sea, and 85 percent of these have balconies. Ocean-view cabins measure 176 square feet, whereas veranda, concierge, and AquaClass staterooms are 194 square feet, with 54-square-foot balconies that can comfortably accommodate a table and two chairs. Suites range in size from 300 square feet with 77-square-foot balconies for the forty-four Sky Suites up to 1,291 square feet with 385-square-foot balconies (complete with an outdoor Jacuzzi) for the two penthouse suites. One hundred and thirty veranda staterooms are designated AquaClass. These staterooms are located in a separate area of the ship, and occupants have unlimited use of AquaSpa's Persian Gardens, priority times for spa therapies, and exclusive dining in the private Mediterranean-themed specialty restaurant named Blu. Every accommodation on board includes all the features listed above for the *Millennium*-class cabins. Although the design and furnishings are extremely tasteful and attractive, storage and counter space in both the staterooms and the bathrooms are a bit sparse.

*Solstice*-class ships feature expanded dining options. Commencing in 2009, Celebrity Select Dining was introduced throughout the fleet. Now, guests can choose traditional, two-seating, assigned-table dining or opt for changing the time and table each evening. The two-level, three-meal-a-day main dining room is especially bright, open, elegant, and inviting. Dinner menus vary by ship but offer a large quality selection typical of Celebrity ships. Specialty dining options include the Tuscan Grille, an Italian steak house; Murano, the elegant, Continental dining restaurant; Bistro on Five, a bistro-style venue serving crêpes, salads, and sandwiches for both lunch and dinner; the Oceanview Café, a large fresh buffet restaurant open throughout the day and evening with both indoor and outdoor seating; the aforementioned Blu; Café al Bacio & Gelateria, serving traditional Italian ices, pastries, and specialty coffees; AquaSpa Café for quick, lighter fare in the Solarium; an outdoor hamburger and hot dog grill; and, of course, twenty-four-hour complimentary room service. An additional specialty restaurant on the *Celebrity Solstice* and *Celebrity Equinox* is Silk Harvest, featuring Asian fusion cuisine. On *Celebrity Eclipse*, *Celebrity Silhouette*, and *Celebrity Reflection*, this space is occupied by Qsine, a uniquely unordinary venue offering classic and contemporary dishes presented in playful, engaging ways, complete with menus and wine lists on iPads. There is an additional charge for the specialty restaurants, and reservations are often hard to come by unless booked well before embarkation. Our dining experience in Murano was the best we have found on any ship at sea and easily equal to any *Michelin*-rated three-star restaurant ashore.

Two unique imbibing venues are the attractive oval-shaped Martini Bar and Crush, with its frozen countertop and performing bartenders, and the elegant Cellarmasters, a wine bar featuring an impressive array of wine selections by the glass and the bottle.

The public areas are expansive and include a giant three-level theater for production and cabaret entertainment; a movie theater; a large fully stocked casino; an art gallery; an airy observation lounge; a clubby disco; more than a dozen retail shops featuring fine jewelry, watches, clothing, crystal, liquors, and sundry items; several additional bars and lounges; an Internet facility; an impressive fitness center with dozens of state-of-the-art cardio machines, exercise equipment, an aerobic studio, a spinning room, and his and her locker areas with sauna, steam room, and showers; AquaSpa by Elemis, a large spa with numerous treatment rooms, a beauty salon, and a relaxation area; two outdoor pools surrounded by two levels of lounge chairs; an additional pool permanently protected by a glass roof; a jogging/walking track a level above the pool; and the Lawn Club, 23,000 square feet of real grass, the venue for croquet, bocce ball, a three-hole putting course, the Sunset Bar, and the Hot Glass Show, where glass-blowing demonstrations are offered daily on *Celebrity Eclipse*, *Equinox*, and *Solstice*.

The daily schedule of activities is also extensive and includes numerous health and fitness workshops, language classes, wine and spirit tastings, cooking demonstrations, dance classes, Hot Glass Shows, and the usual bingo, table tennis, shuffleboard, and similar tournaments. For those who prefer a large variety of facilities, dining options, activities, and entertainment, the *Solstice*-class ships will certainly meet their expectations.

The fourth and fifth *Solstice*-class ships, *Celebrity Silhouette* and *Celebrity Reflection*, have some changes in comparison with the other three. The glass-blowing area has been replaced with a new interactive dining venue, the Lawn Club Grill; the Porch, a casual outdoor venue offering pastries, coffees, wines, salads, and sandwiches; private outdoor lounging cabanas called the Alcoves; the Art Studio; and oversized Adirondack chairs and hammocks. The new AquaClass suites with 79-foot verandas include butler service and complimentary access to Restaurant Blu. Also, there are eight new Sky Suites, additional Concierge Class staterooms, and additional inside staterooms. On the *Celebrity Reflection*, the Reflection Suite measures 1,636 square feet with two bedrooms that can accommodate up to six people with a 194-square-foot wraparound veranda and private whirlpool. The five Signature Suites measure 441 square feet with 118-square-foot verandas and can accommodate four people.

During a dry dock in 2012, all of the *Millennium*-class ships received many of the facilities that debuted on the *Solstice*-class ships, including the ice-topped Martini Bar and Crush, AquaClass staterooms, Cellarmasters, Tuscan Grille, Bistro on Five, Café al Bacio & Gelateria and refurbished suites, staterooms, and software in public areas. Celebrity frequently varies its itineraries; therefore, it is best to obtain their most recent brochures before making your travel plans. Celebrity is currently focusing on Asian, Caribbean, Bermuda, Alaskan, Hawaiian, Panama Canal, South American, Mediterranean, and Northern European destinations.

## Strong Points

Celebrity Cruises' ships have been well received by their guests, travel writers, and travel agents. The spacious, full-amenity staterooms and suites, fine dining, concerned service, dedication to passenger satisfaction, innovative entertainment options, and vast array of facilities make Celebrity one of the better buys and one of the top contenders in the premium-cruise market. The ships offer good all-around cruise experiences, with the option to purchase suites as sumptuous as those offered on the more expensive luxury cruise ships.

*Main Dining Room Celebrity Solstice, courtesy Celebrity Cruise Line*

*Aqua Class stateroom, courtesy Celebrity Cruise Line*

*Celebrity Reflection, courtesy Celebrity Cruise Line*

*Atrium lobby, courtesy Celebrity Cruise Line*

# Celebrity Equinox

Jacques Van Staden

The Silhouette Dining Room menu is designed to provide a "two menus in one" experience. Our changing "Nightly" menu, on the right side, provides the opportunity for you to explore new culinary boundaries through our blend of contemporary, globally inspired menu offerings. On the left hand side, our "Classic Favorites" menu offers more approachable, classically inspired cuisine to enjoy any evening of your cruise. We wish you "Bon Appetit"!

Chef Jacques Van Staden

## *Appetizers*

♡ Grenadine Scented Pineapple
Fresh Hawaiian Pineapple Paired with Honeydew Melon
and Grenadine; Served with Raisin Salad

Cold Smoked Atlantic Salmon
with a Cucumber Dome, Herbed Cream Cheese,
Toasted Bagel Chip and Broken Salmon Caviar Cream

Beef Carpaccio
Delicate Filet Mignon, Thinly Sliced and Layered
with Dijon Aioli, Arugula Salad and Parmesan Shavings

Buffalo Style Frog Legs
Dredged in Rustic Garlic-Parsley Butter;
Served with Carrot-Celery Spears
and Blue Cheese Dressing

## *Soups & Salads*

The Captain's Fish Bisque
with Saffron Essence and Herb Croutons

♡ ❧ Vegetable Consommé
with Cellophane Noodles and Mushrooms

Chilled Tangerine
and Granny Smith Apple Soup
Topped with Grand Marnier Cream

Baby Spinach Salad
with Bacon Bits, Chopped Eggs and Crispy Shallots

♡ ❧ Crisp Romaine Lettuce
with Julienne Carrots, Sliced Button Mushrooms,
Chopped Radish and Toasted Pumpkin Seeds

*Our homemade dressings tonight are:* Shallot Vinaigrette • Tarragon • Bacon Ranch • Citrus Herb

## *Entrées*

Penne Poulet Aux Truffes
Our Signature Pasta Featuring Tender Chunks of
Boneless Chicken Breast, Coated in Chardonnay
Cream Sauce and Mixed with Basil, Spinach, Sun
Dried Tomato, White Truffle Oil and Grana Padana;
Served over Penne Pasta with Parmesan Crown
and Herb Salad

BBQ Glazed Chilean Sea Bass
Pan Seared Sea Bass Glazed with Homemade BBQ
Sauce; Served on Sweet Yellow Corn-Chive
Mashed Potatoes with Crispy Shoestrings,
Wilted Spinach and Horseradish Demi

❧ Vegetable Paella Israeli Couscous
Paella Style Steamed Vegetables
with Israeli Couscous and Cilantro Aioli Crostini

♡ Quail Delight
Roasted California Raised Quail with Wild Rice
and Black Truffle Stuffing; Served Over Braised
Savoy Cabbage, Smoked Apple Wood Bacon,
Sautéed Wild Mushrooms and Sage Jus

✳ Roasted Colorado Rack of Lamb
Dijon Crusted Rack of Lamb, Oven Roasted to
Perfection; Served with Garlic Spiked Mashed
Potatoes, Steamed Broccoli Florettes, Cinnamon
Glazed Baby Carrots and Rosemary Lamb Jus

Classic Chateaubriand Brillat-Savarin
Broiled Angus Beef Tenderloin Served with Roasted
Parisienne Potatoes, Glazed Haricots Verts,
Carrot Batonettes, Shiraz Braised Shallots
and Choice of Béarnaise or Madeira Sauce

• A selection of Domestic and Imported Cheeses Served with Crackers and Biscuits •

## *Your Sommelier Recommends*

Our highly skilled Cellar Master has selected the following wines to complement tonight's Culinary Selections:

### By the Bottle

White
Chablis, Premier Cru, Laroche
59

Red
Château Coufran, Bordeaux
60

### By the Glass

White
Chardonnay, St. Francis, Sonoma
8

Red
Shiraz, Peter Lehman, Barosso, Australia
8

# Classic Dinner Favorites

## Appetizers

Chilled Jumbo Shrimp Cocktail
with Horseradish Cocktail Sauce

Escargots à la Bourguignonne
with Shallots, Garlic, Parsley and Pernod Butter

Celebrity Antipasti Platter
Selection of Cured Meats & Artisan Cheese
with Marinated Olives and Roasted Red Peppers

## Soups & Salads

Baked French Onion Soup
with Herb Croutons & Melted Gruyère Cheese

Creamy Lobster Bisque
with Cognac Cream and Finely Chopped Tarragon

♡ Caprese Salad
Vine Ripe Tomatoes, Layered with Buffalo Mozzarella,
Peppers and Arugula, Tossed in Extra Virgin Olive Oil
and Balsamic Vinaigrette

Classic Caesar Salad
Crispy Hearts of Romaine Lettuce
with Garlic Croutons & Parmesan Cheese

also available entrée-size with
Grilled Chicken Breast or Poached Shrimp

## Entrées

♡ Broiled Atlantic Salmon
with Boiled Potatoes and Grilled Asparagus,
Served Plain or with Classic Hollandaise Sauce

Herb Marinated Grilled Chicken Breast
with Red Bliss Mashed Potatoes, Steamed Broccoli,
Honey Glazed Carrots and Thyme Jus

Grilled New York Sirloin Steak
with Loaded Baked Potato, Caramelized Shallots,
Tender Green Beans and Beurre Maître d'Hôtel

"Choice of" Side Dishes:
Baby Peas, Steamed Green Beans, Broccoli, Rice Pilaf,
Mashed Potatoes or Loaded Baked Potato
with Traditional Toppings

## Desserts

New York Cheesecake
with Fresh Homemade Berry Compote

Apple Pie à la Mode
Our One of a Kind Blend of Golden Delicious Apples
in Seasoned Brown Sugar; Baked in a Crispy Dough

Crème Brûlée
Delightfully Balanced Vanilla Infused Custard
with Caramelized Sugar Topping

⊹ Chef Jacques Van Staden's Recommendation
♡ "Renew" Heart Healthy ❧ Vegetarian

*courtesy Celebrity Cruises*

## Activities & Events

To take part in our signature Celebrity Life series events look for the ★ below.

| Time | Event | Location & Deck |
|---|---|---|
| 7:00am | Celebrity Equinox is scheduled to arrive in Cozumel, Mexico | |
| 7:30am | ★ Freshly Squeezed | Fitness Center 12 |
| 8:00am | ★ Total Body Conditioning | Fitness Center 12 |
| 9:00am | Toddler Time (until 11:00am) | Fun Factory 15 |
| 9:00am | ★ Celebrity Classics: Motown Musical Challenge | Sky 14 |
| 9:45am | Wii Dart Tournament | Quasar 4 |
| 10:30am | ★ Let's Dance: Modern Line Dance | Passport Bar 3 |
| 11:15am | Bocce 101 | The Lawn Club 15 |
| 12 Noon | ★ Celebrity Life Pool Experience by AquaSpa (until 3:00pm) | Solarium 12 |
| 1:00pm | Featured Film: Slumdog Millionaire, R, 120 mins. | Celebrity Central 4 |
| 1:30pm | Golf Putting Practice | The Lawn Club 15 |
| 2:15pm | Table Tennis Tournament | Sky 14 |
| 3:00pm | Blongo | The Lawn Club 15 |
| 3:45pm | ★ Language Learning with Rosetta Stone: Spanish 2 | Celebrity Central 4 |
| 4:45pm | ★ Celebrity Classics: Fun in the Sun Trivia | Oceanview Bar 14 |
| 5:00pm | Lawn Club at Night (until 8:00pm) | The Lawn Club 15 |
| 5:00pm | ★ Molecular Cocktails with Liquid Chef Galleria Tastings 5 | |
| 5:00pm | Catholic Mass | Celebrity Central 4 |
| 5:00pm | Martini Flights** (until 9:00pm) | Martini Flights 4 |
| 5:00pm | Friends of Bill W. | Sky Conf. A 14 |
| 6:00pm | Rock the Lawn Sail Away (until 8:00pm) The Lawn Club 15 | |
| 6:45pm | All guests onboard please | |
| 7:00pm | Celebrity Equinox is scheduled to sail for Fort Lauderdale, Florida | |
| 7:00pm | ★ Hot Glass Show (until 9:30pm) | Hot Glass Studio 15 |
| 7:00pm | Digital Camera Sale | Photo Gallery 5 |
| 7:30pm | ★ Jameson Whiskey Tasting** | Michael's Club 5 |
| 7:30pm | Digital Camera Demonstration | Photo Gallery 5 |
| 7:45pm | Ballroom Dance Hour | Grand Foyer 3 |
| 8:00pm | $10 Bingo | Celebrity Central 4 |
| 8:45pm | Celebrity Headliners Variety Show | Equinox Theatre 4, 5 |
| 10:00pm | ★ Decco – A Night Under the Stars | Poolside 12 |
| 10:00pm | Karaoke (until late) | Sky 14 |
| 10:00pm | ★ StarGazer Series: Stargazing | Solstice Deck 16 |
| 10:45pm | Celebrity Headliners Variety Show | Equinox Theatre 4, 5 |
| 11:00pm | Featured Film: Slumdog Millionaire, R, 120 mins. | Celebrity Central 4 |
| 11:30pm | Club Q | Quasar 4 |

**Indicates a fee is applicable for this event. Refer to the Today's Features Insert or inquire with our friendly staff for more details.

## Culinary Delights

This Evening's Attire: Smart Casual
Ladies: Skirt or Pants, complemented by a sweater or blouse
Gentlemen: Pants with sports shirt or sweater. Shirt must have sleeves.

**Silhouette Dining Room** • Decks 3 & 4

| | |
|---|---|
| Open Seating Express Breakfast (Deck 3) | 7:30am – 9:00am |
| Open Seating Regular Breakfast (Deck 3) | 7:30am – 9:00am |
| Lunch | Closed |
| Fixed Seating Dinner | 6:00pm |
| Fixed Seating Dinner | 8:30pm |
| Celebrity Select Dining (Deck 4) | 6:00pm – 9:30pm |

Note: For Fixed Seating Dinner, entrance to Silhouette Dining Room will remain open for 30 minutes after the assigned dining time.

**Blu** • AquaClass Dining Room Deck 5

| | |
|---|---|
| AquaClass Breakfast | 7:30am – 9:00am |
| Open Seating Dinner | 6:00pm – 9:30pm |

**Oceanview Café** • Deck 14

| | |
|---|---|
| Coffee, Tea & Juices | 24 hours |
| Breakfast Buffet | 7:00am – 10:30am |
| Late Breakfast | 10:30am – 11:30am |
| Lunch Buffet | 12 Noon – 2:30pm |
| Ice Cream | 7:00am – 9:30pm |
| Pizza & Pasta | 12 Noon – 9:00pm, 9:30pm – 1:00am |
| Afternoon Snacks | 4:00pm – 5:00pm |
| Sushi Selection | 5:30pm – 9:30pm |
| Casual Dining | 6:00pm – 9:30pm |
| Late Night Snacks | 9:30pm – 1:00am |

Note: Swimsuits are not allowed in the Oceanview Café. Guests are expected to adhere to this policy at all times.

**Mast Grill** • Deck 14

| | |
|---|---|
| Grilled Specialties | 11:30am – 6:30pm |

**AquaSpa Café** • Deck 12

| | |
|---|---|
| Healthy Alternative Breakfast | 6:30am – 9:30am |
| Healthy Alternative Lunch | 12 Noon – 2:30pm |

**Bistro on Five** • Deck 5

| | |
|---|---|
| Crêperie | 6:00am – 2:00am |
| Cover charge applies. | |

**Gelateria** • Deck 5

| | |
|---|---|
| Italian Gelato | 11:00am – 11:00pm |
| Cover charge applies. | |

**Specialty Restaurants** • Deck 5

| | | |
|---|---|---|
| Murano • Contemporary French Cuisine | 6:00pm – 10:00pm |
| Silk Harvest • Asian Cuisine | 6:00pm – 10:00pm |
| Tuscan Grille • Italian Steakhouse | 6:00pm – 10:00pm |

Cover charge applies. Please call ext. 7000 between 9:00am and 6:00pm to make reservations for specialty dining.

## Hours of Operation

Art Gallery ........................................................ Deck 5
    8:00pm – Midnight
AquaSpa .......................................................... Deck 12
    8:00am – 10:00pm: Spa
    4:00pm – 8:00pm: Acupuncture Clinic
    8:00am – 8:00pm: AquaClass Concierge
    9:00am – 7:00pm: Equilibria
    8:00am – 11:00pm: Fitness Center (Guests 16+ yrs)
    8:00am – 8:00pm: MedlSpa Clinic
    8:00am – 11:00pm: Salon & Barber Shop
Captain's Club Host ........................................... Deck 5
    9:00am – 11:00am, 6:00pm – 8:00pm
Concierge Desk ................................................. Deck 3
    7:00am – 10:00am, 6:00pm – 8:00pm
Cruise Sales Manager ........................................ Deck 5
    6:00pm – 8:00pm
Florist ........................ To order flowers contact Guest Relations
Fortunes Casino (Guests 18+ yrs) ........................... Deck 4
    7:15pm – Late: Slot Machines
    7:15pm – Late: Tables
Galleria Boutiques ............................................. Deck 5
    7:00pm – Midnight
Guest Relations: Open 24 Hours ............................ Deck 3
Library: Open 24 Hours .............................. Deck 10 & Deck 11
Medical Center .................................................. Deck 2
    9:00am – 11:00am, 5:00pm – 7:00pm
Online@Celebrity: Open 24 Hours ......................... Deck 6
    8:30am – 10:30am, 4:30pm – 9:00pm: Staffed
Photo Gallery & Deep Blue Studios ........................ Deck 5
    6:00pm – 11:00pm
Port & Shopping Desk ........................................ Deck 5
    Closed
Shops on the Boulevard ...................................... Deck 4
    7:00pm – Midnight
Shore Excursions Desk ....................................... Deck 3
    7:00am – 10:00am
Solarium & Inside Whirlpools ................................ Deck 12
    7:30am – 10:00pm
    (Children under 16 yrs must be under adult supervision)
Special Occasions Consultant ............................... Deck 5
    7:00pm – 9:00pm
Swimming Pool .................................................. Deck 12
    7:30am – 9:00pm
Team Earth: Open 24 Hours ................................. Deck 7
Outside Whirlpools ............................................ Deck 12
    7:30am – 10:00pm
    (Children under 16 yrs must be under adult supervision)

## Bar Hours

Café al Bacio, Deck 5 ..................................... 7:00am – 1:00am
Cellar Masters, Deck 4 .................................. 5:00pm – Midnight
Ensemble Lounge, Deck 5 ............................. 5:00pm – 1:00am
Galleria Tastings, Deck 5 ............................... 5:00pm – Midnight
Martini Bar & Crush, Deck 4 ............................... 4:00pm – Late
Mast Bar, Deck 14 (weather permitting) ........... 11:30am – 8:00pm
Michael's Club, Deck 5 ................................. 6:30pm – 1:00am
Oceanview Bar, Deck 14 (weather permitting) ... 11:00am – Midnight
Passport Bar, Deck 3 ................................... 4:00pm – 12:30am
Pool Bar, Deck 12 (weather permitting) ............... 8:30am – 9:00pm
Quasar, Deck 4 ............................................ 9:00pm – Late
Sky, Deck 14 ............................................... 4:00pm – 1:00am
Sunset Bar, Deck 15 (weather permitting) .......... 10:30am – 11:00pm
Only guests 21+ yrs will be served alcoholic beverages.

## Cocktail Special

Toast the Holiday Season today. Available in all Bars and Lounges.

### The Mayflower
*Bombay Sapphire Gin, Earl Grey Tea, Raspberry Preserve, Ginger and Lemon Juice*

---

### Saturday, November 21st, 2009

#### ★ Celebrity Life

**Savor: Jameson Whiskey Tasting**
7:30pm      Michael's Club, Deck 5
Sample selected whisky from Green Island of Ireland.

**Renew: Pool Experience by AquaSpa**
12 Noon – 3:00pm      Solarium, Deck 12
Enjoy an afternoon of wellness with the AquaSpa.

**Discover: Language Learning with Rosetta Stone – Spanish 2**
3:45pm      Celebrity Central, Deck 4
Learn how to speak Spanish.

#### ⊕ Equinox Nights

Celebrity Showtime:
**Celebrity Headliners Variety Show**
Featuring Virtuoso Guitarist/Singer Mario D'Andrea
with Comedian Troy Thirdgill.
8:45pm | 10:45pm      Equinox Theatre, Decks 4 & 5
Accompanied by the Equinox Orchestra. Hosted by your Cruise
Director, Gary Walker.

**Decco – A Night Under the Stars**
10:00pm – Late      Poolside, Deck 12
South Beach comes alive with this interactive production. Featuring the
Celebrity Dancers, Cruise Director's staff and Party Band Top Secret.

#### ♪ Equinox Live

**Grand Foyer • Deck 3**
Inspiration Strings: Classical .................................. 5:30pm – 6:15pm
Jefferson Ang: Guitarist ......................................... 6:30pm – 7:30pm
Manny Kellough: Jazz Quartet ................................ 7:45pm – 8:45pm

**Cellar Masters • Deck 4**
Inspiration Strings: Classical ................................. 9:45pm – 10:45pm

**Entertainment Court • Deck 4**
David Clarke: Steel Pan Player .................... 9:45pm & 10:30pm

**Ensemble Lounge • Deck 5**
Peter James: Piano Performer . 5:45pm – 6:30pm, 6:45pm – 7:45pm
Inspiration Strings: Classical ................................. 7:45pm – 8:45pm
Manny Kellough: Jazz Quartet ................................ 9:45pm – 1:00am

**Michael's Club • Deck 5**
Lloyd Baskin: Piano & Vocals. 8:00pm – 8:45pm, 10:00pm – 1:00am

**Oceanview Café • Deck 14**
Jefferson Ang: Guitarist ....... 8:00pm – 9:00pm, 10:00pm – 10:45pm

**Poolside • Deck 12**
Top Secret: Dance Band ...... 5:30pm – 6:30pm, 10:00pm – 12:15am
David Clarke: Steel Pan Player ............................... 6:30pm – 7:30pm
*Note: Live performers may take short breaks in between sets.*

# CLUB MED CRUISES

75 Valencia Avenue
Coral Gables, FL 33134
(800) CLUB MED
(800) 258-2633 or (305) 925-9000

*Club Med II:* entered service in 1992; 14,000 GRT; 614 × 66 feet; 392-passenger capacity; 196 cabins; European officers, international crew, and international Club Med social staff; cruises in the Caribbean and Mediterranean (Category B—not rated)

Club Med's first cruise venture, *Club Med I,* initiated service in February 1990. *Club Med II* followed in 1992. At 542 feet, these two graceful ladies represented the cruise industry's largest sailing vessels, carrying five masts and seven computer-controlled sails. *Club Med I* was sold to Windstar Cruises in 1998 and now sails as the *Wind Surf.* During the fall, winter, and early spring, *Club Med II* sails in the Caribbean, but in the late spring and summer, she shifts to the Mediterranean, offering cruises that vary between three and twelve days to islands and ports around the Mediterranean.

Prices for U.S. passengers start at $2,700 for a seven-day cruise but are somewhat higher for a suite and single occupancy. Reasonable air/sea packages including land options at Club Med Villages are available.

All of the spacious ocean-view cabins measure 195 square feet and are located on the bottom three decks. There are also six suites that measure approximately twice as much. Thirty-five of the cabins can accommodate passengers, and six can accommodate four. All cabins have twin beds that can be converted to king size, and every stateroom includes a telephone, four-channel TV, radio, refrigerator, minibar, private safe, large mirrors on showers, large sinks and vanities, separate toilet compartment, numerous shelves, and bathrobes and beach towels.

The ship carries its own sailboats, scuba gear, windsurf boards, wake boards, water skis, snorkel equipment, launches, sports platform, and expert staff to give lessons. All sports are free except diving. There are two saltwater swimming pools. A spa with three treatment rooms, massages, saunas, and facials are offered, and a well-equipped fitness center is located atop the ship.

Two open-seating restaurants provide a variety of dining options, from lavish Club Med-style breakfast and lunch buffets (with both indoor and outdoor seating available in the top-deck restaurant) to more formal waiter service in the mid deck. On a recent Mediterranean cruise, I found freshly baked bread, rolls, fresh fruits, and cheeses especially outstanding. There are very acceptable French house wines provided gratis at lunch and dinner as well as an à la carte wine list. A no-tipping policy prevails, as at other Club Meds. Room service and minibars in the rooms are available.

The ship also offers four bars, including a piano bar and lounge and pool bars. Other public facilities include a boutique, a hairdresser/beauty salon, and a small meeting/cardroom. After dinner, the genteel organizers/social staff provide you with typical Club Med-style entertainment, followed by late-night dance music in the disco. Club Med provides a very good cruising experience with maximum time spent in each port of call; however, I found that activities and entertainment are not as well developed as those found on more conventional cruise ships.

## Strong Points

An upscale Club Med experience at sea, offering comfortable cabins and great water sports, French food, and the opportunity to visit tropical islands and great beaches in the Caribbean or some unusual ports in the Mediterranean.

*Courtesy Club Med Cruises*

*courtesy Club Med Cruises*

# *Menu*

"SAINT GERMAIN" SOUP (Pea Soup)
or
ICED CAROTTS CREAM SOUP WITH ORANGES

★★★★

SMOKED SALMON WITH GRAPEFRUITS
or

SHRIMPS AND FRESH MUSHROOMS SALAD WITH COGNAC

★★★★

FROG LEGS IN "PROVENCALE" STYLE
WITH PUREE OF TOMATOES WITH BASIL
or
SWEETBREADS IN "PERIGOURDINE"STYLE

★★★★

GRILLED BEEF RIBEYE WITH "BORDELAISE" SAUCE
or
DUCK FILLET WTIH SHERRIES
or
BROCHETTE OF LEG OF LAMB WITH HERBS

★★★★

CHEESE BOARD

★★★★

SABAGLIONE WITH CHAMPAGNE

or

FRUITS WITH THE 2 SHERBETS

# COMPAGNIE DU PONANT

408 avenue du Prado
13008 Marseilles, France
+33 4 88 66 64 00

United States
2 South Biscayne Blvd, Suite 2470
Miami, FL 33131
1-888-400-1082
http://en.ponant.com/

*Le Boreal, L'Austral,* and *Le Soleal:* entered service in 2010, 2011, and 2013, respectively; 10,700 GRT; 466 × 59 feet; 264-passenger capacity; 132 cabins; French and international officers and crew; cruises to diverse destinations around the world (Category B—five stars)

*Le Ponant:* entered service in 1991; 1,443 GRT; 289 × 39 feet; three-mast sail cruiser; sixty-four-passenger capacity; thirty-two cabins; French and international officers and crew (Category B—not rated)

Established in 1988, Compagnie du Ponant is owned by a private equity firm based in London. The cruise ships have a French environment, specializing in French cuisine and French joie de vivre. Although the clientele is predominantly French, American tour operators, such as Tauck Tours, frequently book blocks of staterooms for English-speaking passengers. The U.S. reservations office is now open to book individual travelers as well. All announcements and written materials are in both French and English; and the cruise line seeks to attract a greater number of English-speaking passengers in the future. The officers are European, and the crew is from Mauritius, the Philippines, and Indonesia. All speak both French and English.

Cruise grounds include the Mediterranean, Adriatic, Black Sea, Aegean Sea, Middle East, Indian Ocean, Red Sea, Caribbean, South America, Southeast Asia, North Sea/Baltics, Norwegian fjords, Arctic (including Spitsbergen, Iceland, Greenland), Antarctica, Falkland Islands, South Georgia, and the South Atlantic.

The 264-passenger capacity, 10,700-ton *Le Boreal, L'Austral,* and *Le Soleal* are sister ships that entered service in 2010, 2011, and 2013, respectively, and feature staterooms that measure from 200 square feet with 56-square-foot balconies to 398 square feet with 86-square-foot balconies for luxury suites and 484 square feet with 97-square-foot balconies for the owner's suite. Forty staterooms can also be converted to twenty two-bedroom suites, accommodating families. All in all, ninety-five percent of the accommodations sport balconies. All accommodations include a king-size or twin beds, bathtub and/or shower, a separate enclosed toilet compartment, stocked refrigerator (with charges for the beverages), complimentary bottled water, a flat-screen satellite TV, a desk, an iPad dock, a safe, a hair dryer, bathrobes and slippers, a direct line telephone, Internet access, Wi-Fi, and 110/220-volt outlets. The TVs offer several French stations, CNN, and a selection of in-house movies and music videos. The accommodations on the top passenger deck have butler service and coffee/espresso machines.

Public areas include a theater for live entertainment and conferences, a main lounge and bar for music, dancing, cocktails and afternoon tea, a fitness and beauty center, a full-service spa, steam rooms, a panoramic lounge/library with a cocktail bar, Internet café with computers, outdoor terrace and musical entertainment, an open-seating main restaurant, and an open-seating grill room serving all three meals buffet style (reservations necessary at dinner), a small outdoor heated pool with deck chairs, and atop ship a sundeck and open-air bar. Room service is available around the clock, and cruise fares now include a 24-7 open bar, gratuities, and all port, safety, and other charges and fees.

In the evening, there is musical entertainment in the lounges and production shows in the theater.

In 2012, the 198-passenger capacity, 8,282-ton *Le Diamont* (the former *Song of Flower*) and the 90-passenger capacity, 3,504-ton *Le Levant* were sold.

*Le Ponant* is a three-mast sailing ship with a sundeck, a marina, two restaurants, lounges, bars, a medical center, and accommodations ranging in size from 113 to 145 square feet for twenty-seven cabins on Marie Galant Deck and from 134 to 165 for the five king bed cabins on Antigua Deck. All accommodations have flat-screen TVs, wardrobes, minibars, hair dryers and bathrobes, direct-dial telephones, showers in the bathrooms, and 110/220-volt outlets.

## Strong Points

These are attractive, well-appointed, intimate small ships, carrying fewer passengers with many interesting itineraries not accessible by larger vessels, with special appeal to French cruisers as well as English-speaking passengers who appreciate a more French style of cruising.

*Dining Room on Le Boreal, courtesy Companie du Ponant*

*L'Austrial, courtesy Companie du Ponant*

*Pool deck on Le Boreal, courtesy Companie du Ponant*

*Cocktails with the Captain, Le Boreal, courtesy Companie du Ponant*

# YOUR DAY ON BOARD LE BOREAL

**6.30 - 10.30am**    **Early risers coffee,** Main Lounge , Deck 3

**Breakfast is served**
**7.00 - 9.00am**    Restaurant La Boussole, Deck 6
**8.00 - 10.00am**    Restaurant La Licorne, Deck 2

**9.15– 10.15am**    Meet your guest relation, Nadège, Leisure Area, deck 5.
She will be at your disposal to give you information about La Compagnie
du Ponant cruises.

**9.00– 11.00am**    **Photo/ Video**
Meet Florence and Laëtitia who will be pleased to help you in the choice of
your pictures
Leisure Aera, Deck 5

**"Barbecue" Lunch is served**
**12.00 - 1.30pm**    Restaurant La Boussole, Deck 6
**12.30 - 2.00pm**    Restaurant La Licorne, Deck 2

**4.00 - 5.00pm**    **Tea time,** Main Lounge , Deck 3

**6.00-7.30pm**    **The shore excursion desk is open.**
We kindly invite you to pick up your excursion ticket for St Petersburg.
In front of the reception, Deck 3.

**7.00 pm**    **Buffet Dinner Restaurant La Boussole,** Deck 6
La boussole offers innovative, light & varied buffet style dinners in a cosy atmosphere.
Please kindly note that advanced booking is required. You can book your table with
your Maître D' Florent during breakfast and lunch time.

**7.30 pm**    **Dinner is served Restaurant La Licorne,** A La Carte, Deck 2
Join our Maitre d' Florent and his team to taste « à la carte » menus, made of dishes
carefully prepared by our Chef Mickaël Bernot in a sophisticated and warm atmosphere.

---

### 9.00PM MUSIC IN ALL BARS OF LE BOREAL

## 9.45PM « RUSSIAN MEDLEY»
### WITH TAMILA & VLADIMIR
MAIN LOUNGE, DECK 3

## WEATHER FORECAST

**Your morning : 13°C - 55°F**   **Your afternoon : : 20°C - 68°F**   **Ephéméride of the day :**

Ascension

Precipitations : 5 mm   Wind : SouthEast

Sunrise:   4.42am
Sunset:    9.53pm

### JOIN LE BOREAL
### IN CASE OF EMERGENCY

| | |
|---|---|
| **Reception:** | 0047 23 677 262 |
| **Hotel Manager:** | +336 45 33 55 14 |
| **Cruise Director:** | +336 43 92 39 36 |
| **Shorex Manager:** | +336 45 35 48 80 |

**On board Emergency : 998**

### COCKTAIL OF THE DAY
Today, your Bar Team suggests:
**Berry Good Tini**
Absolut, Chambord, Grand Marnier,
Cranberry juice & Lime

### YOUR ITINERARY

| | |
|---|---|
| Monday 14 May 2012: | Copenhagen, Denmark |
| Tuesday 15 May 2012: | At Sea |
| Wednesday 16 May 2012: | Riga, Latvia |
| **=>Thursday 17 May 2012:** | **Tallinn, Estonia** |
| Friday 18 May 2012: | St Petersburg, Russia |
| Saturday 19 May 2012: | St Petersburg, Russia |
| Sunday 20 May 2012: | St Petersburg, Russia |
| Monday 21 May 2012: | Helsinki, Finland |
| Tuesday 22 May 2012: | Stockholm, Sweden |

### PONANT YACHT SPA (Deck 5)  ♪ 550

From 8.00am - 1.00pm & 4.00– 8.00pm
Hammam opening hours
**CARITA** From 10.00am to 8.00pm

Ships positions
COMPAGNIE DU PONANT

Le Ponant
France
Nice

Le Levant
At Sea

L'Austral
Montenegro
Kotor

### OPENING HOURS
**Reception (Deck 3)  ♪ 999**
6.00am - Midnight
**Shop (Deck 3)**
10.00am - 12.00pm & 9.00pm - 11.00pm
**Main Lounge Ispahan(Deck 3)**
From 6.30 am
**Observatory Lounge Astrolabe (Deck 6)**
10.00am-1.00pm
5.00pm - 8.00pm & 9.30pm - Midnight
**Pool Bar Le Copernic (Deck 7)**
10.00am - 8.00pm (weather permitting)
**Hospital (Deck 3)  ♪ 999**
10.00 - 11.00am & 5.00 - 7.00pm

COMPAGNIE DU PONANT

## Menu

Dimanche 20 Mai 2012
2012, Sunday 20th May

Velouté d'asperges vertes
*Green asparagus creamy soup*
Ou, Or
Consommé de bœuf aux petits légumes
*Beef and vegetables consommé*

---

Salade d'asperges vertes, jambon de pays, provolone et sauce vierge
*Green asparagus salad with raw ham, provolone cheese and virgin sauce*
Ou, Or
Gambas à la plancha, spaghettis à l'encre de seiche et tomates
*Pan seared tiger prawns with garlic ink spaghettis and fresh tomato*

---

Filet de cabillaud frais poêlé, réduction de Merlot
Choux chinois farci et risotto de blé
*Seared fresh cod filet, Merlot reduction*
*Stuffed chinese cabbage and wheat risotto*
Ou, Or
Filet mignon de porc rôti, sauce au Cognac
Compote de pommes, rösti et courgettes tournées
*Roasted pork tenderloin, Cognac sauce*
*Apple compote, rösti potatoes and turned zucchinis*
Ou, Or
Fusilli alla primavera
*Fusilli alla primavera*

---

Assiette de fromages
*Cheese platter selection*

---

Entremet aux deux chocolats
*Cake made of two chocolates*
Ou, Or
Mousse de yahourt, espuma aux fruits rouges
*Yogurt mousse, redberries espuma*

Ce soir afin d'accompagner au
mieux votre dîner, le Sommelier
vous recommande ..
*Your Sommelier suggestion for the*
*best food and wine pairing for*
*tonight's dinner...*
Le Cigare Blanc 2008
Bonny Doon California 58 €

Barolo 2005
Gaia Dragons 89 €

### Menu Light
### Lean and Light

Salade verte, bleu d'Irlande et croûtons
Mixed green salad
*Irish blue cheese and croûtons*

Filet cabillaud frais grillé à l'huile d'olive
Choux fleur à la vapeur
*Seared fresh cod filet, steamed cauliflower*

Fruits de la passion et banane en compote
*Banana and passion fruit compote*

Les boissons incluses dans votre diner seront :
*Included beverages with your dinner will be :*

Blanc/White . Château Belle Cure
Bordeaux 2011

Rosé : Mas Neuf 2010

Rouge/Red : Mas Neuf 2009
Cabernet Sauvignon

Eau minérale plate et gazeuse
*Still and sparkling mineral water*

### « L'Alternative »

Coesar salad au poulet grillé
*Grilled chicken Caesar salad*

Entrecôte grillée, beurre Maître d'hôtel et
frites
*Grilled rib eve steak, maître D butter and*
*French fries*

Glace tatin
*Tatin ice cream*

 COMPAGNIE DU PONANT

# COSTA CRUISE LINES

Suite #200
Costa Cociere S.P.A.
Via XII Ottobre 2
16121 Genoa, Italy
Fax: (954) 266-2100

200 South Park Road
Hollywood, FL 33021
(954) 266-5600
www.costacruises.com

*Costa Atlantica* and *Costa Mediterranea*: entered service in 2000 and 2003, respectively; 86,000 GRT; 960 × 106 feet; 2,114-passenger capacity (2,680-passenger capacity when full); 1,057 cabins; Italian officers and international crew; *Costa Atlantica* cruises Western Mediterranean during summer and fall, and the Far East during spring and summer; *Costa Mediterranea* cruises Northern Europe during spring and summer, and the Caribbean during winter (Category C—five stars)

*Costa Classica*: entered service in 1991; refurbished in 2001 and 2005; 53,000 GRT; 722 × 102 feet; 1,308-passenger capacity; 654 cabins; Italian officers and international crew; cruises the Eastern Mediterranean and Western Mediterranean throughout winter—including two new Canary Islands and Morocco itineraries—and spring (Category C—four stars)

*Costa Serena, Costa Pacifica, Costa Favolosa*, and *Costa Fascinosa*: entered service in 2007, 2009, 2011, and 2012, respectively; *Costa Serena*, 114,000 GRT; *Costa Pacifica, Costa Favolosa*, and *Costa Fascinosa*, 114,500 GRT; 951 × 116 feet; 3,780-passenger capacity (3,000 double occupancy); 1,496 cabins; Italian officers and international crew; *Serena* cruises Western Mediterranean during summer and fall and South America during winter; *Pacifica* cruises Western Mediterranean during fall and winter, and Northern Europe during summer; *Costa Favolosa* cruises South America during winter, and Western Mediterranean during spring; *Costa Fascinosa* cruises South America during winter, and Eastern Mediterranean and Western Mediterranean during spring (Category C—five stars)

*Costa Fortuna* and *Costa Magica*: entered service in 2003 and 2004, respectively; 103,000 GRT; 893 × 125 feet; 3,788-passenger capacity (2,720 double occupancy);

1,358 cabins; Italian officers and international crew; *Costa Fortuna* cruises Eastern Mediterranean during summer and fall, and Dubai, United Arab Emirates, and Oman during winter and spring; *Costa Magica* cruises South America during winter and Eastern and Western Mediterranean during spring and summer (Category C—five stars)

*Costa Luminosa* and *Costa Deliziosa*: entered service in 2009 and 2010, respectively; 92,600 GRT; 2,828-passenger capacity (2,260 double occupancy); 1,130 cabins; Italian officers and international crew; *Costa Luminosa* cruises in Dubai during winter and Northern Europe during summer and Western Mediterranean during spring and fall; *Costa Deliziosa* will again set out on a 115-day round-the-world cruise that will touch five continents (Category C—five stars)

*Costa neoRomantica* (formerly *Costa Romantica*): entered service in 1993; refurbished in 2003 and refitted in 2011; 56,000 GRT; 722 × 102 feet; 1,800-passenger capacity; 789 cabins; Italian officers and international crew; cruises Indian Ocean, Dubai and Greece, Turkey and Crete during winter and spring, and Eastern Mediterranean during summer and fall (Category C—four+ stars)

*Costa Victoria*: entered service in 1996; renovated in 2004; 75,000 GRT; 828 × 105.5 feet; 1,928-passenger capacity; 964 cabins; Italian officers and international crew; is deployed in the Far East year-round (Category C—four stars)

*Costa Voyager* (formerly *Olympic Voyager* and *Grand Voyager*): entered service in 2000; 25,000 GRT; 593 × 84 feet; 927-passenger capacity; 416 cabins; Italian officers and international crew; cruises the Red Sea during winter and the Eastern Mediterranean during spring (Category C—five stars)

*Costa Diadema* will join the Costa Cruises fleet in November 2014. The ship, which at 132,500 gross tons will be the largest vessel flying the Italian flag, will be 1,004 feet long and carry 4,947 guests and 1,253 crew. Diadema will sail weeklong Western Mediterranean cruises through the winter.

(Medical facilities: Cruise line indicated there are one physician and two nurses aboard each ship but furnished no additional information.)

Note: Passenger capacity reflects double occupancy except where otherwise indicated. Ships are capable of carrying more passengers.

These ships are rated in eleven separate categories in the second half of chapter 11.

Until 1997, when Costa Cruises was acquired by the Carnival Corporation and Airtours, the controlling owners were the Costa family, whose business ventures date back to 1854. In 2000, Carnival bought out the interest of Airtours. Costa made its entrance into the cruise industry in 1947, when it introduced Italy's first air-conditioned passenger ship, the *Anna C*, which carried clients between Italy and South America. During the 1950s, 1960s, and 1970s, the company added eight more vessels, some named after the grandchildren of its president: *Federico C, Franca C, Carla C, Andrea C, Enrico C, Eugenio C, Giovanni C, and Flavia*. From time to time, it chartered other ships, including the *Leonardo da Vinci* and *Amerikanis*, as well as the *Daphne* and *Danae*. In recent years, Costa has sold its older ships, renovated others, and embarked on a program of new builds, offering transatlantic cruises as well as cruises in the Caribbean, North Cape/Fjords/Baltics/Russia, South America, the Mediterranean, Dubai, Suez Canal and Egypt, the Far East, Canada and New England, and the Indian Ocean.

The first of the Costa new builds, the 53,000-ton, 1,308-passenger capacity *Costa Classica*, entered service in 1991, followed by *Costa Romantica*, a sister ship, in 1993, and the 75,000-ton, 1,928-passenger *Costa Victoria* in 1996. The 53,872-ton *Costa Europa*, formerly *Westerdam* of Holland America Line and Homeric of Home Line, joined the Costa fleet in 2002 and was refurbished in 2003. In 2006, six new suites with balconies were added and forty-eight staterooms were completely redesigned. In 2009, she was transferred to Thomson Cruises on a long-term lease. With the introduction of the magnificently designed and decorated *Costa Atlantica* in 2000, the cruise line moved up several notches against the competition. This ship and her sister ship, *Costa Mediterranea*, are far more attractive vessels with more impressive facilities, more verandas, and larger staterooms than their Costa predecessors. Costa's next step was the order of two new 103,000-ton ships, *Costa Fortuna* and *Costa Magica*, which entered service in 2003 and 2004, respectively.

Opting for larger ships with greater passenger capacity, Costa's parent company, Carnival Corporation, ordered still bigger ships for the future, and in 2006, the 114,500-ton, 3,780-passenger (3,000-passenger double occupancy) *Costa Concordia* entered service, followed by a sister ship, *Costa Serena*, in 2007. In the summer of 2009, *Costa Pacifica*, a 114,500-ton, 3,780-passenger (3012-passenger double occupancy) sister ship to the *Costa Concordia* and *Costa Serena*, made her debut, to be followed by *Costa Favolosa* in 2011 and *Costa Fascinosa* in 2012. Also in 2009, the 92,600-ton, 2,828-passenger (2,264 double occupancy) *Costa Luminosa* entered service with a sister ship, *Costa Deliziosa*, in 2010. In early 2012, *Costa Concordia* met with a well-publicized disaster in the Mediterranean off the coast of Italy and is no longer with the fleet. Also in 2012, the 927-passenger, 25,000-ton *Costa Voyager* (the former *Olympic Voyager* and *Grand Voyager*) joined the fleet cruising the Red Sea during winter and Western Mediterranean during spring.

The keynote for Costa is Italian ambiance and spirit. On all the ships, you will find friendly Italian officers, romantic Italian orchestras, and helpful cruise directors and social staff. The officers and others holding important positions are Italian; however, the waiters, cabin attendants, and remainder of the crew are recruited from India, Goa, the Philippines, and other areas around the world and have varying cruise experience. Generally, you do not find big-name entertainers, and the dining experience in both the main restaurants and the buffets is inconsistent. However, the wine list offers an excellent selection of Italian wines at reasonable prices.

The ships with Caribbean itineraries follow the pattern of other cruise ships in the Caribbean mass market but carry many Spanish-speaking passengers as well as Italian and European families who have crossed the sea to enjoy a warm Caribbean winter cruise. When sailing in the Mediterranean, you will have mostly Italian and a smattering of other European shipmates. On all ships, you will hear announcements in Italian, French, English, German, and Spanish. The food, entertainment, and activities are somewhat more geared to the European clientele. Management advises that recent enhancements have been made in the food and service departments. Most of the stage productions are performed in English. For those wanting a cosmopolitan experience, these cruises offer a unique opportunity to sail "Italian style" with Italians and passengers from around the world on a more intimate basis. In the past, a less formal, less service-oriented, and more party-focused atmosphere prevailed; however, management advises that this is changing. During Christmas holidays and the summer months, you will find many young adults and families traveling with children as well as onboard activities to accommodate them. Available on both Mediterranean cruises (April through October) and on Caribbean cruises (November through April) are special programs and counselors for children three to twelve years of age and a Costa Teens Club for teenagers.

In the summer of 1990, Costa introduced the *Costa Marina*, a 26,000-ton rebuilt container ship. In 2011, she left the fleet.

In early 1991, the *Costa Classica* entered service, the first totally new ship built by Costa since the Eugenio C. At 53,000 tons, with a capacity to accommodate 1,764 passengers (1,308 double occupancy). Two-thirds of the cabins are outside, and 20 percent have double or queen beds. All cabins and the ten veranda suites include radio, cable TV, telephone, private safes, hair dryers, and good storage space. In addition to the main restaurant, there is a pizzeria, a pastry and coffee shop, and an indoor/outdoor lido restaurant. There is also a health spa with a fitness center including exercise equipment, sauna, steam room, whirlpools, massage, and other body treatment facilities; a gambling casino; and a 1,500-square-foot conference center for business meetings. In 2005, she was refurbished. She presently offers cruises in the Far East. An almost identical sister ship, *Costa Romantica*, entered service in November 1993. All cabins are larger than on the older Costa ships, and the suites offer additional space, comfort, amenities, and privacy. The clientele includes many Italians.

In 2011, Costa furnished a 90-million-euro refit for the Romantica, increasing her size by 3,000 gross register tons and adding 111 new staterooms and several more private balconies. Also added were a 45,000-square foot Samsara Spa, a wine and cheese bar, a pizzeria, a cabaret lounge, a chocolate bar, and a nightclub. After the refit, the name of the ship was changed to *Costa neoRomantica*.

In December 1992, *Costa Allegra* was added to the fleet. She was retired in 2011.

The 75,000-ton, 2,464-passenger (1,928 double occupancy) *Costa Victoria* entered service in the summer of 1996. She cruises South America during the winter and offers eastern Mediterranean cruises during the summer, spring, and fall.

The 86,000-ton, 2,680-passenger (2,114 double occupancy) *Costa Atlantica* entered service in 2000, followed by a sister ship, *Costa Mediterranea*, in 2003, representing a giant leap forward for the cruise line in terms of creating more elegantly designed and decorated ships. On the *Atlantica*, the public areas, with their eclectic Italian theme honoring the films of Federico Fellini, are magnificent and include more than four hundred original works of art and a replica of Venice's Café Florian, a landmark in St. Mark's Square. The décor on the *Mediterranea* is even more spectacular. Architect and designer Joseph Farcus has created a floating palazzo in which Italian art, frescoes, murals, and statuary adorn all of the common areas and exquisite granite, marble, and woods enhance every cabin and public room. Many Costa repeat passengers prefer this ship to the line's other vessels.

The 1,057 staterooms and suites on both ships are far more attractive and comfortable than on the earlier Costa new builds. Two-thirds have ocean views, verandas, and measure 210 square feet (which includes a 30-square-foot veranda). Twenty percent are located in the interior of the ship and measure 160 square feet. Every accommodation features a refrigerator/minibar, remote-control TV, hair dryer, personal safe, dresser with a makeup area, small sitting area, and adequate-sized bathroom. Although the six grand suites (measuring 650 square feet including large verandas) are the most desirable, the thirty-four 360-foot (with veranda) panorama suites are also extremely comfortable with enormous storage and closet space, Jacuzzi tub/shower combinations and double vanities in the bathrooms, separate dressing/makeup areas, and large verandas.

Public areas are uniformly exquisite and include two-level restaurants serving all three meals in two sittings. The buffets and pizzerias, attractively furnished, are alternative casual venues with multiple food stations and both inside and outside tables. There are also hamburger/hot dog grills. Club Atlantica and Club Medusa, elegant, glass-enclosed observation lounges, serve both as alternative specialty restaurants (with menus designed by Gualtieri Marchesi) in the evening and late-night spots for romantic dancing. Other public areas include imaginative Greek/Roman-style spa centers with multiple levels of state-of-the-art exercise equipment, hair salons, his and hers locker rooms with steam and sauna, and numerous treatment rooms offering a full therapy program; three central swimming pools, one with a retractable magrodome; children's pools; whirlpools; jogging tracks; basketball areas; shopping streets with upscale boutiques and signature item/sundry shops; conference facilities; casinos; cardrooms; Internet café/libraries; children's facilities; impressive three-deck-high theaters, the locale for production shows; two-level discos; several additional lounges for various entertainments; and the above-mentioned Café Florian on the *Atlantica*. Eastern Caribbean itineraries on both ships include a visit to Costa's private beach on Catalina Island on the coast of the Dominican Republic.

The 103,000-ton, 2,720-passenger (3,788 with every berth occupied) *Costa Fortuna* also joined the fleet in 2003, followed by her sister ship, *Costa Magica*, in 2004. Five hundred and twenty-two of the 1,358 cabins and suites on each ship have balconies, and twenty-seven can accommodate the physically challenged. An inside cabin measures 160 square feet and an ocean view with balcony 210 square feet, a suite with balcony 360 square feet, and the Grand Suite with veranda 650 square feet. The décor of the *Fortuna* incorporates the style and design of the grand ocean liners of the past. The décor on the *Magica* pays tribute to the most beautiful and magical Italian locales. These are beautifully decorated ships; however, the traffic pattern is a bit complicated because of the location of the dining rooms. Facilities on each ship are similar to the *Atlantica* and *Mediterranea*, except somewhat expanded, and include a nine-deck-high atrium; eleven bars; a three-deck theater; three swimming pools, including one covered by a retractable magrodome; a children's pool and a children's play area; a casino; a disco; an enormous, elegant ballroom; an Internet café; a business/conference center; a two-deck gym and spa; unusually comfortable, spacious changing rooms with large sauna, steam, and shower facilities; two two-story main dining rooms; a buffet and pizzeria; and a combination specialty restaurant and observation lounge. The *Fortuna* cruises the eastern Mediterranean during the summer and fall and the eastern Caribbean during winter and spring, whereas the *Costa Magica* cruises Northern Europe and the Mediterranean during the summer and fall and Brazil during the winter and spring.

The 114,000-ton *Costa Serena*, with a 3,780-passenger capacity (and 3,000 lower berths), entered service during 2007, followed by sister ships, *Costa Pacifica*, in 2009; *Costa Favolosa*, in 2011; and *Costa Fascinosa*, in 2012. Sixty percent of the cabins have ocean views, and 40 percent have balconies. Unique features on these ships not presently on the other Costa vessels include two pools with sliding-glass roofs, one of which has a 200-square-foot video screen; five Jacuzzis; the Samsara Spa, a 20,000-square-foot wellness and relaxation center spanning two decks and including a gym, an indoor thalasso pool, treatment rooms, a Turkish bath and solarium, and a specialty health restaurant; and fifty-five staterooms and twelve suites that have direct access to the spa and special spa amenities; specialty restaurants with cuisine by *Michelin*-rated chef Ettore Bocchia; thirteen bars; and a theater spanning three decks. There are numerous venues for listening and dancing in the evenings. *Costa Pacifica* arrived in 2009, *Costa Favolosa* in 2011, and *Costa Fascinosa* in 2012, at 114,500 tons with six additional cabins and sixteen additional verandas. The Samsara Spa was expanded to 23,000 square feet, and there are two pools, one with a retractable magrodome and the other with a giant outdoor movie screen. As mentioned above, the *Costa Concordia* is no longer in the fleet.

The 92,600-ton, 2,828-passenger (2,260 double occupancy) *Costa Luminosa* and a sister ship, *Costa Deliziosa*, entered service in 2009 and 2010, respectively, boasting verandas in 68 percent of the staterooms and a new golf simulator with thirty-seven virtual golf courses.

Guests booking 120 days in advance can take advantage of early-booking fares that can result in up to a 50 percent savings.

## Strong Points

Fun-oriented full-facility ships with Italian themes affording an opportunity to travel with numerous Italian and international passengers; special appeal for Spanish- and Italian-speaking passengers; an abundance of families and children's activities during holidays and summer months; and good value for your cruise dollar

*Costa Favolosa, courtesy Costa Cruises*

*Bar and Lounge, courtesy Costa Cruises*

*Atrium on Costa Favoloso, courtesy Costa Cruises*

*Stateroom, Costa Favolosa, courtesy Costa Cruise Line*

*Pool on Costa Favolosa, courtesy Costa Cruise Line*

# Dinner

## APPETIZERS

### Ceviche di tonno
Tuna ceviche served on a salad bed * #

### Lonza di maiale
Sliced pork loin on Belgian endive, with extra-virgin olive oil and balsamic vinegar #

### Arancini di riso (♡V)
Rice balls with mozzarella and tomatoes

## SOUP

### Zuppa di borlotti con crostini all'Emmenthal (♡V)
Borlotti bean soup with Emmenthal cheese crouton

## PASTA

### Ravioli di ricotta ed erbe con salsa aurora (♡V)
Ravioli pasta filled with ricotta cheese and herbs served with tomato and béchamel sauce

### Linguine alla carbonara
Linguine with bacon and eggs sauce*

## MAIN COURSES

### Fritto misto di pesce in salsa tartara
Mixed platter of fish with tartar sauce #

### Spalla di vitello con salsa di funghi secchi
Veal shoulder with dry mushroom sauce served with roasted potatoes and vegetables #

### Stroganoff di manzo
Beef Stroganoff served with white rice and fried leeks #

### Pasticcio di polenta con salsa al gorgonzola (♡V)
Polenta custard with gorgonzola cheese sauce

## SALAD

### Insalata mista
Romaine, endivie, radicchio, curly green, Boston lettuce, tomato, carrots and olives
Choice of Dressing: French, Italian, Thousand Island

## CHEESES

### Selezione di formaggi
Selection of International cheeses
Ricotta, Maasdam e Gouda
served with walnut bread

(♡V) Vegetarian Diet

## Desserts

**Strudel di mele al miele e noci**
Apple strudel with honey and nuts

**Mousse di frutti di bosca**
Mousse with wild berries

**Eclairs al ciaccolato**
Chocolate éclairs

**Gelato del giorno**
Ice cream of the day: coffe, strawberry

**Sorbetto del giorno**
Sherbet of the day: lemon, orange

**Frutta fresca**
Fresh fruit: apple, melon Canataloupe, pineapple

## Champagne and Sparkling Wines

|  | US $ |
|---|---|
| Moët & Chandon Dom Pérignon | 250.00 |
| Veuve Clicquot Ponsardin Brut | 90.00 |
| Moët & Chandon Brut Impérial | 85.00 |
| Pommery Brut Royale | 80.00 |
| Jaquart Brut Mosaique | 65.00 |
| Berlucchi Cuvèe Imperiale Vintage Brut | 45.00 |
| Asti Spumante Martini | 30.00 |
|  | Flûte 6.50 |
| Moscato d'Asti Bosc dla Rey Batasiolo | 30.00 |
|  | Flûte 6.50 |

## After dinner drinks

|  | US $ |
|---|---|
| Baglio Florio – Vecchioflorio Risena | 6.90 |
| Ruby Port Sundemann – Hurvey's Bristol Cream | 6.30 |
| Counoisier Napoleon | 11.00 |
| Glenfiddich Ancient Reserve 18 years | 11.00 |
| "Grappa Walcher" | 6.90 |
| Limoncello, Disaronno Originale | 6.90 |
| Averna, Jägermeister, Montenegro, Ramazzotti | 6.90 |
| Liquore di Grappa e Miele "Revel Chion" | 6.90 |

# Chef's suggestions

**Linguine alla carbonara**
Linguine with bacon and eggs sauce*

**Spalla di vitello con salsa di funghi secchi**
Veal shoulder with dry mushroom sauce served with roasted potatoes and vegetables #

## Always Available

**Minestrone**
Vegetables soup

**Spaghetti al pomodoro e basilico o alla Bolognese**
Spaghetti with tomato and basil sauce or with meat sauce #

**Feijão (fagioli), Riso, Mandioca**
Beans, white rice, manioc

**(V) Vegetarian Diet**

## Wine Suggestions

Gewürztraminer DOC "Elena Walch" (Trentino, Italia)          US$ 40.00

Teroldego Sgarzon Granato IGT "Foradori" (Trentino, Italia) US$ 43.00

*Courtesy Costa Cruise Line*

**Costa Favolosa**

# Ilhabela

Friday, 25th January 2013

Sunrise: 6.30am
Sunset:: 7.55 pm

Temperature: Min. 22°C - Max. 26°C
Sea: Smooth ~

## Our Captain Massimo Pennisi Informs You:

**2.00pm** Estimated time of arrival in **ILHABELA**

**9.30pm LAST TENDER BOAT ALL ABOARD!**

**10.00pm** The Costa Favolosa sails for **SANTOS (53** nautical miles)

Our Agency
ISS / DEEP SEA AGENCIA MARITIMA LTDA
Rua Duque De Caxias 188 - CJ 15 - 2 Piso /
Centro
Ilhabela, BRAZIL
**EMERGENCY TELEPHONE NUMBER**
☏+55 12 389 32247 ☏+55 12 389 23760
deepsea@deepsea-agency.com

*GANGWAY EXIT: Deck 0 Kyoto (front of the ship)*

### Navigational Highlights

After navigating all the night, far away from the coast, we will pass by Cape Frio versus 2.00am, after the Cape we will follow a southwestern course in direction of Ilhabela. Circa 12.00pm we will start to navigate in vicinity of the Island São Sebastião. Around 12.30pm we will embark the pilot of the port, who will guide us to the anchor zone at Ilhabela. Ilhabela is an Archipel in front on the north coast of the state San Paolo of Brasil. The archipel is rich of mountains. Ilhabela is formed from the same landmass as the island of São Sebastião and Segheria, the island São Sebastião has is one of the highest points on the coast of Sao Paolo, with the peak of São Sebastião with the high of 1397 meters and the peak Papagalo with 1307 meters above sea level. The Island is situated 135 kilometres away from the capital of the state and 140 km away from the boarder to the state of Rio de Janeiro. The Island is southern of the tropic of the Capricorn, which is passing close to the city of Ubatuba. One of the main characteristics of Ilhabela is the Atlantic forest which is covering a big part of this rainforest Island. Ilhabela is rich on preserved nature and has a limited the urbanization to protect the rainforest. Our Stop is foreseen until 10.00pm. Once we left the anchoring Zone of Ilhabela, we will transit the channel of São Sebastiao, which is approx 9 Seamiles long and at the thigrest part only 1.5 Seamiles wide. When we reach the Point Sela, which will be visible o n the left side of the Ship, we will disembark the Pilot who assisted us during the transit of the São Sebastiao Channel and we will sail straight to Santos.

## Tender Boat Service in Ilhabela

DOCUMENTS NEEDED: COSTA CARD

Upon arrival Local Authorities will come onboard to commence immigration procedures. Once completed, the Authorities will declare the ship's clearance and guests may then disembark. Guests going on excursion should proceed to their Meeting Point.

GUESTS NOT TAKING PART IN THE EXCURSIONS BUT WHO WOULD LIKE TO GO ASHORE IN THE PORT OF ILHABELA, MUST COLLECT A NUMBERED TICKET WHICH IS REQUIRED FOR THE TENDER BOAT SERVICE.

Tickets for the Tender Boat will be available at the HORTENSIA THEATRE, DECK 3 HERMITAGE starting from 2.30pm.

After receiving your tender ticket, we kindly ask that you wait in the public areas (lounges or outside deck) until your number is announced over the loudspeaker system. It is important that you pay close attention to the announcements made over the loudspeaker. We also kindly ask for your cooperation in order to achieve an efficient and safe disembarkation.

WE WOULD LIKE TO INFORM YOU, THAT DUE TO ORGANIZATION AND SAFETY REASONS, IT IS FORBIDDEN TO WAIT ON DECK ZERO, IN THE TENDER DISMEBARKATION AREA. Once the majority of guests have exited the ship, an announcement will be made indicating that the collection of numbered tickets will no longer be necessary. After this announcement, guests may then proceed directly to the gangway. The numbered tickets are not required for the return tender to the ship.

Guests going on excursion please proceed to your Meeting Points as indicated in your TODAY programme.

**First tender boat available to go ashore: 2.30pm**
**The last tender service will leave from the Pier: 9.30pm.**

## Important information: Brazilian Federal State Law

We inform all our Guests that according to Federal Law nº 9294/96 and Law nº13.541/09 (for the state o (São Paulo), it is not permitted to smoke on board in closed or covered areas during our stay in the port of Ilhabela. Fines to offenders are from R$ 200 to R$ 3.2 million Brazilian Reais. It will only be possible to smoke on board in areas designated as smoking areas once the ship has left the port. Thank you for your cooperation.

## EXCURSION OFFICE

9.00am-11.30am
Atrio dei Diamanti, Deck 3 Hermitage
Deck 3 Hermitage
You can also book via the Multimedia Totems
situated on decks 3, 5 & 9.

## COCKTAIL OF THE DAY

EXCELLENT
VODKA, PEACH SCHNAPPS, ORANGE &
CRANBERRY JUICE US$ 7
Also available in the XL glass
at just US$ 7.50!

## BELPHÉGOR CINEMA

**4D** 10.00am-12.30pm
3.00pm-7.00pm / 8.00pm-00.00pm
Deck 5, Tivoli.
Tickets on sale via the multimedia totems. (Minimum age: 6 years)

## RACE CAR SIMULATOR

10.00am-8.00pm
Scuderia Costa, Deck 12 El Prado
Don't miss the opportunity to receive
your free personalized certificate and
experience the thrill of racing at 350km/h.
it is compulsory to use closed shoes
(minimum age: 16 years)

## GOLF CLUB

10.00am-1.00pm / 3.00pm-6.00pm
Deck 12 El Prado
(Minimum age: 10 years)
Learn to play golf for the 1st time,
Practice or challenge friends to a round
of Golf. Choose from 37 different golf
courses, (1-4 persons).
Please reserve your time with Jonathan,
our onboard Golf Pro in advance via the
Multimedia Totems.

## ESCLUSIVE ITINERARIES 2013: CRUISE SALES AGENT

Our Cruise Sales Agent Mineia is available to book all your future cruises
from 9.00am to 10.30am in the Grand
Bar Palatino, Deck 5 Tivoli. If you book
on board, you will be entitled of an
additional 3% discount on our offers!

## SHABBAT SERVICE

6.30pm
Bar Classico Montespan, Deck 5 Tivoli

## Good Morning

| | | |
|---|---|---|
| 9.00am | Healthy Walk | Sport court, Deck 12 El Prado |
| 9.00am-12.30pm | Spa Products Promotion, Come and buy your Beauty Product from France and England starting from 12 US$ | Atrio dei Diamanti , Deck 3 Hermitage |
| 10.00am-11.00am | Books and games at your disposal | Library Della Rosa, Deck 5 Tivoli |
| 10.00am | Quiz: Ship Race | Grand Bar Palatino, Deck 5 Tivoli |
| 10.00am-3.00pm | Free footprint clinic – Your footprint can tell us much more than you think... get your complimentary imprint and we will advise you about next steps! | Spa, Deck 11 Luxembourg |
| 10.15am | Art and craft (only for adults) | Balcony dell'Ondina, Deck 10 Escorial |
| 10.30am | Bright eyes – Learn how to take care of dark circles and puffiness around the eyes. Receive a `complimentary` Pro Collagen-Eye application for all who at tend! | Spa, Deck 11 Luxembourg |
| 10.30am | Lets's play Basket | Sportcourt, Deck 12 El Prado |
| 10.45am | Music Quiz: Brasilian Soap Opera | Pompadour Lounge , Deck 5 Tivoli |

---
10.45am - Lido dell'Ondinda, Deck 9 Villa Borghese
### Cha Cha Cha lesson with Dança de Salão
---

| | | |
|---|---|---|
| 11.00am | Relieving back pain – Chiropractic? Medications? Find out a new and effective method to improve your posture and get rid of your pains.. | Spa, Deck 11 Luxembourg |
| 11.15am | The Queen of the 7 Seas | Lido dell'Ondina, Deck 9 Villa Borghese |
| 11.30am | Video Quiz: Traditional Costumes of the World | Sala Carte, Deck 5 Tivoli |
| 11.30pm | Stop my water retention – Why do I retain water? What can I do? This seminar is for you! | Spa, Deck 11 Luxembourg |
| 11.45am | CULINARIC DEMONSTRATION CLUB FAVOLOSA: Fire & Ice Shrimps Cocktail | Lido dell'Ondina, Deck 9 Villa Borghese |
| 12.00pm | **THE SURPRISE OF COSTA FAVOLOSA** | Lido dell'Ondina, Deck 9 Villa Borghese |

## Good Afternoon

| | | |
|---|---|---|
| 3.00-4.00pm | Books and games at your disposal | Library Della Rosa, Deck 5 Tivoli |
| 3.00pm | Quiz: Currencies of the World | Library Della Rosa, Deck 5 Tivoli |
| 3.15pm | Hit the target | Lido dell'Ondina, Deck 9 Villa Borghese |
| 4.00pm | Game with the cruise staff | Lido dell'Ondina, Deck 9 Villa Borghese |
| 4.15pm | Quiz: General Culture | Grand Bar Palatino, Deck 5 Tivoli |
| 5.15pm | Quiz: Geography | Grand Bar Palatino, Deck 5 Tivoli |
| 5.30pm | Have fun with the cruise staff | Lido dell'Ondina, Deck 9 Villa Borghese |
| 6.15pm | Walk under the Sun of Ilhabela | Sports Court, Deck 12 El Prado |

## Fitness

| | | |
|---|---|---|
| 09.00am | Bike class | front of the ship, Deck 12 |
| 10.00am | Step | Lido dell'Ondina, Deck 9 Villa Borghese |
| 11.00am | Postural Strengh | Grand Bar Palatino, Deck 5 Tivoli |
| 4.00pm | Gymstick | Disco Etoile, Deck 4 Versailles |
| 5.00pm | Jump | Lido dell'Ondina, Deck 9 Villa Borghese |
| 5.00pm | Bike Class | Front of the Ship, Deck 12 |

## Hospitality Desk

11.30am-noon - Grand Bar Palatino, Deck 5 Tivoli
Your English Host Stephan is available for your questions, any assistance you may need!
**LAST CHANCE TO GET THE INFORMATIONS ABOUT YOUR FINAL DISEMBARKATION YOU MIGHT NEED!**

## WELLNESS CENTRE

Spa: 8.00am-9.00pm - Deck 11 Luxembourg ☎ 0151

EXPRESS SPA SERVICES
Short, sweet and absolutely sumptuous Spa services.
Choose between an array of 26 treatments between 10-minute and 25-minute indulgences.
Prices starting at only US$12 per treatment!

9.00am - Yoga (US$11)

## PHOTO SHOP

9.00am-10.30pm - Deck 4 Versailles

Come and discover at our Photo Shop our
SPECIAL PACKAGE.
Discover how to pay less then US$ 7 for a picture

And finally the Video of the Cruise is ready, come and buy
the DVD of the Cruise and the Excursions and receive a free
DVD of the Ship.

## Good Evening

DRESS CODE: INFORMALE

---

### Hortensia Theatre

Deck 3 Hermitage, Deck 4 Versailles and Deck 5 Tivoli

**8.30pm**

For Guests with the 2<sup>nd</sup> Dinner Sitting

**10.15pm**

For Guests with 1<sup>st</sup> the Dinner Sitting

Your Cruise Director

### NAIM JOSÉ AUYB

presents

# ENCHANTED CASTLE

starring the Singers and Dancers of Afro Arimba Productions

For the safety of the performers and to guarantee the quality of the special effects, the use of flash photography and video cameras with auxiliary light is not permitted. We request that you switch off your mobile phone before the beginning of the show.

---

**11.45pm - Grand Bar Palatino, Deck 5 Tivoli**

# ITALIAN PARTY

**with the cruise staff, Dança de Salão
and the Magic Sound Band**

**12.30am - Salão Moliere, Deck 5 Tivoli**

# BRASILIAN PARTY

**with the cruise staff,, Dança de Salão
Lizzi Band and Quibele Band**

---

## MUSICAL ENTERTAINMENT

▶ *Atrio dei Diamanti,*
  *Deck 3 Hermitage*     6.00pm-2.00am
  Pianobar and international music
  with Antonio and the Simple Duo

▶ *Grand Bar Palatino,*
  *Deck 5 Tivoli*     6.00pm-1.30am
  Music with the Duo Padrón and the
  Magic Sound Band

▶ *Ball room Pompadour,*
  *Deck 5 Tivoli*     9.00pm-1.30am
  Music with Will

▶ *Caffetteria Porta d'Oro,*
  *Deck 5 Tivoli*
         6.30-7.30pm/9.30pm-1.30am
  Music with Danila

▶ *Piano Bar Camelot,*
  *Deck 5 Tivoli*
         6.30-7.30pm / 8.00pm-2.00am
  Italian and international music with
  Dario and Roberto

▶ *Club Favolosa,*
  *Deck 11 Luxembourg*
  7.15pm-10.30pm
  Music with the pianist Fred

▶ *Disco Etoile,*
  *Deck 4 Versailles*     Midnight -.
  with DJ Eduardo

  The musical programme could be
  interrupted by technical intervals.

The Costa Collection Store by Emilio
Robba offers gifts for you and for others,
souvenirs from around the world, fantasy
jewellery, home décor and travel items
that embody the Costa Cruises spirit of
value, quality and design.
**10.00am-18.00pm , Deck 5 Tivoli**

## SQUOK CLUB

Please check our Fun@Sea programme for
more information on our Mini Club
(3-6 years) and Maxi Club (7-12 years)
available at the Squok Club located on
Deck 10 Escorial.
For whom, who is interesting in a Baby
Sitting Service after Midnight, please contact the Chief Children Animateur

### TEEN ZONE (12-17 years)

Cristiano and Kaká are waiting for you
at the Teen Zone, DECK 10

---

## ONBOARD SHOPS

10.00am - 11.00pm, Deck 5 Tivoli

50% Discount day ...
Chose among Fragrances Benetton, Feragamo , Ducatti , Ungaro
(prices starting from US$23.00)
SELECTED Costa T-shirts with 50% discount and more...

Pick up your drinks you have buyed, exclusively on deck 5 with your
receipt and your costa card from 9.00pm to 12.00am for the disembarkation of the beverages the clients are self responsable, the ship
is not offering any assitance

## CASINO

Slots: 9.00am -Arrival/Departure-...
Tables: Departure-.. - Deck 5 Tivoli

For those who are disembarking tomorrow please make
sure to CASH OUT all your remaining funds in your
costa card before Casino closes!

Minors under 18 are not allowed to stay in the Casino
Please do not Smoke Cigars or Pipes in the Casino

## ENJOY YOUR MEAL

### Early breakfast
▶ Ca' d'Oro Self-Service Restaurant, Deck 9 Villa Borghese

### Breakfast      6.30am
▶ Ca' d'Oro Self-Service Restaurant, Deck 9 Villa Borghese
Self-Service      7.00am-11.00am
Egg Station (right side)      7.00am-10.00am
▶ Lido dell'Ondina, Deck 9 Villa Borghese
Central Pool      9.30am-11.30am
▶ Lido di Porpora, Deck 9 Villa Borghese
Aft Pool      9.00am-11.30am
▶ Duca d'Orléans Restaurant, Deck 3 Hermitage
Open Sitting      8.00am-9.15am
▶ Samsara Restaurant, Deck 3 Hermitage
Open Sitting      8.00am-9.15am
*Reserved for Samsara guests only with packages*
▶ In cabin      7.00am-10.00am
(Complete Breakfast = US$ 7.50 per person)
*The order will be charged according to the number of persons occupying the cabin.*

### Lunch
▶ Ca' d'Oro Self-Service Restaurant, Deck 9 Villa Borghese
In the Self-Service Restaurant you will find SEAFOOD
specialties      Noon-4.00pm
Pasta & Soup of the Day (right side)      Noon-4.00pm
Grill (left side)      Noon-4.00pm
Pizzeria      Noon-4.00pm
▶ Lido dell'Ondina, Deck 9 Villa Borghese
Grill (Central Pool)      Noon-5.00pm
▶ Lido di Porpora, Deck 9 Villa Borghese
Grill - Pool Aft of the Ship      12.30pm-5.30pm
▶ Duca d'Orléans Restaurant, Deck 3 Hermitage
Open Sitting      12.00pm-1.30pm
▶ Samsara Restaurant, Deck 3 Hermitage
Open Sitting      12.00pm-1.30pm
*Reserved for Samsara guests only with packages*

### Paninoteca
▶ Sandwich Bar, Central Buffet, Deck 10 Escorial

### Afternoon Tea      1.00pm-5.00pm
▶ Ca' d'Oro Self-Service Restaurant, Deck 9 Villa Borghese
Afternoon Tea Time      4.30pm-5.30pm

### Pizzeria
▶ Ca' d'Oro Self-Service Restaurant, Deck 9 Villa Borghese
Self-service pizza by the slice      12.30pm-6.00pm
     7.00pm-3.00am

### Dinner
▶ Duca di Borgogna Restaurant or Duca d'Orléans Restaurant
Deck 3 Hermitage and Deck 4 Versailles
First Sitting      7.15pm
Second Sitting      9.45pm
In order to guarantee the best service, guests are kindly asked to respect set meal hours. Please contact the Maître D' if you arrive 15 minutes after the sitting has started. In the Restaurant we kindly ask that you do not wear shorts or bermudas.
▶ Samsara Restaurant, Deck 3 Hermitage
Open Sitting      7.15pm -9.45pm

### Club Favolosa Restaurant
▶ Club Favolosa, Deck 11 Luxembourg   7.15pm -9.45pm
Restaurant Club Favolosa offers you a selection of Italian specialities. Scrupulous care is taken over every detail so that you can enjoy the experience and fascination of a voyage into the world of the exquisite Italian kitchen. Reserve a table in our Club Favolosa through the MULTIMEDIA TOTEMS or contact the Maître D'. In the Club Restaurant shorts and tank tops are prohibited.

### Gastronomic Surprises
▶ Saloni, ponte 5 Tivoli
Sweets and Salts      01.00

## INFORMATIONS

### Return of Library Books
We kindly inform all Guests finishing their cruise tomorrow that you must return all library books today at the library or at the Guest Services when the library is closed.
In the event that a library book is not returned on the evening prior to your disembarkation, a US$15.00 charge will be added to your end of cruise account.

### Lost Items
All items found during the cruise are kept at the Guest Services, deck 3 Hermitage.

### On demand movies
Dear Guests, we would like to inform you that any on demand movies purchased through the in cabin interactive television system must be viewed within 48 hours of purchase.

### Questionnaires
We do our best to make our service better than your expectations, therefore we please ask you to dedicate a few minutes of your time for an honest opinion. Your comments are valuable for our continuous effort to improve services on board. We are sure you will be able to judge us sincerely. The questionnaires will be delivered to your cabin, once they are completed please drop the forms in the box in front of Guest Services, Deck 3 Hermitage. Those who return their completed questionnaires, will be entered into the draw could be the winner of one of 5 free cruises for 2 people.

### Onboard purchase means of payment
We wish to inform our Guests that all purchases made onboard must be charged on their shipboard account only (with their Costa Card). For each purchase Guests will be asked to sign a paper receipt. Receipts must be retained as proof of purchase for goods subject to guarantee. Cash payments are allowed only on disembarkation day and require the Costa Card to be used to account for the transaction. No cash transactions are permitted at any other time

## BAR
Guests must be 18 years old in order to purchase alcohol. In case of doubt, proof of identity will be requested.

| | | |
|---|---|---|
| Bar dei Diamanti (Central Hall) | Deck 3 Hermitage | 7.00am-1.30am |
| Disco Etoile | Deck 4 Versailles | Midnight-... |
| Montespan Classic Bar (Cigar Bar) | Deck 5 Tivoli | Closed |
| Grand Bar Palatino | Deck 5 Tivoli | 7.00am-1.45am |
| Caffeteria Porta d'Oro (Chocolate Bar) | Deck 5 Tivoli | 3.00pm-1.30am |
| Club Cavallo Bianco | Deck 5 Tivoli | Closed |
| Pompadour Lounge | Deck 5 Tivoli | 6.00pm-1.00am |
| Piano Bar Camelot (Wine Bar) | Deck 5 Tivoli | 4.00pm-1.30am |
| Molière Lounge | Deck 5 Tivoli | 7.00pm-1.30am |
| Lido dell'Ondina Bar (Central Pool) | Deck 9 Villa Borghese | 7.00am-11.00pm |
| Lido di Porpora Bar (Back Pool) | Deck 9 Villa Borghese | 7.00am-1.00am |
| Bar Scuderia Costa - Solarium Bar | Deck 12 El Prado | 10.00am-8.00pm |

## SERVICE HOURS

| | | |
|---|---|---|
| **Guest Services** ✆ 3333 | Deck 3 Hermitage | |
| Open 24 hours | | |
| Currency Exchange: Closed | Reals not available | |
| **Room Service** | | |
| 24 hours ✆ 6666 | | |
| **Costa Club Point** | Deck 5 Tivoli | |
| 15.00am-17.00am | | |
| We would like to inform all Costa Club members that it is also possible to check their points via the Multimedia Totems. | | |
| **Excursion Office** ✆ 3131 | Deck 3 Hermitage | |
| 9.00am-11.30am | | |
| **Spa** | Deck 11 Luxembourg | |
| 8.00am-9.00pm | | |
| **Fitness centre** | Deck 11 Luxembourg | |
| 7.00am-9.00pm (Guests under 16 years of age are not allowed) | | |
| **Photoshop** | Deck 4 Versailles | |
| 9.00am - 10.30pm | | |
| **Onboard Shops** | Deck 5 Tivoli | |
| 10.00am - 11.00pm | | |
| **Casino** | Deck 5 Tivoli | |
| Slots:09.00am-Arrival/Departure-... | | |
| Tables:Departure-... | | |
| **Cinema 4D Belphagor** | Deck 5 Tivoli | |
| 10.00am-12.30pm/3.00pm-7.00pm/8.00pm-12.00am | | |
| **Golf Club** | Deck 12 El Prado | |
| 10.00am-1.00am / 3.00pm-6.00pm | | |
| **Race Car** (Guests under 16 years of age are not allowed) | Deck 12 El Prado | |
| 10.00am-8.00pm | | |
| **Internet Point** | Deck 4 Versailles | |
| Open 24 hours | | |
| **Delia Rosa Library** | Deck 5 Tivoli | |
| 10.00am-11.00am /3.00pm-4.00pm | | |
| In the event that a library book is not returned on the evening prior to your disembarkation, a US$15.00 charge will be added to your end of | | |

| | | |
|---|---|---|
| **Water Slide** (weather permitting) | Deck 14 Las Dueñas | |
| 10.00am-5.00pm | | |
| For safety reasons, the personnel in charge will verify the minimum height restrictions which must be met (1m and 200cm). | | |
| **Pool (Back)** | Deck 9 Villa Borghese | |
| 8.00am-8.00pm (reserved for adults) | | |
| **Pool (Central)** | Deck 9 Villa Borghese | |
| 8.00am-10.00pm | | |
| **Pool** | Deck 11 Luxembourg | |
| 8.00am-8.00pm | | |
| **Sports Court** | Deck 12 El Prado | |
| 9.00am-Noon / 3.00pm-6.00pm | | |
| **Squok Club** ✆ 0989 | Deck 10 Escorial | |
| 9.00am-12.00am | | |
| **Holy Mess with Wedding Renewal** | | |
| 11.30am | Moliere Lounge, Deck 5 Tivoli | |
| **Hospital** ✆ 0020 | | |
| Emergency ✆ 99 | Deck 0 Kyoto | |
| Doctor's medical hours | 9.00am-11.00am | |
| | 5.00pm-7.00pm | |
| Visits during medical hours | US$ 70.20 | |
| Cabin visit | US$ 101.25 | |
| Visit out of medical hours | US$ 87.75 | |
| Night visit | US$ 121.50 | |
| **Pharmacy** | Deck 0 Kyoto | |
| 8.00am-Noon / 4.00pm-8.00pm | | |
| It is possible also to purchase certain medication (for some you may | | |

## CRYSTAL CRUISES

2049 Century Park East, Suite 1400
Los Angeles, CA 90067
(310) 785-9300
www.crystalcruises.com

*Crystal Serenity*: entered service in 2003; renovated in 2008, 2011, and 2013; 68,870 GRT; 820 × 105.6 feet; 1,070-passenger capacity; 535 staterooms; Norwegian captain and international officers, hotel and dining staff, and crew; cruises in the South Pacific, Australia/New Zealand, Asia, Europe, Mediterranean, Canary Islands, Caribbean, Panama Canal, New England/Canada, transatlantic, and other destinations around the world (Category A—six+ stars)

*Crystal Symphony*: entered service in 1995; renovated in 2004, 2006, 2009, and 2012; 51,044 GRT; 781 × 99 feet; 922-passenger capacity; 461 staterooms; Norwegian captain and international officers, hotel and dining staff, and crew; cruises the Panama Canal, Australia/New Zealand, Europe, Baltics, Antarctica, transatlantic, Southeast United States, Canada/New England, Mexican Riviera, Caribbean, and other destinations around the world (Category A—six+ stars)

(Medical facilities: C-4 on *Symphony* and C-8 on *Serenity*; P-1; EM, CLS, MS; N-3; CM; PD; BC; EKG; TC, PO; EPC; OX; WC; ICU; X; LJ; CCP; TM—telemedicine is limited to fax and e-mail of digital photos)

Note: Six+ black stars is the highest rating given in this edition to ships in the deluxe-market category.

These ships are rated in eleven separate categories in the second half of chapter 14.

Crystal Cruises, a subsidiary wholly owned by Nippon Yusen Kaisha (NYK) of Japan and based in Los Angeles, launched its first luxury-class ship, *Crystal Harmony*, in the summer of 1990, followed by the 51,044-ton, 922-passenger *Crystal Symphony* in 1995. The 68,870-ton, 1,070-passenger *Crystal Serenity* joined the fleet in 2003. *Crystal Harmony* was transferred to the Japanese parent company in late 2005 and now sails as *Asuka II*. The *Crystal Symphony* and *Crystal Serenity* are two of the largest and most spacious ships competing in the luxury-cruise market. Both ships recently received multimillion-dollar refurbishments and renovations. These sleek vessels boast some of the largest luxury penthouses afloat, with outdoor verandas in all penthouses as well as in nearly 60 percent of the staterooms on *Crystal Symphony* and 85 percent on *Crystal Serenity*. Many reviewers and travel publications have rated Crystal Cruises as providing the best service in the industry.

Commencing in 2012, Crystal Cruises adopted an "all-inclusive" policy, whereby premium spirits and fine wines and champagnes are gratis throughout the ship with open bar service in all lounges, as well as prepaid gratuities for housekeeping and bar and dining staff. The complimentary gratuity amenity also includes penthouse butler service and service in the specialty restaurants. (This has been the policy on most other luxury ships.)

The 461 staterooms on *Symphony* are composed of the two 982-square-foot Crystal Penthouses, 19 additional penthouse suites measuring 491 square feet, 44 penthouses at 367 feet, 214 outside deluxe staterooms with verandas, and 182 additional deluxe outside staterooms. All penthouses and staterooms have twin beds that convert to queen-size beds, 100 percent Egyptian cotton sheets, plush duvets, sitting areas, stocked mini refrigerators, hair dryers, Frette robes and slippers, magnified makeup mirrors, private safes, showers and bathtubs, large closets with shoe racks, writing/makeup desks, alarm clocks, Wi-Fi access, voicemail, thirty-channel TV, DVD/CD players and radio systems that include CNN, TNT, Fox News, CNBC, BBC, and ESPN. All accommodations at every price level are tastefully decorated with lush textures and neutral/earth tones, and patrons are supplied with fresh fruit daily as well as twenty-four-hour room service, nightly turn-down service, and twice-daily housekeeping. All nonveranda cabins on *Symphony* have large picture windows, and all bathrooms have double vanities. A "pillow menu" allows guests to select from four kinds of pillows to fit their individual requirements. The penthouse staterooms and suites on both ships feature 24-7 butler service, oversized Jacuzzi bathtubs, an enclosed shower stall, twenty-six- to forty-six-inch flat-screen color TV, DVD, CD player, stereo equipment, walk-in closets, and room service from the specialty restaurants, including Nobu's Silk Road and the Sushi Bar. Crystal Penthouses, the highest category available, also include guest bathrooms, a butler's pantry, a library, complimentary laundry and dry cleaning, and more. Describing the deluxe accommodations on these ships is more akin to describing the accommodations at a luxury resort than on oceangoing vessels.

During its renovation in 2004, *Crystal Symphony* received a new feng shui–designed spa and fitness center, expanded computer facilities, and a new Vintage Room that accommodates twelve guests for the cruise line's exclusive, high-end wine-pairing dinner. Additional renovations in 2006 included redecorating and adding twenty-inch LCD flat-screen TVs to all staterooms, reconstructing the bathrooms, adding a new nightclub, and redesigning the casino, Bistro Café, specialty restaurants, Computer University @ Sea, and shops. In 2008, the Asian restaurant was converted to Silk Road and the Sushi Bar, with menus by master chef Nobu Matsuhisa, mirroring the specialty restaurants on *Crystal Serenity*. This was followed by a $25-million makeover in September 2009. The Crystal Penthouses were remodeled with expanded living space and state-of-the-art audio/visual systems, and glass mosaic tiles and recessed TVs were added to the bathrooms. The additional penthouse suites were also remodeled. The Lido Café was redecorated with both indoor and outdoor extensions and new service islands. Prego was redecorated. In the deluxe staterooms, leather sofas replaced the armchairs, and new mattresses as well as some third berths were added. The Neptune pool was removed and replaced with teak decking for alfresco dining. A large modern whirlpool and resort-style outdoor furniture were also added. The year 2012's renovation saw the completion of a $65 million, five-year plan to redesign every space on board. The

Avenue Saloon, Palm Court lounge, Galaxy showroom, Hollywood Theatre, Bridge Lounge, Fantasia and Waves "junior cruisers" areas, and the Tender Landing/passenger boarding area were all chicly made over in a sophisticated, yet comfortable, elegance. Lighting, audio-visual, and environmental upgrades were also made.

The 535 staterooms and suites on *Crystal Serenity* are composed of 4 1,345-square-foot Crystal Penthouses (one can really spread out here), 33 538-square-foot penthouse suites with verandas, 72 403-square-foot penthouses with verandas, 356 269-square-foot deluxe outside staterooms with verandas, and 70 226-square-foot outside deluxe outside staterooms. Again, 85 percent of the accommodations have private verandas. In 2007, 20 additional third-berth accommodations were added, bringing the total to 165. All the features found on the *Symphony's* staterooms can be found on this ship as well, including an electronic "Do Not Disturb" and lighting system. As on *Crystal Symphony*, all penthouse accommodations include butler service, complimentary fully stocked bar in room upon embarkation, complimentary beverages in room throughout the cruise, complimentary pressing and shoe-shine service, and numerous other amenities. In 2011, the ship was given an extravagant $25+ million renovation with many additions to the suites, restaurants, and public areas. Included were new modern furniture and TVs in the accommodations, new redesigned shopping spaces, new lounge chairs in the lido area and on the verandas, and new carpeting, artwork, and lighting throughout the ship.

The central focus of both ships is the magnificent Crystal Plaza atrium lobby. Leading off this area is a casino; a nightclub; a piano bar; the 202-seat Hollywood Theater, the site for both recent and vintage movies as well as religious services; cabaret lounges and showrooms, for live production shows, dancing, and cocktails; a bistro offering an assortment of international coffees, wines, pastries, gourmet snacks, and "small bites"; and a 3,000-square-foot shopping area (3,692 square feet on *Crystal Serenity*). The top-deck observation lounge, Palm Court, offers 270-degree views for tea, dancing, entertainment, and parties. A library offers more than three thousand books and movies; the Bridge Lounge is a home for supervised games; and the Studio houses many of the hands-on enrichment classes. The Crystal Casino features slot machines, craps, blackjack, baccarat, poker, and roulette tables. Elaborate Broadway-style productions are offered throughout the cruise, in addition to excellent cabaret entertainers, classical concerts, and several dance bands. Crystal offers the best entertainment in the luxury-cruise market.

The recently expanded fitness centers offer yoga, Pilates (including Pilates Reformer on select *Crystal Serenity* cruises), stretch, abs, boot camp, personal training, indoor spinning classes, nutrition seminars, and state-of-the-art kinesis strength-training equipment (coordinated by a full-time fitness director) as well as an assortment of exercise equipment and cardio machines with individual TVs, saunas, and steam rooms. Featured at feng shui-designed Crystal Spa and Salons are a new range of innovative face and body treatments including facials; massages; makeup instruction; eye, hair, skin, and scalp treatments; acupuncture; waxing; men's shaves; teeth whitening; manicures; and hairstyling. On *Symphony*, the Seahorse Pool has an adjacent oversized whirlpool accommodating many guests and surrounded by comfortable lounges, including couples' lounges and some covered by shade for protected lounging and napping.

The snack bar serves beverages, hot dogs, hamburgers, pizza, Ben & Jerry's, ice-cream creations, and deli sandwiches. Both ships have a 360-degree promenade deck that winds around the ship, and there is an outdoor track above the pool for jogging or walking (guests can use complimentary weighted WalkVests and Nordic Walking Poles), a paddle-tennis court, a golf driving net with a golf pro, and shuffleboard.

Additional facilities found on *Crystal Serenity* include a casual evening restaurant on deck, a larger spa and more treatment rooms, expanded gym and aerobics studio, two outdoor whirlpools, a second indoor/outdoor pool covered by a retractable roof, a second paddle-tennis court, a golf driving range, and an expanded Computer University @ Sea classroom.

The Creative Learning Institute features magic classes taught by magicians from Hollywood's supersecret Magic Castle, as part of Crystal's exclusive Magic Castle at Sea program; Digital Filmmaking for the iPad, in partnership with the University of Southern California's School of Cinematic Arts; foreign languages classes from Berlitz; wine appreciation from the Court of Master Sommeliers—certified wine experts; gourmet cooking from *Michelin*-starred chefs; skin care; makeup artistry; tai chi; wellness classes from Cleveland Clinic; enrichment lectures by historians, celebrities, and financial experts; recently released and classic movies; dance classes; and numerous other activities offered daily. The abundance and variety of these complimentary upscale/sophisticated activities, especially on sea days, is possibly the most impressive in the industry.

Crystal has introduced a more extensive children's program to attract family travelers. Additional third berths have been added to all categories of staterooms and suites; a designated children's playroom is available and a video arcade for older children. There are babysitting services, and supervised, age-appropriate programs for guests seventeen years and younger are also featured, with extra Junior Activities Directors on summer and holiday cruises.

Crystal was the first cruise line to offer alternative dinner restaurants at no extra charge. In addition to luxurious main dining rooms, passengers can opt for the superb Italian cuisine in the romantic Prego Restaurants on both vessels, which now feature dishes of the critically acclaimed/*Michelin*-starred Valentino restaurants in Los Angeles and Las Vegas. World-class master chef Nobuyuki "Nobu" Matsuhisa has designed the menus and added his touch of excellence to two specialty restaurants, Silk Road and the Sushi Bar, also on both ships. Dining at the specialty restaurants is complimentary. During each cruise, special Vintage Room dinners are offered for twelve to fourteen guests at a charge of $180 to $210 per person depending on the wines chosen. Crystal's annual Ultimate Vintage Room Dinner features a seven-course, ultragourmet dining experience paired with extremely rare wines, for approximately $1,000 per person.

Casual banquet-style breakfast and lunch are offered both indoors and alfresco at the Lido Café near the pools. On some days at sea, lavish theme buffets are attractively presented by the pool. On select evenings, special dinners are also offered poolside. All meals, as well as snacks, are available around the clock through extensive room-service menus. Penthouse guests can order room service from the specialty restaurants as well as from the dining room. Smoked salmon and other expensive delicacies are offered at the buffets, and hot and cold hors d'oeuvres are served each evening in the lounges.

Breakfast selections include freshly made omelets, Belgian waffles, delicious pastries, fresh fruits, Asian cuisine, and other standard items, whereas the luncheon buffets offer numerous eclectic dishes, freshly made pasta, salads, and a variety of delectable desserts. Tastes, just outside *Crystal Serenity*'s Lido Café, offers specialty comfort food for lunch and dinner. The Bistro provides specialty coffees, beverages, and attractive gourmet snacks throughout the day until late evening hours—ideal for those who missed a meal or just feel like visiting over a cup of cappuccino. Afternoon tea with appropriate teatime fare is offered each afternoon at the Palm Court along with musical entertainment. Passengers ensconced in the penthouses enjoy an initial setup of complimentary liquors, nightly hors d'oeuvres in their rooms, free pressing, shoe shines, personalized stationery, and personal butler services. Butler service on Crystal is the best in the industry.

Since 2004, special low-carb dishes have been offered in all restaurants, including the specialty dining rooms and Lido Café. Gluten-free, sugar-free, and lactose-intolerant diets can be arranged. Guests requiring kosher-prepared cuisine must notify the cruise line ninety days before sailing. In addition, Crystal Cruises offers its own proprietary label, "C Wines," which includes a new pinot noir, plus cabernet sauvignon, chardonnay, and merlot; onboard sommeliers always suggest wine pairings with dinner. In 2007, Crystal became the first cruise line to be trans-fat free.

Commencing in 2011, both ships offer dining by reservation. Guests not opting for the fixed-table early or late sittings can make reservations in the main dining room as well as at the specialty restaurants to dine at a time they choose and with whom they choose.

Other special features available to all passengers include twenty-four-hour front-desk service, two European-trained concierges to assist with travel and land arrangements, a Crystal Ambassador (gentleman) host program to accompany solo women to dinner or on the dance floor, self-service launderettes throughout the ship, satellite telephone service, descriptive videos of all shore excursions, and access to private business offices equipped with computers, faxes, and secretarial services on request. Every cruise features onboard enrichment programs. Both vessels offer Computer University @ Sea, an extensive program enabling passengers to take group and private computer lessons—ranging from desktop basic to iPad tricks and photo editing. More than thirty computers are available around the clock for cruisers who wish to send e-mails or surf the Internet. In 2006, additional wireless Internet and cell phone service was added, allowing passengers to use their laptops, cell phones, and smart phones while at sea. However, certain areas of the ships such as the spa and theaters are designated cell phone free. In 2009, Crystal introduced technology concierges, a complimentary service offered through the Computer University @ Sea, to educate guests about the various gadgets they travel with, such as smart phones, tablets, and GPS devices.

A pre- and postcruise hotel program features luxury hotels in twenty-two embarkation/debarkation cities and includes such world-famous properties as the Dorchester in London, the Peninsula in Hong Kong, and the Alvear Palace in Buenos Aires, as well as several Four Seasons, Ritz-Carltons, and InterContinentals. Extended Land Programs in the middle of select cruises also offer one- to two-night hotel stays combined with exploration of regions farther inland.

During the year, numerous Experiences of Discovery theme cruises are offered: Ballroom-at-Sea; Jazz; Wine and Food; Golf; Film and Theater; Mind, Body and Spirit; Ocean Views; Extreme Thrill Seekers; Explorations in Elegance; Gladiators and Empires; Maritime: Past, Present, and Future; Up Close and Magical; Microbrews; and Emerging Artists.

Crystal's ships visit 194 ports worldwide. More than two thousand Crystal Adventures shore excursions—including customizable off-ship jaunts—are offered. *Crystal Serenity* also offers an around-the-world itinerary of approximately one hundred days (available to be purchased in segments).

Crystal offers a uniquely excellent cruise experience that combines the impeccable service, gourmet dining, and spacious accommodations found on the small luxury, yacht-like vessels with the state-of-the-art facilities, and high-caliber entertainment and activities offered on the major ships of today's most popular cruise lines.

Prices average approximately $500 per day, per person for a deluxe outside stateroom. Crystal Penthouses run more than $2,000. However, lower tariffs are offered frequently on select cruises.

## Strong Points

A large variety of sophisticated activities including excellent educational programs, excellent dining and service, spacious and comfortable accommodations in all categories, special pampering for penthouse category occupants, and the ultimate in luxury on large full-facility ships. The line is considered by many reviewers, surveys, and seasoned cruisers to be the best of the medium size luxury ships afloat.

*Pool area, courtesy Crystal Cruises*

*Balcony stateroom, courtesy Crystal Cruises*

*Lounge, Crystal Symphony, courtesy Crystal Cruises*

*Crystal Symphony, courtesy Crystal Cruises*

*Penthouse Suite, Crystal Serenity, courtesy Crystal Cruises*

# Captain's Gala Dinner

Thursday, March 7, 2013
Crystal Dining Room, Crystal Serenity
At Sea, en Route to Búzios, Brazil

Maître d'Hôtel **Leo Assmair**  Executive Chef **Franz Weiss**

On behalf of the officers, staff and crew of Crystal Serenity, I would like to
bid all guests leaving us "på gjensyn," "au revoir," but not "good-bye."
I sincerely hope you have enjoyed your stay on board with us and that we shall
be shipmates again in the very near future.

For those guests staying on, I hope we will continue to exceed your expectations.

**Captain John Økland,** Master

## VEGETARIAN SELECTIONS

**The Captain's Salad**
Selected Lettuce Leaves Tossed with Mango-Passion Fruit Dressing, Garnished with
Cherry Tomatoes, Cucumbers, Papaya, Palm Hearts and Cassava Chips

**Sweet Corn Bisque** with Pumpkin Seed Oil and Leek Straw

**Vegetable Lasagne** – Layers of Pasta, Fresh Vegetables and Porcine,
Oven Baked with Mozzarella Cheese, Served with Tomato and Creamy Herb Sauce

**Sour Cherry Crumble Tart** with Vanilla Ice Cream

## ON THE LIGHTER SIDE

*Crystal Cruises responds to today's trend toward dishes lighter in cholesterol, carbohydrates, fat and sodium
by offering these special selections:*

**Oxtail Consommé** with Truffles, Vegetables, and Mushrooms

**\*Broiled Rock Lobster Tail**
Served with Fresh Garden Vegetables and Wild Rice

**Low-Fat, Soft Serve Vanilla Ice Cream**

## HEAD SOMMELIER'S SUGGESTIONS

*To complement the fine cuisine of our Crystal Chefs this evening, our Head Sommelier suggests:*

### All-Inclusive Complimentary Wine Recommendations

**White:** Chardonnay, "C," Sommelier's Selection, Crystal Cruises Vineyards & Winery, Arroyo Seco 2011
**Red:** Cabernet Sauvignon, Edge, Napa Valley 2009
**Desert Wine:** Spätlese Cuvee, Kracher, Burgenland, Austria 2011

*For additional available varietals, ask your Sommelier for our All-Inclusive Complimentary Wine List.*

### Recommendations from our Connoisseur Wine List

**White:** Puligny-Montrachet, Premier Cru, "Les Perrières," Etienne Sauzet, Montrachet,
Burgundy, France 2009 $150.00
**Red:** Cabernet Sauvignon, Shafer Vineyards, Hillside Select, Stag's Leap District,
Napa Valley 2008 $155.00

*For a more extensive selection from our Connoisseur wine list, please ask your Sommelier.*

## APPETIZERS

**Seafood Crêpe** with Sauce Mornay and Champagne-Chive Sabayon

**Iced Malossol Caviar** with Sour Cream, Chopped Eggs and Onions, Accompanied Fresh Toast and Buckwheat Blinis

**Chicken Liver Parfait**
With Apple Confit, Ice Wine Gelée, and Warm Pineapple Brioche

## SOUP AND SALAD

**Sweet Corn Bisque** with Pumpkin Seed Oil and Leek Straw

**Oxtail Consommé** with Port, Vegetables, Truffles, and Mushrooms, Baked under a Puff Pastry Dome

*Low-sodium soups are available upon request*

**The Captain's Salad**
Selected Lettuce Leaves Tossed with Mango-Passion Fruit Dressing, Garnished with Cherry Tomatoes, Cucumbers, Papaya, Palm Hearts and Cassava Chips

*Traditional favorite dressings available, plus today's specials:*
**Fat-Free Tomato-Basil or Low-Calorie Ranch Dressing**

## PASTA SPECIAL

**Orecchiette Pasta** with Crabmeat, Tomatoes, Roasted Squash, Roast Garlic and Fresh Basil, Drizzled with Lemon Oil

## SALAD ENTRÉE

*****Roasted Lamb Salad** – Crisp Greens Tossed with Balsamic-Herb Vinaigrette, Topped with Zucchini, Sweet Peppers, Black Olives, Plum Tomatoes, Pink-Roasted Lamb Rack, Tête de Moine Shavings & Honey Glazed Brazil Nuts

## MAIN FARES

*****Broiled Rock Lobster Tail**
Served with Melted Lemon Butter or Sauce Hollandaise, Saffron Rice Pilaf and Fresh Garden Vegetables

*****Olive Oil Poached Pheasant Breast**
Spinach Fondue, Mushroom Ragout, Star Anise Vinaigrette

*****Châteaubriand** – Sliced Black Angus Beef Tenderloin with Crystal's Cabernet Sauvignon Demi-Glaze, Baby Corn, Fresh Asparagus and Dauphine Potatoes

*****Grilled Veal Medallions**
Red Beet Gnocchi, Snow Peas & Creamy Morel Sauce

*Upon your request, this Traditional Main Fare is also available:*
***Grilled Black Angus NY Sirloin Steak** with Sauce Hollandaise,*
*Served with Baked Potato & Vegetables of the Day; or*
***Broiled Sablefish Fillet** with Mashed Potatoes, Fresh Garden Vegetables,*
*and Chardonnay Beurre Blanc with Salmon Caviar*

## SIDE ORDERS

**Steamed Garden Vegetables    Fresh Asparagus    Mushroom Ragout**
**Saffron Rice Pilaf    Mashed Potatoes    Angel Hair Pasta** with Tomato Sauce

*Upon request, dishes are available without sauce and main fares can be served as half portions.*
*Vegetables are also available steamed, without butter or salt.*

---

*\* United States Public Health Advisory: Consuming raw or undercooked meats, poultry, seafood, shellfish or eggs may increase your risk for foodborne illness, especially if you have certain medical conditions.*

# Captain's Gala Dinner Dessert

Thursday, March 7, 2013
Crystal Dining Room, Crystal Serenity
At Sea, en Route to Búzios, Brazil

Maître d'Hôtel **Leo Assmair**   Executive Chef **Franz Weiss**

Executive Pastry Chef **Harald Neufang**

---

## SWEET FINALE

*Our Executive Pastry, Chef, Harald Neufang, has selected these Sweet Creations for this evening:*

**Baked Alaska**
With Chocolate and Strawberry Sauce

**Espresso Nougatine**
Coffee Nougat Mousse with Raspberry Sauce

---

## SUGAR-FREE

Strawberry Napoleon Slice

Raspberry Vanilla Budino

## CLASSIC DESSERTS

*Upon your request, these Traditional Desserts, Ice Creams, Yogurts and Sherbet are also available:*

**Flourless Valrhona Chocolate Cake** à la Mode

**Vanilla Crème Brûlée**

**Sour Cherry Crumble Tart** with Vanilla Ice Cream

**Vanilla, Cookie Dough, Peanut Butter** or **Strawberry Ice Cream**
*With Your Choice of Toppings*

Freshly Frozen, Nonfat Raspberry Yogurt

Low-Fat, Soft Serve Vanilla Ice Cream

Refreshing Kir Royale Sherbet

Petits Fours and Chocolate Truffles

Seasonal Fruits

---

## FROM THE CHEESE TROLLEY

Please request to speak with our Cheese Sommelier for tonight's cheese selection

# Good Morning

| Time | Event | Location | |
|------|-------|----------|---|
| 6:00am – 12 Noon | **"The Morning Show"** with your hosts Cruise Director Paul McFarland and Patricia Kent. | TV Channel 27 | |
| 7:30am ★ | **Morning Walk on Water & Nordic Walking Program** with Fitness Director Brian. | Promenade Deck Aft | 7 |
| 8:00am ★ | **Fitness Class:** *Yoga* with Fitness Director Neil. | Starlite Club | 6 |
| 8:30am | **Catholic Mass** is celebrated by Father John Clark. | Galaxy Lounge | 6 |
| 8:45am ★ | **Fitness Class:** *Tour de Cycle* with Fitness Director Brian. | Fitness Center | 12 |
| 9:00am | **Captain's Update.** The latest weather and navigation information. | PA System & Ch. 52 | |
| 9:15am ★ | **CU@Sea Class:** *Perfecting People in Pictures Using PhotoShop Element 9* with Instructors Michael Newell & Judy Koehler-Newell. *(Space is limited; pre-registration required)* | The Studio | 6 |

| 10:00am | **Crystal Wine & Food Festival Cooking Demonstration.** Join Guest Chefs **Odd Ivar Solvold** and **Ørjan Johannessen** as they prepare signature recipes. Recipe cards are provided so you can try it at home. | Galaxy Lounge | 6 |
|---------|-------|----------|---|

| Time | Event | Location | |
|------|-------|----------|---|
| 10:00am | **Fitness Seminar:** *You Are What You Eat.* Our health & fitness expert teaches you how to increase your ability to burn fat and improve your quality of life. | Avenue Saloon | 6 |
| 10:00am – 11:00am | **Beginners Bridge Lesson** with Instructors Susan Carter & Jean Paul Trudel. At this time, the Bridge Lounge is reserved for lessons only. Thank you. | Bridge Lounge | 6 |
| 10:15am ★ | **CU@Sea Lecture:** *iPad Fun with iPhotos* with Instructors Michael Newell & Judy Koehler-Newell. *(Space is limited; pre-registration required)* | The Studio | 6 |
| 10:45am ★ | **TaylorMade Golf Clinic** with PGA Golf Teaching Professional Mike Smith. "Short Game: Chipping and Pitching." *(Inclement weather: Deck 11 landing, outside Fantasia)* | Golf Nets | 12 |
| 10:45am | **"Russian Lacquer Legends and Fairy Tales – A Colorful Journey Through a Thousand Years of Russia's Artistic Heritage."** Join our guest speaker Ian Tiffen for this fascinating story exploring the history and folklore behind some of Russia's most unique and beguiling native arts and crafts. | Hollywood Theatre | 6 |
| 10:45am – 11:30am | **Dollar Bill Origami Class** with Activities Hostess Mari. (Please bring crisp dollar bills.) | Lido Café, Strbd Side | 11 |

| 11:00am | **Crystal Visions Enrichment Program.** Destination Lecturer **Alec Murphy** presents "Land and Life in Northern Europe: A View through Time. A look at how the physical & human geography of Northern Europe has shaped the peoples, cultures & economies of the region." *(Broadcast live on TV Ch 29; Rebroadcast on TV Ch 28: 12 Noon to 4:00pm.)* | Galaxy Lounge | 6 |
|---------|-------|----------|---|

| Time | Event | Location | |
|------|-------|----------|---|
| 11:00am | **BINGO** hosted by the Crystal Casino. *Please note appropriate daytime dress code is appropriate attire for Bingo; no robes.* (Game starts at 11:15am) | Starlite Club | 6 |
| 11:00am ★ | **USC Digital Filmmaking Course iMovie for the iPad.** "Learn the Basics of Editing with iMovie" with Instructors Wesley Malkin & Robyn Symon. (Pre-registration in CU@Sea & your own iPad with iMovie pre-loaded required. Participation is limited.) | Avenue Saloon | 6 |
| 11:00am ★ | **Paddle Tennis Open-Play** with Fitness Director Neil. *(weather permitting)* | Wimbledon Court | 12 |
| 11:00am – 12 Noon | **Intermediate Bridge Lesson** with Instructors Susan Carter & Jean Paul Trudel. At this time, the Bridge Lounge is reserved for lessons only. Thank you. | Bridge Lounge | 6 |
| 11:15am – 12 Noon ★ | **Berlitz Russian Language, AM Class** with Instructor Diana Kleban. *(Limited space; please register in the Library.)* | The Studio | 6 |
| 11:30am | **Veteran's Get Together** hosted by fellow Veteran Cruise Director Paul McFarland. | Palm Court, Portside | 11 |
| 11:30am – 12:30pm | **Brian Donnelly** plays the Crystal Piano for your midday cocktail pleasure. | Crystal Cove | 5 |

# Good Afternoon

| Time | Event | Location | |
|------|-------|----------|---|
| 12 Noon | **Team Trivia** hosted by Daniel from the Crystal Ensemble. | Starlite Club | 6 |
| 12 Noon – 1:00pm | **Free Gaming Lessons.** Get all the tips from our experts. | Crystal Casino | 6 |

| 1:30pm | **Crystal Visions Enrichment Program.** Special Interest Lecturer **Thomas Henriksen** presents "America and the Rogue States." *(Broadcast live on TV Channel 29; Rebroadcast on TV Channel 28: 4:00pm to 8:00pm.)* | Starlite Club | 6 |
|---------|-------|----------|---|

| Time | Event | Location | |
|------|-------|----------|---|
| 1:30pm | **Emeralds Chat.** Join Karen Dickson, Director of Sales for Hubert, and Jeremy Fratkin to learn more about this rare and mysterious gemstone. | Hollywood Theatre | 6 |

★ Indicates Creative Learning Institute Activity.

# Good Afternoon continued...

| | | | |
|---|---|---|---|
| 1:30pm – 2:30pm | **Poolside Music** with the Crystal Sextet *(weather permitting)*. | Seahorse Pool | 11 |
| 2:00pm | **$20 Slot Tournament.** Register from 10:00am until 1:45pm. | Crystal Casino | 6 |
| 2:15pm★ | **CU@Sea Class:** *Fun with iPhoto Using MAC OS X Lion* with Instructors Michael Newell & Judy Koehler-Newell. *(Space is limited; pre-registration required)* | The Studio | 6 |
| 2:15pm – 3:00pm | **Beginners' Needlepoint Get-Together** with Activities Hostess Mari. *(Please bring your kit.)* | Palm Court, Strbd Side | 11 |
| 2:15pm – 4:15pm | **Duplicate and Social Bridge** with Instructors Susan Carter & Jean Paul Trudel. At this time, the Bridge Lounge is reserved for bridge games only. Thank you. | Bridge Lounge | 6 |
| 2:30pm | **Movie: *The Lucky One***. A Marine travels to Louisiana after serving three tours in Iraq and searches for the unknown woman he believes was his good luck charm. PG-13; 1:41 | Hollywood Theatre | 6 |

| | | | |
|---|---|---|---|
| 2:30pm | **Crystal Wine & Food Festival Wine Tasting.** Join Wine Expert **Christian Moueix** for "Old World Cabernet Versus New World Cabernet." | Crystal Dining Room | 5 |

| | | | |
|---|---|---|---|
| 2:30pm | **Complimentary Dance Class.** Tango & Swing with Instructors Adam and Patricia Kent and the Ambassador Hosts. *(Beginners welcome and no partner required).* | Starlite Club | 6 |
| 2:45pm | **Acupuncture Seminar: *Pain Relief*.** Learn how acupuncture can help reduce or eliminate your symptoms for years to come. | Avenue Saloon | 6 |
| 3:00pm★ | **Odyssey Art at Sea** with Instructor Gail Ivanco. Pastel pencils & Archipelago inspiration. | Lido Café, Port Side | 11 |
| 3:00pm | **Texas Hold'em Tournament.** Register from 10:00am until 2:45pm. | Crystal Casino | 6 |
| 3:00pm | **Table Tennis Open-Play** with Fitness Director Brian. | Horizon Deck Aft | 8 |

| | | | |
|---|---|---|---|
| 3:00pm – 4:00pm | **Crystal Wine & Food Festival Mixology Class.** Join Mixologist **Simon Ford** for "The History of the Cocktail in Five Recipes." Make some of the most important cocktails from the cocktails rich 200 year history and share stories from the golden age. | LUXE | 6 |

| | | | |
|---|---|---|---|
| 3:15pm★ | **CU@Sea Class:** *Moving Objects Among Pictures Using PhotoShop Elements* 9 with Instructors Michael Newell & Judy Koehler-Newell. *(Space is limited; pre-registration required)* | The Studio | 6 |
| 3:15pm★ | **TaylorMade Golf Clinic** with PGA Golf Teaching Professional Mike Smith. "Putting & putting contest." (Inclement weather location: Deck 11, outside Fantasia) | Golf Nets | 12 |

| | | | |
|---|---|---|---|
| 3:30pm | **Crystal Visions Enrichment Program.** Special Interest Lecturer **Dr. Joseph Schwarcz** presents "Humor, Magic and Medicine." *(Broadcast live on TV Channel 29; Rebroadcast on TV Channel 28: 8:00pm to 12 Midnight.)* | Starlite Club | 6 |

| | | | |
|---|---|---|---|
| 3:30pm – 4:30pm | **Crystal Afternoon Tea Time** serenaded by the **Ginger String Quartet**. | Palm Court | 11 |
| 3:45pm★ | **USC Digital Filmmaking Course iMovie for the iPad.** "Enhanced Edit Techniques with iMovie" with Instructors Wesley Malkin & Robyn Symon. (Pre-registration in CU@Sea & your own iPad with iMovie pre-loaded required. Participation is limited.) | Avenue Saloon | 6 |
| 4:00pm★ | **Fitness Class: *Pilates*** with Fitness Director Neil. | Fitness Center | 12 |
| 4:30pm★ | **Fitness Class: *Stretch*** with Fitness Director Brian. | Fitness Center | 12 |
| 4:30pm | **Friends of Bill W.** meet in… | Lido Café Aft | 11 |
| 4:45pm – 5:30pm★ | **Berlitz Russian Language, PM Class** with Instructor Diana Kleban. *(Limited space; please register in the Library.)* | The Studio | 6 |
| 5:00pm | **5 O'Clock Funnies LIVE!** Comedy clips hosted by Cruise Director Paul McFarland. TV Trivia at approx. 5:30pm – win a $25 Crystal Casino Slot Coupon. | TV Channel 27 | |
| 5:00pm★ | **Afternoon Walk on Water & Nordic Walking Program** with Fitness Director Neil. | Promenade Deck Aft | 7 |

**6:00pm & 7:00pm • LUXE** Tiffany Deck 6, Midship

## Magic Castle at Sea

Featuring Master Magician **Mark Haslam**

This exclusive performance is limited to only 20 guests per show.
Please collect your ticket from the Library. Tickets are first come, first served.
Limited to two tickets per guest, please.

★ **Indicates Creative Learning Institute Activity**.

# CUNARD CRUISE LINE

**United States**
24303 Town Center Drive, Suite 200
Valencia, CA 91355-0908
(800) 728-6273
(661) 753-1000
Fax: (661) 284-4749

**United Kingdom**
Carnival House, 100 Harbour Parade
Southampton, England SO15 1ST
0044 8450710300

Fax: 0044 2380657409
www.cunard.com

*Queen Mary 2*: entered service in 2004; refurbished in 2011; 151,400 GRT; 1,132 × 135 feet; 2,682-passenger capacity (3,090 with every berth filled); 1,296 cabins; British officers and international crew; cruises to various areas around the world, including transatlantic crossings between Great Britain and Hamburg, between Germany and New York, and between New England and Canada and world voyages, including South America, Caribbean, Norway, Northern Europe, Iberia and Canary Islands, the Mediterranean, and Australia (Queens Grill, Category A—six+ stars; Princess Grill, Category A—six stars; Britannia Restaurant, Category B/C—five stars)

*Queens Grill*

*Princess Grill*

*Britannia Restaurant*

(Medical facilities: C-30; P-2; EM, CLS, MS; N-2; CM; PD; EKG; TC; PO; EPC; OX; WC; OR; ICU; X; M)

*Queen Victoria* and *Queen Elizabeth*: entered service in 2007 and 2010, respectively; 90,000 and 90,400 GRT, respectively; 964.5 × 106 feet; 2,111- and 2,068-passenger capacity, respectively; 1,007 and 1029 cabins, respectively; British officers and international crew; cruises to various areas around the world, including world voyages, the Mediterranean, Northern Europe, and Iberia and the Canary Islands (Queens Grill, Category A—six+ stars; Princess Grill, Category A—six stars; Britannia Restaurant, Category B/C—five stars)

*Queens Grill*

*Princess Grill*

*Britannia Restaurant*

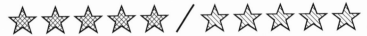

(Medical facilities: Same as *Queen Mary 2*, except twenty wheelchair-accessible cabins)

These ships are rated in eleven separate categories in the second half of chapter 11.

Cunard Line was founded back in 1840 by Samuel Cunard, a merchant from Nova Scotia. His original plan was to provide transatlantic mail service while carrying a few passengers at the same time. The first ship, Britannia, was a 1,135-ton paddle-wheel steamer that made the crossing between continents in fourteen days.

Over the years, the Cunard flag has flown on such well-known vessels as *Aquitania*, *Mauretania*, *Lusitania*, *Caronia*, *Franconia*, *Queen Mary*, and the original *Queen Elizabeth*. Ironically, Cunard Line not only originated transatlantic passenger service more than 173 years ago but also presently, via *Queen Mary 2*, is the last major cruise line offering regular transatlantic crossings.

Cunard, as a wholly owned subsidiary of the British conglomerate Trafalgar House, was acquired by the Norwegian construction and engineering firm of Kvaerner in 1996 and was resold to Carnival Corporation in May 1998. Carnival Corporation then merged Cunard with Seabourn Cruise Line (a company organized in 1987) to form Cunard Line. One hundred percent of the new cruise line is now owned by Carnival Corporation. Seabourn and Cunard continue to operate as separate brands and Cunard's offices have been divided between California and Southampton, England.

Cunard purchased *Sea Goddess I* and *II* in 1986 and in 1994 acquired *Royal Viking Sun* and all rights to the Royal Viking logo. At the time of the merger with Seabourn, the two *Sea Goddesses* and *Royal Viking Sun* were transferred to the Seabourn brand and renamed *Seabourn Goddess I*, *Seabourn Goddess II*, and *Seabourn Sun*. Subsequently, the two *Seabourn Goddesses* were sold to the former owner and CEO of Seabourn and renamed *SeaDream I* and *SeaDream II*, and in April 2002 the *Sun* was transferred to Holland America Line, another subsidiary of Carnival Corporation, and renamed *Prinsendam 2*.

In the mid-1970s, Cunard built *Princess* and *Countess*, two 17,000-ton ships designed to accommodate the then-emerging mass market of first-time and more economy-minded cruisers. Both these ships were sold off in the 1990s. In 1983, it acquired *Sagafjord* and *Vistafjord* (subsequently renamed *Caronia III*) from the now-defunct Norwegian America Cruises. The *Sagafjord* ceased operating for Cunard in 1996 and the *Caronia III* in 2004. Both ships presently sail for Saga Cruises.

*Queen Elizabeth 2* entered service in 1969 and was the flagship of the fleet until the introduction of *Queen Mary 2*. After she underwent numerous renovations and refurbishments, bringing her into the twenty-first century, the cruise line finally decided to retire her in 2008, and she left the fleet to become a floating hotel and tourism attraction in Dubai; however, her future is uncertain.

In January 2004, *Queen Mary 2*, formerly the largest passenger ship in service (before Royal Caribbean's *Freedom*-class and *Oasis*-class ships), debuted at approximately 151,400 GRT, 1,132 feet long, with a 131-foot beam, accommodating 2,604 passengers. The ship operates transatlantic crossings as well as regular cruises, similar to the itineraries formerly operated by *Queen Elizabeth 2*. The accommodating crew is composed of more than fifty different nationalities and is no longer mostly British.

In December 2007, *Queen Victoria* made her debut. Although she is somewhat smaller than *Queen Mary 2*, at 90,000 tons, 964.5 feet long, with a 106-foot beam, accommodating 2,111 passengers, she has similar staterooms, suites, restaurants, and common areas to those of the former vessel, but on a smaller scale. The 90,400-ton *Queen Elizabeth*, which entered service in October 2010, is the second-largest Cunard ship ever built and accommodates 2,068 passengers.

*Queen Mary 2*, *Queen Victoria*, and *Queen Elizabeth* are unique ships in their continuation of a system whereby passengers paying more for their cabins are entitled to an escalating scale of cabin facilities and different dining rooms, all offering a higher caliber of service and gourmet options. Thus, it is possible to travel less expensively in a small cabin and dine in the Britannia Restaurant or cruise in grand luxury in a suite and enjoy meals in one of the elegant Grill dining rooms. Irrespective of which category you book, you will have access to the same ship facilities and participate in the same activities and entertainment.

On *Queen Mary 2*, the least expensive cabins start at 157 square feet with the five most expensive Grand Duplex suites coming in between 1,566 and 2,249 square feet and spanning two levels (featuring three baths and giant balconies). Other top-of-the-line accommodations include four forward Royal Suites, the Queen Elizabeth and Queen Mary suites with private elevators (at 1,194 square feet), the Queen Anne and Queen Victoria suites at 796 square feet, six 758-square-foot penthouse suites, and a plethora of additional Queens Grill and Princess Grill suites, ranging in size from 381 to 506 square feet. Deluxe and premium balcony staterooms measure 248 square feet. Seventy-seven percent of the accommodations have ocean views, and three-quarters of these boast balconies. All Queens Grill suites come with butler service, walk-in closets, flat-screen TVs, entertainment systems, selected beverages, and spirits and wines. Grill guests have access to a special concierge center and exclusive cocktail lounge.

The spa, beauty salon, and wellness and fitness facilities on board, with twenty-four treatment rooms and a staff of fifty-one, are operated by the prestigious Canyon Ranch SpaClub. The facilities are beautiful and among the very best at sea. There is a daily charge of $40 for non-spa treatment guests, entitling them to use the changing rooms, showers, steam room, sauna, and magnificent aqua therapy center. Although the gym is gratis to all guests, there are no changing rooms or showers other than those at Canyon Ranch. Body and therapy treatments at the spa run from $138 to $328.

The onboard enrichment program, Cunard Insights, introduces guests to stimulating experts and accomplished visionaries who reflect the line's heritage of prestige and the quest for oceangoing adventure. Through a series of lectures, QAs, debates, social gatherings, and workshops, guests connect with personalities who have achieved notable distinction in areas including history, world affairs, science, politics, entertainment, the arts, and literature.

*Queen Mary 2* also offers an enrichment program known as ConneXions, with seven classrooms offering a diverse range of educational courses and dozens of computers with e-mail capabilities. Other innovations include a $5 million art collection; the largest ballroom at sea; the only planetarium at sea; the site for a variety of constellation shows, movies, and lectures; certified British nannies for infant care; and a kennel for your favorite dog or cat (during the transatlantic crossings season).

The passengers booking the most luxurious accommodations have a separate lounge and a separate sundeck area, and they dine in the Queens Grill or Princess Grill restaurants, whereas the others dine in the two-seating, 1,351-seat Britannia Restaurant. In 2006, a new "Britannia Club" designation was given to forty-sic deluxe balcony staterooms on deck, twelve of which entitled the occupants to a special single-seating arrangement in an annex to the Britannia Restaurant similar to that in the Grills. King's Court, a buffet restaurant for breakfast and lunch, transforms each evening into four dining venues featuring Asian, Italian, English Grill, and Chef's Galley. At Chef's Galley, guests watch shipboard and guest chefs prepare their meals with a how-to commentary before consumption of culinary treats accompanied by appropriate wines. This is an evening's entertainment for aspiring gourmets. Other alternative dining venues include the outstanding Todd English Restaurant, serving contemporary Mediterranean cuisine, with menus designed by world-famous chef and TV personality Todd English. Two more casual options are the Golden Lion Pub, offering traditional British pub favorites, and Boardwalk Café, for hamburgers, hot dogs, fries, and other snacks (weather permitting).

Starting at the top of the ship, on deck 12, you will find a pool area with a sliding-glass roof, the Boardwalk Café, kennels, and some Princess Grill suites. Most of the other suites are located on decks 9 through 11. The largest library/bookstore at sea, the beauty salon, some staterooms, and the upper level of the Canyon Ranch Spa Club are on deck 8. The lower level of the spa (including the changing rooms and aqua therapy center), a large three-room gym, a lounge, and the Grill Restaurants and buffet restaurants can be found on deck 7. On deck 6 are numerous staterooms and the children's areas and pool. Additional cabins are on decks 4 and 5. Most public areas (including the remaining restaurants, the show lounge, theater, shopping arcade, casino, numerous bars and lounges, and the grand lobby) are located on decks 2 and 3. The various public indoor and outdoor deck areas are somewhat fragmented and not accessible by all elevators. It takes a bit of exploration to become familiar with navigating around the ship. The outdoor lounges and pools are spread among several decks, and there is no single central pool/lido/deck chair area, as on many ships. On deck 7, the promenade deck, passengers can walk or jog around the entire deck or lounge in teak deck chairs. The Pets on Deck program provides twelve kennels. For a $500 to $1,000 fee, your puppy or kitty receives freshly baked biscuits at turn down, a choice of beds and blankets, a name tag and food dish, and a personalized cruise card.

*Queen Mary 2* received a major refurbishment in 2011.

The 90,000-ton, 2,111-passenger (2,504 with every berth filled) *Queen Victoria* joined the fleet in December 2007, well in time for the retirement of *Queen Elizabeth 2*. *Queen Victoria* is a beautifully appointed vessel with public areas exuding style and elegance. As on the other Cunard ships, guests booking the most expensive accommodations dine in the elegant Queens Grill or Princess Grill restaurants with expanded menus and pampered service, while the remaining passengers dine in the larger, two-seating Britannia Restaurant, with a somewhat more limited menu or in the buffet restaurant in the Lido area. Grill passengers share a private bar and lounge with their own concierge and alfresco dining courtyard and can sun in exclusive privacy on their own terrace atop ship. The cuisine and service in the Grills are outstanding.

Of the 1,007 guest accommodations, 86 percent have ocean views and 71 percent have sport balconies, and 20 of these are wheelchair accessible. All include twin beds that convert to queens, flat-screen TVs, hair dryers, private safes, a combination desk/makeup furnishing, and a seating area. As you move up from category to category in price, the size, furnishings, storage space, and amenities increase proportionately. The 143 least expensive inside cabins range in size from 152 to 207 square feet and the 146 ocean-view cabins vary from 180 to 197 square feet and feature a small sitting area. In all of the Britannia-category staterooms, storage space is limited and bathrooms are rather small. However, in 2008, drawers were added under the beds to provide extra storage. The 591 balcony cabins measure 249 square feet, which includes a nice-sized balcony. Those occupying the sixty-one Princess Grill staterooms enjoy 367 square feet, which includes a lounge area, a balcony, and a shower/tub combination in the bathroom. Most of the luxurious sixty Queens Grill suites vary from 508 to 771 square feet and include large marble bathrooms with whirlpool bathtubs, expansive balconies, and a butler. For the big bucks, you can book one of the two 1,100-square-foot master suites or one of the four 2,097-square-foot grand suites.

Outdoor deck space includes a midship pool and an aft pool, each with two whirlpools and comfortable lounging chairs. Numerous areas on multiple levels provide more than adequate lounging space. Sport facilities include a deck tennis court, golf nets, and a shuffleboard.

In the spa/fitness center, you will find a large very-well-equipped gym where cardio machines have their own TVs, an adjoining aerobic area, a thermal suite, a hydrotherapy pool, an aroma spa, a laconicum, a caldarium, a relaxation area (a daily fee applies for nontreatment guests), a men and women's salon, and treatment rooms offering a bevy of spa treatments and rituals.

The classic-style, multilevel, 830-seat Royal Court Theatre features reservation-only private boxes where, for $25 per person, guests can enjoy preshow dessert, coffee, and champagne in a private lounge. The two-deck Queens Room is the spot for traditional English afternoon tea and evening ballroom dancing. For those wishing to imbibe, there are thirteen bars, including the stylish Veuve Clicquot champagne bar serving caviar, a whiskey bar, a wine bar, and the English pub-style Golden Lion Pub featuring typical English fare, music sing-alongs, and TV sports. In addition to a large Internet café, the computer-learning center offers classes throughout each cruise.

The Royal Arcade has four thousand square feet of shops featuring upscale merchandise. The two-story, traditionally styled English library features six thousand books (the first two-story library at sea with a spiral staircase; *Queen Elizabeth* is the second), only exceeded by the eight-thousand-book library on *Queen Mary 2*. Nearby is a well-stocked bookstore offering best sellers and nautically themed books.

Other public areas include several elegant observation lounges atop ship; a cigar room; card, game, and meeting rooms; children's playrooms; a large casino; the first permanent floating museum showcasing Cunard memorabilia; and numerous quiet lounging areas.

The reservation-only, alternative dining restaurant, Todd English, provides innovative, gourmet cuisine at à la carte pricing. Café Carinthia offers pastries and specialty coffees and teas, and English pub food is available at lunchtime at the Golden Lion Pub.

The dress code on Cunard ships is more stringent than that on other cruise lines. Men are expected to wear jackets to dinner, even on casual evenings; and for several evenings each week, formal attire is suggested.

The 90,400-ton, 2,068-passenger ocean liner *Queen Elizabeth* entered service in 2010. She is named after Cunard's first *Queen Elizabeth*, the ship launched in 1938 as the world's largest liner. Although different in décor and featuring various innovations, the ship's layout is quite similar to that of *Queen Victoria*. Beneath the Garden Lounge (with a vaulted glass ceiling, which creates a conservatory feel), guests can enjoy supper club-style dining with dancing under the stars. The Veranda restaurant, displaying artwork and vintage menus inspired by the former *Queen Elizabeth* and *Queen Mary*, replaces Todd English as the upscale specialty restaurant with à la carte pricing. The Lido Restaurant transforms into three eateries at dinner: South American, Mexican, and Pan-Asian, with a $10 cover. The Games Deck offers paddle tennis, croquet, and traditional British bowls under a canopy shielding guests from the sun. The aft outdoor space on deck 9 is the venue for a new concept of entertainment with garden parties reminiscent of those held at British country houses. In addition to the Queens Grill and Princess Grill for the top-suite passengers, the Britannia Club, having first debuted aboard *Queen Mary 2*, features a private dining room with single-seating dining for those guests in the (non-Grill) top Britannia balcony staterooms.

## Strong Points

These are grand ships that exude class and tradition with great facilities, loads of entertainment, and fine dining. For those who can pay the price, the Grill accommodations allow passengers to enjoy greater stateroom comfort, more intimate gourmet dining, more pampering, and an especially elegant, sophisticated experience. Those who believe "bigger is better" will adore *Queen Mary 2*, while those who don't will find very similar amenities on the smaller *Queen Victoria* and *Queen Elizabeth*.

*Balcony Stateroom QM2, courtesy Cunard Cruise Line*

*Illuminations Theater on QM2, courtesy of Cunard Cruise Line*

*QM 2, courtesy Cunard Cruise Line*

*courtesy Cunard Cruise Line*

# BRITANNIA RESTAURANT
Dinner Menu

## ROYAL SPA SELECTIONS
Appetizer—Melon & Pineapple Bisque (V)
Entrée—Grilled Lamb Cutlets, Roasted Vegetables & Bell Pepper Coulis
Dessert—Grand Marnier Crème Brulee

## APPETIZERS & SOUPS
Symphony of Seafood with Salmon Tartare, Seafood Mousse & Shrimp Salad
Baby Vegetable Terrine, Cucumber Sour Cream (V)
Escargots Bourguignon in Garlic Herb Butter
Cream of Celeriac & Porcini, Truffle Oil & Crème Fraiche
Melon & Pineapple Bisque (V)

## SALAD
Radicchio, Snow Peas, Red Beets & Red Onions, Apple Vinaigrette (V)
Caesar Salad with Shaved Parmesan, Artichokes & Anchovies

 *Tio Pepe, Fino Sherry, Jerez, Spain*

## ENTRÉES
Seafood Agnolotti, Lemon Sauce & Rosemary Cream
Lobster Thermidor, with Truffle Scented Pilaf Rice
Grilled Double Lamb Cutlets, Lamb Confit & Feta Strudel, Sweet Onion Jus
Beef Wellington, Dauphine Potatoes & Madiera Truffle Sauce
Wild Mushroom & Young Vegetable Fricasse, Poppy Seed Vol au Vent

 *NV Rondel Rose, Cava, Spain*

 *1999 Great Wall Cabernet Sauvingon*

## DESSERTS
Chocolate Decadence, Kahlua Sauce
Iced Cointreau Souffle
Baked Alaska with Morello Cherries
Sugar Free- Panna Cotta with Strawberry Compote
Cherry Vanilla, Strawberry & Coconut Ice Cream

 *Calvados, Normandy, France*

(V) Indicates dishes suitable for Vegetarians

 Indicates a Chief Sommelier Selection

*Dinner Menu from Brittania Restaurant QM2, courtesy Cunard Cruise Line*

## MORNING ACTIVITIES

**6.00am**   **"Queen Victoria Live"** .......................... TV Channel 21
TV Show with Entertainment Director
Alastair & Gun. Plays until Noon.

**7.30am**   **WALK for Wellbeing Session** ....... Deck 3 Forward, Starboard Side
With your on board Fitness Instructors.

**8.00am**   **PUSH'N'LIFT Conditioning Class** .............. Gymnasium, Deck 9

**9.00am**   **YO'FIT™ Programme (Nominal Fee)** ............. Gymnasium, Deck 9
**Crossword Puzzle and Brainteaser** ........... The Library, Decks 2 & 3

**9.30am**   **Fencing Class Sign Up** ............................ ⌐Queens Room
Today's class starts at 10.00am. With Sports Director Edward.
**Tour of Queen Victoria Public Areas** ...... The Golden Lion Pub, Deck 2
Conducted by the Entertainment Staff.
**Beginners Bridge Class** ......................... Card Room, Deck 3
With Margaret & Roger Chaplin.

**10.00am**   **Enrichment Lecture** ............ ⌐Royal Court Theatre, Decks 1, 2 & 3
"Cunard's Fifth Queen" An informative presentation
by Maritime Historian, John Maxtone-Graham.
**Tour of Queen Victoria Public Areas** ...... The Golden Lion Pub, Deck 2
Conducted by the Entertainment Staff.
**Watercolour Arts Class** .. Britannia Restaurant, Deck 3, Starboard Side
With Norma Rachlin. ($35 one time fee for supplies).
**Bingo Cards go on Sale** ..................... ⌐Queens Room, Deck 2
Cards are $20 for 4 games. Also, purchase an
additional bonus bingo card for $10 more.

**10.15am**   **Spa Seminar** ...................... Royal Spa Fitness Centre, Deck 9
"How to Increase your Metabolism" Learn how you
can improve your health for the year ahead.

**10.30am**   **Tour of Queen Victoria Public Areas** ...... The Golden Lion Pub, Deck 2
Conducted by the Entertainment Staff - last chance!
**Deck Quoits** .................................. Deck 10, A Stairway
With Sports Director Edward.
**Intermediate Bridge Class** ...................... Card Room, Deck 3
With Margaret & Roger Chaplin.

**10.45am**   **Bingo Commences** ..................... ⌐Queens Room, Deck 2

**11.00am**   **Enrichment Lecture** ............ ⌐Royal Court Theatre, Decks 1, 2 & 3
"The Revival of Art Deco and Cunard's Legacy".
With Art Historian, Giancarlo Impiglia.
**Spa Seminar: 10 Years Younger** ........ Royal Spa Fitness Centre, Deck 9
Learn the secrets of the stars with O2 Facials.
**Book Signing with John Maxtone Graham** ........ Grand Lobby, Deck 3
**Introducing Microsoft Office 2007** ............. ConneXions 1, Deck 1
With Computer Instructor Graham Mitchell. Sign up required.
**Pilates Institute Class** .......................... Gymnasium, Deck 9

**11.15am**   **Singles Party** ..................................... Chart Room, Deck 2
For those guests travelling independently. Hosted by
Social Hostess Anja and the Gentleman Dance Hosts.

**11.30am**   **Paddle Tennis** ..................................... Deck 11, Forward
Join fellow guests for a friendly game.

**11.45am**   **Ballroom Dance Class** ..................... ⌐Queens Room, Deck 2
With Dance Instructor Rick Nixon.
**Quizzical Corner** ..................... The Golden Lion Pub, Deck 2
Join the Entertainment Staff for some quizzical fun!

## AFTERNOON ACTIVITIES

**Noon**   **Noon Navigational Announcement from the Bridge** ..... Public Address
**Book Signing** ................................. Grand Lobby, Deck 3
With Art Historian Giancarlo Impiglia.
**Young Adults Get-together** .................... Chart Room, Deck 2
For all young adults ages 18 to 30.

**12.15pm**   **Pub Lunch Melodies** ........................ Golden Lion Pub, Deck 2
Pianist Dezso Farkas.
**Lunchtime Melodies** ........................... Chart Room, Deck 2
With Harpist Chiara Capobianco.

**12.30pm**   **Live Music** ................................... Winter Garden, Deck 9
Enjoy the fabulous sounds of "Stagez".

**1.00pm**   **Shuffleboard Tournament** ...................... Deck 11, A Stairway
Join Sports Director Edward and fellow guests on
deck for this traditional ocean liner game!

**2.00pm**   **Spa Seminar - Acupuncture** .............. The Fitness Centre, Deck 9
For aches, pains, headaches, sinus problems and seasickness.
**Matinee Movie** ................ ⌐Royal Court Theatre, Decks 1, 2 & 3
"No Reservations" A romatic drama starring Catherine
Zeta-Jones, Rated: R, 1 hour 36 minutes.
**Duplicate Bridge Session** ....................... Card Room, Deck 3
With Margaret & Roger Chaplin.
**Watercolour Arts Class** .. Britannia Restaurant, Deck 3, Starboard Side
With Norma Rachlin. ($35 one time fee for supplies).

**2.15pm**   **Spa Seminar: Gravity™** .......... Royal Spa Fitness Centre, Deck 9
The New Way To Exercise.
**Baggo** ..................................... Deck 10, Port Side
Join Sports Director Edward this afternoon for this fun game!

**2.30pm**   **Powerpoint Presentation Plus** .......... ConneXions 1, Grand Lobby
With Computer Instructor Graham Mitchell. Sign up required

**3.00pm**   **Hostess Corner: Needlework & Knitting** ........ Chart Room, Deck 2
Bring along your projects for an informal
gathering. Hosted by Social Hostess Anja.
**Spa Seminar: BeautyTek** ........... Royal Spa Fitness Centre, Deck 9
The latest in slimming and inch loss technology.
**Gravity - Group Exercise** ....................... Gymnasium Deck 9

**3.15pm**   **Table Tennis Tournament** ...................... Deck 10, Port Side
Join fellow guests for a friendly game!

**3.30pm**   **Pub Team Trivia** ........................ The Golden Lion Pub, Deck 2
With the Entertainment Staff.

**4.00pm**   **Spa Seminar: Visea Imaging** .............. The Fitness Centre, Deck 9
Uncover your skin. See the effects that the
environment has been having on your skin. Learn
what you can do to reverse the signs of ageing.
**Friends of Bill W. (unhosted)** ......... The Admiral's Lounge, Deck 10
**Friends of Dorothy (unhosted)** ... Commodore Club, Port Side, Deck 10
**ZUMBA™ Salsa Aerobics Class** ................. Gymnasium, Deck 9
**Absolute Beginners Computers Part I** .... ConneXions 1, Grand Lobby
With Computer Instructor Graham Mitchell. Sign up required.

# TONIGHT'S ENTERTAINMENT

## THE GOLDEN LION PUB
Deck 2 Forward

From 5.00pm to 6.00pm &
7.30pm to 8.30pm
Pianist **DEZSO FARKAS**

From 9.30pm to 10.15pm
& 11.00pm to Late
Pianist
**GREG SAMPSON**

From 10.15pm to 11.00pm
**MUSIC TRIVIA**
Join the Entertainment Staff and
test your musical knowledge!

## THE QUEENS ROOM
Deck 2 Midships

From 9.45pm to 12.15am
**BLACK & WHITE BALL**
with the
**QUEENS ROOM ORCHESTRA**
Under the Direction of
**CHRIS KEARNS**
with
**VOCALIST DOUG ACOSTA**

## HEMISPHERES
Deck 10 Forward

From 9.45pm to Late

**STAGEZ**

&

**DJ SIMON**

From Midnight to 12.30am
"Classic 70s Music" with
**DJ SIMON**
Hemispheres is the place to be!

*No persons under the age of 18 are
permitted after Midnight*

## THE CHART ROOM
Deck 2 Aft

## THE COMMODORE CLUB
Deck 10 Forward

From 7.30pm to 8.15pm & from 9.45pm
International Piano Entertainer
**BARRINGTON "BARTY" BROWN**

From 5.00pm to 6.00pm &
7.30pm to 8.30pm
Pianist
**WISH SEREDYNSKI**

From 9.30pm to 10.30pm
Pianist
**DEZSO FARKAS**

## GRAND LOBBY
Deck 1 Midships

From 5.15pm to 6.00pm, 7.45pm to
8.30pm & 9.30pm to 10.30pm
Harpist
**CHIARA CAPOBIANCO**

## THE ROYAL COURT THEATRE PRESENTS
Decks 1, 2 and 3

At 8.30pm & 10.45pm
Dynamic, Eclectic, Energetic, Fun, Fabulous, Unmissable, Musicals, Golden Voiced, Classics
Vocalist
### MARK O'MALLEY

Hosted by Entertainment Director Alastair Greener
With The Royal Court Theatre Orchestra Directed by Gordon Hough.
Please do not reserve seats prior to Showtime. Audio, video recording and flash photography is prohibited.

*Daily Program on QM2, courtesy Cunard Cruise Line*

# PETER DEILMANN CRUISES

**Am Holm 25**
**23730 Neustadt in Holstein**
**Germany**
**+49(0) 4561 396-100**
**Fax: +49 (0) 4561 8207**
**reservierung@delman.de**

MS *Deutschland*: entered service in 1998; refurbished in 2008; 22,400 GRT; 574 × 82 feet; 513-passenger capacity; 264 cabins; German officers, German and international crew; itineraries all over the world (Category B—five+ stars)

(Medical facilities: C-2; P-1; EM, CLS MS; 2N; CM; PD; BC; EKG; TC; PO; OX; WC; OR; ICU; X; M; CCP; D; TM; LJ)

This ship is rated in eleven separate categories in the second half of chapter 11.

Reederei Peter Deilmann is the owner of the MS *Deutschland*. The clientele on the *Deutschland* is predominantly from German-speaking countries.

The *Deutschland* is a traditional oceangoing cruise vessel offering exotic itineraries (able to be purchased in segments) around the world. The *Deutschland* is one of the more beautifully appointed ships in service and also attracts English-speaking passengers to complement its predominantly German clientele. On the *Deutschland*, all announcements and most written material—including daily programs, shore-excursion information, and menus—are offered in English as well as in German.

Entering service in 1998, the 22,400-ton *Deutschland* accommodates up to 500 passengers in 294 staterooms serviced by a largely European crew of 280. The exterior design is classical with a large funnel, reminiscent of ships built in the mid-1900s. The interior boasts an extremely elegant, tasteful decor with an abundance of burled woods, brass, marble, etched glass, and soft pastels adorning every nook and cranny. Early 1900s-style furnishings and accents include crystal chandeliers, sconces, etched-glass doors, brass balustrades and hardware, potted palms, wooden deck chairs, and a variety of art work. This art deco/grand hotel theme is carried into all staterooms, bathrooms, and hallways, making the *Deutschland* one of the more lovely and extravagantly furnished cruise ships in service.

Of the 294 cabins on the *Deutschland*, 224 are outside with full-size picture windows, and all include radios, telephones, bathrobes, slippers, hair dryers, minibars, and safes. They vary in size from 130 square feet for some inside cabins, 160 square feet for an average outside cabin, up to 240 square feet for a junior suite, 324 square feet for a full suite, and 400 square feet for the most expensive suite. Only the two largest suites have private balconies. Although the lower-priced and standard cabins are not as spacious as those found on other deluxe- or premium-market vessels, the bedroom and bathroom furnishings, appliances, and decor are exquisite.

Atop ship on deck 9 is the lido deck, composed of the midship outdoor pool; a lido bar; the lido terrace, a combination observation lounge, library, and venue for Continental breakfast and afternoon tea; and the casual buffet-style lido restaurant and grill, with adjoining outdoor umbrella-sheltered tables. This restaurant is tastefully and comfortably furnished, a pleasant change from the typical poolside buffet facility.

The suites and more expensive staterooms are found on deck 8, together with the cinema/conference auditorium. Most of the remaining inside and outside cabins are located on decks 4 and 5, along with the reception/shore-excursion desk and the library.

Public rooms found on decks 6 and 7 include the exquisitely designed, two-level Emperor's Ballroom, where passengers sit in comfortable lounge chairs with adjoining small cocktail tables and view the entertainment and gala events; the elegant two-seating Berlin Restaurant; the more intimate, romantic, 104-seat, reservation-only Four Seasons specialty restaurant; the stylish Lili Marleen Lounge; a fitness center that includes a small gym with several treadmills, exercycles, and step machines and connects to an impressive, dual-gender, clothing-optional sauna, steam, shower complex; a boutique and beauty salon; a photo gallery; and the Old Fritz, a warmly furnished, atmospheric, German-style pub.

At the bottom of the ship, on deck 3, is a small indoor pool surrounded by a sauna, a steam room, a sun-bed solarium, massage rooms, showers, and a dressing area. The area serves as the focal point of the vessel's extensive wellness program, which includes such services as thalassotherapy, Ayurveda treatments, and heat therapy. The ship's hospital is also located on this deck.

The ship has no casino or promenade deck where passengers could enjoy an uninterrupted stroll around the entire circumference of the ship without tripping over other guests. There is limited e-mail access through assigned private e-mail accounts.

Dining selections at all meals in all restaurants are numerous, with an emphasis on German-style cuisine. Service is Continental and efficient, and dining is at a more leisurely pace than on most other ships. Dining in the Four Seasons specialty restaurant is by reservation only. There is no cover charge, and participation is not limited.

Activities and entertainment are conducted in German and English, geared primarily to German tastes, and are not nearly as abundant as on ships catering to North American or British clientele. Two TV stations offer English-language movies, whereas the others are in German. Although English-speaking passengers are in a conspicuous minority, the captain, hotel manager, and entire staff are most attentive and make special efforts to accommodate their needs and preferences. The number of passengers from countries other than Germany has been growing each year.

## Strong Points

The *Deutschland* is an upscale, state-of-the-art, beautifully appointed vessel offering exotic itineraries throughout the world. It appeals to those interested in out-of-the-way places and is especially ideal for sophisticated German cruisers.

*Deutschland, courtesy Peter Deilmann cruises*

*Breakfast buffet, courtesy Peter Deilmann Cruises*

*Dining Room, courtesy Peter Deilmann Cruises*

*Junior suite, courtesy Peter Deilmann Cruises*

# FAREWELL
# GALA-DINNER

At Sea – June 26<sup>th</sup> 2012

WINE RECOMMONDATION

DIEL DE DIEL CUVEE 2010
Q.b.A., trocken
Schlossgut Diel

Euro 37,20


CHATEAUNEUF DU PAPE AC 2008
Grenache, Cinsault, Mourvedre, Syrah, Muscardin,
Counoise, Clairette, Bourboulence
Château Mont-Redon, Châteauneuf du Pape

Euro 66,20

# Dear guests,

We will give you lucullan pleasure!

In our restaurant VIERJAHRESZEITEN
we offer you first-class caviar.

## Sibirian
## Sturgeon Caviar

50 g – Euro 85,00

Fine, expressive roe of the world smallest sturgeon.

Beside we serve you
the classical condiments,
blinis and toast

# Menu

Terrine of pigeon and guinea fowl in a parma ham coat
on fried asparagus and parsley cream

Three kinds of sushi with marinated ginger and wasabi

❧❧❧

Essence of game with Royal Tricolore

Champagne-mustard soup with smoked foam

❧❧❧

Fillet of dorado
on wild garlic-barley risotto with saffron sauce
and fillets of tomatoes

❧❧❧

Passion fruit sherbet with cherry juice and mint

❧❧❧

Saddle of venison coated with walnuts on coffee-chocolate gravy
brussels sprouts leaves in
brown butter and potato soufflee

Truffled baby chicken breast in pierogi dough
on sauce perigord with broccoli-almond puree
beetroot in raspberry vinegar
and glazed carrots

❧❧❧

Tarte Tartine of figs with melted Roquefort cheese cream

❧❧❧

"The Grand Ice Parade"

❧❧❧

Homemade truffles and bisquits

❧❧❧

Espresso, coffee, tea

# VEGETARIAN MENU

Créme fraîche on mille feuille of buffalo cheese
and grilled melon with tangerine-star anise jam

❖

Champagne-mustard soup with smoked foam

❖

Asparagus in Parmesan coat on mushroom cream

❖

Passion fruit sherbet with cherry juice and mint

❖

Grilled vegetables with souffléed potatoes
and Riesling wine sabayon

❖

Tarte Tartine of figs
with melted Roquefort cheese cream

❖

"The Grand Ice Parade"

❖

Homemade truffles and bisquits

❖

Espresso, coffee, tea

*Courtesy Peter Deilmann Cruises*

## ETERNAL FIRE AND ICE

---

### SPORT ACTIVITIES WITH ANNIKA WULF

| | | |
|---|---|---|
| 08.00 am | KAISERSAAL | – Abs-Legs-Butt |
| 03.00 – 05.00 pm | FITNESS AREA | – Your Fitness trainer explains the fitness equipment and answers all your questions concerning "fitness". |

---

*Please note, that during the offered exercises there is no support service in our fitness room.*

**MV DEUTSCHLAND lies at Kangerlussuaq, Denmark - at anchor**

| | |
|---|---|
| 06.00 am | On channel 2 of ship's TV<br>Wake up with light music … |

**Dear guests,**
a tender service will start first for the guests going on the excursions. Thank you for your understanding.
The gangway is located on deck 3. For your own safety, please, observe the instructions of our officers. As we have to tender, delays may occur. Thank you in advance for your patience and cooperation.
Please listen to the public announcements which you are able to hear all public announcements in your cabin on TV channel 4.

The tender service for the guests who have booked excursions, is at the following times:

| | |
|---|---|
| 08.00 am | Announcement of the 1. Tender for the guests of excursion no. 33 "Panoramaflug zum Inlandeis" and for the guests of excursion no. 34 „Fahrt zum Inlandeiskap mit Allradfahrzeugen" from deck 4. |
| 08.10 am | Departure of the first tender boat. |
| 08.10 am | Announcement of the 2. Tender for the guests of excursion no. 34 „Fahrt zum Inlandeiskap mit Allradfahrzeugen" from deck 5, deck 7 and deck 8. |
| 08.15 am | Departure of the second tender boat. |
| 08.45 am | Announcement of the 3. Tender for the guests for the guests of excursion no. 35 „Landschaftsfahrt" (Please proceed to bus number 5). |
| 08.55 am | Departure of the third tender boat. |

**After the last excursion tender a regular tender service will be arranged for all guests who want to go ashore individually.**

| | |
|---|---|
| 02.00 pm | CINEMA<br>„Die Schwarzwaldklinik – Die nächste Generation" (app. 103 min., *in German*) |
| 03.30 – 04.30 pm | Tea, coffee, pastries and "Futjes" in the LIDO-Gourmet, deck 9 |
| 03.30 – 04.30 pm | **Elegant tea time** in the LIDO-Terrace, deck 9<br>Musically accompanied by Ciprian Cornita<br>Please observe the recommended dress code! |
| 01.30 pm | **"Last tender from land to ship!"** |

| 02.00 pm | **"Heave up the anchor!"**<br>MV DEUTSCHLAND bids farewell to Kangerlussuaq and sets sail for Nuuk,<br>Dänemark. 244 nautical miles, approximately 451 kilometres lie ahead of us. |
|---|---|
| 03.00 pm | KAISERSAAL<br>Dancing lesson with Mihriban Güler and Martin Kohring |
| 04.30 pm | LILI MARLEEN salon<br>Come and play **Bingo**! The minimum stake is Euro 2,50. |
| 05.15 pm | KAISERSAAL<br>**Captain's Cocktail**<br>Captain Andreas Jungblut invites all guests for a cocktail<br>All frequenters will be honoured. |
| 07.00 pm<br>08.30 pm | ... for the guests of the late seating in the CINEMA<br>... for the guests of the early seating in the CINEMA<br>Life in the ocean –<br>The phantastic creatures in the underwater world<br>Slide show *in German* with ocean biologist Volker Boehlke |
| 09.00 pm | LILI MARLEEN salon<br>The Deutschland Duo plays music to dream and dance. |
| 09.00 pm | ZUM ALTEN FRITZ bar<br>Enjoy the evening with music played by Julius Gürtler. |
| 09.00 pm | KAISERSAAL<br>The Marvin Jones Band plays international dance music. |
| 10.00 pm | CINEMA<br>„Young Victoria" ... a marvellous epos about the young queen Victoria<br>(app. 100 min., *in English*) |
| 10.15 pm | KAISERSAAL |

# „Fiesta"
## An Evening with Els Valldemossa

Afterwards the band entertains you with dance music again.

| 10.45 pm | Late night delicacies are awaiting you in the LILI MARLEEN salon. |
|---|---|

Your movie channel for today:
Channel 5: Travel movies – MV DEUTSCHLAND Winter Destinations –
    *in German*
Channel 6: The best sequels from the famous series of „Das Traumschiff" and
    „Kreuzfahrt ins Glück" – *in German*
Channel 10: „Minority Report" (app. 139 min.) – *in English*
Channel 11: „Snatch" (app. 98 min.) – *in English*

*Courtesy Peter Deilmann Cruises*

# DISNEY CRUISE LINE

**PO Box 10238**
**Lake Buena Vista, FL 32830**
**(800)951-3532 Tel.**
**Fax: (407) 566-3541**
**www.disneycruise.com**

*Disney Dream* and *Disney Fantasy*: entered service in 2011 and 2012, respectively; 130,000 GRT; 4,000-passenger capacity; 1,250 cabins; international officers and crew; *Disney Dream* offers three- and four-night cruises from Port Canaveral, Florida, to Bahamas and Castaway Cay; *Disney Fantasy* offers seven-night cruises to the Caribbean and Castaway Cay from Port Canaveral (Category B—not rated)

*Disney Magic*: entered service in 1998; renovated in 2010 and 2013; 83,000 GRT; 964 × 106 feet; 2,700-passenger capacity; 877 staterooms; international officers and crew; Mediterranean cruises during summer, seven-night cruises from San Juan to the Southern Caribbean, as well as four- and five-night cruises to the Bahamas and western Caribbean from Miami the remainder of the year (Category B—five+ stars)

*Disney Wonder*: entered service in 1999; renovated in 2011; 83,000 GRT; 964 × 106 feet; 2,700-passenger capacity; 877 staterooms; international officers and crew; Alaskan cruises during summer and four- and five-night cruises from Port Canaveral and Miami to the Bahamas and western Caribbean (Category B—five+ stars)

(Medical facilities: C-12; P-2, CLS, MS; N-4; CM; PD; BC; EKG; TC; PO; EPC; OX; WC; OR; ICU; X; M; LJ)

These ships are rated in eleven separate categories in the second half of chapter 11.

The state-of-the-art, unique, 83,000-ton *Disney Magic*, designed to be reminiscent of the classic ocean liners and capable of accommodating 2,700 passengers, entered service in July 1998, followed by *Disney Wonder* in August 1999. The 877 larger-than-average staterooms range in size from 184 square feet up to the 1,072-square-foot Royal Suites. Seventy-one percent of the accommodations are outside and almost half have verandas. All sleep at least three persons, whereas some accommodate four or five persons. All staterooms include tubs and showers (709 out of 877 have split bathrooms), remote control TVs, private safes, hair dryers, phones with voicemail message service, wave phones, and privacy dividers separating bedrooms from the sitting areas that convert to pull-down beds and sofas for the children. In addition, there are two luxurious Royal Suites that can sleep seven persons; two 945-square-foot, two-bedroom suites that can sleep seven persons; and eighteen 614-square-foot, one-bedroom suites, fourteen of which sleep five persons and four are wheelchair accessible. The suites rival those on luxury-category ships. The line offers several stateroom categories, air-sea packages, and early-booking discounts. Staterooms and suites in all categories are a good deal larger and include more amenities than those on most other cruise ships; however, they are designed to accommodate more passengers. The availability of a tub and shower in a split bathroom design in the lower-cost categories is unusual in the cruise industry.

All cruises departing from Port Canaveral include a visit to Castaway Cay, Disney's privately developed one-thousand-acre island in the Bahamas, where guests will enjoy a protected lagoon for water sports, shops, dining pavilions, bicycles, and separate adults-only and family beaches. The ships are able to dock at the island and avoid time-consuming tender service. Programs exclusively for teens and tots are also featured. Among the special activities available for all passengers is Castaway Ray's Stingray Adventure, a supervised, interactive experience with the rays. In 2010, the facilities at Castaway Cay were increased. The family beach was extended, adding bars, buffets, and sixteen 325-square-foot private cabanas. Four cabanas were added on the adults-only beach as well. Several new water attractions were also incorporated, including floating water slides and water play areas.

The dining experience aboard these vessels is unique in that it permits guests to move to a different theme restaurant each night. Dinner companions and their waitstaff move together to three different locations, including Lumiere's, a more traditional, art deco motif dining room; Parrot Cay, sporting a colorful, tropical decor; and Animator's Palate, a totally unique restaurant that transforms over the course of the evening from a room decorated solely in black and white to a kaleidoscope of lights and colors. On the *Disney Wonder*, Lumiere's has been replaced with Triton's, a seafood restaurant with an "under the sea" theme. Dining in these three venues is pleasant and much improved from the cruise line's inception, and the cuisine could be described as eclectic with Continental offerings as well as hearty American fare.

Palo on the *Disney Magic* and *Disney Wonder* is a 120-seat alternative, adults-only, Italian specialty restaurant located atop ship, with windows out to the sea. This is definitely the choice for adults traveling without children and those who can stash them for a few hours with the counselors. Reservations are required, and it is advisable to book immediately upon coming on board. It is also possible to make reservations online at the cruise line's Web site. Here, I found the dining experience top-notch, with gourmet Italian cuisine, an impressive wine list, and excellent presentation and service. Champagne brunches offered here on days at sea are awesome. High Tea is also served here on days at sea. In addition, families can opt for an indoor/outdoor café serving all three meals, snacks, and a buffet lunch and dinner for children; a hamburger, hot dog, and pizza grill near the pool; and an ice-cream bar—Goofy's Galley—offering fresh fruit, salads, wraps, panini, and sandwiches as well as ice cream. Room service is available around the clock.

Public areas (which are traditional and nautical in décor with numerous Disney character and art deco accents) and activities include an entire deck devoted to children and featuring age-specific supervised programs, a children's pool, game arcade, special teen club, play areas, and a full complement of children's counselors and state-of-the-art kids' area; three outdoor pools—one for families, a supervised children's pool fashioned in the image of Mickey Mouse with an impressive waterslide, and a third with adjoining whirlpools exclusively for adults; a 977-seat theater for musical productions and a 268-seat cinema for Disney classics, first-run releases, and live entertainment (3-D technology was added in 2008); a state-of-the-art, jumbo outdoor movie screen for poolside movies; dinner and deck parties with fireworks; shopping opportunities with emphasis on signature Disney items; several themed nightclubs and lounges; a teen club atop ship; a 10,700-square-foot ocean-view equipped gym and Steiner health spa; and a promenade deck for jogging and walking. There is no casino, in keeping with the Disney family image. However, the separate adult pool; private beach on Castaway Cay; lounge areas; spa villas with indoor treatment rooms, outdoor verandas, hot tubs, lounge chairs, and open-air shower; Internet/specialty coffee café; and the excellent, upscale, specialty adults-only Italian restaurant afford some sanctuary for cruisers traveling without children or wishing a few hours of respite. Activities directed to adult singles, couples without children, or older teens are not as extensive as those on other larger cruise ships.

Over the past few years, various renovations were made to the ships, including the addition of an LED movie screen over the family pool for outdoor movies, the expansion of the spa and fitness center, a new toddler splash area, a sports pub, and a new, adults-only specialty-coffee lounge. In 2013, *Disney Magic* received additional renovations, adding many of the features found on the two newer Disney ships.

In early 2007, Disney placed an order to build two new 130,000-ton, 1,250-stateroom vessels. The first entered service in January 2011 and is named *Disney Dream* and followed by the second, *Disney Fantasy*, in 2012. These larger vessels are designed similarly to the original two ships and include a version of all of the venues; however, they have numerous additional features and attractions. One of the most amazing new attractions is the AquaDuck Water Coaster, a 765-foot-long/four-deck high ride that sends guests on a high-speed journey aboard inflatable rafts through drops, twists, uphill climbs, and turns and includes a swing-out loop that launches passengers 12 feet over the side of the ship in a transparent tube. The outside deck area also includes a two-foot-deep children's pool, a family pool that transforms into a dance floor for deck parties at night and includes a giant LED screen, an adults-only pool, and Nemo's Reef, a whimsical water play area/splash pool with characters, pop jets, and fountains.

Dining, too, is similar to the two smaller ships. Rotational dining takes place in three main dining rooms: Animators Palate, Enchanted Garden, and Royal Palace (*Disney Dream*) and Royal Court (*Disney Fantasy*). Cabanas is an indoor/outdoor buffet restaurant, with sixteen specialized food stations, serving all three meals. Palo is the gourmet Northern Italian, adults-only specialty restaurant open for dinner nightly and for brunch on sea days (at a $20 per person charge). Remy features French inspired gourmet cuisine (at a $75 per person charge).

There are several categories of staterooms and suites that can accommodate from three to five passengers. Most have split bathrooms. The largest, the Royal Suites, measure 1,781 square feet, including the verandah. The concierge one-bedroom suites are 622 square feet, the concierge ocean-view family staterooms are 306 square feet, the deluxe family ocean-view staterooms with verandahs are 299 square feet, the ocean-view staterooms are 204-241 square feet, and inside staterooms are 169-204 square feet and include a "virtual port hole" with a view outside the ship provided by video cameras. The five-person family category of suites includes a queen bed, a double-bed convertible couch, and an upper berth. Eighty-eight percent of the accommodations are outside, and of those, 82 percent offer verandas.

Like the other Disney ships, there are adult entertainment areas, high-tech and educational, age-appropriate children's areas and activities, a nursery, and special venues and dedicated indoor/outdoor facilities for teens. The "District" on the *Disney Dream* and the "Europa" on the *Disney Fantasy*, adults-only nighttime entertainment areas, have five venues, which include "Skyline," where the sun sets over the skyline of a different city each evening, a champagne bar, a nightclub, a traditional pub, and a piano/entertainment lounge.

These ships offer a traditional Disney-style experience at sea that will appeal to families who enjoy a Disney vacation and wish to combine a cruise with visits to the theme parks. With itineraries in Europe, these ships offer an attractive cruise vacation for families wishing to expose their children to other cultures. Activities and entertainment are definitely directed to families and the younger set. Different activities are scheduled for the various children's age-groups. However, each year, there is an increasing emphasis on adults-only facilities.

## Strong Points

This is an excellent family-oriented cruise for parents with young children, preteens, and early teens as well as Mickey Mouse junkies. Efforts are made to provide something for all members of the family.

*Disney private island, courtesy Disney Cruise Line*

*Children's pool and water slide, courtesy Disney Cruise Line*

*Veranda stateroom, Disney Dream, courtesy Disney Cruise Line*

*Parrot Cay Dining Room, courtesy Disney Cruise Line*

## Apéritifs

**Kir Royal**
Sparkling Wine with a touch
of Crème de Cassis.  $5.25

**Alizé Passion**
Crafted from Cognac, Passion
Fruit Juice, and Vodka.  $4.50

## Smoothies

Delicious, rich Ice Cream blended with
your favorite flavors. Choose from
Chocolate, Strawberry, Vanilla,
Peach, or Banana.  $3.50
With Rum or Vodka.  $4.50

## Featured Wines

**Mumm Cordon Rouge, Champagne**
A great celebration bubbly, this versatile
Cuvee is fruity, subtle, and refined.
$11.00  Glass    $52.00  Bottle

**Delaporte Sancerre, Loire**
This classic Sancerre features a floral and
slightly grassy bouquet with mineral
notes and is excellent with seafood.
$8.00  Glass    $37.00  Bottle

**Louis Jadot Pouilly-Fuissé,
Burgundy**
Pouilly-Fuissé is America's favorite
French Chardonnay.
$8.75  Glass    $42.00  Bottle

**Louis Jadot Beaujolais-
Village, Burgundy**
Bright Raspberry and Cherry flavors accent
a fruity finish in this lightest of all reds.
$5.25  Glass    $25.00  Bottle

**Chateau Phelan-Segur, St. Estephe**
This Bordeaux is a forceful example of how
blending Cabernet Sauvignon, Merlot, and
Cabernet Franc can produce a wine for
consuming with flavorful meats and pastas.
$14.50  Glass    $69.00  Bottle

## Our Special Layered Liqueur of the Night

**French Flag**
Grenadine, Crème de Cacao,
and Blue Curaçao.  $4.50
In our specialty glass.  $6.50

*We offer a complete array of cocktails,
a full bar, and an extensive wine list.*

## Starters

⬥ **Deep Fried Camembert**
with a Marinara Sauce

**Shrimp Medley**
served with Cocktail Sauce

**Pearls of Seasonal Melon**
with Port Wine

⬥ **Escargot**
with Diced Mushrooms and Garlic Butter

**Cream of Cauliflower Soup**

**Mixed Garden Salad**
tossed with Red Wine Vinaigrette and topped with
Goat Cheese Croutons

## Main Course

**Cheese Ravioli**
served with a Tomato-Basil Sauce

**Garlic-roasted Beef Tenderloin**
served with Mashed Potatoes and a Green Peppercorn Sauce

**Herb-crusted Sea Bass**
with Sautéed Spinach and Champagne Sauce

**Braised Lamb Shank**
served with Portobello Polenta and a Red Wine Sauce

⬥ **Roasted Duck Breast**
with Sautéed Parsnips and an Orange Sauce

**Chef's Vegetarian Selection of the Day**

*Additional selections of Sirloin Steak,
Grilled Chicken Breast, fresh Fish, or "Lighter Fare"
are available. Kindly ask your server.*

## Desserts

**Chocolate Mousse Cake**
served with Rum-Caramel Sauce

**Caramelized Apple Tart**
with Vanilla Sauce

**Grand Marnier Soufflé**
with Chocolate Sauce

⬥ **Crème Brûlée**

**Chef's Sugar-free Dessert**

⬥ **Restaurant Specialty**

*Courtesy Disney Cruise Line*

# DISNEY MAGIC

## ACTIVITIES & ENTERTAINMENT

| | |
|---|---|
| 6:00am - 12:00am | **Goofy's Pool** is open for use. Deck 9, Midship. |
| 6:00am - 12:00am | **The Quiet Cove Pool** is open for use. Deck 9, Forward. *(Guests 18 and older)* |
| 6:00am - 10:00pm | **Mickey's Pool** is open for use. Deck 9, Aft. |
| 8:00am - 12:00am | **Quarter Masters Arcade** is open for your enjoyment on Deck 9, Midship. |
| 8:00am - 4:00pm | **Bridge, Cards & Games**, Fantasia Reading & Game Room, Deck 2, Midship. |
| 8:00am | **Stretch & Relax**, Vista Spa. Deck 9, Forward. |
| 8:30am - 9:00am | **Toddler Time:** Explore the Oceaneer Club with your Toddler, Deck 5, Midship. |
| 9:00am - 6:30pm | **Mickey's Slide** is open for use. Deck 9, Aft. *(Height and age restrictions apply)*. |
| 9:00am - 12:00pm | **Shore Excursion Desk:** Your last opportunity to reserve excursion tickets for St. Maarten, Deck 3, Midship. |
| 9:00am - 11:00am | **Disney Vacation Club:** Stop by to learn the benefits of membership. Deck 4, Midship. |
| 9:00am | **Walk a** *Smile* **Mile:** Join us for a stroll around Deck 4. Meet in Preludes, Deck 4, Forward. |
| 9:30am | **Ballroom Dancing:** Learn the basics of the Foxtrot & Waltz Rockin' Bar D, Deck 3, Forward. |
| 10:00am | **Sign Up Sheets** for Family & Adult Talent Show, limited space available. Sign up at the Shore Excursion Desk, Deck 3, Midship. |
| 10:00am | **Team Trivia:** Join your Cruise Staff in the Promenade Lounge Deck 3, Aft. |
| 10:00am | **Bridge, Cards and Tournaments** in the Fantasia Reading & Game Room, Deck 2, Midship. *(Sign-up sheets available)* |
| 10:00am | **Disney's Art of Entertaining:** "Dazzling Desserts" Our expert chef showcases dessert tips and tricks in Studio Sea, Deck 4, Midship. *(Guests 18 and older)* |
| 10:30am | **Shuffleboard Challenge for Families**, Deck 4, Aft, Port Side. |
| 10:45am | **Jackpot Bingo!** Win Cash Prizes! (First game begins at 11:00am). Rockin' Bar D, Deck 3, Forward. |
| 11:00am - 4:00pm | **Island Music:** Enjoy the sounds of Kool Breeze. Pool Side Gazebo Deck 9, Midship. |
| 11:30am | **Secrets to Beautiful Hair**, Vista Spa, Deck 9, Forward. |
| 11:30am - 12:30pm | **Disney Vacation Club Presentation:** A fun, informative Virtual Open House. Studio Sea, Deck 4, Midship. |
| 12:00pm | **Voice from the Bridge** A navigational update from the Captain. *(Pt. @urni)* |
| 12:15pm | **Family Mini Olympics:** Join the Cruise Staff for fun & games, Sports Deck, Deck 10, Forward. |
| 12:15pm | **Singles, Single Parents or Traveling alone** meet for an informal lunch with the Cruise Staff, Parrot Cay, Deck 3, Aft. |
| 12:30pm | **Island Magic Stage Show** showing in the Buena Vista Theatre, Deck 5, Aft. |
| 1:00pm - 2:00pm | **Disney Vacation Club:** Stop by to learn the benefits of membership. Deck 4, Midship. |
| 1:30pm | **Snorkel Demonstration:** Join the Recreation Staff to learn the basics Goofy Pool, Deck 9, Midship. |
| 1:45pm | **Mickey 200 Sign Up:** first 18 teams to sign up will make a racing car from vegetables for this wild & wacky race, The Off Beat Club, Deck 3, Forward. |
| 2:00pm | **Island Magic Stage Show** showing in the Buena Vista Theatre, Deck 5, Aft. |
| 2:00pm | **The Best "Disney Legs" Contest:** Join your Cruise Staff for this fun game, Goofy Pool, Deck 9 Midship. |
| 2:00pm - 3:00pm | **Disney's Navigator Series:** The Making of the Disney Magic and charting her course. Rockin' Bar D, Deck 3, Forward. *(Guests 18 and older)* |
| 2:00pm - 3:00pm | **Disney's Art of Entertaining:** Innovation, Fun & Creativity in Tablescaping. Studio Sea, Deck 4, Midship. |
| 2:00pm - 3:00pm | **Mickey 200:** Let the racing begin, May the FASTEST VEGGIE WIN! The Off Beat Club, Deck 3, Forward. |
| 2:00pm - 4:00pm | **Shore Excursion Desk:** Your opportunity to reserve excursion tickets for St.Thomas. Deck 3, Midship. |
| 3:00pm | **Jackpot Bingo!** WIN Cash Prizes! (First game begins at 3:15pm). Rockin' Bar D, Deck 3, Forward. |
| 3:00pm | **Back Care Seminar:** Vista Spa, Deck 9, Forward. |
| 3:00pm - 4:00pm | **Stem to Stern Wine Tasting** with our Cellar Master. Sessions, Deck 3, Forward. Reserve your spot at Guest Services $12.00. *(Guests 21 and older)* |
| 3:00pm - 6:30pm | **Disney Vacation Club:** Stop by to learn about benefits of membership. Deck 4, Midship. |
| 3:30pm | **High Tea in Palo:** Space is limited, reservations required. Palo, Deck 10, Aft. *(Guests 18 and older)* |

Disney Character Appearance    Disney's Navigator Series    Shore Excursion

Disney's Art of Entertaining    Disney's Behind-the-Scenes    Guests 18 & Older

## Character Appearances

**Meet some of your favorite Disney Friends:**

12:30pm - 1:00pm
Buena Vista Theatre, Deck 5, Aft.

2:00pm - 2:30pm
Buena Vista Theatre, Deck 5, Aft.

3:00pm - 3:30pm
Mickey Pool, Deck 9, Aft.

5:30pm - 6:20pm
Atrium Lobby, Deck 3, Midship

7:00pm - 7:30pm
Atrium Lobby, Deck 3, Midship.

7:30pm - 8:20pm
Atrium, Deck 3, Midship.

10:00pm - 10:30pm
Atrium Lobby, Deck 3, Midship.

## Movies
### Deck 5, Aft

**Island Magic Stage Show**
12:30pm - Running Time :30
**Island Magic Stage Show**
2:00pm - Running Time :30
**Pearl Harbor (PG13)**
3:15pm - Running Time 3:03
**102 Dalmations (PG)**
6:30pm - Running Time 1:40
**102 Dalmations (PG)**
8:30pm - Running Time 1:40
**Castaway (PG)**
11:15pm - Running Time 2:23

## FAMILY MAGIC QUEST

Join your Cruise Staff for the wildest & wackiest game on the seven seas!

7:45pm
Studio Sea, Deck 4, Midship.

## FAMILY KARAOKE

Join us for some singing FUN!

9:45pm
Studio Sea, Deck 4, Midship
Create your own
COOL Smoothie! $3.50

## Family Activities

**Team Trivia**
10:00am
**Shuffle Board Challenge**
10:30am
**Jackpot Bingo!**
10:45am & 3:00pm
**Family Mini Olympics**
12:15pm
**Magic Quest**
7:45pm
**Cabaret Show Time**
7:45pm
**Family Karaoke**
9:45pm
**Family Dance Music**
11:00pm - 11:30pm

## Trading Cards

Join in on the fun of collecting various trading cards unique to the *Disney Magic* and *Disney Cruise Line*.

Anywhere you see the "card" icon on your *Personal Navigator*, a trading card will be distributed to our younger cruisers.

*Note: A different card is available at each designated time! That's the fun of trading cards, don't miss out!

## Island Magic Stage Show

Don't miss this *FUN* filled stage show featuring some of your favorite Disney Friends.

Captain Mickey takes us on a Magical adventure to Disney's Castaway Cay.

12:30pm & 2:00pm, Buena Vista Theatre, Deck 5, Aft

## SESSIONS

**7:30pm - 8:30pm**
**Joy Wright**
Entertains at the piano.

**9:30pm - 12:30am**
**Joy Wright**
weaves her musical magic at the piano.

Beat Street - Deck 3, Forward
(Guests 18 & older)

## Disney Vacation Club

Welcomes its members and all Guests to a fun & informative, Virtual Open House, 11:30am - 12:30pm Studio Sea, Deck 4, Midship

*If you believe in Magic, you belong!*

## Stem to Stern

"Wine Tasting"

Sample fine wines from around the world 3:00pm - 4:00pm Sessions, Deck 3, Forward. Reverve your place at Guest Services $12.
(Guests 21 and older)

## ADULT ACTIVITIES

**Disney Navigator Series**
2:00pm

**Stem to Stern Wine Tasting**
3:00pm - 4:00pm

**Rock the House**
9:30pm - 10:00pm

**Who's the Boss?**
9:45pm

**Dueling Pianos**
10:15pm & 11:15pm

**Rock and Roll Night**
11:00pm

**Dance Party**
11:45pm - 2:00am

|  |  |
|---|---|
| 3:30pm | **Disney's Navigator Series Ship Tour:** Join us for this walking tour, as we highlight several public rooms illustrating the ship's designing of Disney culture, theming & artistry, The Off Beat Club, Deck 3, Forward. |
| 4:00pm | **Hi/Low Aerobics:** Vista Spa, Deck 9, Forward. |
| 4:00pm - 5:00pm | **Family Basketball Time:** Meet at the Wide World of Sports for informal play. Deck 10, forward. |
| 4:30pm | **Friends of Bill W.** will be meeting in Fantasia Reading & Game Room, Deck 2, Midship |
| 4:30pm | **Seaweed Secrets:** Learn benefits of detoxification for arthritis. Sessions, Deck 3, Forward. |
| 4:30pm | **Mixed Doubles Ping Pong Tournament:** Meet at tables, Deck 9, Forward, Port Side. |
| 5:15pm | **Castaway Club Members:** A special reception for all our returning Disney Cruise Line Guests. Rockin' Bar D, Deck 3, Forward (please bring invitation) |
| 5:15pm - 6:00pm | **Promenade Lounge** presents the smooth & sassy music of *Del & Lynn*, Deck 3, Aft. |
| 5:30pm - 6:30pm | **Family Time:** Explore Disney's Oceaneer Club and Lab, Deck 5, Midship *(Adult accompaniment please)* |
| 5:30pm - 6:30pm | **Portraits** taken in the Atrium Lobby, Deck 3, Midship. |

| | |
|---|---|
| 3:15pm, 6:30pm & 8:30pm | *Disney Cruise Line proudly presents* |

### C'est Magique

Deck 4, Forward

*As a courtesy to all Guests we kindly advise that the seating of seats is not permitted in the Walt Disney Theatre.*

|  |  |
|---|---|
| 7:30pm - 8:30pm | **Pin Trading:** Collect and trade with your fellow guests & Senior Officers in the Atrium Lobby, Deck 3 Midship. |
| 7:30pm - 8:30pm | **Your Shopping in Paradise Guide** *Shelby* is available to answer questions regarding St. Maarten and St. Thomas Duty Free Shopping. Deck 3, Midship, Starboard Side. |
| 7:30pm - 8:30pm | **Sparkling Moments:** Enjoy fine wines and Champagne, available for purchase, Atrium Lobby, Deck 3, Midship. |
| 7:30pm - 8:45pm | **Portraits** taken in the Atrium Lobby, Deck 3, Midship. |
| 7:30pm - 9:00pm | **Disney Vacation Club** Stop by to learn about benefits of membership, Deck 4, Midship. |
| 7:30pm - 12:30am | **Sessions** presents Joy Wright entertaining at the piano. Deck 3, Forward. *(Guests 18 and older)* |
| 7:45pm | **Cabaret Show Time** with the Comedy & Music of *Dan Riley*, Rockin' Bar D, Deck 3, Forward. *(Everyone Welcome)* |
| 7:45pm | **Magic Quest:** Join your Cruise Staff for the wildest & wackiest game on the seven seas for the entire family! Studio Sea, Deck 4, Midship |
| 7:45pm | **ESPN Sports Trivia Challenge** with the Cruise Staff, ESPN Skybox, Deck 11, Midship. |
| 7:15pm - 8:15pm | **Family Pianos:** Craziness for the Kids & You! The Off Beat Club, Deck 3, Forward. *(Everyone Welcome)* |
| 9:30pm - 10:30pm | **Promenade Lounge:** Bring the family and dance to the music of *Del & Lynn*. Deck 3, Aft. |
| 9:30pm - 10:00pm | **Rock the House** with Double Trouble. Rockin' Bar D, Deck 3, Forward. *(Guests 18 and older)* |
| 9:45pm | **Who's the Boss?** Join your Cruise Staff to find out which gender RULES! The Off Beat Club, Deck 3, Forward. *(Guests 18 and older)* |
| 9:45pm | **Disney Behind the Scenes:** Question & Answer session with the Walt Disney Theatre Cast. Walt Disney Theatre, Deck 4, Forward. |
| 9:45pm - 11:00pm | **Family Karaoke:** It's a casting call for all family members in Studio Sea, Deck 4, Midship |
| 10:00pm - 10:30pm | **Character Family Portraits:** Have your portrait taken with Mickey, Minnie, Goofy & Pluto for this one time only opportunity in the Atrium Lobby, Deck 3, Midship. *(No Autographs Please)* |
| 10:15pm | **Cabaret Show Time** with the Comedy & Music of *Dan Riley*, Rockin' Bar D, Deck 3, Forward. *(Guests 18 and older)* |
| 10:15pm - 11:00pm | **Dueling Pianos Tribute:** The Beatles & British Rock Invasion. The Off Beat Club, Deck 3, Forward. *(Guests 18 and older)* |
| 10:30pm - 12:00am | **Promenade Lounge Presents:** Smooth & Sassy music of *Del & Lynn*. Deck 3, Aft. |
| 11:00pm | **Rock & Roll Night!** Rock Around the Clock" with your Cruise Staff & Double Trouble, Rockin' Bar D, Deck 3, Forward *(Guests 18 and older)* |
| 11:00pm - 11:30pm | **Family Dance Music:** Our DJ plays todays hottest hits, Studio Sea, Deck 4, Midship. |
| 11:15pm - 12:00am | **Dueling Pianos Sing Along:** Raise your voices & your spirits in the Off Beat Club, Deck 3, Forward. *(Guests 18 and older)* |
| 11:45pm - 2:00am | **Dance Party** with *Double Trouble & Frankie J*, Rockin' Bar D, Deck 3, Forward. *(Guests 18 and older)* |

*Courtesy Disney Cruise Line*

# FRED. OLSEN CRUISE LINES

Fred Olsen House
White House Road
Ipswich 1P1 5LL
England
+44 (0) 1473 746175
www.fredolsencruises.com

USA
Borton Overseas
5412 Lyndale Ave. S
Minneapolis MN 55419
800-843-0602
www.bortonoverseas.com

*Balmoral* (formerly *Crown Odyssey* and *Norwegian Crown*): entered service in 1988; 34,242 GRT; 614 × 92.5 feet; 1,350-passenger capacity; 710 cabins; Norwegian officers, British cruise staff, and Filipino crew; cruises the Mediterranean, Baltics, Canary Islands, and Norway from the United Kingdom (Category C—not rated)

(Medical facilities: C-2; P-1; N-1; CM, OX, WC)

*Black Watch* (formerly *Royal Viking Star*): entered service in 1972; renovated in 1998 and 2009; 28,492 GRT; 630 × 83 feet; 804-passenger capacity; 423 cabins; Norwegian officers, British cruise staff, and Filipino crew; cruises the North Sea, Baltics, Canary Islands, and around South America (Category C/D—not rated)

(Medical facilities: C-4; P-1; N-2; CM, EKG, OX, WC, OR, X)

*Boudicca* (formerly *Royal Viking Sky*, *Superstar Capricorn*, *Birka Queen*, and *Grand Latino*): entered service in 1973; 25,000 GRT; 593 × 84 feet; 880-passenger capacity; 462 cabins; Norwegian officers, British cruise staff, and Filipino crew; cruises the Canary Islands, Mediterranean, and North Sea (Category C—not rated)

*Braemar* (formerly *Crown Dynasty* and *Norwegian Dynasty*): entered service in 1993; renovated in 2001 and 2009; 19,089 GRT; 537 × 74 feet; 880-passenger capacity; 484 cabins; Norwegian officers, British cruise staff, and Filipino crew; cruises the North Sea, Baltics, Canary Islands, and Caribbean (Category C—not rated)

(Medical facilities: C-4; P-1; N-2: DM, EKG, OX, WC, OR, X)

This family-owned cruise line services a largely British clientele and offers a full-scale, no-frills cruise experience traversing exotic ports around the world at bargain rates.

The *Black Watch* was born in the early 1970s as the luxurious *Royal Viking Star*, and it continues to display much of the wood, brass, and class of the ships of that era. Accommodations are not up to those of the ships built in recent years; however, they are comfortable. Ninety percent of the cabins have portholes or windows. Inside cabins measure up to 140 square feet and escalate in size up to 200 square feet for a superior outside cabin on lido deck. Junior suites measure 240 feet, deluxe suites measure 260 feet, the six marquee suites are 440 feet, and the three premier suites come in at 550 feet. All accommodations have a TV, hair dryer, and bathroom with shower. Superior cabins have picture windows and bathtubs, and the suites include refrigerators and sitting areas. If you require a veranda, your only options are the premier and marquee suites. Single cabins range from inside to balcony and offer a single rate.

There are two main indoor restaurants as well as a casual indoor/outdoor café. Refurbished in 2009, the new Braemar Garden Café, with courtyard area, offers informal dining and themed evenings. Other public areas include numerous lounges; a cabaret show lounge; a fitness center with a gym, sauna, and treatment rooms; Internet facilities, a cardroom; a launderette; a beauty salon; a swimming pool; a splash pool; and an outdoor Jacuzzi.

The 19,089-ton, 900-passenger *Braemar* was built in 1993 and formerly sailed as the *Crown Dynasty* and the *Norwegian Dynasty*. After being acquired by Fred. Olsen Cruise Lines in 2001, it received numerous cosmetic changes, including a wraparound promenade deck for walkers and joggers. In 2008, the ship was lengthened, adding additional cabins. Public facilities include a traditional two-seating restaurant and a casual buffet-style café; a show lounge for nightly cabaret entertainment and several smaller bars/lounges; a swimming pool/lido area with Jacuzzis; a fitness center with a gym, massage, and treatment area and sauna; a library; a cardroom; and an Internet center.

In 2005, the cruise line purchased the 800-passenger *Grand Latino*, formerly *Royal Viking Sky*, from Iberojet Cruceros and renamed her *Boudicca*. The ship is similar to the *Black Watch* (formerly *Royal Viking Star*) and was designed for world cruises. Many cabins have sea views. In 2006, the line acquired the former *Crown Odyssey* from Norwegian and renamed her *Balmoral*. She commenced cruising for the line in January 2008 after a refit. She is the largest ship in the fleet. There are three formal dining rooms, one informal dining room, and several lounges to enjoy evening entertainment and/or tea in the afternoon.

Many of the cruises offer Vistas, a new special interest program that covers a wide range of themes, subjects, and interests, such as weather, photography, ballroom dancing, antiques, classical music, authors and sporting personalities, gardening, wine, history of the royal family, and comedy. On these cruises, guests can enjoy lectures and customized shore excursions.

## Strong Points

Great itineraries at reasonable prices with a full cruise experience on older, non-state-of-the-art vessels. The ships are very popular in the United Kingdom.

*Balcony Stateroom on Balmoral, courtesy Fred. Olsen Cruise Line*

*Atrium Lobby on Balmoral,*
*courtesy Fred. Olsen Cruise Line*

*Pub/Lounge on Braemar, courtesy Fred. Olsen Cruse Line*

*Balmoral, courtesy Fred. Olsen Cruise Line*

# BREADS

*Fresh bread baked daily in our onboard bakery*

# APPETISERS

**TANGY GRAPEFRUIT COCKTAIL**
*Chilled juicy segments and sour cherries spiked with Campari ♥ V*

**HERB MARINATED SALMON**
*Citrus zest, dill, cognac and mild spices, served with asparagus tips*
*and a piquant honey mustard dressing*

# SOUPS

**CHICKEN BROTH**
*A favourite with root vegetables and strips of chicken ♥*

**GREEN PEA SOUP**
*Smooth and silky and served with crunchy croutons ♥ V*

# SALADS

**HOUSE SALAD**
*A selection of market fresh seasonal ingredients ♥ V*

**CLASSICAL NICOISE**
*French beans, potatoes, tomatoes, cucumber, black olives, hard boiled eggs and flaked tuna ♥*

# A CHOICE OF DRESSINGS

*Thousand island, Honey mustard, Italian vinaigrette, Caesar, Balsamic and Creamy French*

## MAIN COURSES

**INDIAN SPICED BAKED BUTTERFISH**
*Curry spiced fillet with a light creamed curry sauce, pilaf rice and steamed vegetables* ♥

**SLOW ROAST DUCKLING CONFIT**
*Slow cooked legs, honey roast parsnips and potato rosti, Madagascan peppercorn sauce*

**GRILLED SIRLOIN STEAK**
*Prime beef, jacket potatoes, balsamic baked tomatoes and herb butter* ♥

**SPAGHETTI "VERDE"**
*Al dente pasta tossed in a basil and light herb sauce, flaked fresh parmesan*

**SCANDINAVIAN HERRING PLATTER**
*Assorted marinated herrings served with dark rye bread and warm dilled new potatoes* ♥

## BRITISH DISH OF THE DAY

**BRAISED BEEF AND SHALLOTS**
*Slow cooked collops of beef with red wine, shallots and cheesy mashed potatoes*

## VEGETARIAN

**OVEN BAKED NUT AND VEGETABLE PIE**
*A rich combination of nuts and vegetables presented in a shortcrust pastry pie,*
*served with crispy vegetables and apple sauce* V

## ALWAYS AVAILABLE

*Grilled Fish of the Day, Rosemary chicken breast, Omelettes,*
*Angel hair pasta with vine ripened tomato ragout* ♥ V
*All served with a selection of daily vegetables and potatoes*

## DESSERTS

**KIWI TART**
*Juicy slices on a sweet cream base, vanilla sauce and blackberry ragout* ♥ V

**BAVARIAN STRAWBERRY CREAM**
*Marinated apricots and a chocolate biscotti* V

**MANDARIN CHAMPAGNE JELLY**
*Plump segments with sweet Champagne jelly topped with Cointreau cream* ♥ V

## SUGAR FREE DESSERT

**MANDARIN CHAMPAGNE JELLY**
*Plump segments, sweet Champagne topped with Cointreau cream* ♥ V

## ICE CREAMS AND SORBETS

*Please ask your waiter for today's selection of ice creams and sorbets*
*Sugar free and soya ice cream is also available*

*A selection of British and International cheeses*
*Grapes, celery, red radish and apricots* V

♥ *Denotes a healthy option*
V *Denotes suitable for vegetarians*

*Some dishes may contain nuts or traces*
*Please contact the Maître d'hôtel for further details*

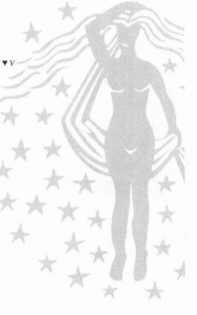

## DESSERT WINE

| | |
|---|---|
| Le Dauphin de Guiraud 2002/2004 | £4.15 |
| Blandy's Alvada Madeira Wine | £2.35 |
| Warre's Otima 10 Year old Tawny | £2.50 |

DD010509RV

*Courtesy Fred. Olsen Cruise Line*

# BLACK WATCH

## GOOD MORNING

| | | |
|---|---|---|
| 8.00am | Daily Quiz available for collection; answers posted at 5.00pm | Library & Braemar |
| 8.15am | Walk a Mile. Meet Sherly Deck 7 aft for a brisk mile walk around the deck | Deck 7 Aft |
| 9.00-11.00am | Library is open for the loan of Books, Videos & CDs | Deck 9 |
| 9.00-9.15am | Navigational Bridge Visit. Collect your ticket for today's visits (15 per visit) | Reception |

| 10.00am | **PORT TALK** | Neptune Lounge |
|---|---|---|
| | Join, Dawn Ramsey for her informative talk on the ports of Valencia & Gibraltar | |
| | *This will be relayed at 4:30pm on Channel 4 of your Cabin TV's* | |

| 10.00am | **BRIDGE CLASS** | Card Room |
|---|---|---|
| | Christine will continue to talk about "Strong Hands & Slam Bidding" | |
| | *(Neil will continue with Beginner's Bridge)* | |

| | | |
|---|---|---|
| 10.00am | Golf Putting with Nick. Meet at the Golf Nets *(Weather Permitting)* | Deck 11 |
| 10.00am | Yoga Class with Carrianne. £5.00 for 30 minutes | Fitness Centre |
| 10.30am | Shuffleboard. Meet Amanda Port Side of Lido Deck *(Weather Permitting)* | Deck 7 |
| 10.30am | Navigational Bridge Visit. *(Weather Permitting)* | Deck 8 Fwd |

| 10.45am | **DOLPHIN RACING AUCTION** | Poolside, Deck 6 |
|---|---|---|
| | An opportunity to become a Black Watch Dolphin Owner & place your 50p bets. | |

| 11.00am | **BLACK WATCH PASSENGER CHOIR!** | Marina Theatre |
|---|---|---|
| | Enjoy the experience of singing all kinds of music with your fellow guests. | |

| 11.00am | **ICE CARVING DEMONSTRATION** - *(Weather Permitting)* | Poolside, Deck 6 |
|---|---|---|
| | Come and watch as our expert ice carver turns a 300lb block of ice into a work of art. | |

| | | |
|---|---|---|
| 11.00am | Morning Quiz with Shelley. More brain teasing questions | Lido Lounge |
| 11.00am | Darts with Julie. (Take the stairs down by the Jacuzzi on Deck 6 aft) | Deck 5 Aft |

| 11.30am | **SANGRIA DECK PARTY** - *(Weather Permitting)* | Poolside, Deck 6 |
|---|---|---|
| | Join us out on deck for sangria & dancing to the music of the | |
| | Black Watch Orchestra | |

## GOOD AFTERNOON

| | | |
|---|---|---|
| Noon - 1.00pm | Piano Melodies. Join Sara Leport at the Grand | Observatory |
| Noon - 1.00pm | Piano Melodies. Dave Johnson takes to the Grand | Lido Lounge |
| 2.00pm | Beginners - Come & learn the basic steps with Professional Instructors Kevin & Debbie | Neptune Lounge |

| | **AFTERNOON BRIDGE** | Card Room |
|---|---|---|
| 2.00pm | Friendly Duplicate and Rubber Bridge with **Christine & Neil Tomkin**. | |
| 2.30pm | Meet in the Card Room if you want a game of *Whist*. | |

| | | |
|---|---|---|
| 2.15pm | Matinee Movie 'Serendipity' Running Time: 90 mins (12) | Marina Theatre |
| 2.30pm | Deck Quoits. Meet Amanda Port Side of Lido Deck *(Weather Permitting)* | Deck 7 |
| 2.30pm | Short Tennis Meet Julie on the Tennis Courts for a friendly game. *(Weather Permitting)* | Deck 11 |
| 2.30pm | Navigational Bridge Visit. *(Weather Permitting)* | Deck 8 Fwd. |

| 2.30pm | **HANDICRAFTS CLASS** | Lido Lounge |
|---|---|---|
| | Join your Handicrafts Instructor **Margaret Taylor** as she continues on | |
| | *"Iris Ribbon Embroidery"* & does | |
| | *"A Demonstration Using Paper Punches & Rubber Stamping for Easter"* | |

| 2.30pm | **AFTERNOON LECTURE** | Neptune Lounge |
|---|---|---|
| | **"From Rags to Riches"** - **They did it their way** | |
| | Today **Barry Marcus** tells the incredible story of Henry Ford, who refused to take | |
| | over his father's farm, founded the Ford Motor Company & put the world on wheels | |
| | despite the slogan *'you can have any colour as long as it's black'* | |

| | | |
|---|---|---|
| 3.00pm | Table Tennis with Joy (Take the stairs down by the Jacuzzi on Deck 6 aft) | Deck 5 Aft |
| 3.30pm | Carpet Boules with Shelley. Roll up for a friendly game. | Star Night Club |
| 4.00pm | Afternoon Quiz with Jon. More brain teasing questions | Lido Lounge |
| 4.00pm | Circuit Training with Carrianne. £3.00 for 30 minutes | Fitness Centre |
| 4.00-6.00pm | Library is open for the loan of Books, Videos & CDs | Deck 9 |

| 4.00pm | **MUSIC & DANCE CONCERT** | Neptune Lounge |
|---|---|---|
| | **"Melodies of the Heart"** | |
| | In this programme, we celebrate *'affairs of the heart'* | |
| | with beautiful romantic music & tales of passionate love. | |
| | With **Robin & Kim Colvill** | |
| | *(Music by Beethoven, Chopin, Grieg, Sibelius, Lecuona & Liszt)* | |

| | | |
|---|---|---|
| 5.00pm | Bingo. Join Joy & Amanda. Win cash prizes. £2 per card for 4 games | Neptune Lounge |
| 5.30pm | Feature Film 'Time Machine' 92 mins (PG) Repeats at 8.00pm & 10.15pm | Marina Theatre |
| 5.30pm | Service Clubs Meeting. An informal gathering of all Lions, Rotarians, etc. | Lido Lounge |

**GOOD EVENING – Evening Dress Code : Formal - Ladies Night**

# Your Evening Entertainment

## Neptune Lounge – Deck 6

**7.30pm - Recorded music for dancing.**
*The Gentlemen Dance Hosts will be available to dance with our Lady Guests*

**8.00pm OFFICERS DANCING**
Ladies tonight is your night to be looked after by the Gentlemen.
Join **Kevin & Debbie, the Captain & his Officers** on the dance floor
for dancing and romancing to the music of the **Black Watch Orchestra**

| 8.45pm<br>First Presentation | **SHOWTIME** | 10.30pm<br>Second Presentation |
|---|---|---|

featuring

*TV Comedy Entertainer* **RIKKI JAY**    &    *The Varied Musical Talents of* **PAUL CONNOR**

**9.30pm - 10.30pm Music for dancing with the Black Watch Orchestra & Kevin & Debbie**
*The Gentlemen Dance Hosts are available to dance with our Lady Guests*

## Braemar Room – Deck 6

6.00pm - 6.30pm & 7.45pm – 8.30pm    **Piano Melodies with "DAVE JOHNSON"**
9.30pm - 11.00pm    **"DE RIBAS STRING QUARTET"**
**Play a variety of easy listening music**

## Observatory Lounge – Deck 9

6.00pm - 6.30pm, 7.45pm - 8.30pm & 10.00pm - 1.00am
**Piano Melodies with "SARA LEPORT"**

## Lido Lounge – Deck 7

| *Resident Duo*<br>**"EDDIE & LINDA"** | **9.30pm – Late**<br>**LIVE ENTERTAINMENT** | *Piano Entertainer*<br>**"DAVE JOHNSON"** |
|---|---|---|

**Continue your Ladies Night with**
**DANCING & ROMANCING**
*Gentlemen, why not treat your Ladies to one of the variety of*
*"Ladies Night Special Cocktails" you will see displayed in the Lido Bar*

## Star Night Club – Deck 7

9.30pm – Late **"DJ JON"** plays your favourite music for dancing
10.00pm - **SCATTERGORIES** with Julie & Jon

*Courtesy Fred. Olsen Cruise Line*

# GENTING HONG KONG

**United States**
7665 Corporate Center Drive
Miami, FL 33126
(305) 436-4000, ext. 1105
(305) 436-4126

**China***
1528 Ocean Centre, 5 Canton Road
Tsimshatsui, Hong Kong SAR
+(852) 2317 7711
Fax: +(852) 2314 1677
www.starcruises.com

*In the United States, passengers wishing to sail on *SuperStar Virgo* can call Norwegian Cruise Line at (305) 436-4000, ext. 1105.

*MegaStar Aries* (formerly *Aurora II*): entered service in 1991; 3,300 GRT; 82.2 × 14 meters; seventy-four-passenger capacity; thirty-six cabins; Scandinavian officers and international crew; cruises in Far East for private charters (Category C—not rated)

*SuperStar Aquarius* (formerly *Norwegian Wind* and *Windward*): entered service in 1993; stretched 1998; 50,760 GRT; 754 × 94 feet; 1,529-passenger capacity; 765 cabins; Scandinavian officers and international crew; overnight cruises from Hong Kong (Category C—not rated)

*Star Pisces* (formerly *Kalypso*): entered service in 1990; 40,000 GRT; 579 × 97 feet; 1,168-passenger capacity; 692 cabins; Scandinavian officers and international crew; cruises from Hong Kong (Category D—not rated)

*SuperStar Libra* (formerly *Norwegian Sea*): entered service in 1988; 42,276 GRT; 709 × 93 feet; 1,472-passenger capacity; 730 cabins; Scandinavian officers and international crew; cruises from various ports in Southeast Asia (Category C—not rated)

*SuperStar Virgo*: entered service in 1999; 76,800 GRT; 880 × 106 feet; 1,960-passenger capacity; 980 cabins; Scandinavian officers and international crew; cruises from Singapore (Category B/C—not rated)

(Medical facilities: all ships equipped with a clinic and medical personnel)

Formed in 1993 by Tan Sri Lim Goh Tong, Star Cruises was the first major cruise line concentrating on meeting the needs and satisfying the tastes of the cruise market in Asia. In late 1999 through early 2000, Star Cruises acquired control of Norwegian Cruise Line. Subsequently, 50 percent of Norwegian was acquired from Star Cruises by the Apollo group, which also owns Oceania and Regent Seven Seas Cruises. In 2008, Star Cruises sold its remaining 50 percent. In 2009, the name of the cruise line was changed to Genting Hong Kong.

Although the top ship officers are Scandinavian and the crew is from all over the world, the passenger mix is 70 percent Asian. The main language spoken on board is

English, and the second languages, such as Mandarin, would depend upon the area of operation.

The line offers three categories of cruise experiences. The *Star Pisces*, a converted ferry liner, is designed to appeal to the Asian mass market of first-time cruisers, vacationing families, and the young-at-heart seeking a less-expensive cruise on a no-frills ship with an abundance of activities and facilities. *MegaStar Aries* is generally booked by private charter groups (up to seventy-four passengers) seeking a more elegant, yacht-like cruise experience. *SuperStar Libra* and *Virgo* are geared to the more traditional, seasoned traveler seeking a more typical cruise experience on longer voyages to multiple destinations, with international standards for food, service, facilities, and so on. *SuperStar Libra*, formerly *Norwegian Sea* of Norwegian Cruise Line, joined the Star Cruise fleet in 2005, and *Virgo* is a 76,800-ton new build that entered service in 1999.

*Star Pisces* was converted from ferry service and offers cruises from Hong Kong. All cabins have small private bathrooms, TVs, and telephones. The junior and executive suites have additional facilities and amenities and would be my recommendation for those requiring more space and comfort. Passengers can dine in a variety of ethnic restaurants serving both Asian and Western cuisine. Public facilities include a cinema, show lounge, several smaller lounges and bars, a Karaoke lounge, an indoor pool, a small gym and health spa, numerous shops, a sundeck, jogging track, video arcade, and child-care center.

*MegaStar Aries* and *MegaStar Taurus* are the former *Aurora II* and *Aurora I* of Classical Cruises. These small yacht-like vessels—which feature more traditional, rather than nautical, decor—are used for private groups and business charters and do not offer regular itineraries.

The second of the line's new builds, *SuperStar Virgo*, debuted in the summer of 1999. The first, *SuperStar Leo*, has been transferred to Norwegian. *SuperStar Virgo* weighs in at 76,800 GRT and can accommodate a maximum of 1,960 passengers (lower berths only) in 980 cabins. This ship offers destination cruises along the Straits of Malacca and is based in Singapore. There are seven 627- to 629-square-foot executive suites on decks 9 and 10 with private balconies, lounging areas, separate bedrooms, master bathrooms with whirlpool tubs and separate shower, guest powder rooms, and two interactive color TVs. There are also eleven 474- to 510-square-foot junior suites. All of the 331 inside cabins have four berths.

Public areas include an atrium spanning six decks, the two-story 824-seat lido show lounge, the 370-seat Galaxy of the Stars observation lounge and disco, an English-style pub with darts and billiards, karaoke rooms, young children's and teen facilities that rival the Disney ships, and Apollo spa and fitness center with pools and Jacuzzis. There are multiple dining venues composed of the 560-seat, three-meal-a-day Bella Vista; the 330-seat, family-style Pavilion Room, serving Chinese dishes; the 516-seat Mediterranean Buffet Terrace, offering international food; the 94-seat à la carte Chinese Noble House; the 26-seat à la carte Italian Palazzo; the 110-seat à la carte Japanese Samurai Restaurant with teppanyaki and tatami rooms; the 132-seat, casual, twenty-four-hour Blue Lagoon Café; the Taj Indian buffet; and the Taverna.

*SuperStar Libra* was transferred from Norwegian Cruise Line in 2005. When based in Mumbai, she offers cruises to Lakshadweep and Goa. When based in Taiwan, she offers cruises to Ishigaki and Naha, Japan, as well as Penghu Island, Taiwan. When based in Singapore, she offers cruises to Penang, Phuket, and Langkawi Island. Public facilities include a variety of restaurants, a pool bar, an ice-cream bar, a karaoke lounge, a discotheque, a show lounge, a pool, a Jacuzzi, a sport deck, a beauty salon, a fitness center, a video arcade, and an Internet café.

Presently, the ships are based in Singapore, Hong Kong, India, China, and Taiwan. Key markets are Singapore, India, China, Malaysia, and Australia.

*SuperStar Aquarius*, formerly *Norwegian Wind* and *Windward* of Norwegian Cruise Line, joined the fleet in Hong Kong in June 2007 and offers one-night gambling cruises.

## Strong Points

Genting Hong Kong offers a variety of cruising styles that are gauged to appeal to Asian and international cruisers.

# BELLA VISTA

## Western Gala Dinner Set Menu

### APPETIZER

Smoked Salmon Tatare
*on bed of cucumber salad finished with raspberry vinaigrette*

or

Duck and Chicken Terrine
*served with white truffle walnut dressing and rocket lettuce*

or

Gala Salad
*mesculin leaves with papaya and mango dressed with
Champagne vinaigrette*

### SOUP

Clear Oxtail Broth
*scented with dry sherry*

or

Cream of Fresh Garden Herbs
*finished with sour cream*

### MAIN COURSE

Beef Wellington
*pink roasted tenderloin wrapped in puff pastry, rich red wine
jus and garden vegetables*

or

Duo of Pan - fried Seabass Fillet & Grilled Tiger Prawn
*set on wok fried vegetables with a sake - lemon grass sauce*

or

Grilled Chicken Breast
*set on casserole of leek, mushroom and artichoke accompanied with
potato gratin and peppercorn cream sauce*

or

Gratinated Shitake Mushrooms Stuffed with Beancurd
*served on crispy taro root roesti with asparagus tips and coriander cream*

### DESSERT

Semi Frozen Blueberry and Baileys Parfait
*served with caramelized orange sauce*

Coffee or Tea
Petit Fours

*courtesy Genting Hong Kong*

# SUPERSTAR VIRGO

## Today At A Glance

| | |
|---|---|
| Crew<br>General Drill | SuperStar Virgo is required by International regulations to conduct Crew General Emergency Drills regularly. Should this happen while you are staying onboard, we ask for your understanding and apologise for any inconvenience this may cause. Your safety is our number one priority; these drills are important as we conduct them for everyone's safety onboard. |

| Time | Activity | Venue | Deck |
|---|---|---|---|
| **Morning** | **(Staying onboard? Port Stay Activities)** | | |
| 7:00am - 7:30am | Early Morning Walk: A perfect way to start your day | Track Oval | 13 Fwd |
| 7:30am - 8:00am | Rise and Stretch* (Pre-registration required. Pls call 12310) | Universal Gym | 12 Fwd |
| 9:30am - 10:00am | Phobia Quiz Challenge | Galaxy of the Stars | 12 Fwd |
| 10:00am - 10:45am | Scrabble Battle & Jenga Challenge | Galaxy of the Stars | 12 Fwd |
| 11:00am - 11:30am | Daytona USA Race Challenge | Video Arcade | 10 Aft |
| **Afternoon** | | | |
| 1:00pm - 2:00pm | Boardgame Mania - Please borrow your favorite boardgames at... (Boardgames are to be played in the Card Room only, Deck 12 Fwd) | Activity Centre | 12 Fwd |
| 2:00pm - 4:00pm | English Blockbuster Movie: **Ocean's Twelve** (Rating - U) | The Lido | 7 Aft |
| 2:30pm - 3:00pm | Single's Club: Giant Chess Challenge | Amphitheatre | 11 Aft |
| 2:30pm - 3:00pm | Boot Scooting Line Dancing | Galaxy of the Stars | 12 Fwd |
| 2:30pm - 3:30pm | Activity-On-Request - Please register at... | Activity Centre | 12 Fwd |
| 3:00pm - 3:30pm | Table Tennis-Double's Competition - Pre-registration required at | Activity Centre | 12 Fwd |
| 3:00pm - 3:45pm | The Art of Cartoon Drawing | Galaxy of the Stars | 12 Fwd |
| 3:00pm - 3:45pm | Coconut Bowling Competition | Parthenon Pool | 12 Mid |
| 3:45pm - 4:15pm | Country & Western Musical Trivia | Galaxy of the Stars | 12 Fwd |
| 5:00pm - 5:45pm | Step Aerobics* (Pre-registration required. Pls call 12310) | Universal Gym | 12 Fwd |
| **Evening** | | | |
| 5:50pm - 6:05pm | 'Gala Fashionista' - A tribute to Costumes of Asia and more! | Grand Piazza | 7 Mid |
| 6:00pm - 9:00pm | Fancy Costume Party (for registered kids only) | Child Care Centre | 10 Aft |
| 6:15pm & 8:30pm | Captain's Gala Cocktail | Grand Piazza | 7 Mid |
| 7:15pm - 8:30pm | Gala Showtime: **SORPRESA - A New Season** (Part 2) (For Late Seating Dinner) | The Lido | 7 Aft |
| 8:00pm - 11:00pm | SSV CNY Lottery :Ticket Promotion | | |
| | Buy 6 Get 1 FREE Topless Show ticket, available at... | Activity Centre | 12 Fwd |
| 8:45pm - 9:30pm | Ballroom Dance Music with the SuperStar Virgo Lounge Band | Galaxy of the Stars | 12 Fwd |
| 9:15pm - 10:30pm | Gala Showtime: **SORPRESA - A New Season** (Part 2) (For Early Seating Dinner) | The Lido | 7 Aft |
| 9:15pm - 1:00am | Continuous Entertainment with the SuperStar Virgo Musicians | Bellini | 8 Mid |
| 9:30pm - 10:15pm | Gala Party for Teens and Kids | Galaxy of the Stars | 12 Fwd |
| 10:00pm - 10:45pm | Karaoke "Singles" Challenge Pre-registration required at 9:45pm, Maximum of 10 participants only. | Out of Africa | 7 Fwd |
| 10:15pm - 11:00pm | Live Music Entertainment with the SuperStar Virgo Big Band | Galaxy of the Stars | 12 Fwd |
| 10:30pm - 11:15pm | **MEGA JACKPOT $24,000 BINGO** | The Lido | 7 Aft |
| 10:15pm - 11:00pm | DJ Mix Class for Teens | Celebrity Disco | 13 Fwd |
| 11:00pm - 11:45pm | Adult Funtime: **NEWLY WED NOT SO NEWLY WED** | Galaxy of the Stars | 12 Fwd |
| 11:45pm - 2:00am | Live Music Hits with the SuperStar Virgo Big Band | Galaxy of the Stars | 12 Fwd |
| 12:00mn - 12:40am | Las Vegas Style Topless Revue: **DESIRE** | The Lido | 7 Aft |

Galaxy of the Stars: For the comfort of others, guests below the age of 18 years shall not be allowed entry after 11:00pm

*Universal Gym: A mininimum of 3 participants must be in attendance for all classes to be held. Pre-registration is required for all classes.

*Courtesy Genting Hong Kong*

## HAPAG-LLOYD CRUISES

**United States**
(800) 782-3924

**Kartagener Associates Inc.**
(877) 445-7447
**ATMS Air Travel Mktg Services**
(800) 888-0200

**Germany**
**Ballindamm 25 D-20095**
**Hamburg, Germany**
+49 (0) 40 3001 4580
Fax: +49 (0) 40 3001 4849

*Bremen* (formerly *Frontier Spirit*): entered service in 1990; 6,752 GRT; 365 × 56 feet; 164-passenger capacity; eighty-two cabins; German officers and staff (all English speaking); expedition cruises to polar regions, rivers, and remote islands (Category B/C—not rated)

*Columbus 2* (formerly *Insignia*): entered service in 2000; refurbished in 2011; 30,277 GRT; 594 × 84 feet; 684-passenger capacity; 342 cabins; international officers and crew; cruises various itineraries around the world (Category B—not rated)

*Europa*: entered service in 1999; 28,890 GRT; 652 × 78 feet; 408-passenger capacity; 204 suites; German officers and staff (all English speaking); cruises to various locations around the world (Category A—six stars for German-speaking passengers; five+ stars for non-German-speaking passengers)

*for German-speaking passengers*

*for non-German-speaking passengers*

*Europa 2*: entered service in May 2013; 42,350 GRT; 225 × 26.7 square meters; 516-passenger capacity; 251 staterooms; German officer and staff (all English speaking); cruises in Eastern and Western Mediterranean, Arabian Peninsula, and Southeast Asia (Category A—six+ stars for German-speaking passengers; five+ stars for non-German-speaking passengers.)

*for German-speaking passengers*

*for non-German-speaking passengers*

*Hanseatic*: entered service in 1993; renovated in 2009; 8,378 GRT; 403 × 59 feet; 184-passenger capacity; ninety-two cabins; German officers and staff (all English speaking); expedition cruises to polar regions, rivers, and remote islands (Category A/B—not rated)

(All ships have hospitals and a physician.)

Some of these ships are rated in eleven separate categories in the second half of chapter 11.

In 1970, Hapag and North German Lloyd lines merged. Both lines date back to the nineteenth century and have played a role in the development of cruising during the twentieth century. The company owns the *Europa*, *Bremen*, *Hanseatic*, and *Columbus*. The four ships are largely sold to the German and European markets, with German being the official language on board and the euro the official currency. The officers and staff are all multilingual, although on most cruises all announcements, programs, menus, and TV channels are exclusively in German. However, on the *Europa*, programs and menus can always be provided in English. Beginning in 2004, the cruise line has indicated that it is interested in attracting the non-German-speaking cruise market by offering select cruises on each of its ships throughout the year in different areas of the world where English as well as German will be the official language, thereby affording an opportunity for non-German-speaking cruisers to enjoy the special Hapag-Lloyd experience.

Hapag-Lloyd Cruises expanded its product in 2012 and 2013, offering two ships to its fleet. In April 2012, the cruise line leased Oceania Cruises' *Insignia*, which formerly was one of the Renaissance ships (see description under Oceania Cruises). The ship sails under the name, *Columbus 2*. In the spring of 2013, the 516-passenger *Europa 2* made its debut accommodating a maximum of 516 passengers in 258 suites.

The current *Europa* is the sixth ship of the original line to receive the same name. The fifth *Europa* was sold in 1999, and the present vessel entered service the same year. Today U.S. bookings are taken through their American marketing/sales offices.

The all-suite *Europa* includes many of the technological advances and creature comforts that appear in ships built in the late 1990s; however, the design and the decor are somewhat atypical of the larger ships built in recent years by other cruise lines in that there is less glitz, glamour, bells, and whistles.

Atop ship on deck 10 are twelve penthouse suites, with fourteen veranda suites below, on deck 9. The remaining suites are located on decks 5, 6, and 7. All in all, 168 of the 204 accommodations have verandas, reflecting today's demand for this feature. All the suites are quite spacious, measuring 290 to 484 square feet (with 64-square-foot verandas). The two top, grand penthouse suites reach 915 square feet. In 2007, four spa suites were added close to the new Ocean Spa area on deck. The spa suites have illuminated whirlpools with ocean views, a rain shower with lateral jets, and scent lamps filled with essential oils. The comprehensive spa package comes with the option of selected in-suite treatments.

Every accommodation has two twin beds with European duvets that can be converted to a double-bed arrangement, a writing desk, a sitting area, a personal safe that can be opened with a credit card, a large walk-in closet, a refrigerator stocked with complimentary soft drinks that is refilled daily, a hair dryer, and bathrooms with terry robes and slippers, tub, and glass-enclosed shower. Standard in each room is an advanced personalized e-mail and video-on-demand system with Internet access via the TV set and a wireless keyboard.

The ten 484-square-foot penthouse deluxe suites are even more spacious, with an entryway, a larger lounging area, two TVs, double bathroom vanities, and Jacuzzi bathtubs. The two penthouse grand suites boast wraparound balconies, a large living room area with a dining table for up to six persons, giant bathrooms with saunas, and an additional guest bathroom. All of the penthouse suites enjoy extraordinarily solicitous, twenty-four-hour butler service, free laundry and pressing, fresh fruit, canapés and caviar upon request, and free in-suite alcoholic beverages and soft drinks. In addition, there are two suites that can accommodate physically challenged passengers.

On deck 9, you will find Sansibar, an observation bar, offering a good view from the stern of the ship, a golf simulator, and a new gym. Deck 8 is the location of the unusually long swimming pool, half of which is covered with a sliding magrodome for inclement weather, a jogging track, a Jacuzzi, numerous lounge chairs, an indoor/outdoor lido buffet restaurant, the Club Belvedere observation lounge, a room that can be used for movies or lectures, and a library. On deck 7 are two newly expanded children's playrooms and the Ocean Spa, which includes a beauty salon, Japanese bath, treatment rooms, solarium, steam room, sauna, and men and women's changing rooms. Deck 4 is the locale for all of the other public rooms, including the reception area, tour desk, grand show lounge, several other lounges and bars, art gallery, cigar-smoking lounge, boutique and jewelry shop, 408-seat main dining room, an Italian specialty restaurant, and the gourmet restaurant of the German award-winning chef Dieter Mueller. The main dining room seats all guests in one sitting at assigned tables for dinner and has open seating for breakfast and lunch. The Italian specialty restaurant is open for both lunch and dinner at no surcharge and requires advanced reservations. Theme lunches with dishes typical of the region are frequently offered at the lido buffet, where a band plays on special occasions. In September 2010, Restaurant Dieter Mueller was added. This new specialty restaurant, serving dinner, features gourmet cuisine with French, Asian, and Mediterranean influences, by German chef Dieter Mueller, who has been awarded three *Michelin* stars.

On the *Europa*, nightly entertainment generally includes musical performers but no production shows. There is no casino on the ship since gambling is not popular with German cruisers.

Food and service are excellent in all of the restaurants. Service throughout the ship is among the most solicitous and efficient in the industry. Cabin attendants will accommodate every reasonable request; pool attendants pamper guests with cold towels, drinks, fresh fruit, and refreshing spray; restaurant waitstaff are always available to accommodate your needs; the information desk staff is knowledgeable and anxious to assist (a rarity in the cruise industry); and the entire staff of officers and crew appear dedicated to leaving each passenger with a positive experience.

In recent years, the *Europa* has received various renovations and added modern amenities such as: Cruise Net, a complimentary TV information network with private e-mail, movies, music on demand, cruise information, and Internet; the Sansibar, a cozy bar with dance floor in the aft of the ship overlooking the ocean; upgrades to the golf area with a computer controlled tee-shot analysis, a newly designed Ocean Spa with four enclosed spa suites for beauty and health treatments; and the enlargement of the fitness loft with ocean views and the addition of two children's areas. In addition, the lido café was redesigned with additional service stations to avoid traffic jams and in the evening offers an alternative dining venue with an open kitchen and grill stations. The size of the gym was significantly increased and moved to a more convenient location on deck 9, and state-of-the-art equipment such as treadmills with personal TVs and exercycles were added. The newly designed Ocean Spa offers four enclosed spa suites for private beauty and health treatments. The children's facilities also were expanded. The number of Zodiacs was increased to thirteen. The area for nude sunbathing was moved to deck 11. Much of the carpeting was replaced, and some of the walls and decor in the common areas were redone.

Itineraries generally run from two to three weeks; however, there are shorter cruises offered at different times of the year. Itineraries include the Mediterranean, North Sea/ Baltics, Southeast Asia, South America, and the South Pacific as well as other itineraries around the world. Passengers can book an entire world cruise if they wish. Most cruises offer a special theme ranging from gourmet cooking or classical music to arts and culture or golf.

The 40,000-ton, 516-passenger *Europa 2* debuted during the spring of 2013, undoubtedly one of the most luxurious ships at sea. The seven categories of accommodations range in size from 301 square feet to 1,066 square feet and include four ultraluxurious Grand Penthouse and Owner's Suites. Sixteen Spa Suites have whirlpool tubs and rain showers, with steam and saunas. Seven family-style suites have separate areas for children connected by a door and shared balcony. All accommodations have verandas (the smallest being 75 square feet) and a free-of-charge minibar and are tastefully furnished with a great deal of storage area and every possible facility and amenity one finds in a cruise ship stateroom. Children younger than eleven years travel free when accompanied by two full-fare adults, and the ship offers an extensive children and teen program with supervised activities for age brackets zero to three, four to ten, and eleven to fifteen years.

There is a greater emphasis on entertainment on *Europa 2* than that on other vessels in the fleet, and in the evenings, there are variety shows and cabaret entertainers, often two each evening. However, the entertainment is more to the taste of the German-speaking guests.

Guests can choose among eight restaurants and six bars. All restaurants are free of charge, with no assigned seating, and include Weltmeere, the main dining room serving international and refined vegetarian menus; the Yacht Club, providing specialties from the grill and a variety of buffet items, with both inside and outdoor seating; Tarragon, featuring French cuisine; Elements, offering Asian fare; Serenissima, with an Italian menu; Sakura sushi restaurant; and a venue where a group of guests can have a private, exclusive gourmet repast for $1,800 for the evening.

The 10,000-plus-square-foot wellness center includes the Ocean Spa, with eight treatment rooms offering numerous massage, beauty, and relaxations treatments; a well-equipped fitness area with cardio and fitness equipment; as well as a room for Pilates and spinning. The spa area—complete with three different varieties of sauna, a whirlpool, relaxation rooms, an ice wall, and specialty showers—is very impressive and open to both genders, clothing optional. The vessel carries twelve Zodiacs for exploration excursions, as well as a fleet of bicycles.

The 15,000-ton, 420-passenger *Columbus* entered service in 1997 but left the fleet in 2012. Taking its place is Oceania's *Insignia*, which has been leased for two years and will be called *Columbus 2*.

The 8,378-ton, 184-pasenger *Hanseatic* entered service in 1993. In 2009, the ship underwent renovations, receiving new bathrooms in the suites, Internet access, and new windows in all staterooms. This is an exploration cruise vessel with the highest ice classification for passenger vessels (E4); her ice-resistant hull and shallow draft enable her to navigate icy waters in the Arctic, Antarctic, White Russian Sea, and the Northwest Passage as well as small harbors in less-traveled waters not available to other ships, such as the Amazon River and Micronesia. She carries fourteen Zodiacs for shore excursions as well as bicycles, Nordic walking gear, and snorkeling equipment. In polar regions, passengers are equipped with warm parkas and rubber boots. These are cruises that explore nature, history, geography, and architecture with onboard lecturers to enhance the experience.

*Hanseatic* is considered luxurious for an expedition ship, and as such, it features cabins with all-outside views that are generally more spacious than the norm. The eighty-eight, 237-square-foot outside staterooms have either two single beds or one double bed, sitting areas, TV/radios, free personal e-mail connections, minibars, marble bathrooms with showers, hair dryers, and bathrobes. There are four 473-square-foot suites. Two cabins can accommodate the physically challenged. Seven have an additional bed, and there are also two four-bedded cabins. The suites and staterooms on bridge deck enjoy butler service.

Atop ship on the observation deck is a small pool, a Jacuzzi, a sauna, a bar, a hairdressing salon, a small gym, a library, and an observation lounge. On the next four decks are the cabins and public facilities, which include the Columbus Lounge with a bar, the Explorer Lounge with a bar and dance floor, the lecture room, the tour office, the reception, and the hospital. There is a single-seating main restaurant and a specialty restaurant serving ethnic cuisine. Snacks are available through twenty-four-hour cabin service. The minibars in all cabins contain soft drinks and are refilled daily at no charge.

In June 2011, the ship went through its regularly scheduled maintenance, which included cabin upgrades on decks 5 and 6, complete modernization and renovation of the spa area, new furniture and fabrics in the Columbus Lounge, a new design for the pool area, wireless Internet access in all rooms and public areas, and DVDs in all cabins.

The former *Frontier Spirit*, built for expedition cruising, now sails as the *Bremen*. The ship has eighty 194-square-foot outside cabins featuring sitting and bedroom areas, closed-circuit TV, refrigerators, minibars, satellite telephone, hair dryers, and bathrobes. The two 258-square-foot suites on deck 7 and the sixteen staterooms on deck 6 have private verandas. Public areas and facilities include a library, two lounges (including a panorama lounge), a sauna, a gym, a swimming pool, a single-seating dining room, a bar, a beauty parlor, an infirmary, and twelve exploration Zodiacs. The ship goes through regular renovations, the most recent being 2008 and 2010, adding additional computers and Internet connections, new carpeting, new bathrooms, and new furniture to all cabins. All cabins also have been furnished with new flat-screen TVs and converted to nonsmoking.

Built to cruise where other ships are unable to go (similar to the *Hanseatic*, with the highest ice classification for passenger vessels), the *Bremen* visits such out-of-the-way destinations as the Arctic, Antarctic, Northwest Passage, and the deep Amazon and Orinoco rivers in South America, as well as the Red Sea, the Mediterranean, the Far East, and the South Pacific.

Cruising on Hapag-Lloyd Cruises offers a very typical German experience with traditional German and international cuisine and will be appreciated most by those travelers wishing to enjoy the flavors, efficiency, excellent service, and spirit of that country.

## Strong Points

*Europa* and *Europa 2:* superior accommodations in all categories, interesting and diverse dining possibilities, exceptional service, and desirable itineraries. *Europa 2* is one of the most unique and elegant ships at sea.

*Hanseatic*: one of the few more upscale, yacht-like cruise ships with comfortable cabins to offer expedition itineraries.

*Europa 2, courtesy Hapag-Lloyd*

*Hanseatic in Antarctica, courtesy Hapag-Lloyd*

*Suite on Europa 2, courtesy Hapag-Lloyd*

*Pool Deck on Europa 2, courtesy Hapag-Lloyd*

*French Restaurant on Europa 2, courtesy Hapag-Lloyd*

# EUROPA

# Daytime activities:

| Sunrise | 04.37 h |
| Sunset | 19.52 h |

**07.00 h**  **Pilot**
The pilot for Copenhagen arrives on board.

**08.00 h**  **Arrival at Copenhagen!**
MV EUROPA moors at the pier of Copenhagen.

**08.30 h**  **Walking**  **Fitnessroom, Sport Deck**
Personal Trainer Heiko Werner will meet you at the gym to start
the day with exercises.

**14.00 h**  **„Cruise from Hamburg to Malaga"**  **TV channel 3**
Our video producer Dr. Manfred Classen shows the variety of the European Atlantic
coast and dramatic scenery in this video.

**16.00 - 17.00 h**  **Relaxing Tea Time**  **Club Belvedere, Lido Deck**
Enjoy the afternoon with piano entertainment by Giorgio di Luca.
At the same time you can experience our wide variety of different teas - taste
another kind of tea each day!

**16.00 - 19.30 h**  **Cruising with Hapag-Lloyd**  **Atrium, Europa Deck**
CRUISING OFF CAPE HOORN - experience this part of the world during
Christmas time, when MV EUROPA sails from Buenos Aires to Valparaiso.
Here, in the south of Argentina the world's biggest flock of Magellan penguins can
be found. Another attraction are the beautiful glaciers of the Chilean fjords.
Ingrid Beyer-Ziegler is available for information. If you book your next cruise
on board you will be granted an additional bonus of 3%!

**17.30 h**  **End of Shore Leave**
We kindly ask you to be on time!

**17.30, 18.30**  **MV EUROPA Board TV**  **TV channel 1**
**and 19.30 h**  Famous German TV presenter Babette Einstmann interviews Joan Orleans,
the Queen of Soul.

**17.45 h**  **Sail Away Brass music**  **Bellevue Deck, Deck 9**
Our New Connection Band plays when MV EUROPA leaves Copenhagen.

**18.00 h**  **Good Bye, Copenhagen!**
MV EUROPA leaves Copenhagen and sets course for Kiel
(172 nautical miles = 319 km).

# Enjoy the evening!

| | | |
|---|---|---|
| 18.00 - 20.00 h | **The gallery is open!** | Gallery, Europa Deck |
| | Enjoy the "Likörelle"- exhibition by german singer and Rock-Legend | |
| | Udo Lindenberg! All pictures are painted with different kinds of liqueurs. | |
| | | |
| 18.00 h | **Sail away** | Lido Pool, Lido Deck |
| | ... with melodies performed by the Rivieras Band. Enjoy the special | |
| | atmosphere on deck when MV EUROPA is leaving Copenhagen. | |
| | The ship's officers look forward to meet you for a glass of Champagne! | |
| | | |
| 18.30 and | **Romantic tunes** | Atrium, Europa Deck |
| 20.45 h | ... at cocktail hour by Giorgio di Luca. | |
| | | |
| 21.00 h | **Would you like to dance?** | Clipper Lounge, Europa Deck |
| | Our Rivieras Quartet invites you to dance. | |

| | | |
|---|---|---|
| 21.00 h | **In the Mood** | |
| | New Connection will get you in the mood for tonight's show. | Europa Lounge, Europa Deck |
| | | |
| 21.45 h | **JOAN ORLEANS: THE VOICE OF LOUISIANA** | Europa Lounge, Europa Deck |
| | 600 appearances with standing ovations in the musical „Mahalia- Queen | |
| | of Gospel" now on stage at MV EUROPA. She was discovered at the famous | |
| | german TV show „Bio's Bahnhof" with Alfred Biolek. He recognized the astonishing | |
| | voice of the „Souls-lady". Tonight she will be accompanied by Jo Kurzweg's | |
| | New Connection- Band. | |
| | | |
| 22.30 h | **FAREWELL** | Europa Lounge, Europa Deck |
| | Captain Friedrich Jan Akkermann invites you for an evening together with | |
| | the crew. Enjoy the sea-chart auction with Staff-captain Peter Losinger and | |
| | the crew choir with traditional German shanties. Join us afterwards in the | |
| | Atrium for a sing-along with the crew. | |

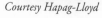

*Courtesy Hapag-Lloyd*

# EUROPA

Russian Ossietra Caviar on Potato Fritters
Tatar of wild Salmon on Lemon-Brioche
Artichokes Tureen with Salmon Caviar

or

Black Truffle flavoured Goose Liver Mousse
presented on Beef Carpaccio

❦

Cream of sweet Potatoes and Saffron with Alaska King Crab Meat

❦

Raspberry Vinegar marinated Barbarie Duck Breast,
served in Red Bell Pepper Soup

❦

Pan fried Dover Sole with Horseradish-Hollandaise,
new Potatoes and white Asparagus

or

Symphony of Reindeer and Venison with Red Wine Espresso,
Chestnuts in Caramel, Gingerbread Polenta and Broccoli

❦

Kir Royal

❦

Selection of Tölzer Kasladen

❦

Harmony of Chocolate, fresh Strawberries
and Champagne

*Courtesy Hapag-Lloyd*

# HOLLAND AMERICA LINE

### 300 Elliott Avenue West
### Seattle, WA 98119
### (800) 426-0327; (206) 281-3535
### www.hollandamerica.com

*Amsterdam*: entered service in 2000; 62,735 GRT; 780 × 105.8 feet; 1,380-passenger capacity; 690 cabins; European and international officers, Indonesian and Filipino crew; cruises the Caribbean, Panama Canal, Alaska, South America, South Pacific, and world voyages (Category B—five+ stars)

*Eurodam*: entered service in 2008; 86,273 GRT; 936 × 105.8 feet; 2,104-passenger capacity; 1,052 cabins; European and international officers and Indonesian and Filipino crew; Caribbean cruises during winter, European cruises during summer, and East Coast of the United States and Canada during fall (Category B—five+ stars)

*Maasdam*: entered service in 1993; 55,575 GRT; 719 × 101 feet; 1,258-passenger capacity; 629 cabins; European and international officers and Indonesian and Filipino crew; cruises the southern and eastern Caribbean, eastern Canada/New England, Canada, Europe, and transatlantic (Category B—five+ stars)

*Nieuw Amsterdam*: entered service in 2010; 86,273 GRT; 936 × 105.8 feet; 2,106-passenger capacity; 1,053 cabins; European and international officers, Indonesian and Filipino crew; Caribbean cruises during fall/winter and European cruises during summer (Category B—six stars)

*Prinsendam* (formerly *Royal Viking Sun* and *Seabourn Sun*): entered service in 1988; renovated in 2008 and 2010; 37,983 GRT; 669 × 106 feet; 835-passenger capacity; 419 cabins; European and international officers and Indonesian and Filipino crew; cruises Western Europe, Mediterranean, Norwegian fjords, Black Sea, transatlantic, Caribbean, Panama Canal, South America, and Amazon River (Category B—five+ stars)

*Rotterdam*: entered service in 1997; 61,859 GRT; 780 × 105.8 feet; 1,404-passenger capacity; 702 cabins; European and international officers, Indonesian and Filipino crew; cruises the Mediterranean Sea, Europe, Far East, and Asia (Category B—five+ stars)

*Ryndam*: entered service in 1994; refurbished in 2010; 55,819 GRT; 720 × 101 feet; 1,260-passenger capacity; 630 cabins; European and international officers and Indonesian and Filipino crew; cruises the Caribbean and Europe (Category B—five+ stars)

*Statendam*: entered service in 1993; refurbished in 2010; 55,819 GRT; 720 × 101 feet; 1,260-passenger capacity; 630 cabins; European and international officers and Indonesian and Filipino crew; cruises Alaska, Pacific Northwest, Panama Canal, and South Pacific (Category B—five+ stars)

*Veendam*: entered service in 1996; refurbished in 2009; 57,092 GRT; 720 × 101 feet; 1,350-passenger capacity; 675 cabins; European and international officers and Indonesian and Filipino crew; cruises, Caribbean, Canada/New England, Panama Canal, Mexico and Hawaii (Category B—five+ stars)

*Volendam* and *Zaandam*: entered service in 1999 and 2000, respectively; 61,396 GRT; 780 × 105.8 feet; 1,432-passenger capacity; 716 cabins; European and international officers and Filipino and Indonesian crew; *Volendam* cruises South Pacific, Australia/ New Zealand, Southeast Asia, and Alaska; *Zaandam* cruises South America and Alaska (Category B—five+ stars)

*Zuiderdam, Oosterdam, Westerdam,* and *Noordam*: entered service in 2002, 2003, 2004, and 2006, respectively; 82,305 GRT; 935 × 105.8 feet; 1,916-passenger capacity on *Zuiderdam, Oosterdam,* and *Westerdam*, 1,924 on *Noordam*; 958-962 cabins; European and international officers and Indonesian and Filipino crew; *Zuiderdam* cruises the Caribbean, Alaska, and Panama Canal; *Oosterdam* cruises Alaska and Australia/New Zealand; *Westerdam* cruises the Caribbean, Panama Canal, and Alaska; and *Noordam* cruises the Caribbean, Mediterranean, and transatlantic (Category B—five+ stars)

(Medical facilities: P-2; EM, CLS; MS; N-2to3; CM; PD; BC; EKG; TC; PO; EPC; OX; WC; ICU; X; M; CCP, D, TM, LJ; twenty-one to twenty-five wheelchair-accessible cabins on *Rotterdam, Volendam, Amsterdam,* and *Zaandam;* twenty-eight on *Zuiderdam, Oosterdam, Westerdam,* and *Noordam;* six to eight on *Statendam, Maasdam, Ryndam,* and *Veendam;* thirty on *Eurodam* and *Nieuw Amsterdam;* and ten on *Prinsendam*

These ships are rated in eleven separate categories in the second half of chapter 11.

Dutch owners started the Netherlands-America Steamship Company in 1872, and its first ocean liner, the original *Rotterdam,* made its maiden voyage to New York in 1873. In 1896, the company became known as Holland America Line (HAL). Westours, based in Seattle, Washington, had sold Alaskan tours since 1947 and frequently leased Holland America ships. In 1974, HAL/Westours became a subsidiary of the Dutch parent company. In 1989, the line was purchased by Carnival Corporation.

All of the ships today have European or international officers holding the top jobs, with a mixed crew of Indonesians and Filipinos holding the positions of waiters, wine stewards, bartenders, and cabin attendants. Most cruisers find the crew attentive, friendly, and anxious to please, but some are disenchanted with the crew's lack of formality and lack of familiarity with European and North American tastes and needs. At times, cabin service and restaurant service can be a bit slow.

The *Rotterdam V,* built in the late 1950s, was retired from service in 1997 and now serves as a conference center, museum, and hotel in Rotterdam. The sister ships *Nieuw Amsterdam* and *Noordam* were two of the more conveniently laid out, attractively designed, and tastefully furbished vessels built in the 1980s. However, with the entry of newer and larger HAL ships, these two did not fit into the fleet and were chartered long term. The *Westerdam* was built by Home Lines as the Homeric in 1986. She was purchased by Holland America in 1988, given an $85 million expansion in 1989, and transferred to Costa Cruise Lines in 2002. This should not be confused with the new 82,348-ton *Westerdam* that entered service in 2004.

Holland America added four new modern vessels in the mid-1990s. Each of these ships is approximately 55,451 tons and carries 1,258 to 1,350 passengers in 630 to 675 staterooms, three-quarters of which are outside. The first of these vessels, the *Statendam,* entered service in January 1993; the second, the *Maasdam,* in December 1993; the third, the *Ryndam,* in October 1994; and the fourth, the *Veendam,* in May 1996. These ships are called the S-class ships and are similar in layout and facilities. Commencing in 2009 and due for completion in 2013, the cruise line began extensive enhancements and upgrades to these vessels.

The 149 deluxe cabins and suites on the S-class vessels are located on navigation and verandah decks near the top of the ships and boast floor-to-ceiling windows, private verandas, whirlpool baths and showers, hair dryers, refrigerated minibars, flat-screen TVs, plush terry cloth robes, Aromapure bath amenities, personalized stationery, hors d'oeuvres in the suites, and maximum space and comfort. The suites also have DVD players. Most of the remaining accommodations are on the three lower decks and include two lower beds convertible to a queen-size bed, small sitting areas, decent closet space, multichannel music systems, telephones with voice mail, flat-screen TVs, private room safes, Elemis Aromapure bath amenities, and hair dryers. Public facilities encompass eight passenger elevators; two outdoor pools; two outdoor, heated whirlpools; an elegant dual-level dining room with tables adorned with fresh flowers, fine crystal, and Rosenthal china; a comfortable lido buffet-style restaurant with exceptional buffets; a health spa with exercise and cardiovascular machines, sauna, steam rooms, masseuse, hair salon, and daily exercise and aerobics classes; a casino; a well-stocked library; card and game rooms; a comfortable movie theater; a large two-level showroom; and numerous more intimate lounges.

The new *Rotterdam* entered service in fall 1997, when the previous *Rotterdam* was retired, and was at that time marketed as the company's flagship. The vessel was built and designed especially for luxurious European and around-the-world voyages with the capability to sustain speeds up to twenty-five knots (20 percent faster than today's average cruise ships) to permit more hours in ports of call and shorter sailing time between ports. Weighing in at 59,652 tons and accommodating 1,316 passengers (increased to 1,404 passengers after renovations), the *Rotterdam* incorporates abundant use of woods and darker colors for a more classic feel. She boasts an entire deck of suites with 180-square-foot verandahs, including 4 penthouse suites that measure 1,159 square feet and 36 556-square-foot suites with special concierge lounge and concierge services. She also offers 121 additional deluxe 292-square-foot cabins with verandahs, whirlpool bathtubs, refrigerators, DVDs, and other conveniences. Included on the ship are a special alternative ninety-seat, reservation-only restaurant that is opulent in decor, a spectacular two-deck main dining room, a two-deck show lounge, expensive art, and various other tasteful public areas and lounges (as are found on all HAL vessels). The layout of the ship is quite similar to the other vessels built in the 1990s. For passengers opting to partake in the "suite life" (on navigation deck), the comfort and special amenities parallel those featured on luxury-market cruises.

The line purchased the 2,400-acre Bahamian island of Little San Salvador and developed a $16 million facility, completed in late 1997, naming it Half Moon Cay. The development includes a most enviable two-mile strand of white-sand beach, snorkel area, stingray lagoon, Wave Runner park, horseback riding on the beach, tender dock, aqua park for kids, and sport area (offering kayaks, banana boats, Hobie catamarans, parasailing, Sunfish sailboats, and floating air mattresses). In addition, there are fifteen private beachside cabanas (each can accommodate up to four people and costs $299), the 1,620-square foot Private Oasis (which can accommodate up to twenty-five people and includes a private sundeck, hot tub, water slide to a private beach area, barbeque area, wet bar, refrigerator, massage table, and indoor and outdoor showers and costs $1,195 for the first twelve guests and $99 for each of the next twelve guests, although prices are subject to change), a Bahamian straw market, a post office, a chapel for vow renewals and/or weddings, a food pavilion, exclusive jewelry shops, several bars, numerous lounge chairs with umbrellas, and hiking trails. Guests to the island will notice five new, colorful, two-story Beach Villas available for rent during each call. The luxury hideaways boast exclusive hot tubs on the second floor and provide private accommodations for guests while they relax and experience the island's highlights.

This is a major port of call for HAL ships with Caribbean itineraries and is considered by many reviewers as the best private island in the cruise industry. This is one of the only private island beaches owned by a cruise line where there are no rocks or pebbles in the water, only firm white sand lapped by clear aqua waters.

In 1999 the *Volendam* and in 2000 the *Zaandam* and the *Amsterdam*, three modified sisters to the *Rotterdam*, came on line as the *Rotterdam*-class of vessels. The new ships, built by Fincantieri Shipyards in Italy at a price tag of approximately $300 million each, are approximately 61,396 gross tons with passenger capacities of 1,380 to 1,432 each. Technically, *Amsterdam* is a sister to the *Rotterdam* and a HAL flagship, and the *Volendam* and *Zaandam* are similar siblings. However, all four ships are quite similar in their design and facilities, and there is little difference between them and the *Statendam*-class ships. *Volendam* and *Zaandam* boast an especially attractive 1,126-square-foot penthouse suite (including veranda), one of the most spacious and desirable at sea.

Joining the industry trend, "as you wish dining" was introduced on all ships of the fleet. All guests can choose between traditional set dining times at a designated table or a flexible schedule permitting them to dine with whomever they please between 5:30 and 9:00 p.m. All HAL ships offer dining alternatives most evenings in their lido restaurants between 6:30 and 8:00 p.m., with casual open seating, piano music, and tables set with linens, stemware, and flatware. Complimentary espresso and cappuccino are offered at dinner. Expanded room-service menus, including items from the main dining room, are also being introduced. Pinnacle specialty restaurants featuring steaks, chops, fish, and seafood (described by the cruise line as Northwest U.S. fare) were added to all ships that did not already have a specialty restaurant and replaced the prior specialty restaurants on those that did. Special wine-taster dinners with set menus will be offered at these restaurants on selected evenings. On all the ships, one evening on each cruise is designated "an evening at Le Cirque," which takes place in the Pinnacle Grill. In partnership with Le Cirque Restaurant in NY, the ship recreates the Le Cirque experience. An additional specialty Pan Asian restaurant, Tamarind, was added to the new Signature-class ships. The casual Canaletto, an Italian-themed restaurant, is available on all HAL ships.

In 2002, the *Seabourn Sun* (formerly *Royal Viking Sun*) was transferred to Holland America and renamed *Prinsendam*. Since the acquisition, many structural renovations have been made. Of the 419 cabins, 388 have ocean views and 151 of these sport verandahs. Deck 13 atop ship is the observation deck. Deck 12, the sports deck, is the location of the Crow's Nest observation lounge, eight deluxe verandah suites, the penthouse verandah suite, a golf net, and the volleyball-basketball court. On deck 11, lido deck, there are ten more verandah suites, the Neptune lounge, a concierge lounge for suite passengers, the pool, lido bar and terrace grill, and lido restaurant. Additional verandah cabins can be found on decks 9 and 10 along with the ocean spa/gym/beauty salon and the aft pool. The main show lounge, shopping and photo arcade, theater, cardroom, casino, Java Café, ten newly added verandah suites, and several additional lounges are located on deck 8. On deck 7 are the outside staterooms, Internet café, pinnacle grill dining room, ocean bar, and an open promenade (four times around to the mile). The remaining inside and outside cabins are located on decks 5 and 6. In January 2010, twenty-two staterooms were added.

In December 2002, the 82,305-ton, 1,916-passenger *Zuiderdam* entered service, the first of the line's Vista-class ships. She was followed by the *Oosterdam* in 2003, the *Westerdam* in 2004, and the *Noordam* in 2006. Eighty-five percent of the accommodations feature ocean views, and two-thirds sport verandahs. Each ship has two penthouse verandah suites measuring 1,000 square feet with 318-foot verandas.

Standard inside and outside cabins range in size from 170 square feet to 200 square feet, and deluxe veranda cabins measure 200 square feet (with 54-square-foot verandas). Verandah suites range in size from 398 to 700 square feet (including the verandah). The furnishings and facilities in the various categories of accommodations are similar to the other HAL ships, with the addition of expanded veranda areas. However, storage area in the nonsuite cabins and bathrooms is somewhat limited. All of the *Statendam-* and Vista-class ships offer concierge lounges for suite passengers, offering special services, free laundry, pressing and cleaning, priority tender boarding and other amenities, espresso, cappuccino, Continental breakfasts, and afternoon and evenings snacks, but no soft drinks or alcoholic beverages.

Public areas are brighter, more eclectic, less classic, with less wood and brass, and are more spread out than those on the prior generation of HAL ships, the *Oosterdam*, *Westerdam*, and *Noordam* being more toned down than the *Zuiderdam*. Facilities on Vista-class ships not found on S-class vessels include glass elevators on port and starboard sides of the ship with views to the sea; additional bars; a cabaret-style show lounge complementing the two-deck production show lounge; a hydrotherapy pool in the greenhouse spa and salon (there is a daily or weekly charge for using the steam rooms and the pool); a new look, location, and menu for the Pinnacle Grill; reservation-only specialty restaurants; and the Explorations Cafe, featuring snacks, pastries, sandwiches, and specialty coffees and cocktails.

In late 2004, the line announced a Signature of Excellence program to be completed on all ships during a thirty-six-month period. The first phase was completed in October 2006, with the innovations for the fleet including upgraded mattresses, bed linens, duvets, towels, bathrobes, and showerheads in the staterooms; DVDs, personalized stationery, fully stocked minibars, and access to the concierge lounge for all suite passengers; an Explorations Café serving coffees while guests enjoy Internet connections, the library, music, and New York Times crossword puzzles; additional dining times in the main dining rooms (four options); enhanced lido dining with a greater variety of international choices and table-side wait service at dinner; greenhouse spas to be added to all ships; expanded fitness facilities and thermal pools; additional culinary and enrichment programs, including a culinary arts center with a "show kitchen" with rotating guest chefs; upgraded children's facilities; new teen venues; a new kids/teens culinary program offering forty-five-minute classes on the preparation of various dishes; and early embarkation programs enabling passengers to board ship by noon.

Additional phases of the program continue: stateroom upgrades including carpets, soft goods, and bathroom enhancements; the addition of verandahs to twelve staterooms on deck 9 forward; an early embarkation program allowing guests to board as early as 11:30 a.m.; expansion of the greenhouse spa; twenty-four-hour concierge service for suite guests; a resort-style aft pool concept called the Retreat; a large LED screen for movies on the aft deck; expansion of the Club HAL, children and teen's programs, including a teens-only lounge connected to a teens-only sundeck; a canopy and windscreens to create additional seating for lido restaurants; an upscale pizzeria called Slice; new Italian restaurants; an expanded menu in the Pinnacle Grills; and two dinner seating times in the upper level of the main dining rooms, with open seating on the lower level. A lounge was added that combines the library, Internet café, cardroom, and premium coffee shop. Staterooms on lower promenade deck had windows replaced with lanai doors that open out to the deck, whereas other staterooms were converted to spa staterooms.

The *Ryndam* was the first of the S-class ships to receive renovations while in dry dock to incorporate the full Signature of Excellence program. Similar renovations are being extended to all the S-class ships. When the *Noordam, Eurodam*, and *Nieuw Amsterdam* were launched, the Signature of Excellence program amenities and additions were already in place.

In 2005, the cruise line announced that it had entered into contracts (through its parent, Carnival) to build two 86,700-ton, 2,104- to 2,106-passenger ships, to be designated Signature class. The first of this new class of ships, the *Eurodam*, came on line in the summer of 2008, followed by *Nieuw Amsterdam* in 2010. They have 1,052 and 1053 (respectively) tastefully appointed staterooms with 86 percent outside, 67 percent with balconies, and thirty wheelchair-accessible rooms. The size of all accommodations is quite generous. The 155 inside cabins range in size from 175 to 200 square feet, the 189 outside cabins are 189 square feet, the 596 verandah cabins are 200 square feet with 22- to 54-square-foot verandahs, the superior and deluxe verandah suites range from 300 to 570 square feet with 89- to 130-square-foot verandahs, and the two penthouse suites come in at 1,000 square feet with 318-square-foot verandahs.

Fifty-six spa staterooms located near the greenhouse spa are available and offer a few special amenities, including exclusive spa and salon services (at an extra cost), direct access to the thalasso pool (at an extra cost), and a special spa breakfast. All of the Signature of Excellence innovations described above are present in all staterooms. Bathrooms in the nonsuite staterooms are small, with limited shelf space.

In addition to the main dining rooms, lido restaurant, and the elegantly appointed Pinnacle Grill, three new dining venues have been added. On the top deck, Tamarind, featuring Pan-Asian fare, is open for both lunch and dinner. Included in the offerings are dim sum and sushi at lunch. Across from Tamarind is an Oriental-style cocktail lounge. The Den offers cozy cubicles for before- or after-dinner libations. The forward section of the lido restaurant converts each evening to Canaletto, tempting with a vast menu of Italian favorites. An assortment of pizzas is offered at Slice until midnight. This is the best pizza at sea. Once each cruise, "An Evening at Le Cirque" is offered in the Pinnacle Grill. At this event, for a reasonable $39, guests can enjoy a truly gourmet repast with a menu from Cirio Maccioni's famous Manhattan restaurant.

Other innovations include a fifty-seat observation lounge featuring panoramic views that connects to a large Internet café atop ship, with an impressive variety of books and DVDs as well as beverages and snacks; a free digital workshop; expanded shopping, spa, gym, youth, and teen facilities; and all of the Signature of Excellence features found on the other vessels. The gym is very large and offers more state-of-the-art cardio machines and equipment than the other HAL ships or ships of competing cruise lines.

Guests wishing to sit out on deck with some privacy can now rent cabanas, either by the day or for the duration of the cruise. Fourteen are located on deck 12 overlooking the midship pool, and eight are located on deck 9 around the pool. Each cabana comes with bathrobes, hand-held Evian spray misters, iPods, frozen grapes in the morning, and a glass of champagne and chocolate-dipped strawberries in the afternoon. On our most recent cruise on *Nieuw Amsterdam*, we were most impressed with the enhancements and especially the dining venues.

The line currently has a new ship on order from Fincantieri shipyard for delivery in February 2016 called the Signature class.

Historically, the cruise line's primary audience has been older, financially secure couples with an average age of fifty-seven years. More than 40 percent of all passengers are repeaters. In recent years, the line has actively sought to increase its share in the family cruise market, and greater numbers of younger adults and couples are opting for HAL ships. Summer cruises especially attract many families with children. Hosting more than twenty-five thousand children and their families each year, the cruise line offers the Club HAL program, which is open to ages three to twelve years with age-specific activities and facilities. A separate teen program is geared for ages thirteen to seventeen years with separate venues. Guests can also expect a full complement of activities and entertainment: movies, numerous live nightclub shows, several orchestras, deck sports, bridge tournaments, dance lessons, gambling at the casinos, disco, romantic orchestras, wine tasting, formal teas, arts, crafts, bingo, and audience-participation games. In addition, the line features an extensive golf program on Caribbean sailings, with tee times at the Caribbean's most acclaimed golf courses. The company has also introduced wheelchair-accessible tenders.

All ships have complete computer facilities and Wi-Fi, permitting passengers to log on and engage in e-mail correspondence for a charge. The Vista- and Signature-class ships are quite impressive, and cabins on these ships have data ports. Complimentary computer courses are offered through the Digital Workshop powered by Windows on all ships.

Among new culinary offerings are a new alternative dining option exclusively aboard MS *Rotterdam* called "Taste of De Librije," featuring the cuisine of Culinary Council member and *Michelin* three-star chef Jonnie Boer. Named after Boer's restaurant in the Netherlands, the menu will showcase a selection of starters, soups, entrees, and desserts from his land-based eatery.

Once per cruise the Pinnacle Grill will be transformed with service staff wearing the uniform livery from De Librije, the restaurant's table setup will be replicated, and the wine list will highlight a selection of labels from the Lady De Librije collection. Reservations can be made for "Taste of De Librije" for a US $69 surcharge per person, including wine parings.

In early 2013 the company introduced "Dancing with the Stars: At Sea" theme cruises, with famed dance professionals and celebrities from the ABC hit show on board as well as shipboard dance contests on all cruises. Events on six themes a year include dance lessons with the shipboard dance professionals; a chance to meet the dance pros and celebrities from the show, ask questions, and take photos; a special fashion show with the glamorous show costumes; and a dazzling production starring the celebrities and dance pros, complete with routines from the TV series.

HAL's fleet of fifteen ships offers more than five hundred cruises to 415 ports in ninety-eight countries, territories, or dependencies. Although HAL is constantly shifting its cruise grounds to accommodate the market, the ships generally sail to

Alaska, Antarctica, Europe, the Panama Canal, Mexico, Hawaii, South America, the Caribbean, Australia/New Zealand, Asia, and Eastern Canada/New England as well as a Grand World Voyage.

## Strong Points

The physical layout and décor of the vessels make the HAL vessels among the more classically attractive ships afloat; activities, facilities, dining, excellent specialty restaurants, and itineraries make for a solid cruise experience—considered by many as one of the best in the premium-market category. Luxury veranda and penthouse suites are very large and comfortable, affording a superior experience similar to ships competing in the luxury-cruise market.

*Nieuw Amsterdam, courtesy Holland America Cruises*

*Explorations Lounge, courtesy Holland America Cruises*

*Balcony stateroom, courtesy Holland America Cruises*

*Rotterdam Lido pool area, courtesy Holland America Cruises*

*Pinnacle Grill, courtesy Holland America Line*

*Dining Room, courtesy Holland America Line*

# Appetizers

**Citrus Delight with Amaretto** GOURMET VEGETARIAN
Glistening oranges, pineapple and grapefruit with an
autumn-scented cranberry apple vinaigrette

**Jumbo Shrimp Cocktail**
With American cocktail sauce

**\* Prosciutto, Genoa Salami, Melon and Figs**
Served with crostini, olives and sun-dried tomato

**Tomato and Goat Cheese Tart** GOURMET VEGETARIAN
Baked in a flaky crust with herbs, tomato and
cheese, served with fresh greens and basil oil

# Soups and Salad

**Chicken and Corn Soup**
A rich chicken broth fortified with corn kernels, diced
smoked chicken, scallions, bell pepper and mushrooms

**Cream of Pumpkin Soup** GOURMET VEGETARIAN
Lightly flavored with brown sugar, cinnamon, ginger and nutmeg,
thickened with puréed pumpkin and served with a drizzle of cranberry

**Chilled Peach and Ginger Soup** GOURMET VEGETARIAN
Refreshing blend of peach and ginger with buttermilk and apple juice

**Heart of Romaine Lettuce Niçoise** GOURMET VEGETARIAN
Flakes of tuna, crisp green beans, cucumbers, sun-ripened tomato, olives, red
onion rings and tender diced potato, marinated in fresh oregano vinaigrette

*Choice of Dressing: Olive Oil & Balsamic Vinegar, House Italian,
Thousand Island, Blue Cheese, Balsamic Vinaigrette, or fat-free Blue Cheese*

# Entrées

**Meat Tortellini with Sautéed Spinach**
Olive oil, garlic, julienne of bell peppers, scallions and fresh spinach sautéed
together, tossed with hearty stuffed pasta and a Roma tomato basil sauce

**Avocado Citrus Salad** GOURMET VEGETARIAN
Sliced avocado and Meyer lemon slices on a bed of mixed lettuces with
fresh basil, dressed with a citrus zest and sherry vinaigrette

*Add seasoned grilled shrimp on request*

**Baked Southwestern-Style King Crab Cakes**
Topped with black bean-mango salsa and
served over creamy jalapeno jack cheese grits

**\* Hazelnut-Crusted Salmon**
Served with creamy chive sauce, asparagus spears,
sautéed cherry tomatoes and wild rice

**\* Filet of Beef Wellington**
Mouthwatering tenderloin of beef topped with a duxelles of duck liver and mushrooms,
wrapped in a puff pastry, served on a mirror of Madeira sauce with duchess potatoes
and a medley of green asparagus and Chinese pea pods

**Herb-Crusted Rack of Lamb with Mint Basil Pesto**
Served over a Cabernet reduction with potatoes gratin and braised zucchini

**Oven-Roasted Quail**
Plump quail, deboned, then stuffed with spinach and goat cheese,
served on a bed of shiitake mushroom risotto with glazed pineapple

**Roasted Vegetable Tart** GOURMET VEGETARIAN
Accented with tomato fondue and Parmesan cheese

Culinary Council Featured Menu Item

*Dinner Menu, courtesy Holland America Cruises*

Forecast: Clear Skies
Dress Code: Formal

## SAILING TOWARD HAWAII

Bringing the cultures, tastes and unique Holland America experiences to life, both on board and off.

Today's highlights include:

**Aloha Ka-Pua Crafts - 8am**
LIDO POOLSIDE, DECK 4, MIDSHIP
Learn to make a fresh, floral lei. Space is limited.

**Hawaiian Highlights - 10am**
MONDRIAAN LOUNGE, DECK 4, MIDSHIP
Learn how to make the most out of your time ashore with Shore Excursions Manager Michael and Location Guide Kainoa.

**Cooking Show: E mai'ai - 11am**
CULINARY ARTS CENTER, DECK 4
Celebrate the flavors of Hawaii! Learn to prepare Pork Loin Chops with Pineapple Salsa and the retro-classic Blue Hawaii cocktail.

**Learn to do the Hula - 1pm**
LIDO POOLSIDE, DECK 4, MIDSHIP
Learn a Hawaiian hula, with its movements and meaning.

**Ukulele Presentation: Hawaiian Legend and Henry Kaleialoha Allen - 1:30pm**
MONDRIAAN LOUNGE, DECKS 4 & 1
The history and origin of the ukulele and how the ukulele plays an important part in Hawaiian music and culture.

**Geology and Geography of Hawaii - 2:30pm**
MONDRIAAN LOUNGE, DECKS 4 & 1
Location Guide Kainoa discusses the once isolated island group in the world and highlights the most active volcanoes that formed the Hawaiian Archipelago.

**Ukulele Lesson - 3:30pm**
CROW'S NEST, DECK 9
Learn to play the ukulele in this hands on class.

### Did you know?
Holland America Line's commitment to sustainable seafood programs means that our seafood is caught in a manner that does not harm the surrounding ecosystem and ensures enough fish remain in the sea to feed future generations and support local fishing communities. www.marineconservation.org

---

### Today's Sailing toward Hawaii — SUNDAY, FEBRUARY 17, 2013

- **2:30pm** — ON LOCATION The Geology and Geography of Hawaii with Location Guide Kainoa — Mondriaan Lounge, 4 & 1
- **2:30pm** — Digital Scavenger Hunt — Meet in Atrium, 3
- **3:30pm** — Dance Class: Learn to Waltz — Crow's Nest, 9
- **3:30pm** — ON LOCATION Mixology Class: Learn to mix our signature cocktails. No charge to attend, mix and drink for $12.50 — Crow's Nest, 9
- **3:00pm** — Captain Tea — Dining Room, 5
- **3:30pm** — Team Trivia with Cruise Director Kismet. Come as group or come solo and get ready to have some fun. — Mondriaan Lounge, 4 & 1
- **3:30pm** — ON LOCATION Ukulele Lesson with Henry Allen — Crow's Nest, 9
- **3:30pm** — Brush Up on PC Basics. Discover issues and touch gestures in Windows 8 that make it easy for you to navigate your PC — Digital Workshop, 5
- **3:30pm** — Cruise Classics: Bing Tess — Atrium, 3
- **4:00pm** — $25,000 Jackpot Bingo cards on sale at 4:00pm. Games begin at 4:15pm, $25 for 3 cards, $20 for six cards. — Mondriaan Lounge, 4 & 1
- **4:00pm** — ON LOCATION Hawaiian Location Guide Kainoa helps plan your day ashore — Explorations Cafe, 5
- **4:30pm** — Keep Your Photos Organized! Discover how Photo Gallery can manage, view, and organize photos through tags, captions, and ratings. — Digital Workshop, 5
- **4:30pm** — ON LOCATION A Little Something. Join us for a pre-dinner appetizer perfectly paired with the Cellar Master's wine of the day. Wine by the glass $4.50 — Wine Cellar, 4
- **4:30pm** — Friends of Bill W. Meet — King's Room, 1
- **5:00pm** — ON LOCATION Aloha Music Hour with Henry — Crow's Nest, 9
- **5:00pm** — Total Body Conditioning — Fitness Center, 2
- **5:30pm** — Techspert Time: Techspert Team is available to answer your questions about Windows 8? & Windows Live Essentials — Digital Workshop, 5
- **6:00pm** — Pub Trivia Grab a drink and join Show Host Jay and our bartenders for general knowledge trivia! — Piano Bar, 5
- **7:00pm** — LGBT Gathering — Crow's Nest, 9
- **7:45pm / 8:30pm** — Captain's Welcome Toast followed by SHOWTIME: Lens, Broadway. Featuring the Zaandam Singers & Dancers — Mondriaan Lounge, 4 & 1
- **8:45pm** — 80s & 90s Night with Show Host Jay — Crow's Nest, 9
- **9:00pm** — Texas Hold'em Players Meet Right before games — Crow's Nest, 9
- **10:00pm** — SHOWTIME: Lens, Broadway. Featuring the Zaandam Singers & Dancers — Mondriaan Lounge, 4 & 1
- **9:00pm** — Generation Next Meet for guests 14 - 25 years old — Crow's Nest, 9
- **10:00pm** — All Request Hits with Show Host Jay — Crow's Nest, 9
- **12:00am** — Show Host Jay Keeps the Party Going — Crow's Nest, 9

---

### DRINKS

**DRINK OF THE DAY**
Blue Hawaii $6.95

| LOCATION | HOURS | HAPPY HOUR | DECK |
| --- | --- | --- | --- |
| Explorations Cafe | 7a-10p | — | 5 |
| Lido Bar | 7a-6p | — | 8 |
| Ocean Bar | 11a-12m | — | 5 |
| Crow's Nest | 11:30a-close | 4-6p, 11p-12m | 9 |
| Cellar Bar | 5:30p-close | 5p-6p | 4 |
| Piano Bar | 5p-11p | — | 5 |
| Explorer's Lounge | 7p-11p | — | 5 |

### TODAY'S SPECIALS

**MERABELLA LUXURY BOUTIQUE, DECK 5**
9:00am - 11:00pm

Diamonds & Tanzanite Seminar
12:00pm, Piano Bar, 5

**MINIATURE SHOPS**
Fine Jewelry Refill
40% off U.S. retail prices on Diamonds and Tanzanite
Signature Shops, Deck 5
12:00pm

Gold by the Inch
14K Gold or Sterling Silver Chains
Signature Shops, Deck 5
9:00am - 10:00pm

### TODAY'S SALON PACKAGE

Cleopatra's Treatment
Full Body Exfoliation
Skin Nourishing Milk Wrap
30 Minute Full Body Massage
Scalp or Foot massage

Valued at $281 - Today $149

Visit the Greenhouse spa, Deck 8 or dial 94 to schedule an appointment

### SERVICES

| LOCATION | HOURS | DECK |
| --- | --- | --- |
| Explorations Cafe Library | 8a-10p | 5 |
| Fitness Center | 6a-10p | 2 |
| Front Office | 24 hours | 1 |
| Future Cruise Consultant | 9a-11a, 3p-6p | 5 |
| Greenhouse Spa & Salon | 8a-8p | 8 |
| Sauna | 8a-8p | 8 |
| Thermal Suite | 8a-8p | 8 |
| Medical Center | 8a-12p, 3p-6p | 1 |
| Doctor's Hours | 11a-11a, 5p-6p | 1 |
| Pools | 7a-9p | 8 |
| Hot Tubs | 8a-10p | 8 |
| Port & Shopping Ambassador | 9a-5p | 5 |
| Shore Excursions Desk | 8a-5p | 5 |

**FUTURE CRUISE**
Get a history ticket to win a free cruise! Book your next cruise by Feb 21st to receive dinner entry for $25 shipboard credit! Visit your Future Cruise Consultant Michelle. Future Cruise Desk, Deck 5, aft

**FINE ART**
Art Seminar: Art Collecting 101. Learn how to spot a great deal on how different types of art are created. Ocean Bar, 5. 12:00am

**CASINO**
Gaming Lessons. Learn Blackjack, Roulette and more. $30 Texas Hold'em Registers. Tournament 12:30pm.
Slot Tournament — Win up to $500. 1:00pm-2:00pm, $20 Tickets on sale at the casino. Casino, Deck 5. Cashier: 10:00am. Tables: 10:30am. Slots 24 hours.

**PHOTO GALLERY**
JC Black Label Art Photography. See your onboard JC Black Label Artist Dauan for details. Lowest appointments available. Photo Gallery, Deck 4. 6:00pm - 10:30pm

**INTERNET**
Receive up to 100 free additional minutes. Ask your Internet Manager for details. Explorations Cafe, Deck 5. Internet Services Open 24 hours

# HURTIGRUTEN

**405 Park Avenue, Suite 904**
**New York, NY 10022**
**(212) 319-1300; (800) 323-7436**
**Fax: (212) 319-1390**
**www.hurtigruten.us**

MS *Finnmarken*: entered service in 2002; 15,000 GRT; 138.5 × 21.5 meters; 643-passenger capacity; fifty cars; Norwegian officers and crew

MS *Fram*: entered service in 2007; 12,700 GRT; 371 feet long; 318-passenger capacity; cruises Iceland, Greenland, and Disco Bay during summer, Antarctica during winter, and North American and European cruises during spring and fall

MS *Kong Harald*: entered service in 1993; 11,200 GRT; 121.8 × 19.2 meters; 490-passenger capacity; fifty cars; Norwegian officers and crew

MS *Lofoten*: entered service in 1964; renovated in 2003; 2,661 GRT; 87.4 × 13.5 meters; 171-passenger capacity; four cars; Norwegian officers and crew

MS *Midnatsol* and MS *Trollfjord*: entered service in 2003 and 2002, respectively; 15,000 GRT; 135.7 × 21.5 meters; 674-passenger capacity; fifty cars; Norwegian officers and crew

MS *Nordkapp*: entered service in 1996; 11,386 GRT; 123.3 × 19.5 meters; 490-passenger capacity; fifty cars; Norwegian officers and crew

MS *Nordlys*: entered service in 1994; 11,200 GRT; 121.8 × 19.2 meters; 482-passenger capacity; fifty cars; Norwegian officers and crew

MS *Nordnorge*: entered service in 1997; 11,386 GRT; 123.3 × 19.5 meters; 464-passenger capacity; fifty cars; Norwegian officers and crew

MS *Nordstjernen*: entered service in 1960; renovated in 2000; 2,568 GRT; 87.4 × 13.2 meters; 164-passenger capacity; four cars; Norwegian officers and crew

MS *Polarlys*: entered service in 1996; 12,000 GRT; 123 × 19.5 meters; 482-passenger capacity; fifty cars; Norwegian officers and crew

MS *Polar Star*: entered service in 1969; renovated in 1988 and 2000; 3,500 GRT; 86.5 × 21.2 meters: 100-passenger capacity; Norwegian officers and crew

MS *Richard With*: entered service in 1993; 11,205 GRT; 121.8 × 19.2 meters; 490-passenger capacity; fifty cars; Norwegian officers and crew

MS *Vesteralen*: entered service in 1983; renovated in 1995; 6,261 GRT; 108.6 × 16.5 meters; 318-passenger capacity; forty cars; Norwegian officers and crew

The cruise line also leases the 120-passenger, 6,336-ton MS *Expedition* for service in Spitsbergen.

(Medical facilities: generally no physicians except in Antarctica on *Fram* and *Polar Star* in Spitsbergen; no medical facilities aboard the ships)

Hurtigruten has been operating for more than one hundred years and calls at thirty-four Norwegian ports daily. The line has fifteen ships, most of which were built since 1993, with passenger capacities between 114 and 674. Each ship has lounges, dining rooms, twenty-four-hour cafeterias, and souvenir and sundry shops. The newer vessels have children's playrooms, conference facilities, Internet cafés, elevators, and cabins for disabled passengers. In 2005, outdoor Jacuzzis were installed on the newer vessels.

The ships offer cruises along 1,250 miles of the fjord-indented western coast of Norway. Cruises are six days southbound, seven days northbound, and twelve days round trip. Itineraries include the cultural cities of Bergen and Trondheim; small arctic towns such as Tromso, Oksfjord, and Hammerfest; and passages through narrow straits and past magnificent fjords.

The newest ship in the fleet, the MS *Fram*, is one of the most deluxe expedition ships, designed to make shore excursions easier and to offer the same amenities as upscale cruise ships, including a wellness center with saunas, a conference facility, outdoor whirlpools, and a guest bridge. She offers cruises in Antarctica and the Chilean fjords between October and March. This is a unique itinerary with unforgettable experiences to an area of the world largely undiscovered by tourists.

During the summer months, the MS *Nordstjernen*, MS *Polar Star*, and MS *Expedition* offer service in Spitsbergen. Expeditions to Greenland are also offered.

Other larger and newer ships of the line, the 15,000-ton *Trollfjord*, *Midnatsol*, and *Finnmarken* entered service in 2002, 2003, and 2002, respectively. The first two ships can accommodate 674 passengers and fifty cars, whereas the *Finnmarken* accommodates 643 passengers and fifty cars. These new builds have added upscale suites for passengers willing to pay a bit more for more space and comfort. There are thirty-two on *Finnmarken*, twenty-three on *Midnatsol*, and twenty-three on *Trollfjord*. Five suites on *Midnatsol* and *Trollfjord* have balconies and fourteen have balconies on *Finnmarken*. All accommodations on *Finnmarken* have TVs, safes, refrigerators, and telephones. Public areas include numerous dining venues, a conference area, a children's area and arcade, a library, an Internet café, shops, and several lounges. The two-story panoramic lounges provide spectacular views of the coastal scenery, and even the saunas and glass elevators have sea views. The top decks contain fitness rooms, two saunas, a large sundeck, a bar, and the observation-lounge balcony. These ships cruise round trip from Bergen, Norway, to Kirkenes, close to the Russian border, and back to Bergen in twelve days.

Cruise rates range from $115 per day, per person up to $915 per day for a suite (depending on the ship, season, and cabin category). Various all-inclusive cruise programs are available, including air, train journeys, hotels, and sightseeing.

All expedition programs offer shore landings, expert guides, and lecturers.

## Strong Points

These ships offer expedition cruising as well as a definitive Norwegian fjord itinerary in a true Norwegian environment, with the potential for upscale accommodations for cruisers wishing to experience uniquely beautiful parts of the world.

*Courtesy Hurtigruten*

*MS Fram, Courtesy Hurtigruten*

# MSC CRUISES (USA) INC.

**6750 North Andrews Avenue, Suite 100**
**Fort Lauderdale, FL 33309**
**(877) 665-4655**
**Fax: (908) 605-2600**
**www.msccruisesusa.com**

MSC *Armonia* (formerly *European Vision*): entered service in 2001 and joined MSC in 2004; 58,625 GRT; 824 × 94 feet; 1,544-passenger capacity (2,199 when every berth full); 777 staterooms; Italian officers and international crew; seven-night cruises in the Red Sea and seven-night cruises in Eastern Mediterranean (Category C—four+ stars)

MSC *Divina* and MSC *Preziosa:* entered service in 2012 and 2013, respectively; 139,400 GRT; 3,502-passenger capacity (4,345 when every berth full); 1,751 staterooms; Italian officers and international crew; MSC *Divina* offers three- to eleven-night cruises in the Caribbean from the late fall to the early spring and seven-night cruises in the Eastern Mediterranean during the remainder of the year. MSC *Preziosa* offers three- to seven-night cruises in South America during the late fall through the winter and seven-night cruises in the Eastern Mediterranean during the other months (Category C-5—five stars)

Yacht Club (Category B—six stars)

MSC *Fantasia* and MSC *Splendida:* entered service in 2008 and 2009, respectively; 137,936 GRT; 1,094 × 124 feet; 3,274-passenger capacity; 1,637 staterooms; Italian officers and international crew; MSC *Fantasia* offers eleven-night cruises in Eastern Mediterranean from late fall through early spring and seven-night cruises in Western Mediterranean during the remainder of the year; MSC *Splendida* offers seven-night Western Mediterranean cruises year-round (Category C-5—four stars)

Yacht Club (Category B—6 stars)

MSC *LIRICA*: entered service in 2003; 59,058 GRT; 824 × 94 feet; 1,560-passenger capacity (2,199 when every berth full); 780 staterooms; Italian officers and international crew; seven-night cruises in United Arab Emirates from late fall through the winter and seven- and eleven-night Eastern Mediterranean cruises during the remainder of the year (Category C—four+ stars)

MSC *Musica* and MSC *Orchestra*: entered service in 2006 and 2007, respectively; 92,409 GRT; 964 × 121 feet; 2,550-passenger capacity (3,223 when every berth full); 1,275 staterooms; Italian officers and international crew; MSC *Musica* offers seven-night deep Southern Caribbean sailings from late fall to early spring and seven- and eleven-night cruises in Western Mediterranean during the remainder of the year; MSC *Orchestra* offers three- to eight-night cruises in South American from late fall through the winter, in the summer three- to nine-night Western Mediterranean and seven-night Northern Europe, as well as three- and eleven-night cruises in the Black Sea in early fall (Category C—five stars)

MSC *Opera*: entered service in 2004; 59,058 GRT; 824 × 94 feet; 1,712-passenger capacity (2,199 whenever berth full); 856 staterooms; Italian officers and international crew; two- to ten-night South African cruises from late fall through early spring and seven- to ten-night Northern Europe cruises during the remaining months (Category C—four+ stars)

MSC *Poesia* and MSC *Magnifica*: entered service in 2008 and 2010, respectively; 92,627 GRT for *Poesia* and 95,128 for *Magnifica*; 964 × 121 feet; 3,223-passenger capacity (2,550 lower berths) for *Poesia* and 3,013-passenger capacity (2,518 lower berths) for *Magnifica*; 1,275 staterooms for *Poesia* and 1,259 for *Magnifica*; Italian officers and international crew; MSC *Poesia* offers three- to nine-night South American cruises from late fall to early spring, seven-night Northern Europe during summer, and eight-night Western Mediterranean during early fall; MSC *Magnifica* sails six- and seven-night South American cruises during winter and two- to fourteen-night Northern Europe cruises during summer (Category C—five stars)

MSC *Sinfonia* (formerly *European Star*): entered service in 2002 and joined MSC in 2005; 58,625 GRT; 824 × 94 feet; 1,544-passenger capacity; 777 staterooms; Italian officers and international crew; two- to fourteen-night cruises in South Africa from late fall through winter, twelve-night Black Sea during spring, seven-night cruises in Western Mediterranean during summer, and eleven-night cruises in Eastern Mediterranean in early fall (Category C—four+ stars)

(Medical facilities: C-2 *Armonia* and *Sinfonia;* C-6 *Lirica, Opera*; C-17 on *Musica* and *Orchestra*; P-2 *Lirica* and *Opera*/P-1 on others; N-1; CM; PD; EKG; TC; OX; WC; OR; ICU; CCP; LJ; some medical facilities on all ships)

Some of these ships are rated in eleven separate categories in the second half of chapter 11.

Note: Itineraries are subject to frequent changes.

MSC Cruises is part of the giant shipping group Mediterranean Shipping Company (MSC), which also operates a global fleet of container vessels with a corporate presence in Geneva, Switzerland, and Naples, Italy. In 1990, the privately owned and family-run MSC purchased an Italian cruise company, Starlauro, which owned one vessel, MV *Achille Lauro*. Between 1990 and 1995, Starlauro acquired MV *Monterey*, MV *Symphony*, and MV *Rhapsody*. In 2001, the name of the cruise line was changed to MSC Italian Cruises to take advantage of the reputation associated with the parent company. In 1997, it purchased the Star/Ship *Atlantic* from Premier Cruise Line and renamed her MSC *Melody*. The *Achille Lauro*, *Symphony*, *Rhapsody*, *Monterey*, and *Melo*dy are no longer with the cruise line. The line subsequently changed its name to MSC Cruises.

Since 2003, MSC Cruises has taken delivery of an average of one newly built vessel a year. The company's first new build, the MSC *Lirica*, joined the fleet in 2003, followed by a sister ship, the MSC *Opera*, in 2004. Also in 2004, MSC purchased the 1,544-passenger *European Vision* and *European Star* from the bankrupt First European/Festival Cruises and renamed them MSC *Armonia* and MSC *Sinfonia*. Several larger new builds, the 92,409-ton, 2,550-passenger MSC *Musica*, MSC *Orchestra*, and 92,627-ton MSC *Poesia* joined the fleet in 2006, 2007, and 2008, and sister ship MSC *Magnifica* debuted in 2010. The MSC *Fantasia* and MSC *Splendida*, two 137,936-ton sisters with 3,274 lower berths, entered service in 2008 and 2009. MSC *Divina* entered service in 2012, and MSC *Preziosa* followed in 2013. Legendary screen actress Sophia Loren is godmother to all but two MSC ships.

In 2004, the cruise line hired industry veteran Rick Sasso to head its North American operations. Sasso, formerly CEO of Celebrity Cruises, proceeded to hire many of the people who worked with him at Celebrity with the aspiration to make MSC Cruises a major competitor in the North American as well as European markets. The company has grown over 800 percent in the past eight years.

Overall, the line emphasizes Mediterranean and international ambiance and entertainment and in past years has largely serviced the European market in the Mediterranean, South American, and South African cruise areas. During the winter, the line offers cruises in the Caribbean, South America, United Arab Emirates, Red Sea, and Mediterranean. In the summer the ships are deployed in the Mediterranean and Northern Europe. Prices on the various vessels range from $90 per person per night for a minimum inside cabin with upper and lower berths to $325 for an outside suite.

During sailings in Europe and the Mediterranean, the demographics of the ships are overwhelmingly European, with English-speaking passengers in the minority (often

15 to 20 percent). "Our menus offer Mediterranean cuisine with many American favorites—a change since you last sailed." Dining, service, and entertainment will appeal more to European tastes. Room service is on an à la carte basis on European sailings and complimentary in the Caribbean. MSC has what they call a quiet ship policy, in which only necessary announcements are made (such as arrival to a port, departure from a port, etc.). Announcements are in five different languages and vary according to the composition of the guests on board; however, most of the officers and crew speak English. Most officers and supervisors are of Italian heritage, and the crew is composed of South Africans, Indonesians, Indians, Filipinos, and Eastern Europeans.

In the cruise line's desire to encourage families, children eleven years and younger sail free when sharing a stateroom with two adults paying full fare; and children twelve to seventeen years of age sail at a reduced rate. Special counselors organize age-appropriate activities for children three to six years old in the Mini Club, seven to eleven years old in the Juniors Club, twelve to fourteen years old in the Y-Team Club, and fifteen to seventeen years old in the MSC Generation Teen Club. The line also offers special activates for babies (ten to thirty-six months old) accompanied by their parents. In addition, there are children's menus in the restaurants and special cruise charge cards for guests twelve to seventeen years of age, allowing them to charge inexpensive items such as soft drinks. Happy Dinners are available for children in the Mini and Junior Club, in which children dining with their parents are picked up by the youth staff when they are done eating to allow parents to enjoy a leisurely meal. Four times a week, children in this age-group can dine in a specially decorated area of the buffet with the entertainment team so that parents can dine alone.

With the building of the *Fantasia*-class ships (MSC *Fantasia*, MSC *Splendida*, MSC *Divina*, and MSC *Orchestra*), MSC Cruises introduced MSC Yacht Club. A ship within a ship featuring sixty-nine to seventy-one suites (varying by ship) with butler and concierge service; complimentary select wines, spirits, soft drinks, mineral waters, and juices; private pool area, lounge, library, and dining room. With the introduction of MSC *Preziosa*, the line partnered with Eataly, the popular Turin-based chain, with locations throughout Italy, Japan, New York City, to introduce the first Eataly restaurants at sea, Eataly and Ristorante Italia. The ship also features the longest single rider slide at sea, Vertigo.

The 59,058-ton MSC *Lirica* entered service in 2003, followed by a sister ship, MSC *Opera*, in 2004. Although the same exterior frame, the MSC *Lirica* has 780 staterooms, 132 of which are 290-square-foot balcony suites, whereas the MSC *Opera* has 856 staterooms with twenty-eight 269-square-foot balcony suites and 172 162- to 178-square-foot balcony staterooms. Numerous cabins can accommodate a third and/ or fourth passenger. Four on MSC *Lirica* and five on MSC *Opera* can accommodate wheelchairs, and more than half have ocean views. All accommodations on both ships have satellite TV, a minibar, a private safe, a radio, a telephone, 110/220-volt electric current, and a makeup area. Average cabins measure 140 square feet with small bathrooms. The twenty-eight accommodations sold as suites atop each ship are larger with a small sitting area, bathtub/shower combination, small walk-in closet, and additional storage. However, they would only be designated deluxe staterooms on many other cruise lines.

Public areas are traditional in décor, very tastefully designed and decorated with an Italian flare without being glitzy. They include a fitness center with several massage rooms, men and women's changing rooms, saunas and steam rooms, a relaxation area, and a medium-size gym and aerobics area; two-deck show lounge and several other nightclub venues for musical groups, including an observation lounge/disco atop the ships; two swimming pools connected by two whirlpools surrounded by two decks of lounges and a walking/jogging track; miniature golf course atop ship; supervised children's club; virtual-reality center; shopping gallery; Internet café; casino; two main dining rooms; buffet restaurant with outside grill and pizzeria and protected outside seating; and main lobby with an information desk, tour desk, and money-changing facility. In addition to nightly variety and cabaret shows, there are several listening/dancing venues and musical entertainment is outstanding throughout the ship. Activities are plentiful and could be described as Club Med style.

The 58,625-ton MSC *Armonia* (formerly *European Vision*) and MSC *Sinfonia* (formerly *European Star*) accommodations include 132 290-square-foot minisuites with balconies. Standard cabins measure 140 square feet. Public areas include two pools, a basketball court, rock-climbing wall, two-deck theater, seven lounges, a large main dining room, buffet restaurant, casino, English pub on MSC *Armonia* and an Irish pub on MSC *Sinfonia*, cigar-smoking lounge, golf simulator, miniature golf course, health spa/fitness center, children's playroom, teen club, video arcade center and Internet café, and conference meeting space. Activities, entertainment, dining, and service are similar to that found on MSC *Lirica* and MSC *Opera* but are more geared to European tastes.

The 92,409-ton, 2,550-passenger MSC *Musica* and MSC *Orchestra* and the 92,627-ton MSC *Poesia* and 95,128-ton MSC *Magnifica* provide sea views in 80 percent of the accommodations, and 65 percent of these have balconies. Each accommodation includes two twin beds convertible to a European king size, and many can accommodate a third and/or a fourth person. There are seventeen cabins for the physically challenged. Interior staterooms measure 140 square feet, ocean-view staterooms are 167 square feet, balcony staterooms range from 185 to 275 square feet, and the eighteen balcony suites are 330 square feet. All balconies measure 32-78 square feet. There are forty-four 290-square-foot family suites on MSC *Magnifica*.

The vessels feature a three-deck waterfall in the central foyer; 12,500-square-foot spa/beauty center; 7,000-square-foot casino; children's pool, play area, and program; LED movie screen at the main pool; two main restaurants; a specialty Japanese restaurant and sushi bar on MSC *Musica* and MSC *Poesia*; a specialty Asian fusion restaurant on MSC *Orchestra*; and MSC *Magnifica*, a surcharge gourmet specialty restaurant; pizza grill; wine-tasting bar; coffee bar; cigar room; two outdoor swimming pools; four whirlpools; special children's facilities; a solarium; golf simulator and minigolf (on MSC *Musica* and MSC *Orchestra*); jogging track; a three-deck-high theater seating 1,240; and panoramic disco. Also there is a deck tennis court on MSC *Orchestra*. All of these ships have a sports area with game courts. MSC *Magnifica* features a retractable magrodome over the secondary pool area and a 4-D cinema.

The 133,796-ton, 3,274-passenger MSC *Fantasia* and MSC *Splendida* are extremely attractive ships, eclectic in their design and décor. Each features the MSC Yacht Club—seventy-one suites ranging between 278 and 572 square feet in exclusive private areas available only to those passengers booking the most expensive accommodations. The MSC Yacht Club (a ship within a ship) is a new concept for MSC, one similar to the courtyard villas of Norwegian Cruise Line and the Grill-class area of Cunard's ships. The 46,000-square-foot MSC Yacht Club area is accessible by a private elevator and includes its own pool, two Jacuzzis, an outdoor bar-patio sunning area, and a panoramic, multipurpose VIP observation lounge. Privileges include priority embarkation and debarkation, private access to the spa; twenty-four-hour room service; butler and concierge services; your choice of morning newspaper; complimentary select fine wines, beers, name-brand liquors and aperitifs; English high tea and hot and cold hors d'oeuvres daily in the lounge; and dining in the private restaurant (breakfast, lunch, and dinner). In addition to the standard stateroom amenities, these suites include Internet access, Wi-Fi, Nintendo Wii, interactive TV, full bath and shower combination with marble accents in the bathrooms, ergonomic mattresses, Egyptian cotton sheets, a Dorelan pillow menu, and a complimentary minibar. The butlers are extremely efficient and helpful.

Staterooms on the ship range from 171 to 318 square feet and suites are 346 square feet. The twenty-two Panoramic Aurea Suites on each ship range from 223 to 549 square feet. Seventy-seven percent have balconies and forty-three are wheelchair accessible. The accommodations have all the facilities and amenities previously described for the other vessels; however, the non-MSC Yacht Club suites would not be considered suites on most other cruise lines.

In addition to the two bi-level main dining rooms and two casual buffet-style eateries, MSC *Fantasia* and MSC *Splendida* offer a Tex-Mex restaurant, pizzeria, sports bar for snacks, and Italian cantina for wines and tapas. At the central piazza, there is a patisserie café and gelato stand. Dining in the themed restaurants is a la carte.

The large spa complex is very impressive and offers a state-of-the-art gym, a spot for yoga classes, relaxation rooms, treatment rooms, steam rooms and several saunas, and a spa bar for smoothies and healthy snacks. There are two swimming pools, one with a magrodome, an Aqua Park with 150 fountains, and twelve whirlpools. The game arcade includes a four-dimensional cinema and a Formula 1 simulator.

MSC *Divina* and MSC *Preziosa*—larger sister ships at 139,400-tons, 3,502 passengers (4,345 when every berth is full), and 1,751 staterooms—came on line in 2012 and 2013, respectively. Staterooms on these ships range from 130 to 275 square feet and Aurea Suites are 399-549 square feet. The MSC Yacht Club has sixty-nine suites ranging from 278 to 572 square feet. The MSC Yacht Club, casino, disco, and adults-only area surrounding the aft pools have been expanded from those areas on the MSC *Fantasia* and MSC *Splendida*. Guests have access to three restaurants and an alternative dining restaurant (Tex-Mex on MSC *Divina*; Eataly and Ristorante Italia on MSC *Preziosa*), Aqua Park, MSC Aurea Spa with Balinese-inspired treatments, children and teen areas, interactive 4-D Cinema, virtual Formula 1 auto racing, and international entertainment in the Theater. MSC *Preziosa* also features the longest single rider waterslide, Vertigo, at sea.

Aurea Suites on board MSC *Fantasia*, MSC *Splendida*, MSC *Divina*, and MSC *Preziosa* offer upgraded staterooms with Aurea Spa offerings such as a welcome herbal tea, complimentary consultation with the spa doctor, and complimentary use of the thermal spa for the duration of the cruise.

## Strong Points

Interesting itineraries, including areas of the world not regularly visited by many other cruise lines; Mediterranean spirit, ambiance, and regional cuisine; and a chance to mingle with passengers from other countries. Rates are reasonable, and children sail free when sharing cabin with two adults. The newer ships offer some unique and very desirable features. Those who opt for the MSC Yacht Club, on the MSC *Fantasia*, MSC *Splendida*, MSC *Divina*, and MSC *Preziosa* are rewarded with a luxury-style cruise experience.

*Balcony stateroom on MSC Fantasia, courtesy MSC Cruises*

*MSC Divina, courtesy MSC Cruises*

*Lounge on MSC Fantasia, courtesy MSC Cruises*

*Dining Room on MSC Splendida, courtesy MSC Cruises*

*MSC* Orchestra, *courtesy MSC Cruises*

*MSC* Orchestra, *courtesy MSC Cruises*

*MSC* Opera, *courtesy MSC Cruises*

## Appetizers

Tropical sea scallop mango cocktail*
with tomatillo sauce

"Vol-au-vent Regina"
puff pastry nest filled with diced chicken and sautéed Portobello mushrooms
in a creamy sauce

Vegetable Maki Roll*
Nori seaweed roll with Japanese rice, avocado, asparagus,
carrot sticks and cream cheese, topped with Unagi sauce and sesame seeds

## Salad & Soups

Greek salad
sliced tomatoes and cucumbers, topped with Feta cheese crumbles,
julienne bell peppers, red onions and Kalamata olives
SERVED WITH YOUR CHOICE OF DRESSING:
Ranch, Blue Cheese, Thousand Island, Italian, French and low-calorie Yogurt

Creamy leek and potato soup
garnished with a seared shrimp

Oriental vegetable consommé
with rice noodles, Chinese mushrooms, cabbage, bamboo shoots and coriander

## Pasta

Homemade fresh pasta
"Tagliatelle al ragù di vitello"
Tagliatelle pasta in a creamy veal and Porcini mushrooms sauce

## Main Courses

Seared fillet of sea bass*
served with golden brown butter, fried sage and pumpkin risotto

Roast rack of lamb*
served with oven-roasted Red Bliss potato wedges and confit tomatoes,
bell peppers and zucchini in olive oil

Surf & Turf*
seared lobster tail and juicy beef tenderloin medallion
served with Béarnaise sauce and melted butter
accompanied by fried sweet potato sticks and grilled asparagus

Vegetable Lasagna with Ricotta au gratin
in a creamy tomato sauce and Parmesan cheese

# Bread
Bread of the day, Focaccia,
Six-grain mini-baguette with sesame seeds,
Semolina bread roll, Knot-shaped bread with semolina

# Cheese
Cheese selection
served with grissini and grapes

# Desserts & Fruit
Baked Alaska
traditional cake made with sponge cake layered with different ice cream flavors,
topped with caramelized meringue
Ice cream or sorbet of the day
Fresh fruit platter
No sugar added
Lemon Jello with diced fresh fruit
Ice cream of the day
American coffee and tea are always available

# Suggested Wines
Conundrum Caymus s $ 49.00
Napa Valley, California
Château Rolland-Maillet Sainte-Émilion Grand Cru s $ 54.00
Bordeaux, France
By the glass
Müller Thurgau Palai delle Dolomiti DOC s $ 7.50
Pojer e Sandri—Trentino Alto Adige, Italy
Bordeaux Rouge Supérieur AOC s $ 7.25
Château Majureau-Sercillan—Bordeaux, France

A 15% bar service charge is automatically added to all purchases

*If you have any allergies or sensitivity to specific foods, please notify our Maître d'Hôtel before ordering.*

*\* Public Health advisory: We advise that eating raw or undercooked meats (poultry, beef, lamb, pork, etc.), seafood, shellfish or eggs may increase your risk of food borne illness, especially if you have certain medical conditions.*

MSC Signature   GB Dish   Light   Vegetarian

*MSC Dinner Menu, courtesy MSC Cruises*

# MSC ORCHESTRA

**DAILY PROGRAM**

MSC ORCHESTRA
Monday, 23rd March 2009

Sunrise 7:48am - Sunset 7:59pm

## Welcome to... COZUMEL

*Expected arrival time in **Cozumel** approx 10:00am*
*All aboard: 4:30pm*
*Departure time for **Georgetown**: 5:00pm   (334 Nautical Miles)*

### IMPORTANT INFORMATION
**We kindly ask all our Guests to keep their watches set to ship time**
even though there is a two hour difference in Cozumel (Ship time is two hours ahead).

### EXCURSION MEETING POINTS

| | | |
|---|---|---|
| COZ09 - FURY CATAMARAN SNORKEL & BEACH | 10:00am | Savannah Bar, Deck 6 |
| COZ23 - TULUM MAYA RUINS EXPRESS | 10:00am | Covent Garden Theatre, Deck 6 |
| COZ10 - COZUMEL HIGHLIGHTS & SHOPPING | 10:15am | Covent Garden Theatre, Deck 6 |
| COZ12 - CLEAR KAYAK, SNORKEL AND BEACH SNORKEL COMBO | 10:15am | Savannah Bar, Deck 6 |
| COZ24 - PUNTA SUR ECO-PARK, MAYAN RUIN & SNORKEL | 10:45am | Savannah Bar, Deck 6 |
| COZ14 - DUNE BUGGY & BEACH SNORKEL AT PUNTA SUR | 10:45am | Covent Garden Theatre, Deck 6 |
| COZ20 - ATV JUNGLE ADVENTURE | 10:45am | Savannah Bar, Deck 6 |
| COZ21 - 3 REEF SNORKELING BY BOAT | 11:15am | Savannah Bar, Deck 6 |
| COZ22 - DOLPHIN SWIM | 12:45pm | Savannah Bar, Deck 6 |

Passengers on excursion: Don't forget to hand your **excursion ticket** and **MSC Cruise Card**. Do you take part in the excursions? Don't forget to have mineral water, which you may purchase at the bars of the meeting point lounges. You will get 25% discount showing your excursion ticket. The bottle will cost only $ 1,50.

---

**We inform all passengers that smoking is forbidden at the excursions meeting points.**

---

### ATTENTION!
We would like to inform our passengers that a **general emergency drill** will take place today during the morning **for crew members only**. Passengers are not required to participate. We inform you that during the drill all the services on board will be closed. Thank you for your understanding.

### EXCURSION OFFICE  DECK 6
We are waiting for you at the Excursion desk (Deck 6) from 4:00pm to 8:00pm to book the last available tickets for Georgetown in the Cayman Islands, the land of the stingrays!

### DIAMOND POWER HOUR Take your Maps ashore!
MSC's number one recommendation for diamonds this cruise is Diamonds International, #1 on your map! If you missed them in Key West, this is your chance!! Meet Valerija at Diamonds International from **11:00am – 12:00pm Free Diamond & Sapphire Necklace Raffle!** Remember to bring your VIP card as it will guarantee you the manager's best price on jewellery and watches.
See Valerija at the gangway for last minute Tips **9:30am-10:30am**

**FOLLOW THE MSC FLEET** - Here's where the MSC Cruise fleet is today

| MSC FANTASIA | MSC POESIA | MSC MUSICA | MSC LIRICA | MSC OPERA | MSC SINFONIA | MSC ARMONIA | MSC MELODY | MSC RHAPSODY |
|---|---|---|---|---|---|---|---|---|
| Naples | At sea | At sea | At sea | Ilhabela | Ilha Grande | Recife | Durban | Messina |

**TONIGHT'S DRESS CODE:** *CASUAL*

**MSC** CROCIERE

## TODAY ONBOARD

### POOLS, DECK 13
**10:00am-12:00pm & 3:00pm-5:00pm**
**Meeting point with the Entertainment Team:**
Sports equipment available: mini-golf, tennis & ping-pong, racquets, balls, table soccer, playing cards, shuffle-board decks

#### Morning

| | | |
|---|---|---|
| 9:00am | Morning walk | Pools, Deck 13 |
| 9:30am | Aerobics | Pools, Deck 13 |
| 10:00am | Stretching | Pools, Deck 13 |
| 10:30am | Quiz time | Pools, Deck 13 |
| 11:15am | Aperitif game | Pools, Deck 13 |

#### Afternoon

| | | |
|---|---|---|
| 3:00pm | Ability game | Pools, Deck 13 |

**3:30pm** Pools, Deck 13
**Zankys vs Pankys– Team game**

| | | |
|---|---|---|
| 3:30pm | Shuffleboard tournament | Deck 14 |
| 4:00pm | Basketball tournament | Deck 16 |

**4:00pm** Pools, Deck 13
**Towelball– Team game**

| | | |
|---|---|---|
| 4:30pm | Caribbean line dancing | Pools, Deck 13 |
| 5:00pm | Aerobics & stretching | Pools, Deck 13 |

Sports equipment, mini-golf, tennis & table-tennis, racquets, balls, playing cards, table soccer, will be available from **12:00pm** to **3:00pm** and from **5:00pm** to **7:00pm** at the towel distribution (**Deck 13**) showing the MSC Cruise Card.

**10:15pm Bar l'Incontro, Deck 5, portside**
### FRIENDS OF BILL W. MEETING

# Our night on board

With The Entertainment Team

## Savannah Bar, Deck 6

**7:45pm** **Elvis Game**

**9:30pm** **Bachata Dance Lesson**

**10:30pm** *Miss Orchestra*

**Women: it's your moment!**
With a surprise from the Entertainment Team

## Shaker Lounge, Deck 7

**11:15pm** **Karaoke**

---

## INFORMATION

##### NAUTICAL INFORMATION
Around 5:20pm, once left the pilot, we will take a North East route. Keeping a distance of 3 nautical miles from the Mexican Island, we will take as a still point the Punta Molas lighthouse (Northest part of Cozumel) and around 5:50pm we will sail along the coast in direction of Georgetown.

### IMPORTANT NOTICE
Please do not occupy the sun beds with towels once having left the pool area. Thank you for your co-operation.

### Today Free Movie on your ITV
"CHARLIE WILSON'S WAR" Comedy
and **Tonight** at 10:00pm
**Pools, Deck 13**
**(on the maxi-screen)**

## Miniclub Activities
8:00pm  R32 Disco, Deck 14
**BABY CRAZY DISCO**
8:45pm  Cafeteria La Piazzetta, Deck 13
**ICE-CREAM PARTY**

**Teenagers Meeting Point**
**(13-18 Years old)**
3:30pm R32 Disco, Deck 14 **MEETING POINT**
4:00pm Barracuda Bar, Deck 13 **TABLE TENNIS**

### MUSIC IN THE LOUNGES

**L'Incontro Bar, Deck 5 & The Purple & Zaffiro Bar, Deck 6**
5:00pm-5:45pm; 7:15pm-8:30pm; 9:00pm-10:00pm; 10:30pm-11:30pm
Latin american music with *Los Paraguayos*

**The Amber Piano Bar, Deck 6**
5:00pm-6:00pm; 7:00pm-8:30pm; 9:00pm-10:00pm
Evergreen with *Fabrizio e Ivana*
10:00pm-1:00am          Pianobar with *Edo*

**The Savannah Bar, Deck 6**
6:30pm-7:00pm; 11:45pm-1:00am
Pianobar with *Ottawa Duo*
7:15pm-8:30pm; 9:00pm-9:30pm; 10:00pm-10:30pm;
11:00pm-11:45pm   International music with *Ocean Band*

**The Shaker Lounge, Deck 7**
8:00pm-9:00pm; 10:30pm-11:15pm
Pianobar wirh *Ottawa Duo*
9:00pm-10:30pm; 12:00am-1:00am
Music for dancing with *Popcorn Band*

**La Cantinella Wine Bar, Deck 7**
5:00pm-5:30pm; 7:30pm-8:15pm; 9:15pm-10:15pm;
10:30pm-11:15pm; 11:30pm-12:00am
Notes on the waves with *Igor*

**DISCO DANCE - R32 Disco, Deck 14**
11:45pm-...          with *Dj Mike*
The entrance of underage is not reccomended.

| YOUR EVENING'S EVENTS | SPECIALS TODAY |
|---|---|

## "COVENT GARDEN" THEATRE
(Entrance from Deck 6 & 7)

**7:00pm**  2<sup>nd</sup> Seating of Dinner

*7:00pm  2nd Seating of Dinner*

**8:30pm**  1<sup>st</sup> Seating of Dinner

*Your Cruise Director Marco presents:*

*No video cameras, video telephones, drinks or food in the Theatre. The Theatre is a no Smoking Area. In some scenes, laser effects, artificial and non-toxic smoke will be used.*
**Seats may not be reserved.**

---

### CHEF'S SURPRISE
11:30pm          served in the lounges

### *FRIED FANTASIES*

---

## DAILY COCKTAIL
Served in all bars

### "COSMOPOLITAN N. 2" $ 5.50
*Vodka, Cointreau, raspberry Brandy, Rose's Lime*

### NOT ALCOHOLIC COCKTAIL
### "ALICE IN WONDERLAND" $ 3.50
*Pineapple & Orange juice, grenadine, cream*

### DAILY COFFEE -"SPANISH COFFEE" $ 4.60
*Spanish Brandy, Cointreau, coffee and whipped cream*
**From 4:30pm to 8:00pm all Martini cocktails will be available at the Savannah Bar!**
**Shaker Lounge, Deck 7**
*Tonight you're the Bar Tender! It's your night! Our staff will bring at your table all you need and will guide you at the preparation. If you will do a good job we will hire you as Bar Tender!*

---

**Coffee Bars, Decks 5 and 6**
**All liqueurs will be served in a MSC glass that you can keep as souvenir!**

---

## BODY & MIND SPA Deck 13

**RELAX DAY**
Today with the purchase of 3
Sun Tanning
**You will pay just $ 25 instead of $ 39**
3 Sessions of Press therapy
for tired legs one session $ 52; 3 for $ 126

### SPECIAL OFFER !!!!!!
### Only today
30 Min. Hot stones therapy massage
For two $ 139 instead of $ 178 (save $ 39)
Shampoo and Blow-dry
$ 29 instead of $ 37 (save $ 8)
Men's cut $ 25 instead of $ 31 (save $ 6)

**For information and bookings, call 2732**

---

### SERVICES AND ENTERTAINMENT
*AT THE PRESS OF A BUTTON*
All cabins on MSC Orchestra are equipped with Interactive television (ITV). Select "Menù", and have fun! Using your remote control, you are able to book all excursions, purchase movies, order room services, and acess all the information you need. We remind you kindly to check your daily "free messages".

---

## DUFRY SHOPS

**TAX & DUTY FREE SHOPS ON BOARD, Deck 6**
**Discover our large selection of custom jewellery**
**DESIGNER COCKTAIL RINGS** from only **$13.95**
R.S.Covenant's fashion is unconditionally guaranteed for life! R.S.Covenat fashion is crafted in the same manner as 14/18k gold jewellery .
*Tequila tasting* From 7-8 pm Get 10% discount on your Tequila purchase
**COLOMBIAN EMERALDS INTERNATIONAL, deck 6**
**Fresh Water Pearls** – Treasures form the Sea, Fantastic collection started from as little as $14.99! Take part into the game 'find the fake Amber!'.

---

## PHOTOSHOP Deck 7

We inform you that at the Photo shop Deck 7 aft, you'll find the pictures of your cruise and all the photo-items that you may need during your vacation. My cruise DVD– We remind you that you can purchase the DVD of the MSC Orchestra translated in 5 languages with scenes of the ship and of the excursions.

## TODAY'S DINING TIMES

- **BREAKFAST**

| | | |
|---|---|---|
| Villa Borghese Restaurant | Deck 5 | 7:30am-9:30am |

- **BUFFET**

| | | |
|---|---|---|
| Self Service | Deck 13 | 6:30am-10:30am |

- **LUNCH (OPEN SEATING)**

| | | |
|---|---|---|
| Villa Borghese Restaurant | Deck 5 | 12:00pm-1:30pm |

- **BUFFET**

| | | |
|---|---|---|
| Self Service | Deck 13 | 12:00pm-3:00pm |

- **GRILL**

| | | |
|---|---|---|
| Caffetteria la Piazzetta | Deck 13 | 12:00pm-4:30pm |

- **TEA & SNACK**

| | |
|---|---|
| Caffetteria la Piazzetta-right side, Deck 13 | 3:30pm-4:30pm |
| **PIZZERIA**　　　Deck 13 | 5:00pm-9:00pm |

- **CASUAL DINNER**

*Cafeteria La Piazzetta-Portside*

| | | |
|---|---|---|
| | Deck 13 | 6:00pm-7:30pm |

- **DINNER**

*Villa Borghese Restaurant* Deck 5

| | |
|---|---|
| 1st Seating | 5:30pm |
| 2nd Seating | 8:00pm |

*Ibiscus Restaurant*　　Deck 6

| | |
|---|---|
| 1st Seating | 5:30pm |
| 2nd Seating | 8:00pm |

**We kindly remind you that it is not allowed to enter into the Restaurant with shorts and vests.**

*To offer you the finest service, please respect the above times. Restaurant doors will close 15 min. after opening.*

- **FRIED FANTASIES**

| | |
|---|---|
| Served in the lounges | 11:30pm |

---

### RESTAURANTS FOR AN UNFORGETTABLE EXPERIENCE

| | | |
|---|---|---|
| La Cantinella Wine Bar | Deck 7 | 4:00pm-1:00am |

**RESERVATIONS REQUIRED, CALL 99:**

| | | |
|---|---|---|
| Shanghai Chinese Restaurant | Deck 7 | 12:00pm-2:30pm |
| | | 7:00pm-11:00pm |
| Restaurant 4 Seasons (à la carte) Deck 13 | | 6:30pm-9:00pm |

For guests with reservation, the Restaurant will be open until 10:30pm.
Extra Services

---

## TODAY'S BAR OPENING HOURS

| | | |
|---|---|---|
| L'Incontro Bar (Starboard side) Coffee Bar Deck 5 | | 6:30am-12:00am |
| L'Incontro Bar(Port side) Coffee Bar | Deck 5 | 12:00pm-12:00am |
| Purple Bar - Coffee Bar | Deck 6 | 4:00pm-12:00am |
| Zaffiro Bar - Coffee Bar | Deck 6 | 4:00pm-12:00am |
| Amber Bar | Deck 6 | 8:00am-1:30am |
| Savannah Bar | Deck 6 | 4:30pm-1:00am |
| The Shaker Lounge Martini Bar | Deck 7 | 8:00pm-1:00am |
| La Cantinella Wine Bar | Deck 7 | 4:00pm-1:00am |
| La Cubana - Cigar Room | Deck 7 | 7:00pm-1:00am |
| Palm Beach Casino | Deck 7 | 6:00pm-... |
| Spa Bar - Vitamin Bar | Deck 13 | 9:00am-7:00pm |
| Barracuda Bar - Tropical Bar | Deck 13 | 10:00am-7:00pm |
| El Sombrero Bar-Ice Cream Parlour | Deck 13 | 8:00am-1:00am |
| La Piazzetta Cafeteria | Deck 13 | 6:30am-5:00pm |
| R32 Disco | Deck 14 | 11:00pm-... |

---

### OUR AGENT IN COZUMEL

ACS S.A. DE C.V.

*CALLE 6 NORTE ENTRE 10 Y 15 AV. APARADO 161 COZUMEL, Q. ROO MEXICO 77600*

Tel. 00 52 - 987 - 87 23779

---

## SERVICE DIRECTORY
### MEDICAL EMERGENCY NUMBER: 115

| | | |
|---|---|---|
| • **Front Desk - Reception** tel. 99 Deck 5 | | 24 hrs |
| - *Concierge* | tel. 99 | 5:00pm-10:00pm |
| • **Wake up calls** | | 24 hrs |
| tel. 99 | | |
| • **Room Service** | | 24 hrs |
| tel. 2720,2781 | | |
| • **Medical Centre** | Deck 5 | 8:00am-12:00pm |
| tel. 2660 | | 4:00pm-8:00pm |
| • **Tour Desk** | Deck 6 | 4:00pm-8:00pm |
| tel. 2804/2805 | | |
| • **Accounting Desk** | Deck 5 | 8:00am-11:00am |
| tel. 2807 | | 4:00pm-7:00pm |
| • **Exchange Office** | Deck 5 | 8:00am-11:00am |
| tel. 2806 | | 4:00pm-7:00pm |
| • **Shops** | Deck 6 | 5:00pm-12:00am |
| - *Jewellery* | tel. 2778 | |
| - *Cosmetics* | tel. 2773 | |
| - *Duty Free* | tel. 2774 | |
| - *Logo shop* | tel. 2775 | |
| - *Watch shop* | | |
| • **Internet Cafè** | Deck 7 | 24 hrs |
| • **Photo Shop** | Deck 7 | 5:00pm-11:30pm |
| Tel. 2706 | | |
| • **Palm Beach Casino** | Deck 7 | 5:20pm-... |
| Tel. 2698 | | |
| • **Slot Machines** | Deck 7 | 5:20pm-.... |
| Tel. 2868 | | |

*We remind you that only 18 and over are welcome in the Palm Beach Casino.*

| | | |
|---|---|---|
| • **Art Gallery** | Deck 7 | 8:00pm-10:00pm |
| tel. 6037 | | |
| • **Shopping guide** | Deck 5 | 7:00pm-9:00pm |
| • **Library** | Deck 7 | 3:30pm-6:30pm |
| Tel. 2868 | | |
| • **Swimming Pool** | Deck 13 | 7:00am-6:30pm |
| • **Jacuzzi** | Deck 13 | 7:00am-6:30pm |
| • **Tennis Court** | Deck 16 | 7:00am-8:00pm |

*Body & Mind Spa Beauty Farm, Deck 13*

| | | |
|---|---|---|
| • **Beauty Salon** | | 8:00am-8:00pm |
| tel. 2732 | | |
| • **Sauna - Steam Room** | | 9:00am-7:00pm |
| tel. 2732 | | |
| • **Massage Booking Desk** | | 8:00am-8:00pm |
| tel. 2732 | | |
| • **Gymnasium**, tel. 2875 | | 7:00am-7:00pm |

\* to be allowed to workout in the gym please fill in the health form that you can find at the Fitness Centre, deck 13.
Please come to the gym with sneakers.
*For over 14 only*

---

### MINI, JUNIOR & TEENS CLUB

- **Mini club** (3-6 years old)
9:00am-12:00pm; 3:00pm-6:00pm; 7:00pm-11:00pm
- **Juniors club** (7-12 years old) Deck 14
10:00am-12:00pm; 3:00pm-6:00pm; 7:00pm-11:00pm
- **Teens club** (13-18 years old) R32 Disco, Deck 14
3:30pm

For information and communications
Tel. 2877 / 2879

---

### UNFORGETTABLE DINING EXPERIENCE

We invite you to enjoy the view from a very special panoramic dinner table tonight, in the Restaurants:

| | |
|---|---|
| **4 Seasons** | Paying Menu<br>Deck 13  6:30pm-9:00pm<br>**Menu 'à la carte' $ 25.00** |

# NORWEGIAN CRUISE LINE

**7665 Corporate Center Drive**
**Miami, FL 33126**
**(800) 327-7030**
**(305) 436-4000**
**www.ncl.com**

*Norwegian Breakaway*: entered service in 2013; 144,017 GRT; 1,062 × 130 feet; 4,000-passenger capacity (double occupancy); 2,000 cabins; international officers and crew, cruises to Bermuda and Caribbean from New York (Category C—not rated)

*Norwegian Dawn*: entered service in 2002; renovated in 2011; 92,250 GRT; 965 × 105 feet; 2,244-passenger capacity (double occupancy); 1,112 cabins; international officers and crew; cruises Bermuda and the Caribbean from Boston, Miami, and Tampa (Category C—four stars)

*Norwegian Epic*: entered service in 2010; 155,873 GRT; 1,081 × 133 feet; 4,100-passenger capacity (double occupancy); 2,050 cabins; international officers and crew; cruises from Miami to the Caribbean and in Europe from Barcelona (Category C—five+ stars)

Courtyard Suites (Category B—six stars)

*Norwegian Jade* (formerly *Pride of Hawaii*): entered service in 2006; renovated in 2011; 93,502 GRT; 965 × 106 feet; 2,402-passenger capacity (double occupancy); 1,201 cabins; international officers and crew; year-round cruises in Europe (Category C—four+ stars)

*Norwegian Jewel*, *Norwegian Pearl*, and *Norwegian Gem*: entered service in 2005, 2006, and 2007, respectively; 93,502 GRT; 965 × 105 feet; 2,376-, 2,394-, and 2,394-passenger capacity, respectively; 1,188 to 1,197 cabins; international officers and crew; *Jewel* cruises to the Bahamas, Florida, Caribbean, and Alaska; *Pearl* cruises to Alaska, Bahamas, Florida, the Panama Canal, and the Caribbean from Miami; *Gem* cruises the Caribbean, Canada, New England, Bahamas/Florida, and Bermuda (Category C—five stars)

*Norwegian Sky* (formerly *Pride of Aloha* and *Norwegian Sky*): entered service in 1999; rechristened in 2008; renovated in 2009; 77,104 GRT; 848 × 105 feet; 2,002-passenger capacity (double occupancy); 1,001 cabins; international officers and crew; three- and four-night cruises from Miami to the Bahamas (Category C—not rated)

*Norwegian Spirit* (formerly *Super Star Leo*): entered service in 1998; rechristened in 2004; renovated in 2008 and 2011; 75,338 GRT; 881 × 105 feet; 2,018-passenger capacity; 1,009 cabins; international officers and crew; cruises to the Mediterranean from Barcelona and Venice (Category C—not rated)

*Norwegian Sun*: entered service in 2001; refurbished in 2011; 78,309 GRT; 848 × 105 feet; 1,936-passenger capacity (double occupancy); 968 cabins; international officers and crew; cruises to Alaska from Vancouver and to Caribbean from Miami (Category C—four+ stars)

*Norwegian Star*: entered service in 2001; refurbished in 2010; 91,740 GRT; 965 × 105 feet; 2,348-passenger capacity (double occupancy); 1,174 cabins; international officers and crew; cruises the Caribbean from New Orleans, Europe from Copenhagen, Panama Canal from Mexico, and the Mexican Riviera from Los Angeles (Category C—four+ stars)

*Pride of America*: entered service in 2005; 80,843 GRT; 921 × 105 feet; 2,138-passenger capacity; 1,069 cabins (double occupancy); American officers and crew; seven-night cruises in Hawaiian Islands from Honolulu (Category C—not rated)

(Medical facilities on all ships: C-0; P-1; EM; CLS; N-1; CM; PD; EKG; PO; OX; X)

Miami-based Norwegian Cruise Line (Norwegian) was formerly a subsidiary of the Oslo-based Norwegian Cruise Line Holding ASA/NRW, formerly Klosters Rederi A/S, a shipping company owned by the Kloster family since the turn of the nineteenth century. In 1996, the name of the parent company was changed to Norwegian Cruise Line Ltd. During the period extending from late 1999 through early 2000, the stock was acquired by the Asian-based Star Cruises, renamed Genting Hong Kong. In August 2007, a private equity group, Apollo Management LP, agreed to make a $1 billion cash equity investment in Norwegian. Under the terms of the investment, which closed in January 2008, Apollo became a 50 percent owner of Norwegian Cruise Line. Apollo Management LP also owns Prestige Management, parent company to Oceania Cruises and Regent Seven Seas Cruises. Today, Norwegian has eleven ships in service and two four-thousand-berth vessels for delivery in the spring of 2013 and the spring of 2014, respectively.

From 1968 to 1971, Norwegian introduced four similarly designed bread-and-butter cruise ships. First came the MS *Starward* in 1968, followed by the MS

*Skyward* in 1969, and the MS *Southward* and MS *Sunward II* in 1971. All four ships were intended to bring the cruise experience to upper-middle-class and middle-class America. Passengers received numerous meals and loads of food, continuous activities and entertainment, several popular ports of call, adequate service and accommodations, and the excitement of cruising at reasonable prices. All four ships ceased being operated by Norwegian during the 1990s and were replaced with newer vessels.

The cabin stewards and waiters are a mixture of Filipino, Romanian, Caribbean, Asian, and Central and South American. They are generally friendly, competent, and efficient.

In 2000, Norwegian became an innovator for the industry by announcing its intention to eventually convert all of its vessels in order to offer Freestyle Cruising. This allows passengers to dine in any of the dining venues aboard ship whenever and with whomever they want. Although this has been the agenda on the smaller luxury-class ships for decades, Norwegian Cruise Line is the first cruise line to offer this widely desired dining program on large mass-market vessels. In addition to one or more main dining rooms, lido buffet, and outdoor grill areas, there are six additional specialty restaurants on the *Sun* and *Dawn*, seven additional on the *Star*, and eight or more additional on the *Pride of America*, *Norwegian Jade*, *Jewel*, *Pearl*, and *Gem*. On *Norwegian Epic*, there are approximately twenty venues. The dining experience on all ships has greatly improved since the takeover of the cruise line by Star Cruises (now known as Genting Hong Kong). Gratuities of $12 a day per person are added to the passengers' onboard account and can be prepaid or paid on the last day of the cruise.

The itineraries have shifted over the years, but when cruising in the Caribbean, the ships normally cover three or four ports, including a beach party at Norwegian's privately owned island paradise in the Bahamas, Great Stirrup Cay. This island received a $20 million upgrade in facilities that was completed in 2011, including a new tender facility, new food stations, additional bars, private beachfront cabanas, and a kids' play area.

All Norwegian ships feature a Dive In program, where passengers receive instruction and supervision in snorkeling, both aboard ship and while ashore. The Sports Afloat program offers a variety of exercise, aerobic, yoga, and fitness classes throughout the day as well as organized walks both on the ships and at various ports of call.

In 1988, the 42,000-ton MS *Seaward* joined the fleet, accommodating 1,518 passengers, double occupancy. In 1998, she was renamed *Norwegian Sea*, but in 2004, she was transferred to parent company Star Cruises (now Genting Hong Kong).

At 50,764 GRT each, the MS *Dreamward* and MS *Windward* entered service in December 1992 and June 1993, respectively. In 1998, both ships were stretched, and now each carries 1,747 passengers. The ships were then renamed *Norwegian Dream* and *Norwegian Wind*. In 2007, *Norwegian Wind* was transferred to parent company Star Cruises. In 2008, *Norwegian Dream* was sold to Louis Cruises along with the *Norwegian Majesty*. The 34,242-ton, 1,078-passenger *Norwegian Crown* was sold off to Fred. Olsen Cruise Line in 2007.

The 77,104-ton, 2,002-passenger *Norwegian Sky* joined the fleet in August 1999, the first new ship to be built by Norwegian since the early 1990s. She was reflagged into the U.S. registry and renamed *Pride of Aloha* in 2004. In 2008 she was transferred to Star Cruises (now Genting Hong Kong) and then transferred back to Norwegian

Cruise Line. In 2009, she was refurbished with new furnishings and upholstery in the public areas, fourteen suites, and Adagio, the Italian restaurant. Also new food stations were installed in the Garden Café.

The *Norwegian Sun*, sister ship to *Norwegian Sky*, entered service in the fall of 2001 with numerous innovations, including larger cabins with greater storage space, more lovely and tasteful décor in the public areas, and an abundance of specialty restaurants, all with panoramic ocean views. Most accommodations measure 150 to 173 square feet with 48-foot balconies. The inside cabins are 145 square feet and outside cabins without balconies are 150 square feet. Suites range in size from 215 to 355 square feet with balconies from 48 to 149 square feet. The four top-of-the-line owner's suites come in at 502 square feet with 258-foot balconies sporting outdoor Jacuzzis. The recent refurbishment in 2010 included updated décor in all thirty-three of the ship's suites; improvements to the Kids Crew area, which offers complimentary children's programs; the addition of Moderno Churrascaria, the line's new Brazilian steak house; and overall replacement of carpets and wall coverings in public areas.

In the fall of 2001, the 91,000-ton, 2,240-passenger *Superstar Libra*, originally intended to sail for Star Cruises (now Genting Hong Kong), was transferred to Norwegian, named *Norwegian Star*, and positioned for Hawaiian cruises. Today, she offers itineraries in the Caribbean and Bermuda from Tampa, New York, and New Orleans. Although not as traditionally decorated as the *Sun* and possessing a somewhat confusing traffic pattern, she boasts many alternative specialty restaurants at sea, as well as two of the largest, most indulgent courtyard villas and garden villas afloat (each suite measuring 5,000 square feet with 1,722 square feet of rooftop terrace gardens).

*Norwegian Dawn* joined the fleet in 2002. She offers itineraries to Bermuda and the Caribbean from Miami, Boston, and Tampa. The ship went into dry dock during the spring of 2011, and fifty-eight new staterooms were added including four new deluxe owners suites and ten new family suites.

Two sister ships with numerous modifications, *Norwegian Jewel* and *Norwegian Pearl*, joined the fleet in 2005 and 2006. A third, *Norwegian Gem*, joined the fleet in 2007. The *Jewel* has sixty-eight additional cabins and can carry 2,376 passengers (double occupancy), whereas the *Pearl* and *Gem* have 2,394 lower berths. Many of the staterooms can interconnect to create two-, three-, four-, or five-bedroom areas. In addition to the two giant garden villas at 5,000 square feet each, these ships offer the Haven by Norwegian, a ship within a ship complex consisting of ten exclusive 572-square-foot courtyard villas and two 928-square-foot deluxe owner's suites that include numerous amenities and share their own private pool, Jacuzzi, sundeck, and small gym. The main accommodations include 412 inside cabins (143 square feet), 243 ocean-view cabins (161 square feet), 360 ocean-view with balcony cabins (205 square feet), 134 minisuites (284 square feet), 4 romance suites (460 square feet), 10 penthouse suites (572 square feet), and 2 deluxe owner's suites (928 square feet). Twenty-seven accommodations are equipped for the physically impaired. The full suites and villas enjoy butler service. Both full suites and minisuites have a special concierge who will make arrangements for services and dining reservations on board ship and for shore excursions. The inside, ocean-view, and balcony cabins (nonsuite) are not as desirable and offer few stateroom amenities.

There are ten dining venues: two main dining rooms; an upscale steak house; a French and an Italian restaurant; Moderno Churrascaria, the line's new Brazilian steak house; an Asian complex featuring Japanese and Thai/Chinese selections, sushi and sashimi, and a teppanyaki room; an indoor/outdoor buffet-style restaurant; and a twenty-four-hour food-court-style restaurant. The numerous dining options and the dining experiences are excellent and the strong point of these ships.

Public areas include a new bar central, which features a martini bar, champagne and wine bar, and beer and whisky pub all connected but unique in their own way; a three-story art nouveau-styled theater; a large casino; an art gallery; a library; a cardroom; seven thousand square feet of shopping area; a sports bar/nightclub; seven additional bars and lounges; a cigar club; a chapel; a medical center; several meeting rooms; and two pools, one with a waterfall and three Jacuzzis and the other with a water slide and two Jacuzzis. Internet connections are in all staterooms, and wireless Internet is available around the ship. There is also an Internet café. Guests can rent laptops (but there is limited availability). The spas feature twenty treatment rooms, thermal suites with steam, sauna, Jacuzzis, thalassotherapy pools, and relaxation areas (all available at a surcharge for those not taking a spa treatment). The fitness centers are quite large and well equipped, and each piece of cardio equipment has its own flat-screen TV. The sports deck includes a combination full tennis court/basketball court, shuffleboard, golf nets, ping pong, and a jogging track. The Kid's Club includes a cinema, nursery, and sleep/rest areas. In addition, there is a theme teen club for ages thirteen to seventeen years and a video arcade. The *Pearl* and *Gem* also feature rock-climbing walls and bowling alleys.

The line formerly had a big presence in the Hawaiian cruise market with the *Pride of Aloha*, *Pride of Hawaii*, and *Pride of America* offering seven-day cruises. However, in 2008, various problems and lack of bookings resulted in the *Pride of Hawaii* being renamed and reflagged *Norwegian Jade* and transferred out of the Hawaiian market. The *Pride of Aloha* was transferred to parent company Star Cruises (now Genting Hong Kong) and then back again to Norwegian, where it adopted its original name, *Norwegian Sky*.

Of the 1,069 cabins on *Pride of America* (the only remaining ship of the Norwegian Cruise Line America fleet), 661 sport balconies. The average cabin is 178 square feet with two lower beds that convert to queen size, a small sitting area, a TV, a private safe, and a hair dryer. The suites are quite a bit larger and include a concierge lounge and butler service. The "best of America" theme and décor are carried throughout the ship.

There are eight restaurants, including the 496-seat Liberty and 628-seat Skyline main dining rooms, Jefferson's Bistro, Lazy J Texas Steakhouse, East Meets West (offering Asian cuisine with a teppanyaki room), the Cadillac Diner, Aloha Café (with numerous buffet islands), and Little Italy (located in a section of the buffet restaurant and featuring Italian favorites at dinnertime). Key West Bar Grill serves up burgers and grilled chicken. A reservation service with monitors located around the ship provides waiting times and seating information.

Public facilities include the Santa Fe Spa and Fitness Center, numerous lounges, a cardroom, shops, an Internet center, children's and teen areas, a children's cinema, a conference area with breakout rooms, a large pool area, whirlpools, a bungee trampoline, and a gyro-chair.

*Pride* of *America* offers seven-day destination-oriented itineraries from Honolulu on Oahu, calling at Hilo and Kona on the Big Island of Hawaii and at the Islands of Kauai and Maui.

*Norwegian Jade*, originally named *Pride of Hawaii*, sister ship to the *Jewel, Pearl,* and *Gem*, has some variations in décor. Ten restaurants are featured, including Cagney's Steak House, Blue Lagoon, Le Bistro, Moderno Churrascaria, the line's new Brazilian steak house, Papa's Italian Kitchen, buffet restaurants, Jasmine Garden Restaurant (featuring a sushi bar and a teppanyaki table), and a Pacific fusion restaurant. Like the other sister ships, there are two 5,000-square-foot garden villas and ten courtyard villas sharing a private courtyard and sundeck with interconnecting cabins to create two-, three-, four-, or five-bedroom areas. She also includes four Romance Suites, which are 460 square feet, with a special romantic décor. In 2008, the ship was shifted to the European market.

Pricing can be a bit confusing on all the ships since the brochure prices, though relatively high for mass-market ships, are generally heavily discounted for early bookings or during slow seasons.

Norwegian has announced that over the next few years, the bulk of the company will consist solely of recently constructed ships, and eventually, the older, less competitive vessels will be transferred to service less demanding markets.

*Norwegian Epic*, a 155,873-ton, 4,100-passenger ship with 1,315 outside cabins featuring balconies, was delivered in 2010, offering eastern Caribbean itineraries from Miami in the winter and Mediterranean cruises during the warmer months. The ship has numerous innovative venues. On open deck, there is an aqua park with tube slides and a rock-climbing wall; rappelling wall; bungee trampoline line; a sport court for basketball, volleyball, and soccer; and pools, whirlpools, and lounge areas. In addition, there are six bowling alleys, three separate kids' and teens' activity areas, twenty dining venues, a comedy club, a jazz club, and multiple entertainment venues.

The Ice Bar, with temperatures below 17F, is literally a frozen vault with walls, tables, stools, glasses, and a bar of solid ice. Passengers are given fur coats, gloves, and hats as well as iced vodka. Spice $H_2O$, located around the aft swimming pool, is an adults-only area. It consists of terraced decks and a giant movie screen. In the morning, spicy Bloody Marys are served accompanied by music; at noon, Asian-inspired food is served; and at sunset, guests can luxuriate with glasses of champagne as a floor covers the pool, allowing passengers to dance under the stars.

The Haven by Norwegian is a private club composed of sixty private suites and villas ranging in size from 322 to 852 square feet on two private decks atop ship in a courtyard villa complex featuring two whirlpools, a gym, a sauna, a sundeck, an indoor/outdoor dining, a bar/nightclub, and a concierge lounge. This is truly a ship within a ship, and sailing in this complex is a quite different experience from sailing elsewhere on the ship.

The *Epic* introduces a new category of inside staterooms for budget travelers—the Studios. These staterooms, at one hundred square feet, maximize space and feature a large round window that looks out into the corridor with customized changing light effects that mirror different stages of the day. These accommodations occupy two decks and have key-card access to the Living Room, a two-story shared private lounge. The lounge has its own concierge, bar, room service, and two large TV screens.

The spa balcony, deluxe balcony staterooms, and suites located within the spa have complimentary access to the ship's thermal center and state-of-the-art fitness center.

The 851 balcony staterooms enjoy a unique design with curved walls, extensive storage, and unusual split bathrooms, the subject of varied opinions.

The *Epic* features more dining venues than on the other Norwegian ships and, in addition to the traditional main dining rooms and buffet facilities, offers a dinner theater with a Cirque Dreams and Dinner show; a supper club with music; Italian, French, and Brazilian restaurants; the signature Cagney's Steak House; and several Asian restaurants. Numerous evening entertainment options include such well-known acts as the Blue Man Group, Second City Comedy Troupe, Howl at the Moon, and Legends in Concert. Other entertainment options include a jazz and blues club, the largest casino at sea, disco dancing, a total of six bowling alleys, and the above-described Spice H$_2$O and the Ice Bar. All Norwegian ships offer around the clock pizza delivery service to the cabins.

Two new 143,000-ton vessels were delivered in 2013 and 2014. The first was named *Norwegian Breakaway* and the second *Norwegian Getaway*. Each has 1,024 balconies and 238 minisuites and have a more traditional cabin design than the *Epic*. The ships also have studio staterooms for single passengers as well as the deluxe area known as "The Haven," the ship within a ship concept. All staterooms have beds with faux-leather headboards with recess lighting accommodating books and electronic reading devices and computers and twenty-six-inch flat-screen TVs adjustable between the beds and the sofas. There are seventeen dining venues and twelve bars.

Innovations on these ships include a new seafood restaurant, "Ocean Blu" featuring traditional seafood, a raw bar and sushi; a new area called "The Waterfront," an outdoor promenade where eight restaurants, lounges, and entertainment areas open to the open deck providing outdoor seating as well as indoor seating; and a three-deck-high atrium connected to all of the dining and amusement areas on the ship.

In 2012, Chef's Table was added fleet-wide and is offered once per cruise to a limit of twelve passengers at a cost of $89 per person.

## Strong Points

The ships built since 2000 are attractive modern ships with a plethora of facilities and are welcome additions to the mass cruise market. Freestyle Cruising, as it is executed on Norwegian, offers a uniquely large number of dining possibilities, with excellent cuisine, making the cruise experience akin to dining out at a different shore-side restaurant each evening. Passengers receive a good deal more for their money on Norwegian than on some competing cruise lines. Passengers opting for the full suites and villas enjoy the luxury and pampering offered by more expensive cruise lines. *Pride of America* offers a cruise for all members of the family wishing to visit the Hawaiian Islands. The new *Norwegian Epic, Norwegian Breakaway*, and *Norwegian Getaway* are three of the more innovative ships launched this century.

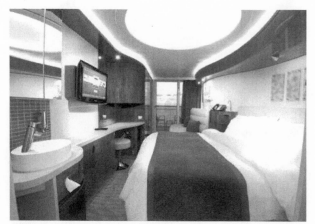

*Balcony Stateroom on Norwegian Epic, courtesy Norwegian Cruise Line*

*Aqua Park on Norwegian Epic, courtesy Norwegian Cruise Line*

*Cagney's Steakhouse, Norwegian Epic, courtesy Norwegian Cruise Line*

*Courtyard lido area, Norwegian Epic, courtesy Norwegian Cruise Line*

*Norwegian Breakaway, courtesy Norwegian Cruise Line*

# FAVORITE SELECTIONS

## Starters

Crispy Fried Pork and Vegetable Spring Roll
SWEET AND SPICY DIP

✓ *Norwegian Smoked Salmon Tartare
AVOCADO, CUCUMBER, LEMON MUSTARD DRESSING

Wild Mushroom Quesadilla
GUACAMOLE, PICO DE GALLO

French Onion Soup
CHEESE CROUTON

Garden Broccoli Bisque
WHITE CHEDDAR CHEESE

✓ Mixed Seasonal Greens
CHOICE OF 1000 ISLAND, BLUE CHEESE DRESSING
OR BALSAMIC VINAIGRETTE

Caesar Salad
ROMAINE LETTUCE, HERB CROUTONS

## Entrées

*Beef Rib-Eye Steak
BAKED POTATO, SPINACH,
GARLIC ROASTED ROMA TOMATO

✓ Grilled Chicken Breast
MASHED POTATOES, BROCCOLI FLORETS

*Pork Tenderloin Medallions
ROASTED BLISS POTATOES, SPINACH,
MUSHROOM CREAM SAUCE

✓ *Fillet of Salmon
MASHED POTATOES, FRESH GREEN BEANS,
LEMON CAPER BUTTER

Spaghetti with Grated Parmesan
CHOICE OF BEEF BOLOGNESE,
CREAMY BACON CARBONARA
OR TOMATO MARINARA SAUCE

# FAVORITE SELECTIONS

## Starters

Crispy Fried Pork and Vegetable Spring Roll
SWEET AND SPICY DIP

✓ *Norwegian Smoked Salmon Tartare
AVOCADO, CUCUMBER, LEMON MUSTARD DRESSING

Wild Mushroom Quesadilla
GUACAMOLE, PICO DE GALLO

French Onion Soup
CHEESE CROUTON

Garden Broccoli Bisque
WHITE CHEDDAR CHEESE

✓ Mixed Seasonal Greens
CHOICE OF 1000 ISLAND, BLUE CHEESE DRESSING
OR BALSAMIC VINAIGRETTE

Caesar Salad
ROMAINE LETTUCE, HERB CROUTONS

## Entrées

*Beef Rib-Eye Steak
BAKED POTATO, SPINACH,
GARLIC ROASTED ROMA TOMATO

✓ Grilled Chicken Breast
MASHED POTATOES, BROCCOLI FLORETS

*Pork Tenderloin Medallions
ROASTED BLISS POTATOES, SPINACH,
MUSHROOM CREAM SAUCE

✓ *Fillet of Salmon
MASHED POTATOES, FRESH GREEN BEANS,
LEMON CAPER BUTTER

Spaghetti with Grated Parmesan
CHOICE OF BEEF BOLOGNESE,
CREAMY BACON CARBONARA
OR TOMATO MARINARA SAUCE

*Dinner Menu, courtesy Norwegian Cruise Line*

## NCL Freestyle Daily Activities

### Stuff for "morning people"...

| | | |
|---|---|---|
| Early Morning Stretch (Free) | Fitness Center, Deck 12, Fwd | 7:30am |
| Total Body Conditioning (Free) | Fitness Center, Deck 12, Fwd | 8:00am |
| Tennis Play with your Fellow Guests | Sports Court, Deck 13, Aft | 8:00am-10:00am |
| Golf Clubs Available | Great Outdoors Bar, Deck 12, Aft | 8:00am-5:00pm |
| Common Skin & allergy problems of Cats and Dogs | Spinnaker Lounge, Deck 13, Fwd | 9:00am |
| Service Club Meets | Whiskey Bar, Deck 6, Mid | 9:00am |
| Library (Sudoku & Trivia Available) | Deck 12, Fwd | 9:00am-11:00am |
| Origami with your Host Elwyn - bring a crisp dollar bill | Whiskey Bar, Deck 6, Mid | 9:45am |
| Morning Trivia | Bar City, Deck 6, Mid | 10:00am |
| Rock Climb Wall (Weather Permitting) | Deck 14, Aft | 10:00am-1:00pm |
| Aqua Kid's Club: Port Play Group Fun ($5/hour) | Deck 12, Mid | 10:00am-5:00pm |
| Sport Court | Deck 13, Aft | 10:00am-5:00pm |
| 2 for 1 Bowling while in port | Deck 7, Aft | 10:00am-6:00pm |
| Bowling Alley (Must be 6 years or older to play) | Bliss Ultra Lounge, Deck 7, Aft | 10:00am-Close |
| Board Games with your Fellow Guests | Card Room, Deck 12, Fwd | 10:15am |
| Nintendo Wii - On the Big Screen | Crystal Atrium, Deck 7, Mid | 10:30am-Noon |
| Golf Putting Challenge | Bar City, Deck 6, Mid | 11:00am |

### Add pizzazz to your afternoon...

| | | |
|---|---|---|
| Casino Pool Deck Gaming | Deck 12, Fwd | Noon |
| Ping Pong Challenge | Deck 12, Fwd, Portside | 12:30pm |
| Rock Climbing Wall (Weather Permitting) | Deck 14, Aft | 1:00pm-5:00pm |
| Shuffleboard Challenge | Deck 7, Promenade, Starboard | 1:30pm |
| NFL Live: Jacksonville vs. Pittsburgh | Crystal Atrium, Deck 7, Mid | Satellite Pending, 2:00pm |
| Library (Sudoku & Trivia Available) | Deck 12, Fwd | 2:00pm-4:00pm |
| Bridge Play with your Fellow Guests | Card Room, Deck 12, Fwd | 3:00pm |
| Fun Trivia | Bar City, Deck 6, Mid | 4:45pm |
| Spin to Win Free Pull for CAS members | Pearl Club Casino, Deck 6 Fwd | 4:00pm-6:00pm |
| Trio Los Hernandez - Harmonies & Guitars | Tahitian Poolside, Deck 12, Mid | 4:00pm-7:00pm |
| Frank's Place - Continuous Music of Sinatra | Star Bar, Deck 13, Mid | 4:00pm-Close |
| Bingo on the H₂O | Spinnaker Lounge, Deck 13, Fwd | 5:00pm |
| NFL Live: Detroit vs. San Diego | Crystal Atrium, Deck 7, Mid | Satellite Pending, 5:15pm |
| Friends of Bill W. | The Chapel, Deck 13, Fwd | 5:00pm |
| Mihail Polak - Mellow Piano and Cocktails | Bar City, Deck 6, Mid | 5:30pm-8:45pm |

### Everything's hotter when the sun goes down...

| | | |
|---|---|---|
| Guess the Picasso | Art Gallery, Deck 7, Aft | 6:30pm-9:30pm |
| Pearl Showband Ballroom Dancing | Spinnaker Lounge, Deck 13, Fwd | 6:45pm-7:30pm/7:45pm-8:30pm |
| Aqua Kid's Club | Deck 12, Mid | 7:00pm-10:00pm |
| Magical Showtime: featuring Richard Burr and Josette | Stardust Theater, Decks 6 & 7, Fwd | 7:30pm |
| NFL Live: Washington vs. New York | Crystal Atrium, Deck 7, Mid | Satellite Pending, 9:00pm |
| Trio Los Hernandez - Harmonies & Guitars | Tahitian Poolside, Deck 12, Mid | 8:00pm-10:00pm |
| Battle of the Sexes Game Show | Spinnaker Lounge, Deck 13, Fwd | 8:30pm |
| Sailing Solo and Singles Mix | Star Bar, Deck 13, Mid | 8:30pm |
| Ron Arduini - Lyric Elegance | Bar City, Deck 6, Mid | 9:00pm-Close |
| Great Dance Music with Harmony & Rhythm | Spinnaker Lounge, Deck 13, Fwd | 9:30pm-10:15pm |
| Magical Showtime: featuring Richard Burr and Josette | Stardust Theater, Decks 6 & 7, Fwd | 9:30pm |
| Friends of Dorothy a gathering for our GLBT guests | Bliss, Port VIP section, Deck 7, Aft | 9:30pm |
| DJ Patrick – plays the hits | Bliss Ultra Lounge, Deck 7, Aft | 10:00pm-Close |
| "Name That Tune" with Ron Arduini | Bar City, Deck 6, Mid | 10:15pm |
| 70's Groove Party | Spinnaker Lounge, Deck 13, Fwd | 10:30pm |
| Bliss Ultra White Party | Bliss Ultra Lounge, Deck 7, Aft | 11:30pm |
| Paradise Lotto Drawing- Jackpot over $139,000! | Pearl Club Casino, Deck 6, Fwd | 11:30pm |
| Double Bonus Points to be earned on slots | Pearl Club Casino, Deck 6, Fwd | Midnight-2:00am |

**Ok, we know this looks like a schedule (gasp!)**
**But, remember, you're free to whatever!**

## Bar Services

| | |
|---|---|
| **Java Café & Juice Bar** Deck 7, Mid | 7:00am-Close |
| Morning Specials and Fresh Juices | |
| **Great Outdoors Bar** Deck 12, Aft | 7:00am-Close |
| **Topsiders Bar** Deck 12, Mid | 8:00am-Close |
| **Bliss Ultra Lounge** Deck 7, Aft | 2:00pm-Close |
| **Sky High Bar** Deck 13, Fwd | 3:00pm-Close |
| **Star Bar** Deck 13, Mid | 4:00pm-Close |
| **Spinnaker Bar** Deck 13, Fwd | 4:00pm-Close |
| **Bar City** Deck 6, Mid | 4:00pm-Close |
| **Champagne Bar** Deck 6, Mid | 4:00pm-Close |
| **Maltings Bar** Deck 6, Mid | 4:00pm-Close |

## Guest Services

| | |
|---|---|
| **Metro Video Arcade** Deck 12, Mid | Open 24 Hours |
| **Reception Desk** Deck 7, Mid (#00) | Open 24 Hours |
| **Internet Café** Deck 7, Aft | Open 24 Hours |
| **Body Waves Fitness** Deck 12, Fwd | Open 24 Hours |
| **Onboard Credit Desk** Deck 7, Mid | 8:00am-10:00am / 6:00pm-8:30pm |
| **Internet Manager** Deck 7, Aft | 8:00am-10:00am / 4:00pm-6:00pm / 7:00pm-10:00pm |
| **Tahitian Pool\*** Deck 12, Mid | 8:00am-10:00pm |
| **Jacuzzis\*** Deck 12, Mid | 8:00am-Midnight |
| **South Pacific Spa & Salon** Deck 12, Fwd | 8:00am-10:00pm |
| **Medical Center** Deck 4, Mid | 8:30am-10:00am / 4:00pm-5:00pm |
| **Photo Gallery** Deck 7, Aft | 8:30am-Arrival / 5:00pm-11:00pm |
| **Water Slide** Deck 12, Mid | 9:00am-6:00pm |
| **Pearl Club Casino** Deck 6, Fwd | 2:00pmApprox-Close |
| **Cruise Consultant** Deck 7, Mid | 5:00pm-9:00pm |
| **Port Shopping Representative** Deck 7, Aft | 6:30pm-8:00pm |
| **Art Gallery** Deck 7, Aft | 6:30pm-9:30pm |
| **Gift Shops** Deck 7, Fwd | 6:00pm-11:00pm |
| **Shore Excursions Desk** Deck 7, Mid | 7:00pm-9:00pm |

*Pools and Jacuzzi will be open as long as it is weather permitting. Forward Jacuzzis and Pool, Deck 12, are for adults only. Please, no reserving of deck chairs. Items left on deck chairs for more than 30 minutes will be removed and placed at Reception, Deck 7, Mid

**Walking & Jogging:** Deck 13 is a walking/jogging track open 24/7. Deck 7 is a walking-only track; it's open 9am-9pm. Remember, all sports play is at your own risk.
**Jacuzzis & Pools:** Glass & bottles can't be brought into any of the pools or hot tubs; neither can children in diapers or pull-ups, including swimmers.
**Casino:** You have to be 18 (and have ID) to gamble or be in the casino. Sorry, but no winnings can be paid to any person or bets in violation. Also, drinks or glassware can't be taken out; pipes or cigars can't be taken in, but cigarette smoking is ok. Slot winnings of $1200 and above are subject to W2-G tax withholding.
**Liquor Purchased Ashore:** Any liquor purchased in our ports of call will be collected and returned to you at the end of the voyage.
**Restaurant Cancellations:** To ensure each of our guests receive our best service, we can cancel your dinner reservation for 15 minutes. If you need to cancel, please do so by 5:00pm on the day of your reservation to avoid having the cover charge for up to two guests applied to your account.
**Smoking Policy:** Smoking is only allowed inside the Casino, staterooms, Corona Cigar Club and designated outside deck areas. Cigars are only permitted in the Corona Cigar Club, Deck 6, Mid.

## Freestyle Dining

Specialty Restaurants reservations can be made for the day of or the next day before dinner time. To make your reservations, call extension number 050 or visit us on the desk located at Mambo's Restaurant, Deck 8, Mid.

**Getting Started-Breakfast**

| | |
|---|---|
| **Early Risers** Deck, 12, Mid | 5:30am |
| **Garden Café** Dec k 12, Mid | 6:30am-10:30am |
| **Great Outdoors** (weather permitting) Deck 12, Mid | 7:00am-11:30am |
| **Summer Palace** Deck 7, Aft | 7:30am-9:00am |
| **The Grill** (weather permitting) Deck 12, Mid | 8:00am-10:30am |

**Satisfy Your Afternoon Appetite-Lunch**

| | |
|---|---|
| **Summer Palace** Deck 7, Aft | Noon-1:30pm |
| Five-course meals, two-story windows | |
| **Garden Café** Deck 12, Mid | 11:30am-3:30pm |
| Various (and delicious) Food Action Stations | |

**What Are You In The Mood For?-Dinner**

| | |
|---|---|
| **Garden Café** Deck 12, Mid | 5:00pm-9:00pm |
| **Main Dining Rooms:** | |
| **Summer Palace** Deck 7, Aft | 5:30pm-10:00pm |
| Five-course meals, two-story windows | |
| **Indigo** Deck 6, Mid | 5:30pm-10:30pm |
| Five-courses, more intimate | |
| **Specialty Restaurants:** | |
| **Mambo's Restaurant** Deck 8, Mid | 5:30pm -10:30pm |
| Tex Mex delights | |
| **La Cucina** Deck 12, Aft, Portside | 5:30pm -10:30pm |
| Now that's Italian! | |
| **Lotus Garden ($10)\*** Deck 7, Mid | 5:30pm -10:30pm |
| Fusion of exotic Asian flavors | |
| **Shabu-Shabu ($10)\*** Deck 7, Mid | 5:30pm -10:30pm |
| Mongolian hot pot | |
| **Sushi Bar ($15)\*** Deck 7, Mid | 5:30pm -10:30pm |
| It doesn't get any fresher | |
| **Cagney's Steakhouse ($20)\*** Deck 13, Mid | 5:30pm -10:30pm |
| Grilled perfection, elegant setting | |
| **Le Bistro ($15)\*** Deck 6, Mid | 5:30pm -10:30pm |
| French cuisine that's magnifique | |
| **Teppanyaki ($20)\*** Deck 7, Mid | 5:30 / 7:30 / 9:30pm |
| All fresh for your enjoyment | |

**For Whenever You Are Hungry**

| | |
|---|---|
| **Blue Lagoon Café** Deck 8, Mid | Open 24 hours |
| Lite bites/burgers & fast wok dishes | |
| **Great Outdoors** (weather permitting) Deck 12, Aft | 3:30pm-5:00pm |
| **Topsiders** Deck 12, Aft | 9:00pm-11:00pm |

*These restaurants charge a cover, and for what you get, you'll find it's well worth it. Resort casual dress gets you into every bar, lounge and dining venue. Want to get all decked out? A fun choice anywhere on the ship. In the mood for casual shorts? Have a relaxing dinner in the buffet. Your favorite nice jeans? They're welcome in almost all of our restaurants. Hey, it's your vacation, so dress comfortably, and you'll find a there's venue that suits your style.

**Door Decorations:** Be safe – overly decorated stateroom doors can pose a fire hazard, so please keep your decorations inside your room.
**Environmental Hotline:** You can report environmental incidents by calling 1-877-501-5976, the ship's Reception Desk, Deck 7, Mid or via e-mail to Environmentalhotline@ncl.com. Reports are confidential.
**Customer Advisory:** Eat Smart: In case you didn't know, there's a certain level of danger to eating raw or undercooked animal products. It's also risky to drink juices that haven't been pasteurized. So if you have any immune system disorders, you should talk with your doctor.
**Customer Relations:** Got a service problem? We'll do our best to solve it! Dial '00' while onboard or write Norwegian Cruise Line, 7665 Corporate Center Drive - Miami, Florida 33126.
**Safety Equipment:** Please don't remove or meddle with any safety equipment onboard (such as smoke detectors or fire extinguishers). And, please follow safety instructions from the crew members.
**Announcements:** All announcements can be heard on channel 24 on your stateroom television.
**Open Flames:** Open flames (like burning candles and incense) are strictly forbidden.
**Sharps Containers:** If you've got any type of needles to throw away, please ask for a special container from the Reception Desk, your Room Steward or the Medical Center.

*Courtesy Norwegian Cruise Line*

## OCEANIA CRUISES

**8300 NW 33rd Street, Suite 100
Miami, FL 33122
(800) 531-5658; (305) 514-2300
Fax: (305) 514-2222
www.oceaniacruises.com**

*Marina* and *Riviera*: entered service February 2011 and May 2012, respectively; *Marina* is 66,172 GRT, and *Riviera* is 66,084 GRT; 785 × 106 feet; 1,250-passenger capacity (double occupancy); 625 cabins; European officers and international crew; cruises to the Mediterranean, Northern Europe, the Caribbean, Central America, South America, and the South Pacific (Category A/B—six star)

*Regatta, Insignia,* and *Nautica* (formerly *R-2, R-1,* and *R-5*): entered service in 1998 and 2000; last refurbished in 2010 and 2011; 30,277 GRT; 594 × 84 feet; 684-passenger capacity; 342 cabins; European officers and international crew; cruises to the Mediterranean, Scandinavia and the Baltics, Asia and the Far East, Africa Central and South America, the Caribbean, Alaska, New England/Canada, and Panama Canal (*Insignia* leased to Hapag-Lloyd for two years commencing May 2012; Category B—six stars)

(Note: Six stars is the highest rating given ships in the premium-market category.)

(Medical facilities: C-0; P-1, CLS, MS; N-1; CM; PD; BC; EKG; OX; TC; PO; EPC; WC; ICU; X; CP; TM)

These ships are rated in eleven separate categories in the second half of chapter 11.

In 2002, two former cruise line executives, Joe Watters (formerly with Crystal Cruises) and Frank Del Rio (formerly with Renaissance Cruises) along with a conglomerate of other investors created this new cruise company. Upon acquiring long-term leases on the 30,277-ton, 684-passenger former *R-1* and *R-2* of the now-defunct Renaissance Cruises, they renamed these two sister vessels *Regatta* and *Insignia* and conducted various renovations and refurbishments. Subsequently, the cruise line acquired the former *R-5*, renamed her *Nautica*, and placed her in service in late 2005. In 2007, Apollo Management, a private equity firm with holdings in the travel industry, became the majority shareholder in the company. After Apollo purchased Regent Seven Seas Cruises in 2008, that cruise line and Oceania became part of Prestige Cruise Holdings and continue to operate as separate brands. In 2011, the cruise line's first new build, *Marina*, entered service, followed by sister ship *Riviera* in 2012. After a two-year charter, *Insignia* returns to the fleet in May 2014.

These four beauties (five if you count *Insignia*) are among the more elegantly and tastefully decorated vessels currently in service and could be described as a Ritz-Carlton or Four Seasons at sea. The traditional décor in the various public rooms is quite unique for a cruise ship. Corridors are laden with floral runner-style carpets similar to those found in grand hotels; stairways are adorned with antiques and works of art; and lounges, the main dining room, the library, and public areas are furnished with rich, dark woods as well as expensive classical-period French and English furnishings and elegant wall and window treatments. The décor throughout the vessel is ingeniously orchestrated to create a feeling of understated elegance and grand refinement without a hint of glitz or ostentation.

On the *Regatta*, *Insignia*, and *Nautica*, there are 170 similar 173-square-foot outside accommodations with 43-square-foot verandas that include a queen or two twin beds with thick mattresses covered with posh sheets and duvets, a small sitting area, a satellite TV, a hair dryer, and a bathroom with a single vanity, toilet, and shower. Of these staterooms, 104 are designated concierge staterooms and have a refrigerator and minibar, a DVD player, and additional amenities. Other accommodations aboard include 110 standard outside and inside cabins (143-165 square feet); 52 minisuites (260 square feet) with 72-foot verandas, larger sitting areas, and both a bathtub and shower; and 10 full suites ranging in size from 533 to 598 square feet with 253- to 364-foot wraparound verandas, separate living rooms with dining areas, guest baths, and all-marble master bathrooms with whirlpool tubs. Twenty cabins and suites can connect for families and friends traveling together, sixty can accommodate a third person, and thirty-eight can sleep four passengers. The minisuites and full suites are considerably more comfortable with more storage than the other staterooms.

Atop each ship on decks 9 and 10 are the Terrace Café buffet restaurant, the centrally located swimming pool surrounded by comfortable lounges (including several built for couples), two outdoor whirlpools, the spa and fitness center, a walking/jogging path, the panoramic observation lounge and bar, the library, Internet café, cardroom, and two of the specialty restaurants, Polo Grill and Toscana. On all three ships, guests can book private cabanas with special services and amenities by the day for a fee. Suites and minisuites are located on deck 8 and the remaining accommodations on decks 3, 4, 6, and 7. Conveniently located on deck 5 is the elegant Grand Dining Room, several bars and lounges, the casino, two shops, and the show lounge with its comfortable traditional-style lounge chairs set around cocktail tables (unlike the theater-style arrangement on most cruise ships).

Certainly one of the strongest suits on each of the ships is the variety of superior dining experiences offered to guests. First, there is no assigned seating and passengers can dine where they want and with whom they want in any of the numerous dining venues without any surcharge. The elegant Grand Dining Room features a multicourse menu designed by master chef Jacques Pépin that changes daily and includes numerous gourmet and regional specialties artistically presented and impeccably served.

In addition to the main dining facility, there are three specialty restaurants open each evening. Polo Grill is a clubby, New York-style chophouse specializing in giant cuts of prime beef (sixteen- and thirty-two-ounce portions of prime rib, as well as porterhouse, filet, and New York strip steaks), double-cut lamb and pork chops, lobster tail, scampi, ahi tuna with all the accoutrements, and a nice choice of appetizers, soups, salads, and desserts. Toscana is a romantic, gourmet, multicourse Italian restaurant with a wide selection of antipasti, pastas, veal dishes, seafood, and all of your typical Italian favorites. Both Polo Grill and Toscana serve Maine lobster and have their own bars. In the evening, the Terrace Café features a variety of themed menus. Of course, guests can opt to dine in their cabins, where there is twenty-four-hour room service and choices include items offered in the dining rooms. Suite guests can order complete course-by-course meal service from any of the restaurant menus. Country club casual attire is suggested, and jackets and ties are never required (although some passengers will occasionally dress for dinner). There is no extra charge for the specialty restaurants.

The breakfast and lunch buffets served at the buffet-style Terrace Café and adjoining outdoor Waves Grill are outstanding and feature an enviable variety of ever-changing ethnic selections as well as high-quality more-traditional fare. Many items such as pasta, pizzas, salads, and grilled hamburgers and fish are made to order (rather than prepared in advance and left standing in steam tables).

Service in all of the restaurants is among the most solicitous and professional of any ship sailing today. We found service throughout the ships exceptional.

Commencing in 2011, the ships feature small-scale productions shows in addition to cabaret entertainment and musicians for listening and dancing in the various lounges. Each day, numerous recently released movies are offered on the TV stations as well as current cable programs, CNN, port talks, and descriptions of upcoming ports of call. Daily activities include cooking demonstrations, cultural lectures, card tournaments, exercise classes, beauty classes, art auctions, bingo, trivia, and other usual shipboard diversions.

The three smaller ships underwent multimillion-dollar refurbishments in 2010 and 2011 wherein the top suites were rebuilt and lavishly furnished; bathrooms in the penthouse suites were completely rebuilt; the other accommodations received new décor, carpeting, 1,000-thread-count Egyptian cotton linens, duvets, plush down comforters, custom-tufted headboards, refrigerator/minibars, and flat-screen LCD TVs and DVD players; the public areas were recarpeted, reupholstered, and teak decks were constructed; eight luxury cabanas were added on the top deck; menus in the specialty restaurants and Terrace Café were enhanced; Canyon Ranch Spa cuisine was offered in the main dining room; and the communication equipment was revamped both for high-speed Internet and to enable the use of cell phones at sea.

*Nautica* provides Mediterranean, Scandinavian-Baltic Sea, Asian, and African itineraries, whereas *Regatta* cruises Alaska and New England/Canada during the warmer months and repositions to the Caribbean and South and Central America during the late fall and winter. The emphasis is on itineraries to the most desired destinations on somewhat longer cruises with special appeal to seasoned cruisers. In 2007, the line announced that it had ordered two new 66,084-ton, 1,250-passenger ships. The first, *Marina*, entered service in February 2011, and the second, *Riviera*, entered service in May 2012. Each category of accommodations is considerably larger than that on the other three vessels and features twin tranquility beds convertible to queen size, flat-screen TVs, wireless Internet access, refrigerated minibars with soft drinks and bottled water replenished daily, security safes, cotton robes and slippers, direct-dial satellite telephones, hair dryers, glassed-in showers, full-sized bathtubs (except in the inside cabins), and sitting areas with sofas and makeup/writing desks. Three Owner's Suites (2,000 square feet), eight Vista Suites (1,200-1,500 square feet), twelve Oceania Suites (1,000 square feet), and 124 penthouse suites (420 square feet) enjoy butler service, a special concierge lounge, free soft drinks and bottled water in the minibars, priority check-in and luggage delivery, priority restaurant reservations, a complimentary iPad for onboard use, and many more stateroom amenities. The Owner's, Vista, and Oceania Suites have whirlpools both in their bathrooms and on their verandas. Ninety-eight percent of the 625 staterooms and suites have ocean views, and 96 percent include verandas. The 244 veranda staterooms measure 282 square feet (many designated "concierge level" with access to a concierge lounge and extra amenities), the 20 ocean-view staterooms measure 242 square feet and include floor-to-ceiling panoramic windows, and the 14 inside cabins measure 174 square feet. There are self-service launderettes on several decks.

In addition to the elegant Grand Dining Room, the posh Polo Grill steak house, the charming Toscana Italian restaurant, the Terrace Café buffet, Waves Grill, and ice-cream bar found on the smaller three ships, there are several additional dining and imbibing venues on the *Marina*. Red Ginger, with a stunning themed interior, offers a contemporary interpretation of Asian classics; Jacques, resembling a classic Parisian Bistro, is an attractive gourmet venue offering French cuisine designed by Jacques Pépin; the intimate Privee is a private dining room reserved for parties of up to ten guests who can choose from the Polo Grill or Toscana menus or a combination of both ($250 for the entire table); Bon Appétit Culinary Center offers hands-on cooking classes with twenty-four fully equipped work stations; La Reserve by Wine Spectator is a new wine bar with wine pairing dinners at $112 per person including gratuities; and Canyon Ranch Spa cuisine is available in the Grand Dining Room. The offerings in each of the specialty restaurants as well as in the main dining room exceed what you would find in most stateside restaurants in variety, quality, and presentation. We noted on our recent cruise that the service in the buffet restaurant and in the cabins was not up to the service on the smaller Oceania vessels.

Other features of note include the Artist Loft for art classes and Canyon Ranch Spa, which offers numerous massage, aromatherapy, and skin care treatments and a beauty salon as well as a large fully equipped, state-of-the-art fitness center; two outdoor whirlpools, sauna, and steam rooms; small "his" and "her" changing rooms, near but not connected to the steam and saunas; and aerobic, step, spinning, yoga, and Pilates classes. Public areas also include a large Internet café, a large library with a specialty coffee bar, three boutiques, a rambling casino, nine bars and lounges, a large heated pool and two whirlpools (thalassotherapy pool on *Riviera*) surrounded by comfortable lounges including couples beds, a jogging track, movies under the stars, a show lounge with musical reviews and cabaret-style performances, and an observation lounge with nightly dancing and disco music.

Although competing in the upper-premium category, the ship has many of the features and services offered on luxury-class vessels. The cruise line describes itself as "affordable luxury" at the upper end of the premium-cruise market. I would agree wholeheartedly with this assessment.

## Strong Points

Highly desirable itineraries on beautifully appointed ships with numerous fine-dining options at competitive prices—one of the top contenders in the upper-premium market. Good value.

*Jacques restaurant on Marina, courtesy Oceania Cruises*

*Lobby staircase on Marina, courtesy Oceania Cruises*

*Marina, courtesy Oceania Cruises*

*Veranda stateroom on Marina, courtesy Oceania Cruises*

*Pool area on Marina at night, courtesy Oceana Cruises*

*Dining room on Riviera, courtesy Oceania Cruises*

## The GRAND DINING Room

### Jacques Pépin Signature Dishes

**Steak Frites:** *New York Strip Steak, Hand-Cut French Fries and Garlic Butter Rosette*
**Poulet Rôti:** *Herb Crusted Roasted Rôtisserie Free Range Chicken with Red Bliss Mashed Potatoes and Pan Gravy*
\\**Suprême de Saumon au Court-Bouillon:** *Norwegian Poached Salmon Supreme with Rice Pilaf and Sauce Choron*

### Light Cuisine Menu

**Appetizer, Soup and Salad**

*Risotto al Radicchio e Fromaggini di Capra, Tender Arborio Rice with Goat Cheese and Radicchio*
*Chicken Consommé Bellini garnished with Baby Semolina Diamond*
*Green Salad tossed with Light Olive Oil and Lemon Juice Dressing*

**Entrée**

*Broiled Butterfly Tiger Shrimps with Star Anise Cream and Steamed Jasmine Rice*
*Roast Black Angus Strip Loin with Natural Jus and Steamed Vegetables*

### Vegetarian Selections

**Appetizers, Soup and Salad**

*Marinated Artichoke with Mushroom Medley and Parmesan Shavings*
*Papaya, Mango and Kiwi with Red Berry Coulis*
*Vegetable Consommé*
*Assorted Green Leaves with Your Choice of Dressing*

**Entrées**

*Tagliatelle Verde tossed in Tomato Vodka Sauce and Chili Flakes*
*Vegetarian Bean Chili in Baked Potato Barquette delicately cooked in its own Juices*

### The Cellar Master suggests the following wines served for tonight's menu:

**White Wine**
*Chardonnay, Delatite Winery, Mansfield 2001 Australia*

**Red Wine**
*Shiraz "The Barossa" Peter Lehmann, Barossa Valley 2000*

---

*Dinner Menu on Riviera, courtesy Oceania Cruises*

Tuesday, January 31, 2012

*Daily Activities*

| | GOOD MORNING | |
|---|---|---|
| Continuous | The Daily Program with your Cruise Director, Dottie Kulasa | Channel 4 |
| Continuous | Shopping the World: Your Guide to Port Shopping with Elizabeth Sterne | Channel 5 |
| 8:00 am | M/S Marina is scheduled to dock in Road Harbor (Tortola), B.V.I. | |
| 10:00 am | Marina's Links to the World 18 Hole Golf Course BIG⊖POINTS | Sports Deck Fwd (16) |
| 10:45 am | Croquet Anyone? with your Entertainment Team BIG⊖POINTS | Sports Deck Aft (15) |
| 11:30 am | Ping Pong with your Entertainment Team BIG⊖POINTS | Pool Deck (12) |
| | GOOD AFTERNOON | |
| 2:00 pm | Marina's Links to the World 18 Hole Golf Course BIG⊖POINTS | Sports Deck Fwd (16) |
| 2:00 pm | Social Bridge (non hosted) | Polo Grill (14) |
| 2:45 pm | Shuffleboard Test your skills with your Entertainment Team BIG⊖POINTS | Sports Deck Aft (15) |
| 3:00 pm | CanyonRanch Spa Enrichment Seminar: The Benefits of Reflexology | Horizons (15) |
| 3:30 pm | Paddle Tennis with your Entertainment Team BIG⊖POINTS | Sports Deck Fwd (16) |
| 4:00 pm | Tea Time Featuring the music of the Tatra String Quartet | Horizons (15) |
| 4:30 pm | Team Trivia with your Cruise Director, Dottie BIG⊖POINTS | Marina Lounge (5) |
| 5:00 pm | Friends of Bill W | Terrace Cafe (12) |
| 5:30 pm | Snowball Jackpot BINGO with J.R. - jackpot expected to be over $1,500<br>Cards on sale from 5:30 to 5:45 pm only. Games begin at 5:45 pm - 2 for 1 Cocktails | Marina Lounge (5) |
| 5:30 pm | All On Board! All guests are required to be back on board! | |
| 5:45 - 6:30 pm | Sailaway Melodies with The Mark Band | Pool Deck (12) |
| | GOOD EVENING | |
| 6:00 pm | M/S Marina is scheduled to sail for San Juan, Puerto Rico, U.S.A. *(a distance of 145 nautical miles)* | |
| 6:15 pm - 7:00 pm | Canadian Get Together (non-hosted) | Horizons (15) |
| Tony Payne at the Piano 5:30 - 6:00 pm • 6:30 - 7:15 pm • 9:15 - 9:45 pm • 10:30 pm - Closing | | Martinis (6) |
| The Celebration Band 6:00 - 6:45 pm • 9:00 - 9:45 pm • 10:30 - 11:15 pm • 11:30 pm - 12:15 am | | Horizons (15) |
| The Tatra String Quartet 6:00 - 6:45 pm • 7:30 - 8:15 pm • 8:30 - 9:00 pm | | Grand Bar (6) |
| 7:15 - 8:00 pm | The Sounds of the Mark Band for your listening and dancing pleasure | Horizons (15) |
| 7:30 pm | Single Malt Tasting (nominal fee of $10) | Horizons (15) |
| 8:30 pm | Evening Trivia with your Entertainment Team BIG⊖POINTS | Martinis (6) |
| 9:00 pm | Texas Hold'em Cash Game with your friendly Casino Team ($50 buy in) | Casino (6) |
| 9:00 pm | Movie Under the Stars (weather permitting): Fool's Gold (112 minutes, 2008)<br>PG 13. Matthew McConaughey, Kate Hudson and Donald Sutherland | Pool Deck (12) |
| 9:00 - 9:30 pm | Pre-Showtime Dancing with The Mark Band | Marina Lounge (5) |

"Classics"
*Standards, Rat Pack, and Broadway with*

# J.R. Lustig

9:45 pm • Marina Lounge (5)

*Please be advised that the taping of tonight's performance or the use of flash photography is strictly prohibited.*

| 10:30 pm - 12:15 am | Late Night Dancing with The Celebration Band | Horizons (15) |

*Courtesy Oceania Cruises*

# P&O CRUISES

**United Kingdom
Carnival House, 100 Harbour Parade
Southampton SO15 1ST, UK
0843 374 0111
Fax: 023 80 657030
www.pocruises.com**

*Adonia* (formerly *R8* of Renaissance Cruises and *Royal Princess*): entered service in 2001; renovated in 2007; 30,277 GRT; 181 × 26 meters; 710-passenger capacity; 355 cabins; exclusively for adults; offers a world cruise/Asian Grand Adventure, exotic-fly cruises, and cruises to the British Isles, Ireland, Guernsey, France, Mediterranean, Iberia, Canary Islands, Baltics, Fjords, Iceland, Middle East, South East Asia, Burma, Philippines, China, Japan, India (category B—not rated)

*Arcadia*: entered service in 2005; renovated in 2008; 83,781 GRT; 286 × 32 meters; 2,016-passenger capacity; 976 cabins; exclusively for adults; offers a world cruise, exotic-fly cruises, and cruises to Guernsey, Belgium, Mediterranean, Iberia, Baltics, Fjords, Iceland, Canary Islands, Canada and New England, Caribbean, Panama Canal, USA, French Polynesia, Fiji, New Zealand, Australia, Indonesia, South East Asia, India, Middle East (category B—not rated)

*Aurora*: entered service in 2000; renovated in 2009; 76,152 GRT; 272 × 32 meters; 1,874-passenger capacity; 939 cabins; offers a world cruise, exotic-fly cruises, and cruises to Guernsey, Belgium and the Netherlands, Mediterranean, Iberia, Black Sea, Canary Islands, Baltics, Fjords, Arctic Circle, Caribbean, Panama Canal, Hawaii Islands, American Samoa, Tonga, New Zealand, Australia, Philippines, China, South East Asia, South Africa, Namibia (category B—not rated)

*Azura*: entered service in 2010; 115,055 GRT; 289 × 36 meters; 3,100-passenger capacity; 1,524 cabins; cruises to Belgium, Mediterranean, Iberia, Baltics, Fjords, Canary Islands, Caribbean (category B—not rated)

*Oceana* (formerly *Ocean Princess*): entered service in November 2000; renovated in 2012; 77,499 GRT; 261 × 32 meters; 2,016-passenger capacity; 1,008 cabins; cruises to Guernsey, Belgium and the Netherlands, Mediterranean, Iberia, Fjords, Canary Islands, Caribbean (category B—not rated)

*Oriana*: entered service in 1995; renovated in 2011; 69,840 GRT; 261 × 32 meters; 1,880-passenger capacity; 914 cabins; exclusively for adults; cruises to Belgium and Germany, Mediterranean, Iberia, Baltics, Iceland, Fjords and North Cape, Arctic Circle, Canary Islands, Caribbean (category B—not rated)

*Ventura*: entered service in 2008; 116,017 GRT; 289 × 36 meters; 3,096-passenger capacity; 1,524 cabins; Mediterranean fly-cruises during summer and Caribbean fly-cruises during winter (category B—not rated)

P&O (the Peninsular and Oriental Navigation Company) dates back to 1837 and is one of the oldest, most prestigious lines in the history of cruising. P&O purchased Princess Cruises in 1974 and ran most of its ships under the Princess flag during the 1980s but now markets its vessels under the P&O Cruises banner, with the major promotion to British and European cruisers.

Principal cruise areas include the Mediterranean, Baltics and Norwegian fjords, Canary Islands, Adriatic, and the Caribbean. *Adonia, Arcadia,* and *Aurora* typically offer world voyages and exotic-fly cruises during the winter. *Ventura* will offer year-round fly-cruises to the Mediterranean in the summer months and the Caribbean in the winter months, both serviced by UK charter flights, whereas *Azura* offers Caribbean fly-cruises in the winter and a variety of cruises from the United Kingdom in the summer. *Oriana* and *Oceana* will both offer year-round cruises departing from the UK.

In 2000, P&O split the company's cruise business from its noncruise vessels and noncruise interests and formed a separate public company. In 2003, the shareholders of Carnival Corporation and P&O/Princess approved the formation of a new public company (which acquired all of the P&O/Princess assets, with the stock in the new corporation split up between the shareholders of Carnival and P&O/Princess) to be traded on the New York and British stock exchanges. Thereafter, P&O Cruises and Princess Cruises became brands under the Carnival corporate umbrella.

*Oriana* was the first P&O (non-Princess division) ship built in decades and was designed to be marketed primarily to the British as an upscale, more modern vessel than the other P&O ships. At 69,000 tons, 850 feet long, and with accommodations for up to 1,822 passengers, it debuted as the largest ship in the P&O fleet and has received a most enthusiastic reception by British cruisers wishing to sail on this more updated high-tech vessel capable of speeds up to twenty-five knots. The ten-passenger decks are serviced by ten elevators and include eight categories of cabins and suites, including eight suites measuring 400 square feet with private balconies, sixteen deluxe 300-square-foot minisuites with private balconies, and all cabins feature twin beds that are convertible to a king size bed. One hundred and thirty cabins have balconies, three hundred twenty-eight cabins are inside, and ninety-two cabins can accommodate third or fourth berths. A selection of cabins have bathtubs, and all have color TVs, refrigerators, direct-dial telephones, and personal safes—all in keeping with the ships built in the 1990s.

In late 2011, she was refurbished and became a ship exclusively for adults. Twelve new balcony cabins and two single cabins were added. Sorrento, a stylish, new Italian restaurant with ocean views and an outdoor dining area, and Ocean Grill by Marco Pierre White, a specialty dining restaurant, were added; and the Oasis Spa was updated.

At the top of the ship at the forward end is the Crow's Nest observation lounge. Immediately beneath is the health spa with sauna, steam, whirlpools, massage and beauty-treatment rooms, and exercise and aerobics facilities. Adjacent are two swimming pools, a vast sundeck area, and an indoor-outdoor lido buffet breakfast-and-lunch restaurant with an adjoining bar. Most cabins and suites are located on the next three decks.

Then comes D deck, where you will find the Ocean Grill at the Curzon Room by Marco Pierre White; the library; Crichton's, the cardroom; the writing room; Tiffany's, Costa Coffee bar and a 189-seat tiered cinema. On promenade deck, next below, is the 650-seat production theater, a photo gallery, several bars and lounges, a casino, a slot machine area, and a disco. Below that, E deck is the site of eighty-three cabins, the two dining rooms, and the bottom of the atrium area, where the shops are located. The remaining cabins and reception desk are located on F deck, and the medical center is on G deck.

In the spring of 2000, the 76,000-ton, 1,874-passenger ship named *Aurora* entered service. The 939 cabins encompass two-deck penthouse suites, 10 suites with balconies, 18 minisuites with balconies, 376 additional staterooms and cabins with balconies, and 22 cabins that accommodate disabled passengers. All cabins include coffee and tea-making facilities, refrigerators, private safes, color TVs, direct-dial telephones, and twin beds convertible to king size. Among several dining options, a bistro-style restaurant is open twenty-four hours a day. Café Bordeaux offers a unique French bistro-style menu created by *Michelin* three-star chef Marco Pierre White. The ship also features facilities for children and teens. Other facilities include a sidewalk café, a champagne bar, a Costa Coffee bar, a virtual-reality game room, a movie theater, eleven bars, a gymnasium and aerobics studio, a beauty and health service salon, and a library.

In late 2002, the *Ocean Princess* was transferred from the Princess fleet and renamed *Oceana*. On board, Café Jardin offers a special grill-style menu with Italian-inspired dishes created by Marco Pierre White.

The 83,000-ton, 2,534-passenger *Arcadia* joined the fleet in 2005. Originally intended to be a Cunard ship named *Queen Victoria*, parent corporation Carnival decided in 2004 to send the new vessel to P&O Cruises and build another ship for Cunard for delivery in 2007. She is a child-free ship with a striking modern design, and the interior includes three thousand pieces of modern art. Of the 976 accommodations, 758 face the sea and 685 of these include balconies. All cabins have flat-screen TVs and duvets. There are six restaurants, including Ocean Grill by Marco Pierre White and Orchid, featuring an Asian/Oriental-fusion menu.

In the spring of 2008, *Ventura* came into service and underwent a major multi-million-pound refurbishment in March 2014. At 116,000 tons, with a maximum passenger capacity of 3,096, it is the largest ship ever built for the cruise line. Seventy-one percent of the accommodations are outside, and 57 percent have balconies. The ship offers numerous dining venues, including three main restaurants (one with freestyle dining and two with traditional fixed seating); the White Room, the fine-dining restaurant created by celebrity chef Marco Pierre White; East, a new Asian-Fusion restaurant by *Michelin*-star chef Atul Kochhar; the Glasshouse, a wine bar with wines selected by British TV expert Olly Smith; a pizzeria; two buffet dining rooms; room service; and balcony dining. For children and teens, there are five different age-group areas and programs. The 785-seat main theater features variety and cabaret shows. In addition, there are four pools, one with skydome, six Jacuzzis, a large spa with thermal suite, shops, a nightclub, and numerous bars and lounges offering entertainment.

In the spring of 2010, a sister ship, *Azura*, joined the fleet. The ship offers several innovations and is designed with the needs of British holiday travelers in mind. These include Sindhu, an Indian fine-dining restaurant by *Michelin*-star chef Atul Kochhar; the Glass House, an award-winning wine bar developed by British TV wine expert Olly Smith; eighteen single staterooms; a spa with thermal suite and the Retreat, a private adults-only outdoor spa terrace; and Sea Screen, an open-air cinema by the Aqua Pool.

In 2011, the *Royal Princess* from Princess Cruises was transferred to P&O and renamed *Adonia*. The overall experience on this ship is different from that on P&O Cruises other ships. Sorrento, an Italian restaurant, and Ocean Grill by Marco Pierre White, are the specialty venues.

*Oriana*, *Arcadia*, and *Adonia* are adults-only ships. *Aurora*, *Azura*, *Oceana*, and *Ventura* are family-friendly ship.

## Strong Points

Exceptional around-the-world itineraries at considerably better value than on the more luxurious cruise lines. The ships especially appeal to a British clientele.

*Pool on Ventura, courtesy P&O Cruises*

*Deluxe balcony Cabin on Ventura, courtesy P&O Cruises*

*Atrium on Azura, courtesy P&O Cruises*

*Ventura, courtesy P&O Cruises*

*Ocean Grill Oriana, courtesy P&O Cruises*

# ORIANA

❀ Gravadlax of Salmon with a Light Dill and Mustard Sauce

❧ Corn on the Cob with Melted Butter

Caesar Salad

◆

❧ Cream of Asparagus

Essence of Beef with Oxtail and toasted Pine Kernels

◆

Medallions of Monkfish with Noodles
*enriched with butter, lemon zest and parsley*

❀ Roast Rib of Beef with Yorkshire Pudding, Gravy and Roast Potatoes

❀ Sauté of Lamb's Kidneys with Creamed Spinach and Dijon Mustard Sauce

Panfried Breast of Chicken
*with ginger, spring onions and braised bok choy topped with sesame seeds*

❧ Vegetable Roulade with a Tomato Coulis

Fine Beans          Panache of Vegetables          Savoyarde and Boiled Potatoes

◆

❀ Warm Apple and Cherry Strudel with Crème Anglaise
Banana and Pecan Nut Sundae
❀ Peppered Pineapple with a Sauce of Crème de Cacao with Vanilla Ice Cream
Vanilla, Mint Choc Chip and Strawberry Ice Creams
Sweet Sauces: Butterscotch Chocolate Melba
Fresh Fruit Salad
Mango Sorbet

◆

A selection of British and Continental Cheeses with Biscuits

Fresh Fruit

◆

Freshly Brewed Coffee     De-Caffeinated     Espresso     Cappuccino     Speciality Teas
After Dinner Mints

***Fresh from the Bakery***
White, Wholemeal, Malted Wheat and Sun Dried Tomato Rolls

D5

*Dinner Menu on Oriana, courtesy P&O Cruises*

# ORIANA

## TODAY'S EVENTS

**7.55am  Navigator's Early Morning Call**
Tune into TV channel 8 for the *Navigator's* early morning broadcast with up to date weather, geographical details and other points of interest. This will also be broadcast over the open decks.

**9.00am  Social Short Tennis**
A chance to make a racket and have a ball. Any players wishing for a friendly game should meet in the *Sun Deck Nets* at this time.

**9.45am  Choir Practice**
Let's hear those harmonies. *Cathy* takes you through the hymns for this morning's service. *Theatre Royal*

**9.45am  Keep Fit**
No time to waste, so just make haste and lose those inches from your waist. Join *Alison* in *Harlequins*.

**10.00am  Walk & Talk**
Ramble as you amble around the Promenade. Meet outside the *Pacific Lounge*.

**10.00am  Games Handout**
A chance for you to monopolise the games cupboard as you search for your favourites. *Library*

**10.00am  Hand and Nail Care Demonstration**
Dry, brittle or cracked nails, or your nails simply won't grow? Join Steiner the nail care experts today and find a way to beautiful hands. *Medina Room*

**10.15am**
*Theatre Royal*
**Ship's Church Service**
This morning's service will be conducted by *Captain Colin Campbell*. There will a collection made for marine charities.

**10.30am  Coffee Chat**
Thirsty for conversation. Time to relax for a while with a cuppa and a chat with some of the team in the *Curzon Room*

**10.30am  Travelling Alone Get Together**
Don't sit there feeling all alone, we're here to make you feel at home. *Tiffany's*

**10.30am  American Line Dancing for First Sitting Passengers**
Calling all Beginner Bootscooters. Hold on to your holster and make for *Harlequins* as today *Chris* will be revising what you learnt yesterday before starting on a fun new dance. Yeehah!

**10.45am  Ship in a Bottle with Ted Machin and Norman Rogers**
Assembly of the ship continues with the mainsail and rigging lines being finalised and secured. *Crow's Nest*

**11.00am  Wine Talk**
Head Wine Steward *Bisht Santinder* will be giving an informative illustrated talk on the wine served on Oriana with particular reference to some of the interesting bin ends available. *Curzon Room*

**11.00am  Deck Quoits**
Make it your target to compete in this morning's game. *Deck 13 Aft*

**11.00am  Shuffleboard**
Shuffle along and try your luck, will yours be the winning puck. *Deck 13 Aft*

**11.00am**
*Pacific Lounge*
**'Madeira Wine'**
An informal lecture by *Ana Isabel Dantas* of The Old Blandy Wine Lodge Madeira Wine Company. Win a fabulous prize of some Madeira wine. Complete the quiz sheet in your cabin and return it to the Reception Desk by 6.00pm on the 18th October. Prizes will be announced at 10.30am on the 19th in the *Pacific Lounge*.

**11.00am  Short Tennis Competition**
See if you can net yourself a prize in this morning's game. Suitable footwear must be worn. *Sun Deck Nets*

**11.00am  Couples Massage Demonstration**
Let our experts teach you how to ease away those aches and pains. *Oasis Spa*

**11.00am  Masonic Meeting**
All Brethren are invited to meet at this time in the *Iberia Room*.

**11.15am  American Line Dancing For Second Sitting Passengers**
Calling all Beginner Bootscooters. *Chris* repeats his earlier class in *Harlequins*. Yeehah!

**11.15am  Daily Tote**
Come and guess how far Oriana has steamed from noon yesterday until noon today. 50p a go. Cash only please - bet you win! *Lord's Tavern*

**11.15am  Port Enhancement Talk - Tenerife and Gran Canaria**
*Greville Rimbault* gives an informative, illustrated talk on Tenerife and Gran Canaria. This will be repeated at 4.45pm and can also be seen on channel 3 of your cabin circuits. *Chaplin's Cinema*

**11.30am**
*Lord's Tavern*
**Singalong with Checkmate**
The trio choose those cheery songs that'll get you humming along.

**Noon  Announcement from the Bridge**
Details of ship's position, present and predicted weather, and mileage report. Have you won the Daily Tote? If so collect your winnings from *Lord's Tavern*.

**Noon  Golf Get Together**
*Crichton's*

**Noon**
*Crow's Nest*
**Sounds of Jazz**
*The Rick Laughlin Trio* jazz up your lunchtime as they play for your listening pleasure.

**2.00pm  Eye and Neck Care Seminar**
The eyes and neck area are very delicate and unfortunately show visibly early signs of the ageing process. Join your on board therapist for the correct advice today. *Medina Room*

**2.30pm  Bridge Get Together**
Anyone wishing to play rubber bridge should meet in *Crichton's* at this time.

**2.45pm  Adult Cricket**
Don't be caught out. Join us for an afternoon game in the *Sun Deck Nets*.

**2.45pm  Whist Drive**
It's on the cards you'll be able to get a game in *Crichton's Aft*.

**2.45pm  Make-up Made Easy with Viv Foley**
*Viv* shows you how to do make-up easily with no fuss. *Viv* will also look at eye shapes. Please bring a lipstick with you. *Crow's Nest*

**2.45pm  Advanced Line Dancing with Dawn Jordan**
*Dawn* revises what you learnt yesterday before tackling another new dance. *Harlequins*

**2.45pm  Shuffleboard**
Paddle up and make your way to *Deck 13 Aft* where you can try your luck with the puck.

**2.45pm  Beginner's Dance Class**
If you missed yesterday's class, it's not too late. Join *Ian* and *Ruth* as they continue their light hearted instruction. Today they will revise your basic steps in the Social Foxtrot and Cha Cha Cha. Also at today's class, have fun with the Merengue. *Pacific Lounge*

**3.00pm  Perfume Talk**
Join *Hayley* as she describes the various perfumes available from the Knightsbridge Shop on board. *Iberia Room*

**3.00pm  Deck Quoits**
Make it your aim to join one of the team for this competition and you could be on target for a prize. *Deck 13 Aft*

**3.15pm  Aromaspa Demonstration**
The ultimate in body wraps, using the richness of seaweed combined with aromatherapy oils. This is followed by a facial and half body massage. Learn more about it with our specialist. *Oasis Spa*

**3.30pm  Games Handout**
All of your favourites will be available from the *Library*.

**4.00pm  Social Short Tennis**
See if you can meet your match and maybe net yourself a P&O prize. *Sun Deck Nets*

**4.00pm  Ship in a Bottle with Ted Machin and Norman Rogers**
This afternoon's class is devoted to those who require a little help. *Crow's Nest*

**4.15pm  Jackpot Bingo**
*Hughie* and the team will be calling out the lucky numbers and today it could be you. *Pacific Lounge*

**4.15pm  Captain's Coketail Party**
*Captain Colin Campbell* meets our younger cruisers in *Harlequins*. All adults are welcome to attend.

**4.45pm  Port Enhancement Talk- Tenerife and Gran Canaria**
*Greville Rimbault* repeats his informative talk on Tenerife and Gran Canaria. *Chaplin's Cinema*

**5.15pm  Colours for Men and Women with Viv Foley**
*Viv* repeats her talk on colours and how the right colours make you look healthy and successful. *Medina Room*

**5.30pm  Individual Quiz**
Twenty teasers to test the grey matter and if you have the highest score a prize could be yours. *Crichton's*

**5.30pm  Football**
Can we corner you into joining in a fun kick around in the *Sun Deck Nets*?

**5.45pm  Cocktail Set**
*Alan Christie's* music takes you to new heights in the *Crow's Nest* as you enjoy an aperitif and *Rick Laughlin* plays in *Tiffany's*

**6.00pm  Radio Oriana**
The *Pete Le Gros* radio show will be playing your requests and keeping you up to date with the activities on board so tune into channel 6 on your cabin circuits and 7317 is the number to call.

**7.45pm  Cocktail Melodies**
*Alan Christie* makes the music in the room at the top' as you enjoy the sounds and the views around and *Gary Jones* plays in *Tiffany's*.

**8.30pm & 10.30pm**
*Theatre Royal*
**The Stadium Theatre Company presents BEST OF BRITISH**

**9.00pm - 12.45am**
*Pacific Lounge*
**COUNTRY MUSIC SPECIAL with Kenny Johnson & Northwind and Neon Moon**

**9.00pm  A Step in Time**
*Checkmate* ask you to put on your dancing shoes and dance the night away in *Harlequins*.

**9.30pm  Tunes in Tiffany's**
Stave off your thirst as you hear **Alan Christie** tinkle those ivories tonight in *Tiffany's*.

**9.45pm  With a View to Dancing**
*By Design* will be pleased to have your company in the *Crow's Nest* whether you are dancing or enjoying their great sound.

**9.45pm  Boulevard Entertain**
In the mood for dancing? *Boulevard* make some of the best sounds around that'll get you up on your feet dancing to the beat.
*Harlequins*

**10.30pm  Syndicate Quiz**
Get the fizz if you win the quiz. Come and join in the fun at tonight's teaser. *Crichton's*

**10.45pm  Checkmate**
Continue dancing the night away to more great music in *Harlequins*.

**10.45pm  Alan Christie's Request Time**
More music from our superb pianist as he plays familiar favourites in the *Crow's Nest*.

**11.15pm  Prepare to Party with Boulevard**
Our guest band pull out all the stops to keep you up on your feet dancing to their fabulous beat in *Harlequins*. Remember the night is still young!

**11.30pm  Dance to the Duo**
Sweet sounds from *By Design* as they take you through to a brand new day. *Crow's Nest*

**12.15am  Disco Dance Date**
Our Debonair DJ will be spinning the discs as all you disco dollies boogie into tomorrow. *Harlequins*

**12.30am  Late Night Date**
Scale the heights to the Room with a View where *By Design* make the midnight melodies. *Crow's Nest*

## MEDICAL CENTRE

Granada Deck [4], forward, staircase Number 1 (green carpet).
The Medical Centre will be open today from 10.00am to noon and from 5.00pm to 6.00pm. **For medical attention 24 hours please dial '0' and wait for the operator. In an emergency only dial '999'.**

In the unlikely event of rough weather, effective treatment for motion sickness is available in the form of an injection.

## SUPERLATIVE TRAVEL

**Clive Peterson**, Tour Director will be available in the *Crow's Nest* between 10.00am and 11.00am to answer any queries you may have.

## GOLF GET TOGETHER

Although we do not officially organise golf tours, any passengers who wish to play in port or borrow any clubs should meet **Pete** at noon in *Crichton's*.

## WITHOUT RESERVATIONS

'Without reservations' means you may sit at any table on either sitting in either restaurant, subject to availability. When meals are served without reservations the port side window tables are designated smoking areas.

## TOURS OFFICE

Open 8.30am to noon, and 3.30pm to 5.30pm. **Jackie** and **Nikki** will be available to assist you with bookings.

**BOOKINGS FOR TOURS IN TENERIFE MUST CLOSE AT 5.30PM THIS EVENING**

**TENERIFE**
**Tour E** - Taganana Village and Mercedes Forest, due to a landslide this tour has had to be cancelled.

**PORT ENHANCEMENT TALKS - TENERIFE AND GRAN CANARIA**
*Chaplin's Cinema* 11.15am and 4.45pm.
Today **Greville** will describe in his illustrated talk our visits to the Canary Islands of Tenerife and Gran Canaria. There are two large cities to explore and also some spectacular tours to consider.
These talks can also be viewed on channel 3 of the cabin TV circuit.

## FOOD COMMENT FORMS

For your convenience we have installed outside the Peninsular and Oriental Restaurants passenger comment boxes and forms so that should you wish to express a concern or some satisfaction you are more than welcome.
There is also a box in the Conservatory on the port side by the doors to the lifts.

## WINE TALK

At 11.00am in the *Curzon Room*, Head Wine Steward **Bisht Satinder** will be giving an informative illustrated talk on some of the wines served on Oriana.

## SPECIAL OFFER

Later in the cruise we will be offering the following special take ashore bottle offers.

Whyte & MacKay Special Scotch Whisky
£6.50 per litre

Beefeater London Gin
£6.50 per litre

Please hand a completed and signed bar chit to your Cabin Steward who will deliver the bottle to your cabin towards the end of the cruise.

## CHAPLIN'S CINEMA

11.15am & 4.45pm
**Port Enhancement Talk - Tenerife and Gran Canaria**

2.30pm
**Songwriter**
Drama starring Willie Nelson and Kris Kristofferson
Running time 91 minutes, certificate 15

6.00pm
**Children's Magic Show**

8.30pm & 10.30pm
**A Perfect Murder**
Drama with Michael Douglas and Gwyneth Paltrow
Running time 105 minutes, certificate 15

## DINING HOURS

**CONSERVATORY**

| | |
|---|---|
| Early Bird | 6.30am to 7.00am |
| Hot Breakfast | 7.00am to 10.00am |
| Continental Breakfast | 10.00am to 11.00am |
| Buffet Luncheon | noon to 2.00pm |
| Afternoon Tea | 3.30pm to 4.30pm |
| Children's Tea | 5.15pm to 5.45pm |
| | (starboard side only) |

**PENINSULAR & ORIENTAL RESTAURANTS**
Breakfast - *without reservations*
First sitting - *Doors close at 8.15am* ... 8.00am
Second sitting - *Doors close at 9.15am* .. 9.00am

Luncheon - *without reservations*
First sitting - *Doors close at 12.30pm* .. 12.15pm
Second sitting - *Doors close at 1.45pm* .. 1.30pm

Afternoon Tea
Peninsular Restaurant only . 4.00pm to 4.45pm

Dinner - *with reservations*
First sitting ... 6.30pm
Second sitting ... 8.30pm

Oriana Sandwich Bar
Peninsular Restaurant only
... 11.30pm to midnight

**PIZZERIA AL FRESCO**

Continuous service ...... from Noon to 7.00pm

## LIBRARY

9.00am - 12.30pm
2.30pm - 5.30pm
9.30pm - 10.30pm

## IN THE BARS

| | |
|---|---|
| **Andersons** | 11.00am until 2.00pm & 5.00pm until late |
| **Crow's Nest** | 11.00am until 2.00pm & 5.00pm until late |
| **Harlequins** | 10.30am to noon & 8.30pm until late |
| **Lord's Tavern** | 11.00am until late |
| **Pacific Lounge** | 4.00pm to 5.00pm & 8.30pm until late |
| **Riviera Bar** | 9.00am until 7.00pm |
| **Splash Bar** | 11.00am until 6.00pm |
| **Terrace Bar** | 9.00am until 7.00pm |
| **Tiffany's** | 9.00am until noon & 5.00pm until midnight |

Passengers under 18 years of age will not be served alcoholic beverages. Please understand that you may be requested to show identification indicating date of birth.

**Cocktail of the Day**
Brandy Alexander    £1.50
Smooth and creamy, with brandy, Creme de Cacao and cream.

**Virgin Cocktail**
Orchard Dream Fizz    90p
A blend of apple juice, grapefruit juice, a dash of Grenadine and soda.

**Speciality Coffee**
French Café    £1.20
Cointreau

*Daily Program on Oriana, courtesy P&O Cruises*

# P&O CRUISES AUSTRALIA

**203 Pacific Highway Level 7**
**St. Leonards, NSW 2065, Australia**
**001161 2 8424 8800**
**www.pocruises.com.au**

*Pacific Dawn* (formerly *Regal Princess*): entered service in 1991; 70,000 GRT; 805 × 115 feet; 2,020-passenger capacity; 795 cabins; international officers and crew; cruises from Brisbane, Australia (Category C—not rated)

*Pacific Jewel* (formerly *Ocean Village Two* and *Crown Princess*): entered service in 1990; 70,000 GRT; 805 × 115 feet; 1,900-passenger capacity; 830 cabins; international officers and crew; cruises from Sydney, Brisbane, Melbourne, and Fremantle, Australia (Category C—not rated)

*Pacific Pearl* (formerly *Ocean Village, Star Princess*, and *Star Majesty*): entered service in 1989; 64,000 GRT; 1,800-passenger capacity; 770 cabins; international officers and crew; cruises from Auckland, New Zealand, and Sydney and Melbourne, Australia (Category C—not rated)

Formerly a division of P&O/Princess Cruises, P&O Cruises Australia became a Carnival Corporation brand following Carnival's acquisition of P&O/Princess in 2003. The division was formed to service the growing Australian cruise population. The vessels trace their heritage to the 1980s and 1990s, when they sailed for other cruise lines.

In late 2007, Princess Cruises' *Regal Princess* was transferred to P&O Cruises Australia and renamed *Pacific Dawn*. Having entered service in 1991 at 70,000 tons with a 1,590-passenger capacity, she was renovated in 2000. In December 2009, *Pacific Jewel* (the former *Crown Princess* and sister to the *Regal Princess*) joined the fleet, the first of two ships to be transferred from the UK-brand Ocean Village. *Pacific Pearl* joined the fleet in December 2010. Other than the sister ships *Pacific Dawn* and *Pacific Jewel*, all the vessels are different in design and layout. They are somewhat typical of mass-market ships built from 1980 to the early 1990s, with one-third to one-half of the cabins in the interior of the ship and only a few suites sporting balconies. Public areas on each ship include main dining rooms, fine-dining specialty restaurants, casual buffet-style restaurants, pizza stations, large show lounges, casinos, nightclubs, numerous bars and lounges, Internet facilities, gyms, attractive outdoor pool areas, shops, cardrooms, hospitals, and all the other facilities typically found aboard cruise ships of their vintage.

## Strong Points

These are reasonably priced, full-facility vessels offering unusual itineraries in a part of the world not frequently visited by other cruise lines. A comfortable way to explore Australia, New Zealand, and nearby islands in the South Pacific.

*Balcony stateroom, Pacific Dawn, courtesy P&O Cruises Australia*

*Pacific Dawn, courtesy P&O Cruises Australia*

*Dining Room Pacific Pearl, courtesy P&O Cruises Australia*

*Lobby, Pacific Pearl, courtesy P&O Cruises Australia*

# everyday a la carte

### entree

**sesame crusted chicken wings**
with sweet and spicy glass noodles

**cured and seared tasmanian salmon**
with creamy dill potatoes and honey mustard dip

**aussie pumpkin soup with damper** (v)

**grilled vegetable salad** (v)
with persian feta, garlic ciabatta croutons

**beetroot and red apple salad** (v)
with horseradish and red wine vinaigrette

**clear chicken broth with vegetable wontons**

### pasta

**pumpkin ravioli** (v)
with pecorino and parsley pesto

**beef lasagne**
topped with mozzarella and provolone cheese, basil and truss tomato sauce

### main

**grilled red snapper fillet**
with garlic and olive butter, three bean casserole and silverbeet

**barbequed pork belly and roasted sea scallops**
with capsicum gazpacho and parmesan chips

**homemade pot pie (choice of chunky lamb or beef)**
topped with puff pastry and served with mash and peas

**grilled 250g beef striploin steak**
240 days grain-fed, marble score 3+, with potato wedges and roasted mushrooms

**butter chicken**
with coriander raita and steamed rice

**parmesan crusted eggplant** (v)
with artichoke and pear risotto

### sides

all main dishes are complemented by specially selected sides, should you require additional vegetables, please order from the selection below:

**honey and thyme roasted carrots, turnips and parsnips** (v)

**steamed white cabbage wedge with bacon strips**

**brussels sprouts with caramelised onions** (v)

**minted english garden peas** (v)

**steamed vegetable** (v)

**chips, mash or roast potatoes** (v)

### dessert

**caramelised cardamom and cherry crème brulee**

**warm belgian chocolate delight with vanilla ice cream**

**seasonal fresh fruits**

*Dinner Menu, courtesy P&O Australia*

## PAUL GAUGUIN CRUISES

**1100 Main Street, Suite 300**
**Bellevue, WA 98004**
**(800) 848-6172**
**www.pgcruises.com**

MS *Paul Gauguin*: entered service in 1998; renovated in 2009 and 2012; 19,200 GRT; 513 × 71 feet; 332-passenger capacity; 166 staterooms; European officers and international crew; cruises in French Polynesia, Cook Islands, Marquesas Islands, Tuamotus, Fiji, Australia, and Southeast Asia (one wheelchair-accessible cabin) (Category B—six stars)

MV *Tere Moana* (formerly *Le Levant*): entered service in 2003; 3,504 GRT; 330 × 46 feet; renovated in 2012; 90-passenger capacity; 45 cabins; European officers and international crew; cruises in Caribbean and Latin America in the winter and in Europe in the summer (Category B—not rated)

In January 1998, the 19,200-ton, 332-passenger *Paul Gauguin* joined the Regent Seven Seas (formerly Radisson Seven Seas) fleet, offering seven-night Polynesian cruises. The ship is now owned by Pacific Beachcomber Company. The 166 staterooms, including nine suites, all have ocean views, and two-thirds sport private balconies. They measure from 200 square feet up to 531 square feet (not including verandas). All accommodations include full-size bathtub with shower; cotton robes and slippers; hair dryers; TV with in-house movies and programs; DVD players; private safes; direct-dial telephones; refrigerators replenished daily with beer, soft drinks, and bottled water; wardrobes; and a vanity/desk. Vanities, in both the staterooms and bathrooms, include numerous mirrors affording multisided views. Six million dollars was spent in 2009 to renovate and enhance the vessel. She was outfitted with a new lounge/piano bar and fourteen additional staterooms, seven of which have private balconies.

Thereafter, in January of 2012, the ship was dry docked for three weeks for a major facelift. Substantial innovations were made, including new carpeting, upholstery, headboards and furnishings in the staterooms and suites, new carpeting and new upholstery in most of the public areas and dining venues, and redesign of the restaurants and Le Grand Salon, increasing the size of the La Palette Lounge, Le Casino, and Grand Suites.

Onboard gratuities are included in the cruise fare, as are select wines, spirits, soft drinks, bottled water, and hot beverages throughout the ship. These perks are generally only offered by expensive, luxury cruise ships. Thus, passengers on *Paul Gauguin* receive a more enjoyable cruise experience without being nickel and dimed.

The staterooms on *Paul Gauguin* are not similar in size. There are eight categories, and the space and comfort levels are directly proportionate to what you pay. Thus, passengers booking in category F share a 200-square-foot stateroom with two portholes, a small sitting area, and reduced storage space; category E has windows rather than portholes; category C and D guests receive a 37-square-foot veranda, tub/shower combination, and additional storage; and category B veranda staterooms are 249 square feet with 56-square-foot verandas. Those guests opting for a 300-square-foot category A veranda suite with 28-square-foot veranda, one of the 332-square-foot grand suites with 197-square-foot verandas, or one of the 457- to 531-square-foot owner's suites with 53- to 77-square-foot verandas receive more closet and storage space, more spacious sitting areas, larger bathrooms, and more amenities. All categories of accommodations are cleverly designed and decorated with attractive dark wood and chrome cabinetry, floor-to-ceiling mirrored walls, and tasteful fabrics. Occupants of the suites and veranda stateroom on deck 8 have butler service.

Single open-seating dining is offered in three restaurants. The opulent L'Etoile is reminiscent of a grand Parisian restaurant and features multicourse Continental dinner menus. The specialty restaurant, La Veranda, with menus and cuisine designed by celebrity chef Jean-Pierre Vigato (whose restaurant Apicus in Paris boasts two *Michelin* stars) offers French provincial cuisine and a tasting menu. Several of Chef Vigato's signature dishes also appear on the menu at L'Etoile. La Veranda, a casual buffet venue, is also open for breakfast and lunch, as is the indoor/outdoor Le Grill by the pool. In the afternoon, Le Grill features afternoon high tea. In the evenings, Le Grill features South Pacific-inspired cuisine under the stars.

A late-riser's Continental breakfast is served at La Palette, an observation lounge that converts to a disco late in the evening. Select wines from around the world are offered at lunch and dinner in all restaurants, and classified vintages are available at an additional charge. As mentioned earlier, wines and liquor, along with all nonalcoholic beverages, are complimentary throughout the ship. The quality of the cuisine throughout the vessel is exceptional. Hors d'oeuvres are featured in all lounges before dinner, and numerous complimentary cocktail parties take place during each cruise. Complimentary twenty-four-hour room service is also available.

Facilities aboard include Le Grand Salon, the setting for lectures, movies, dancing, and nightly entertainment; a small casino; a photo shop; a boutique; the restaurants and lounges described earlier; an outdoor pool surrounded by lounge chairs; several bars including a cozy piano bar/lounge; a sea-level marina; a small fitness center; the Deep Nature Spa, which offers massage and beauty treatments, a steam room, and a hairdressing facility; and an Internet center. From the ship's water-sports platform, guests can kayak, windsurf, paddleboard, or take Zodiacs for dive excursions. Also offered is an optional PADI dive program and certification.

Although there are no production shows and somewhat limited entertainment and activities (as compared with larger vessels), the cruise director puts together a nightly cabaret show that may feature a piano artist, the Gauguins, local dancers, or himself. The band is outstanding and accompanies the evening entertainment and plays music in La Palette Lounge for listening and dancing. The Gauguins are a troupe of talented Polynesian entertainers. During each cruise, among their other duties, they entertain; give talks and demonstrations on local lore, Tahitian language and dancing, crafts, and Pareo tying; and assist on shore excursions—embellishing the feeling that passengers are traveling in French Polynesia. The emphasis of the ship is on the destinations and providing a comfortable, carefree, romantic cruise experience.

Itineraries explore exotic ports in the South Pacific. They include seven-night voyages throughout the Society Islands with overnights in Moorea and Bora Bora; ten-night cruises that add the Tuamotus group; eleven-night cruises that add the Cook Islands; and fourteen-night cruises that include the Society Islands, Tuamotus, and Marquesas. In 2014, itineraries will also include Fiji, Australia, and Southeast Asia. Numerous shore excursions are offered at each stop—most are quite expensive.

While on Bora Bora, guests have access to the company's private beach on a motu (islet) where they can swim, snorkel, and sunbathe on a white sand beach lapping a crystal clear turquoise lagoon. Guests can also spend a complimentary day on a picturesque private motu off the coast of Taha'a and enjoy snorkeling, water sports, and barbecues along with full bar service. The beach party held here is phenomenal.

In December 2012, the former ninety-passenger *Le Levant* from Compagnie Du Ponant cruises commenced cruises for Paul Gauguin as the MV *Tere Moana*. After renovations in the fall of 2012, the ship now accommodates ninety guests in forty-five staterooms. She sails in the Caribbean and Latin America during the winter and in Europe in the summers.

The sleek, ninety-passenger, 3,504-ton *Tere Moana* accommodations range from 194 square feet to 298 square feet, and all have a king-size or twin beds, a minibar, a flat-screen satellite TV, a DVD/CD player, a desk, a safe, a dressing table, a hair dryer and bathrobes, a satellite direct-line telephone, 110/220-volt outlets, and Wi-Fi. Eight staterooms have balconies.

Deck 6 is a sundeck with a hot tub and Balinese sun beds. There is a pool, an outside bar, a fitness center, and the Deep Nature Spa on deck 5. On deck 4, La Veranda offers breakfast and lunch during the day. Also located on deck 4 is a library. Deck 3 is the location of Le Salon, the main lounge, La Boutique, an infirmary, and the marina. Kayaking and paddleboarding are available from the ship's marina or from the beach in select ports. On deck 2 is the main dining room, L'Etoile, featuring multicourse Continental dinner menus, along with several signature dishes by celebrity chef Jean-Pierre Vigato. Gratuities, soft drinks, select wines, and spirits are included in the cruise fare.

## Strong Points

*Paul Gauguin* features exotic itineraries in the South Pacific with plenty of time to explore the various islands on a comfortable, full-facility, upscale ship with Polynesian flavor, and many gratis perks.

*The Gauguins on Paul Gauguin, courtesy Paul Gauguin Cruises*

*Author with Captain, Paul Gauguin, courtesy Paul Gauguin Cruises*

*La Veranda Dining Room, courtesy Paul Gauguin Cruises*

*L'Etoile Restaurant, courtesy Paul Gauguin Cruies*

*Salon, courtesy Paul Gauguin Cruises*

*Veranda stateroom, courtesy Paul Gauguin Cruises*

# Dinner menu

## Appetizers

**Classic vitello tonnato**
Thinly sliced roast veal loin, served a with tuna cream sauce and capers

**Corn fritters (Hush puppies)**
Served with a sweet and sour cucumber dipping sauce

**Polynesian pineapple fruit cup**

**House made gravlax**
Salmon fillet cured with dill, cracked black pepper, salt and sugar
Accompanied by rye bread and mustard dill sauce

## Soups

**Chilled mango bisque**

**Cream of Cauliflower**
Topped with cheddar cheese garlic croutons

**Caldo verde**
Portuguese cabbage and chorizo soup with coriander

## Salads

**Rustic garden salad**
Beets, celery root, pumpkin and turnips combined with champagne herb vinaigrette resting
on a bed of fresh lettuce

**Crisp mixed greens with cream cheese fritters**
Tossed with ginger tomato dressing

## From the pasta corner

**Fusili alla matriciana**
Famous dish from Amatrice with tomatoes, onions and pancetta

**Fresh spaghetti pasta**
Italian tomato sauce, bolognaise sauce or pesto sauce

## Intermezzo

**Refreshing sorbet of the day**

## Specialities

**Polynesian fresh mahi mahi with almond crust**
On a light butter sauce, parsley potatoes and bouquet of vegetables

**Tonight Chef's Daniel suggestion:**
**Roasted striploin of black angus beef**
Accompanied by vanilla glazed root vegetables, country style potatoes and lemon black pepper butter

**Blackened cajun rubbed porkloin**
With a three bean salsa and house made tropical fruit chutney

**The famous chicken cordon bleu**
Thin slices of chicken escalope stuffed with ham and Comte cheese
Finished with natural jus, sautéed artichokes, carrots and cranberry garnish

**New Zealand salmon**
Prepared to order: plain grilled, sautéed or poached
Served with drawn butter or béarnaise sauce

**Marinated chicken breast**
Prepared to order: grilled, sautéed or poached
Served with natural gravy or béarnaise sauce

## Vegetarian menu

**Polynesian pineapple fruit cup**

**Rustic garden salad**
Beets, celery root, pumpkin and turnips combined with champagne herb vinaigrette resting on a bed of fresh greens

**Cream of cauliflower**
Topped with cheddar cheese garlic croutons

**Cauliflower, potato and lentil patek**
With saffron rice, golden onions and tomato raita

## Light & healthy

**Classic vitello tonnato**
Thinly sliced roast veal loin, served with tuna cream sauce and capers

**Chilled mango bisque**

**Oven roasted mahi mahi with almond crust**
Parsley potatoes and bouquet of vegetables

## No salt added

**Polynesian pineapple fruit cup**

**Cream of cauliflower**
Topped with cheddar cheese garlic croutons

**Crisp mixed greens with cream cheese fritters**
Tossed with ginger tomato dressing

**Oven roasted mahi mahi with almond crust**
On a light butter sauce, parsley potatoes and bouquet of vegetables

*Dinner Menu, courtesy Paul Gauguin Cruises*

# la Orana

## MORNING

|  |  |  |
|---|---|---|
| 8:00 | **BOARD GAMES ENTHUSIASTS** – Board Games are available all day long. | Fare Tahiti –Deck 6 aft |
| 8:00 – 6:00 | **SHUFFLEBOARD GAME** – An informal gathering to play Shuffleboard. | Muster Station C(5) |
| 8:30 | **WALK A MILE with a smile!!! 20 laps = one mile. Join your Tahitian Hostess on the Sun Deck.** | Sun Deck (9) |
| 10:00 | **SHIP'S BRIDGE TOUR** – Sign up in advance at Reception (*maximum of 10 passengers per group allowed*). *Please meet your Escort at the Reception desk.* | Reception (4) |
| 10:30 | **TAHITIAN SONGBOOK** – Join **Les Gauguines** to learn some Tahitian songs. | La Palette (8) |
| 10:30 | **VOLLEYBALL**– Available at the Motu. Please, see **Les Gauguines**. | Bora Bora Motu |
| 10:30 – 1:45 | **NATURALIST BEACH HOURS** – **Meagan** will be available on the Motu to answer any questions. | Bora Bora Motu |
| 11:00 | **UKULELE LESSON** – Join **Les Gauguines** for a music lesson with this typical Polynesian instrument. | La Palette (8) |
| 11:00 | **NATURALIST CORNER – "BIRDS OF THE SOUTH PACIFIC"** For an introduction to Birding! This discussion will inform you of the most common birds you can hope to encounter. With **Meagan.** | Bora Bora Motu |
| 11:00 – 2:00 | **PING-PONG** is available. | Grand Salon (5) |

## AFTERNOON

|  |  |  |
|---|---|---|
| 1:30 | **PICTIONARY FANS GET TOGETHER** – Meet new friends and start your own game. | Piano Bar (5) |
| 2:00 | **DOCUMENTARY MOVIE – "MARQUESAS "** There are many ways to approach the Marquesas. This film features the land, the people and it's ocean. Duration: 52 minutes. | Grand Salon (5) |
| 2:30 | **FRENCH PETANQUE** – Enjoy the most popular French game in these islands. **Les Gauguines** teach you how to play. | Bora Bora Motu |
| 2:30 – 5:00 | **SOCIAL BRIDGE** – Players get together for an informal game. | L'Etoile (5) |
| 3:00 | **MEANING OF THE MOVEMENT** – Learn the meaning of Tahitian dance with **Les Gauguines.** | Piano Bar (5) |
| 3:30 | **BADMINTON** – Enjoy a game on the beautiful Bora Bora Motu. | Bora Bora Motu |
| 3:30 | **APARIMA DANCE CLASS** – Join **Les Gauguines** as they teach you some of the slow Tahitian dance steps. | Piano Bar (5) |
| 4:00 | **BOOK CLUB** – Meet fellow guests to discuss your favorite books & authors or exchange paperbacks. | Library (6) |
| 4:00 – 5:00 | **TI NO AVATEA** – Afternoon Tea is served to the melodies of **Adrian.** | La Palette (8) |
| 5:00 | **SERVICE CLUB** – Members of Rotary, Lions, Kiwani. Please meet **Verity** to receive your certificate. | La Palette (8) |
| 5:00 | **NATURALIST LECTURE – "ISLAND FORMATION"** What is the difference between a volcanic island a motu and an atoll. Learn how these beautiful islands came to be. | Grand Salon (5) |

## EVENING

|  |  |  |
|---|---|---|
| 6:30 – 7:30 | **COCKTAILS & MUSIC** – Music played by **Siglo Trio.** | La Palette (8) |
| 6:30 – 7:30 | **COCKTAILS** – The best melodies played by **Ruben.** | Piano Bar (5) |
| 6:50 – 7:50 | **TAHITIAN PHOTO TIME** – **Pierre** will take a photo of you with two of **Les Gauguines.** | Outside L'Etoile (5) |
| 8:45 – 9:30 | **AFTER-DINNER DRINKS** – Enjoy your after-dinner drink at the Piano Bar. Music by **Ruben.** | Piano Bar (5) |
| 9:30 | **AFTER-DINNER DANCING** – Come join in the rhythm's of **Siglo** ! | Grand Salon (5) |
| 10:00 | **GRAND SALON SHOWTIME – "KREW KAPERS": Starring the Crew of the m/s Paul Gauguin.** Come and support your favorite crew members in their very special performance. | Grand Salon (5) |
| 10:15 – 11:00 | **LA PALETTE** – Have a drink with friends under the stars. | La Palette (8) |
| 10:45 – 11:30 | **PIANO BAR** – Ruben serenades you into the night. | Piano Bar (5) |
| 11:00 | **LA PALETTE DISCO** – Party into the night at La Palette Disco. | La Palette (8) |

# TONIGHT

### Krew Kapers!
10:00pm | Grand Salon (5)

Featuring the Crew of the m/s *Paul Gauguin* The Crew is excited to entertain you tonight with their very own show!

# EVENTS

### Guest Lecturer, Mark Eddowes — "Trails of the Ancients"
6pm | Grand Salon (5) | LIMITED SPACE: Sign-up at the Travel Concierge Desk (4)

Mark is an acknowledged authority and researcher in the field of Polynesian anthropology. Originally from New Zealand, much of his knowledge was gained in the field on archaeological digs. He has been honored with the title of National Geographic expert in the archeology of French Polynesia and the Cook Islands. He has also been invited to head an archaeological research committee charged with classifying Raiatea as a UNESCO World Heritage Sites. Fluent in French and Tahitian, as well as his native English, Mark makes his home in Huahine, the "Garden Island" of the Society Islands chain. Don't miss this opportunity to attend this entertaining and enlightening lecture given by this renowned archaeologist and scholar—and gifted raconteur!

# ANNOUNCEMENTS

### Notes for Motu Mahana
- Although precautions are taken to ensure your safety from falling coconuts on our private motus, please be aware of this very real risk, which increases as you leave our private areas.
- Please exercise caution when snorkeling
- Please do not stand on the coral and be aware of the current at all times as they can be very strong.
- It is recommended to wear reef shoes

# TENDER SCHEDULE

Priority is given to passengers with excursions. Please refer to your ticket for meeting time and place.

| Destination | First tender | Last tender | Frequency |
|---|---|---|---|
| To Viatape | 8:30am | 5:00pm | 30 mins |
| To Ship | – | 5:00pm | – |
| To Motu | 10:15am | 4:15pm | 60 mins |
| To Ship | – | 5:00pm | – |

Please note that there are no restrooms and no food available on the Motu. However, drinks will be available at the Motu Bar.
Please use the beach towels from your stateroom.

*Daily Program, courtesy Paul Gauguin Cruises*

# PEARL SEAS CRUISES

**741 Boston Post Road, Suite 250
Guilford, CT 06437
(800)983-7462
(203)458-5280
www.pearlseascruises.com**

*Pearl Mist*: entered service in 2014; 5,062 GRT; 335' × 56'; 210-passenger capacity; 108 staterooms; American captain and international crew; seven-, ten-, eleven-night Great Lakes/St. Lawrence Seaway, Canadian Maritimes, New England cruises, Caribbean, and South America (No ratings)

*(Complete information for the ship was not available at publication, and therefore, some features and amenities may be left out of this article.)*

Pearl Seas Cruises is owned by the same group that owns American Cruise Lines, a company founded in 1974 that has operated a number of all-American vessels over the years. Originally intended to enter service in 2008, and after overcoming several delays, the *Pearl Mist* will launch in 2014, as the first of several vessels planned by the company to offer luxury, small-ship cruising in areas normally serviced by less-upscale vessels.

All of the eight suites and one hundred staterooms on the *Pearl Mist* have sliding glass doors opening to private balconies. Most of the staterooms measure 300+ square feet, and the suites measure 580 square feet. All of the spacious accommodations include twin- or king-size beds, hair dryers, satellite TVs, DVD players, private safes, refrigerators, sitting areas, showers, robes, and slippers.

Public areas include a sundeck atop ship with lounge chairs and tables, various exercise equipment, and a putting green; the staterooms and suites are located on the next four decks along with several lounges, a library, Internet facilities, and open passenger deck space. The lobby, dining room, hospital, and spa are located on the bottom deck. The main lounge is the venue for lectures, cocktail hour, and nightly entertainment. An elevator services all decks.

All meals are served in a single-seating dining room with panoramic views. Complimentary wines are served with lunch and dinner, and complimentary coffees, espresso, and snacks are available throughout the day. Before dinner each evening, complimentary cocktails and hors d'oeuvres are served in the main lounge. Room service and laundry service are available.

The *Pearl Mist* will showcase some of the most beautiful, historic, and exotic destinations in Canada and the United States. Guests will have a choice of dozens of magnificent destinations, a few being Québec City, Georgian Bay, Prince Edward Island, Newport, Halifax, Thousand Islands, Saguenay Fjord, Nantucket, Cape Breton Island, Percé, St. Pierre-Miquelon, Martha's Vineyard, and Bar Harbor. Initial itineraries will be Halifax to Quebec and reverse, Quebec to Toronto and reverse, and Toronto to Chicago and reverse.

The demographics of the passengers tend to be fifty years in age or up. The average age of the service staff is in the early twenties. Prices roughly range between $530 to $810 per person per night.

## Strong Points

The *Pearl Mist* is an intimate small more upscale ship aspiring to compete in the luxury cruise market category, initially offering destinations in the Northeastern United States and Canada. I look forward to personally reviewing the ship.

*Pearl Mist, courtesy Pearl Seas Cruises*

*Courtesy Stateroom Pearl Seas Cruises*

## PEARL SEAS
## C R U I S E S™

*Dinner Menu*

### *Appetizers*

New England Clam Chowder
served in a Freshly Baked Bread Bowl

*Or*

Roasted Red Pepper Bisque served with Tomato and Goat Cheese Crostini

*Or*

Heirloom Tomato Mozzarella Salad with Balsamic Dressing

### *Entrees*

Roasted Prime Rib of Beef Au Jus
Accompanied by Wild Mushroom Risotto and Steamed Baby Squash

*Or*

Chicken Breast stuffed with Fresh Mozzarella, Prosciutto di Parma and Baby Spinach
served with a Rustic Herb Tomato Sauce Accompanied by Wild Mushroom Risotto
and Steamed Baby Squash

*Or*

Traditional Maine Lobster Dinner
served with Drawn Butter Fresh Corn on the Cob and Herb Roasted Red Potato

### *Desserts*

Maine Blueberry Pie à la mode

*Or*

Molten Chocolate Lava Cake with Fresh Raspberry Sauce

*Or*

A choice of Butter Pecan, Pistachio, Strawberry, Mint Chocolate Chip,
Chocolate, Vanilla, or Sugar Free Vanilla Ice Cream

*Pearl Seas' chefs will specially design
a menu to accommodate food allergies*

050213

*Dinner menu, courtesy Pearl Seas Cruise*

# PRINCESS CRUISES

**24305 Town Center Drive
Santa Clarita, CA 91355
(800) PRINCESS; (661) 753-0000
Fax: (661) 284-4771
www.princess.com**

*Caribbean Princess, Crown Princess, Emerald Princess,* and *Ruby Princess*: entered service in 2004, 2006, 2007, and 2008, respectively; 113,000 GRT; 951 × 118 feet; 3,080-passenger capacities, 1,532 cabins, 1,557 on *Caribbean Princess*; British and Italian officers and international crew; *Caribbean Princess* cruises the Caribbean, Canada/New England, and Europe; *Crown Princess* cruises the Caribbean, Europe, and in 2014 will sail to South America, the West Coast, and Alaska; *Emerald Princess* sails the Caribbean, Canada/New England, and Europe; *Ruby Princess* sails the Caribbean and Europe (Category B—five+ stars)

(Medical facilities: C-26; P-1 or 2, EM, CLS, MS; N-2 to 5; CM; PD; BC; EKG; TC; PO; EPC; OX; WC; OR; ICU; X; M; CCP; L)

*Coral Princess* and *Island Princess*: entered service in 2003; 92,000 GRT; 964 × 106 feet; 1,970-passenger capacity; 987 cabins; British and Italian officers and international crew; cruises Alaska, West Coast, and Panama Canal (Category B—five stars)

(Medical facilities: C-20; P-2, EM, CLS, MS; N-5, CM; PD; BC; EKG; TC; PO; EPC; OX; WC; OR; ICU; X; M; TM; CCP, J)

*Diamond Princess* and *Sapphire Princess*: entered service in 2004; 116,000 GRT; 952 × 123 feet; 2,670-passenger capacity; 1,337 cabins; British and Italian officers and international crew; itineraries in Alaska, Hawaiian Islands, the California Coast, Mexican Riviera, Australia, New Zealand, and Asia (Category B—five+ stars)

In summer 2014, *Diamond Princess* will be based in Japan.

(Medical facilities: same as *Caribbean Princess* except C-28)

*Grand Princess, Golden Princess,* and *Star Princess*: entered service in 1998, 2001, and 2002, respectively; renovated in 2008 and 2009; *Grand Princess* had major renovation in 2011; 107,500 GRT for *Grand Princess* and 109,000 GRT for *Golden* and *Star*

*Princess*; 935 × 118 feet; 2,600-passenger capacity; 1,300 cabins; British and Italian officers and international crew; all three ships offer cruises in the Caribbean, South America, Mexican Riviera, Pacific Coast, Alaska, Hawaiian Islands, South Pacific, Mediterranean, and other European itineraries (Category B—five stars)

(Medical facilities: C-28; P-2; EM, CLS, MS; N-5; CM; PD; BC; EKG; TC; PO; EPC; OX; WC; OR; ICU; X; M; TM CCP)

*Pacific Princess* and *Ocean Princess* (formerly *Tahitian Princess*): entered service in 1999; renovated in 2010 and 2009, respectively; 30,277 GRT; 594 × 84 feet; 670-passenger capacity; 334 cabins; British and Italian officers and international crew; *Pacific Princess* offers various itineraries, including Alaska, South America, Europe, and the Holy Land, and world cruises sold in segments; *Ocean Princess* offers sailings in Asia, India, Africa, and Europe (Category B—five stars)

*Royal Princess* and *Regal Princess*: entered service in 2013 and 2014 respectively; 141,000 GRT; 1,083 × 126 feet; 3,600-passenger capacity; 1,780 cabins; British and Italian officers and staff; international crew; Europe and Caribbean cruises (Category B—five+ stars)

(Medical facilities: same as *Caribbean Princess* except C-36)

*Sun Princess*, *Dawn Princess*, and *Sea Princess*: entered service in 1995, 1997, and 1998, respectively; renovated in 2009; 77,000 GRT; 856 × 106 feet; 1,950-passenger capacity; 975 cabins; British and Italian officers and staff, international crew; *Sun Princess*, *Dawn Princess*, and *Sea Princess* offer sailings from Australia to the South Pacific, Asia, Australia/New Zealand, and world cruises; in summer, *Sun Princess* is based in Japan, offering sailings in that market (Category B—five stars)

(Medical facilities: C-19; P-2; EM, CLS, MS; N-3; CM; PD; BC; EKG; TC; PO; EPC; OX; WC; OR; ICU; X; M; CCP; and TM on Sea)

Note: All ships can accommodate passengers performing peritoneal dialysis as well as hemodialysis groups accompanied by a nephrologist, dialysis nurses, and technicians.

These ships are rated in eleven separate categories in the second half of chapter 14.

The London-based Peninsular and Oriental Steam Navigation Company (P&O) dates back to the early 1800s and is one of the oldest, largest, and most prestigious lines in the history of cruising. During the first three quarters of the twentieth century, numerous vessels sailed under the P&O flag. However, most of them were sold after P&O purchased Princess Cruises in 1974.

Princess was originally formed by Stanley McDonald. In 1965, he chartered the six-thousand-ton *Princess Patricia* and initiated cruises from California to ports on the west coast of Mexico. Thereafter, in 1967, with the charter of the *Princess Italia*, the itineraries were expanded to include spring and summer sailings to Canada and Alaska.

The *Princess Carla* was chartered in 1968 for a short period. In 1971, a major upgrade came when McDonald chartered Flagship Line's *Island Venture*, renaming her *Island Princess*. When P&O acquired Princess in 1974, they purchased the *Island Princess* and soon afterward also purchased her sister ship, the *Sea Venture*, which subsequently became famous as the *Pacific Princess*—TV's *Love Boat*. During the same period, P&O changed the name of its *Spirit of London* to the *Sun Princess* and designated her for seven-day cruises in the Caribbean and Alaskan markets.

The *Love Boat* TV series brought cruising into the living rooms of millions of Americans whose prior nautical experience had not gone beyond a rowboat. The show not only gave a gigantic shot in the arm to the cruise industry as a whole but also made Princess Cruises a household word. Although on most sailings passengers did not rub elbows with Captain Stubing, Julie, Gopher, Doc, or Isaac, the TV series did film several segments each year on board. Ironically, over the years, I have found the real-life captains, officers, and crew on Princess ships to be among the most friendly and efficient staff sailing.

The success of the line gave rise to the addition of the popular all ocean-view accommodation, 44,000-ton *Royal Princess* in 1984.

In 1988, Princess acquired Sitmar Cruises, changed the name of its vessels, and instantaneously added four new ships to its rapidly expanding empire. At the same time, the *Sun Princess* was transferred to Premier Cruise Line (not to be confused with the *Sun Princess* that entered service in 1995).

Sitmar had entered the North American cruise industry in 1971 with two refurbished Cunard ships: the *Fairsea* (*Fair Princess*) and the *Fairwind* (*Dawn Princess*). Their spacious cabins, friendly and efficient Italian service, excellent cuisine, and special children's facilities and programs combined to make these two of the most popular ships of the 1970s. The 46,000-ton *Fairsky* (*Sky Princess*) was added in 1984, and in 1989, the 62,500-ton *Star Princess* became the largest vessel in the then-combined Princess-Sitmar fleets. Two new 70,000-ton vessels, the *Crown Princess* and the *Regal Princess*, were added in 1990 and 1991, respectively. All of these ships have since left the fleet.

In the mid-1990s, Princess committed more than $1 billion to the construction of its next generation of gigantic superliners. The 77,000-ton *Sun Princess*, *Dawn Princess*, *Sea Princess*, and *Ocean Princess* entered service in 1995, 1997, 1998, and 2000, respectively. The 109,000-ton *Grand Princess* commenced cruising in 1998, and two sister ships—*Golden Princess* and *Star Princess*—entered service in 2001 and 2002, respectively. Two 88,000-ton ships named *Coral Princess* and *Island Princess* (not to be mistaken with the prior ship from the *Love Boat* series, which left the fleet) were delivered in 2003. Eighty percent of the outside cabins on these ships have balconies. In 2004, two 116,000-ton ships, *Diamond Princess* and *Sapphire Princess*, joined the fleet as well as the 113,000-ton *Caribbean Princess*. The *Ocean Princess* was transferred to P&O in the fall of 2002, and *Sea Princess* followed in 2003, only to be returned in 2005. In 2006, the new *Crown Princess* and in 2007 the *Emerald Princess* entered service, ships similar in dimensions to *Caribbean Princess*. *Ruby Princess*, a sister ship to the others, was delivered in 2008.

Itineraries for the ships vary from year to year and include more than 280 different ports around the globe. The line offers not only Caribbean, Mexican Riviera, Panama Canal, Alaskan, Bermuda, South America/Amazon, Canada/New England, and colonial America cruises but also Mediterranean, North Sea/Baltics, Hawaii/Tahiti, South Pacific, Indian, African, Holy Land, Far East, and world cruises as well. Since Princess makes a practice of following the pulse of the marketplace, it is best to recheck itineraries each season.

In 2000, P&O split off the company's cruise business from its noncruise vessels and noncruise interests and formed a separate public company. At that time, the new company, P&O Princess Cruises, owned and operated all of P&O's cruise ships under six separate brands: P&O Cruises, P&O Cruises Australia, Princess Cruises, Swan Hellenic, Seetours International, and AIDA Cruises (these last two brands concentrate on a largely German clientele).

In 2003, the shareholders of Carnival Corporation and P&O/Princess finally approved the formation of a new public company (which acquired all of the P&O/Princess assets with the stock in the new corporation split up between the shareholders of Carnival and P&O/Princess) to be traded on the New York and British stock exchanges. Subsequently, the P&O brands were spun off and now are separate brands of Carnival.

When the sleek, 856-foot, 14-story, 77,000-ton *Sun Princess* made its debut in December 1995, it was the largest cruise ship in service. Passenger capacity was limited to 1,950 (somewhat less than its behemoth competitors), which is in keeping with Princess Cruises' intention to provide a more intimate, less crowded cruise experience aboard a large ship while still offering more dining, entertainment, and lounging options. The abundance of soft woods, brass, fine fabrics, and artwork—together with the dramatic central atrium area and design in the public rooms—made this ship, and its sister ships, the most attractive in the then Princess fleet.

In terms of cabins, 603 of the 975-passenger accommodations are outside, 410 have balconies, and 19 are wheelchair accessible. Standard staterooms are not large; however, they are cleverly designed and tastefully appointed and include two twin beds that convert to a queen-size bed; electronic wall safes; refrigerators; remote-control color TV with CNN, in-house movies, and three music channels; hair dryers; and ample drawer and closet space. The thirty-two deluxe minisuites and six ultradeluxe full suites are considerably more spacious, have larger balconies, and include bathrooms with Jacuzzi tubs. There are self-serve laundry facilities on every stateroom deck.

The *Sun Princess* offers several dining and entertainment options, which include two elegant, formal dining rooms; a twenty-four-hour lido café featuring breakfast, lunch, and teatime buffets and an alternative à la carte dinner menu as well as a special children's menu; a pizzeria; a patisserie; a hamburger/hot dog grill; an ice-cream bar; twenty-four-hour room service; and a champagne, wine, and caviar bar that is one of the seven more intimate lounges aboard. Two five-hundred-seat show lounges provide a diversity of evening entertainment while avoiding crowding passengers into a single multilevel facility. Other public rooms and areas adorned with $2.5 million of art include an attractive casino, a library, a cardroom, seven duty-free shops, five swimming pools and five whirlpools, an expansive walking/jogging track (three and a half times around to a mile), and a marvelous spa/fitness area with a fully equipped gym, aerobics room, his and hers sauna and steam rooms, a variety of massage and spa treatment rooms, whirlpools, a beauty salon, and computerized golf simulator.

In its tradition of appealing to the family trade, on all of its ships except the three smaller vessels, Princess has built unique centers for teens and fully equipped and supervised age-appropriate fun zones and educational centers for ages three to seven, eight to twelve, and thirteen to seventeen years.

The *Dawn Princess*, the *Sea Princess*, and the *Ocean Princess*, the *Sun's* sister ships, commenced service in 1997, 1998, and 2000, respectively, and are identical except for the art, decorations, and nomenclature of the various public rooms. The *Ocean Princess* was transferred to P&O in the fall of 2002 and the *Sea Princess* in 2003; however, in 2005, the *Sea Princess* was returned to the Princess fleet, and the *Royal Princess* was transferred to P&O. Currently, both the *Dawn Princess* and the *Sun Princess* are offering cruises from Australia and are marketed in the Australian market as well as in the United States. Both ships sail from Australia year-round, offering an onboard experience geared to Australian tastes. *Sea Princess* is also based in Australia. In 2013, *Sun Princess* inaugurated the company's first Japan-based cruise program—the largest deployment in that market by a global cruise line.

The 109,000-ton *Grand Princess* entered service in the spring of 1998. Seven hundred and ten of the 1,300 staterooms boast private balconies and include 28 full suites and 180 minisuites. Twenty-eight accommodations are wheelchair accessible. The 372 inside cabins, at 160 square feet, seemed a bit small, especially when they are occupied by a third or fourth passenger. Standard outside cabins vary from 165 to 210 square feet and increase by an additional 45 square feet if they have balconies. Although the cabins and bathrooms are not very large, all have twin beds that convert to queens, refrigerators, color TVs with CNN and in-house movies, hair dryers, and electronic safes. The minisuites, measuring 325 square feet (balcony included), have a second TV, larger sitting area with sofa bed, and a walk-in dressing area adjacent to a bathroom with tub and shower. For a few hundred dollars more per cruise, the minisuites are the more desirable accommodations. The full suites have separate parlors, wet bars, larger split bathrooms, and walk-in closets and, as expected, are the most desirable accommodations aboard ship.

The *Grand Princess* offers a wide range of dining venues, which include three Italian Renaissance-style main dining rooms with sitting areas divided for greater intimacy: Sabatini's, an outstanding Italian trattoria featuring an eight-course extravaganza of seafood and Italian specialties; Sterling Steakhouse, which was replaced by Crown Grill in 2011; and the twenty-four-hour Horizon Court, an alternate dining facility offering buffet breakfasts and lunches and bistro-style, full-service dinners. On lido deck, passengers can enjoy the hamburger/hot dog grill and the pizza counter as well as ice-cream creations. Room service is available around the clock.

Indoor and outdoor public facilities are mind boggling and include the 748-seat Princess Theater, with lavish nightly productions, a 13,500-square-foot casino, numerous additional lounges offering entertainment, dancing, and piano music; dozens of bars; a library; a writing room; a cardroom; a business center; a wedding chapel for marriages and vow renewals; a sports bar; a coffee-champagne-caviar bar; several boutiques; three regular swimming pools (one of which has a retractable dome for inclement weather), a children's pool and playground area, a pool with infused current for exercise swimming, and several whirlpools; a golf center with a nine-hole putting green and golf simulator machine; a fitness center with cardiovascular equipment, aerobics rooms, massage and beauty treatment rooms, a beauty salon, sauna and steam rooms, and locker facilities; a sport court for tennis, basketball, and volleyball; a small jogging track; youth and teen centers; a hospital with telemedical machines; and atop ship, a glass-enclosed moving sidewalk ascending to Skywalkers Disco and Observation Lounge, providing the feeling of entering a spaceship. This was removed on *Grand Princess* in 2011, and a new dance club, the One 5, was added on deck 15 as well as Alfredo's Pizzeria and Leaves Tea Lounge and Library.

Most public areas are broken up into multiple sections in order to downplay the immensity of the vessel. Despite multiple exits for disembarkation of the ship and tenders and numerous elevators, traffic can be heavily backed up at peak times. Many of the areas, such as the sauna-steam-shower complex, the fitness center, the outside deck lounges, the jogging track, and the outside lido dining tables, could be insufficient to accommodate all passengers on a day at sea. However, overall this is truly a "resort at sea," with vast facilities and options offering something that will appeal to all age-groups and a diverse segment of the cruising population.

The 109,000-ton *Golden Princess* and *Star Princess*, sister ships to the *Grand Princess*, entered service in spring 2001 and spring 2002, respectively. These ships boast wedding chapels that offer sea weddings conducted by the ship's captain. Various improvements not found on the other two vessels were also made on the *Star Princess*, including an improved spa featuring the new Lotus Spa as well as expanded children's facilities. The three *Grand*-class ships were renovated in 2008 and 2009 with the addition of the piazza-style atrium, which includes the International Café, Vines Wine Bar, and a new Internet café/library; a three-hundred-square-foot Movies Under the Stars screen over the pool; an adults-only sanctuary; and LED flat-screen TVs in all staterooms. In 2011, *Grand Princess* received a twenty-four-day makeover, adding a piazza atrium; a new nightclub that replaces Skywalkers; Alfredo's, a full-service pizzeria; a new tea lounge/library; ten new suites; a new martini bar; and a Crown Grill steak/chophouse.

The 116,000-ton, 2,670-passenger *Sapphire Princess* and *Diamond Princess* entered service in 2004. Similar to the *Grand Princess* series of ships in design, public facilities, and accommodations, additional features include Club Fusion (a high-tech lounge featuring various entertainments), five main dining rooms, five pools, and eight spas. Similar to the *Grand*-class ships, standard balcony and outside cabins are not very large and the bathrooms are quite small. Passengers desiring more living and storage space are best advised to opt for a mini or full suite. One of the most innovative features on these ships is the expanded dining possibilities. In addition to the casual, twenty-four-hour Horizon Café and the signature specialty restaurant, Sabatini's restaurant, the two main dining rooms have been divided into five different venues: one traditional two-seating, assigned-table dining room with the typical Princess Continental menu and four "anytime" dining rooms. Each of these dining rooms is elegantly furnished in a décor reflecting its theme. Passengers can make dining reservations each evening through a concierge service. A reservation-only (surcharge) Sterling Steakhouse specialty restaurant, similar to that on the other Princess ships, is also available.

The 113,000-ton, 3,100-passenger *Caribbean Princess* also joined the fleet in the spring of 2004 with a magnificent décor and such innovative features as a three-hundred-square-foot LED poolside movie screen for watching movies under the stars, expanded Internet, children and teen centers, an extended fitness area featuring twenty treadmills and numerous cardiovascular machines with personal TVs, improvements in the Lotus Spa areas with additional exotic treatments and massages, numerous premium TV channels, many additional activities including the Scholarship at Sea program, and new, innovative entertainment venues. The ship also offers a new dining venue, Café Caribe, with nightly themed buffets of Caribbean cuisine.

The Movies Under the Stars program takes place in two levels around the pool, where passengers sit in comfortable lounges with blankets (if needed) and can enjoy popcorn, drinks, and other snacks. The program has been extended to all the ships in the fleet except the three smaller vessels.

Of the 1,557 accommodations, 1,105 face the sea, 881 have private balconies, 25 are wheelchair accessible, and 682 have additional upper berths. The square footage of the cabins, bathrooms, and suites is similar to the other *Grand*-class ships (as described earlier).

Sister ships in dimension to the *Caribbean Princess*, the *Crown Princess*, the *Emerald Princess*, and the *Ruby Princess* entered service in 2006, 2007, and 2008, respectively, with numerous changes to the public areas. The atrium lobby is designed to look like a street café with a piazza-style atrium. Located here is a twenty-four-hour international café offering specialty coffees, drinks, rotating snacks, and desserts throughout the day; a wine and seafood bar featuring an extensive list of wines by the glass and a variety of seafood and tapas; and an Internet café. Sabatini's has been relocated to deck 16, featuring panoramic ocean views and a warm, intimate lounge, Adagio, for passengers to enjoy a more sophisticated atmosphere, cocktails, and live music. Crown Grill, a new specialty steak and chop restaurant with additional Continental favorites located on deck 7, features a theater-style kitchen, rich leather booths, and superior cuisine. The Lotus Spa facility occupies two decks. The Sanctuary, a special adults-only, semishaded outdoor area offers lounges, cabanas for a private massage, healthy food and beverages, and special service at a cost of $10 per person for a half day. The Sanctuary has been expanded to all but the two smaller ships.

When *Ruby Princess* entered service in 2008, new shipboard services were introduced, many of which are now available on other ships in the fleet. At lunch on sea days, the Wheelhouse Bar converts to an English-style pub (similar to those on Cunard's vessels), and suite passengers can enjoy an exclusive gourmet breakfast in

Sabatinis. Other innovations include tapas at Vines, the atrium area wine bar; additional enrichment programs, audience-participation events, and children's activities; wireless and cell phone connectivity around the vessel and in the staterooms; and ship tours to back-of-the-house areas for a maximum of twelve passengers offered twice each week for $150 per person.

The 92,000-ton, 1,950-passenger *Coral Princess* entered service in 2003, followed by a sister ship, *Island Princess*. Of the 987 staterooms and suites, 879 have ocean views, and all but 144 of these have private balconies. The inside cabins measure 156 square feet and the outside cabins without balconies measure 162 square feet. Balcony cabins range in size from 217 to 232 square feet, minisuites from 285 to 302 square feet, and the sixteen full suites come in at 470 square feet. (All measurements include the balcony.) Twenty cabins are wheelchair accessible, and 616 can accommodate a third or fourth passenger. There are no ultradeluxe grand suites as on the *Sun*-class and *Grand*-class vessels.

Public areas include three pools, five whirlpool spas, two main dining rooms, the signature Sabatini's Trattoria, Bayou Café and Steakhouse (a New Orleans-style restaurant), poolside pizza, ice-cream and hamburger facilities, the main showroom, numerous other lounges, a Las Vegas-themed martini bar, a casino, three duty-free shops, a fitness center and spa, children and teen centers, a library, an Internet café, a wedding chapel, an art gallery, and a golf putting green and simulator.

Princess acquired the former 30,277-ton, 670-passenger *R-3* and *R-4* of the now-defunct Renaissance Cruises and put them back in service in 2002 and 2003 after renaming them *Pacific Princess* and *Tahitian Princess*. The *Tahitian Princess* sailed year-round throughout French Polynesia, but in 2009, her name was changed to *Ocean Princess*, and she now cruises Asia, India, Africa, and Europe. A sister ship, the former *R8* of Renaissance Cruises, which sailed as *Minerva II* for Swan Hellenic, was transferred to Princess in April 2007 and renamed *Royal Princess*. In 2011, she was transferred to P&O Cruises and renamed *Adonia*. These ships, being considerably smaller than the other Princess vessels, are able to navigate ports not available to the rest of the fleet. They lend themselves to longer and more exotic itineraries.

These vessels are attractively designed and decorated to emulate the great ocean liners of the past with corridors laden with floral runner-style carpets similar to those found in grand hotels, stairways adorned with antiques and works of art, and lounges, libraries, and dining rooms done in rich dark woods and filled with expensive French and English furnishings and wall and window treatments. Most of the furnishings, equipment, and soft goods throughout the ships remain from their former days with Renaissance Cruises. However, various technical replacements, equipment upgrades, carpet replacement, and decorating took place on each ship between 2009 and 2011.

Ten suites on each ship range in size from 583 to 598 square feet with 283- to 364-square-foot private wraparound balconies, two TVs, separate living rooms with dining areas, a guest bath, and all marble master bathrooms with whirlpool tubs. Fifty-two suites on *Pacific Princess* and *Ocean Princess* average 260 square feet with 70-square-foot balconies, and an additional 170 outside staterooms average 173 square feet with 43-square-foot balconies.

In January 2001, Princess Cruises introduced Personal Choice Dining aboard *Grand Princess* and expanded the concept to its entire fleet over the remainder of that year. In essence, it allows passengers the choice between the traditional cruise dining, during which they sit at the same table with the same waiters and table mates each evening at a scheduled time, and the alternative, which entails dining any time between 5:30 and 10:00 p.m. at any table with anyone in the main dining room. Of course, the option to dine in buffet restaurant (which turns into an evening bistro) or through room service is always available. A steak house named Sterling Steakhouse on some ships and Crown Grill on others, featuring special cuts of Angus beef (at a surcharge), is also available on all ships. We found the quality of the beef and overall dining experience at these steak houses exceptional. Sabatini's restaurant, offering a multicourse Italian feast, is also available on most ships. Dividing the main dining rooms into several venues was inaugurated on the *Diamond Princess* and *Sapphire Princess* ships.

An additional innovation, Internet cafés debuted on the *Golden Princess* and were expanded to the entire fleet. With up to twenty-five computer stations open twenty-four hours, the facilities on these ships are among the largest and most impressive at sea. On the *Diamond* and *Sapphire Princess*, there are twenty-nine stations, and coffee and pastries are available to passengers while on line.

In 2004, new amenities were added throughout the fleet for those repeat passengers with significant sailing days aboard Princess ships and for suite passengers. Included are, laundry, dry cleaning, and shoe polishing, as well as afternoon tea and before-dinner hors d'oeuvres in the suite, an initial setup of liquors and soft drinks, and a corsage on formal nights. Cell phones work aboard all of the ships.

For $50 per person, balcony-cabin guests can opt for the "ultimate balcony dinner," wherein a multicourse dinner is elegantly served on their balcony. For $28 per cabin, a special champagne breakfast will be served in all staterooms. This is in addition to the standard room-service breakfast menu.

Available on all ships (other than on *Sun Princess*, *Dawn Princess*, and *Sea Princess*) is a new dining experience, the Chef's Table, where for $75 per head passengers can enjoy predinner cocktails and hors d'oeuvres in the ship's galley, hosted by the executive chef, followed by a multicourse tasting dinner with special wines in the dining room and dessert and discussions with the chef, which include the Princess cookbook.

In 2010, Princess brought back the Bon Voyage Experience from days gone by. The new version allows up to fifty guests to make advance arrangements to come on board the day of sailing in order to wish their passenger friends goodbye. For a $39 charge, they are treated to a four-course lunch with wine in the dining room and a tour of the ship.

Prices vary somewhat from ship to ship, being higher on European and Far East sailings. There is only a supplement for single occupancy of double cabins, and there are sizable reductions for third and fourth passengers sharing a room. Numerous air-sea packages are available, and Princess features significant discounts on early bookings (often as high as 40 to 50 percent). In addition, the Captain's Circle program offers numerous perks for frequent cruisers on the line.

Princess offers its passengers the opportunity to visit the top destinations around the globe with sailings ranging in length from seven to 107 days. In recent years, Princess has placed more emphasis on shore excursions. In addition to numerous active and adventurous options, the line makes available an array of air, sea, and land tours that afford opportunities to get close to the natural environs and sample the best sightseeing each area has to offer.

All sixteen ships presently in the fleet were delivered after 1995, making Princess one of the most modern lines in the premium-cruise market. There is an overall ambiance, desire to please, and lack of stuffiness not present on many other luxury liners. The larger Princess ships have exceptional special facilities and programs for youngsters and a full range of activities and entertainment, making them ideal choices for families. The adult clientele is an even mix of passengers from their twenties to seventies, making the demographics of the cruise line more diverse than that of other premium cruise lines. Most passengers are very pleased with the blend of luxury, fun, food, service, entertainment, activities, and personal-choice dining.

Two 141,000-ton, 3,600-passenger new builds joined the fleet in 2013 and 2014. The first is named *Royal Princess* and the second *Regal Princesss* (not to be confused with earlier Princess ships with the same names). Eighty percent of the staterooms on both ships have private balconies. Among the new features found on board is a greatly expanded atrium, the social hub of the ship; the dramatic overwater SeaWalk, a top-deck, glass-bottomed enclosed walkway on the ship's starboard side extending more than twenty-eight feet beyond the edge of the vessel; plush private poolside cabanas that appear to be floating on the water; a dazzling water and light show; an expanded version of Princess's signature adults-only haven, the Sanctuary; and the popular poolside theater, Movies Under the Stars. On these ships, special dining experiences include Chef's Table Lumiere; Crown Grill, which is combined with the Wheelhouse Bar; Sabatinis, which is adjacent to Vine's Wine Bar; and Alfredo's Pizzeria. In the expanded Horizon Court, there is a special area just for kids, new action stations, and a dedicated pastry shop.

## Strong Points

Attractive vessels, activities, entertainment, ambiance, itineraries, good service, and varied dining choices add up to a well-rounded, upscale cruise experience. The *Grand*-class ships are extremely well-appointed and offer a plethora of facilities. The innovations on the *Caribbean, Crown, Diamond, Emerald, Regal, Ruby, Royal* and *Sapphire Princess* vessels make them some of the most desirable of the megaships presently in service. The line offers attractive perks for repeat passengers.

*Royal Princess, courtesy Princess Cruises*

*Atrium lobby, courtesy Princess Cruises*

*Sanctuary area, courtesy Princess Cruises*

*Balcony stateroom, courtesy Princess Cruises*

# Captain's Welcome Dinner

*Sapphire Princess*

## Appetizers

**Applewood Smoked Duck Breast\***
with a zesty cranberry-blackberry relish and baby green salad

(V)  **Stilton Mousse and Waldorf Salad**
fluffy cheese mousse enhanced with sour cream and apple & celery slaw

**Crabmeat and Monterey Jack Cheese Quiche**
baked in savory pie crust and served with charred red pepper salsa

## Always Available

**Shrimp Cocktail**
an American classic with horseradish-spiked cocktail sauce

(V)  **Classic Caesar Salad**
crisp romaine lettuce, caesar dressing, parmesan cheese and herb croutons;
anchovies upon request

**Grilled Salmon with Herb & Lemon Compound Butter\***
vegetables of the day and parsley potatoes

**Pan-Seared Corn-Fed Chicken with Thyme Jus**
lightly seasoned boneless breast, vegetables of the day and roast potatoes

**Grilled Beef Filet Medallions, Tarragon Jus\***
market fresh vegetables and roast potatoes

**Spice-Rubbed Tri Tip Roast\***
marinated choice American beef, slow roasted, served medium-well
with chimichurri or BBQ sauce, vegetables of the day and steak fries

(V) Vegetarian

If you have any food related allergies or special dietary requirements, please
make sure to contact only your Headwaiter or the Maitre d'Hôtel.

*\*Consuming undercooked or raw meats, poultry, seafood, shellfish or eggs may
increase your risk of foodborne illness, especially if you have certain medical conditions.*

## Soups and Salad

**French Onion Soup**
gratinated with gruyère cheese crouton

**Creamy Asparagus Soup**
a recipe from Master Chef Alfredo with poached salmon dumplings

(V) **Chilled Sweet Corn and Potato Soup**
flavored with jalapeno, shredded basil and smoked tomatoes

(V) **Butter Lettuce, Curly Endive, Radicchio & Arugula Salad**
choice of homemade and low-fat dressings

## Signature Pastas
Available as an appetizer or main course and served with freshly grated parmesan cheese

**Farfalle alla Rustica**
bowtie pasta with tender veal, morel mushrooms and green peas
in cream sauce

(V) **Fettuccine Alfredo in Crisp Parmesan Basket**
**An All-Time Princess Favorite**
rich, comforting and entirely satisfying

## Main Courses

**Pan-Seared Barramundi with Chive & Mustard Seed Butter Sauce**
over melted leeks with green asparagus and potato batons

**Shrimp "Daniele"**
broiled tiger shrimp glazed with Café de Paris butter, broccoli
and vegetable fried rice

**Roasted Cornish Game Hen with Pan Jus**
on a bed of potato & mushroom ragout with pea pods

**Grilled Medallions of Beef Tenderloin**
**with Madeira-Truffle Demi-Glace***
an array of glazed carrots, pattypan & zucchini squash, almond croquettes

Home-Style Cuisine: **Rosemary Rubbed Roast Leg of Lamb**
**with Mint Jelly***
on natural pan juice with string beans, provencale tomato
and chateau potatoes

(V) **Crustless Spinach & Potato Flan with Spicy Tomato Sauce**
asparagus spears, zucchini batons, cherry tomatoes and roast potatoes

*Dinner Menu, courtesy Princess Cruises*

# EMERALD PRINCESS

## Let Princess be your Consummate Host®

| | |
|---|---|
| 2:00pm | **Champagne Art Auction** (1:00pm Preview) Enter Free Early Bird Raffle to win! Explorers Lounge, Deck 7 Midship — Crew's Choice |
| 2:00pm | **Detox For Health, Energy And Weight Loss** Aerobics Studio, Deck 16 Fwd |
| 2:00pm– 4:00pm | **Scholarship@Sea: Ceramics Painting** (Fees Apply) Deck 16 Forward Portside (Near Tradewinds Bar) |
| 2:15pm | **Tropical Rum Tasting & Raffle!** Enjoy the taste of tropical rum flavors. Enter to win a bottle of Captain Morgan. Club Fusion Deck 7 Aft |
| 2:30pm– 3:30pm | **Sea Waves Radio with Mike & Ben in the Arvo** Neptune's Reef & Pool, Deck 15 Midship |
| 2:45pm | **Water Volleyball** With the Cruise Director's team. Neptune's Reef & Pool, Deck 15 Midship |
| 2:45pm | **Robin Hood** Starring: Russell Crowe (Rated PG-13 · 2hrs 20mins) |
| 3:00pm | **Acupuncture Seminar – Back Pain and Sciatica Solutions.** Hearts and Minds, Deck 16 Fwd |
| 3:15pm | **Aurora Ammolite Seminar!** Join Kevin & learn about this rare gem. Enter to win an ammolite pendant valued at $200. Wheelhouse Bar, Deck 7 Fwd |
| 3:30pm | **$1250 Diamond Snowball Jackpot Bingo** may go in 51 numbers. Purchase a $40 pack and receive a raffle ticket to win a diamond and sapphire necklace. All participants will receive a gift card for a Caribbean charm bracelet. Cards available from 2:30pm. Club Fusion, Deck 7 Aft — Crew's Choice |
| 3:30pm– 4:30pm | **Afternoon Tea - A Tradition At Sea** Da Vinci Dining Room, Deck 6 Midship |
| 3:30pm– 4:30pm | **Easy Listening Melodies With DJ Dollar** Neptune's Reef & Pool, Deck 15 Midship |
| 3:45pm | **Wrinkle Remedies Seminar** Hearts and Minds, Deck 16 Fwd |
| 3:45pm | **Line Dance Class** With the Cruise Director's team. Piazza, Deck 5 Midship |
| 4:00pm– 6:00pm | **Paddle Tennis Play** (Unhosted) Sports Court, Deck 19 Aft |
| 4:30pm | **Afternoon Trivia** With the Cruise Director's team. Club Fusion, Deck 7 Aft |
| 4:45pm & 8:45pm | *In the Piazza:* **Duo Alia - Adagio / Body Balancing** Deck 5 Midship |

## Enchanting Evening

| | |
|---|---|
| 5:00pm– 10:30pm | **Formal Portraits Tonight!** Nine studio locations to choose from! Decks 5, 6 & 7 |
| 5:15pm | **Music For Listening & Dancing With Emerald Princess Orchestra** - Wheelhouse Bar, Deck 7 Fwd |

| | |
|---|---|
| 5:15pm | **Heart Of Alaska** (27mins) Calypso Pool, Deck 15 Midship |
| 7:00pm– 9:00pm | **The Piano Stylings Of Steven Mehaffey** Adagio Bar, Deck 16 Aft |
| 7:15pm & 9:00pm | **Dance To Gypsy Moon** Wheelhouse Bar, Deck 7 Fwd |
| 7:30pm | **Captain's Party Live on the Red Carpet Coverage** Explorers Lounge & Channel 21 |
| 7:30pm– 8:15pm | *In the Piazza:* **Captain's Welcome Aboard Party** Piazza, Decks 5, 6 & 7 |
| 7:30pm onwards | **Champagne Waterfall** Photographers will be there for the Captain's event! |
| 8:00pm & 10:30pm | **The Tourist** Starring: Johnny Depp & Angelina Jolie (Rated PG-13 · 1hr 44mins) |
| 8:15pm | **Ballroom Dance Hour** Club Fusion, Deck 7 Aft |
| 8:15pm & 10:15pm | **SHOWTIME:** **Production Show Spectacular:** "What A Swell Party" Princess Theater, Decks 6 & 7 Forward |
| 8:30pm & 10:30pm | **SHOWTIME:** **Comedy Showtime** Starring: Comedian Jeff Bradley Explorers Lounge, Deck 7 Midship — Crew's Choice |
| 9:00pm– 11:00pm | **"Jazzio in the Adagio"** With the Orchestra Jazz Cats Adagio Bar, Deck 16 Aft |
| 9:00pm– 11:00pm | **Hot Seat Slots** - Your chance to win random prizes simply by playing with your cruise card in your favourite slot machine. Gatsby's Casino, Deck 6 Fwd |
| 9:15pm | **Music Trivia With DJ Clinton** Club Fusion, Deck 7 Aft |
| 9:15pm & 11:15pm | **Dance To The Music of Icon** Explorers Lounge, Deck 7 Midship |
| 9:15pm Onwards | **It's Always Showtime With Barrington 'Barty' Brown** Crooners, Deck 7 Midship |
| 10:00pm | **Singles And Solos Get-Together** Skywalkers Nightclub, Deck 18 Aft |
| 10:15pm | **Princess Popstar Karaoke Contest** Join us for Heat #1. The audience judges. Club Fusion, Deck 7 Aft |
| 11:00pm Late | **Wild Bunch Party** Join the Cruise Director's staff and DJ Dollar. Skywalkers Nightclub, Deck 18 Aft |
| 11:30pm Close | **DJ Clinton's Formal Night Dance Party** Club Fusion, Deck 7 Aft |
| 12:00am | **Slot machines & PokerPro** are open all night. Casino Cashier opens tomorrow at 10:00am. Gatsby's Casino, Deck 6 Fwd |

---

### Captain's Welcome Aboard Party

Meet Captain Nicoló Binetti and his Senior Officers. Pose for a picture with the Champagne Waterfall. Enjoy complimentary champagne, mimosas and orange juice.
**Piazza, Decks 5, 6 & 7 · 7:30pm–8:15pm**

### PRINCESS CRUISES PRESENTS
### What A Swell Party

"Taking a step back in time with Cole Porter, this is a tongue in cheek look at this naughty but fun era."
**8:15pm & 10:15pm · Princess Theater**

### Food & Beverage
### British-Style Pub Lunch

Experience traditional pub fare and beers in a relaxed atmosphere.
**11:30am–2:30pm · Wheelhouse Bar, Deck 7**

## ☎ How will you escape completely?

### Refreshing Morning

**6:00am–Noon** — **The Wake Show** With Cruise Director Billy. Stateroom TV Channel 21

**Passover Service** In observance of Passover, a Seder Service will be conducted by Cantor Saltzman at 7:30pm. In order to prepare correct food quantities, those passengers who wish to attend must register at the Passenger Services Desk on Deck 6 Midships before 2:00pm today. Thank you.

**9:00am** — **Crochet@Sea** Come and meet fellow passengers and start your projects with the Cruise Director's team. Adagio Bar, Deck 16 Aft

**9:00am** — **Tour of Emerald Princess Public Areas** Join the Cruise Director's team for an orientation. Bring your map! Skywalkers Nightclub, Deck 18 Aft

**9:15am** — **Dr. Bob & Bill W. Meeting** - Hearts and Minds, Deck 16 Fwd

**9:15am** — **Veterans Get-Together** Crooner's Bar, Deck 7 Midship

**9:30am** — *In the Piazza* **Floral Demonstration With Our Florist Ferdinand.** Deck 5 Midship

**9:30am** — **Ballroom Blitz Dance Class: The Merengue** with the Cruise Director's team. Club Fusion, Deck 7 Aft

**9:45am** — **Basketball Free Throw Competition** With the Cruise Director's team. Sports Court, Deck 19 Aft

**10:00am** — **Acupuncture Seminar: A Life Changing Introduction** Hearts and Minds, Deck 16 Fwd

**10:00am** — **Extreme Pictionary** With the Cruise Director's team. Wheelhouse Bar, Deck 7 Fwd

**10:00am** — **Bridge Lecture** With Guest Lecturer, Martin Finver. Crown Grill, Deck 6 Aft

**10:00am–11:00pm** — **Citizen, Guess & Fossil Watches...** Receive 10% off any contemporary watch, when you spend over $50. Today Only. Piazza, Deck 7

**10:00am–11:00pm** — **Valerio 888 Amber Trunk Event!** Enter to win a piece of Amber jewelry when you "spot the fake". Meridian Bay, Deck 6

**10:00am–Noon** — **Scholarship@Sea: Ceramics Painting** (Fee's Apply) Deck 16 Forward Portside (Near Tradewinds Bar)

**10:15am** — **Morning Trivia** With the Cruise Director's team. Club Fusion Deck 7 Aft

**10:15am** — **movies under the stars** **An Affair to Remember** Starring: Cary Grant & Deborah Kerr (Rated NR • 1hr 54mins)

**10:30am** — **Jacqueline Kennedy Event!** - Join Sarah and learn all about the exquisite jewelry worn by Jacqueline Kennedy. Wheelhouse Bar, Deck 7 Fwd

**10:30am** — **$60 Texas Hold' Em Tournament** Followed by a $1/$2 No Limit cash game. Register for tomorrow's tournament from 12:00pm. Gatsby's Casino, Deck 6 Fwd

**10:30am** — **Caribbean Port & Shopping Show** - Detailed info on your duty & tax free shopping and excursions ashore! $5000 in prizes to be won including a $500 Tanzanite Necklace! Princess Theater, Deck 6 & 7 Forward — *Crew's Choice*

**10:45am** — **Emerald Princess Great Boat Building Competition Registration** Library, Deck 7

**10:45am** — **Closest To The Pin Competition** With the Cruise Director's team. Cybergolf Simulator, Deck 19 Aft

**11:00am** — **$1000 Snowball Jackpot Bingo** may go in 51 numbers. Avoid the lines - buy tickets early from 10:00am at Club Fusion Deck 7 Aft

**11:00am** — **Martini Demonstration** - Watch the creation of popular martinis as featured in our Crooners Bar Menu. Piazza, Deck 5, 6 & 7 Midship — *Crew's Choice*

**11:00am** — **How To Look 10 years Younger In 10 minutes** Hearts and Minds, Deck 16 Fwd

**11:00am** — **Secrets To A Flatter Stomach** Aerobics Studio, Deck 16 Fwd

**11:30am–2:30pm** — **British-Style Pub Lunch** Wheelhouse Bar, Deck 7 Fwd

### Relaxing Afternoon

**12:00pm** — **18-20's Wii Bowling** With the Cruise Director's team. Club Fusion Deck 7 Aft

**12:00pm** — **Gaming Lessons – Blackjack, Roulette, & Three Card Poker** All attendees receive a $5 match play ticket. Gatsby's Casino Deck 6 Fwd

**12:10pm** — **movies under the stars** **Barry Manilow In Concert** (59mins) Calypso Pool, Deck 15 Midship

**12:15pm** — **Zumba Class Intro** - Adon your workout clothes with Alicia & Miko. Piazza, Deck 5 Midship

**12:15pm–1:15pm** — **Live Poolside Music with Icon** Neptune's Reef & Pool, Deck 15 Midship

**1:00pm** — **Arts & Craft@Sea** - With Guest Instructor, Christine Peterson. Conference Room, Deck 6 Fwd

**1:00pm–3:30pm** — **Bridge Play** With Guest Lecturer, Martin Finver. Crown Grill, Deck 7 Aft

**1:30pm** — **movies under the stars** **Pavarotti in Concert** (89mins) Calypso Pool, Deck 15 Midship

**1:30pm** — **Emerald Princess Masters Championship Round #1** With DJ Clinton. Princess Links, Deck 19 Aft

**2:00pm** — **Afternoon Movie: Secretariat** Starring: Starring: Diane Lane & John Malkovich (PG - 2hrs. 4mins.) Princess Theater, Deck 6 & 7 Fwd

**2:00pm** — **Princess Pop Choir Rehearsal And Sign-Up** Join Miko of the Cruise Director's staff and find out what all the fun is about. Piazza, Deck 5

**2:00pm** — **Bar Wars** - Join us for a cool cocktail competition. Neptune's Reef & Pool, Deck 15 Midship

*Courtesy Princess Cruises*

# REGENT SEVEN SEAS CRUISES

**(800) 477-7500**
**Miami, FL 33122**
**www.rssc.com**

*Seven Seas Mariner:* entered service in 2001; renovated in 2011; 48,075 GRT; 709 × 93 feet; 700-passenger capacity; 350 suites (all with verandas); European and international officers and crew; cruises the Mediterranean and South America (Category A—six+ stars)

*Seven Seas Navigator:* entered service in 1999; renovated in 2012; 28,803 GRT; 565 × 81 feet; 490-passenger capacity; 245 suites; European and international officers and crew; cruises in the Caribbean, Panama Canal, Canada/New England, and Alaska (Category A—six stars)

*Seven Seas Voyager:* entered service in 2003; renovated in 2011; 42,363 GRT; 670 × 94.5 feet; 700-passenger capacity; 350 suites; European and international officers and crew; cruises Mediterranean, Baltics, Asia, Arabia, India, and Australia/New Zealand (Category A—six+ stars)

(Medical Facilities: C-4; P-1, EM, CLS, MS; N-1; CM; PD; BC; EKG; TC; PO; WC; OR; ICU; X; M; CCP)

Note: Six+ black stars are the highest ratings given in this edition to ships in the deluxe-market category.

These ships are rated in eleven separate categories in the second half of chapter 11.

In 2012, Regent Seven Seas Cruises celebrated its twenty-year milestone, tracing its origins to 1992. In 1995, the Seven Seas Cruises brand merged with Diamond Cruise Line and became Radisson Seven Seas Cruises. In 1998, the cruise line embarked upon a joint venture with Monte Carlo-based Vlasof Group, which formerly owned Sitmar Cruises, to build a series of new ships. In March 2006, the cruise line was rebranded Regent Seven Seas Cruises. In early 2008, the Apollo investment group, which owns 50 percent of Norwegian Cruise Line, purchased Regent Seven Seas Cruises following an earlier purchase of Oceania Cruises. Both companies are now part of Prestige Cruise Holdings; however, they are operated as separate brands. The emphasis of the brand is ultraluxury and service, along with destination cruising.

Included in the cruise fares on all of the ships are shore excursions, alcohol and all beverages throughout the ship, in-suite minibar replenished daily, gratuities, round-trip airfare, ground transfers, gourmet dining specialty restaurants without surcharges, complimentary shore excursions, and precruise hotel stay. When comparing prices with other cruise lines, these items must be taken into consideration.

Radisson Hotels Worldwide made its debut into the cruise industry in May 1992 with the revolutionary $125 million, twin-hull, ultradeluxe *Radisson Diamond*. The ship left the fleet in 2005. *Song of Flower*, which sailed for over a decade for Radisson Seven Seas, was retired from the fleet in October 2003. In January 1998, the 19,200-ton, 330-passenger *Paul Gauguin* joined the fleet, offering seven-night Polynesian cruises. The ship is now owned and operated by Pacific Beachcomber Company.

In November 1999, the *Seven Seas Navigator* debuted. This 28,803-ton, 565-foot-long vessel accommodates 490 guests in 245 suites. All of the standard suites measure 301 square feet (add an additional five feet for suites with balconies). In addition to the main dining room, the vessel offers three alternative dining venues: Prime 7 Steakhouse, La Veranda/Sette Mari at La Veranda, and a casual pool grill. This ship includes a variety of itineraries, including a series of destination-intensive cruises in the Caribbean, Canada/New England, and Alaska.

All accommodations include extremely generous storage areas, a large walk-in closet with unattached wooden hangers, a private safe, terry cloth robes, a makeup area with a hair dryer, an entertainment/sitting section with a writing desk, couch, small table for in-suite dining, TV with DVD player, refrigerator initially stocked with soft drinks and beer and bottled water, replenished daily, two twin beds or a European king bed, and marble bathrooms with a separate glassed-in shower stall, separate bathtub, large vanity with abundant storage, a toilet, and various toiletries. The suites have two separate rooms with larger balconies and two master suites, and two grand suites include a powder room and balconies that wrap around the front of the ship.

Located on decks 11 and 12, atop the ship, are the fitness center, a Canyon Ranch Spa Club, a beauty salon, a jogging track, nineteen suites, an observation lounge, and the romantic Galileo's Lounge, the best spot on the ship for cocktails, and late-night dancing and listening. The pool, outdoor whirlpools, additional suites, Prime 7, and La Veranda can be found on deck 10. La Veranda is open during the day and offers breakfast and lunch buffets. In the evening, La Veranda transforms into Sette Mari at La Veranda, a casual, intimate Italian dining experience. Prime 7 restaurant features steaks, chops, lobster, and seafood. The pool grill features a hot and cold buffet, panini sandwiches, and barbecue items as well as an ice-cream station. The remaining suites are located on decks 5 through 9 (only those on deck 5 do not include balconies).

Most of the public rooms are spread along decks 6 and 7 and include an elegant casino; a glamorous two-story show lounge; two boutiques; the central information/travel concierge area; a fully stocked library complete with books, videos, computers, printers, and e-mail/Internet capacities; a cardroom; and several other cocktail lounges. The main, single-seating Compass Rose dining room is on deck 5. Complimentary fine wines and liquor are served throughout the ship.

In 2001, the 48,075-ton, 700-passenger *Seven Seas Mariner* entered service. The ship has European senior officers, a 445-person international crew, and four different dining venues. It operates Mediterranean, South America, and Grand Crossing itineraries. This is the first all-suite, all-balcony vessel in the cruise industry.

Whether you opt for one of the 130 standard, deluxe, or concierge suites (301 square feet) or treat yourself to one of the 220 ultradeluxe accommodations—ranging in size from 449 to 2,002 square feet—you will be delighted with the large private balcony as well as the roominess, design, and tasteful furnishings. (Measurements include balconies.) Each suite features your choice of twin or matrimonial beds with down comforters, a makeup area with hair dryer, spacious walk-in closet with a private electronic safe and terry cloth robes, separate lounging section with a writing desk, remote-control TV and DVD, refrigerator stocked gratis (with your choice of soft drinks, beer, and bottled water), marble bathroom with a large vanity/storage area, bathtub/shower combination (some with a large marble-accented shower stall with a seat and rain shower head), upscale toiletries, and toilets situated so that you do not crunch your knees against the door. Of course, the more expensive suites not only afford greater space but also have additional facilities and amenities. Six suites accommodate wheelchairs.

In keeping with its dedication to culinary excellence, the cruise line has provided an excellent open-seating main dining room featuring exquisitely prepared epicurean selections as well as a nightly tasting menu, Canyon Ranch spa cuisine, and vegetarian alternative menus.

For a change of scenery, guests can select from three additional and distinctly different dining venues. Signatures, an elegantly furnished private dining room with panoramic sea views, features haute and nouvelle French cuisine. This is one of the finest gourmet specialty restaurants at sea. Prime 7 is a steak and chophouse featuring prime meats, lobster tails, and other steak house fare. The more casual Mediterranean bistro, La Veranda, transforms into Sette Mari at La Veranda each evening, offering authentic antipasti and Italian specialties served both buffet-style and à la carte. Complimentary yet excellent red and white wines from around the world are served in all four dining areas with dinner.

Public areas include a two-tiered show lounge, several observation lounges and bars, a nightclub, casino, cardroom, conference room, library, computer learning center and Internet café, health and fitness center, state-of-the-art spa operated by Canyon Ranch, large outdoor swimming pool and whirlpools, shuffleboard, and golf nets. The high ratio of space-to-passenger capacity results in no area of the ship ever feeling crowded.

The 42,363-ton, 700-passenger *Seven Seas Voyager* came on line in the spring of 2003. Similar in facilities to the *Seven Seas Mariner*, all accommodations are balcony suites, the smallest (called "Deluxe Category") measuring 306 square feet (plus a 50-square-foot balcony). The two largest master suites are a whopping 1,216 square feet, plus a 187-square-foot balcony, and the remaining suites range in size from 370 square feet to 1,403 square feet, including the balconies. Four suites can accommodate wheelchairs. All of the balconies can accommodate lounge chairs and small tables.

All accommodations feature separate lounging areas; walk-in closets; private safes; refrigerators stocked with soft drinks, beer, and bottled water as well as an initial bar setup; hair dryers; telephones; cotton bathrobes; high-tech interactive TV systems with free movie channels, CD and DVD players, and e-mail capabilities; and marble bathrooms with separate glass-enclosed showers and full bathtubs. Butler service is included in Penthouse Suite categories or higher.

Most of the public areas can be found on decks 4, 5, 6, and 11, with guest suites occupying decks 6 through 11, all with enviable ocean views. Although many of the public facilities and restaurants are similar to those described earlier for the *Mariner*, the Internet café and learning center have been expanded. The menus at Prime 7, Signatures, and Sette Mari specialty restaurants on *Seven Seas Voyager* are the same as on *Seven Seas Mariner*.

Beginning in 2008, all three ships commenced a multiyear, multimillion dollar refurbishment program, which included extensive renovations in public areas as well as a new pizza station and ice-cream bar. *Seven Seas Navigator*, the last scheduled to undergo renovations, emerged from dry dock in May 2012.

Wines and spirits are complimentary at all bars and restaurants throughout the fleet.

In December 2009, Canyon Ranch commenced operation of the spas on all three ships. Facilities include a state-of-the-art spa, a wellness center, a fully equipped fitness facility with weight-training equipment and cardio machines, a full-service beauty salon, men's and women's locker rooms with sauna and steam, thalasso-therapy pools, a juice bar, and a relaxation lounge.

A comprehensive selection of shore excursions are included in the cruise fare on all voyages. The Destination Services Department also plans unusual upscale explorations such as helicopter rides and meals at luxury restaurants ashore.

A new 54,000-ton, 738-passenger ship to to named, *Seven Seas Explorer* is scheduled to enter service in the summer of 2016. She will have 369 sites ranging insize between 300 and 1,500 square feet, a Canyon Ranch spa and six open-seating restaurants.

## Strong Points

With continuous upgrading in dining and service, Regent Seven Seas has become one of the top contenders in the luxury-cruise market. *Seven Seas Navigator*, *Seven Seas Mariner*, and *Seven Seas Voyager* boast the most spacious, comfortable, and livable accommodations at sea (from the lowest to the highest category). Larger than the former Regent Seven Seas' ships, they offer exceptional cuisine, additional facilities, and entertainment without sacrificing service and concern for passenger satisfaction.

*Dining Room, Seven Seas Voyager, courtesy Regent Seven Seas Cruises*

*Seven Seas Voyager, courtesy Regent Seven Seas Cruises*

*Suite on Seven Seas Voyage, courtesy Regent Seven Seas*

*Pool area on Seven Seas Voyager, courtesy Regent Seven Seas Cruises*

# Compass Rose

## Appetizers

Tiger Prawns, Remoulade Sauce and Celery

Goat Cheese and Golden Delicious Apple Tart Tatin with Watercress

Cantaloupe Melon and Grapefruit Segments, Sweet Côteaux du Layon Wine

Fresh Black Mussels with White Wine, Tomato and Onions, Garlic Herb Baguette

Orecchiette alle Verdure, Pasta Sautéed with Shallots and Crunchy Baby Vegetables in a Light Cream Sauce

## Soups

Cream of Cauliflower and Potatoes with Chicken Quenelle

Beef Consommé Diablotine, Parmesan Croutons with Cayenne Pepper

## Salads

Sicilian Salad, Arugula, Baby Greens, Onion, Tomato, Black Olives, Capers and Red Wine Vinaigrette

Boston Lettuce with Sweet Spiced Walnuts, Stilton Cheese and Fig-Vinegar Dressing

Caesar Salad with Traditional Garnish

## Intermezzo

Passion Fruit Sorbet

## Main Courses

Capellini alla Emilio, Angel Hair Pasta with Cherry Tomatoes, Artichokes and Melted Buffalo Mozzarella

Stir-fried Tofu with Glass Noodles, Tomatoes, Lima Beans, Green Peas and Shiitake Mushrooms

Striped Bass Fillet, Vegetable Stuffed Calamari Wrapped in Pancetta, Duo of Green Peas and Fish Jus

Broiled Cornish Hen on Barley Risotto with Cranberries and Chanterelle Mushrooms

Pork Medallions with Asparagus Spears, Snow Crab Meat and Hollandaise Sauce

Roast Black Angus Beef Strip Loin with Natural Jus and Paprika Potato

## A Taste from Prime 7 and Signatures Restaurant

Scallops with Smoked Bacon, Savoy Cabbage, Mashed Potatoes, Brouilly Cream

New Zealand Lamb Chops 6 oz, Lyonnaise Potatoes, String Beans with Bacon, Chimichurri

Please ask your Waiter if you prefer a dish from the menu prepared Plain, Low Fat, Low Sodium, without Sauce, Grilled or Poached. Also, if you require a special diet please ask our Restaurant Manager one day in advance.

## Menu Degustation

Our Executive Chef's invites you to sample a perfectly portioned gourmet tasting menu.

Tiger Prawns, Remoulade Sauce and Celery

Cream of Cauliflower and Potatoes with Chicken Quenelle

Fresh Black Mussels, with White Wine, Tomato and Onions, Garlic Herb Baguette

Passion Fruit Sorbet

Striped Bass Fillet, Vegetable Stuffed Calamari Wrapped in Pancetta, Duo of Green Peas and Fish Jus

Creamy Pistachio Croquant, Orange Segments

## Dessert Sensations

*9-Minute Baked "Valrhona" Chocolate
Cake with Raspberries, Vanilla Ice Cream

Strawberry Sablé
Shortbread with Passion Fruit Cream & Strawberries

Iced Cappuccino Parfait
In Chocolate Cup with Chantilly Cream

Seasonal Fresh Fruit Plate

## Canyon Ranch Selection

Classic Lemon Bars
Blueberry Puree 120/5/tr

## Old Time Favorite

Apple Crumble Pie

## Sorbet

Kir Royal

## Premium Ice Cream

Spumoni—Macadamia Nut

*Vanilla

Strawberry Frozen Yogurt

## Gourmandises

*No Sugar Added

# ONBOARD ACTIVITIES

Saturday, April 20, 2013 - ADRIATIC AND AEGEAN ESCAPES • Sunrise: 6:38am • Sunset: 7:57pm

### GOOD MORNING

|  |  |  |
|---|---|---|
| All Day | THE MARINER TODAY: An overview of the day's events with Cruise Director Paul Reynolds | TV Channel 1 |
| All Day | PORT PARTICULARS & EXCURSION INFORMATION will play continuously on your In-Suite TV | Channels 5 & 6 |
| All Day | ENRICHMENT LECTURES: Re-runs of the most recent presentations in the theater play in a loop | Channel 9 |
| 7:00am | ♥WALK A MILE! Join fellow guests for a mile walk around deck 12 (11 laps = 1 mile) | Sports Deck (12) |
| Until 6:00pm | * DAILY QUIZ: A winner will be chosen randomly. The PUZZLE PAGE is also available for fun! A sign-up book for BRIDGE is available for those guests that want to meet for informal games | Library (6) |
| 8:00 – 9:00am | ARRIVAL: Seven Seas Mariner is scheduled to anchor off the island of Santorini, Greece IMPORTANT INFORMATION: Local Tender Boats will be used to take you ashore today. These transfer guests on tour to the port of Athinios to meet local transportation which is not accessible from the pier in Thira. Guests not on a Regent excursion should therefore remain on board until the ship relocates. Tender boats will then run to the pier below the main town of Thira for the remainder of the day. Guests on Regent excursions will end their tour in Thira and should make their own way down to the pier using the cable car tickets provided. Only guests on a Regent excursion should meet in the theater upon arrival. Guests with independent arrangements should wait for a public announcement confirming the ship has relocated | |
| 9:30am approx | INDEPENDENT GUESTS: An announcement will be made when the ship has relocated to Thira and that tender boats are now running to the pier. Access to the town of Thira is by cable car, by foot or by donkey. Complimentary cable car tickets are available from Destination Services after 9:00am and until 11:00am, only for those guests not joining a Regent excursion. Those who are will receive these from the tour guide | |
| 10:00am | COFFEE CONNECTION: Still finalizing plans for your day? Get together with other independent travelers to exchange ideas and make plans for your time ashore | Coffee Corner (6) |
| 10:30am | BOARD GAME ENTHUSIASTS: Get together with fellow guests informally for a board game challenge | Card Room (6) |
| 11:15am | * BOCCE: Enjoy a relaxed morning game & some fresh air with members of the Entertainment Team | Sports Deck (12) |
| 11:30am | LIBRARY CORNER: Meet fellow fans to swap stories and discover your next good read | Library (6) |

### GOOD AFTERNOON

|  |  |  |
|---|---|---|
| 1:45 – 4:00pm | INFORMAL BRIDGE PLAY: Join fellow guests for an afternoon of unsupervised play | Card & Conference Room (6) |
| 2:00pm | DECK SPORTS ENTHUSIASTS MEET: Meet at the pool bar and join fellow guests to arrange an informal game of Shuffleboard, Bocce, Ping Pong, or Paddle Tennis with other interested players | Pool Bar (11) |

## IMPORTANT SAFETY PROCEDURES WHEN USING THE TENDER BOATS

These safety guidelines will increase your safety and comfort when riding a tender boat in ports where the ship is anchored.

- The service operates at the discretion of the Safety and Security Officers. Please await instructions from the officer on duty before disembarking towards the tender platform.
- Do not crowd the landing platform or the gangway area during the arrival process - this will only hinder the operation and delay matters. All guests should meet in the Constellation Theater.
- Both arms must be free when getting on or off a tender boat. Loose articles should be handed over to the crew before trying to get on or off.
- When stepping on or off you should extend "forearm to forearm" to the person assisting you. Never grip hands as this immobilizes the helper.
- Wait for the signal from the crew to board or exit the tender boat.
- Obey orders given by the crew, who are aware of certain sea conditions for safe operation. Please do not try in any way to help unless asked to do so.
- Never jump on board. Sit down as soon as you can, and stand up when requested.
- To avoid the danger of fire and discomfort to others, smoking is not permitted on tenders or while waiting in boarding lines.

## ONBOARD ACTIVITIES

| | | |
|---|---|---|
| 2:15pm | * SHUFFLEBOARD: Enjoy this cruise ship classic and challenge fellow guests for some Regent Rewards | Sports Deck (12) |
| 2:30pm | PADDLE TENNIS FANS get together for an un-hosted afternoon on the court | Sports Deck (12) |
| 3:15pm | * INDOOR SKITTLES: Take the challenge with the Entertainment Team for some Regent Rewards | Outside Boutique (6) |
| 4:00 - 5:00pm | AFTERNOON TEATIME: Enjoy a spot of tea with soothing music from guitarist Jakub until 4:30pm | Horizon Lounge (6) |
| 4:30pm | * TEATIME TRIVIA: Join fellow guests in teams of up to six to take the daily challenge in a fun round of fifteen questions, and a chance to win some Regent Rewards | Horizon Lounge (6) |
| 5:30 - 6:00pm | FRIENDS OF BILL W. are invited to get together | Card Room (6) |
| 5:30pm | LAST TENDER from shore to ship as *Seven Seas Mariner* prepares to set sail *We strongly advise guests to leave sufficient time to ride the cable car down to the pier* | |

* Signifies a "Regent Reward" will be awarded to the winner ♥ Signifies a "Fitness Afloat" activity

### GOOD EVENING – DRESS CODE: ELEGANT CASUAL
*A skirt, or slacks with blouse or sweater, pant suit or dress for ladies; slacks and collared shirt for gentlemen.*

| | | |
|---|---|---|
| 6:00pm | DEPARTURE: *Seven Seas Mariner* sets sail for Rhodes, Greece *(146 nautical miles)* | |
| 6:15 - 7:00pm | ENRICHMENT LECTURE WITH TIIU LUKK: EPHESUS! Steeped in the history of the Greeks and the Romans, Ephesus once had a population of 250,000, making it one of the largest cities in the Mediterranean. Join Tiiu for a "walk" through another time, from the Library of Celsus to the Roman Theater, discovering the largest collection of Roman ruins in this fascinating historical insight | Constellation Theater (5/6) |
| 6:15 - 7:30pm | SAILAWAY SERENADE: Resident Pianist Alexey presents melodies in the room with a view | Observation Lounge (12) |
| 6:30 - 7:45pm | TRIO DELIGHTS: Enjoy upbeat melodies from the Nature Rhythm Trio & refreshing treat from the bar | Mariner Lounge (5) |
| 6:30 - 7:30pm | HORIZON ROMANCE: Enjoy smooth romantic moods with the Regent Signature Orchestra | Horizon Lounge (6) |
| 6:30pm – Late | CENTURY CASINO: BLACKJACK ATTACK: Our special promotion continues through the evening | Casino (7) |
| 6:45 - 7:15pm | SOLO & SOCIAL TRAVELERS: Join Hostess Terese and fellow guests for cocktails; and plan the evening | Horizon Lounge (6) |
| 8:45 - 9:30pm | MARINER MELODIES: with Resident Pianist Alexey – perfect after dessert and before the show | Mariner Lounge (5) |
| 9:30pm | REGENT PROUDLY PRESENTS "LE CIRQUE MARINER" Starring the JEAN ANN RYAN SINGERS & DANCERS who transport you to the world of Cirque as they travel east to India, exploding in color and excitement onto the streets of Bombay with dynamic Bollywood choreography, an amazing musical score and set design by an award-winning scenic designer from the team of *Slumdog Millionaire*. Enjoy authentic Indian costumes as the flavors of this rich culture come to life with flying aerial ballet and stunning Specialty Artist performances from Caroline Warwick-Oliver and Denys Petrenko | Constellation Theater (5/6) |
| 10:00 - 11:15pm | ALEXEY'S PIANO BAR: Enjoy conversation & a nightcap as Resident Pianist Alexey serenades | Observation Lounge (12) |
| 10:15 - 11:15pm | DIXIELAND JAZZ NIGHT: The Regent Signature Orchestra present a Dixieland special as they take a journey to the deep south for your late-night entertainment | Horizon Lounge (6) |
| 10:15 - 11:30pm | STARS OF THE STRINGS: The Nature Rhythm Trio entertain into the night with upbeat sounds | Stars Night Club (6) |
| 11:30pm –Late | JUKEBOX DISCO: You to choose the hits, take to the dance floor and party into the night! | Stars Night Club (6) |

# DIXIELAND JAZZ NIGHT

## WITH THE REGENT SIGNATURE ORCHESTRA

### 10:15pm • Horizon Lounge (6)

## RESIDENSEA MANAGEMENT LTD.

### 14471 Miramar Parkway, Suite 401 Miramar, FL 33027
### (954) 538-8400
### Fax: (954) 431-7151
### www.aboardtheworld.com

*The World*: entered service in 2002; 43,524 GRT; 644 × 97.8 feet; 657-passenger capacity; 106 apartments and 59 studio apartments and veranda studios; Norwegian officers and international crew; itineraries around the world (Category A—not rated)

A residential community at sea offering itineraries around the world, it was conceptualized several years ago by Knut Kloster Jr., whose father founded Norwegian Caribbean Line in 1966. After years in the planning stages, his vision became reality when *The World* entered service in March 2002. In 2003, the resident owners took over total ownership of the vessel. *The World* is managed by Florida-based ResidenSea Management Ltd., which is responsible for the sales, marketing, operations, and administration of the vessel.

Sports deck and pool deck atop ship are the locations of many of the public areas, including the pool and outdoor lounging facilities; a full tennis court; paddle-tennis court; jogging track; golf club with putting green, golf simulator, and pro shop; the Mediterranean-style Tides Restaurant; Asian-style East Restaurant; sushi bar; pool grill; and beverage bar.

Immediately below these facilities on decks 7 through 10 are the 106 luxury apartments, ranging in size from 1,106 square feet (two-bedroom, two-bath apartment) to 3,242 square feet (three-bedroom, three-bath apartment). As in any private community, a select number of apartments are available for resale. The average price of those currently available for sale is $2 million. Most of the apartments can be rented by guests at rates of around $2,000 per night. Meals, select beverages, gratuities, and port charges are included, and a six-night minimum stay is required.

The nineteen one- and two-bedroom studio apartments ranging in size from 675 to 1,011 square feet and forty veranda studios averaging 340 square feet (for the traditional cruiser) can be found on deck 6, with a few in the higher categories on deck 7. Each includes two twin beds that convert to a queen; a separate sitting area with a writing desk, dressing table, and hair dryer; a marble bath with separate tub and shower; a refrigerator and cocktail cabinet stocked with complimentary beverages; a remote-control TV/VCR; a five-disc CD player; and direct-dial telephones. Eighty-four percent have private verandas and many have walk-in closets.

In addition to the apartments located on deck 6, there is a library, gallery, and the Garden tearoom.

Most of the remaining public areas can be found on deck 5, including the seven-thousand-square-foot Banyan Tree Spa, which includes treatment rooms, a sauna, and a beauty salon operated by Clinique La Prairie; a fitness center with exercise and cardiovascular machines, aerobics classes, and personal trainers; gift boutiques; the main theater for movies and live entertainment; a business and conference center; the

Marina restaurant, featuring seafood, steaks, and rotisserie specialties; Fredy's Deli, which triples as a gourmet market, street café, and deli; Portraits, the most upscale dining venue, offering French-fusion cuisine with themes highlighting the ship's destinations; and the casino.

On the lowest passenger deck, deck 4, there is a medical center and retractable marina and pool.

Dinner is offered in the various venues between 7:00 and 10:30 p.m., and guests can dine whenever they wish and with whomever they wish. All meals, except those in Portraits, are included for guests. Portraits is an à la carte restaurant where guests order from a set menu with dishes of varying prices. Evening entertainment is limited and there are no production shows or cabaret entertainers as on cruise ships. Daytime activities include lectures, classes in dance, navigation, language, cooking, arts and crafts, music, computers, and photography as well as tea service.

Representatives of the owners advise that the average occupancy is two hundred residents and guests, resulting in a high service staff-to-passenger ratio. Central to *The World's* unique concept is the flexibility afforded to residents and guests. Passengers can disembark the ship at any port and then rejoin at another, allowing extended visits ashore. A concierge is available to help with all shore-side arrangements.

# ROYAL CARIBBEAN INTERNATIONAL

1050 Caribbean Way
Miami, FL 33132
(800) 327-6700
Fax: (800) 722-5329
www.royalcaribbean.com

*Enchantment of the Seas*: entered service in 1997; lengthened 2005; 82,910 GRT; 989 × 105.6 feet; 2,730-passenger capacity (2,252 double occupancy); 1,126 cabins; international officers and crew; three- and four-night Bahamas cruises year-round from Port Canaveral, Florida (C-14)* (Category C—five stars)

*Freedom of the Seas, Liberty of the Seas,* and *Independence of the Seas*: entered service in 2006, 2007, and 2008, respectively; refurbished in 2011; 154,407 GRT; 1,112 × 185 feet; 4,375-passenger capacity (3,634 double occupancy); 1,817 cabins; international officers and crew; *Freedom of the Seas* offers seven-night eastern and western Caribbean cruises from Port Canaveral, Florida; *Liberty of the Seas* offers four- and five-night Caribbean itineraries in the winter and spring and seven-night itineraries in the Western Mediterranean in summer and autumn from Barcelona, Spain; *Independence of the Seas* offers three- to fourteen-night Mediterranean itineraries in the summer and six- and eight-night Caribbean itineraries in the winter and spring (C-32)* (Category C—five+ stars)

*Grandeur of the Seas*: entered service in 1996; 73,817 GRT; 916 × 105 feet; 2,446-passenger capacity (1,950 double occupancy); 975 cabins; international officers and crew; seven-night Bermuda, Bahamas, and Canada itineraries in summer and autumn and nine- and twelve-night Caribbean itineraries in winter and spring from Baltimore, Maryland (C-14)* (Category C—five stars)

*Legend of the Seas*: entered service in 1995; 63,100 GRT; 867 × 106 feet; 2,074-passenger capacity (1,804 double occupancy); 902 cabins; international officers and crew; seven- to eleven-night Northern Europe and Baltic itineraries from Copenhagen, Stockholm, and Hamburg in summer and autumn and ten- and eleven-night Caribbean and Panama Canal itineraries from Fort Lauderdale, Florida (C-17)* (Category C—five stars)

*Majesty of the Seas*: entered service in 1992; renovated in 2007; 74,077 GRT; 880 × 106 feet; 2,763-passenger capacity (2,350 double occupancy); 1,829 cabins; international officers and crew; three- and four-night cruises to the Bahamas from Miami, Florida (C-4)* (Category C—four stars)

*Oasis of the Seas* and *Allure of the Seas*: entered service in 2009 and 2010, respectively; 225,282 GRT; 1,187 × 215 feet; 6,318-passenger capacity (5,400 double occupancy); 2,700 cabins; international officers and crew; seven-night eastern and western Caribbean cruises from Fort Lauderdale, Florida (Category C—not rated)

*Quantum of the Seas*: entered service 2014; 167,800 GRT; 1,141' × 136'; 4,905-passenger capacity (4,180 double occupancy); international officers and crew; itineraries to be determined (Category C—not rated)

*Radiance of the Seas, Brilliance of the Seas, Serenade of the Seas,* and *Jewel of the Seas* entered service in 2001, 2002, 2003, and 2004, respectively; *Radiance of the Seas* was refurbished in 2011; 90,090 GRT; 965 × 106 feet; 2,501-passenger capacity (2,110 double occupancy); 1,055 cabins; international officers and crew; *Radiance* offers cruises to Alaska in summer and Australia and Hawaii in winter; *Brilliance* offers four- and five-night Caribbean cruises from Tampa, Florida, in winter, twelve-night Northern Europe and Baltic cruises from Harwich, England, in summer, and seven-night Canada and New England cruises from Boston, Massachusetts, in autumn; *Serenade* sails to the western Caribbean from New Orleans, Louisiana, during winter and offers ten- to twelve-night Mediterranean cruises from Barcelona, Spain, and Venice, Italy, in summer; *Jewel* sails year-round from San Juan on seven-night southern Caribbean cruises (C-14)* (Category C—five stars)

*Rhapsody of the Seas*: entered service in 1997; revitalized 2012; 78,491 GRT; 915 × 105.6 feet; 2,416-passenger capacity (1,998 double occupancy); 1020 cabins; international officers and crew; cruises in Hawaii, Alaska, and Australia/New Zealand (C-14)* (Category C—five stars)

*Splendour of the Seas*: entered service in 1996; revitalized 2011; 69,130 GRT; 867 × 105 feet; 2,074-passenger capacity (1,830 double occupancy); 915 cabins; international officers and crew; Brazil cruises from Sao Paolo and seven-night Mediterranean cruises from Venice, Italy (C-17)* (Category C—five stars)

*Vision of the Seas*: entered service in 1998; revitalized 2000; 78,340 GRT; 915 × 105.6 feet; 2,416-passenger capacity (1,998 double occupancy); 999 cabins; international officers and crew; seven-night southern Caribbean cruises from Colon, Panama, in winter and four- and five-night Caribbean cruises from Fort Lauderdale, Florida, in summer (C-14)* (Category C—five stars)

*Voyager of the Seas, Explorer of the Seas, Adventure of the Seas, Navigator of the Seas*, and *Mariner of the Seas* entered service in 1999, 2000, 2001, 2002, and 2003, respectively; 138,279 GRT; 1,020 × 157.5 feet; 3,807-passenger capacity (3,114 double occupancy); 1,557 cabins; international officers and crew; *Voyager* sails Australia and New Zealand cruises from Sydney in winter and the Asia-Pacific from China in summer; *Mariner* offers year-round Asia-Pacific cruises from China and Singapore; *Navigator* offers seven-night Caribbean sailings from Galveston, Texas, in winter, as well as seven-night Mediterranean cruises from Rome, Italy, in summer (C-26)* (Category C—five+ stars)

(Medical facilities: The wheelchair-accessible cabins [noted by *] are indicated for each ship after its listing. For all Royal Caribbean ships, the following applies: P-2, CLS, MS; N-3; CM; PD; EKG; TC; PO; EPC; OX; WC; ICU; X; M; LJ.)

Note: Actual passenger capacity on all ships will vary and, on most cruises, is less when there are only two passengers in a cabin. Thus, doubling the number of cabins is reflective of usual passenger capacity.

These ships are rated in eleven separate categories in the second half of chapter 14.

Royal Caribbean International was founded in 1969 by three Norwegian shipping companies. In the 1990s, it became a publicly held company traded on the New York and Oslo stock exchanges under "RCL."

Its first vessel, *Song of Norway*, entered service in 1970 (sold in 1996), followed by *Nordic Prince* in 1971 (sold in early 1995), *Sun Viking* in 1972 (sold in 1998), and *Song of America* in 1982 (sold in 1998). All four ships were built in Finland and designed for cruising the Caribbean. The first of Royal Caribbean's new breed of ships, *Sovereign of the Seas*, entered service in 1988, followed by *Nordic Empress* (renamed *Empress of the Seas*) in 1990, *Monarch of the Seas* in 1991, and *Majesty of the Seas* in 1992. Commencing with *Legend of the Seas* in 1995, Royal Caribbean introduced its *Vision*-class fleet with many improvements and innovations from prior vessels. *Splendour of the Seas* and *Grandeur of the Seas* followed in 1996, along with *Enchantment of the Seas* and *Rhapsody of the Seas* in 1997 and *Vision of the Seas* in 1998. The first of its mammoth 3,114-passenger, 142,000-ton *Voyager*-class (formerly *Eagle*-class) ships, *Voyager of the Seas*, entered service in 1999, followed by *Explorer of the Seas* in 2000, *Adventure of the Seas* in 2001, *Navigator of the Seas* in 2002, and

*Mariner of the Seas* in 2003. Four 90,000-ton *Radiance*-class ships came on line over the next few years. The first of this genre, *Radiance of the Seas*, entered service in the spring of 2001, followed by *Brilliance of the Seas* in 2002, *Serenade of the Seas* in 2003, and *Jewel of the Seas* in 2004. *Freedom of the Seas*, at 160,000 tons with a maximum passenger capacity of 4,370, the first of the *Freedom*-class vessels, entered service in the spring of 2006, followed by *Liberty of the Seas* in 2007 and *Independence of the Seas* in 2008. The 225,282-ton, 5,400-passenger *Oasis of the Seas* made its debut in December of 2009, the largest cruise ship ever built by far. A sister ship, *Allure of the Seas*, entered service in late 2010. In 2014, the first of the *Quantum*-class vessels, *Quantum of the Seas*, debuts, to be followed by *Anthem of the Seas* in 2015.

In June 1997, Royal Caribbean's parent company, Royal Caribbean Cruises Ltd. (RCL), acquired the highly acclaimed Celebrity Cruises; in 2006, RCL acquired Pullmantur, a Spanish cruise line; and in 2007, it created the boutique cruise line Azamara Cruises, which subsequently rebranded and changed its name to Azamara Club Cruises in 2010. However, each line continues to operate as a separate brand.

The company also launched a new cruise brand, CDF Croisieres de France, tailored for the French market. The first ship for the new brand, *Bleu de France* (formerly *Europa* and *Holiday Dream*), began sailing in May 2008, following a refit. During the warmer months, she sails from Marseille in the Mediterranean and during the winter from La Romana, Dominican Republic, in the Caribbean. RCL also entered into a joint venture with TUI AG, which services the German market. The new TUI Cruises commenced operations in 2009 with one ship, the *Galaxy* from Celebrity Cruises. Two new builds are planned for 2011 and 2012. The intention is for TUI Cruises to position itself as a premium cruise line between such luxury ships as Hapag-Lloyd's *Europa* and Peter Deilmann's *Deutschland* and economy, mass-market ships of AIDA Cruises.

Cruise fares vary slightly from ship to ship and for different itineraries. Unlike most cruise lines, there are numerous suites, staterooms, and cabins in each price category, and the gradual increase in price from one category to the next buys you more space and not just a more desirable location. The brochure price for the least expensive inside cabin on all the ships goes for approximately $190 per person per day, graduating to $250 to $320 per day for an average cabin without a veranda and $450 to $550 per day per person for a deluxe stateroom or minisuite with a veranda. The top-of-the-line royal suite on each ship will set you back from $650 to $1,000 per day per person. Add approximately $36 per day per person ($250 per week) for the air-sea packages. Additional parties sharing cabins pay approximately $100 per day. Prices on the *Oasis*-class, *Freedom*-class, *Voyager*-class, and *Radiance*-class ships run slightly higher, and discounts (ranging from 20 to 33 percent) are available for early bookings (nine to twelve months in advance). However, based on special promotions and other discounts, prices generally are often somewhat lower.

Breaking from a long tradition of assigned table dining, in 2009 the cruise line provided an option they refer to as My Time Dining, allowing passengers to dine wherever and with whomever they wish during normal dining hours. In addition, My Family Time Dining offers expedient forty-minute dining during the first seating in the main dining room for the benefit of children three to eleven years of age.

In recent years, Royal Caribbean has expanded its marketing program throughout the world, visiting more than 250 ports of call worldwide and providing daily programs, shore-excursion lists, and other onboard material in Spanish, German, Italian, French, and Portuguese. As a result, the line has attracted a more international mix of passengers. The number of non-United States/Canadian cruisers will vary between 10 and 33 percent, depending upon the itinerary and port of embarkation.

In 1988, the 73,192-ton *Sovereign of the Seas* joined the fleet as the largest cruise ship then in service. Sister ships *Monarch of the Seas* and *Majesty of the Seas* followed in 1991 and 1992, respectively. These ships are capable of carrying 2,773 passengers (2,292 double occupancy) in 1,146 cabins, 722 of which are located outside the ships. In 2008, *Sovereign of the Seas* was transferred to Pullmantur followed by *Monarch of the Seas* in 2012. *Majesty of the Seas'* ship design is similar to *Sovereign of the Seas*, with several innovations and improvements, including the addition of balconies in sixty-two of the suites and superior staterooms. In 2007, *Majesty of the Seas* was renovated, adding expanded dining options, new entertainments, upgraded spa/fitness areas, and three teen-only locations, and the staterooms and bathrooms were refurbished, including upgraded bedding.

In May 1995, the 69,130-ton, 2,076-passenger *Legend of the Seas*, the first of the *Vision*-class ships, entered service with emphasis on windows overlooking the sea, a seven-deck atrium topped off by a two-deck skylight attached to a 250-seat observation lounge/nightclub, facilities that include an eighteen-hole miniature golf course, a state-of-the-art spa and fully equipped fitness center, a 118-foot swimming pool, an indoor-outdoor pool with sliding-glass roof, special youth and teen facilities, and public areas, with numerous innovations and improvements over the line's prior vessels. Twenty-five percent of the staterooms and suites have private verandas, and all cabins convert to queen-bed configurations. In 1996, the sister ship, *Splendour of the Seas*, joined the fleet. *Grandeur of the Seas*, which entered service in late 1996, *Enchantment of the Seas* and *Rhapsody of the Seas*, which entered service in 1997, and *Vision of the Seas*, in 1998, are all somewhat similar to *Legend of the Seas* and boast extremely exquisite designs, fabrics, and artwork.

These are attractively furnished ships. Passengers can appreciate the elegant main lobbies, stairwells, and wide corridors with their abundance of wood, brass, marble, glass, and exquisite sculptures and artwork; the spacious elevators and public washrooms; the unique casinos; the lavish spa area with its numerous facilities; the opulent shopping plaza; the selection of theme lounges and bars; the lovely, comfortable two-story dining rooms and show lounges; giant panoramic observation lounges; special facilities for children and teens; and gigantic lido-pool complexes. A standard cabin is quite adequate and includes a small sitting area, two single beds or one queen bed, a private safe, a remote-control TV, a mirrored makeup area, a refrigerator, and a small bathroom. All outside staterooms and suites on decks 7 and 8 are spacious and include nice-sized balconies. The twenty-one grand suites, owner's suites, Royal Family suites, and one Royal Suite on deck 8 have larger sitting areas and balconies, refrigerator/minibars, and beautiful marble bathrooms with double vanities, tubs, showers, and robes. All accommodations on *Rhapsody of the Seas* and *Vision of the Seas* are a bit larger. On all of the *Vision*-class ships, the smallest inside cabin is at least 135 square feet. Average outside cabins without balconies range from 153 to 193 square feet, staterooms and regular suites with balconies from 241 to 630 square feet, and the Royal Suites more than 1,100 square feet.

In 2005, *Enchantment of the Seas* was stretched, adding a seventy-three-foot midsection, 151 additional staterooms (many with balconies), two seventy-five-foot-long suspension bridges spanning the pool deck, and additional pool/lido areas that include a splash deck with interactive fountains for kids and four bungee trampolines. Dining attractions include a new coffee and ice-cream shop serving Ben and Jerry's ice cream and Seattle's Best coffee, Chops Grill specialty restaurant, and additional food islands in the buffet restaurant, offering a more diverse range of items from different regions of the world. There is also an enhanced shopping area. The expanded spa facility added additional treatment rooms but eliminated the sauna and steam rooms. She offers five- and nine-night voyages to the Caribbean from Baltimore, Maryland.

In 2011, *Splendour of the Seas* underwent an extensive revitalization, adding more than one hundred balcony staterooms, new dining venues, new entertainment offerings, and aerial acrobatics in the signature centrum atrium. The revitalization of *Splendour of the Seas* is part of a fleetwide ship-by-ship revitalization initiative to introduce some of the most popular dining concepts and innovative onboard amenities from its most recent *Oasis* class of cruise ships, as well as new cutting-edge entertainment. In 2012, *Rhapsody of the Seas* underwent a similar revitalization. Many ships in other classes also have been revitalized, with the remaining also scheduled to enter dry dock through 2016.

Common enhancements aboard each ship include oversized LED movie screens overlooking the main pool deck, bow-to-stern Wi-Fi service, flat-panel LED televisions in staterooms, the Royal Babies & Tots Nursery for six- to thirty-six-month-olds, new exclusive lounges for loyalty program members and suite guests, and a multitude of specialty dining options—ranging from Park Café gourmet deli, to Giovanni's Table Italian family restaurant, to an intimate eighteen-guest Chef's Table degustation and wine-pairing experience.

All of Royal Caribbean's 69,000+-ton ships offer the same caliber of cruise experience; that is, they are large ships lavishly furnished and boasting a multitude of activities, facilities, and entertainment options. The dining rooms feature a variety of items nightly with multicourse, rotating menus, and concerned service. The Windjammer Cafés offer a casual dining alternative for all three meals, with a good selection of choices.

In November 1999, the 142,000-ton *Voyager of the Seas*, at that time the world's largest cruise ship, arrived in its home port of Miami, offering year-around cruises to the western Caribbean. Although the facilities, entertainment, and activities are similar to Royal Caribbean's other vessels, her increased size permits vastly expanded facilities and features. Public areas include the Royal Promenade, an open, four-deck atrium in the interior of the ship lined with a wide selection of shops, bars, cafés, and spontaneous entertainment; the 1,350-seat state-of-the-art theater, spanning three decks and offering nightly production shows and guest artists; the 900-seat Studio B, an ice rink featuring ice-skating by day and professional ice shows in the evening; the Vault, a unique disco off the Royal Promenade; youth facilities that include an enviable variety of video games, a teen nightclub, a children's water slide, outdoor games, supervised programs for youngsters three to seventeen years old, and more; a conference center; a fully stocked library with an abundance of computers and e-mail facilities for guests; the Spa, an upscale facility as luxurious as the finest resort spas, offering numerous beauty and body treatments, steam, sauna, hydrotherapy pool, aerobics classes, and a large well-equipped gym, one of the most impressive at sea; unparalleled outdoor sport options including basketball, paddleball, volleyball, golf simulators, an attractive vegetated, nine-hole putting course, a rock-climbing wall, an in-line skating track, a jogging track, and several swimming pools and spas; a helipad to accommodate helicopters for emergency medical services; a fully equipped medical facility with two physicians and three nurses; a most impressive $12-million art collection disbursed throughout the ship; a chapel; and numerous lounges including a jazz club and an observation lounge.

Nine hundred and thirty-nine of the 1,557 cabins and suites spread throughout the ship have ocean views and 707 have balconies. One hundred and thirty-eight of the 618 inside cabins, called "promenade view" staterooms, have bowed windows overlooking the Royal Promenade, the unique four-story central area in the interior of the ship. Twenty-six staterooms are wheelchair accessible, and four cabins can accommodate families up to eight persons. Every accommodation includes twin beds that convert to a queen, a sitting area, a vanity area with a hair dryer, a refrigerated minibar, a radio, an interactive TV, and a bathroom with screen-enclosed showers. Most cabins measure 160 square feet; the superior outside cabins come in at 202 feet including a balcony; and a variety of suites range from 277 to 506 feet, with the elaborate Royal Suite (with grand piano) at 1,088 feet.

The immense, yet extremely elegant, main dining room spans three decks and is connected by a dramatic grand staircase. For a $15 service charge, eighty-eight passengers can reserve tables for dinner at the tastefully decorated Giovanni's Table, the Italian specialty restaurant. The 310-seat Windjammer Café and the 454-seat Island Grill, located near the pool area, offer buffet breakfasts and lunches and casual buffet dinners with specials from the dining rooms. Johnny Rockets, the very popular 1950s-style diner, is open around-the-clock. The sidewalk café/brasserie on the Royal Promenade is the place to enjoy a Continental breakfast and specialty coffees, as well as pizza, pastries, and finger sandwiches throughout the day and evening. In addition, there is an ice-cream/yogurt parlor; a champagne bar; a sports bar; the English-style pub; the Connoisseur Club selling cigars, brandies, and cordials; and twenty-four-hour in-cabin room service.

Sisters to the *Voyager of the Seas*, *Explorer of the Seas* entered service in 2000, *Adventure of the Seas* in 2001, *Navigator of the Seas* in 2002, and *Mariner of the Seas* in 2003. In addition to aesthetic and structural differences in the public rooms, *Explorer of the Seas* is the first cruise ship to boast a working oceanographic and atmospheric laboratory with research being conducted by government and academic researchers. *Navigator of the Seas* and *Mariner of the Seas* have added an interactive wine bar, expanded venues for teens, a Southeast Asian/fusion buffet restaurant adjacent to the casual multi station Windjammer Café, a Ben & Jerry's ice-cream parlor, Chops Grill Steak House, Bolero's (a Latin jazz bar), and enhanced balconies.

Although many of Royal Caribbean's competitors extol the virtues of their private islands, Labadee is the most scenic private beach destination, offering the best (and the most) beaches for swimming and the best variety of water sports. The facility added a pirate-themed water playground in 2005 and has since launched a 2,600-foot zip line, private cabanas, craft market, among many other activities and amenities.

For the twenty-first century, Royal Caribbean introduced four 90,090-ton ships, which they refer to as *Radiance* class. Eighty percent of the accommodations have sea views, 60 percent with balconies. The first ship of this class, *Radiance of the Seas*, entered service in 2001; the second, *Brilliance of the Seas*, in 2002; the third, *Serenade of the Seas*, in 2003; and the fourth, *Jewel of the Seas*, in 2004. These elegant and beautiful ships feature nine-deck atrium lobbies and glass elevators that travel twelve decks facing out to the sea, and they are propelled by gas and steam turbine power rather than the more traditional diesel and diesel electric. These are the most luxuriously appointed of the line's cruise ships.

The smallest inside cabin measures 165 square feet and an average veranda cabin 179 square feet with a 41-square-foot veranda. The largest suite measures 1,001 square feet with a 215-square-foot veranda and includes a grand piano, wet bar, forty-two-inch flat-screen TV with stereo and VCR, a whirlpool bath, and steam shower. Although accommodations in all categories (as well as bathrooms in the nonsuites) are not particularly large, all are beautifully decorated and contain every necessary amenity.

The elegant two-level main dining room serves breakfast and lunch in an open seating and dinner in two seatings. Alternative dining includes Park Café, Boardwalk Dog House, Giovanni's Table, Izumi Asian Cuisine, Rita's Canteen, and Samba Grill Brazilian steak house. Some new specialty dining options are complimentary; others require a cover charge, ranging from $15 to $75 per guest inclusive of gratuities; while Izumi offers an a la carte menu, and the Windjammer buffet restaurant serves all three meals and snacks both indoors and outdoors. The buffet restaurants on these ships have a more convenient floor plan, with more service stations and better offerings than those I found in the buffet restaurants on many other ships.

Facilities aboard these ships include a state-of-the-art, attractive 15,500+-square-foot spa/fitness center, a rock-climbing wall, a golf simulator and nine-hole miniature golf course, a basketball court, a jogging track, an Internet café, a three-level theater for productions, a movie theater, a casino, a billiard club, cardrooms, the Viking Crown Lounge, an observation lounge by day and a combination nightclub and disco at night, a library, a champagne bar, a conference center, and numerous other bars and lounges. In 2011, *Radiance of the Seas* received an expansive revitalization. Hardware and software were upgraded in the staterooms and public areas.

As on all of Royal Caribbean's ships, the youth program and facilities are outstanding, with different levels of activities depending on age. The age groupings are from three to five, six to eight, nine to eleven, twelve to fourteen, and fifteen to seventeen years. The ship also now features a Royal Babies & Tots Nursery added during its revitalization. Facilities include a computer lab, play stations, video games, children's pool with a water slide, and a special teen disco/coffeehouse. Activities for children are also offered on Royal Caribbean's private beach and babysitting services are available. In 2005, the cruise line entered into an arrangement with Fisher-Price

Inc. to provide interactive educational programs for children six months to thirty-six months old, along with their parents, known as Aqua Babies (six to eighteen months) and Aqua Tots (eighteen months to three years). This includes special in-cabin TV programs as well. Royal Caribbean offers some of the best all-around facilities and boasts one of the best all-around children's programs in the industry.

Royal Caribbean and its sister line, Celebrity Cruises, entered into a joint venture with Cingular Wireless Maritime Communication Network to provide a service to allow guests to receive phone calls on their own cell phones at their personal numbers while in international waters. The service was initiated on *Majesty of the Seas, Navigator of the Seas*, and Celebrity Cruises' *Summit* and was thereafter extended to all the ships of both fleets. The two cruise lines also offer an online check-in program throughout both fleets, greatly speeding up the check-in process upon boarding ship.

In 2006, *Freedom of the Seas*, the first of the *Freedom*-class ships—accommodating up to 3,634 passengers (double occupancy 4,375 with every berth full), with a tonnage of approximately 160,000 GRT—came on line. *Liberty of the Seas*, a sister ship, entered service in 2007, and *Independence of the Seas*, a third sister ship, entered service in 2008. *Freedom of the Seas'* combined pool area is 43 percent larger than on *Voyager*-class ships and features an $H_2O$ Zone with innovative water attractions, an adults-only, jungle-themed solarium with cantilevered whirlpools that hang out 12 feet from the sides of the ship and a pool with piped-in underwater music, a dedicated sports pool, and a main pool area that transforms in the evening into an open-air nightclub. The 1,215-square-foot Presidential Family Suite, with an 810-foot patio area with an outdoor Jacuzzi and private bar, can sleep up to fourteen people. Also, there is a 1,406-square-foot Royal Suite with a 377-foot balcony, and thirty-two accommodations are wheelchair accessible. The ship also features the first boxing ring at sea. She offers seven-night western Caribbean itineraries. *Freedom of the Seas* and *Liberty of the Seas* were revitalized in 2011, with both ships headlining the DreamWorks Experience and *Liberty of the Seas* uniquely featuring Broadway-musical *Saturday Night Fever*.

In December 2009, *Oasis of the Seas*, the first of the 225,282-ton, 5,400-passenger (double occupancy) ships from STX in Finland, entered service, followed in 2010 by sister ship *Allure of the Seas*. The ships feature countless innovations never seen previously on cruise ships, including a unique neighborhood concept with seven distinct areas, numerous dining options and entertainment venues, the largest spa/fitness facility at sea, imaginative pools and water attractions, and expanded facilities for children of all ages. However, the most amazing aspect of these two giants is the décor throughout the ships. Every public area is cleverly designed to accommodate the large population and is still adorned with the most tasteful and impressive materials and furnishings.

The Opus main dining room spans three decks and features traditional seating as well as My Time Dining and My Family Time Dining for families with children ages three to eleven years. Opus is open for both lunch and dinner. The stateroom menus have been expanded and are available around the clock with a $3.95 service charge between midnight and 5:00 a.m.

The "neighborhood" of Central Park is the first open-air park at sea and is planted with tropical foliage, flowers, grass, shrubs, and trees surrounded by dining and drinking venues and shops. Included in the dining venues are the Chops Grille steak house (with a $30 cover charge); the Italian trattoria, Giovanni's Table (cover charge of $15 for lunch and $20 for dinner); and 150 Central Park, the fine-dining restaurant (with a $40 cover charge). The Park Café offers a complimentary breakfast and lunch menu with both indoor and outdoor seating.

A neighborhood for families is the Boardwalk, with a Coney Island theme, recreating the atmosphere of a seaside-pier entertainment area. The centerpiece is the first carousel at sea. Lining the sides of the Boardwalk are a candy store, an ice-cream parlor, a Johnny Rockets diner, the Seafood Shack, teen and children's retail stores, and a temporary-tattoo parlor. Suspended above is a zip line giving passengers a ride 82 feet above the Boardwalk atrium. The Boardwalk also features the first-of-its-kind AquaTheater amphitheater, which doubles as a performance venue and as the largest swimming pool at sea (21.9 feet wide by 51.6 feet long and 17.9 feet deep) with two diving towers.

The Royal Promenade neighborhood is an expanded version of the shopping mall found on other Royal Caribbean ships and includes numerous cafés, pubs, and bars. The Pool & Sports Zone includes a split-level pool deck with four main pool areas, two FlowRiders, a dozen Jacuzzis, an area dedicated to children, a full basketball court, and a miniature golf course. Other neighborhoods include the Vitality at Sea Spa and Fitness Center, a truly impressive facility with dozens of cardio and strength-building machines, cycles for spinning classes, an aerobics room, a spa offering numerous massage therapy and beauty treatments, and the Vitality Café, a bistro featuring light lunches and snacks. The Youth Zone offers age-appropriate facilities and activities for children of all ages. There are varying separate charges for several of the dining venues and for use of certain of the spa facilities for those not taking a treatment.

There are six entertainment venues, including Dazzles Nightclub (a two-story lounge and music venue), a comedy club, a jazz lounge, and the 1,300-seat Opal Theater. Similar to the *Freedom-* and *Voyager*-class ships, the Studio B ice rink features spectacular ice shows and ice-skating for passenger during the day. Numerous bars and lounges are sprinkled throughout the ship, including the Rising Tide Bar, which appears to levitate on jets of water, and the signature towering Viking Crown Lounge.

Accommodations include fabulous bi-level loft suites, two-bedroom/two-bath AquaTheater suites, staterooms with balconies facing Central Park and the Boardwalk, and a variety of balcony and sea-view staterooms as well as inside cabins.

Passengers on *Oasis* have been impressed with its size, indescribable beauty, and plethora of facilities. Although it sails like other ships, it is more akin to a giant sprawling resort or Las Vegas hotel, and enjoyment of the facilities and entertainments is more important than the destinations and the sail experience. In 2010 and 2011, many of the *Oasis of the Seas* features were added to *Freedom of the Seas* and *Liberty of the Seas* during their respective dry docks.

Although virtually identical to its sister, *Allure of the Seas* has certain innovations. Having negotiated an alliance with DreamWorks, a DreamWorks Experience has been created including encounters with some of the children's favorite film characters. Also new to this ship are Samba Grill Brazilian Steakhouse, Starbucks, Boardwalk Dog House, a cirque-style Blue Planet dance and aerobic spectacular, a musical production of *Chicago* (on *Oasis*, the musical production is *Hairspray*), and Rita's (a Mexican cantina with live music and dancing each evening). In 2011, many of the *Allure of the Seas* innovations were added to *Oasis of the Seas*.

In 2005 and 2006, Royal Caribbean instituted a program called Luggage Valet, which allows disembarking passengers to check in for same-day flights and to check their luggage right on the ship, thereby avoiding long lines at the airport. This service, which costs from $20 per passenger plus applicable airline luggage fees, is available for ships arriving at Fort Lauderdale, Miami—excluding *Majesty of the Seas*—Port Canaveral, Seattle, and Seward.

In 2009, the cruise line introduced enhanced service and amenities for suite passengers throughout the fleet. Suite passengers receive a special gold "sea pass" card allowing for priority check-in and disembarkation, admittance to the Concierge Club, special suite amenities, the ability to order off a full dining-room menu in their suites, and reserved seating poolside and in the theaters. Tipping is added to guest statements daily, $12.00 per day per person for nonsuite guests and $14.25 per person for suite guests.

With all of the new builds, Royal Caribbean will continue to expand its itineraries around the world. Caribbean cruises depart from ten different ports, including Miami, Fort Lauderdale, Port Canaveral, Tampa, New Orleans, Galveston, San Juan, Boston, New York, and Baltimore.

Two additional 4,100-passenger *Quantum*-class ships and a third *Oasis*-class ship are on order. The 167,800-ton *Quantum of the Seas* is expected to enter service in November of 2014 and *Anthem of the Seas* in the spring of 2015, with many new innovations. Among these are designated single staterooms (some with balconies), inside staterooms with virtual balconies showing the view from outside of the ship provided by a camera, studio staterooms for single passengers, a multilevel great room with 270-degree panoramic sea views, a two-story jewel-shaped glass capsule suspended atop ship where up to fourteen passengers can enjoy dramatic views, a skydiving simulator, a circus school with flying trapeze, and roller-skating and bumper cars.

## Strong Points

Beautifully appointed megaships offering attractive spacious accommodations, a large variety of facilities, activities, and entertainment, as well as enjoyable dining experiences. The *Oasis*-class, *Voyager*-class, *Freedom*-class, and *Radiance*-class ships are awesome, with exquisite décor and incredible appointments. Offering some of the most activities, entertainment, dining options, and facilities at sea makes them ideal for families of all ages. The *Oasis*-class ships are the most innovative and well-appointed ships in the cruise industry, offering the greatest number of amusements and facilities. Royal Caribbean is a very strong competitor in the mass cruise market, with a wide appeal to a diverse population of cruisers.

*Dining Room on Freedom of the Seas, courtesy Royal Caribbean Cruise Line*

*Oasis of the Seas and Allure of the Seas, courtesy Royal Caribbean Cruise Line*

*Balcony stateroom, courtesy Royal Caribbean Cruise Line*

**Shrimp Cocktail**
With traditional American cocktail sauce

**Dungeness Crab and Shrimp Cake**
Rémoulade sauce

**Smoked Duck Salad**
Orange confit, baby lettuce, green asparagus and zesty Cointreau dressing

**Oyster Duet**
Rockefeller, spinach and Hollandaise gratin
Kilpatrick, baked with bacon and a tangy BBQ-Worcestershire sauce

**Asian-Inspired Spicy Tuna***
On crisp black sesame seeds and parmesan crisps,
with cucumber and avocado salsa, unagi sauce and micro greens

**Warm Goat Cheese and Basil Soufflé**
Double baked soufflé served with portabella mushroom confit
and creamy sage reduction

**Cheese N' Onion Soup**
Topped with Gruyère cheese

**Forest Mushroom Soup**
Scented with white truffle oil

**Not So Traditional Caesar Salad**
Romaine hearts, garlic croutons, and chive-Caesar dressing

**Beefsteak Tomato and Purple Onions**
Sprinkled with blue cheese crumbles

**Chops Signature Salad**
Caramelized baby beetroots, bacon chips, mixed lettuces,
tomatoes and red wine vinaigrette

## SEAFOOD & CHICKEN

**Pan-fried Barramundi Fillet** (∅)
On fondant potatoes, butternut squash purée and a crispy tempura vegetable bundle

**Alaskan Halibut**
Baked on a cedar plank

**Herb-crusted Jumbo Shrimp**
Asparagus, grape tomatoes and

lime-crab beurre blanc

**Free-range Chicken Breast** (∅)(⅋)
Wrapped in crispy pancetta

> **New York Strip Steak\*** (∅)(⅋)
> 12 ounces of an all time favorite

## STEAK & CUTS\* (∅)(⅋)

**Petit Filet Mignon**
7 ounces of a thick and flavorful cut from the tenderloin

**Broiled Veal Chop**
10 ounces, served on the bone

**Chops-style Mixed Grill**
Combination of a grilled lamb chop, apple-chicken sausage, veal tournedos, bacon, bubble & squeak and veal reduction

**Broiled Porterhouse Steak**
18 ounces, served on the bone

**Boneless Beef Short Rib**
Slowly braised in rich Burgundy-veal sauce

**Filet Mignon**
10 ounces of a thick and flavorful cut from the tenderloin

## SIDES & VEGETABLES
◇ Rock Salt Baked Idaho Potato V (∅)(⅋)
◇ Double Whipped Mashed
  Potatoes V (∅)
◇ Roasted Potatoes with Prosciutto
  and Parmesan (∅)

◇ Sautéed Broccolini V (∅)(⅋)
◇ Crimini Mushrooms and Leek V (∅)(⅋)
◇ Green Beans with Dijon mustard
  sabayon and feta cheese crumble V
◇ Steamed Asparagus V (∅)(⅋)
◇ Fried Onion Rings V (⅋)

## SAUCES
◇ Classic Béarnaise (∅)
◇ Chimichurri Sauce (⅋)

◇ Green Peppercorn Sauce
◇ Cabernet Reduction (∅)(⅋)

\*Consuming raw or undercooked meats, seafood, shellfish, eggs, milk, or poultry may increase your risk of foodborne illness, especially if you have certain medical conditions.

(∅) Gluten-free available   (⅋) Lactose-free available   V Vegetarian

Please inform your waiter if you have any food allergies or dietary needs.
Royal Caribbean International galleys are not food allergen-free environments.

*Dinner Menu for Chops, courtesy Royal Caribbean Cruise Line*

| | | |
|---|---|---|
| Airbrushed Tattoos | 7:15 pm – 10:00 pm (Royal Promenade) | Deck 5 |
| Pets At Sea | 7:15 pm – 10:00 pm | Deck 5 |
| Baby Splash Zone* | 8:00 am – 6:00 pm (starboard, inside the H2O Zone) | Deck 15 |
| Box Office (show reservations) | 8:30 pm – 9:00 pm (Comedy Live) | Deck 4 |
| | 10:00 pm – 10:30 pm (Comedy Live) | Deck 4 |
| Carousel | 5:00 pm – 10:30 pm | Deck 6 |
| Casino Royale (slots & Tables) | 7:15 pm – late | Deck 4 |
| Explorations! Desk | 8:00 am – 11:00 am / 6:00 pm – 8:00 pm | Deck 5 |
| Floral Cart | 4:00 pm – 9:30 pm | Deck 5 |
| Focus Camera Store | 7:15 pm – 11:00 pm | Deck 5 |
| H2O Zone* | 8:00 am – 8:00 pm | Deck 15 |
| Loyalty & Cruise Sales | 9:00 am – 11:00 am & 4:00 pm – 8:30 pm | Deck 6 |
| Medical Facility (dial 51) | 8:00 am – 11:00 am & 4:00 pm – 7:00 pm | Deck 2 aft |
| Parkside Art Gallery | 7:00 pm – 11:00 pm | Deck 8 |
| Photo Gallery | 6:00 pm – 11:00 pm | Deck 6 |
| Picture This | 6:00 pm – 10:30 pm | Deck 8 |
| Rising Tide | 5:00 pm – 1:00 am | |
| | (enter starboard side, after 10:00 pm Adults Only.) | Deck 5 |
| SeaTrek Dive Shop (2684) | 8:30 am – 9:30 am | Deck 15 |
| Shopping Guide | 10:00 am – 11:00 am (gangway) | Deck 2 |
| | 7:30 pm – 8:30 pm (dial 4453) | Deck 5 |
| Shops Onboard | 7:15 pm – 11:00 pm | Decks 5, 6, 8 |
| Smile Photo Studio | 6:30 pm – 10:30 pm | Deck 6 |
| Sports Court* | 8:00 am – 11:00 pm | Deck 15 |
| Sports Desk* | 8:00 am – 11:00 am / 3:00 pm – 6:00 pm | Deck 15 |
| **FlowRiders**\*\* | | |
| Boogie Boarding | 9:00 am – 11:00 am / 3:00 pm – 6:00 pm; (starboard side) | |
| Advance Stand-up Surfing | 8:00 am – 9:00 am; (port side) | |
| Stand-up Surfing | 9:00 am – 10:00 am/ 3:00 pm – 6:00 pm; (port side) | |
| Teen Stand-up Surfing | 10:00 am – 11:00 am; (port side) | Deck 16 |

*(Please remove all jewelry items. Ladies are advised to wear a T-shirt. A FlowRider waiver must be completed. Minimum height requirement: Boogie Boarding is 52", Stand Up Surfing is 58").*

| | | |
|---|---|---|
| Oasis Dunes Golf* | 8:00 am – 11:00 pm | Deck 15 |
| **Rock Climbing Walls**\* | | |
| Open Climbing | 3:00 pm – 7:00 pm; Starboard Side | Deck 7 |

*(Please bring socks, t-shirt and shorts/pants and clothing must be dry. A Rock Climbing Wall waiver must be completed once a cruise vacation. Children must be 6 years of age or older to climb. Parents must be present to sign a waiver for children under the age of 18 and must stay to supervise children under the age of 13 years. Adults must be able to fit into the XXL harness to climb. Sign ups will close 15-30 minutes before closing time.)*

| | | |
|---|---|---|
| Shuffleboard Courts* | 9:00 am – 11:00 pm | |
| | Closed During Performances & Rehearsals (behind AquaTheater screen). | Deck 6 |
| Zip Line* | 3:00 pm – 5:30 pm | Deck 16 |

*Please bring only your SeaPass Cards, remove all loose articles including watches, wallets, jewelry, glasses, wallets, and glasses and ensure pockets are completely empty. Please tie back long hair and wear closed, secure shoes or bring socks. (Sign-ups will close 15-30 minutes before closing time.)*

| | | |
|---|---|---|
| Tuxedo Rentals | (contact guest services by dialing 0) | Deck 5 |
| Vitality at Sea Spa (dial 4600) | 8:00 am – 10:00 pm | Deck 6 |
| Vitality at Sea Fitness Center | 6:00 am – 11:00 pm | Deck 6 |

**The Following Services and Venues are Open 24 Hours:**

Emergency Only (dial 911) / Guest Services (dial 0), Deck 5 / Jogging Track, Deck 5 / Library, Deck 11 / Operator (dial 0) / Photo Kiosk, Deck 6 / RCTV (View, spa and excursion reservations available) / royal caribbean online\*\*, Decks 7, 9, 14 / Selected Swimming Pools & Hot Tubs, Deck 15 / Solarium Hot Tubs, Pools & Area (16 years & older only), Decks 15, 16 / Table Tennis, Deck 15.

*\*For rules and restrictions and sign up requirements; please see the staff at the appropriate venue.*

## DAY 4

Tuesday, June 12, 2012
**FALMOUTH, JAMAICA**
ARRIVAL: 10:00 am (Ship's time)
ALL ABOARD: 6:30 pm (Ship's time)
Please stay on Ship's time

### DINING SCHEDULE & AFTERNOON SNACKS

**Check the Dining Availability Screens
located throughout the ship and on your stateroom TV**

| BREAKFAST | | DECK |
|---|---|---|
| 7:00 am – 11:00 am | Breakfast ..........Windjammer Marketplace | 16 |
| 7:30 am – 10:30 am | Solarium Bistro....................Solarium | 15 |
| 7:30 am – 11:00 am | Park Café....................Central Park | 8 |
| 8:00 am – 10:00 am | Express Breakfast Buffet | |
| | ....................Opus Dining Room | 3 |
| 8:00 am – 10:15 am | Johnny Rockets....................Boardwalk | 6 |

| LUNCH | | |
|---|---|---|
| 11:30 am – 3:30 pm | Windjammer Marketplace | 16 |
| 11:30 am – 6:00 pm | Park Café....................Central Park | 8 |
| Noon – 2:30 pm | Solarium Bistro....................Solarium | 15 |
| 1:00 pm – midnight | Johnny Rockets ($)....................Boardwalk | 6 |
| 2:00 pm – 5:30 pm | Seafood Shack ($)....................Boardwalk | 6 |
| 2:00 pm – 6:00 pm | Vintages/Tapas ($)....................Central Park | 8 |

| SNACKS | | |
|---|---|---|
| 24 hours | Room Service – Please note a $3.95 service charge | |
| | will be applied for Room Service orders between midnight | |
| | and 5:00 am. | |
| 24 hours | Café Promenade .......Royal Promenade | 5 |
| 7:00 am – 10:30 am | Donut Shop ....................Boardwalk | 6 |
| 7:00 am – 6:00 pm | Park Café....................Central Park | 8 |
| 7:00 am – 9:00 pm | Vitality Spa Café ..........Vitality Spa | 6 |
| 7:00 am – 11:00 pm | Starbucks Coffee ($)......Royal Promenade | 5 |
| 11:30 am – 6:00 pm | Frozen Yogurt....................Pool Deck | 15 |
| 11:30 am – 3:00 am | Sorrento's ............Royal Promenade | 5 |
| 1:00 pm – 9:00 pm | Boardwalk Bar ....................Boardwalk | 6 |
| 3:00 pm – midnight | Ice-Cream Parlor ($) ........Boardwalk | 6 |
| 3:00 pm – midnight | Cupcake Cupboard ($)......Royal Promenade | 5 |
| 3:30 pm – 5:30 pm | Wipe Out Café.............. Sports Deck | 15 |
| 4:00 pm – 7:00 pm | Donut Shop ....................Boardwalk | 6 |

### BAR OPEN HOURS

For an early drink the Promenade Bar opens at 7:00 am and the Pool Bar at 9:00 am. The Casino Bar, Boleros, the Schooner Bar, Dazzles, Blaze and Jazz on 4 remain open later than other bars.

*Daily Program on Oasis of the Seas, courtesy Royal Caribbean Cruise Line*

# SEABOURN CRUISE LINE

**300 Elliot West**
**Seattle, WA**
**(800) 929-9391**
**www.seabourn.com**

*Seabourn Legend* (formerly *Royal Viking Queen* and *Queen Odyssey*): entered service in 1993; refurbished in 2010; 10,000 GRT; 440 × 63 feet; 208-passenger capacity; 104 suites; European officers, international staff and crew; cruises the Mediterranean, Arabia, India, Indonesia, and Malaysia as well as other destinations around the world (Category A—six+ stars)

*Seabourn Odyssey, Seabourn Sojourn,* and *Seabourn Quest*: entered service in 2009, 2010, and 2011, respectively; 32,000 GRT; 654 × 84 feet; 450-passenger capacity; 225 suites; Norwegian and British officers and international staff and crew; *Seabourn Odyssey* cruises Eastern Mediterranean, Arabia, India, Southeast Asia, Australia/New Zealand, and South Pacific; *Seabourn Sojourn* cruises South America, Eastern and Western Mediterranean, North Sea/Baltics, Northern Europe, Canada/New England, Caribbean, and a world cruise; *Seabourn Quest* cruises Eastern and Western Mediterranean, South America, and Antartica (Category A—six+ stars)

*Seabourn Pride*: entered service in 1988; refurbished in 2010; 10,000 GRT; 440 × 63 feet; 208-passenger capacity; 104 suites; European officers, international staff and crew; cruises Southeast Asia, Mediterranean, Baltics, and Norwegian fjords (The ship will commence sailing for Windstar Cruises in April 2014; Category A—six+ stars)

*Seabourn Spirit*: entered service in 1989; refurbished in 2010; 10,000 GRT; 440 × 63 feet; 208-passenger capacity; 104 suites; European officers, international staff and crew; varying itineraries, including South America, the Mediterranean, Southeast Asia, the Orient, India, and Arabia (Category A—six+ stars)

(Medical facilities: C-4; P-1; EM, CLS, MS; N-1; CM; PD; EKG; TC; PO; OX; WC; ICU; X; M)

*Note*: Six+ black stars is the highest rating given in this edition to ships in the deluxe-market category.

These ships are rated in eleven separate categories in the second half of chapter 11.

The three original 208-passenger, 10,000-ton, all-suite vessels of Seabourn are positioned at the top of the luxury-cruise market and are designed to offer the most elegant, luxurious cruise experience afloat, with spacious suite accommodations, open-seating dining with top-of-the-line service and gourmet cuisine, tasteful and elegantly appointed public rooms, excellent water-sport and spa facilities, and some of the most desired destinations. Although dress during the day is casual, on most evenings gentlemen are expected to wear jackets in the dining room, and the atmosphere is more formal and sophisticated than on other ships. However, in the evening, guests may opt to have dinner at the new, more casual venue Restaurant 2, located at the Veranda Café or at the Sky Grill on sundeck, where the dress code is more casual.

In May 1998, Carnival Corporation acquired Cunard Line Ltd., merged Cunard with Seabourn Cruise Line, and transferred the two *Sea Goddesses* and the *Royal Viking Sun* from Cunard to the Seabourn brand, renaming the ships *Seabourn Goddess I* and *II* and *Seabourn Sun*. Subsequently, the two *Sea/Seabourn Goddesses* were sold to the former owner and CEO of Seabourn, and the *Sun* was transferred to Holland America Line, another subsidiary of Carnival Corporation, and renamed *Prinsendam*. Thereafter, corporate management decided that there was little similarity between the sleek, yacht-like Seabourn vessels and the original Cunard ships. Presently, Seabourn is operated as an entirely separate brand from Cunard and is marketed to a somewhat different cruise population.

The original Seabourn ships, the *Pride* and *Spirit*, entered service in 1988 and 1989, respectively, and were heralded throughout the industry as the most magnificent and luxurious smaller vessels ever built. Seabourn ordered a third ship built in 1991 but exercised its option not to buy it. The shipyard, in turn, sold it to Royal Viking Line, where it entered service in 1992 as the *Royal Viking Queen*. When Royal Viking Line was dismantled by its owners, the ship was transferred to the Royal Cruise Line and renamed *Queen Odyssey*. Royal ceased operating in 1996, at which time the ship was repurchased by Seabourn and became known as *Seabourn Legend*.

Cruise-only prices in the brochure range from $400 to $2,000 per person, per day (double occupancy), depending on location of cabin and cruise area. Tips are included in the cruise fare. There is no charge for liquors or soft drinks throughout the ships, and wines, champagne, and caviar are served gratis at lunch and dinner and at any other time. The line also offers past passengers substantial discounts (often as high as 40 or 50 percent) and any passenger accruing 140 days on board receives a complimentary seven-day cruise on a Seabourn ship and any passenger accruing 250 days receives a complimentary fourteen-day cruise on any Seabourn ship. In 2012, the line introduced a tiered loyalty rewards program that starts offering onboard benefits such as free laundry, Internet service, discounts on shore excursions, and much more after as few as twenty days sailed. Guests are invited to choose the rewards that mean the most to them, from a menu of benefits.

Itineraries for all ships include Northern Europe, the Orient, and the Mediterranean during spring, summer, and early fall and the South Pacific, Southeast Asia, the Middle East, India, the Caribbean, South America, and Panama/Costa Rica during the remainder of the year, with several transatlantic positioning cruises. Passengers can select a variety of air and pre- and postcruise land arrangements. Seabourn's comprehensive air program features competitively priced, negotiated tariffs with major carriers in economy, business, and first class as well as on luxurious private jets. Land packages include most prestigious hotels and custom-designed Signature Series shore excursions.

Most suites are approximately 277 square feet, with a large 3 × 5 feet picture window looking out to the sea; twin beds that convert to a queen; flat-screen color TV with DVD player; richly appointed armchairs, sofa, and coffee table; a refrigerator and minibar (fully stocked with the choices of the guests) upon embarkation, free of charge; a hair dryer; a large walk-in closet with a private safe; and a marble bathroom with twin-sink vanities (except the *Legend*, which has single-sink vanities); a shower or shower/tub combination; luxurious bathroom and well-being amenities from Molton Brown; and ample storage space. There are also larger suites that range in size from 400 to 575 square feet; several have small private verandas. Small French-style balconies were added to approximately 35 percent of the suites in 2000, allowing passengers to peek out and enjoy the sunshine and fresh sea air. They are too small to lounge on; however, they do provide views along the side of the ship.

In 2007 the *Pride* and in 2008 the *Spirit* and *Legend* received various renovations, including an expansion of the outdoor dining venues, upgraded bedding, and new carpets and furnishings. Additional renovations took place in 2009 and 2010 with a refurbishing of all public areas, giving them a more modern look.

The health spa on each vessel offers massages and herbal body wraps and includes an exercise room (recently doubled in size) with state-of-the-art equipment and treadmills with personal TVs, in addition to a steam room, a sauna, three outdoor whirlpools, and an outdoor swimming pool. At the fold-out marina, off the rear of the ship, passengers can swim, windsurf, water-ski, banana boat, and sail.

The observation lounges at the top of each ship are glass enclosed and afford a panoramic view for passengers enjoying coffee, tea, or drinks. The club has a piano bar and is the location for evening cocktails and hors d'oeuvres as well as late-night dancing. There also is a large showroom that can accommodate all passengers; an indoor/outdoor café where imaginative buffet breakfasts, lunches, and dinners are served (possibly the best casual restaurants in the industry); a casino; a hospital; a boutique; an Internet café with four terminals; a tiny self-service launderette; and laundry and dry-cleaning service.

One of the highlights of the Seabourn experience is the elegant, open-seating dining room featuring some of the best Continental cuisine at sea as well as an extensive wine list. Several bottles of wine are offered gratis with each meal; however, there is a charge for the other options on the wine list.

The constantly evolving menus may include appetizers of flash-cooked striped bass with toasted garlic/lemon juice and capers; an extravagant entrée called "Lobster, Lobster, Lobster and Lobster Sauce"; grilled venison with aged balsamic vinegar and foie gras sauce; vegetarian delights such as soy-glazed shiitake and gingered greens, crunchy Vidalia onions, and onion soubise; and fanciful desserts such as warm lemon soufflé tart and honey-lemon sorbet or a trio of crèmes brûlée (including jasmine, cappuccino, and classic vanilla). Commencing in 2006, the Veranda Café on all the ships was transformed during the evenings to a reservation-only, casual dining venue called Restaurant 2, serving innovative, five-course tasting menus of creative, paired, small dishes. Also, a steak and seafood menu is offered a few times each week alfresco at the Sky Grill near the Sky Bar.

Service at the cafés in the main dining rooms and throughout the ships is impeccable, the most attentive at sea. This may be the ultimate cruise experience for well-heeled, sophisticated cruise aficionados. During afternoon tea, the ships feature rare estate teas and blends. In addition, there is a prepurchase premium wine program called "Vintage Seabourn" that allows oenophiles to choose bottles from the ship's extensive wine cellars at substantial savings.

Seabourn offers a personal valet service program wherein passengers can arrange to have their personal luggage shipped directly from their homes to their suites on the ship. Although the service costs extra, passengers with a large amount of luggage may find that it is not much more expensive than paying to take extra luggage on airplanes (under the new airline regulations).

In February 2013, Seabourn entered into a contract to sell these three 10,000-ton ships to Windstar Cruises. *Seabourn Pride* will join Windstar in April 2014, *Seabourn Legend* in April 2015, and *Seabourn Spirit* in May 2015. Until their transfer dates, the vessels will continue on their planned Seabourn itineraries.

Three new 32,000-ton, 458-passenger ships were delivered in 2009, 2010, and 2011. The first, *Seabourn Odyssey*, entered service in June 2009, followed by *Seabourn Sojourn* in the summer of 2010 and *Seabourn Quest* in June 2011. Ninety percent of the 225 luxury suites feature verandas, and accommodations range in size from 295 to 1,207 square feet. Most suites are designated veranda suites, and they measure 300 square feet with 65-square-foot verandas. The twenty-two penthouse suites come in at 436 square feet and the Owner's, Signature, Wintergarden, and Grand Suites range in size from 760 to 1,207 square feet. In May 2013, four new Penthouse Spa Suites were added to *Seabourn Quest*. These large accommodations will be accessed through the spa lobby and share the decor with the spa; fares will include entry to the Spa Serene Area. The same suites are to be added to the other two sister ships at their next dry dockings. All suites on the ships include separate living areas, walk-in closets, flat-screen interactive TVs with a large selection of movies, fully stocked refrigerator/minibars replenished daily, writing desks, direct-dial telephones, electronic safes, spacious granite/marble bathrooms with separate tub and shower, twin sinks and vanities, hair dryers, and 110/220 electrical outlets. None of the suites have butler service, and guest requests are made through the cabin attendants (who perform many of the services that a butler would perform), room service, and guest relations. Two fully equipped launderettes are available to guests gratis.

Public areas and dining venues are somewhat similar to the original three ships but greatly expanded. There are four open-seating dining alternatives, which include the elegant, open-seating main Restaurant, offering gourmet cuisine (jackets recommended on most nights and several on each cruise are elegant casual and others formal optional); Restaurant 2, where very unusual, unique dishes with unfamiliar combinations are prepared individually by the chef in tasting portions (dress is elegant casual and the cuisine is different from that offered on the smaller ships); Colonnade, an attractive indoor/outdoor venue serving breakfast and lunch buffet style with attentive assistance from the staff and serving dinner with table service, linen-clad tables, and changing themes for dinner (dress is elegant casual); the casual Patio Grill by the pool, serving all three meals and a variety of grilled steaks, chops, and seafood at dinner; and, of course, in-suite service, including the option to have dinner served course by course in your suite, complete with fine linens and personal service.

Other public areas include five lounges and bars, an expansive pool and sunbathing area, and a spectacular two-deck indoor/outdoor expansive spa facility with a state-of-the-art exercise room and a vast range of innovative programs and treatments. When weather permits, the ship's built-in marina offers swimming, snorkeling, windsurfing, banana boat rides, kayaking, and water-skiing off the stern of the ship or at the ship's private beach party. In the evenings, there is musical entertainment, cabaret shows, dancing to live bands, a casino, and movies under the stars. Unfortunately, the ships provide very little port information for the independent traveler, and day-time activities are limited.

Although three times larger than the three smaller vessels, these ships carry only twice the number of passengers, allowing for more room in both public areas and staterooms. They boast the highest space-per-guest ratio in the cruise industry and are possibly the most beautifully designed and decorated ships afloat.

## Strong Points

Top-of-the-line luxury (at top-of-the-line prices except when special offers are available on selected cruises), superb food, impeccable service, and elegant spacious accommodations as well as the most desired itineraries. The three original sisters are the most spacious and comfortable of the yacht-like cruise ships and offer the most guest pampering. The new 450- to 458-passenger ships, though less intimate, offer similar exceptional dining, service, and accommodations with additional space and facilities. Most seasoned cruisers (who have experienced other cruise lines) consider these the best ships in service today.

*Suite on Seabourn Odyssey, courtesy Seabourn Cruise Line*

*Captain and Hotel Manager with Author, Seabourn Odyssey,
courtesy Seabourn Cruise LIne*

*Suite on Seabourn Odyssey, courtesy Seabourn Cruise Line*

*Pool Area, Seabourn Odyssey, courtesy Seabourn Cruise Line*

*Seabourn Odyssey in Venice, courtesy Seabourn Cruise Line*

*Main Dining Room on Seabourn Odyssey, courtesy Seabourn Cruise Line*

## THE RESTAURANT

### FIRST COURSE

CAVIAR TARTS, SMOKED SALMON CREME FRAICHE
malossol caviar, warm blini lemon vinaigrette

FOIE GRAS TRUFFLE AND VANILLA TERRINE
preserved strawberry, aged balsamic

TWICE BAKED BOURSIN CHEESE SOUFFLE
roasted sweet garlic veloute

PUFF PASTRY BAKED PARMESAN & PROSCIUTTO
CONSOMME
navy beans, black truffle essence

WHITE PLUM TOMATO SOUP
basil foam

BABY ROMAINE WITH CAESAR STYLE VINAIGRETTE
garlic croutons, parmesan cheese

TRUFFLED BABY CORN SALAD WITH MACHE & ARUGULA
crisp red onions

### MAIN COURSE

GRILLED SWORDFISH, CHINEESE CABBAGE RAGOUT
green apple and onion, grain mustard beurre blanc

SAUTEED NIGERIAN SHRIMP, GAMBAS & CALAMARI
watercress risotto, semi dried tomato coulis

PINK GRILLED LAMB LOIN
cauliflower - zucchini semolina, potato gratin, lamb jus

FILET OF BEEF WELLINGTON
sauteed vegetables, pommes dauphine, madeira jus

VEGETARIAN - THREE CHEESE RAVIOLI
corn puree, herb oil

**Available Through Room Service**

**During Restaurant Opening Hours**

## RESTAURANT 2

CHEF'S COCKTAIL: CRISPY FOIE GRAS, PORT WINE SPLASH

LOBSTER ROLL, YOGURT CAVIAR SAUCE
BACALAITO FRITTER, AVOCADO & TOMATO SALAD
SEARED PANELA SALMON, WHITE BEAN SALSA, PIQUILLO COULIS

SHIRAZ BRAISED OXTAIL PRESSE, MANCHEGO POTSTICKERS
WHITE ASPARAGUS VANILLA CAPPUCCINO, MUSHROOM TOAST

DRUNKEN TURBOT, PORCINI & SWISS CHARD, HAZELNUT VINAIGRETTE
TUSCANY BRAISED VEAL, MASCARPONE MASHED POTATO

LIMONCELLO TIRAMISU FOAM, MARINATED ORANGES

DARK CHOCOLATE GANACHE, ESPRESSO CITRUS PANNA COTTA, CONDENSED MILK ICE CREAM

NIGHT CAP: KAHLUA FRAPPE

The innovative tasting menus at Restaurant 2 are served in a casual, friendly style. Seating is limited and reservations are required. Touch
Guests may be seated together at tables for six, another way to ensure a fun, informal dining experience at our most unusual dinner option.

# THE COLONNADE·ELEGANT BISTRO

## STARTERS

### COLD APPETIZER/SALAD

Foie Gras Truffle and Vanilla Terrine
preserved strawberry, aged balsamic

or

Baby Romaine with Caesar Style Vinaigrette
garlic croutons, parmesan cheese

### HOT APPETIZER/SOUP

Twice Baked Boursin Cheese Souffle
roasted sweet garlic veloute

or

Puff Pastry Baked Parmesan & Prosciutto Consomme
navy beans, black truffle essence

## MAINS

Pan Fried Turbot Fillet
lemon caper butter, young spinach, new potatoes

or

Filet of Beef Wellington
sauteed vegetables, pommes dauphine, madeira jus

## DESSERTS

Creme Brule En Parade
jasmine, cappuccino, classic vanilla

or

Red Wine Poached Peaches, Balsamic Strawberry Sorbet

**NOT AVAILABLE VIA ROOM SERVICE**

# PATIO GRILL

Closed

*Today* AT-A-GLANCE

## GOOD MORNING

**7:00AM**    **ARRIVAL:** Seabourn Odyssey arrives in Istanbul, Turkey.

**9:30AM**    **BOOK GIVE-AWAY & EXCHANGE**
Conference Room 3, Deck 5
Exchange a book you've finished or pick one up.

**10:00AM**    **BOARD AND CARD GAMES AVAILBLE**
Card Room, Deck 7
*(Sign-up sheet available throughout the day)*

**10:30AM**    **DECK SPORTS (NON-HOSTED)**
The Retreat, Deck 11
Golf, Table Tennis and Shuffleboard available (until 6.00PM)

## GOOD AFTERNOON

**3:00PM**    **PORT EXPERT MEET & GREET**
Seabourn Square, Deck 7
Meet our Port Expert Abilio Menendez for information on our
upcoming ports of call. (until 4.00PM)

**4:15PM**    **ALL ABOARD:** As Seabourn Odyssey prepares to set sail. All
services will be suspended in preparation for the Guest Emergency
Drill.

**4:30PM**    **GUEST EMERGENCY DRILL**
It is mandatory that all Guests (including in-transit Guests) on
board attend this drill. Please listen to the announcements
made from the Bridge. Thank you for your cooperation.
**Please note: Lifejackets are not required during this drill.**

**5:00PM**    **SAIL-AWAY PARTY**
Pool Deck, Deck 8 & Sky Bar, Deck 9
Cruise Director John Howell invites you to join your fellow
Guests for a special sail-away event. Accompanied by The Band
featuring vocalist Liana (*weather permitting*).

         **DEPARTURE:** Seabourn Odyssey Sails for Myrina, Greece

**5:30PM**    **FRIENDS OF BILL W.**
Conference Room 1, Deck 5.

---

**IMPORTANT INFORMATION:**
For reasons of safety and security, all Guests must carry a personal
identification card when leaving the vessel. In addition, each Guest is
required to present your suite key card at the gangway. This card will
be scanned as you exit, thus recording that you are off the vessel.
Upon your return, it will be scanned to confirm that you are back on
board. The security staff may also ask to inspect your belongings
either by X-ray or manually.
We appreciate your cooperation in this important matter.

---

## GOOD EVENING

**6:00PM**    **DRESS THIS EVENING IS 'RESORT CASUAL'. NO JACKET
REQUIRED FOR GENTLEMEN.**
**Gentlemen:** Slacks with a shirt.
**Ladies:** Blouse with skirt or slacks.
Jeans are not considered appropriate in the Restaurant.

**6:30PM**    **PORT LECTURE: MYRINA AND IZMIR**
Grand Salon, Deck 6
Seabourn Port Expert Abilio Menendez delivers fascinating
insight into our first ports of call.

         **PANORAMIC PIANO BAR**
Observation Bar, Deck 11
Enjoy scenic cocktails with music by Pierre. (until 8.00PM)

         **GUITAR SELECTIONS**
The Club, Deck 5
Guitarist Chris Bartlett entertains (until 8.00PM)

**7:00PM**    **SOLO TRAVELLERS GET-TOGETHER**
The Club, Deck 5
Meet Social Hostess Melissa for a cocktail and meet fellow solo
travelers.

**8:15PM**    **GUITAR MELODIES UNDER THE STARS**
Poolside, Deck 8
Guitarist Chris Bartlett entertains (until 9.00PM)

**9:30PM**    **PIANO MELODIES WITH PIERRE**
Observation Bar, Deck 10
Piano Entertainer Pierre plays (until midnight).

         **GUITAR MELODIES**
The Club, Deck 5
Guitarist Chris Bartlett plays (until 10.00PM)

**10:00PM**    **SHOWTIME: LIMELIGHT**
Grand Salon, Deck 6
Tonight the Seabourn Singers deliver an unforgettable live
music experience. Accompanied by The Band and introduced by
Cruise Director John Howell.

**11:15PM**    **WELCOME ABOARD DANCE PARTY**
The Club, Deck 5
Cruise Director John Howell and the Cruise Staff invite you to an
evening of music and dancing with The Band featuring Liana on
vocals.

         **THE ENTERTAINMENT CONTINUES...**
Enjoy Piano Entertainer Pierre in the Observation Bar
(until midnight) and dance to the tunes of The Band featuring
Liana in The Club (*until close*).

---

### SHIP'S ANNOUNCEMENTS CAN BE HEARD IN YOUR SUITE ON TELEVISION CHANNEL 16

| GUEST SERVICES | | SHOPS & SPA | | MEDICAL & CASINO | |
|---|---|---|---|---|---|
| **Guest Services** | Hours | **Shopping, Deck 7** | Hours | **Casino, Deck 5** | |
| Seabourn Square, Deck 7 | 24 hours | | 6.00PM – 11.00PM | Slots | 6.30PM till Close |
| | | ONBOARD TAX AND DUTY FREE SHOPPING | | Tables | 6.30PM – 8.00PM/ 9.00PM – Close |
| **Destination Services** | | Check your inter-active TV for promotions. | | | |
| Seabourn Square, Deck 7 | 24 hours | **Health and Beauty, Deck 9** | Hours | **Medical Center, Deck 3 fwd** | |
| Please contact Guest Services by dialing ext. 9 | | Spa | 1.00PM – 10.00PM | 9.00AM – 11.00AM / 4.30PM – 6.00PM | |
| **Cruise Sales Specialist** | | Fitness Center | 6.00AM – 10.00PM | Sharps containers are available | |
| Seabourn Square, Deck 7 | 24 hours | Please refer to your inter-active TV for | | from your stewardess | |
| Please contact Guest Services by dialing ext. 9 | | fitness class schedule. | | | |

*Daily Progam, courtesy Seabourn Cruise Line*

# SEA CLOUD CRUISES

**United States**
**282 Grand Ave.**
**Englewood, NJ 07631**
**(888) 732-2568; (201) 227-9404**
**Fax: (201) 227-9424**

**Germany**
**An der Alster 9**
**20099 Hamburg, Germany**
**+49(0) 403095920**
**Fax: +49(0) 4030959222**

**www.seacloud.com**
**info@seaclould.com**

*Sea Cloud*: entered service in 1931 as private yacht; frequently renovated and refurbished; 360 × 50 feet; thirty-two cabins; sixty-four-passenger capacity; international crew; cruises primarily in Mediterranean, Adriatic, Aegean, and the Caribbean/Central America (Category A/B—not rated)

*Sea Cloud II*: entered service in 2001; frequently refurbished; 384 × 53 feet; forty-seven cabins; ninety-four-passenger capacity; international crew; cruises primarily in Mediterranean, Adriatic, Aegean, Atlantic, British Isles, North Sea, the Baltics, and the Caribbean/Central America (Category A/B—not rated)

Launched in 1931 as a private yacht, *Sea Cloud* was a home away from home for millionaires Edward Hutton and Marjorie Merriweather Post. This legendary four-masted vessel captures the elegance of the rich and famous during that period in the U.S. history with its mahogany superstructure, teak decks, polished brass fixtures, and brilliant tapestry of more than 32,000 square feet of sails. She was acquired in 1978 by a group of Hamburg ship owners and business executives who proceeded to install additional cabins, new rigging, and state-of-the-art navigation, communication, and safety systems. Modern amenities and upgrades notwithstanding, the ship still offers the charm and charisma of the romantic spirit in which she was conceived over eighty years ago.

The six original guest chambers on the main deck and the two owner's suites and two cabins (formerly crew quarters) have been skillfully restored and the furnishings recall the era of the early 1900s. Twenty-two additional staterooms were added on the two above decks.

Atop ship are the lido deck, lido bar, bridge, and eight luxury accommodations. On the promenade deck below are fourteen additional staterooms, a lovely lounge, and the elegant main dining room that accommodates all passengers in a single seating with no assigned tables. There is piano music during dinner and afterward in the lounge. When weather permits, lunch is served buffet style on the lido deck.

Although more modern in design, *Sea Cloud II* retains much of the old-world charm of her elder sister. Atop ship on sundeck is the captain's bridge. Below on lido deck are the two owner's suites, the elegant main lounge, the lido bar, and a library. On promenade deck are the single-seating dining room, boutique, purser's office, reception area, and eighteen staterooms. The remaining cabins are one more deck down on cabin deck, along with a gym, sauna, hospital, and water sports deck. All accommodations include a sitting area, minibar, TV and video player, and marble baths appointed with gold fittings and inlays.

These sailing yachts can be found cruising the Mediterranean, Adriatic, Aegean, Atlantic, British Isles, North Sea, the Baltics, and the Caribbean/Central America.

The company's riverboat, *River Cloud II* is covered in chapter 10.

## Strong Points

Upscale sailing yacht experiences on elegantly appointed vessels.

*Sea Cloud, courtesy Sea Cloud Cruises*

*Sea Cloud II, courtesy Sea Cloud Cruises*

*Dining Room, Sea Cloud II, courtesy Sea Cloud Cruises*

*Stateroom Sea Cloud II, courtesy Sea Cloud Cruises*

*Lounge on Sea Cloud II, courtesy Sea Cloud Cruises*

# *Dinner Menu*

◢ ◢ ◢

Scallops with Baby Asparagus
or
Piccata of Zucchini

◢ ◢ ◢

Tomato Consommé with Basil Quenelles

◢ ◢ ◢

Rock Lobster Tail with
Sautéed Vegetables

or

Filet Mignon with
Onion Confit & Potato Purée

or

Mushroom Medley Risotto

◢ ◢ ◢

Dark Chocolate Crème Brûlée

◢ ◢ ◢

Cheeseboard with assorted international cheeses

◢ ◢ ◢

Coffee, Tea and Pralines

*Courtesy Sea Cloud Cruises*

## SEADREAM YACHT CLUB

**601 Brickell Key Drive, Suite 1050
Miami, FL 33131
(800) 707-4911; (305) 631-6100
Fax: (305) 631-6110
www.seadream.com**

*SeaDream I* and *II* (formerly *Sea Goddess I* and *II* and *Seabourn Goddess I* and *II*): entered service in 1984 and 1985, respectively; both redesigned in 2002; 4,250 GRT; 344 × 48 feet; 112-passenger capacity; fifty-six staterooms; international officers and crew; mostly seven- and fourteen-day voyages in the Caribbean, the Mediterranean, the Black Sea, Costa Rica, Asia, and the Baltics (Category A—five+ stars)

(Medical facilities: C-1; P-1, EM, CLS, MS; N-0; CM; PD; BC; EKG; TC; PO; EPC; OX; WC; OR; ICU; X; M; CCP; TM; LJ)

These vessels are rated in eleven separate categories in the second half of chapter 11.

SeaDream Yacht Club was launched in 2001 by Norwegian entrepreneur Atle Brynestad, founder and owner. Mr. Brynestad was also the original founder of Seabourn Cruise Line. Robert Lepisto is the president of the company and has been part of the original SeaDream team since its inception. Pamela Conover was recently appointed the company's CEO. These twin luxury megayachts offer mostly seven- to fourteen-night Caribbean, Mediterranean, Costa Rica, Asia, and the Baltic yachting voyages. Possibilities for longer back-to-back voyages are available. They are sometimes under private charter, so it is best to check ahead with the SeaDream as to their availability on any given date.

SeaDream states that although the yachts depart their first port and arrive at their last port as scheduled, the captains have authority to adjust for local opportunities and make unscheduled calls at smaller yachting ports, harbors, and secluded bays, allowing guests to indulge in water sports and unique sightseeing adventures.

SeaDream offers custom-designed land adventures and other shore activities and often features late departures or overnight stays in port to enable passengers to enjoy the nightlife. Shoreside casual excursions are limited to a few choices in each port and are frequently hosted by yacht officers or members of the crew. The highlight of each Caribbean voyage is the Champagne & Caviar Splash™ beach party, held at a pristine beach. During this event, yacht crew immersed in the sea offer guests champagne and caviar. A highlight of Mediterranean and other voyages is the Shaken not Stirred cocktail and caviar party held on the pool deck.

There is no formal dress code, and country-club casual attire is acceptable throughout the voyage. Guests dine open-seating either in the elegant, indoor dining salon or alfresco at the partially sheltered Topside Restaurant. In addition, there is a twenty-four-hour simplified menu, "Small Bites," as well as elegantly prepared snacks available at the Top of the Yacht Bar and at the pool deck. It is possible to arrange a romantic tête-à-tête dinner in other areas of the yacht as well. Appropriate snacks are available around the clock throughout the yacht. The dining experience at all meals is exceptional, with an abundance of high-quality, gourmet preparations imaginatively presented and impressively served. Alcoholic drinks, including premium brands, are gratis throughout the yacht, and a nice assortment of wines is complimentary at mealtime. The wine cellar menu has a wide selection of new and old-world wines for purchase, and French champagne is available at all of the bars.

Of the fifty-six ocean-view guest accommodations, fifty-four are Yacht Club staterooms and measure 195 square feet. Sixteen of the Yacht Club staterooms can be combined to make Commodore Suites, doubling their size. In addition, travelers can opt for the 447-square-foot Owner's Suite, with its lavishly appointed private bedroom and bath and elegant living and dining room with its own half bath, or the Admiral Suite, which is 375 square feet with one-and-a-half baths and three panorama windows. Every accommodation includes a small lounge area, closet with dresser space and a hanging area (wooden hangers provided), private safe, hair dryer, refrigerator, iPod docking station, CD/DVD player, and flat-screen TV (channels depend on the sailing region but also include in-room movies). Guests can select queen or single beds, down or synthetic pillows, and blankets or duvets. All staterooms are Internet ready, and guests can request a laptop for use while on board. Bathrooms are small with little storage space but include a well-sized glassed-in shower with multiple jets and Bulgari bath amenities. There are no balconies, and standard staterooms are smaller than on other luxury vessels.

The vessels were redesigned and refitted after their acquisition from Seabourn. Public areas include the SeaDream Spa with massage rooms, steam shower, and tiny sauna; fitness center with various equipment, including four treadmills with attached TVs, DVD players, and views looking out to sea; outdoor pool; whirlpool and pool bar; water sports marina and floating dock perfect for swimming (offering personal watercraft, stand-up paddleboards, snorkel gear, glass-bottom kayaks, Hobie Cat, Zodiacs for water-skiing, banana boat rides, and a floating island on which to relax or sunbathe); mountain bikes available for shoreside explorations; small casino with a blackjack table; beauty salon; boutique; thirty-course golf simulator; cardroom; library with two computers for Internet access; medical facility staffed by a doctor; main dining salon; Topside Restaurant; piano bar; main lounge; and Top of the Yacht Bar with 360-degree views. The signature Balinese Dream Beds are very comfortable sun beds atop ship for sun worshippers and star gazers. There are large umbrellas for those who prefer the shade. On overnights in port, arrangements can be made to have a bed with pillows, linen, and cozy duvets made up topside for those who wish to sleep under the stars.

In contrast to cruise ships, the company describes their vessels as "yachts" and the experience as "yachting" and therefore there are fewer onboard organized activities and entertainment than on conventional vessels. Cocktail hour offers live piano music, lavish hors d'oeuvres, and a short talk about the next day's port of call. After dinner guests can enjoy live guitar at the Top of the Yacht Bar or starlit movies poolside or in the main salon on a giant screen. Alternatively, guests can congregate at the piano bar with their own musical requests and libations, play blackjack in the casino, or select a DVD for their staterooms from a well-stocked viewing library.

## Strong Points

A magnificent dining experience with gourmet cuisine prepared a la minute and impeccable service, great bar service, and a lot of pampering by an award-winning crew of ninety-five. This line will appeal most to passengers who enjoy unstructured elegance and do not require an abundance of group activities, entertainment, or a strong shore program. This is truly an intimate yacht-like experience highly recommended for loving couples and discerning guests.

*Breatfast by the Sea, SeaDream II, courtesy SeaDream Yacht Club*

*Breakfast Table on SeaDream II,*
*courtesy SeaDream Yacht Club*

*Top of the Yacht on SeaDream II, courtesy SeaDream Yacht Club*

*SeaDream II, courtesy SeaDream Yacht Club*

# SEADREAM YACHT CLUB DINING ROOM

## Starters

Thai Style Beef Salad with Fresh Mango and Cilantro

•

Grilled Spiced Shrimps with Blood Orange Segments and Chili Dressing

•

Gratinated Escargots with Aubergine Compote and Champignon de Paris*

## Soups

Cream of Garlic with Seven Grain Croutons

•

Lime and Coriander with Chicken Flakes

•

Chilled Raspberry Flip

## Salads

Caesar Salad with Chilli Croutons and Anchovy Fillet

•

Sweet Cucumber Salad with Fresh Dill

*An Assortment of Salads is always Available with your Favourite Dressings*

## World Flavour

Lemongrass and Ginger marinated Monkfish
on Spinach and Rocket Salad with Cherry Tomato Vinaigrette

## Chef's Main Dishes

Grilled Lobster Tail on Black and White Rice, Green Vegetables,
Crispy Shallots and Crustacean Sauce*

•

Whole Roast Rack of Lamb
with Pommes Gratin, Ratatouille and Rosemary infused Demi Glace

•

Pappardelle Pasta with Parma Ham, Sautéed Spinach,
Roasted Garlic and Fresh Pesto

*SeaDream Signature Dish

## This Evening's Vegetarian Alternative

Sweet Cucumber Salad with Fresh Dill

•

Cream of Garlic with Seven Grain Croutons

•

Porcini Mushroom Risotto with Arugula Lettuce and Balsamic Nage

*A Selection of Steamed Vegetables and Baked Potatoes is always available*


## SeaDream Oriental Wellness Cuisine

*In Combination with SeaDream Spa, Our Chefs have created a daily selection
of dishes from the Oriental wellness Cuisine*

Lemongrass and Ginger marinated Monkfish
on Spinach and Rocket Salad with Cherry Tomato Vinaigrette

•

Lime and Coriander with Chicken Flakes

•

Lean Beef Curry with Basmati Rice, Mango Chutney and Crispy Poppadum*

•

Grilled Pineapple with Coconut Frozen Yoghurt

•

Oriental Ginger Tea


## À la Carte

Consommé Double with "Battonet au Fromage"

•

Caesar Salad served with Croutons and Grated Parmesan Cheese

•

Linguini al Pesto or with Chunky Tomato Sauce

•

Broiled Fillet of "Organic" Salmon with Caper Butter

•

Chicken Breast with Herbs, Lemon and Virgin Olive Oil

•

Grilled N.Y. Cut Strip-Loin Steak, Madagascar Pepper Sauce

•

Rosemary Marinated Lamb Chops

*All dishes may be ordered with your choice of French Fried Potatoes,
Baked Potato, Rice and Vegetables of the day.*

# Desserts

**Pastry Chef Garfield Anderson's Signature Dessert**

"Fondant au Chocolat" with Vanilla Ice Cream*

∽∼

Pistachio Cheese Cake with Sour Cream Topping and Strawberry Compote
•
Grilled Pineapple with Coconut Frozen Yoghurt

**Healthy and Delicious**

Red Wine Poached Pear with Crème Fraîche Sorbet

**Garfield's Selection of Homemade Ice Cream, Sorbets**

Vanilla, Rum and Raisin, Maple Walnut Ice Cream,
Crème Fraîche Sorbet and Coconut Frozen Yoghurt

**From The Cheese Board**

Assorted European Cheeses
Served with Home Made Cheese Bread

SeaDream I Exclusive Selection of Herbal and Exotic Teas from "Mhai Diva Teas",
Espresso, Cappuccino, Regular and Decaffeinated Coffee accompanied by an assortment of
Homemade Petits Fours with Chocolate Truffles

## SeaDream
### YACHT CLUB

*Courtesy SeaDream Yacht Club*

Partly Cloudy
High: 79°F / 26°C
Low: 72°F / 22°C

**SEADREAM**
YACHT CLUB

# Daily program

Gustavia, St. Barts, FWI
Tuesday, February 17th 2009

Next Port:
Sandy Ground
Anguilla, BWI
Distance:
33 Nautical Miles

Sunrise: 06:39

| | | |
|---|---|---|
| 07:00 | Early Riser's Coffee is available at the Top of the Yacht Bar. | Deck 6 |
| 08:00 – 10:30 | Breakfast is served at the Topside Restaurant. | Deck 5 |
| 07:30 | SEADREAM I anchors off Gustavia, St. Barts, FWI. | |
| | A tender service will be established and operate on a continuous basis throughout our stay. | |

Sunset: 18:14

## MORNING ACTIVITIES

| | | |
|---|---|---|
| 08:00 | "Crew Shoreside Casual" – Join your Club & Activities Director **Richard** for a morning hike to Fort Gustav & Fort Carl ruins; followed by swimming at Shell Beach. Please meet at the gangway and wear comfortable walking shoes and a swim suit. | Deck 3 |
| 08:00 | **Yoga Session** with Khun Yuu, please meet at the SEADREAM Spa. | Deck 4 |
| 09:00 | A limited selection of Mountain Bikes and Snorkel Equipment is available at the gangway. | Deck 3 |
| 09:30 | Yachting Land Adventure - '**The Independent Explorer**' departs from the gangway. | Deck 3 |
| 09:30 – 11:30 | Yachting Land Adventure - '**Island Tour by ATV**' departs from the gangway. | Deck 3 |
| 10:15 – 12:15 | Yachting Land Adventure - '**Fast & Fun**' departs from the gangway. | Deck 3 |
| 11:30 – 12:30 | Swimming is available from the marina platform. (Port Authority & weather permitting) Please sign a waiver form and collect a wrist band from the Concierge. | Deck 2 / Marina |

| | | |
|---|---|---|
| 12:30 – 14:00 | Luncheon is served at the Topside Restaurant. | Deck 5 |

## AFTERNOON ACTIVITIES

| | | |
|---|---|---|
| 13:45 – 14:45 | Yachting Land Adventure - '**St. Barth Semi - Submersible**' departs from the gangway. | Deck 3 |
| 13:45 – 15:45 | Yachting Land Adventure - '**Blue Cat Snorkeling**' departs from the gangway. | Deck 3 |
| 14:00 – 16:00 | Water Sports are available from the marina platform. (Port Authority & weather permitting) Please sign a waiver form and collect a wrist band from the Concierge. | Deck 2 / Marina |
| 15:00 | **Stretch & Tai-Chi Session** with Khun Ticha, please meet at the SEADREAM Spa. | Deck 4 |
| 16:00 – 16:30 | Swimming is available from the marina platform. (Port Authority & weather permitting) Please sign a waiver form and collect a wrist band from the Concierge. | Deck 2 / Marina |

| | | |
|---|---|---|
| 18:00 – 20:00 | The SEADREAM Yacht Boutique is open with assistance from **Rose**. | Deck 4 |
| 18:30 | Cocktails are served poolside. | Deck 3 |
| 19:15 | A brief review of tomorrow's port of call in Sandy Ground, Anguilla with your Club & Activities Director, **Richard Jones** poolside. | Deck 3 |
| 19:30 – 21:30 | '**Starlight Dinner**' is served at the Topside Restaurant. | Decks 5/6 |

## AFTER DINNER ACTIVITIES

| | | |
|---|---|---|
| 21:30 – 23:00 | The SEADREAM Yacht Boutique is open with assistance from **Rose**. | Deck 4 |
| 21:30 | The Piano Bar is open with Chief Bartender **Jamie** serving 'After Dinner' drinks & **George** on the Piano. | Deck 4 |
| 21:30 | The Top of the Yacht Bar is open with your Bartenders **Danny & Sebastian** serving your favorite Cocktails. | Deck 6 |
| 21:30 | **Take 777 and win your prize!** The Casino is open with your casino dealer **Elena**. | Deck 4 |
| 21:30 | *Movie under the stars* | |
| | *'Mama Mia'* | |
| | *starring Pierce Brosnan, Meryl Streep, and Colin Firth* | Deck 3 |

| | | |
|---|---|---|
| 24:00 | The last tender departs from the pier. | |

Early Morning SEADREAM I sails for Sandy Ground, Anguilla.

In the Family – SEADREAM II is in San Juan, Puerto Rico.
**DRESS CODE THIS EVENING IS 'YACHT CASUAL' AFTER 18:30**

| | | | | | | |
|---|---|---|---|---|---|---|
| Concierge Desk | 08:00 – 23:00 | Deck 3 | **ON BOARD RECREATION** | SEADREAM Spa | 08:00 – 20:00 | Deck 4 |
| Gymnasium | 07:00 – 20:00 | Deck 4 | | Hospital | 09:00 – 10:00 | Deck 5 |
| Golf Simulator | 08:00 – 22:00 | Deck 6 | | Hospital | 17:00 – 18:00 | Deck 5 |
| Boutique | 18:00 – 20:00 | Deck 4 | | Casino | From 21:30 | Deck 4 |
| Boutique | 21:30 – 23:00 | Deck 4 | | Future Bookings | see Richard or Dial 9 | |

>>>SEADREAM I telephone number: + 47 23 67 59 30<<<

*Courtesy SeaDream Yacht Club*

## SILVERSEA CRUISES LTD.

**110 E. Broward Boulevard**
**Fort Lauderdale, FL 33301**
**(800) 722-9955**
**Fax: (954) 356-5881**
**www.silversea.com**

*Silver Cloud*: entered service in 1994; refurbished in 2004 and 2012; 16,800 GRT; 514 × 71 feet; 296-passenger capacity; 148 suites; Italian officers, European staff, and international crew; cruises the Mediterranean, Northern Europe, the Baltics, the Caribbean, South America, and other worldwide destinations (Category A—six stars)

*Silver Explorer* (formerly *Prince Albert II*, *Delfin Clipper*, and *World Discoverer*): entered service in 1989; totally renovated and refurbished in 2008; 6,072 GRT; 132-passenger capacity; sixty-six cabins; European officers and staff and international crew; expedition cruises in Arctic Circle, Iceland, and Greenland during summer and Antarctica and South America during winter (Category A—not rated)

*Silver Galapagos* (formerly *Galapagos Explorer II, Renaissance III*): entered service in 1990, totally renovated and refurbished in 2013; 4,077 GRT; 289 × 50 feet; 100-passenger capacity; 50 suites; Ecuadorian officers and crew; expedition cruises in the Galapagos Islands (Not rated)

*Silver Shadow* and *Silver Whisper*: entered service in 2000 and 2001, respectively; refurbished in 2011 and 2010, respectively; 28,258 GRT; 610 × 82 feet; 382-passenger capacity; 194 suites; Italian officers, European staff, and international crew; *Silver Shadow* cruises Alaska, Australia, New Zealand, and Far East; *Silver Whisper* cruises the Baltics, Northern Europe, the Arabian Peninsula, Indian Ocean, South Pacific, Far East, Canada, New England, and other worldwide destinations (Category A—six+ stars)

*Silver Spirit*: entered service in 2009; 36,000 GRT; 642 × 86 feet; 540-passenger capacity; 270 suites; Italian officers and international crew; varied worldwide itineraries, including the Mediterranean and the Caribbean (Category A—six+ stars)

*Silver Wind*: entered service in 1995; refurbished in 2008; 16,800 GRT; 514 × 71 feet; 296-passenger capacity; 148 suites; Italian officers, European staff, and international crew; cruises the Mediterranean, Africa, the Seychelles, and other worldwide destinations (Category A—six stars)

(Medical facilities: C-all; P-1; EM, CLS, MS; N-1; CM; PD; BC; EKG; TC; PO; EPC; WC; OR; ICU; X on *Whisper* and *Shadow* only; M; CCP; LJ)

*Note*: Six+ black stars is the highest rating given in this edition to ships in the deluxe-market category.

These ships are rated in eleven separate categories in the second half of chapter 14.

In 1994, the Lefebvre family of Rome, previously a co-owner of Sitmar Cruises, entered the deluxe cruise market with two new 16,000+-ton vessels that compete with Seabourn, Cunard, Crystal, and Regent Seven Seas. *Silver Cloud* and *Silver Wind* entered service in 1994 and 1995, respectively. Every accommodation on these ships is a suite, and three-quarters of them feature spacious teak verandas. Although most of the line's staterooms are veranda suites (295 square feet in size, including the veranda), other suites on these two ships range in size from 240 to 1,314 square feet. Air-sea fares are among the industry's most inclusive and are somewhat less than many of the line's competitors.

The intent of Silversea Cruises was to create the optimum ship—small enough to sail intriguing waterways unavailable to most of the larger vessels while also providing a smooth, comfortable ride in deep-water cruising. In addition, these ships offer the intimacy, service, and nuances found on many of the smaller deluxe cruise ships while also affording all of the facilities, amenities, and activities available on the larger cruise ships.

These ships have the most advanced nautical architecture and maritime equipment, which renders them very steady at high speeds and highly maneuverable. Design and decor were conceived by Norwegian architects whose credits include most of the other small luxury cruise ships as well as Royal Caribbean's megaliners. In addition to glass doors leading out to verandas in 85 percent of the suites and large picture windows in the remaining 15 percent, each suite features spacious storage; a walk-in closet; mirrored dressing table; writing desk; twin beds (convertible to queen); a separate sitting area; stocked refrigerator; electronic wall safe; remote-controlled TV with videocassette player; a large umbrella; all-marble bathrooms with tub, shower, hair dryer, and 110- and 220-volt outlets; and plush terry cloth robes and slippers. Guests desiring more space than the standard vista or veranda suites can opt for a silver suite (541 square feet), the two-bedroom owner's suite (827 square feet), a two-bedroom royal suite (1,031 square feet), or a two-bedroom grand suite (1,314 square feet).

During 2008, extensive refurbishments were completed on the *Silver Wind*. Included among these additions are new carpeting and some new furnishings in the public areas, a new ocean-view spa and fitness center, a new observation lounge, eight new larger suites on decks 7 and 8, and reduction of some vista suites on deck 4.

All suites received new flat-screen TVs, sofas, armchairs, desks, vanities, night tables, headboards, carpeting, drapes, and bed coverings as well as new fixtures, bathtubs, and marble countertops, walls, and flooring in the bathrooms.

Featuring the highest space-to-guest and crew-to-guest ratios of any ship in the industry, the 28,258-ton, 382-passenger *Silver Shadow* was launched in 2000, followed in the summer of 2001 by its sister ship, *Silver Whisper*. Every suite on these newer vessels includes the facilities described above for the *Cloud* and *Wind*, plus a few innovations, such as double marble vanities in the bathrooms. Except for twenty-six vista suites measuring 287 square feet, all other accommodations sport verandas. These include nine additional vista suites with shared verandas, 128 veranda suites measuring 345 square feet, and twenty-three larger suites ranging in size from 521 square feet up to 1,435 square feet for one of the grand suites with an optional second bedroom. The six largest suites sell for considerably more than the vista or veranda suites and feature additional amenities, such as whirlpool tubs, greater private veranda space, CD player/ stereo systems, comfortable dining areas, deluxe bathroom amenities, guest powder rooms, giant closets, flat-screen TVs, and complimentary laundry and butler service.

As with the refurbishment of sister ship *Silver Whisper* in 2010, the enhancements made aboard *Silver Shadow* in 2011 echo the sophisticated contemporary design themes and warm color palettes of Silversea's newest ship, *Silver Spirit*. Some of the highlights of *Silver Shadow's* makeover include refreshed public areas, upgraded outdoor spaces, and a new look for suites—replacement of all carpets, headboards, curtains, and veranda furniture; new upholstery for the sofas and chairs; new mattress (custom-made for Silversea), featuring an individual spring system with a soft and firm side that can be reversed to suit each guest's preference; and new memory foam pillow tops that cover the mattress when configured as a queen-sized bed.

The line offers attractive inclusive-cruise packages. Fares include all gratuities, alcoholic and nonalcoholic beverages (both in your suite and throughout the ship), fine wines with lunch and dinner, and complimentary shuttle-bus service to the city center in many ports of call. Although there is a charge for shore excursions, select sailings feature a special complimentary Silversea Experience—a customized shore event available only to Silversea guests—which can range from a traditional street party in Mykonos with wine, dancing, and singing to a formal soirée in one of St. Petersburg's lavish nineteenth century palaces. Also included in the fare are special in-suite touches such as fresh fruit and flowers, a pillow menu, personalized stationery, lunch and dinner menus and satellite newsletters delivered daily, and a bottle of chilled Pommery Brut Royal champagne to greet you upon arrival. In addition, your cruise tickets, baggage tags, and itineraries arrive before the cruise in a handsome leather portfolio. Another innovation for passengers is the option to board or disembark at any port they choose during every cruise itinerary.

Dining options range from casual to elegant, with open seating in both the more casual indoor/outdoor La Terrazza and in the more formal restaurants, including the ultragourmet Le Champagne. Twenty-four-hour in-suite dining is also offered, with course-by-course dinner service available. Both the more formal restaurant and La Terrazza are elegantly furnished and afford a good deal of space between tables, a well-controlled sound level, and fine food and service. La Terrazza takes on an Italian accent for dinner, offering an innovative à la carte menu showcasing classic Italian Slow Food and rustic Tuscan cuisine.

The main dining rooms on each ship feature selected menu items created in conjunction with the famed chefs of Relais & Chateaux. One of the alternative specialty restaurants on all ships (except *Silver Explorer*) is Le Champagne. Developed in collaboration with Relais & Chateaux, the restaurants offer seasonally inspired menus showcasing regional specialties prepared with fresh locally sourced produce and products, featuring a collection of dishes designed specifically to compliment great wines. Gratuities are not expected in any of the restaurants.

Special theme parties and dinner dancing are featured on each sailing, and mature gentlemen hosts are available as dance and bridge partners on selected sailings. Public areas also offer guests a great variety of choices and include a multilevel show lounge with full-scale entertainment throughout the cruise; a panorama lounge; a library stocked with books, computers with Internet access, periodicals, and reference materials as well as videos and DVDS; a bar/nightclub; a full casino with roulette, blackjack, and slots; a health spa with masseuse, beauty salon, sauna, and well-equipped exercise facility; a cardroom; an outdoor pool and two heated whirlpools; and a sundeck observation area.

Public areas on the *Shadow* and *Whisper* are similar to those on the *Cloud* and *Wind*, with various innovations available due to their increased size, including a larger casino; a larger, more fully equipped exercise facility and spa; a poolside grill; the Connoisseur's Corner, a cigar bar, and a scenic observation lounge atop ship.

Worldwide itineraries offer cruises that can be booked from 6 to 115 days. Frequent cruisers can earn points resulting in significant savings and extra amenities when booking future cruises.

Officers and staff on board Silversea ships are highly experienced, and many have extensive tenure with other upscale and premium cruise lines. Italian officers create a warm and friendly onboard ambiance, Asian butlers provide efficient and hospitable suite service, and a Northern European hotel staff, together with an international support staff, provide gracious onboard dining.

A partnership with Wireless Maritime Services allows passengers to use their mobile phones and other wireless devices aboard ship. Silversea also offers remote wireless Internet access (Wi-Fi) in designated locations aboard its ships.

Notable guest lecturers on each voyage offer definitive views of the history, culture, and geography of the countries the ships visit. The line will also continue its Wine Cruises, hosted by some of the world's finest vintners, as well as its Culinary Arts cruises, featuring renowned chefs.

In 2007, the cruise line purchased the former 6,072-ton, 132-passenger *World Discoverer*, upgraded and refurbished her, and commenced operating her as *Prince Albert II* in June 2008. In 2011, the name was changed to *Silver Explorer*. The expedition ship has a strengthened hull and can operate in remote locations around the world such as the Arctic and Antarctica. All accommodations have ocean-view rooms ranging in size from 175 to 675 square feet and flat-screen TVs with DVD players, and many also have balconies. Included in accommodations are two owner's suites, two grand suites, and six silver suites similar to the cruise line's other vessels. There is Wi-Fi and cell phone access throughout the ship. The main restaurant features single-seating dining and serves breakfast and lunch buffet style and dinner à la carte. Other public areas include a cigar lounge, library/Internet café, theater for shows and lectures, boutique, beauty salon, fitness center, full-size spa, two Jacuzzi pools, launderette, medical center, and the Panorama and Observation lounges. The ship has six Zodiac crafts and offers complimentary shore excursions.

The 36,000-ton, 540-passenger *Silver Spirit* joined the fleet in late 2009. All but twelve of the 270 ocean-view suites have verandas. Accommodations are exceptionally comfortable, beautifully furnished, and have generous sitting areas, walk-in closets, fine bed linens, choice of pillows, personal safes, flat-screen TVs with DVD players, beverage cabinets stocked with choice of beverages (including alcoholic), a bottle of Pommery champagne upon arrival, fresh fruit, flowers, personal butlers, and marbled bathrooms with full-size tubs, separate showers, robes, slippers, and European bath amenities.

The 224 veranda suites measure 376 square feet; the 26 silver suites, 742 square feet; the six grand suites, 990 square feet; and the two owner's suites, 1,292 square feet. (Measurements include the veranda.) The owner's and grand suites can be joined with a veranda suite and include butler service, laundry service, pressing, and cleaning.

Guests can choose between the three-meal-a-day sophisticated main dining room, the Restaurant, with open seating and exclusive menus by Relais & Chateaux; La Terrazza, the more casual indoor/outdoor venue that serves buffet style for breakfast and lunch and offers Italian fare à la cart at dinner; the Pool Grill at lunch and dinner, featuring grilled meats and fresh-from-the-oven pizza (in the evenings, the upper level is designated the Grill; there passengers can grill their own chops and steaks on hot rocks at their tables); a lobby bar serving Italian coffees, champagne, wine, and spirits gratis; Le Champagne, by Relais & Chateaux (described previously); Seishin, offering Asian/Fusion cuisine; and Stars Supper Club, where a multicourse tapas-style dinner is accompanied by music, dancing, and entertainment. There is a charge at Le Champagne and Seishin. In-suite dining service includes dinner served course by course with selections, linens, crystal, and china from the Restaurant. We were most impressed with the excellence and gourmet quality of our dinner at Le Champagne as well as the unique cuisine and style of presentation at Stars Supper Club.

Public venues include the show lounge, with double banquet seating, where full-scale productions and classical soloists are featured; the panorama lounge for music and dancing; the observation lounge atop ship; the Connoisseur's Corner for cigars and cognacs; a library/Internet café; three duty-free shops with upscale merchandise; a large casino; a swimming pool and lido area which includes three whirlpools, the Pool Grill, a bar, a jogging track, and movies on deck; an 8,300-square-foot spa with nine treatment rooms, a beauty salon, indoor/outdoor relaxation areas, sauna, steam room, and an outdoor whirlpool only available to guests booking a treatment or those paying $25 per day; a fitness center with two aerobics studios and the latest cardio and weight equipment; and small locker rooms and mixed gender sauna and steam rooms available to all guests.

In 2009, butler service was extended to all suites on every ship in the fleet. Also, the Silver Shore Concierge program provides one-on-one consultations to assist passengers in designing their one-of-a-kind shore excursions as well as pre- and postcruise land adventures.

## Strong Points

The *Silver Cloud* and *Silver Wind* offer the ultimate in a luxury yacht-like cruise experience with imaginative gourmet cuisine, sumptuous accommodations, impeccable service, and exotic itineraries. The *Silver Shadow*, the *Whisper*, and the *Spirit* offer a similar luxurious, pampered cruise experience; however, being somewhat larger, there is more public area space and expanded facilities, activities, and entertainment. Many critics rate Silversea as the best in the luxury-cruise market.

*Silver Spirit, courtesy Silversea Cruises*

*Silver Spirit veranda stateroom, courtesy Silversea Cruises*

*Pool on Silver Spirit, courtesy Silversea Cruises*

*Dining Room Silver Spirit, courtesy Silver Sea Cruises*

*Suite amenities on Silver Shadow, courtesy Silversea Cruises*

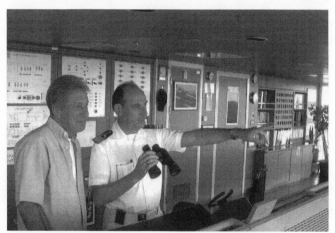

*Author with Captain on Silver Shadow, courtesy Silversea Cruises*

Always Available from our Steakhouse Menu

###### —— APPETISERS ——

Black Angus Beef Tartare *
Side Salad · Balsamic Dressing · Traditional Condiments

Swordfish Carpaccio *
Arugula and Cherry Tomato Salad · Basil Olive Oil

Shrimp 'Ritz' Martini
Baby Shrimps · Eggs · Avocado · Marie Rose

###### —— SOUPS ——

Lobster Bisque
Fresh Cream · Lobster Bits

Tomato Velouté ❧
Home-made Pesto

###### —— GRILL SPECIALS ——

Fillet of Atlantic Salmon *
Steamed | Grilled | Broiled

Fish of the Day *
Steamed | Grilled | Broiled

Whole-roasted Free-range Baby Chicken
Mushroom Fricassee

Grilled Fillet Mignon (6oz.) *
Your Choice of Side Offerings

New York Strip Steak (8oz.) *
Your Choice of Side Offerings

Charred Pork Chop
Apple Compote

###### —— CHOICE OF SIDE OFFERINGS ——

Condiments & Sauces
Natural Gravy | Grainy Mustard Sauce | Five-Pepper Sauce
Drawn Butter | Creamy Mushroom Sauce | Tomato Relish
Herb Beurre Blanc | Mint and Coriander Relish | Apple Sauce

Vegetables
Mash Potatoes | French Fries | Parsley Potatoes
Vichy Carrots | Broccoli and Cauliflower Medley | Green Asparagus
Wilted Greens | Shallot Green Beans | Mushroom Fricassee

| Head Sommelier | Executive Chef | Restaurant Manager |
|---|---|---|
| Cosmin Rusu | Ricardo Dotti | Marcelo Affonso |

*Silver Spirit*

En Route to: Gustavia, St. Barts
Friday, 29 March 2013

Our Chef's Selection for Tonight

—— APPETISERS ——

Fried Chicken Puffs ✦
Coconut Chutney

Conch Fritters ✦*
Mojo and Island Slaw

Tomato Terrine ✿
Arugula Coulis

—— SOUP, SALAD & PASTA BAR ——

Sweet Potato Soup ✦ ✿
Plantain Crisps · Shredded Spinach

Blue Crab & Mango Salad ✦
Citrus Dressing

Sun-dried Tomato Risotto ✿
Fresh Herbs

—— SORBET ——

Guava
Tropical Coulis

—— MAIN COURSES ——

Grilled Ginger & Habanero-glazed Swordfish Steak ✦*
Smoked Bacon · Papaya · Citrus Salad

Colombo ✦
Curried Island Lamb Stew · Fragrant Rice · Plantain

Rum-Glazed Baby Back Ribs ✦
Oven-roasted Sweet Potato · Caribbean Slaw

Chefs Cut *
Ask your Waiter for Today's Chef Special · Choice of Side Offerings

Involtini di Melanzane ✿
Eggplant Rolls · Provolone

---

✦ REGIONAL FARES A regional selection of recipes and dishes based on local produce sourced by your Executive Chef in our ports of call.

✿ VEGETARIAN FARES A mix & match of nutrient non-meat substitutes for vegetarians and non-vegetarians alike.

* At Silversea Cruises, we take maximum food precautionary measures to ensure the safest quality product is offered to our guests. The United States Public Health Service advises that consuming raw or undercooked meats, seafood, shell fish, eggs, milk or poultry may increase your risk of food-borne illness, especially if you have certain medical conditions.

*Menu Silver Spirit dining room, courtesy Silversea Cruises*

## THURSDAY, 28 MARCH 2013

### Sunrise 7:03am · Sunset 7:16pm

### GOOD MORNING

| | | |
|---|---|---|
| 7:30 | Morning Walk with Personal Trainer Nenad | Jogging Track (11) |
| 8:00 | **Silver Spirit is scheduled to dock in Castries, St. Lucia** | |
| | Once the vessel has been cleared by local authorities, Cruise Director Don will give weather and gangway location information. | Public Address System / TV Channel I |
| 8:00 | **Preferred Shopping Partner Philip** is available to assist with shopping in port | Lobby (5) |
| 8:00 | International Hostess is available to assist non-English speaking guests (until 9:00am) | Main Lobby (5) |
| 8:00 | IT Concierge Andrei is available to assist you with any computer questions (until 11:00am) | Internet Cafe (7) |
| 8:30 | Today's Crossword puzzle and Sudoku are available | Library (7) |
| 8:30 | Silversea Quiz. Prize points will be awarded to whomever has the most correct answers before 3:00pm | Library (7) |
| 9:00 | Table Tennis (Deck 10 Mid.) and Shuffleboard (Deck 8 Aft.) will be set up for your enjoyment throughout the day. | |
| 10:30 | Coffee Chat with the Artists of Silversea | Panorama Lounge (9) |
| 10:30 | Informal Cards & Games available (unhosted) | Card Room (9) |

### GOOD AFTERNOON

| | | |
|---|---|---|
| 2:00 | Bridge Play (unhosted) | Card Room (9) |
| 3:00 | **Acupuncture Seminar:** "Pain Solutions with Acupuncture" with Acupuncturist Filipa Rodrigo | Conference Room (5) |
| 4:00 | **Fitness Seminar:** "How to Increase your Metabolism" with Personal Trainer Nenad | The Bar (5) |
| 4:00 | **Bingo** for fun and prize points with International Hostess | Panorama Lounge (9) |
| 4:00 | IT Concierge Andrei is available to assist you with any computer questions (until 7:00pm) | Internet Cafe (7) |
| 4:00 | Afternoon Tea is served accompanied by our resident Pianist's music (until 5:00pm) | La Terrazza (7) |
| 4:45 | **Team Trivia** with Cruise Director Don for fun and prize points | Panorama Lounge (9) |
| 5:00 | Power Yoga Class with Personal Trainer Nenad | Fitness Centre (6) |
| 5:30 | **ALL ABOARD! Silver Spirit prepares to sail** | |
| 5:30 | Sundowner Cocktails (weather permitting) | Pool Deck (9) |
| 5:30 | Friends of Bill W meet | Observation Lounge (11) |
| 5:30 | Golf Putting Competition with the Artists of Silversea | Lobby of Panorama Lounge (9) |

### GOOD EVENING · DRESS CODE: FORMAL

| | | |
|---|---|---|
| 6:00 | **Silver Spirit sets sail for Roseau, Dominica** | |
| 6:00 | Relaxing Stretch Class with Personal Trainer Nenad | Fitness Centre (6) |
| 6:00 | Easy listening music by Pianist Florandy Fijer | The Bar (5) |
| 7:00 | **CAPTAIN'S MINO PONTILLO WELCOME RECEPTION** | The Bar (5) |
| | You'll be introduced to the Senior Officers of Silver Spirit. Music provided by the Silver Spirit Trio | |
| 7:00 | Enjoy a cocktail with music by Pianist Amedeo | Panorama Lounge (9) |
| 7:00 | Solo Travellers meet for cocktails (unhosted) | Panorama Lounge (9) |
| 7:30 | Dance to the music of The Duo, Alvin & Angie as they play during dinner poolside (weather permitting) | Pool Deck (9) |
| 8:00 | Enjoy the melodies of pianist Florandy Fijer | The Bar (5) |
| 8:30 | Piano melodies with TC Chandler | Stars (7) |
| 9:00 | The Silver Spirit Trio plays dance music (until 11:00pm) | Panorama Lounge (9) |
| 9:00 | Amedeo delights you with unforgettable melodies | The Bar (5) |
| 9:15 | Easy Jazz with Singer Mickki Brown & TC Chandler (until 11:00pm) | Stars (7) |
| 10:00 | **Nightclub Dancing!** Dance the Night Away with our Resident DJ | Panorama Lounge (9) |
| 10:00 | Pianist Florandy Fijer plays music for your listening and dancing pleasure | The Bar (5) |
| 10:15 | **SHOWTIME! Silversea proudly presents: SIGNED, SEALED, DELIVERED** | The Show Lounge (5) |
| | Performed by the Artists of Silversea | |
| 11:00 | **Stars Showtime!** Starring Singer Mickki Brown with TC Chandler on piano | Stars (7) |
| 11:00 | Amedeo delights you with late night melodies | The Bar (5) |

*Silver Spirit daily program, courtesy Silversea Cruises*

# STAR CLIPPERS

**760 NW 107th Street, Suite 100
Miami, FL 33172
(800) 442-0551
www.starclippers.com**

*Royal Clipper:* entered service in 2000; 5,000 GRT; 439 × 54 feet; 227-passenger capacity; 114 cabins; European officers and international crew; seven-day Caribbean cruises during winter from Barbados and seven-, ten-, and eleven-day Mediterranean cruises during summer from Civitavecchia (Rome) and Venice, Italy (Category B—four+ stars)

*Star Clipper:* entered service in 1992; 2,298 GRT; 360 × 50 feet; 170-passenger capacity; eighty-five cabins; European officers and international crew; seven-, ten-, and eleven-day Mediterranean cruises from Athens and Venice during summer and winter cruises in Caribbean from St. Maarten (Category C—four+ stars)

*Star Flyer:* entered service in 1991; 2,298 GRT; 360 × 50 feet; 170-passenger capacity; eighty-five cabins; European officers and international crew; a variety of European cruises during summer and seven-day Costa Rican cruises during winter (Category C—four+ stars)

(Medical facilities: C-0; P [on trans-ocean cruises only]; N-1—medical facilities and equipment are very limited)

These ships are rated in eleven separate categories in the second half of chapter 11.

In 1991, Mikael Krafft, a Swedish shipping and real-estate entrepreneur and the founder and managing owner of Star Clippers, embarked on bringing to the cruise market yacht-like sailboats that sail more than they operate their engines. The cruise line emphasizes enjoying a sailing vessel, being close to the sea, participating in water sports, and visiting great beaches in a casual yet comfortable shipboard environment.

When *Star Flyer* and *Star Clipper* entered the cruise market in 1991 and 1992, they were (and still are) the tallest sailing ships afloat, with 36,000 square feet of Dacron sail flying from four towering masts, the highest rising to 226 feet. The ships feature a unique antirolling system designed to keep them upright and stable for sailing and while at anchor.

Eighty-five air-conditioned staterooms accommodate 170 passengers. Six are small inside cabins with upper and lower berths. The remainder measure approximately 120 square feet and are outside, with two twin beds that convert to a double bed, TV that plays in-house DVDs, radios, lighted dressing table with mirror and stool, small closets with shelving and built-in personal safes, cellular satellite telephone with direct dialing, and small bathrooms with showers, toilets, hair dryers, and mirrors. The eight more-expensive cabins located on main and sundecks are a wee bit larger and include refrigerators, full windows, and larger bathrooms with Jacuzzi tubs and shower attachments.

Public areas, entertainment, and onboard activities are limited. However, every day the officers permit passengers to participate in hoisting and lowering the sails and steering the vessel. The captains and other senior staff give nautical talks on deck daily, and other classes are offered, such as knot tying. In the evening there are audience-participation events and dancing, or local entertainment comes on board when the ship is in port. Atop ship on sundeck, surrounded by the sails, are two small swimming pools and the lounge chairs. The main deck, below, is the location of six of the larger cabins, the piano bar lounge, the library, and the sheltered outdoor tropical bar—the hub of activity on the ship. The dining room and half of the remaining cabins are on clipper deck; the other cabins are located on commodore deck.

The attractive dining room seats all passengers at an open sitting. Breakfast and lunch are served buffet style, and a five-course dinner features a choice of four entrees, including a vegetarian offering. The diverse selection of ethnic and Continental cuisines is excellent and the service is warm, friendly, and efficient. The atmosphere is casual, and jackets are never required. At midnight, the chef prepares a special snack that is served in the piano bar.

At least once in each cruise in the Caribbean and Costa Rica, there is a barbecue lunch and beach party at a private, secluded beach, with water sports and games. An extensive water sport program is available daily as well, at no extra cost. The water sport staff supervises kayaking, snorkeling, small-craft sailing.

The ships are sometimes under charter to private groups, and you must check in advance to be certain the cruise date you select is open to the public. Itineraries for the two ships are not written in stone; however, the ships cruise in the Caribbean or Costa Rica during the winter months and in the Mediterranean during the summer. I have found the sailings in southeast Asia from Phuket, Thailand, to be spectacular, calling at small pristine, scenic islands seldom visited by the average tourist. Recently, this itinerary was discontinued because of problems in this area of the world. All of the itineraries are a beach, snorkel, and water sport lover's paradise.

Rates run from approximately $240 per person per day for a standard outside cabin with double or twin beds up to $370 per person per day for one of the larger cabins on main or sundecks. A third passenger sharing a cabin pays only $53 per night. The cruise line will arrange air from most U.S. cities for an average cost of $865 to the Caribbean and $1,290 to the Mediterranean. Star Clippers is also marketed throughout Europe, so you can expect a large percentage of the travelers to be European, even in the Caribbean. Announcements are in English, followed by German and French, depending on the passenger mix of each cruise.

The 5,000-gross-ton, 227-passenger, 42-sail *Royal Clipper* entered service in spring 2000 as the largest sailing ship afloat. A total of 56,000 square feet of sails fly from her five great steel masts. Considerably larger and more elegantly appointed than the other vessels, she offers two 355-square-foot owner's suites and fourteen 215-square-foot deluxe suites with verandas. The remaining standard cabins measure 108 to 145 square feet and include marble bathrooms with shower stalls, remote-control TVs, radio channels, satellite telephones, private safes, and elephant-trunk hair dryers. (Six of these are interior accommodations, and two are somewhat larger and open onto the deck.) The seven-day itineraries cover the Caribbean from Barbados during the late fall and winter, and the ship offers seven-, ten-, and eleven-day cruises from Rome and Venice throughout the remainder of the year. Overall, the accommodations and public areas are a great deal more upscale than on the two smaller vessels and are enhanced by the use of brass, rich dark woods, attractive fabrics, mirrors, and nautical art and accents.

Public areas include an indoor main lounge with a piano bar midship, an observation lounge, an outside but protected Tropical Bar, and a library, all similar to those on the two smaller ships but on a much larger scale. In addition, there is a two-level, paneled dining room (accessible from staircases that descend from a dynamic atrium) featuring open seating, with buffet offerings for breakfast and lunch and dishes served at the table for dinner, a lower-deck complex that includes a gym with antiquated equipment, a spa offering various massage and body treatments, a Turkish bath, a sundeck with three tiny pools and scattered lounge chairs, and a hydraulic platform at the rear of the ship for water sports and access to the tenders. Rates range from approximately $200 to $400 per person per night for the six categories of standard cabins, up to $500 to $600 for the sixteen deluxe suites, and $630 to $690 for the two owner's suites.

The cruise line announced that it intends to build a new 7,400-ton, 296-passenger, five-masted, thirty-seven-sail barque that will be 518 feet long by 61 feet wide. She will be 50 percent larger than the *Royal Clipper* and have an ice-class hull. The ten inside cabins will measure 129 square feet, whereas the 140 standard outside cabins will measure 162 square feet. For more space and amenities, there are thirty 323-square-foot deluxe suites, two deluxe 215-square-foot deck cabins, and two 592-square-foot owner's suites. All deluxe accommodations have balconies. Public areas include a two-level, one-seating main restaurant, a piano lounge, a two-level tropical bar, a dive/spots bar, an observation room, a multipurpose room that can convert to a 160-person conference room, a library, a spa, a gym, three pools, and a retractable marina at the stern of the ship for water sports.

## Strong Points

A more intimate, hands-on sail/cruise experience to great beach destinations and offbeat small ports in a casual environment at middle-market prices and enviable dining and service—but with less entertainment, service, creature comforts, and amenities than those found on the more traditional smaller cruise ships. A must for real sailors and beach/water sport lovers. The *Royal Clipper* offers more space, facilities, pampering, and comfort as well as several more upscale deluxe suites with verandas.

*Piano Lounge on Royal Clipper, courtesy Star Clippers*

*Stateroom Royal Clipper, courtesy Star Clippers*

*Royal Clipper and Star Clipper, Courtesy Star Clippers*

*Dining Room on Royal Clipper, courtesy Star Clippers*

## STAR CLIPPERS

### *Les Entrées*

**Bresaola et sa salade d'orge**
Thinly sliced dried beef served with a barley salad
Bresaola, luftgetrocknetes Rindfleisch, mit Graupensalat

**Crêpes au saumon, sauce au safran**
Salmon pancakes with saffron sauce
Crepes gefüllt mit Lachs in Safransauce

### *Le Potage*

**Velouté de carottes á l'orange**
Cream of carrot soup with Orange slices
Karottencremesuppe mit Orangenspalten

### *Le Sorbet*

**Sorbet Tomate Vodka**
Tomato - Vodka sorbet
Tomatensorbet mit Vodka

### *Les Plats*

**Queue de homard grillée, beurre aux fines herbes**
Grilled lobster tail with herb butter
Gegrillter Hummerschwanz mit frischer Kräuterbutter

**Filet de bœuf « Chateaubriand »**
Filet of beef "Chateaubriand" with truffle sauce
Rinderfilet "Chateaubriand" mit Trüffelsauce

### *Le Vegetarien*

**Quiche aux Champignons**
Mushroom quiche
Champignon Quiche

### *Caribbean Chef Special*

**Magret de canard au curry**
Duck breast with curry sauce
Entenbrust mit Currysauce

*Vous pouvez également commander un Consommé, des Pâtes ou une Entrecôte, Pommes frites*
If you wish, you may order a Consommé, a Pasta dish or a Sirloin steak with French Fries
Auf Wunsch servieren wir Ihnen eine Kraftbrühe, ein Nudelgericht oder ein Entrecote mit Pommes frites

 Convient aux Végétariens / Suitable for Vegetarians / Empfehlung für Vegetarier

## STAR CLIPPERS

### *La Salade*

**Salade de Radicchio aux pignons, vinaigrette à la crème**
Radicchio salad with pine nuts and cream dressing
Radicchiosalat mit Pinienkernen und Rahmsauce

### *Le Fromage*

***Une sélection de fromages, accompagnée de fruits et biscuits salés***
A selection of international cheeses served with fresh fruit and biscuits
Kleine Käseauswahl mit frischem Obst und Salzgebäck

### *Les Desserts*

***Omelette Norvégienne***
Baked Alaska
Flambierte Eistorte "Alaska"

~ * ~

### *Le Conseil du Sommelier*

**Louis Jadot, Puligny Montrachet AOC, Burgundy 2004.**
*Fresh, clean citrussy nose - still quite closed.*
*Rounded and medium-bodied with ripe, warm citrus and toasted oak flavors.*
75 cl € 48.00

**Château La Chapelle de Calon, St. Estephe AOC 2004, Bordeaux.**
*Appealing ripe prune fruit, spicy oak bouquet. Full bodied,*
*balanced tannins and good finish.*
*75 cl € 36.00*

*Star Clippers a consulté le chef Jean Marie Meulien, honoré de trois étoiles au*
*guide Michelin, pour la création de ces menus.*

*For the creation of these menus Star Clippers has consulted the chef Jean Marie Meulien*
*who has been awarded 3 stars in the Michelin guide throughout his career.*

*Star Clippers konsultierte den mit drei Michelin Sternen ausgezeichneten*
*Chef Jean Marie Meulien zur Gestaltung der Menus*

| **Rodolfo Soledad** | **Francesco Mazzoni** | **Emmanuel Abella** |
|---|---|---|
| Executive Chef | Hotel Manager | Maitre d' Hotel |

# SPV Royal Clipper

*Barbados – Union Island – Grenada – Tobago Cays – St. Vincent/Bequia – Martinique – St. Lucia – Barbados*

| | | |
|---|---|---|
| *08:00 – 08:30* | **Morning Gymnastics** *with Tanja* | *Tropical Bar* |
| *08:00 – 20:00* | ***Captain Nemo Lounge (Spa / Wellness / Fitness Centre) is open for you!*** | |
| *09:00* | **Port Information on Tobago Cays** *with Timoteo* | *Bridge* |

| | |
|---|---|
| *09:30* | **SPV Royal Clipper anchors off the Tobago Cays !** <br> **A continuous tender service will be at your disposal** *to the beach and back.* <br> *Do not forget to take some money (ECS or US$) for the local t-shirts!* |

*South of Canouan and West of Mayreau lie the Tobago Cays Islands like giant turtle shells rousing from the crystal clear water The white sand beaches and the turquoise blue water are withstanding for those who like swimming, snorkelling and diving. The coral reefs are an unforgettable experience for all visitors!*

| | | |
|---|---|---|
| *09:30* | **„Southern Grenadines by Powerboat"** <br> *(do not forget to put your swimsuit & to take towel, hat, sun lotion and camera!)* <br> **Tour ends at +/- 13:00 on the beach for the beach barbeque** | *Meet at the* **Tropical Bar** |

| | | |
|---|---|---|
| *10:00 – 15:30* | **The Sports Team** *awaits you* **at the Beach** *with water sports activities (weather permitting)* | |
| *10:30* | **Certified Dive** *with the Dive instructors* | *Marina Platform* |
| *13:00* | **Discover Scuba Dive** *with the Dive instructors* | *Beach* |
| *14:00* | **Aqua Gymnastics** *with Tanja* | *Beach* |

| | |
|---|---|
| *15:30* <br> *16:00* | **Last tender back to the SPV Royal Clipper ! All guests back on board !** <br> **SPV Royal Clipper sets sail for St Vincent !** <br> *Join Captain Sergey and Crew for the sail away maneuvers by the bridge.* <br> *Enjoy the afternoon sailing on deck !* |

| | | |
|---|---|---|
| *16:45* | **Captain Sergey's Story time following by Sailing maneuvers** <br> *(weather permitting)* | *Bridge* |
| *19:00 – 20:30* | **Piano melodies** *with Laszlo* | *Piano Bar* |
| *21:30 – 22:00* | *After-dinner music with our musician Laszlo* | *Tropical Bar* |

| | |
|---|---|
| **22:00** | *Night of music*          *Tropical Bar* |

*AFTERWARDS DANCING UNDER THE STARS...*

**Captain Sergey and the entire Crew wish you a fantastic day in Tobago Cays!**

*courtesy Star Clippers, Inc.*

# WINDSTAR CRUISES

**2101 Fourth Avenue, Suite 210
Seattle, Washington 98121
(800) 258-7245
www.windstarcruises.com**

*WIND SPIRIT*: entered service 1988; renovated 2007, 2010 and 2012; 5,703 GRT; 440' × 52'; four masts 204' high; six sails and three engines; 148-passenger capacity; 74 cabins; British officers, Indonesian and Filipino crew; seven-day cruises in the Caribbean from Barbados during winter and in the Mediterranean and Greek Islands during summer and early fall, plus two transatlantic repositioning cruises; commencing in May 2014, seven-day cruises in French Polynesia (Category B—5+ stars)

*WIND STAR*: entered service 1986; renovated 2007, 2010 and 2012; 5,703 GRT; 440' × 52'; four masts 204' high; six sails and three engines; 148-passenger capacity; 74 cabins; British officers, Indonesian and Filipino crew; seven-day cruises Costa Rica and the Panama Canal during winter and the Mediterranean and Greek Islands during summer and early fall, plus two transatlantic repositioning cruises (Category B—5+ stars)

*WIND SURF* (formerly *Club Med I*): entered service 1990; renovated 2006, 2010, 2011 and 2012; 14,745 GRT; 617' × 66'; 312-passenger capacity; 156 cabins; British officers, Indonesian and Filipino crew; seven-day cruises in the Mediterranean during summer and early fall and in the Caribbean during winter and spring, plus two transatlantic repositioning cruises (Category B—5+ stars)

*STAR PRIDE* (formerly *Seabourn Pride*): entered service 1988; refurbished 2010 and 2014; 10,000 GRT; 440' × 63'; 208-passenger capacity; 104 suites; international officers and crew; varying itineraries (Category A—not rated)

(Medical Facilities: C-0; P-1; EM, CLS; N-0; BC; CM; PD; EKG; TC; PO; EPC; OX; WC; ICU; LJ, except *Wind Surf*, which also carries a nurse)

These ships are rated in eleven separate categories in the second half of chapter 11.

Windstar Cruises was founded in 1984 by Finnish-born Karl Andren, who put the uniquely designed *Wind Star* into Caribbean service in 1986. Thereafter, *Wind Star* was joined by her two identical sister ships, *Wind Song* in July 1987 and *Wind Spirit* in 1988. In 1997, Windstar purchased *Club Med I* from Club Med Cruises, renamed the ship *Wind Surf,* and conducted extensive renovations, including the addition of thirty-one new suites, a ten-thousand-square-foot spa, and a Mediterranean-style restaurant. *Wind Surf* commenced service for its new owners in the Mediterranean in the spring of 1998. In late 2002, the *Wind Song* was destroyed in an unfortunate fire. The line decided not to rebuild the ship and discontinued itineraries in French Polynesia; however, in May 2014 the cruise line returned to this area with the newly renovated *Wind Spirit.*

Windstar Cruises was purchased by Holland America Line in 1988, and Holland America was subsequently purchased by Carnival Cruise Line. In February 2007, Carnival sold the cruise line to Ambassadors International, Inc. In 2010, the three ships each received "Degrees of Difference" enhancements in the areas of dining, activities, accommodations, spas, fitness centers, and shore excursions. In May 2011, the cruise line was sold to Xanterra Parks and Resorts. The new owners renovated the vessels in 2011 and 2012 to give them a more stylish, luxurious décor.

The unique feature of these vessels is motorized sailing systems with diesel-electric back-up propulsion. However, the ships are not under sail the duration of the cruise.

All of the seventy-four cabins on the two original ships are outside, virtually identical, and located on the lower two decks. (There is also one larger suite.) They are 188 square feet in area and are designed in a modern interpretation of the nautical tradition, with mixed woods and rich fabrics. Actually the clever layout and utilization of storage space makes the cabin seem larger. Each includes a flat-screen color television with a DVD/CD player built in, a lockbox, a three-channel radio, a desk and sitting area, a fully stocked refrigerator and minibar (soft drinks are gratis, but alcoholic beverages are expensive for a cruise ship), waffle-weave robes, slippers, L'Occitane bath amenities, a direct-dial ship-to-shore telephone, two twin beds that convert to queen size, and a nice-sized bathroom with separate toilet compartment, sink, shower, and generous cabinet space. All cabins have portholes, and none have verandas. Room service is available around the clock. Several cabins offer a third berth. All rooms also have Bose SoundDock speakers for docking Apple iPods and wireless Internet. The ship has Wi-Fi in the staterooms and in public areas. Packages can be purchased $89 for 60 MBs of data or $159 for 120 MBs of data.

Public areas are located on the top two decks, with the exception of the small gym, infirmary, and water sports platform, which are located on the first deck down from the top (designated deck 2). The public areas include a sundeck with a small pool and hot tub, a small casino, an intimate yet elegant wood-paneled dining room, a lounge and bar, a spa, a boutique, an infirmary, and a library. Excellent breakfasts and lunches are served partially buffet style and partially with table service in the glass-enclosed Veranda Lounge, or alfresco on the adjacent deck area. Dinner takes place in the romantic main dining room from 7:00 to 9:30 p.m. without preassigned seating. The line describes its cuisine as a combination of French, European, and New American. In the evening, the Pool Deck bar area transforms into Candles, a reservation-only specialty restaurant featuring various cuts of beef as well as fish and seafood. Previously there was a no-tipping policy; however, today $12 per person, per day is added to your shipboard account in lieu of personal tipping. Guests do have the right to adjust this amount up or down if they so choose.

In the evening, a piano player entertains, and (once per cruise) a gala deck barbecue under the stars is offered. A large selection of DVDs and CDs are available in the library and can be aired in individual cabins. There is also a small casino with a black jack and a poker table and thirteen slot machines. Guests can send e-mails on a computer in the library or they can rent laptops at reception. Wireless Internet is available throughout the ship at the above described charges. Hot and cold hors d'oeuvres are served at cocktail hour, also the occasion for a lecture on the following day's excursions.

Complimentary water sports, including water-skiing, sailboating, kayaking, and windsurfing, are available off the marina deck.

During the winter, the itineraries for the *Wind Spirit* include some of the more picturesque islands in the Caribbean; the ships sail to a number of French, Italian, Greek, and other Mediterranean islands and ports during the spring, summer, and fall. However commencing in May 2014, the ship will ply the waters of French Polynesia, home based in Papeete, Tahiti. The unique ability of these vessels to navigate shallow waters and to tender passengers to beaches and harbors permits these ships to call on more unusual destinations that the larger cruise ships cannot negotiate.

The emphasis of all three vessels is on beaches; complimentary water sports; quaint small ports; and making the most of the beauty of the natural surroundings. Each ship is equipped with Zodiac-type inflatable motor launches for water-skiing and transportation to shallow beaches, as well as water skis, snorkel equipment, kayaks, wind-surfing boards, and small sailboats. A water sport platform extends from deck 2 (second deck from the bottom of the ship).

The most enjoyable features of cruises on this line are the impressive comfort, special features, and storage space in all cabins; the intimate dining experience that permits passengers to dine alone or with other passengers of their choice and alfresco for breakfast and lunch (with waiters rather than cafeteria style); the option to dress casually and comfortably; the relaxed and unregimented program; and the ability to visit numerous exotic ports seldom offered by other cruise lines. The Indonesian and Filipino service staff is friendly and efficient.

The line offers attractive air-sea packages. Cruise fares are the same for every cabin, ranging from about $285 per day per person to $665, depending on the ship, cruise grounds, and season. Special discount values are available on various cruises throughout the year.

*Wind Surf* offers two recently constructed 495-square-foot suites, 31 suites that measure 376 square feet, twice the size of the 123 deluxe, 188-square-foot cabins. All accommodations are outside with queen beds that convert to twins, flat-screen color televisions with DVDs, CDs, safes, minibar/refrigerators, international direct-dial telephones, wireless Internet, cell phone service, Bose SoundDock speakers, L'Occitane bath amenities, hair dryers, and waffle-weave robes. The 31 suites are actually double cabins where one has been converted to a parlor while retaining its storage space and bathroom, affording exceptional space and comfort for its occupants.

Following a second refit completed in December of 2000, the *Wind Surf* has an intimate, small-ship feel like the other members of the fleet. The most visible change is found in the lounges and casino, where the innovative new design creates a more comfortable and sociable gathering place. In addition to the single-seating main dining room, there is Stella Bistro, featuring French fare, which has been expanded to seat ninety guests. A specialty restaurant, Candles, is now available on all three ships featuring steaks and chops. Veranda Bistro with a central wine bar. Breakfast and lunch are served atop ship at the Veranda restaurant or alfresco immediately outside. Most items appear on the buffet but additional items from the menu will be served at your table. Hot appetizers are served each evening in the lounges and snacks, pastries, and special treats are served late each afternoon at Compass Rose, the indoor/outdoor lounge/bar overlooking one of the pools. (These are also served on the other two vessels).

The ten-thousand-square-foot spa features treatment rooms for body wraps, facials, and massages. The locker room and sauna are shared by both sexes and are located near the marina. A well-stocked, glassed-in fitness center sits atop ship, permitting those exercising to enjoy interesting panoramas. Complimentary water sports—including water-skiing, sailboating, kayaking, paddleboarding, wakeboarding, and windsurfing—are available off the marina deck, and the ship has one outdoor swimming pool, two Jacuzzis, and several lido/lounge/bar areas. Meeting facilities can accommodate up to sixty people with special audiovisual equipment. Other public facilities include a large main lounge; a signature boutique, the Yacht Club, featuring a sandwich and espresso bar; eight computers with Internet access; DVDs, CDs, and books that can be checked out; a casino; a fitness center with new equipment as of 2010; and an infirmary. *Wind Surf*, being almost three times the size of the other two vessels, offers more indoor public areas and far more generous outdoor deck space.

Between 2006 and 2007, the ships underwent a multi-million-dollar fleet enhancement project with improvements to public areas, soft goods, and pool and deck areas. Known as the "Degrees of Difference" incentive, new additions include Apple iPod Nanos, Bose SoundDocks, personal laptops and wireless connectivity throughout public areas, new flat-screen TVs and DVD/CD players in all staterooms as well as luxury soft goods and mattresses, an array of bathroom amenities by L'Occitane, and hammocks built for two located on deck under the sails. Additional enhancements were added in 2010 to 2012, which provided enhancements in the areas of dining, activities, accommodations, spa, fitness, and shore excursions. Soft drinks and nonalcoholic beverages are now complimentary on all three vessels.

*Wind Surf* will offer seven-day cruises in the Mediterranean during the spring and summer and Caribbean cruises from Barbados the remainder of the year.

In February 2013, the owners of the cruise line finalized a contract to purchase three 10,000-ton, 208-passenger ships from Seabourn Cruises. The former *Seabourn Pride* joined Windstar in April 2014 as the *Star Pride*. The *Seabourn Legend* will join Windstar in April 2015; the *Seabourn Spirit*, in May 2015.

Most suites on these three ships are approximately 277 square feet, with a large 3 × 5 feet picture window looking out to the sea; twin beds that convert to a queen; flat-screen color TV with DVD player; richly appointed armchairs, sofa, and coffee table; a refrigerator and minibar; a hair dryer; a large walk-in closet with a private safe; and a marble bathroom with twin-sink vanities (except the *Legend*, which has single-sink vanities); a shower or shower/tub combination; luxurious bathroom and well-being amenities from Molton Brown; and ample storage space. There are also larger suites, which range in size from 400 to 575 square feet; several have small private verandas. Small French-style balconies were added to *approximately* 35 percent of the suites in 2000, allowing passengers to peek out and enjoy the sunshine and fresh sea air. They are too small to lounge on; however, they do provide views along the side of the ship.

In 2007 the *Pride* and in 2008 the *Spirit* and *Legend* received various renovations, including an expansion of the outdoor dining venues, upgraded bedding, and new carpets and furnishings. Additional renovations took place in 2009 and 2010, with a refurbishing of all public areas, giving them a more modern look. Each ship will receive additional renovations prior to entering service for Windstar.

The health spa on each vessel offers massages and herbal body wraps and includes an exercise room (recently doubled in size) with state-of-the-art equipment and treadmills with personal TVs, in addition to a steam room, a sauna, three outdoor whirlpools, and an outdoor swimming pool. At the fold-out marina, off the rear of the ship, passengers can swim, windsurf, water-ski, banana boat, and sail.

The observation lounges at the top of each ship are glass enclosed and afford a panoramic view for passengers enjoying coffee, tea, or drinks. The club has a piano bar and is the location for evening cocktails and hors d'oeuvres as well as late-night dancing. There also is a large showroom that can accommodate all passengers; an indoor/outdoor café where imaginative buffet breakfasts, lunches, and dinners are served; a casino; a hospital; a boutique; an Internet café with four terminals; and a tiny self-service launderette.

## Strong Points

Unique, beautiful design; attractive staterooms; water sports; casual, tasteful atmosphere; a more intimate dining experience; and super itineraries for beach and water sport lovers wishing to travel in comfort and luxury. The newly renovated *Wind Surf* offers an attractive suite option for the more affluent traveler and greater indoor and outdoor public areas. The acquisition of the three former Seabourn ships enables Windstar to boast the most luxurious small ships afloat.

*Stateroom on Wind Surf, courtesy Windstar Cruises.*

*Lido area Wind Star, courtesy Windstar Cruises*

*Dining Room on Wind Star, courtesy Windstar Cruises*

*Wind Star, courtesy Windstar Cruises*

# DINNER MENU WINDSURF

## Starters

Antipasti Platter (*)
salami, prosciutto, marinated red pepper, Kalamata olives, basil pesto
and roasted cherry tomatoes, served with a dash of virgin olive oil
and toasted herbed focaccia bread

Vitello Tonnato
seared seasoned veal loin served with fresh tuna dressing,
fried capers and arugula lettuce
Portobello mushrooms gratin
stuffed with crab meat, topped with melted Mozzarella cheese

## Soup and Salads

Butternut squash soup
freshly made soup with duck rillette

Pear and goat cheese salad
on shaved mixed lettuce served with prosciutto

Market greens (v)
with choice of dressing:
French, Italian, Thousand island, Blue cheese
and Hot honey mustard or light dressings

## Main Course

Oven baked Herb crusted Merluza
on plum tomato flavored pilaf rice, with pan-fried mixed zucchini,
topped with diced tomatoes and basil pesto

New York strip steak
rosemary skewered cherry tomatoes, creamed potatoes
and green peppercorn sauce

Roasted pork loin (*)
on mushrooms pilaf rice, complemented with wilted spinach, carrot flan
and a drizzle of course grain mustard sauce

Basque chicken
roast chicken breast on herb smashed fingerling potatoes and wilted greens, topped
with seared diced tomatoes, capers, red onions and cilantro

## Seafood risotto
risotto of seafood stock and cream, topped with sautéed scallops, shrimps,
mussels and fish, finished with a splash of basil pesto and fennel juice

## Vegetable Wellington (v)
layered roasted vegetables, baked in puff pastry
and served with shallot cream sauce and steamed bok choy wedge

### Available daily:
grilled or broiled sirloin steak, chicken breast or salmon

### Dinner wine selection,
to enjoy a special food and wine pairing, our executive chef selected for you 3 wines
by the glass to compliment your appetizer, entrée and dessert for only $32.00

### Side dishes:
roasted asparagus with sea-salt and lemon zest
steamed mixed broccoli, cauliflower, carrot and green beans
wilted spinach
smashed potatoes
crispy fries (truffle oil and parmesan cheese optional)
sweet potato fries with Cajun seasoning

(V) = vegetarian
(*) = chef's recommendation
(+) = no sugar added dessert

Please ask your waiter for assistance for any allergies, diets or food intolerance you
might have, we are happy to adjust our dishes to your personal needs


# Desserts

## After eight surprise
minted mousse and ganache in chocolate sponge, almond tuile and syrup

## Caramel flan
with fresh berries in a sugar snap basket

## Chocolate and coconut cake
with pan-fried bananas and banana coulis

## Apple Aumonière (+)
almonds and honey marinated apple wrapped in phyllo pastry,
served with vanilla sauce

## Cheese plate of the day
with Edam, Brie, Montrachet (goat) cheese,
pistachio nuts and sundried apricots


*Dining Room Menu, courtesy Windstar Cruises*

# Le Marin, Martinique

Monday, December 10, 2012

**Arrival: 8:00 AM**

**Last Tender:  9:45 PM**

Wind Surf prepares to sail for Pigeon Island, St. Lucia

**Where is the Fleet Today?**

Wind Star: Panama Canal Transit

Wind Spirit : At Sea

## Tender Service

Tenders will run continuously to and from the pier ashore

For your safety, Guest bags may be subject to random checks by our yacht's security team, we appreciate your understanding.

**A Friendly Reminder From Housekeeping**

Beach towels will be available at the gangway on port days, kindly return them at the gangway when you arrive back from shore side.

## Shore Excursions

Main Deck, Aft

**5:00PM - 6:00PM**

**Excursion Departure Times:**

**8:15AM** Martinique Heritage with Rum Tasting

**8:30AM** Jeep Tour of Southern Martinique

**Kindly meet in The Lounge 10 minutes prior to departure time**

## Today's Highlights

**9:00 PM – 4:00 PM Water Sports Marina** Visit our Marina on Deck 2, Aft.  Marina opening is subject to local restrictions and sea conditions. We thank you for your understanding.

**6:30 PM Port Talk in the Lounge**

Guest Services Manager January will present general information about your day tomorrow in Pigeon Island, St. Lucia. Destination Manager Geoff will be in the Lounge to present an overview of Shore Excursions.

**7:00 PM – 9:00 PM (Weather Permitting)**

**Deck BBQ Dinner Under The Stars**

Join Jump Duo & their enjoyable music at the Compass Rose. Terrace Bar & Flying Bridge offer a more private & relaxed venue & music. Top Society will provide entertaining music on the Star Deck.

**Followed by the Crew Line Dancing**

Put on your dancing shoes and join the Wind Surf Crew for Line Dancing. This will be followed by our Dance Party, with more fun and music on the Star Deck.

## Navigational Information from the Bridge

Duration Sails have been up since the beginning of the cruise until midnight last night: 51.60 hours.

Captain Alan MacAry

Hotel Manager Henri Lemay

**Port Agent Emergency Contact**

Agent : Plissonneau Shipping

Tel : + 596 596 633 004 & + 596 596 450 385

Contact : Mr. Olivier Georges & Mr. Olivier de Reynal

**Yacht Mobile Number**

+ (37) 259 238 634

## Places to Lounge

| | |
|---|---|
| Lounge Bar: | 5:00 PM – Closing |
| Pool Bar: | 9:30 AM – 6:30 PM |
| Compass Rose: | 9:30 AM – 5:30 PM & 7:00 PM – Closing |
| Yacht Club: | 7:00 AM – 6:30 PM |
| Terrace Bar: | 9:30 AM – 5:30 PM & 7:00 PM – Closing |

**Cocktails of the Day**: Shark Bite $7.75

Strawberry Cooler (Non-alcoholic)

## Places to Eat

**Breakfast**

6:00 AM – 8:30 AM in the Compass Rose (Continental)

7:00 AM – 9:30 AM in the Veranda

**Lunch**

12:30 PM – 2:00 PM in the Veranda

**Cookies & Tea**

4:00 PM – 5:00 PM in The Compass Rose

**Appetizers**

6:00 PM – 7:00 PM in the Lounge and Compass Rose

## Dinner

**Deck BBQ Dinner Under The Stars 7:00 PM – 9:00 PM**

Star Deck and Compass Rose

Room Service is available 24 hours - dial "3450".

**If you have any dietary restrictions please notify Reception**

## Specialty Sandwich Bar

Be sure to visit our Specialty Sandwich Bar located in The Yacht Club! Treat yourself to one of our eight freshly prepared delicious Signature Sandwiches!

## Weather

Sky      Scattered showers

Temp    High   82°F / 28°C   Sunrise:  6:20 AM

Temp    Low     74°F / 23°C   Sunset:  5:38 PM

*Daily Program on Wind Surf, courtesy Windstar Cruises*

# MISCELLANEOUS ADDITIONAL CRUISE LINES

## Blue Lagoon Cruises
## (877) 252-3454
## www.bluelagooncruises.com

MV *Fiji Princess*: 1,228 GRT; 179 × 44 feet; sixty-eight passenger capacity; thirty-four cabins.

MV *Mystique Princess*: 1,533 GRT; 188 × 44 feet; sixty-four-passenger capacity thirty-six cabins.

(These ships have not been rated.)

Blue Lagoon Cruises was founded in 1950 by a New Zealand stockbroker and an Australian aviator in hopes of establishing a tuna-fishing industry. The venture failed and both men having fallen in love with Fiji went on to establish Fiji Airways (the forerunner of Air Pacific) and Blue Lagoon Cruises, offering cruises to the picturesque Yasawa Island group. In 1966, the cruise line was sold to a New Zealand ship owner and the line acquired various vessels over the years.

Presently, the two boutique ships offer three-day/two-night, four-day/three-night, and seven-day/six-night cruises from Lautoka on Viti Levu, Fiji, to the Manuka Islands and the Yasawa Islands, truly some of the most pristine island paradises to be found anywhere in the world. Cruise rates fluctuate depending on the length of cruise and ship. In general, they range from approximately $860 per cabin per night to $1,200 per cabin per night for the largest suite on sky deck. There are early-booking discounts. The vessels can also be chartered.

On the flagship of the line, MV *Mystique Princess*, there are thirty-six air-conditioned staterooms ranging in size from 179 square feet to the 296-square-foot owner's suite on sky deck. Some staterooms have twin beds and others, king-sized beds. Many have convertible day beds for additional passengers. Each accommodation has an ocean view, a minibar, a sofa, an international self-dial telephone, a personal safe, a TV/DVD/audio system, a vanity table, and a hair dryer. Public areas include a one-hundred-seat dining salon, a lounge, two cocktail bars, a guest laundry, a small boutique, a spa, and three decks for sunbathing.

MV *Fiji Princess* is a catamaran and the latest addition. It is 179 × 44 feet wide, with a weight of 1228 tons, and she carries sixty-eight passengers in thirty-four cabins in a twin share configuration on four decks—Hibiscus, Frangipani, and Orchid, with the Sky Deck at the top, with no accommodations. Facilities include a foyer, eighty-seat dining saloon, Sky Deck Cocktail Bar, upper deck Lounge Bar, onboard beauty spa, small boutique, four sundeck areas, and a small swimming pool

The main attraction of these cruises is the destinations. Pristine beaches, blue lagoons, swimming, snorkeling, fish feeding, windsurfing, outdoor island feasts, and other activities taking advantage of the unique geography of this region are featured.

# CAPTAIN COOK CRUISES

**No. 6 Jetty Circular Quay**
**Sydney NSW 2000, Australia**
**+61 2 9206 1111**
**Fax: +61 2 82770 5107**
**International tel. 612-9206 1100**
**www.captaincook.com.au**

*Coral Princess*: 730 GRT; 35 × 13 meters; fifty-passenger capacity; twenty-five cabins; Australian officers and international crew; cruises to the Great Barrier Reef.

*Coral Princess* II: 884 GRT; 35 × 12 meters; forty-six-passenger capacity; twenty-four cabins; Australian officers and international crew: cruises to the Great Barrier Reef.

MV *Captain Cook's Explorer*: 1160 GRT; fifty-three meters long; 116-passenger capacity; sixty-one cabins; Australian officers and international crew; overnight cruises in Sydney Harbor.

MV *Reef Endeavor*: 3,125 GRT; 73 × 14 meters; 130-passenger capacity; 65 cabins; Australian officers and international crew; cruises from Port Denarau in Fiji to Yasawa Group of Islands.

PS *Murray Princess*: built in 1986 and refitted in 2004; 1,500 GRT; 67 × 15 meters; 120-passenger capacity; sixty cabins; Australian and British officers and international crew; stern paddle-wheeler riverboat offering river cruises on Murray River in Australia.

(These ships have not been rated.)

On all the vessels, dress is country club casual at dinner, there are no facilities for the physically challenged or for children, and tipping is not required.

The 120-passenger *Murray Princess* is a stern paddle-wheeler riverboat offering three-, four- and seven-night cruises from Adelaide on the Murray River. Fifty-one of the sixty cabins are outside, average approximately 120 square feet, and open to the outside deck. Nine are inside. There is no pool; however, there are two Jacuzzis, two saunas, two bars, two lounges, a sundeck, an elevator, a library, a shop, a guest laundry, and a single sitting dining room serving buffet breakfasts and lunches and table service dinners.

The 130-passenger *Reef Endeavor* sails from Port Denarau Fiji offering three-, four-, and seven-night cruises to the pristine Yasawa Islands. The sixty-five cabins are all outside, and twenty-one cabins located on deck A open out onto the outer deck and have picture windows. The four Tubua Suites measure twenty-eight square meters and the rest approximately fourteen square meters. Public areas include a pool, two spas, a sport deck, a gym, a sauna, two lounges, two bars, a gift shop, a guest laundry, an elevator, and a glass bottom boat for explorations as well as snorkeling and diving vessels. The dining salon has a dance floor with live entertainment nightly. As on the other Captain Cook vessels, breakfast and lunch are buffet style and there is table service at dinner.

The *Coral Princess* and the *Coral Princess II* are small special-purpose ships built to cruise the Great Barrier Reef. All accommodations are air-conditioned and have private bathrooms. Common facilities on each include a dining room, two modern lounges, a sundeck and spa pool, phone and fax facilities, a cocktail bar, a gift shop, and a dive shop.

The cruise line also offers day cruises on five modern passenger ferries. The *Captain Cook's Explorer* also offers overnight cruises in Sydney Harbor. The ship is also used for meetings.

# CDF CROISIERES DE FRANCE

## 0891 362 233
### www.cdfcroisieresdefrance.fr

*L'Horizon* (formerly *Horizon* and *Pacific Dream*): entered service in 1990; renovated in 2009 and 2011; 47,000 GRT; 682 × 95 feet; 1,875-passenger capacity (1,440 double occupancy); 721 cabins; international officers and crew (Category C—not rated)

Royal Caribbean Cruises Ltd. created this new cruise line aimed at the French market. The new company began operations in May 2008 with *Bleu de France*, formerly Pullmantur Cruises' *Holiday Dream*. Originally built in 1982 as Hapag-Lloyd's *Europa*, the ship was also with Star Cruises as *SuperStar Aries* before being bought by Pullmantur. In 2010, the ship was sold to Saga Cruises. The line acquired *L'Horizon* (formerly *Horizon* of Celebrity Cruises) from Pullmantur. The ship commenced sailing as the CDF Admiral in the spring of 2012. Before entering service with CDF, the ship underwent various renovations. The onboard experience of *L'Horizon's* guests is totally French, from cuisine to entertainment to decor. French is the language used on the ship as well. Sixty-eight of the 721 cabins and suites have balconies. The ship operates Mediterranean cruises from Marseille and repositions to La Romana, Dominican Republic, for Caribbean cruises during the winter.

On the upper deck is the AquaSpa facility that houses a beauty salon, treatment rooms, fitness area and changing rooms with steam and sauna, a jogging track, and an upper level of deck chairs overlooking the pool. The next deck below features a swimming pool and thalasso pool surrounded by lounge chairs, a bar, and a music bandstand as well as the lido restaurant, outdoor grill, and panoramic observation lounge.

The next two decks contain the higher-priced staterooms, with the remaining accommodations being located on the lower decks of the ship, below the two main public deck areas. The main public deck areas include the large two-level theater/show lounge, several other smaller show and cocktail lounges, a disco, a large casino, an electronic game room and an attractive dining room.

# CLASSIC INTERNATIONAL CRUISES

**Level 3, 3-5 Young Street**
**Neutral Bay 2089**
**NSW Australia**
**(800) 990-857**
**www.classicintcruises.com**

*Athena* (formerly *Stockholm*): entered service in 1948; rebuilt 1994 and refurbished in 2004; 16,144 GRT; 160 × 21 meters; 650-passenger capacity; 276 cabins; Portuguese, Australian, and international crew (Category D—not rated)

*Arion* (formerly *Istra*): entered service in 1965; refurbished in 2000; 24,351 GRT; 330-passenger capacity; 163 cabins; Portuguese, Australian, and international crew (Category D—not rated)

*Funchal*: entered service in 1961; refurbished in 2003; 9,562 GRT; 153 × 19.5 meters; 577-passenger capacity; twenty-four cabins; Portuguese, Australian, and international crew (Category D—not rated)

*Princess Danae* (formerly *Danae*): entered service in 1955; rebuilt 1972; 16,335 GRT; 162 × 21 meters; 479-passenger capacity; Portuguese, Australian, and international crew (Category D—not rated)

*Princess Daphne* (formerly *Daphne*): entered service in 1955; rebuilt 1972 refurbished in 2008; 15,833 GRT; 162.37 × 21.3 meters; Portuguese, Australian, and international crew (Category D—not rated); chartered for three years to Ambiente Kreuzfahrten commencing April 2012

The cruise line offers cruises of varying durations from Freemantle and Adelaide, Australia, to ports in Australia, Southeast Asia, Europe, and the Middle East on older, renovated ships at bargain prices. Some cruises are from Rome.

# CRUCEROS AUSTRALIS

**4014 Chase Avenue, Suite 215**
**Miami Beach, FL 33140**
**(877) 678-3772; (305) 695-9618**
**Fax: (305) 534-9276**
**www.australis.com**

*Mare Australis*: entered service in 2002; 2,664 GRT; 292 × 47.8 feet; 130-passenger capacity; sixty-four cabins

*Stella Australis*: entered service in 2010; 4,500 GRT; 233 × 42 feet; 210-passenger capacity; 100 cabins

*Via Australis*: entered service in 2005; 2, 664 GRT; 292 × 47.8 feet; 136-passenger capacity; sixty-four cabins

(These ships have not been rated.)

Cruise grounds include cruises to Patagonia and Tierra del Fuego between Ushuaia, Argentina, and Punta Arenas, Chile, with visits to Magdalena Island, Cape Horn, Ainsworth Bay, Wulaia Bay, Pia, Aguila, Piloto and Nena Glaciers, Straights of Magellan, and the Beagle Channel including Glacier Alley. Many of the cruises are marketed by My Exclusive Journeys. Passengers enjoy daily excursions via Zodiac boats, accompanied by expert guides. The official languages aboard are Spanish and English.

*Mare Australis* and *Via Australis* have sixty-four 161-square-foot cabins, two lounges, a dining room, exercise room, library, infirmary, open deck, and Zodiacs for explorations, visiting glaciers, forests, bays and the southernmost cities of the world. *Stella Australis* has ninety-six 177-square-foot cabins and four 220-square-foot cabins and similar facilities, in addition to a third lounge and an exercise room. All meals, as well as soft drinks, liquor, wine, and beer, and all shore excursions are included in the cruise fare.

This company also markets *Premium*, a fifteen-cabin riverboat offering two-, three-, and five-night cruises on the Amazon from Manaus, including Rio and Salvador da Bahia, Brazil.

Presently, the *Mare Australis* is being used by a sister company that operates it in Northern Chilean Patagonia.

# FTI CRUISES

**FTI Touristik GmbH**
**Landsberger Straße 88**
**D-80339 München**
**FTI-cruises.com**

*FTI Berlin* (formerly *Berlin* and *Spirit of Adventure*): entered service in 1980; 9570 GRT; 458 × 56 feet; 456-passenger capacity; 206 cabins; German officers and international crew; cruises in Eastern Mediterranean and Black Sea (Not rated)

FTI, a travel operator in Germany, leased the ship from Saga Cruises and commenced operations in May of 2012. The ship was originally built and operated by Peter Deilmann Cruises. One hundred and fifty-eight of the cabins face outside. There are two full suites and four junior suites. Public areas include a main dining room, a veranda restaurant by the swimming pool, a beer garden on sundeck, several lounges, and a library.

The company intends to acquire more ships in the future.

## HEBRIDEAN ISLAND CRUISES

**1850 S.E. 10th Avenue, Suite 205**
**Fort Lauderdale, FL 33316**
**(877) 600-2648; (954) 315-1170**
**www.hebrideancruises.com**

*Hebridean Princess*: entered service in 1964; refurbished on an annual basis during her winter off-season; 2,112 GRT; fifty-passenger capacity; thirty staterooms; cruises around the British Isles and Northern Europe (Category B—not rated)

*Royal Crown*: entered service in 2012; eighty-five passenger capacity; forty-two staterooms; cruises on the Rhine, Mosel, Danube, and Main rivers in Europe (no category—not rated)

The *Hebridean Princess* offers four- to ten-night cruises around the British Isles and Northern Europe. Cruises are more of an upscale, yacht-like experience visiting scenic ports. Although formerly attracting a mostly British clientele, the cruise line is now reaching out to North Americans. This is an all-inclusive cruise experience wherein all meals (including picnics ashore), beverages and select wines, spirits, and champagne are included as well as privately escorted tours and all port charges and gratuities. Also included are a variety of activities such as the use of the ship's bicycles to explore ashore, fishing, and speedboat rides. There are formal nights and fine dining in the panoramic Colomba Restaurant.

Of the thirty staterooms, ten are designated for single occupancy. Public areas include an all-purpose lounge with a decorative inglenook fireplace, a library, gift shop, a waterfront deck gym, another lounge, a conservatory and a restaurant.

In 2012, the company introduced river cruises aboard the eighty-five-passenger riverboat *Royal Crown*, which offers a variety of cruises on the rivers of Europe. On the top deck are sun lounges and a bar. Located on the Panorama Deck are five Royal Suites, the restaurant, main lounge, reception area, fitness, and sauna. On the Select Deck are the remaining accommodations.

All accommodations are "art deco" style and include satellite TV, Wi-Fi, showers, hair dryers, slippers, bathrobes, and safety deposit boxes. The five Royal Suites measure 195 square feet and include sitting areas and large windows. The other staterooms measure 145 or 150 square feet and have portholes. There are no balconies or French balconies.

The cruise is all-inclusive, with shore excursions, gratuities, port fees, and alcoholic drinks and nonalcoholic beverages included. Breakfast is served buffet style with eggs to order; lunches offer four courses with items from the buffet table as well; and at dinner, there are five-course menus. Tables accommodate either four or eight passengers. The cuisine is a combination of British and European fare.

# HNA CRUISES

*Henna* (former *Jubilee* and *Pacific Sun*): entered service in 1986; 47,262 GRT; 733' × 92'; 1.900-passenger capacity; 743 cabins; Chinese officers and crew; cruises from Sanya and Tianjin in China to South Korea and Vietnam

(No ratings)

The first local Chinese cruise company purchased the *Pacific Sun* (formerly *Carnival Jubilee*) from P&O Australia in 2012 and put her in service in January 2013 with home ports in Sanya and Tianjin. Initially she will offer cruises to Vietnam and South Korea and mainland China ports. She will concentrate upon the growing Chinese market. HNA Cruises is a subsidiary of HNA Tourism.

# IBERO CRUCEROS

**+902282221**
**www.ibercruceros.es**

*Grand Celebration* (formerly *Celebration*): entered service in 1987; 47,262 GRT; 733 × 92 feet; 1,486-passenger capacity; 743 cabins; Italian officers and international crew; seven-night cruises from Barcelona (Category C/D—not rated)

*Grand Holiday* (formerly *Carnival Holiday*): entered service in 1985; refurbished in 2010; 46,053 GRT; 727 × 92 feet; 1,452-passenger capacity; 726 cabins; Italian officer and international crew (category C/D—not rated)

*Grand Mistral* (formerly *Mistral*): entered service in 1999; 47,900 GRT; 708 × 95 feet; 598 cabins; 1,715-passenger capacity; seven-night Baltic and Norwegian fjord cruises from Copenhagen (Category C/D—not rated)

This Spanish cruise line caters mostly to passengers from Spain and Portugal. In 2007, Carnival entered into a joint venture with Iberojet and now owns 75 percent of the renamed cruise line. Carnival transferred the *Celebration* in 2008 and the *Holiday* in 2010, and it is expected that Carnival will transfer additional ships from its other holdings to Ibero Cruceros.

# LINBLAD EXPEDITIONS

96 Morton Street
New York, NY 10014
(800) 397-3348; (212) 765-7740
Fax: (212) 265-3770
www.expeditions.com

*National Geographic Endeavor*: entered service in 1966; rebuilt 1998; 3,132 GRT; 295 feet long; ninety-six-passenger capacity; fifty-six cabins; cruise grounds in Galapagos Islands

*National Geographic Explorer* (formerly *Lyngen* and *Midnatsol*): entered service in 1982; renovated in 2007; 367 feet long; 148-passenger capacity; eighty-one cabins; cruise grounds include Arctic, Iceland, Greenland, Arctic Canada, Antarctica, South America, North America's Atlantic Coast, Newfoundland, the Baltics, and North Cape

*National Geographic Islander*: entered service in 1994; 164 feet long; forty-eight-passenger capacity; twenty-four cabins; Galapagos Island cruises

MV *Orion*: entered service in 2003; 4,000 GRT; 103 × 14.25 meters; ice-reinforced hull; 106-passenger capacity (double occupancy); fifty-three staterooms; ten Zodiacs; exploration cruises to Antarctica, Papua New Guinea, Micronesia, Melanesia, Kimberly, Borneo, Spice Islands, Pacific Islands

*Sea Bird* and *Sea Lion*: entered service in 1981 and 1982, respectively; 100 GRT; 151 × 31 feet; sixty-two-passenger capacity; thirty-one cabins; cruises Alaska, British Columbia, Costa Rica, Panama, Columbia and Snake rivers, Baja, and Sea of Cortés

*Sea Voyager*: entered service in 1982; 354 GRT; 174 feet long; sixty-four-passenger capacity; thirty-two cabins

(These ships have not been rated.)

The cruise line commenced operations in 1979 as a division of Linblad Travel. In 2005, it formed a partnership with National Geographic. All meals are single seating at unassigned tables. A naturalist and/or a historian give lectures and lead expeditions. All vessels have kayaks, snorkel equipment, underwater video cameras, and Zodiacs. Cruise areas include Baja California, Galapagos Islands, Antarctica, Falkland Islands, Patagonia, Chilean fjords, Panama, Costa Rica, the Arctic, Coastal Norway, Baltics, Canary Islands, and the Columbia and Snake rivers. The two major vessels are the *National Geographic Explorer* and the *National Geographic Endeavor*. Published per diem rates for these two ships start at $460 to $850 and go as high as $790 to $1,600.

In March 2013, Linblad Expeditions acquired Orion Expedition Cruises and its one remaining ship, M/V *Orion*.

The *Orion* is a purpose-built expedition vessel designed to explore various destinations worldwide, currently stationed in the Southern Hemisphere, near Australia and Antarctica. The fifty-three staterooms are composed of thirty-one suites and twenty-two staterooms. The ocean-view staterooms measure 175 to 180 square feet, whereas the suites range in size from 218 to 345 square feet. All accommodations have a flat-screen TV, DVD/CD player, Internet connectivity, a personal safe, hair dryer, a mini-refrigerator continuously stocked with complimentary bottled water, and marble bathrooms with robes. Nine of the most expensive have French balconies.

Common areas include a show lounge, a lecture theater, a health spa with a dry sauna and a range of massage/spa treatments, a small gymnasium with life-fitness equipment and free weights, a sundeck with Jacuzzi and outdoor bar, a hair and beauty salon, a boutique, a well-stocked library, a main dining room and an outdoor café, a marina platform from which guests can board the Zodiacs, an observation lounge, an elevator, and a medical center.

# LOUIS CRUISE LINE

Sterling Vacations
5213 Doc Valley Line
Austin, TX 78759
(512) 345-7755
Fax: (512) 345-7722

2 Nikis 3-5
Karagiorgi Serevias Street
10563 Athens, Greece

www.louiscruises.com

*Ausonia*: 12,609 GRT; 159 × 21.3 meters; 701-passenger capacity; 254 cabins (Category D—not rated)

*Coral* (formerly *Cunard Adventurer*, *Sunward II*, and *Triton*): entered service in 1971; refurbished in 2005; 14,000 GRT; 491 × 71 feet; 945-passenger capacity; 378 cabins (Category D—not rated)

*Crystal*: 25,611 GRT; 162 × 25 meters; 1,200-passenger capacity; 480 cabins; cruises from Greece (Category D—not rated)

*Louis Majesty* (formerly *Norwegian Majesty* and *Royal Majesty*): 40,876 GRT; 680 × 91 feet; 1,462-passenger capacity; 731 cabins (Category D—not rated)

*Orient Queen*: 15,781 GRT; 160 × 23 meters; 912-passenger capacity; 364 cabins; cruises from France and Italy (Category D—not rated)

*Perla*: 16,710 GRT; 163 × 23 meters; 1,095-passenger capacity; 395 cabins; cruises from Greece (Category D—not rated)

*Princesa Cypria*: built 1968; refurbished in 1990; 9,984 GRT; 124.9 × 19 meters; 733-passenger capacity; 274 cabins (Category D—not rated)

*Sapphire*: 12,163 GRT; 149 × 21.5 meters; 650-passenger capacity; 300 cabins (Category D—not rated)

*Sun Bird* (formerly *Song of America*): entered service in 1982; 37,584 GRT; 214.8 meters long; 1,611-passenger capacity; 725 cabins (Category D—not rated)

This is a Cyprus-based company operating budget cruises on older ships; however, the cruise line is in the process of building new ships and may eventually sell off some of the older vessels. In the spring of 2008, the cruise line acquired the 1,460-passenger *Norwegian Majesty* and 1,750-passenger *Norwegian Dream* from Norwegian Cruise Line. Several of the ships they own are frequently on charter to other companies. Louis Cruises also owns the *Calypso*, *Emerald*, *Thomson Destiny*, and *Thomson Spirit*, which are all under lease to Thomson Cruises.

# PAGE AND MOY

**Compass House, Rockingham Road, Market Harborough**
**Leicester, LE167QD, UK**
**0800 0430 234**
**www.pageandmoy.com**

MV *Athena*: 16,000 GRT; 550-passenger capacity (Category D—not rated)

*Ocean Majesty* (formerly *Homeric*): 10,417 GRT; 535-passenger capacity; 273 cabins (Category D—not rated)

*Ocean Monarch* (formerly *Daphne*): 15,739 GRT; 420-passenger capacity; 211 cabins (Category D—not rated)

*Black Prince*: entered service in 1966; renovated in 1998; 11,209 GRT; 451-passenger capacity; 241 cabins (Category D—not rated)

Page and Moy is a large British cruise agent active in the cruise charter business. Cruise grounds include the Mediterranean, Black Sea, Northern Europe, and European rivers.

The clientele are British adults older than fifty years.

Some of the riverboats that the company charters include the 142-passenger MS *Infante D Henrique*, built in 2003; the 285-passenger MS *Furmanov*, built in 1985; the 118-passenger MS *Jasmin*, built in 1988; the twenty-eight-passenger MS *Mekong Sun*, built in 2006; the 158-passenger MS *Michelangelo*, built in 2000; the 136-passenger MV *Serenade I*; the 104-passenger MV *Tamr Henna*; and the 285-passenger MV *Victoria Sophia*, built in 1994.

# PULLMANTUR CRUISES

C/Orense 16
Madrid, Spain
00 34 91 418 88 91/92
Fax: 00 34 91 418 87 79
www.pullmantur.es

MS *Empress* (formerly *Empress of the Seas*): entered service in 1990; renovated in 2004; 48,563 GRT; 692 × 100 feet; 1,840-passenger capacity (1,620 double occupancy); 814 cabins, international officers and crew (Category C—not rated)

MS *Monarch* (formerly *Monarch of the Seas*): entered service in 1991; renovated in 2003 and 2012; 73,397 GRT; 880 × 106 feet; 2,744-passenger capacity (2,390 double occupancy); 1,195 cabins; international officers and crew; three- and four-night cruises to the Bahamas from Port Canaveral, Florida (Category C—not rated)

*Sovereign* (formerly *Sovereign of the Seas*): entered service in 1988; renovated in 2008; 73,192 GRT; 880 × 106 feet; 2,850-passenger capacity (2,280 double occupancy); 1,140 cabins; international officers and crew (Category C—not rated)

MS *Ocean Dream* (formerly *Tropicale*, *Costa Topicale*, and *Pacific Star*): entered service in 1982; renovated in 2001; 35,000 GRT; 1,400-passenger capacity; 511 cabins; international officers and crew (Category D—not rated)

*Zenith*: entered service in 1992; refurbished and renovated in 1999 and 2006; 52,090 GRT; 679 × 95 feet; 1,440-passenger capacity; 670 cabins; international officers and crew (Category C—not rated)

Pullmantur is a subsidiary of Royal Caribbean International servicing the Spanish cruise market. Spanish is the primary language on board; however, many staff members also speak English, and announcements are in both languages. The largest Spain-based cruise line, it began operations in the 1990s. Royal Caribbean has transferred several of their older vessels as well as *Zenith* of Celebrity Cruises to this cruise line. Subsequently, it acquired *Horizon* from Island Cruises, also a former Celebrity ship, but transferred her to CDF Croisieres de France in 2010. Formerly, it owned three of Renaissance Cruise's *R*-class ships but they were sold to Oceania and Azamara. Most itineraries are in the Mediterranean; however, some are in the Caribbean and Baltics.

Pullmantur offers all-inclusive prices that include all carbonated beverages, water, juice, and coffee and most alcoholic beverages such as beer, wine, and liquor. Premium label liquor is available for an additional charge.

The 1,440-passenger *Zenith* commenced cruises for Celebrity Cruise Line in 1992 and was considered one of the most desirable premium class ships of its day. Subsequently, it has been refurbished. There are ten suites and forty-seven cabins with verandas. All accommodations have safes, telephones, TVs, and hair dryers. Dinner is served in two sittings at assigned tables. Public facilities include bars, lounges, a casino, a disco, a library, shops, a spa, swimming pools, a fitness center, a children's playroom, a teen center, and an Internet center.

The 1,400-passenger *Ocean Dream*, the former *Tropicale*, was the first new-build by Carnival back in 1982. It had several stints with other cruise lines and was renovated in 2001 and 2008. Twelve suites have verandas. All accommodations have safes, telephones, TVs, and hair dryers. Dinner is served in two sittings at assigned tables. Public facilities include a showroom, bars, lounges, a casino, a library, shops, a spa, three hot tubs, three swimming pools, a fitness center, a jogging track, children's playroom, a teen center, and a kiddie pool.

The 2,850-passenger *Sovereign*, the former Royal Caribbean *Sovereign of the Seas*, entered service in 1988 and has received several refurbishments, the most recent being in 2008. Of the 1,140 accommodations, 67 are considered suites and have verandas. All accommodations have TVs, telephones, and hair dryers. As on the other Pullmantur ships, dining is in two sittings at assigned tables. Public facilities include a showroom, ten bars and lounges, a spa, a video arcade, a casino, a disco, four elevators, an Internet center, a library, shops, two hot tubs, two swimming pools, a rock climbing wall, a fitness center, a basketball court, a children's playroom, a kiddie pool, and a teen center.

The 2,020-passenger *Empress*, the former Royal Caribbean *Empress of the Seas*, entered service in 1990 and was most recently refurbished in 2008. Of the 814 accommodations, 69 have balconies, and there are six suites. All staterooms have telephone, TVs, safes, and hair dryers. Here again dining is in two sittings at assigned tables. Public facilities include a showroom, six bars and lounges, a beauty salon, a casino, a disco, shops, a library, three elevators, four hot tubs, two swimming pools, a fitness center, a spa, a jogging track, a rock climbing wall, a children's playroom, a teen center, and a kiddie pool.

# QUARK EXPEDITIONS

**93 Pilgrim Park Ste#1**
**Waterbury, VT 05676**
**Tel.888-892-0334**
**Fax: 203-857-0427**
**www.quarkexpeditions.com**

*Sea Adventurer* (formerly *Clipper Adventurer*): entered service in 1975; renovated in 1998; 4,364 GRT; 101 × 16.2 meters; 120-passenger capacity; 58 outside cabins and three suites, all with private facilities; dining room, multipurpose lounge, two bars, a gift shop, library, fleet of Zodiacs, exercise room, and a licensed doctor

*50 Years of Victory*: 150.7 × 30 meters; 128-passenger capacity; world's largest and most sophisticated nuclear-powered icebreaker; all cabins have exterior views and private facilities; helicopter for aerial sightseeing; full fitness facilities, including gym, sauna, and small swimming pool; all-inclusive bar and beverage package; and a licensed doctor

*Ocean Diamond* (formenly *Song of Flower* and *Explorer Starship*): 124 × 16 meters; 189-passenger capacity; 105 outside cabins, including 10 balcony suites and 10 nonbalcony suites, all with facilities and flat-screen TVs and DVD players; theater-style auditorium; lounge; gift shop; restaurant; elevator; massage and wellness program; observation lounge; polar library; pool; fitness room; and licensed doctor

*Sea Spirit* (formerly *Renaissance 5*, *Spirit of Oceanus*, and *Bleu de France*): entered service in 1991; remodeled 2001; 4,500 GRT; 90.6 × 15.3 meters; 112-passenger capacity; fifty-six cabins; fifteen suites have balconies; all staterooms measure from 215 square feet to 353 square feet, except owner's suite—which measures 550 square feet and has a separate living room and a private deck and a Jacuzzi tub; all accommodations have outside views, private facilities, TVs and DVD players, safe, refrigerator, telephone, and hair dryers; common areas include a multipurpose presentation room, library, game room, restaurant, bistro, Internet access, hot tub, two lounges, elevator, and licensed physician

*Sea Explorer* (formerly *Renaissance 7*, *Island Sky*): sister ship to the *Sea Spirit*; 4,500 GRT; 90.6 × 15.3 meters; 111-passenger capacity; all staterooms face outside, and several have private balconies; the ship has an exercise area, a polar library, Internet access, lounges, outdoor decks and a spacious restaurant for all guests, elevator, fleet of Zodiacs, and an onboard licensed physician

Quark Expeditions is the only company in the world to offer voyages exclusively to the Arctic and Antarctic. This expedition and adventure cruise line offers cruises to the North Pole, Russian Arctic, Canadian Arctic, Spitsbergen, Greenland, Iceland, Antarctica, South Georgia, and the Falkland Islands. All the vessels have dining rooms, a bar, a lounge, a library, small exercise room, an observation deck, and Zodiacs. *Sea Spirit* is the most upscale of the vessels with a luxury owner's suite. Brochure prices range from roughly $450 to $2,000 a night per person.

## SAGA CRUISES

### The Saga Building, Folkestone
### Kent CT20 3SE, England
### (800) 343-0273; +44 (0) 1303 771 111; 0800 096 0079
### www.sagacruises.com

*Saga Pearl II* (formerly *Astoria* and *Sagafjord*): 18,591 GRT; 446-passenger capacity (Category C—not rated). This ship is to be transferred to sister brand *Spirit of Adventure* in May 2012 and renamed *Quest for Adventure*. It will replace *Spirit of Adventure*. (Category C—not rated)

*Saga Ruby* (formerly *Vistafjord* and *Caronia*): entered service in 1973; refurbished in 1999; 23,492 GRT; 763-passenger capacity (Category C—not rated)

*Saga Sapphire* (formerly *Europa*, *Holiday Dream*, and *Bleu de France*): entered service in 1981; refitted in 2008; 37,301 GRT; 658 × 95 feet; 752-passenger capacity; 316 cabins (Category C—not rated)

A British tour operator, Saga Cruises specializes in cruise-tour packages exclusively for mature British cruisers older than fifty years, with seventy years being the average age. Cruise grounds include more than forty cruises to more than one hundred ports in Northern Europe, the Mediterranean, the Caribbean, South America, the Indian Ocean, Australia, the Canary Islands, Greenland, Iceland, and the Arctic as well as around-the-world cruises.

# SILJA LINE

United States
SeaEurope Holidays Inc.
2500 Quantum Lakes Drive, Suite 203
Boynton Beach, FL 33426
(800) 533-3755
Fax: (561) 491-5156

Finland
Erottajankater 19
00130 Helsinki, Finland

+358(0)9-18041
Fax: +358(0)9-1804-402

www.tallinksilja.us

M/S *Baltic Princess*: entered service 2008; 212 meters x 29 meters; 2,800-passenger capacity; 927 cabins; Finnish officers and crew; operates between Turku and Stockholm (D—not rated)

M/S *Galaxy*: entered service 2006; 212 meters x 29 meters; 2,800-passenger capacity; 1,000 cabins (D—not rated)

*Silja Europa*: entered service in 1993; 59,914 GRT; 662 × 105 feet; 3,013-passenger capacity; 1,152 cabins; Finnish officers and crew (D—not rated)

*Silja Festival*: entered service in 1986; refurbished in 1992; 34,419 GRT; 551 × 90.5 feet; 2,023-passenger capacity; 588 cabins; Finnish officers and crew (Category D—not rated)

*Silja Serenade*: entered service in 1990; 58,376 GRT; 660 × 130 feet; 2,852-passenger capacity; 986 cabins; Finnish officers and crew; day and night cruises between Helsinki and Stockholm (Category D—not rated)

*Silja Symphony*: entered service in 1991; 58,376 GRT; 660 × 130 feet; 2,852-passenger capacity; 986 cabins; Finnish officers and crew; overnight cruises between Helsinki and Stockholm (Category D—not rated)

(Medical facilities: No information was provided by the cruise line.)

Silja Line is part of the Silja Group, owned by Tallink, a Baltic ferry operator.

The *Baltic Princess* and *Galaxy* offer either day or night sailings between Turku, Finland, and Stockholm, Sweden (taking nine to twelve hours), and range in price. Cars are additional.

The *Silja Europa* is the world's largest cruise ferry. All cabins are air-conditioned and include telephone, radio alarm clocks, TV (except in the lowest category), and toilets with showers. Cabins are small and storage space is limited. I would not recommend anything less than a *Silja*-class cabin for cruisers requiring a modicum of comfort.

Dining options aboard the *Europa* range from a self-serve café, a McDonald's at sea, an all-you-can-eat Food Market with up to a 670-seat smorgasbord-style buffet, and à la carte steak, seafood, and gourmet restaurants. The Bon Vivant, the most upscale and expensive dining room, offers Continental cuisine and fine wines.

After dinner, cruisers can enjoy a movie, mediocre live entertainment, disco and pop dancing, a music pub, gambling at a casino, or duty-free shopping. The facilities aboard include a small indoor swimming pool, sauna, three whirlpools, a children's pool, conference rooms and VIP meeting facilities, and a children's playground.

The voyage between Helsinki and Stockholm offered on the *Symphony* and *Serenade* departs at 5:30 p.m. and arrives at 9:30 a.m. the next morning.

On all the ships, Scandinavians make up most the passengers, with a smattering of travelers from other European countries, Asians, and North Americans. Announcements are in numerous languages. There is an abundance of families with small children.

The above sailings offer an economical alternative means of transportation between the countries they service and are especially ideal for travelers with automobiles. The seasoned cruiser must be prepared to make many allowances. Overall comfort, food, and service are not comparable to that found on typical cruise ships.

# SWAN HELLENIC

**1850 S.E. 10th Avenue, Suite 205
Fort Lauderdale, FL 33316
(866) 923-9182; (954) 315-1170
www.swanhellenic.us**

MV *Minerva* (former *Explorer II*): entered service in 1996; renovated in 2011/2012; 12,500 GRT; 437 × 66 feet; 350-passenger capacity; 181 staterooms; British and European officers; international crew (Not rated)

Swan Hellenic entered the cruise business in 1954 and has owned and operated various ships over the years. P&O purchased the company in 1983. After Carnival Corporation acquired P&O/Princess, Swan Hellenic became a brand of Carnival. Thereafter, in 2006, Carnival decided to drop this brand; however, a former CEO of P&O/Princess, Lord Sterling, reacquired the original *Minerva*, which had been sailing as *Explorer II*, and the cruise line lives again under the ownership of the All Leisure Group. The ship has a loyal guest following in Great Britain and also targets the North American cruise market.

There are 144 outside staterooms and thirty-seven inside staterooms. Twenty-three percent have balconies. All have TVs, safes, hair dryers, and telephones. During the 2012 major renovation, additions included new en suite bathrooms; thirty-two additional balconies; a new dedicated Internet lounge; Wi-Fi throughout the ship; a new walk-around promenade; and a new observation lounge and bar at the front of the ship, a venue for dancing and entertainment. Other common areas include two restaurants, several lounges, a library, a cardroom, a gift shop, a pool, a gym, beauty salon, spa services, a complimentary launderette, a medical center, and telephone, fax, and e-mail facilities. Prices start at $130 per person per night for an inside stateroom and from $340 for a balcony accommodation.

Core to Swan Hellenic's cruise experience is the signature guest speaker program, with lecturers who are each selected for their high level of expertise, which include respected historians, archaeologists, geologists, military and art historians, ambassadors, and writers. Three or four guest speakers accompany each cruise.

# THOMSON CRUISES

**London NW1 7SD, England**
**0870 0602277**
**www.thomson-cruises.co.uk**

*Calypso*: 11,162 GRT; 486-passenger capacity; cruises Black Sea and eastern Mediterranean (adults only); leased from Louis Cruise Lines (Category D—not rated).

*Emerald*: entered service in 1958; refurbished in 1992; 26,431 GRT; 1,198-passenger capacity; leased from Louis Cruise Lines (Category D—not rated)

*Thomson Destiny* (formerly *Song of America*): entered service in 1981; 37,000 GRT; 705 × 93 feet; 1,522-passenger capacity; 701 cabins; leased from Louis Cruises Lines (Category D—not rated)

*Thomson Dream* (formerly *Westerdam*, *Homeric*, and *Costa Europa*): entered service in 1986; lengthened 1990; refurbished in 2003 and 2005; 55,000 GRT; 798 × 101 feet; 1,494-passenger capacity; 733 cabins (Category D—not rated)

*Thomson Spirit* (formerly *Nieu Amsterdam*): entered service in 1983; refurbished in 2003; 33,900 GRT; 1,254-passenger capacity; 627 cabins; leased from Louis Cruise Lines (Category D—not rated)

*Thomson Celebration* (formerly *Noordam*): entered service in 1884; refurbished in 2004; 33,930 GRT; 1254-passenger capacity; 627 cabins (Category D—not rated)

Thomson is Britain's largest tour operator. The ships offer seven- to fourteen-day itineraries in the Mediterranean and Canary Islands. *Destiny*, *Calypso*, and *Spirit* are owned by Louis Cruise Line and chartered to Thompson.

The 1,254-passenger, 33,900-ton *Spirit* and *Celebration*, sister ships, formerly sailed for Holland America as the *Nieu Amsterdam* and *Noordam* and have very attractive interiors and public facilities. All accommodations have two wardrobes, TVs, hair dryers, bathrooms with showers and WC, and safes (at a charge). Standard cabins measure 13-16 square meters; deluxe cabins are 19 square meters and have minibars, a table and chair; and suites measure 26 or 27 square meters and have both bathtubs and showers and small sitting areas. On the *Spirit*, there is a 38-square-meter Presidential Suite as well. There is open seating in the main restaurants, a specialty restaurant with a cover charge, a twenty-four-hour buffet-style restaurant with an open area, and an outdoor grill area for lunchtime barbeques, pizzas, and salads. Other public areas on both ships include five bars, two lounges, a nightclub, a casino, two swimming pools, whirlpools, a cinema, a cardroom, a spa, gym and beauty salon, a library, a children's club, a gift shop, and an Internet lounge.

The 1,522-passenger, 37,000-ton *Destiny*, formerly Royal Caribbean's *Song of America*, originally entered service in 1981 but has since been refurbished. Standard cabins measure from 10 to 15 square meters, deluxe cabins 15 to 22 square meters, suites are 25 square meters and have private balconies, and the Grand Suites are 32 square meters and also have balconies.

There is open seating in the main dining room for breakfast and lunch but dinner is in two sittings at assigned tables. A self-service buffet restaurant is located near the pool. Other public areas include five bars, two lounges, a casino, two swimming pools, a library, a beauty salon, a kid zone, a video arcade, a gym, a sauna a medical center, and an Internet area.

The 1,494-passenger, 55,000-ton *Dream* has four restaurants, five bars, three lounges, a nightclub, a casino, two whirlpools, two swimming pools, a fitness center, a kid zone, a library, an Internet lounge, a cardroom, and shops. There is open seating for all meals in the Orion Restaurant, an alternate main dining room service buffet style; the Grill, a cover charge steak and seafood specialty restaurant; a twenty-four-hour lido buffet restaurant; and an outside grill for lunch serving barbeque, pizza, and salads.

# TUI CRUISES

**Karl-Wiechert-Allee 4**
**30625 Hanover, Germany**
**+49(0)511 566-00**
**Fax: +49(0)511 566 1901**
**www.tui-group.com**

Cruise ships:

*Mein Schiff* (formerly *Celebrity Galaxy*): entered service in 1996; renovated in 2009; 77,713 GRT; 866 × 105 feet; 1,870-passenger capacity; 956 cabins; German and international officers and crew (Category B—not rated)

*Mein Shiff 2* (formerly *Celebrity Mercury*): entered service in 1997; renovated in 2010; 77,713 GRT 866 × 105 feet; 1,870-passenger capacity; 956 cabins; German and international officers and crew (Category B—not rated)

TUI Cruises is a German-based cruise line that is a joint venture between the German tour firm, TUI AG and Royal Caribbean Cruise Line. Operations were started in 2009 when the former *Celebrity Galaxy* was transferred, renamed *Mein Schiff*, and renovated to be more compatible with German tastes. *Celebrity Mercury* followed in 2011 and was renamed *Mein Schiff 2*. These ships are marketed exclusively to a German clientele, and German is the language used on the ships. The ships are typical of luxury ships built by Celebrity Cruise Line in the 1990s and have a variety of accommodations, including eight 534-square-foot Royal Suites with 94-square-foot balconies and two 1,219-square-foot penthouse suites with large balconies with outdoor Jacuzzis.

The ships cruise in European waters during the summer and the Caribbean in the winter. The cruise line plans to build two new 100,000-ton, 2,000-passenger ships in the future.

Coverage of the companies' riverboats is covered in chapter 10.

# UN-CRUISE ADVENTURES

**3826 18th Ave W**
**Seattle, WA 98119**
**888-862-8881 Tel.**
**206-283-9322 Fax**

SS *Legacy* (formerly *Spirit of 98, Pilgrim Belle, Colonial Explorer, Victorian Empress*): entered service 1984; renovated 2012; 96 GRT; 192' × 40'; 88-passenger capacity; 45 cabins; cruises to Alaska and the Columbia and Snake rivers (Not rated)

*Safari Endeavour* (formerly *Spirit of Endeavour, Sea Spirit, Newport Clipper*): entered service 1983; 99 GRT; 232' × 37'; 86-passenger capacity; 43 cabins; cruises in Alaska and Mexico's Sea of Cortés (Not rated)

*Safari Explorer* (formerly *Rapture*): entered service 1998; renovated 2008; 97 GRT; 145' × 36'; 36-passenger capacity; 18 cabins; cruises in Alaska and Hawaiian Islands (Not rated)

*Safari Quest* (formerly *Obsession*): entered service 1992; renovated 2006; 97 GRT; 120' × 29'; 22-passenger capacity; 11 cabins; cruises to Alaska, Columbia and Snake rivers, Washington State and British Columbia (Not rated)

*Safari Voyager* (formerly *Sea Voyager, Temptress Voyager, The America*): entered service 1982; renovated 2013; 174' × 36'; 64-passenger capacity; 33 cabins; cruises in Mexico's Sea of Cortés, Costa Rica, Panama, and Belize (Not rated)

*Wilderness Adventurer* (formerly *Caribbean Prince*): entered service 1984; renovated 2011; 89 GRT; 60' × 39'; 60-passenger capacity; 30 cabins; cruises in Alaska (Not rated)

*Wilerness Discoverer* (formerly *Mayan Prince*): entered service 1992; renovated 2011; 99 GRT; 176' × 39'; 76-passenger capacity; 38 cabins; cruises in Alaska (Not rated)

*Wilderness Explorer* (formerly *Spirit of Discovery, The Independence, Columbia*): entered service 1976; renovated 2012; 94 GRT; 186' × 38'; 76-passenger capacity; 38 cabins; cruises in Alaska (Not rated)

In 1997, American Safari Cruises pioneered yacht cruising in Alaska, while InnerSea Discoveries, a sister brand, enjoyed its inaugural season of expedition-style active exploration of Southeast Alaska's Inside Passage in the summer of 2011. In January 2013, the company changed its name to Un-Cruise Adventures.

Headquartered at historic Fishermen's Terminal in Seattle, Washington, Un-Cruise Adventures offers an alternative to traditional cruises by taking guests into areas inaccessible to large ships and on excursions that are exclusive and private. The company offers several styles of cruising to choose from:

- Active Adventures are launched from three expedition vessels. The sixty-guest *Wilderness Adventurer*, the seventy-six-guest *Wilderness Discoverer*, and the seventy-six-guest *Wilderness Explorer* offer destinations in Southeast Alaska.
- Luxury Adventures are operated aboard four upscale yachts. The twenty-two-guest *Safari Quest*, the thirty-six-guest *Safari Explorer*, the sixty-four-guest *Safari Voyager*, and the eighty-six-guest *Safari Endeavour* offer destinations in Southeast Alaska, Columbia and Snake rivers, Coastal Washington and British Columbia, Mexico's Sea of Cortés, and the Hawaiian Islands.
- Heritage Adventures operate from the eighty-eight-guest *Safari Legacy*, a replica of a Victorian-style steamer, with cruises to Southeast Alaska and the Columbia and Snake rivers.
- Charter Adventures provide explorations for a private group that charters the entire ship on any of the above explorations.

Breakfast, lunch, and dinner are served in single-seating dining rooms. Meals are buffet style for breakfast and lunch and plated for dinner on the three Active Adventure expedition vessels, and alcoholic beverages are available at a charge. The other vessels have table service and spirits; wines and beers are included in the cruise fare.

All of the vessels have a book library, fitness equipment, yoga classes and saunas (except the *Safari Quest*), hot tubs, hair dryers, en suite bathrooms, and iPod docks. Active and Luxury Adventure vessels have inflatable skiffs, kayaks, and paddleboards. The *Legacy* has an elevator. On the *Safari Explorer* and *Safari Quest*, guests must be thirteen years or older or travel on a Kids in Nature departure.

There are four step-out balconies on the *Safari Endeavour*, two on the *Safari Explorer*, and four on the *Safari Quest*. Four cabins on the *Safari Endeavour* have private Jacuzzi tubs, six on the *Safari Explorer*, and one on the SS *Legacy*. One cabin is wheelchair accessible on both the *Wilderness Explorer* and the SS *Legacy*.

# VOYAGES TO ANTIQUITY

### 1800 SE 10th Ste. 240
### Ft. Lauderdale, FL 33316
### (877) 398 1460
### www.voyagestoantiquity.com

*Aegean Odyssey* (formerly *Aegean Dolphin*): entered service in 1975; rebuilt 2010; 11,563 GRT; 461 × 67 feet; 378-passenger capacity; 198 cabins; international crew; cruises in Mediterranean and Southeast Asia (Not rated)

The thrust of this cruise line is educational journeys to places of historical and cultural interest with tours and lectures to enhance the experiences. The ship was rebuilt in 2010, and twenty-two balconies were added to the top-priced cabins. All cabins have flat-screen TV, safes, hair dryers, and quality bedding. The balcony-class accommodations are larger with more amenities. In 2012, eight single cabins were added, bringing the total to twenty-four cabins.

Public areas consist of a main, open-seating dining room serving free wines, beer and soft drinks with dinner, an indoor/outdoor terrace café, a small pool, a Jacuzzi, a small gym, a beauty salon, a lecture theater, three lounges, four bars, an Internet center, a library, a small shop, but no disco or casino.

## VOYAGES OF DISCOVERY

**1800 SE Tenth Avenue, Suite 205
Fort Lauderdale, FL 33316
(866) 623-2689; (954) 761-7878
www.voyagesofdiscovery.com**

MV *Voyager* (formerly *Alexander von Humboldt,* built in 1990): entered service for cruise line in 2012 as their new flagship vessel after extensive refits and renovations; 540-passenger capacity; 270 staterooms; worldwide destinations, including Mediterranean, Adriatic and Black Sea, Northern Europe, Arctic Circle, Iceland, the Baltics, British Isles, Middle East, Far East, India, Africa, South America, and the Caribbean (Category C—not rated)

This cruise line offers 9- to 125-day enrichment itineraries with their signature guest speaker program on days at sea. Cruises include shipboard overnights with a focus on longer port visits. Grand voyages are offered to exotic places around the world. *Voyager's* staterooms are 87 percent ocean view, with thirty-five suites (thirty with balconies), and are equipped with a bath and/or shower, TV, hair dryer, and safes. All ocean-view staterooms have two or more portholes, or windows. *Voyager* suites have both a bath and shower (some with spa baths) and include fridges, bathrobes, slippers, a basket of fruit, and a bottle of champagne.

*Voyager* offers open-seating dining in one of three restaurants—the main Discovery Restaurant or the casual Veranda Restaurant, which also offers alfresco dining. The Explorer Club is a specialty restaurant offered at no additional charge, by reservations only. Other public areas include two lounges, four bars, a library, a pool with two hot tubs, a medical center, an Internet center, a gift shop, a beauty center, and a gym.

The line offers a full cruise experience. Rates start from $95 per day for inside staterooms and from $300 per day for balcony staterooms. Fares include the guest speaker program and enrichment workshops, and service fees are included in bar purchases and spa services. Beginning in 2014, the cruise line will include gratuities in the cruise fare.

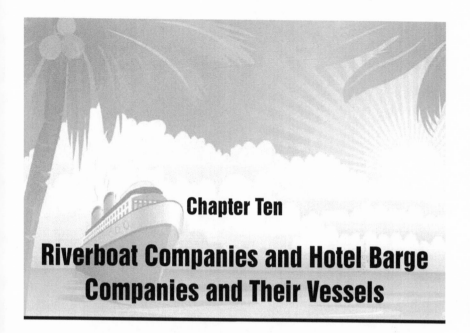

# Chapter Ten

# Riverboat Companies and Hotel Barge Companies and Their Vessels

For those cruisers who would appreciate a more relaxing, intimate, low-key experience sailing down scenic rivers and inland waterways while visiting charming noncoastal cities and villages, a riverboat or hotel barge sojourn may be the perfect solution.

Numerous riverboat companies operate in Europe, traversing the Rhine, Main, Moselle, Elbe, Havel, Danube, Seine, Saône, Rhône, Douro, and Volga rivers, as well as other waterways in Russia, Holland, and Belgium. Some of the companies offer riverboat cruises in Egypt and Southeast Asia. American Queen Steamboat Company and American Cruise Line have riverboats sailing on rivers in the United States. The most well-known riverboat cruise lines that own their own riverboats and seek to interest passengers outside of Europe are described in this chapter. Generally, riverboats carry from 110 to 160 passengers with voyages that vary in duration from seven to twenty-eight days.

Hotel barges, on the other hand, generally accommodate from four to twelve passengers; they traverse smaller rivers, canals, and waterways not accessible to riverboats. Most operate throughout France; however, there are several that explore waterways in Holland, Belgium, Great Britain, and Ireland. The majority of these vessels are privately owned, though marketed, and often operated through companies specializing in hotel barge cruising. Traditionally, they offer six-night excursions in specific areas with tariffs quite a bit higher than prices on riverboats. It is possible to book the entire vessel for friends, families, or associates, as well as to book an individual cabin and sail with other passengers.

The three major hotel barge companies are covered in this chapter. However, there are dozens of independently owned hotel barges that are available for cruises and charters, and these are covered in my *Stern's Guide to European Riverboats and Hotel Barges*.

(Note: *Official Steamship Guide International*, available by subscription as a magazine or on the Internet, now includes a comprehensive directory listing the dates of sailing and complete itineraries for every European riverboat. This is an indispensable tool in assisting you to select the cruise that will best suit your riverboat travel plans. Go to OfficialSteamshipGuide.com.)

*Slip away to the French countryside...*

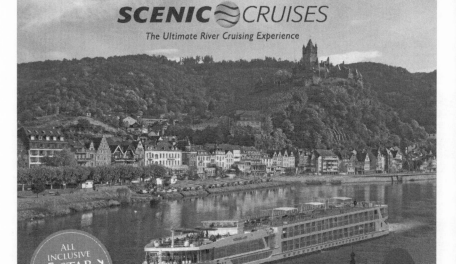

# THE RIVERBOAT AND HOTEL BARGE CRUISE LINES
# AND THEIR VESSELS

AmaWaterways

American Queen Steamboat Company

A-Rosa Cruises

Avalon Waterways

CroisiEurope

European Waterways

French Country Waterways

Grand Circle Cruises

Lueftner Luxury River Cruises

Nicko Tours

Orient-Express

Scenic Cruises

Scylla AG

Sea Cloud Cruises

Tauck River Cruises

TUI Premicon Cruises

Uniworld

Vantage Travel

Victoria Cruises

Viking River Cruises

# AMAWATERWAYS

**21625 Prairie Street**
**Chatsworth, California 91311**
**(800) 626-0126; (818) 428-6198**
**(818) 772-7335 Fax**
**www.amawaterways.com**

MS *AmaCello*, MS *AmaDagio*, MS *AmaDante*, MS *AmaDolce*, MS *AmaLegro*, and MS *AmaLyra*: entered service in 2008, 2006, 2008, 2009, 2007, and 2009 respectively; 360' × 38'; 148- to 150-passenger capacity; 77 cabins; international officers and crew; cruises on the Danube, Main, Rhine, Moselle, Rhône, and Saône rivers, as well as waterways of Belgium and Holland

MS *AmaBella*, MS *AmaVerde*, MS *AmaCerto*, and *AmaPrima*: entered service in 2010, 2011, 2012, and 2013 respectively; 443' × 38'; 162-164 passengers; 82 cabins; international officers and crew; cruises on the Danube, Main, Rhine, Moselle, Rhône, and Saône rivers, as well as waterways of Belgium and Holland

MS *AmaKatarina*: entered service in 2011; 443' × 52'; 212 passengers; 106 cabins; international officers and crew; cruises on Volga River and Baltic Waterways between St. Petersburg and Moscow

MS *AmaLotus:* entered service 2010; 62 cabins; 124-passenger capacity; international officers and crew; cruises on the Mekong River

MS *AmaRena*, MS *AmaSonta*: entered service 2014; 164-passenger capacity; 82 cabins; International officer and crew; Cruises on European rivers

MS *AmaVida*: entered service in 2013; 260' × 37'; 108-passenger capacity; 54 cabins; international officers and crew; cruises on the Douro River in Portugal

MS *La Marguerite*: entered service 2009; 235' × 41'; 92-passenger capacity; 46 cabins; international officers and crew; cruises on the Mekong River

MS *Zambezi Queen*: entered service 2012; 28-passenger capacity; 14 cabins; international officers and crew; cruises the riverbands of the Chobe River, Botswana

In 2002, Rudi Schreiner (former president of Viking River Cruises), Kristin Karst, and Jim Murphy (former owner and CEO of Brendan Worldwide Vacations) launched Amadeus Waterways. Subsequently, the line changed its name to AmaWaterways. From 2006 through 2009, the company introduced six new deluxe riverboats designed to traverse the various rivers and waterways of Europe. Between 2010 and 2012, five even more upscale riverboats joined the European fleet, along with two new boats on the Mekong River and the waterways of Russia. Additionally, the cruise line leases or charters four additional riverboats that offer cruises on the rivers of Russia, France, and the Mekong River in Southeast Asia. The cruise line partners with APT Waterways, an Australian tour operator who operates cruises on the AmaWaterways ships.

The 148-passenger MS *AmaDagio*, MS *AmaDante*, MS *AmaDolce*, MS *AmaLegro*, and MS *AmaLyra* are sister ships that entered service between 2006 and 2009 and are among the newer and more modern vessels cruising on the rivers of Europe.

Seventy-one of the cabins on these ships measure 170 square feet, and the four junior suites on each ship measure 255 square feet. Of the accommodations, 82 percent sport French balconies, and each includes two twin beds convertible to queen size, plush bedding, down duvets, a cozy sitting area, a safe, terry cloth bathrobes, a hair dryer, flat-screen TVs with English-language stations, satellite telephones, and Internet access. The junior suites have larger sitting areas and a bathtub and shower. There is Wi-Fi throughout the ship.

Public areas feature a well-appointed, panoramic, open-seating dining room offering a champagne breakfast buffet daily, as well as multicourse lunch and dinners. Complimentary wine, beer, and soda are available with dinner; and cappuccino and espresso are complimentary with all meals. Other venues include a lounge and bar with panoramic river views, the location for afternoon tea and snacks and evening lectures and entertainment; a library; a glassed-in wellness area encompassing a fitness center, sauna, and massage and beauty salon; and a sundeck with whirlpool, lounges, and a walking track. Bicycles are available for passengers wishing to explore the cities and villages in this fashion.

The line's newest, most modern and upscale vessels (162- to 164-passenger capacity) MS *AmaBella*, MS *AmaVerde*, MS *AmaCerto*, MS *AmaPrima*, MS *AmaReena*, and MS *AmaSonata* joined the fleet in 2010, 2011, 2012, 2013, 2014, and 2014 respectively. Unique to these ships are the twin balconies in many of the accommodations (i.e., French balconies and full outside balconies). French balcony suites measure 170 square feet; twin balcony suites, 210-235 square feet; twin balcony owners' suites, 255 square feet; and the top owner's suite, 350 square feet. There are four of these 350-square-foot suites on *AmaReena* and *AmaSonata*. There is complimentary Internet and first-run movies in the staterooms, as well as Wi-Fi throughout the vessel.

These ships offer an array of dining options, including the main restaurant serving Continental cuisine and, occasionally, an additional Italian menu for dinner; a chef's table where up to twenty-four passengers watch a private chef prepare a special tasting menu; private dining for six in the wine room; and an outdoor lunch on the sundeck when weather permits. Room service at breakfast and dinner is available for the top suites.

Public areas include a main lounge and bar; a library; an observation lounge at the front of the vessel; an elevator; a twenty-four-hour coffee/tea station; a small fitness center; a sauna (not on *AmaCerto*); a massage, hair, and beauty salon; a lower sundeck; and a topside sundeck with teak lounges, a walking track, putting green, giant chessboard, and heated pool.

All-inclusive shore excursions are conducted by knowledgeable English-speaking tour guides. About 70 percent of the passengers are from the United States or Canada, and the rest are from Australia, New Zealand, and other parts of the world. The ships offer varying itineraries on such European rivers as the Danube, Main, Rhine, and Moselle. Prices range from $1,700 per person for a seven-night cruise in a standard stateroom to $8,800 per person for a thirty-night cruise and land package.

In 2010, the 220-passenger MS *AmaKatarina* debuted as the line's second riverboat on Russian waterways, sailing between St. Petersburg and Moscow. The ship was stripped to the hull and completely rebuilt by AmaWaterways before its first voyage in 2011. Sixty-seven percent of the 114 staterooms have balconies. Standard cabins range from 110 to 135 square feet, deluxe staterooms with balconies 238 square feet, and suites from 280 to 434 square feet. All have bathrooms with separate shower areas. Common areas include a panorama lounge, a bar/nightclub, a conference hall, an elevator, a gift shop, an infirmary, and a sauna and solarium.

The 92-passenger MS *LA MARGUERITE* and the 124-passenger MS *AMALOTUS* are very modern riverboats with spacious accommodations. Of the thirty-eight 226-square-foot deluxe staterooms on *LA MARGUERITE*, thirty have balconies. The six 284-square-foot suites also have balconies, and the two 443-square-foot suites have both balconies and whirlpool tubs. Common areas include a panoramic restaurant, lounge and library, business center, sundeck with lounges, whirlpool and bar, lobby-reception area, small fitness room, spa for treatments, and beauty salon. Beer, soft drinks, spirits, bottled water, coffee, and tea are all complimentary. MS *LA MARGUERITE* is the first modern riverboat plying the waters of the Mekong River, which flows through Vietnam, Laos, and Cambodia.

In 2010, the 124-passenger MS *AMALOTUS* joined the MS *LA MARGUERITE*, offering cruises on the Mekong River. Staterooms measure 226 square feet, ten junior suites 290 square feet, and two top suites measure 624 square feet. Ninety percent of the staterooms have balconies. All staterooms have two twin beds, a small sitting area, a writing desk, a minibar, a private safe, a TV with in-house movies, an in-house telephone, and bathrooms with a shower, a bathrobe, slippers, and a hairdryer. Public areas include two restaurants (local beers, house spirits, soft drinks, coffee, tea, and bottled water served with meals), a lounge, a fitness room, library, and sundeck with its own bar and outdoor whirlpool.

The *ZAMBEZI QUEEN* was specifically designed for Safari River cruising on the Chobe River, Bostwana and offers a sophisticated design to maximize animal sightings. The fourteen staterooms have balconies. The top deck of the ship has a dining room, lounge, bar, and pool area.

## Strong Points

The riverboats owned by the cruise line and built during the past seven years are among the more modern, comfortable, and upscale vessels to offer cruises on the European waterways. All the vessels operated by AmaWaterways and its partner, APT Waterways, offer interesting itineraries with excellent service staff and cruise directors. The newest ships boast real balconies and French windows in many of the cabins.

*Stateroom, courtesy of AmaWaterways*

*Lounge on AmaCerto, courtesy of AmaWaterways*

*Dining room of AmaCerto, courtesy of AmaWaterways*

*The Danube, courtesy of AmaWaterways*

# VIENNA DINNER
*Saturday, 13th October 2012*
Freshly Home Baked Bread with Garlic Butter
Or with Regular Butter on Request

## APPETIZERS
Tatar of Smoked Salmon Served on Potato Salad
Accompanied with Honey Mustard Sauce
Mixed Garden Greens * #
With Onions, Tomatoes, Carrot and Balsamic Dressing
Cocktail of Plums with Apricot Liqueur #

## SOUPS
Creamy Pumpkin Soup with Roasted Seeds * #
Beef Consommé with Sliced Pancake * #

## MAIN COURSES
Grilled Fillet of Pike Perch with Roasted Almond Butter, * #
Sautéed Spinach, Glazed Carrots and Potato Pearls
"Schnitzel Vienna Style" #
In Butter Fried, Breaded Escalope of Pork Loin or Turkey Breast
With Mixed Vegetables and Parsley Potatoes
Breaded Camembert with Onion Confit,
Cranberry Jam and Salad Garnish

## DESSERTS
Warm Apple Strudel with Vanilla Sauce #
Ice Cup "Opera"
Walnut Ice with Meringue and Caramel Sauce
With Whipped Cream
Fresh Fruits *
Local and International Cheese Selection
    Healthy Choice* / Local Choice *#

## CHEF'S RECOMMENDATION
Tatar of Smoked Salmon Served on Potato Salad
Accompanied with Honey Mustard Sauce
Creamy Pumpkin Soup with Roasted Seeds
"Schnitzel Vienna Style" #
In Butter Fried, Breaded Escalope of Pork Loin or Turkey Breast
With Mixed Vegetables and Parsley Potatoes
Warm Apple Strudel with Vanilla Sauce

## OUR WINE RECOMMENDATION

### WHITE
**Weiss Family**
**Country**: Austria **Area**: Burgenland **Grape**: Welschriesling
**Characteristics:** "A Fine Yellow Color with Greenish Tints Pronounced Primary Fruit Aromas, Hint of Lemon and Green Apples, Light and Fruity White Wine"

### RED
**Weiss Family**
**Country**: Austria **Area**: Neusiedlersee **Grape**: Zweigelt
**Characteristics:** "Deep and Dark Fruit and at the Same Time with its Soft Character, Zweigelt Grape is an Austrian Unique, its Main Flavors Include Blackberry and Wild Raspberry, Dry and Full Bodied"

### STANDING ORDER
Grilled Entrecote Steak, Salmon Steak or Chicken Breast,
Caesar's Salad, Coleslaw and French Fries

### COBB SALAD
*Chicken Breast, Avocado, Blue Cheese, Bacon, Tomato,
Egg and Mixed Greens Tossed in Vinaigrette


Courtesy of AmaWaterways

## Your program today—Amacerto

Cruise schedule is subject to change due to navigational conditions beyond our control WELCOME ABOARD THE *MS AMACERTO*

| | |
|---|---|
| **ALL DAY** | Tea and Coffee are available in the Strauss Bar & Main Lounge |
| **11:00 AM-3:00 PM** | Sandwiches and Soup in the Strauss Bar & Main Lounge |
| **2:00-5:00 PM** | For "Erlebnis" Restaurant reservation, please see our Headwaiter Karoly in the "Erlebnis" Restaurant, deck 3 Aft |
| **3:00 PM** | Cabins are ready. Move in and get cozy! |
| **3:00-5:00 PM** | Tea time in the Strauss Bar & Main Lounge |
| **5:30-6:00 PM** | Strauss Bar & Main Lounge is closed in preparations for the Captain's Welcome Reception |
| **6:00 PM** | Please join us in the Strauss Bar & Main Lounge for our "Captain's Welcome Reception" and our important safety and information briefing! |
| **7:00 PM** | Welcome Dinner is served in our main Restaurant (to the accompaniment of local Hungarian musicians) who will get us in the right mood! Enjoy your dinner! The "Erlebnis" Restaurant is also ready for those who made reservations. |
| **9:15 PM** | *ALL ABOARD!* |
| **9:30 PM** | MS *AmaCerto* sails from Budapest. Join us on the sundeck and enjoy the wonderful sight of illuminated Budapest as we "set sails" for our next port of call—Bratislava, the capital of Slovakia |
| **10:00 PM** | Late night snack will be served in the Strauss Bar & Main Lounge while our on board musician Mathias entertains! |

Daily program, courtesy of AmaWaterways

## AMERICAN QUEEN STEAMBOAT COMPANY

**(formerly Great American Steamboat Co.)**
**One Commerce Square, 40 South Main Street, 21st floor**
**Memphis, TN 38103**
**Tel. 888-749-5280; 901-654-2600;**
**Fax 901-654-2541**
**www.AmericanSteamboatCompany.com**

*American Queen*: entered service in 1995; renovated in 2012, reentered service in April 2012; 3,707 GRT; 418 × 109 feet; 436-passenger capacity; 222 staterooms; American officers and crew; cruises on Mississippi and other U.S. inland rivers

The *American Queen* originally entered service in 1995 as the pride of the Delta Queen Steamboat Company, the largest steam-driven riverboat ever built. Its parent company was the American Classic Voyages, who filed under chapter 11 in 2001. In 2006, the Delta Queen Steamboat Company was sold to Ambassadors International who formed a new cruise line called Majestic America Line. However, in 2008, this line also went under, and the ship ceased operation. Rising from the ashes, this beautiful ship was acquired in the summer of 2011 by its present owners, received various renovations, and reentered service in the spring of 2012. Originally, the cruise line was named Great American Steamboat Company; however, in July 2012, the name was changed to American Queen Steamboat Company.

These are nostalgic, all-American cruises, where melodic riverboat tunes emanate from calliopes, a bright-red paddlewheel churns up a frothy wake, Dixieland jazz bands entertain in the lounges, and Southern regional and Creole dishes are served in the dining room. A "riverlorian" offers historic lectures throughout the cruise. Complimentary shore excursions are offered at each stop with in-depth immersion into the history, culture, and cuisine of America's heartland. One of the most unique features of a cruise on *American Queen* is the one-night precruise stay at a first-class hotel, which is included in the cruise fare.

Her public rooms, décor, and accommodations seek to portray the opulence and ambiance of the American Victorian era. All of the staterooms are furnished with faux Victorian-period pieces, floral fabrics, a great deal of wood, and feature plush bedding, fine linens, large mirrors, storage space (that varies with cabin categories), a flat-screen TV, Wi-Fi accessibility, a private bathroom with a shower (suites have tubs and showers), robes and slippers, ice buckets, telephones, piped-in music, period art, Starbucks coffee, and complimentary bottled water and fresh fruit. Some of the most expensive accommodations have French doors that open onto the deck or veranda, others have bay windows. Three-quarters are outside. As you move up in categories from I to AAA, overall cabin size, sitting areas, and abundance of antiques increase. However, the single cabins, although attractively priced, are quite small. None of the accommodations have refrigerators, private room safes, lock drawers, hair dryers, or robes. Overall, the accommodations are not as desirable as those found on European riverboats.

The elegant, "grand-hotel style" main dining room features the cuisine of acclaimed American chef, Regina Charboneau, with a multicourse menu in two sittings with tables for two, four, six and eight. The restaurant's stained glass-topped windows provide magnificent river views. We found the abundance of Creole and Cajun dishes a bit rich for our taste; and felt that the layout and presentation at the buffet table could use improvement.

Alternative dining was available around the clock at the Front Porch, offering simpler fare and snacks (help yourself), as well as a full-service bar and an espresso/cappuccino machine. This was a welcome venue for those seeking their first cup of coffee without having to go to the dining room. During the warmer months, casual alfresco dining was available at the River Grill atop ship. Po' boys and salads are offered in the Engine Room, a location for nightly sing-alongs and musical entertainment. Café Beignet serves beignets and coffee in the morning and casual food from 11:00 a.m. to 11:00 p.m. The weekly New Orleans jazz brunch is the culinary event of each cruise. Wine, beer, and soft drinks are provided gratis with dinner. Soft drinks are free throughout the ship. Afternoon tea and late-night suppers are also available. Elegant, casual attire is suggested throughout the cruise, and there are no formal nights. Service, for the most part, by the all-North American staff was attentive and excellent.

Public areas include a movie theater, a small bathing pool, a small gym (with preponderance of the guests being well over seventy, there was not much call for additional equipment), several bars and lounges, shops, a library, and the elegant Grand Salon, with a mezzanine level made up of private box seats, reminiscent of the famous Ford Theater.

The ship carries a fleet of bicycles that passengers can use to tour in ports. Most passengers are most interested in the daily tours to the historical and cultural destinations featured on the various itineraries offered by the cruise line. In addition to those excursions for which there is a charge, gratis shore excursions, known as "hop on/hop off" experiences, are offered wherein the company's steam-coaches transport passengers on tours around the various cities.

There is an abundance of additional entertainment which includes a Dixieland/jazz band that plays at various times at the lounge outside of the main dining room; a duo that plays nightly in the Engine Room lounge for sing-alongs and dancing; cabaret acts and a full orchestra for dancing in the Grand Salon alternating as a back-up for the nightly production shows. Depending on the theme of the cruise, music could be Dixieland, jazz, swing, big band, and/or music of the fifties and sixties.

Itineraries include historical stops along the Mississippi River and its tributaries. Three-, five-, six-, seven-, eight-, and ten-night cruises may embark from New Orleans, Memphis, Cincinnati, St. Louis, St. Paul, Louisville, Vicksburg, or Chattanooga. The themes for the various cruises include Southern Culture, Epic Civil War, Big Band, Music of the 1950s, Music of the 1960s, Springtime on the River, Kentucky Derby, Fall Colors, Old Fashioned Holidays, and New Year's Big Band.

Some of the well-known names in entertainment that will appear on select cruises include the Platters, Bill Haley's Comets, Lovin' Spoonful, B. J. Thomas, and the Glenn Miller Orchestra.

## Strong Points

An authentic, nostalgic, and wholesome "all American" experience for mature adults who appreciate steamboating and U.S. history. Décor, dining excursions, and entertainment are true to its Americana theme.

*courtesy American Queen Steamboat Company*

*Dining Room, courtesy American Queen Steamboat Company*

*Grand Staircase, courtesy American Queen Steamboat Company*

*Stateroom on American Queen, courtesy American Queen Steamboat Company*

*Author with Captain, on Bridge of American Queen*

## ONBOARD SERVICES

**PURSER'S OFFICE**
DECK 2, LOBBY
*Dial 0 or 280 for information*
*& assistance.*
*Open 24 hours a day*

**AQ EMPORIUM**
DECK 2, LOBBY
*Dial 270 during opening hours for*
*information & assistance.*
*8:00 am - 8:00 pm*
*Closed from 12:00 pm - 2:00 pm*

**CHART ROOM**
DECK 4
*River, history and more:*
*Our Riverlorian will:*
*Check out books, answer questions,*
*check out bicycles*

**AQ SPA**
MAIN DECK
*(Facing Main Deck Lounge)*
*Dial 280 for information*
*8:00 am - 8:00 pm*

**SELF-SERVICE**
**LAUNDRY**
DECK 4
*Open Daily*
*7:00 am - 10:00 pm*

**STEAMBOAT AMBASSADOR**
DECK 2, LOBBY
*8:30 am - 10:00 am*
*4:00 pm - 7:00 pm*

**FITNESS CENTER**
DECK 6, FORWARD
*Open Daily*
*9:00 am - 10:00 pm*

*Towels and bottled water*
*are available in the Fitness*
*Center*

**SWIMMING POOL**
DECK 6, FORWARD
*Due to inclement weather the*
*pool will be closed*

**SHORE EXCURSIONS**
DECK 2, LOBBY
*See Desk for office hours*

**MORNING COFFEE**
*Your stateroom attendant will*
*be happy to provide morning*
*coffee service to you in your*
*room; please contact them*
*should you wish to have this*
*service.*

**PRINTING SERVICES**
*We are pleased to offer a pc with*
*internet and printing functionality*
*for guests. Please visit the Mark*
*Twain Gallery to use this service.*
*Instruction can be found on the*
*desk which is located at the*
*forward port side corner of the*
*Mark Twain Gallery*

## PHONE DIRECTORY

| | |
|---|---|
| PURSER'S OFFICE | 280 |
| SHORE EXCURSIONS | 286 |
| AQ EMPORIUM | 270 |
| AQ STEAMBOAT AMBASSADOR | 250 |

## DINING OPTIONS

**SNACKS & COFFEE SERVICE**

| | |
|---|---|
| FRONT PORCH OF AMERICA | 24 HOURS |

*Light snacks and sweets will be available all day*

**BREAKFAST**

| | |
|---|---|
| J.M. WHITE DINING ROOM | 7:00 AM - 9:30 AM |
| *(buffet and a la carte options)* | |
| FRONT PORCH OF AMERICA | 6:00 AM - 10:00 AM |

**LUNCH**

| | |
|---|---|
| J.M. WHITE DINING ROOM | 11:30 AM - 1:30 PM |
| *(buffet and a la carte options)* | |
| FRONT PORCH OF AMERICA | 11:00 AM - 3:00 PM |

**TEA TIME**

| | |
|---|---|
| MAIN DECK LOUNGE (1) | 4:00 PM - 4:30 PM |

**DINNER**

**J.M. WHITE DINING ROOM**

*First seating dinner guests are invited to the dining room at*
*5:15 pm*

*Second seating dinner guests are invited to the dining room at*
*7:45 pm*

**FRONT PORCH OF AMERICA**

*Casual dining option from 5:00 pm - 8:00 pm*

## BAR HOURS

| | |
|---|---|
| CAPTAIN'S BAR | 11:30 AM – CLOSING |
| ENGINE ROOM BAR | 3:00 PM – CLOSING |
| GRAND SALOON<br>BAR SERVERS BEFORE CURTAIN | 6:45 PM (1ST SHOW)<br>8:15 PM (2ND SHOW) |

## HAPPY HOUR

| | |
|---|---|
| CAPTAIN'S BAR | 5:00 PM – 6:00 PM |
| ENGINE ROOM BAR | 6:00 PM – 7:00 PM |

*1/2 PRICE AMARETTO SOURS*

WEATHER

PARTLY CLOUDY

THURSDAY
NOVEMBER 29, 2012

PORT OF
VICKSBURG

SUNRISE 7:02 AM
SUNSET 5:06 PM

| | |
|---|---|
| ARRIVAL | 8:00 AM |
| DEPARTURE | 1:00 PM |
| ALL ABOARD | 12:30 PM |

AMERICAN QUEEN
SETS SAIL TOWARDS
MEMPHIS

DAILY SPECIALS

AQ EMPORIUM
20% OFF SHORT SLEEVE
POLO'S

AQ SPA
FREE PEVONIA KIT WITH
COFFEE WRAP

## Vicksburg

Charming Vicksburg is deceptively bucolic for an area that has been the site of several bloody battles. The French were the first inhabitants and by 1719 had built Fort Saint-Pierre on the bluffs above the Yazoo River to protect their fur trading post from Native Americans. That theory was put to the test on November 28, 1729, when the Natchez waged a battle against the fort and many of the plantations in the area and several hundred people were killed. Although the French retained control, the colony never fully recovered.

The Choctaw Nation helped the French eventually defeat the Natchez and the Yazoo. Several years later, the Choctaw laid claim to the area. The Spanish were next, and by 1790, a small military outpost had been founded. Americans took over the small fort eight years later and the area grew quickly, incorporating in 1825 as Vicksburg in honor of Newitt Vick, a Methodist minister.

Vicksburg's prosperity came to a horrific end during the Civil War. After a siege lasting 47 days, Union General Ulysses S. Grant finally forced the surrender of Confederate General John C. Pemberton on July 4, 1863, with more than 37,000 soldiers either killed or wounded. The day before, General Robert E. Lee lost the battle of Gettysburg in a dark time for the Confederate States of America that became recognized as the turning point of the Civil War. While July 4 was known as Independence Day across America, the citizens of Vicksburg viewed that date as a day of defeat and did not celebrate the 4th of July again until 1945.

But Vicksburg's place in history is also owed to less deadly events. Few people know that local candy store owner Joseph Biedenharn made history on March 12, 1894 when he bottled the first batch of Coca-Cola in the city.

*Daily Program, courtesy American Queen Steamboat Company*

# Dinner
## J.M. White Dining Room

## AQ CLASSIC STARTERS

**Crispy Fried Frog Legs**
Frog legs dusted in a seasoned flour, fried to
a crisp golden brown served with a
sweet-tart okra and tomato chutney

**Shrimp and Avocado Tower**
Gulf shrimp, fresh avocado salad
and crusty French bread crostini

## AQ SOUP

**Corn and Crab Chowder**
Creamy corn chowder with blue crab topped with crisp bacon

## AQ SALAD

**Petite Wedge of Lettuce**
A petite wedge of crisp lettuce, topped with ripe tomato,
crumbled blue cheese, cucumber, and lemon vinaigrette

## AQ ENTRÉES

**Pan Seared Catfish with a Smoked Tomato Coulis**
Seasoned farm raised Mississippi catfish pan seared and served on a
a bed of smoked tomato coulis, topped with a black eyed pea vinaigrette

**Prime Rib of Beef**
Salt and pepper crusted prime rib of beef served with Au Jus
and pomme duchesse with chefs choice of vegetable

**Chicken Coq au Vin**
Marinated chicken in red wine sauce with pearl onion, tomato concassee
and crisp pancetta

**Cauliflower and Macaroni au Gratin**
A creamy cauliflower and macaroni gratin served with a mini, spinach stuffed tomato

---

### ALWAYS AVAILABLE
*Our culinary team are pleased to present our always available selections*
*Chicken broth*         *Caesar salad*
*Grilled chicken breast*    *Catch of the day*    *Petite steak*
*Steamed vegetables*      *Baked potato*

---

*Dinner Menu, courtesy American Queen Steamboat Company*

# A-ROSA

## Tel. +49(0) 381 202 6006
service@a-rosa.de

*A-Rosa Aqua*: entered service, 2009; 2,000 GRT; 135 m × 11.4 m; 202-passenger capacity; 99 cabins

*A-Rosa Bella*: entered service, 2002; 1,850 GRT; 124 m × 14.4 m; 242-passenger capacity; 100 cabins

*A-Rosa Brava*: entered service, 2011; 2,000 GRT; 135 m × 11.4 m; 202-passenger capacity; 99 cabins

*A-Rosa Donna*: entered service, 2002; 1,850 GRT; 124.5 m × 14.4 m; 242-passenger capacity; 100 cabins

*A-Rosa Luna*: entered service, 2005; 1,387 GRT; 125.8 m × 11.4 m; 174-passenger capacity; 86 cabins

*A-Rosa Mia*: entered service, 2003; 1,850 GRT; 124.5 m × 14.4 m; 242-passenger capacity; 100 cabins

*A-Rosa Riva*: entered service, 2004; 1,850 GRT; 124.5 m × 14.4 m;

242-passenger capacity; 100 cabins

*A-Rosa Stella*: entered service, 2005; 1,387 GRT; 125.8 m × 11.4 m; 174-passenger capacity; 86 cabins

*A-Rosa Silva*: entered service, 2012; 2,553 GRT; 135 m × 11.4 m; 186-passenger capacity; 83 cabins

*A-Rosa Viva*: entered service, 2011; 2,000 GRT; 135 m × 11.4 m;

202-passenger capacity; 99 cabins

A-Rosa was developed from 2000 to 2002 by Seetours, a joint venture of the British shipping company P&O and DSR. The cruise line was created to serve the German cruise market, alongside the AIDA Cruises fleet, which had been acquired by P&O in 1999. A-Rosa was modeled loosely on the AIDA concept and began life with three ships. *A-Rosa Blu* was the sole cruise ship of the fleet, accompanied by *A-Rosa Bella* and *A-Rosa Donna*, two newly built riverboat cruise ships. In 2003, P&O Princess merged with Carnival Corporation to form Carnival Corporation & PLC.

The A-Rosa brand was sold soon after the merger and was purchased by DSR. In the spring of 2009, the company was taken over by private investors.

By 2013, A-Rosa will have a fleet of ten riverboats cruising the Danube, Rhine, Main, Moselle, Rhône, and Saône rivers between March and January, terminating with the New Year's Eve cruise. All the ships have German/Austrian/international officers and crew. The *Luna* and *Stella* sail on the Rhône and Saône rivers; the *Bella*, *Donna*, *Mia*, *Riva*, and *Silva* on the Danube and Main-Danube Canal; the *Aqua*, *Viva*, and *Brava* on the Rhine, Main, and Moselle rivers.

The official language aboard is German; however, English menus and programs are always available. Although the majority of passengers speak German, non-German-speaking passengers are welcome, and they generally come from a variety of European countries. On select cruises, there is an international host to look after the international guests. The ships can be chartered by groups from other countries.

Accommodations on all the vessels of A-Rosa are air-conditioned, have a private bathroom with a toilet and glassed-in shower, a hair dryer, a double bed, two night tables, a telephone, a TV with satellite, an option for Wi-Fi connections, a wardrobe, and a safe.

The four oldest ships—the 242-passenger *A-Rosa Bella*, *A-Rosa Donna*, *A-Rosa Mia*, and *A-Rosa Riva*—each have one hundred outside cabins, several with an extra bed. The cabins on deck 2 measure 172 square feet and have floor-to-ceiling windows that open to the river, referred to as Juliet windows; those on deck 3, 177 square feet with panorama windows; and those on deck 1, 156 to 166 square feet with small windows that do not open.

The *A-Rosa Aqua*, *A-Rosa Brava*, and *A-Rosa Viva* each accommodate 202 guests in ninety-nine outside cabins. All cabins measure 156 square feet, and those on the top-two passenger decks have Juliet windows. There are no suites on these three ships.

*A-Rosa Luna* and *A-Rosa Stella* accommodate 174 passengers in eighty-six outside cabins, each measuring 156 square feet. Those on the top-two passenger decks have Juliet windows.

On the newest 186-passenger *A-Rosa Silva*, the two-bed outside cabins measure 156 square feet; the four two-bed junior suites, 226 square feet; and the two full suites, 312 square feet. The cabins and suites on the top-two passenger decks have Juliet windows and full balconies.

Each of the ships has its own onboard Spa-Rosa, where you will find exercise machines, cardio equipment, massage cubicles, and a relaxation area, as well as sauna and steam. Personal trainers are available, and cycling and Nordic walking tours are offered. Guests have the opportunity to be part of guided tours or to hire an individual bike to discover the countryside or a city on their own.

A heated pool can be found on the sundeck of the following ships: *A-Rosa Bella*, *Donna*, *Luna*, *Mia*, *Riva*, *Silva*, and *Stella*; and a heated whirlpool can be found on *A-Rosa Aqua*, *Brava*, and *Viva* in the spa outdoor area on deck 3. Bath towels are located in the cabin.

On *A-Rosa Luna*, *Stella*, and *Silva*, there is an outdoor bar situated on the sundeck, as well as a café bar and lounge bar on deck 2. On *A-Rosa Aqua*, *Brava*, and *Viva*, there is an indoor and outdoor bar on deck 3, as well as a café and lounge bar. *A-Rosa Bella, Donna, Mia*, and *Riva* have a café bar and a lounge bar on deck 3.

All meals are served buffet-style with open seating. When weather permits, some meals are served on sundeck. Wine, soft drinks, and specialty coffees *are not* included; however, bottled water is free of charge.

Guests who sign up for the "wine and dine" package at an extra charge can enjoy regional specialties and wines in a reserved part of the restaurant on special evenings. After dinner, there is music and occasional guest artists and entertainers.

Shore excursions in different languages are offered in most ports of call. Most last a few hours. An explanation of each excursion will be presented during the onboard information event on the first evening. A daily program is placed in each passenger's cabin the night before. There is a charge for all shore excursions that varies depending upon the excursion.

## Strong Points

These ships are good choices for more active German travelers, who prefer a dinner buffet in the evening, do not require table-service dining, can appreciate the sport and spa facilities not found on most other riverboats, and prefer to pay as they go for drinks, tours, and other items in exchange for lower cruise fares.

*Courtesy of A-Rosa Cruises*

**A cabin aboard the A-Rosa Bella.**
*Courtesy of A-Rosa Cruises*

*Dining buffet, courtesy of A-Rosa Cruises*

# AVALON WATERWAYS

**5301 S. Federal Circle**
**Littleton, Colorado 80123**
**(877) 797-8791**
**www.avalonwaterways.com**

*Avalon Ankor*: entered service 2012; 131' long; 32-passenger capacity; 16 cabins; cruises on Mekong River, and cruises in Vietnam and Cambodia and Thailand

*Avalon Affinity, Avalon Creativity, Avalon Felicity, Avalon* Luminary, and *Avalon Scenery*: entered service 2009, 2009, 2010, 2010, and 2008, respectively; 2,150 GRT; 361' long; 138- to 140-passenger capacity; 65 to 68 cabins; international officers and crew; *Affinity* and *Creativity* cruise Rhine, Moselle, and other rivers of Europe; *Felicity* and *Luminary* cruise various rivers of Europe; *Scenery* cruises rivers of France

*Avalon Imagery, Avalon Tapestry,* and *Avalon Tranquility*: entered service 2007, 2006, and 2007, respectively; 2,150 GRT; 443' long; 170-passenger capacity; 81, 80, and 81 cabins, respectively; international officers and crew; cruises on Rhine, Moselle, and Danube rivers and Main Canal

*Avalon Panorama*: entered service 2011; 443' long; 166-passenger capacity; 83 cabins; international officers and crew; cruises on the various rivers of Europe

*Avalon Visionary*: entered service 2012; 361' long; 128-passenger capacity; cruises European waterways

*Avalon Vista, Avalon Artistry II, Avalon Expression, Avalon Illumination, Avalon Impression, Avalon Poetry*: entered service 2012, 2013, 2013, 2014, 2014, and 2014 respectively; 443' long; 166-passenger capacity; cruises European waterways

This cruise line, a part of the Globus family of brands, commenced service on the waterways of Europe in 2004 with the introduction of the *Avalon Artistry*. Eleven additional small ships were added in Europe by the close of 2011, and two additional vessels came on line in 2012, and another two in 2013. The oldest vessel in the European fleet has been cruising for only six years. The cruise line boasts one of the youngest fleets of river cruise ships plying the waters of the Rhone, Saone, Seine, Rhine, Moselle, and Danube rivers, as well as the Main Canal and waterways in Belgium and Holland.

Itineraries generally vary from eight to fourteen days, but in 2010, the cruise line also began offering four- and five-day itineraries on the Danube River between Vienna and Budapest starting at less than $1,000. Typically, passengers book a complete package that includes air, pre- and posthotel, transfers, and most land tours. An expert guide meets passengers at the precruise hotel and stays with them for the entire cruise until they depart from their postcruise visit. I have found this Avalon Waterways package one of the best offered in the cruise industry.

On the pre-2011 vessels, the modern, streamlined staterooms measure a minimum of 172 square feet, whereas junior suites are 258 square feet, a decent size for a river cruise ship. Accommodations on the top two passenger decks have floor-to-ceiling sliding glass windows that open out to the river. All have two twin beds that can be reconfigured to queen size, European-style duvets, flat-screen satellite TV and radios, stocked minibars, hair dryers, safes, writing desks, high-speed Internet service, adequate closets, and generous storage both in the cabins and bathrooms. Laundry and ironing services are available. There are two suites on the *Scenery, Creativity,* and *Tapestry,* and four on the *Affinity* and *Imagery.* There are elevators on the *Scenery, Creativity, Panorama, Vista, Visionary,* and *Affinity.* Virtual tours of the river cruise ships are available on Avalon's Web site.

The *Avalon Panorama* entered service in May 2011 with sixty-four panorama suites at 200 square feet on the upper two passenger decks, seventeen 172-square-foot staterooms on the lower deck, and two 300-square-foot Royal Suites on the top deck. Each of the sixty-six suites has a small seating area adjacent to floor-to-ceiling, wall-to-wall panoramic windows that open out to the river. Two new "Suite Ships" entered service in 2012—*Avalon Visionary* and *Avalon Vista.* The top two decks have 200- and 300-square-foot suites, featuring panoramic windows similar to those on the *Avalon Panorama* described above.

Two additional "Suite Ships," *Avalon Artistry II* and *Avalon Expression,* entered service in 2013 and three additional "Suite Ships," *Avalon Impression, Avalon Illumination* and *Avalon Poetry* will enter service in 2014. Two of the older ships, *Avalon Tranquility* and *Avalon Imagery* left the fleet at the end of 2013. Thus, almost all of the Avalon vessels are only a few years old.

Public areas on these ships include a partially covered sky deck with deck chairs, a walking track and the navigation bridge, a reception area, a large main lounge and bar, a small beauty salon/massage facility, the main, open-seating restaurant, an observation lounge at the rear of the ships, complimentary Wi-Fi and Internet access, and a small fitness center with four cardio machines. On the six newest ships there is a small whirlpool on the sky deck. On the "Suite Ships," there is an open-air bistro on Sky Deck open for grill lunches. Onboard electrical outlets are 220 volts.

Breakfast and lunch are served buffet style. Complimentary sparkling wine is served during breakfast for Mimosas, and made-to-order egg dishes are available at a special egg/omelet station. A Continental breakfast can be ordered through room service. At dinner, there is open seating and table service. At each dinner, there are two choices of appetizer, soup, salad, entrée, and dessert and complimentary wine, beer, or soft drinks. Late-evening snacks are served at ten thirty and complimentary specialty coffees, espresso, and cappuccino are available throughout the day. There is nightly piano music (and sometimes a singer) for listening and dancing, occasional regional entertainment, and turn-down service each evening. Avalon offers more entertainers and artists than one finds on most riverboats. Daily walking tours in each port of call are offered gratis. More elaborate tours by bus can be purchased. The escorted pre- and postcruise package, as well as the organization of the programs and tours aboard ship, are excellent.

The thirty-two-passenger *Avalon Angkor*, which entered service in 2012 with 172-square-foot staterooms with sliding-glass doors and balconies, offers cruises on the Mekong River. This is the first and only passenger ship built to cruise all the way from Ho Chi Minh City to Siem Reap, exclusively eliminating seven hours of drive time on land for travelers. The Sun Deck affords panoramic views and public areas include a twenty-four-hour bar as well as a spacious dining room, relaxing massage area, and fitness equipment.

Avalon Waterways also offers Nile and Lake Nasser cruises on the MS *Mayfair* and MS *Kasr Ibrim*; Yangtze River cruises on the *Victoria Anna* and *Victoria Jenna* (see Victoria Cruises); and Galapagos Island cruises on the forty-four-cabin *Santa Cruz*.

## Strong Points

This is one of the most modern, well-designed riverboat lines with excellent precruise, postcruise, and onboard tour programs, with an excellent service staff and cruise directors.

*Courtesy of Avalon Waterways*

*Dining room, courtesy of Avalon Waterways*

*Stateroom on Panorama, courtesy of Avalon Waterways*

Wall-to-Wall Panoramic Window measuring 11 feet – 50% wider than industry standard.

*Suite, courtesy of Avalon Waterways*

*Lounge, courtesy of Avalon Waterways*

# WELCOME GALA DINNER

**AMUSE BOUCHE** – Salmon Rose
Greetings from the Kitchen

**Appetizer**  **"SALADE COMPOSÉE"** - Green Leaves with Pears, Walnuts and Fourme de Ambert

**Soups**  **BEEF CONSOMME** with Semolina Dumplings
—————— or ——————
**CREAM OF HERBS DE PROVENCE** with Smoked Salmon

**Hot Appetizer**  **PAN FRIED SCAMPI WITH CHAMPAGNER RISOTTO**

**Sorbet**  **ORANGE SORBET WITH CAMPARI**

**Main Course**  **SLOW ROASTED VEAL LOIN** - with Morel Mushroom Sauce
Served with Truffle Mashed Potatoes and Vichy Carrot
—————— or ——————
**CRISPY PAN FRIED PIKE PEARCH**
on Light Pommery Mustard Sauce with Wild Rice and Fennel
—————— or ——————
**VEGETABLE GRATIN** - with Potato Noodles

**Dessert/Cheese**  **YOGHURT-BERRIES -TERRINE** - on Fruit Coulis
—————— or ——————
**RHUBARB RAGOUT** with Vanilla Ice Cream, Served with Whipped Cream and Strawberry Sauce
—————— or ——————
**FRESH SLICED FRUITS**
—————— or ——————
**CHEESE PLATE** – Fougerous, Munster and Brie Coeur de Lion
Served with Nuts and Grapes

**Coffee / Tea**  **COFFEE** - Regular or De-caffeinated
—————— or ——————
**TEA**

**Always available for you ...**  **CEASAR'S SALAD**
**Standing Orders**
—————— or ——————
**GRILLED FILLET OF CHICKEN BREAST** - with Morel Mushroom Sauce
Served with Truffle Mashed Potatoes and Vichy Carrot
—————— or ——————
**GRILLED BEEF RUMPSTEAK**
Served with Baked Potato with Sour Cream, Green Vegetables and Herbed Butter
—————— or ——————
**GRILLED SALMON FILLET**
on Light Pommery Mustard Sauce with Wild Rice and Fennel

*Dinner menu, courtesy of Avalon Waterways*

# DAILY NEWSLETTER

### Strasbourg, France / Sunday, September 9, 2012

*Situated on the border of France and Germany, Strasbourg is influenced by the culture of both countries and the capital of the Alsace region. It is the seat of the Council of Europe and the European Parliament. Noteworthy sights are the Gothic Cathedral, the lovely La Petite France district, Place Kleber, and Place Gutenberg, with the statue of the inventor of the printing press.*

**Weather Forecast:**

Partly Cloudy, Chance of Rain, 20°C/70°F
www.acouweather.com

1 USD = 0.76 EUR
1 AUD = 0.78 EUR
1 GBP = 1.21 EUR
1 CAD = 0.77 EUR
1 NZD = 0.62 EUR

*These rates may change without any previous notice. Bank and exchange commission fees apply. Substantial commissions apply for re-exchange into Euros or US Dollars and other major currencies.*

'No one realizes how beautiful it is to travel until he comes home and rests his head on his old, familiar pillow.'
Lin Yutang

## TIME SCHEDULE

| | | |
|---|---|---|
| 6-6:30 am | Early Riser Breakfast | Lounge |
| 6:30-8:30 am | Champagne Buffet Breakfast | Restaurant |
| 8:15 am | Included Strasbourg City Tour with Canal boat | Pier |

**Please take your earpieces and pick up the headsets from Reception Desk!**

*Your program starts with a canal cruise of Strasbourg, then proceed on foot to the Cathedral with your local experts. After some free time, your guides will walk you to the COACHES on Place de la Republique for your return transfer to the Luminary.*

| | | |
|---|---|---|
| 8:30-9:30 am | Late Riser Breakfast | Lounge |
| 12 noon | Buffet Lunch | Restaurant |
| | BBQ (please sign up at Reception! Weather permitting) | Sky Deck |
| 1:30 pm | Optional Alsace Wine Tasting / Black Forrest excursions | Pier |

**Please pick up your tickets for the excursions! Headsets are needed!**

| | | |
|---|---|---|
| 1:30 pm | Shuttle to Strasbourg downtown | Pier |
| | *Shuttle available for all those who did not book the optional tours!* | |
| 3:30-4 pm | Coffee & Cake | Lounge |
| 4:30 pm | Coach transfer from Place de la Republique to the Luminary | |
| 6-7 pm | Happy Hour | Lounge |
| | *Cocktails and drinks in the bar on the special menu cards at reduced price!* | |
| 6:30 pm | Port Talk with Cruise Director Barbara | Lounge |
| 7 pm | Welcome Gala Dinner (DC: smart) | Restaurant |
| 9 pm | French Chansons with Armand Jehle.. | Lounge |
| | *Followed by some Piano and Dancing Music* | |
| 10:30 pm | Call All Aboard! Avalon Luminary sails to Speyer | |
| 10:30 pm | Late Night Snack | Lounge |

### Overnight Cruise to Speyer, Germany

## TECHNICAL INFORMATION

*The Avalon Luminary is docked at the Port of Strasbourg some 15 minutes drive away from the Old Town! Our docking position address is Quai de Belges.*

*The above schedule has been put together to our best plans, but, because of unforeseen events, it might have to be modified. These changes will be advised through the PA system or the onboard Information Channel. In some ports due to the ever increasing number of river cruise ships, our vessel may have to dock next to other vessels which may block the view from the stateroom. We apologize for the inconvenience!*

*Daily program, courtesy of Avalon Waterways*

# CROISIEUROPE

**12 Rue de la Division Leclerc**
**67000 Strasbourg, France**
**Tel. 00 33 388 76 44 44**
**Fax 00 33 388 32 49 96**
**info@croisieurope.travel**

*Beethoven*: entered service, 2004; renovated, 2010; 110 m × 11.4 m; three decks; 180-passenger capacity; 90 cabins; cruises on the Danube

*Belle de Cadix*: entered service, 2005; renovated, 2010; 110 m × 11.4 m; three decks; 176-passenger capacity; 88 cabins; cruises on Guadiana, Guadalquivir, and Atlantic Coast

*Boheme*: entered service, 1995; renovated, 2011; two decks; 162-passenger capacity; 81 cabins; cruises on the Rhine and Danube

*Botticelli*: entered service, 2004; refurbished, 2010; 110 m × 11.4 m; two decks; 151-passenger capacity; 75 cabins; cruises on the Seine

*Camargue*: entered service, 1995; renovated, 2006; 110 m × 10 m; two decks; 146-passenger capacity; 76 cabins; cruises on Rhône and Saône

*Douche France*: entered service, 1997; renovated, 2011; 110 m × 11.4 m; two decks; 160-passenger capacity; 79 cabins; cruises on Rhine and its tributaries

*Europe*: entered service, 2006; renovated, 2011; 110 m × 11.4 m; three decks; 180-passenger capacity; 90 cabins; cruises on the Danube

*Fernao De Magalhaes*: entered service, 2003; refurbished, 2011; 75 m × 11.4 m; three decks; 142-passenger capacity; cruises on Douro River

*France*: entered service, 2001; renovated, 2010; 110 m × 11.4 m; two decks; 159-passenger capacity; 78 cabins; cruises on Rhine, Danube, and Seine

*Gerard Schmitter*: entered service, 2012; 110 m × 11.4 m; three decks; 176-passenger capacity; 88 cabins; cruises on the Rhine and its tributaries

*Infante Don Henri*: entered service, 2003; refurbished, 2010; three decks; 75 m × 11.4 m; 142-passenger capacity; 71 cabins; cruises on Douro River

*Leonard de Vinci*: entered service, 2003; refurbished, 2011; 110 m × 11.4 m; two decks; 144-passenger capacity; 72 cabins; cruises on Rhine and its tributaries

*Modigliani*: entered service, 2001; refurbished, 2011; 110 m × 11.4 m; two decks; 160-passenger capacity; 78 cabins; cruises on the Danube

*Mona Lisa*: entered service, 2000; refurbished, 2010; 82 m × 9.5 m; two decks; 100-passenger capacity; 49 cabins; cruises on Elbe

*Mistral*: entered service, 1999; refurbished, 2007; two decks; 110 m × 10.4 m; 158-passenger capacity; 75 cabins; cruises on Rhône and Saône

*Princess d'Aquitane*: entered service, 2001; refurbished, 2011; 110 m × 11.4 m; 138-passenger capacity; 69 cabins; cruises on Garonne

*Renoir*: entered service, 1999; refurbished, 2011; 110 m × 11.4 m; two decks; 158-passenger capacity; 78 cabins; cruises on Seine

*Seine Princess*: entered service, 2002; refurbished, 2010; 110 m × 11.4 m; two decks; 138-passenger capacity; 67 cabins; cruises on the Seine

*Van Gogh*: entered service, 1999; refurbished, 2007; 110 m × 11.4 m; two decks; 158-passenger capacity; 78 cabins; cruises on Rhône and Saône

*Michelangelo*: entered service, 2000; refurbished, 2011; 110 m × 11.4 m; two decks; 158-passenger capacity; 78 cabins; cruises on Po River and Venetian Lagoon

*Vasco de Gama*: entered service, 2002; refurbished, 2009; 75 m × 11.4 m; three decks; 142-passenger capacity; 71 cabins; cruises on Douro River

*Courtesy of CroisiEurope*

# EUROPEAN WATERWAYS

**The Barn, Riding Court, Riding Court Rd.**
**Datchet, Berkshire SL3 9JT, United Kingdom**
**US Tel. 1-877-879-8808; Canada Tel. 1-877-574-3404**
**UK Tel. 44(0) 1753 598555; AUS Tel. 1-800-828050**
**www.GoBarging.com**

On all European Waterways barges, alcoholic and nonalcoholic drinks are complimentary with open bars, and each barge has at least one van or minibus that follows the barge and is available for excursions; most have Wi-Fi, hi-fi systems, compact discs, and docking stations for iPhones, and all have AC and central heating (unless otherwise noted) and hair dryers. Cabin square footage includes en suite bathrooms. Prices may vary with the season, and the per-person prices are based upon double occupancy.

*Anjodi*: converted, 1983; refurbished, 2006 and 2011; 200 GRT; 100' × 16.6'; eight-passenger capacity; four French- and English-speaking crew; four cabins (91, 87.5, 98, and 98 square feet) with en suite bathrooms; Wi-Fi; sundeck and heated spa pool; eight touring bikes and one tandem bike; cruises in Canal du Midi/Corbieres/Minervois, France, from March to November; $4,390 pp/$31,000 charter; owned and operated by European Waterways

*Enchante*: converted, 2009; renovated, 2008; refurbished, 2011; 200 GRT; 100' × 16.6'; eight-passenger capacity; four English- and French-speaking crew; four 200-square-foot cabins with en suite bathrooms; sundeck and heated spa pool; Internet; eight touring bikes; cruises Canal du Midi/Corbieres/Minervois, France, from March to October; $5,540 pp/$38,700 charter; exclusively marketed by European Waterways

*La Bella Vita*: converted, 1995; refurbished, 2010; 140' × 46'; twenty-passenger capacity; five to eight Italian and international crew (some speak English); ten 100- to 110-square-foot cabins with en suite bathrooms; Wi-Fi and computer; ten touring bikes; large rooftop sundeck; cruises Venetian Lagoon and Bianco Canal from Venice to Mantua (Italy) from March to October; $3,840 pp/$62,700 charter; exclusively marketed by European Waterways

*La Belle Epoque*: converted, 1995; refurbished, 2011; 2,000 GRT 128' × 16.6'; twelve-passenger capacity; six English- and French-speaking crew; six cabins (165, 150, two at 130, two at 125 square feet, and a single cabin at 90 square feet) with en suite bathrooms; Wi-Fi; sundeck and heated spa pool; ten touring bikes and one tandem bike; cruises upper Burgundy Canal/Chablis, France, from March to October; $4,750 pp/$47,400 charter; owned and operated by European Waterways

*L'Art de Vivre*: converted, 1998; refurbished, 2006 and 2008; 200 GRT; 100' × 16.6'; eight-passenger capacity; four French- and English-speaking crew; four 100-square-foot cabins with en suite bathrooms and with safes; Wi-Fi; sundeck and heated spa pool;

eight touring bikes and one tandem; cruises in Burgundy/Chablis, France, from March to October; $4,150 pp/$29,000 charter; owned and operated by European Waterways

*L'Impressionniste*: converted, 1996; refurbished, 2007 and 2011; 200 GRT; 128' × 16.6'; twelve-passenger capacity; six French- and English-speaking crew; seven cabins (two at 127, two at 110, one at 143, one at 152 square feet, and a single cabin at 87 square feet) with en suite bathrooms; Wi-Fi; DVD player and TV; sundeck and heated spa pool; ten touring bikes and one tandem; cruises in Burgundy/Côte de Beaune/Côte de Nuits, France, from March to October; $4,750 pp/$47,400 charter; owned and operated by European Waterways

*Nymphea*: converted, 1980; refurbished, 2003; 200 GRT; 81' × 14'; six-passenger capacity; two to three French- and English-speaking crew; three cabins (65, 75, and 91 square feet) with en suite bathrooms; Wi-Fi; deck salon and dining salon; six mountain bikes; cruises Loire Valley, Western Burgundy, and Upper Loire in France from June to October; $4,150 pp/$21,000 charter; marketed exclusively by European Waterways

*Panache* (formerly *Marjorie II*): converted, 1998; refurbished, 2007 and 2011; 200 GRT; 129' × 16'; twelve-passenger capacity; six 150-square-foot cabins with en suite bathrooms; sundeck and heated spa pool; Wi-Fi; twelve touring bikes; piano; five French- and English-speaking crew; cruises Holland from March to May (tulip season) and Alsace-Lorraine in France from June to October; $4,890 pp/$47,400 charter; owned and operated by European Waterways

*Renaissance* (formerly *La Bonne Humeur*): converted, 1997; refurbished, 2006; 200 GRT; 128' × 17.6'; eight-passenger capacity; four 260- to 270-square-foot suites with large bathrooms, with flat-screen TV and DVD player, and abundant storage space; sundeck and heated spa pool; Wi-Fi and laptop computer in salon; eight touring bikes and one tandem bike; five British crew; cruises Loire Valley, Upper Loire, and Western Burgundy in France from March to October; $6,090 pp/$42,000 charter; owned and operated by European Waterways

*Rosa*: converted, 1990; refurbished, 2010; 2,000 GRT; 100' × 16.4'; eight-passenger capacity; four cabins (92, 104, 107, and 110 square feet) with en suite bathrooms; sundeck; eight touring bikes; four French- and English-speaking crew; cruises Gascony and Bordeaux, France, from March to November; $4,050 pp/$28,000 charter; marketed exclusively by European Waterways

*Scottish Highlander*: converted, 2000; renovated, 2006; 200 GRT; 117' × 16.6'; eight-passenger capacity; four English-speaking crew; four cabins (one at 147 square feet and three at 115 square feet) with en suite bathrooms; no AC, but heated; eight touring bikes; sonic fish finder; Scottish and English crew; cruises the Caledonian Canal and Loch Ness, Scotland, from March to October; $3,690 pp/$27,000 charter; owned and operated by European Waterways

*Courtesy European Waterways*

*Courtesy European Waterways*

*Courtesy European Waterways*

# LA BELLE EPOQUE
## MENU

### LUNCH

*CONTAL CHEESE AND MUSTARD MARINATED
TOMATOES IN A PASTRY CRUST
COUSCOUS SALAD
MARINTATED CABBAGE WITH SHALLOTS AND
PARSLEY
PROSCIUTTO WRAPPED MELON
CHEESES:
PAPILLON ROQUEFORT. DELICE DE BOURGOGNE*

### DINNER

*WILD MUSHROOMS IN PUFF PASTRY
DUCK BREAST IN A CASSIS SAUCE WITH CARROT
PUREE AND BRAISED ENDIVE
MIXED GREENS
CHEESES:
GAPARON, BUCHONS DE CHEVRE
ICED HAZELNUT MOUSSE WITH RASPBERRY COULIS*

*Courtesy European Waterways*

## FRENCH COUNTRY WATERWAYS

PO Box 2195
Duxbury, MA 02331
Tel. 800-222-1236
www.fcwl.com

On all of the French Country Waterways barges, alcoholic and nonalcoholic drinks are complimentary with open bars, and each barge has at least one minibus that follows the barge and is available for excursions. Most have hi-fi systems, compact discs, and docking stations for iPhones and Wi-Fi; and all have AC and central heating, elegant furnishings in the common areas, and hair dryers. One dinner each cruise is at a *Michelin*-starred restaurant. Cabin square footage includes en suite bathrooms. Prices may vary with the season, and the per-person listed prices are for double occupancy.

*Adrienne*: Built in 2005; renovated continuously; 250 GRT; 128' × 16'; twelve-passenger capacity; six English- and French-speaking crew; six 157-square-foot cabins with en suite bathrooms, good storage space, and robes; elegant French provincial furnishings in common areas; 110/120V outlets; partially covered sundeck with canopy and deck chairs; Wi-Fi; bikes; cruises April through October in Cote d'Or region of Burgundy, France; $5,295 to $6,295 pp/$61,140 to $75,540 charter.

*Horizon II*: Rebuilt in 2005; renovated continuously; 190 GRT; 128' × 16'; eight-passenger capacity; six English- and French-speaking crew; four 161-square-foot cabins with en suite bathrooms and good storage space and robes; elegant British decor; large sundeck; Wi-Fi; eight bikes; cruises April through October on Upper Loire Valley in France; $5,495 to $6,495 pp/$42,360 to $51,960 charter.

*Nenuphar*: Rebuilt in 2007; frequently refurbished; 240 GRT; 128' × 16'; twelve-passenger capacity; six English- and French-speaking crew; six 157-square-foot cabins with en suite bathrooms, robes, and good storage; Wi-Fi; partially covered sundeck; bikes; elegant decor in common areas; cruises from April through October in Central Burgundy, France; $5,095 to $6,295 pp/$59,940 to $74,340 charter.

*Princess*: Built in 1973; frequently renovated and refurbished; 280 GRT; 128' × 16'; eight-passenger capacity; six English- and French-speaking crew; two 180-square-foot suites and two 210-square-foot suites, all with en suite bathrooms, robes, and good storage; Wi-Fi; partially covered sundeck and canopy; bikes; elegant decor in common areas; cruises April through June in Champagne region and from July through October in Alsace-Lorraine; $5,495 to $6,695 pp/$43,160 to $52,760 charter.

Horizon II *on Burgundy Canal, courtesy French Country Waterways, Ltd.*

*Dining room on* Horizon II, *courtesy French Country Waterways, Ltd.*

Horizon II *on Burgundy Canal, courtesy French Country Waterways, Ltd.*

Adrienne, *courtesy French Country Waterways, Ltd.*

Adrienne, *courtesy French Country Waterways, Ltd.*

Adrienne, *courtesy French Country Waterways, Ltd.*

# ADRIENNE

Nemours         *le 1ᵉʳ Septembre 2006*

*Foie gras de canard poêlé accompagné de ses pommes aux épices*
*Réduction balsamique*

✶ ✶ ✶ ✶ ✶ ✶ ✶ ✶ ✶ ✶ ✶ ✶ ✶ ✶

*Noix de St Jacques et sa julienne de légumes*

✶ ✶ ✶ ✶ ✶ ✶ ✶ ✶ ✶ ✶ ✶ ✶ ✶ ✶

*Filet de bœuf, sauce aux morilles*
*Pomme Paillasson et fagot de haricots verts*

✶ ✶ ✶ ✶ ✶ ✶ ✶ ✶ ✶ ✶ ✶ ✶ ✶ ✶ ✶

*Plateau de fromages*
*Salade*

✶ ✶ ✶ ✶ ✶ ✶ ✶ ✶ ✶ ✶ ✶ ✶ ✶

*Farandole de desserts*

*Vin Blanc*          *Vin Rouge*

*Alsace Sylvaner vieilles vignes 2003*    *Clos-Vougeot Grand Cru*
             *1998*

*Corton Charlemagne Grand Cru 2000*

Courtesy French Country Waterways, Ltd.

# GRAND CIRCLE SMALL SHIP CRUISES

**347 Congress Street**
**Boston, Massachusetts 02210**
**(617) 350-7500**
**(800) 248-3737**
**(617) 346-6840 Fax**
**www.gct.com or www.oattravel.com**

MS *River Adagio* and MS *River Aria*: entered service in 2003 and 2001 respectively; 1,935 GRT; 410' × 38'; 164-passenger capacity; 82 cabins; international crew; up to fourteen-night cruises on various rivers in Europe

MS *River Allegro*: entered service in 1991; refurbished in 2011; 1,219 GRT; 90-passenger capacity; international crew; eleven-night river cruise tour from Hamburg to Prague

MS *River Bizet*: entered service in 2002; 1,900 GRT; 363' × 37.6'; 120-passenger capacity; 60 cabins; international crew; up to fourteen-night cruises on various rivers in Europe

*River Chardonnay*: entered service in 1999; 822 GRT; 260' × 28'; 50-passenger capacity; 27 cabins; international crew; up to fourteen-night cruises on Saône and Rhône rivers and from Burgundy and Provence to the Côte d'Azure

MS *River Concerto*, *River Harmony*, *River Melody*, and *River Rhapsody*: entered service in 2000, 1999, 1999, and 1999 respectively; 1,642-1,949 GRT; 361' × 38'; 140-passenger capacity; 70 cabins; international crew; seven- to fourteen-night cruises on various rivers in Europe

MS *Tikhi Don*: entered service in 1977; refurbished in 2006; 3,570 GRT; 425' × 54'; 220-passenger capacity; 112 cabins; Russian and international crew; fourteen-night cruises between Moscow and St. Petersburg along Volga and Svir rivers and through Lakes Onega and Ladoga

MS *Rossia*: entered service in 1978; refurbished in 2007; 3,570 GRT; 425' × 54'; 220-passenger capacity; 112 cabins; Russian and international crew; fourteen-night cruises between Moscow and St. Petersburg along Volga and Svir rivers and through Lakes Onega and Ladoga

Grand Circle Travel was launched in 1958 to serve AARP members. In 1985, the company was acquired by Alan and Harriet Lewis, who began offering Grand Circle's international itineraries to United States citizens over the age of fifty. In 1993, Grand Circle added a second brand, Overseas Adventure Travel, also for mature Americans. In 1998, the company created Grand Circle Cruise Line, now called Grand Circle Small Ship Cruises.

Grand Circle Small Ship Cruises owns fourteen river ships and three fifty-passenger oceangoing ships (and more than forty exclusive charters). Grand Circle Travel (GCT) and Overseas Adventure Travel (OAT) brands take travelers to Europe, Egypt, the Red Sea, the Suez Canal, the Panama Canal, Russia, China, the Galapagos, and beyond.

All the riverboats feature air-conditioned outside cabins with closets, storage space, private bath and showers, color TV with CNN and movies, radios, direct-dial telephones, and in-room safes. Public areas include a restaurant with a single open seating, a bar and lounge, and a sundeck. Some have fitness rooms and saunas. The international crew all speak English, and four-course dinners are featured with two choices of entrées.

The riverboats stop at cities, towns, and villages along the waterways they traverse.

Grand Circle Cruises packages these sailings with international round-trip air arrangements, all transfers, and pre- and postland tours.

*Courtesy of Grand Circle Tours*

*Seine River, courtesy of Grand Circle Tours*

## LUEFTNER LUXURY RIVER CRUISES

**Amraser See Strasse 56, Menardi Center
6020 Innsbruck, Austria
+43512365781
+43512365781-6 Fax
www.lueftner-cruises.com**

*Amadeus*: entered service, 1997; 1,560 GRT; 110 m × 11.4 m; 146-passenger capacity; 73 staterooms; international officers and crew

*Amadeus Brilliant*: entered service, 2011; 1,566 GRT; 110 m × 11.4 m; 150-passenger capacity; 76 staterooms; international officers and crew

MS *Amadeus Classic*: entered service, 2001; 1,560 GRT; 110 m × 11.4 m; 142-passenger capacity; 71 staterooms; international officers and crew

MS *Amadeus Diamond*: entered service, 2009; 2,000 GRT; 295' × 148'; 146-passenger capacity; 77 staterooms; international officers and crew

*Amadeus Elegant*: entered service, 2010; 1,566 GRT; 110 m × 11.4 m; 150-passenger capacity; 76 staterooms: international officers and crew

MS *Amadeus Princess*: entered service, 2006; 1,560 GRT; 110 m × 11.4 m; 160-passenger capacity; 80 staterooms; international officers and crew

MS *Amadeus Rhapsody*: entered service, 1998; 1,560 GRT; 110 m × 11.4 m; 142-passenger capacity; 71 staterooms; international officers and crew

MS *Amadeus Royal*: entered service, 2005; 1,560 GRT; 110 m × 11.4 m; 144-passenger capacity; 72 staterooms; international officers and crew

MS *Amadeus Symphony*: entered service, 2003; 1,560 GRT; 110 m × 11.4 m; 146-passenger capacity; 73 staterooms; international officers and crew

MS *Danubia*: Joined cruise line in 2007 and totally renovated and redecorated; 102 m × 11.4 m; 71 staterooms; international officers and crew

Since this riverboat line entered the market in 1997, it has been increasing its fleet, each new entry being more modern and better equipped than the previous vessel. Three of the more recent riverboats—MS *Amadeus Diamond* (2009), MS *Amadeus Princess* (2006), and MS *Amadeus Royal* (2005)—are considered premium ships with very elegant decor, large floor-to-ceiling wall-to-wall windows opening to the sea on the top-two passenger decks, and more spacious public areas. The two newest sister ships,

*Amadeus Elegant* and *Amadeus Brilliant*, entered service in 2010 and 2011 respectively. These are the most upscale with the most suites of the fleet.

All the vessels have well-appointed cabins, 161 square feet in size. Each ship has a limited number of suites measuring 236 square feet (nine of these on the *Elegant* and on the *Brilliant*).

Public areas on the vessels include a foyer/reception area, panoramic lounge and bar, panoramic dining room, an Amadeus Club with Internet stations, fitness center, observation deck with lounges (some with whirlpools), library, and hairdresser.

Itineraries include the various rivers of Europe, including the Rhine, Moselle, Main Canal, Danube, Rhône, Saône, Seine, and waterways of Holland and Belgium.

*Courtesy of Lueftner River Cruises*

# NICKO TOURS

**D-70499 Mittlerer Pfad 2**
**Stuttgart, Germany**
**Tel. +497112489900**
**Fax. + 4971124899028**

MS *Alemannia*: 110 m × 11.6 m; 184-passenger capacity; cabins are 12 and 24 sq m

MS *Bellissima*: entered service, 2004; 110 m × 11.4 m; 134-passenger capacity; cabins are 13 and 24 sq m

MS *Britannia*: 110 m × 11.6 m; 184-passenger capacity; cabins are 12 and 24 sq m

MS *Casanova*: 103 m × 9.7 m; 96-passenger capacity; cabins are 12 and 16 sq m

MS *Cezanne*: 118 m × 11.6 m; 102-passenger capacity; cabins are 15 sq m

MS *Classica*: 111.2 m × 11.4 m; 157-passenger capacity; cabins are 12 and 15 sq m

MS *Deltastar*: 107.3 m × 12.8 m; 168-passenger capacity; cabins are 11 and 20 sq m

MS *Dnepr*: 105.9 m × 16.1 m; 160-passenger capacity; cabins are 8, 11, and 14 sq m

MS *Donaustar*: 107.3 m × 12.8 m; 168-passenger capacity; cabins are 11 and 20 sq m

MS *Duoro Queen*: 78.11 m × 11.4 m; 130-passenger capacity; cabins are 15 sq m

MS *Fedin*: 125 m × 16.7 m; 240-passenger capacity; cabins are 8, 10, 13, and 30 sq m

MS *Flamenco*: 135 m × 11.4 m; 200-passenger capacity; cabins are 13 sq m

MS *Frederic Chopin*: 83 m × 9.5 m; 80-passenger capacity; cabins are 12 and 13 sq m

MS *Heidelberg*: 109.4 m × 11.4 m; 110-passenger capacity; cabins are 18 sq m

MS *Heinrich Heine*: 106.6 m × 11.1 m; 110-passenger capacity; cabins are 12 and 17 sq m

MS *Johannes Brahms*: 81.95 m × 9.5 m; 80-passenger capacity; cabins are 11 sq m

MS *Katharina von Bora*: 83 m × 9.52 m; 80-passenger capacity; cabins are 12 and 13 sq m

MS *Koenigstein*: 68.5 m × 8.1 m; 68-passenger capacity; cabins are 11 sq m

MS *Moldavia*: 116 m × 17 m; 180-passenger capacity; cabins are 11 sq m

MS *Princesse de Provence*: 110 m × 11.2 m; 150-passenger capacity; cabins are 11 sq m

MS *River Art*: 110 m × 11.4 m; 128-passenger capacity; cabins are 11 and 17 sq m

MS *Rousse*: 113.5 m × 16 m; 192-passenger capacity; cabins 11 are and 17 sq m

MS *Simonov*: 125 m × 16.7 m; 240-passenger capacity; cabins are 8, 10, 13, and 30 sq m

MS *Chicherin*: 125 m × 16.7 m; 240-passenger capacity; cabins are 8, 10, 13, and 30 sq m

MS *Viktoria*: 126.7 m × 11.4 m; 184-passenger capacity; cabins are 16 sq m

MS *Vatutin*: 129.1 m × 16.7 m; 280-passenger capacity; cabins are 8, 10, 13, and 30 sq m

MS *Volga*: 105.9 m × 16.1 m; 164-passenger capacity; cabins are 11 and 14 sq m

Between 1999 and the present, Nicko Tours has developed into the largest German operator specializing in river cruises. The company is situated in Stuttgart. Nicko tours organizes river cruises on chartered vessels on the following rivers: Danube, Rhine, Moselle, Saar, Neckar, Elbe, Vltava, Oder, Rhône, Saône, Seine, Po, Douro, Volga, Neva, Dnieper, Yangtze, and Nile.

In 2012, there were twenty-six ships cruising in European waters that were chartered exclusively by Nicko Tours. Ekkehard Beller is the sole owner and managing director of Nicko Tours GmbH (Ltd).

The ships span a wide range of categories from standard to premium. All were built some years back and were originally operated by other companies prior to their being chartered by Nicko.

All cabins of the Nicko Tours ships are outside cabins, most of which offer an excellent view of passing scenery through the panorama windows. The latest ships, such as MS *Flamenco*, MS *Serenity*, MS *River Navigator*, and MS *Bellissima* have floor-to-ceiling windows that can open to the river on the upper decks. All Nicko Tours vessels have a panorama lounge, affording excellent views; a panorama restaurant; and a sundeck, an inviting place to sit and view the passing scenery.

In the spacious onboard restaurants, all meals are served at a single sitting. Lunch and dinner are served at the table by the waitstaff. This method spares guests the necessity of queuing at a buffet and allows them to enjoy their meals at leisure.

On all Nicko Tours ships, the cruise director, who also speaks English, looks after the passengers' well-being and provides an efficient and helpful personal service throughout the whole stay on board.

The excursion program is an integral part of any river cruise. In the case of many operators, these tours can be booked only once on board. With Nicko Tours, the major excursions are formed into a package, which guests can easily book in advance and receive a discount. Selected local agents guarantee high-quality guides and a high quality of local transport.

# ORIENT EXPRESS/AFLOAT IN FRANCE

Orient-Express Trains & Cruises
Central Reservation Office
205 Meeting Street
Charleston, SC 29401

USA
Tel: 1-800-524-2420
Fax: 843 937 9036
www.afloatinfrance.com/

On all these barges, alcoholic and nonalcoholic drinks are complimentary with open bars, and each barge has at least one van or minibus that follows the barge and is available for excursions. Most have hi-fi systems, compact discs, and docking stations for iPhones, and all have AC and central heating and hair dryers. Cabin square footage includes en suite bathrooms. Prices may vary with the season, and the per-person listed prices are for double occupancy.

*Alouette*: converted, 1986; renovated, 1999; refurbished, 2008; 98' × 17'; four-passenger capacity; four English- and French-speaking crew; two cabins (205 and 269 square feet) with en suite bathroom and satellite TV; Internet; Bose iPod docking station; four bikes; tennis rackets and balls; sundeck with lounges and umbrella; cruises Canal de Midi, France; charter only, $23,800 to $28,600

*Amaryllis*: converted, 2001; refurbished, 2007; 129' × 16.6'; eight-passenger capacity; six English- and French-speaking crew; four cabins (one at 135 square feet, one at 179 square feet, and two at 222 square feet) with en suite bathroom; sundeck with heated pool; eight touring bikes; cruises Burgundy Canal, Saône River, and Canal du Centre, France; charter only, $51,700 to $63,600

*Fleur de Lys*: converted, 1996; refurbished frequently; 129' × 16.6'; six-passenger capacity; six English- and French-speaking crew; three staterooms (one at 254 square feet, one at 179 square feet, and one at 191 square feet), all with en suite bathroom with double sinks, large shower, and two with bathtubs; lavish decor and piano in salon; sundeck with spa pool; cruises on Saône River and Burgundy Canal, France; $7,950 pp in May, otherwise for charter only, $47,700

*Hirondelle*: converted, 1992; frequently refurbished; 128' × 17'; eight-passenger capacity; five English- and French-speaking crew; four cabins (two at 124 square feet and two at 104 square feet) with en suite bathroom; sundeck with lounge chairs and an umbrella; cruises Canal du Rhône au Rhin, Saône River, and Canal du Centre, France; $5,400 pp/$43,300 charter **(Category B)**

*Napoleon*: converted,1963; frequently renovated and refurbished; 128' × 16.5'; twelve-passenger capacity; six English- and French-speaking crew; six cabins (one at 92 square feet and five at 103 square feet), all with en suite bathroom; twelve touring bikes; sundeck with outdoor dining, exercise equipment, and spa pool; Bose iPad docking station; TV; guest computer with Internet access; tennis rackets and balls; cruises Canal du Midi, France; $6,050 pp/$72,600 charter

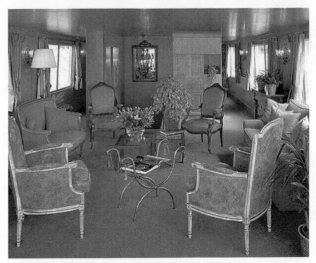

# SCENIC CRUISES

**United States**
**320 120th Ave NE Suite 100**
**Bellevue, WA 98005**
**Phone: 1-888-824-2418**
**www.scenictours.com**

**Australia**
**Level 2, 11 Brown St.**
**Newcastle, NSW 2300**
**Phone: 1-300-136-001**
**Fax: (02)4929-4943**
**www.scenictours.com.au**

*Scenic Sapphire, Scenic Emerald, Scenic Diamond, Scenic Ruby, Scenic Pearl, Scenic Crystal* and *Scenic Jewel* : entered service 2008, 2008, 2009, 2009, 2011, 2012 and 2013 respectively; 2,721 GRT; 443' long; 169-passenger capacity; 85 staterooms; International officers and crew; cruises on Rhine, Moselle, Danube, and Main/Danube Canal

Scenic Cruises, a division of Australia based Scenic Tours, owns seven largely identical ships offering eight- to thirty-day cruise/land tours on the Rhine, Moselle, Main/Danube Canal, and Danube rivers. In addition, the company charters the *Amadeus Symphony* for cruises in Southern France between Beaune and Arles, the *Scenic Tsar* for cruises between St. Petersburg and Moscow, and the M/S *Sun Ray* and M/S *Darakun* for Nile River Cruises between Luxor and Aswan. Options with all cruises include pre- and postcruise stays at deluxe hotels as well as extended land tours to cities and countries near the cruise region.

Scenic Cruises emphasizes the fact that their cruises are all inclusive. Included in the cruises fare are all sightseeing, beer, wine and soft drinks in your mini bar, with meals and throughout the ship, complimentary snacks, espresso, cappuccino, coffees and teas all day, complimentary Wi-Fi throughout the ship, airport transfers, all tipping and gratuities, meals while on tours, and wine tastings and special events ashore. Although many other riverboat companies offer complimentary sightseeing, most exact an extra charge for the more upscale optional tours. On Scenic Cruises, all tours and excursions are covered in the fare. This is the only riverboat company that uses its own buses for the stops between Budapest and Nuremberg.

Each of the 2,721-ton Scenic "Space Ships" accommodates 169 passengers in eighty-five staterooms, 82 percent of which have full-size outdoor balconies. The private balcony suites range in size from 205 to 250 square feet; the four Royal Suites from 300 to 315 square feet; and the nonbalcony staterooms on the lowest deck measure 160 square feet. All staterooms and suites include a flat-screen TV, wireless Internet access, a minibar, a personal safe, bathrobes, hairdryers, a lounge area, and L'Occitane bath products. The thirty-six accommodations on Danube Deck enjoy butler service, two complimentary items pressed daily, a complimentary shoe shine, and in-room dining at breakfast. The four Royal Suites also enjoy a complimentary bottle of Veuve Clicquot and a minibar restocked daily, in-room dining for all meals, daily service of canapés and petit fours, and a larger bathroom with a separate shower, bathtub, and twin basins. As on all riverboats, storage in the nonsuite accommodations is limited. On many of the vessels, the private balconies have a feature that enables passengers to press a button which encloses the outside balcony with a sealed glass window so as to create a glassed-in indoor lounge area.

Located atop ship on Sun Deck are the wheelhouse, lounge chairs, an open-air lounge, a chessboard and a walking track. The top passenger deck, Danube Deck, is the location of the most expensive suites, the Observation Lounge, the Portobello's specialty restaurant, the Panorama Lounge and Bar, the all-day River Café by the bar toward the front of the Lounge, a gift shop, and the reception/information area. The Rhine Deck contains the remaining balcony suites and the Crystal Dining Room. The lowest passenger deck, Moselle Deck houses the standard staterooms and the wellness center. On the latest Scenic ships there is also a small fitness room with limited equipment. An elevator connects the Rhine and Danube Decks.

For breakfast and lunch in the dining room, guests can enjoy a bountiful buffet table, as well as, a la carte specials served by waiters. At the five-course dinner, all guests can be seated at one time and choose between tables for two, four, six or eight. Complimentary beer, local wines, and soft drinks are included at lunch and dinner, as they are throughout the ship. Portobello's is the thirty-guest fine-dining Italian/international restaurant offering a seven-course menu and Italian wines. On selected days, open-air barbeques are served on Sun Deck. On *Scenic Crystal* there is a special gourmet chefs'-table-style restaurant, *Table la Rive,* in a section of the main dining room that serves a seven-course dinner which is more upscale than the dining room fare, and is by invitation only for the guests booking the most expensive suites.

After dinner, there is music and dancing nightly, and occasionally the ship brings aboard local entertainers. Cultural activities, enrichment lectures and games are also offered.

A program referred to as "Scenic Enrich" provides exclusive events such as a private dinner at the twelfth-century Marksburg Castle, a private Viennese concert at the Majestic Palais Liechtenstein, an organ recital in Melk Abbey, a full day excursion into the beautiful Black Forest, and access to several special villages off the beaten track where passengers can mix with the locals, visit their homes, sample local wines and learn about their way of life.

Complimentary bicycles are available for those wishing to explore on their own. The bicycles on *Scenic Crystal* are electronic.

The "Scenic Free Choice" program allows guest to have the freedom to choose from a range of exciting activities and excursions that may interest them, allowing them to customize their holiday all at no extra cost. For example: a visit to Anne Frank House in Amsterdam; an excursion to the Alsatian wine region: or a visit to the prestigious Spanish Riding School in Vienna.

Typical per person fares for fourteen-night cruise range from $5,300 to $6,000 for a standard stateroom, $7,000 to $9,000 for a balcony suite, and $8,900 to $9,600 for a Royal Suite.

## Strong Points

These are all-inclusive river cruises with a large range of upscale excursions, on vessels with attractive decors in the common areas and many accommodations with full balconies.

*Rhine Gorge, courtesy of Scenic Tours*

*Suite, courtesy of Scenic Tours*

*Sun Deck, courtesy of Scenic Tours*

*Dining room, courtesy of Scenic Tours*

*Dinner menu, courtesy of Scenic Tours*

# SCENIC CRUISES

## DAILY PROGRAM
### Friday, October 12, 2012

**Ship's docking times**

**YAROSLAVL**

| Arrival | Departure |
|---------|-----------|
| 8:00PM | 12:00 NOON |

**Weather forecast:**
changeable,
possible rains
**Temperature:**
Day +9° C
Night +4°C

**Movie program:**
Channel 4 – The
Russian Revolution
(1917)
Channel 5 – Amadeus

**Daily Cocktail:**
Orange Grapefruit
Red Devi
**Martini:**
Waldorf Martini

**Gift shop
working hours:**
12:00 – 2:00 PM
3:00 – 6:45 PM

**Emergency contacts:**
Scenic Tsar:
+79152824714

Cruise Director:
+79164909131

| Timing | Schedule | Location |
|--------|----------|----------|
| 6:30 – 7:00 AM | Early Riser | Tsar Lounge |
| 7:00 – 8:30 AM | Breakfast | Tsar Dining Ro |
| 8:30 – 9:00 AM | Late Riser | Tsar Lounge |
| 8:00AM | *Arrive in Yaroslavl* | Tsar Lounge |
| 8:30AM | Bus city tour of *YAROSLAVL* | |
| | • Bus ride with photo stops | |
| | • visit to the Transfiguration Monastery (a museum) | Tsar Lounge |
| | • Church of Elijah the Prophet (a UNESCO site) | |
| | • Free time at the local market and downtown o Yaroslavl | Tsar Lounge |
| 11:45AM | *All aboard!* | |
| 12:00 noon | *Ship sets sail for GORITSY* | |
| 12:00 AM | Lunch buffet on board | |
| | | Tsar Dining Ro |
| 2:00 PM | Scenic Product Presentation followed by a tour of the ship's cabins with Hotel Manager Ludmila by groups | Tsar Lounge |
| 3:00 PM | *Tour of the ship's cabins for guests from cabins 200 – 226* | Meet in Lounge |
| 3:30 PM | *Tour of the ship's cabins for guests from cabins 226 – 317* | |
| 4:30 PM | Russian Cooking Class 1 – BLINI Making with Hotel Manager Ludmila | Tsar Lounge |
| | *Enjoy time at leisure!* | |
| 6:45 PM | Port talk on *GORITSY* with Cruise Director Diana | Tsar Lounge |
| 7:00 PM | Dinner | |
| 9:00PM | All You Wanted To Know About Russia Interactive Presentation and a folk costume show with your Scenic Ambassadors and Cruise Director Diana followed by | Tsar Lounge |
| 10:15PM | Live music and dancing with our on-board musician | Tsar Lounge |

## SCENIC TOURS

*Daily program, courtesy of Scenic Tours*

## SCYLLA AG

**Uferstrasse 90**
**CH-4019 Basel**
**Tel. +41 (0) 61 638 81 81**
**Fax +41 (0) 61 638 81 80**
**www.scylla.ch**

MS *Alina*: entered service in 2011; 135 m × 11.45 m; 220-passenger capacity; 108 cabins; European and international officers and crew; cruises on European waterways

MS *Amelia*: entered service in 2011; 135 m × 11.45 m; 220-passenger capacity; 108 cabins; European and international officers and crew; cruises on European waterways

MS *Aurelia*: entered service in 2007; 110 m × 11.4 m; 159-passenger capacity; 76 cabins; European and international officers and crew; cruises on European waterways

MS *Saxonia*: entered service in 2001; 82 m × 9.5 m; 89-passenger capacity; 45 cabins; European and international officers and crew; cruises on European waterways

MS *Swiss Corona* and *Swiss Gloria*: entered service in 2004 and 2005 respectively; 110 m × 11.4 m; 155-passenger capacity; 76 cabins, 1/3 with French balconies; European and international officers and crew; cruises on European waterways

MS *Swiss Crown*: entered service in 2000; 110 m × 11.4 m; 154-passenger capacity; 76 cabins, some with French balconies; European and international officers and crew; cruises on European waterways

MS *Swiss Crystal*: entered service in 1995; 101.3 m × 11.4 m; 125-passenger capacity; 63 cabins; European and international officers and crew; cruises on European waterways

MS *Swiss Diamond*: entered service in 1996; 101.3 m × 11.4 m; 125-passenger capacity; 63 cabins; European and international officers and crew; cruises on European waterways

MS *Swiss Emerald* (see Tauck Tours)

MS *Swiss Jewel* (see Tauck Tours)

MS *Swiss Pearl*: entered service in 1993; renovated in 2006; 110 m × 11.4 m; 123-passenger capacity; 62 cabins; European and international officers and crew; cruises on Rhône and Saône rivers

MS *Swiss Ruby*: entered service in 2002; 85 m × 10.6 m; 88-passenger capacity; 44 cabins, 22 with French balconies; European and international officers and crew; cruises on European waterways

MS *Swiss Sapphire*: (see Tauck Tours)

MS *Swiss Tiara*: entered service in 2006; 110 m × 11.4 m; 153-passenger capacity; 76 cabins, 64 with French balconies; European and international officers and crew; cruises on European waterways

MS *Treasures* (see Tauck Tours)

MS *Vista Prima*: entered service in 2010; 110 m × 11.4 m; 158-passenger capacity; 76 cabins; European and international officers and crew; cruises on European waterways

The Swiss shipping company Scylla AG's first riverboat, MS *Scylla*, entered service in 1974. Today the company operates seventeen vessels spanning all the major waterways of Europe. Four of their ships, the *Swiss Emerald*, *Swiss Sapphire*, *Swiss Jewel*, and *Treasure* are chartered exclusively by Tauck Tours and marketed largely to the English-speaking market. Tauck offers all-inclusive cruise tours, and the company is considered by many to be the best riverboat-tour operator in Europe. (See Tauck Tours for details on these ships.)

Many of their riverboats, in addition to the standard lounge, bar, restaurant, lobby, and shop, have wellness centers with whirlpools or a swimming pool, sauna, and steam room, as well as whirlpools on the sundeck.

Scylla operates their other vessels on the various waterways of Europe, including the Elbe and Elbe-Havel Canal, the Rhine and its tributaries, the Rhône and Saône, and the Danube.

*Courtesy of Scylla AG*

*Dining room, courtesy of Scylla AG*

*Stateroom, courtesy of Scylla AG*

*Lido Bar, courtesy of Scylla AG*

## SEA CLOUD CRUISES

**In the United States**
**282 Grand Ave.**
**Englewood, New Jersey 07631**
**(888) 732-2568; (201) 227-9404**
**(201) 227-9424 Fax**
**www.seacloud.com**

**In Germany**
**An der Alster 9**
**Hamburg, Germany 20099**
**+49(0) 403095920**
**+49(0) 4030959222 Fax**
**info@seacloud.com**

*River Cloud II*: entered service, 2001; refurbished annually; 338' × 32'; 44 cabins; 88-passenger capacity; international crew; cruises on rivers in Europe

Built in 2001, the eighty-eight-passenger *River Cloud II* previously cruised in Italy, up and down the Po River between Cremona and Venice. Currently, it travels the Rhine, Main, Moselle, and Danube rivers, as well as the Dutch waterways. The twenty 118-square-foot double-bedded and the ten 118-square-foot twin-bedded outside cabins located on cabin deck are beautifully finished with architectural details and colorful fabrics and include closet space, private safes, dressing tables, a TV/DVD combination, and marble baths with glass-enclosed shower stalls, hair dryers, magnifying mirrors, and terry cloth bathrobes and slippers. Fresh fruit and soft drinks are provided by cabin stewardesses free of charge as is a welcome bottle of champagne. The thirteen 150-square-foot panorama cabins on promenade deck have queen beds, separate sitting areas, a TV and video player, a writing desk, marble bathrooms, and large windows, and are the better choice for guests desiring larger accommodations.

Atop ship on sundeck are the bridge, Lido Bar, and a large sunning and observation area with wood-backed lounges, shuffleboard, and a giant chess set. On promenade deck are the dining room, the thirteen panorama cabins, the reception, main lounge, and library. On the cabin deck are the boutique, hairdresser, and remaining cabins.

The attractive open-seating dining room with tables for two, four, six, and eight people is the locale for breakfast and lunch buffets, featuring a vast array of regional dishes. Multicourse dinners offer a set menu with two choices for the main course. Complimentary red and white wines are offered at all meals, as well as espresso and cappuccino. When weather permits, alfresco barbeques are offered atop ship. Soft drinks, juices, bottled water, coffee, and tea are available around the clock free of charge on all Sea Cloud Cruises yachts. A piano player entertains in the main lounge during cocktail hour and after dinner.

*Courtesy of Sea Cloud Cruises0*

*Stateroom, courtesy of Sea Cloud Cruises*

*Lounge, courtesy of Sea Cloud Cruises*

*Dining room, courtesy of Sea Cloud Cruises*

Dinner Menu

Cocktail of king prawn
with avocado and corn crème

or

Tasting of three different kinds of Gazpacho with parmesan cheese
Beef consommé
Pike perch pan fried with Szechuan pepper on spinach and saffron foam

or

Rosa roasted fillet of beef with
glazed snow peas & mille feuille of celery

or
Tomato olive risotto
Variations on mandarins
Cheeseboard with assorted international cheeses
Coffee, Tea and Pralines

Dinner menu, courtesy of Sea Cloud Cruises

# SONESTA NILE CRUISE COLLECTION

**c/o Sonesta Collection Hotels-Resorts-Cruises**
**116 Huntington Avenue**
**Boston, MA 02116**
**(800) 766-3782**
**www.sonesta.com/Nilecruises/**

*Moon Goddess*: entered service in 2000; renovated in 2009; 220 × 43 feet; 112-passenger capacity; 52 staterooms; Egyptian crew; three-, four-, and seven-night cruises up and down the Nile

*Nile Goddess*: entered service in 1989; renovated in 2008; 118-passenger capacity; 53 cabins; Egyptian crew; three-, four-, and seven-night cruises up and down the Nile

*St. George I*: entered service in 2006; 74.5 meters long; 118-passenger capacity; 56 cabins; Egyptian crew; three-, four-, and seven-night cruises between Luxor and Aswan

*Star Goddess*: entered service in 2006; 72 meters long; 66-passenger capacity; 33 cabins; Egyptian crew; three-, four-, and seven-night cruises between Luxor and Aswan.

*Sun Goddess*: entered service in 1993; 124-passenger capacity; 62 cabins; Egyptian crew; three-, four-, and seven-night cruises up and down the Nile

(Medical facilities: C-4; P-1; EM; CLS; MS; N-O; OX; LJ)

*Nile Goddess* was built in 1989 and totally renovated in 1995 and 2008. Its five decks include a pool with an adjoining lounge, recreation area, barbecue area, show lounge, bar, game room, shop, disco, and restaurant. The one-sitting restaurant provides buffet meals.

There are forty-seven cabins, two junior suites, and four full suites. All cabins are air-conditioned and feature panoramic windows to view the Nile and passing scenery. All accommodations include private direct-dial telephones, hair dryers, safety-deposit boxes, minibars, music, wireless Internet access, plasma TVs with movies, and bathrooms with full-size bathtubs.

The *Sun Goddess* was built and added to the fleet in 1993, then completely renovated in 2009. The public areas are similar to the *Nile Goddess* and include a Turkish bath. The ship has fifty-eight cabins and four suites with the same facilities and amenities as its sister ship.

The *Moon Goddess* came on line in 2000 and offers forty-eight junior suites, each with sliding-glass doors opening to a private balcony and two presidential suites with private lounges. All staterooms feature private direct-dial telephones, in-room safes, hair dryers, remote-control TV and video, and bathrooms with bathtubs. Amenities on board include an outdoor pool, pool bar, lounge, casino, disco, jogging track, table tennis, and gym.

All three ships sail between Luxor and Aswan, Egypt, on alternate three-, four-, and seven-night cruises. Shore excursions visit the Temples of Karnak and Luxor, the Valley of Kings and Queens, the Temple of Queen Hatshepsut, the Colossi of Memnon, the Temple of Dendera in Kena, the Temple of Horus in Edfu, the Temple of Sobek and Haroeis in Kom Ombo, the Agha Khan Mausoleum, the High Dam granite quarries, and the Temple of Philae in Aswan.

In 2006, two new ships joined the fleet, *Star Goddess* and *St. George I*. They operate three-, four-, and seven-night cruises between Luxor and Aswan with the same shore excursions as those listed.

The *Star Goddess* has four decks and thirty-three suite accommodations that feature private direct-dial international telephone lines, Internet access, individual climate control, hair dryers, minibars, safety-deposit boxes, TV and movie programs, and bathrooms with full-size tubs. Facilities include an outdoor swimming pool with bar service, jogging track, spa offering massage, sauna and Jacuzzi, gym, dining room and outdoor barbecue area, discotheque, main lounge, and several bars. On each cruise, there are theme nights, shows, and a captain's welcome cocktail party.

The *St. George I* has five decks, forty-nine cabins, nine presidential suites, and one royal suite. All accommodations feature double-glassed open panoramic windows, private direct-dial telephones, wireless Internet access and laptops, safety-deposit boxes, hair dryers, minibars, twenty-one-inch LCD TVs with satellite programming, and bathrooms with Jacuzzis and showers with music and water massage. Facilities and entertainments are similar to those described for *Star Goddess*.

In 2009, the *Amirat Dahabeya* joined the fleet. This upscale cruiser offers six cabins and two full suites and is designed for small groups or extended families traveling together. This is a sailing barge that is towed behind the crew vessel, providing a leisurely seven-night excursion between Luxor and Aswan.

## Strong Points

New, modern riverboats offering in-depth Nile cruises. The three newest ships are especially upscale for Nile riverboats.

*Moon Goddess cabin, courtesy Sonesta International Nile Cruises*

*Amirat Dahabeya, courtesy Sonesta International Nile Cruises*

*Sun Goddess, courtesy Sonesta International Nile Cruises*

# TAUCK RIVER CRUISING

**10 Norden Place**
**Norwalk, Connecticut 06855**
**(800) 468-2825**
**www.tauck.com**

MS *Swiss Emerald,* MS *Swiss Sapphire,* MS *Swiss Jewel,* and MS *Treasures*: entered service in 2006, 2008, 2009, and 2011 respectively; 361' × 37'; 118-passenger capacity; 59 staterooms; European captain and crew; Tauck directors American and European; various itineraries on the Danube, Rhine, Moselle, Rhône, Saône, Main Canal, and waterways of Belgium and Holland

Tauck River Cruising is a division of Tauck, a large tour operator. The river-cruising division is composed of four modern riverboats, which Tauck leases exclusively from Scylla, a Swiss company. The company's four vessels are true sister ships with virtually identical features and amenities; thus guests' choices depend mostly upon the itinerary they prefer.

Each has fourteen 300-square-foot suites. The remaining junior suites and cabins range from 150 to 183 square feet. Eighty-five percent of the accommodations have panoramic floor-to-ceiling windows that open to the river. All have river views, 100 percent goose down pillows, thick pillow-top mattresses, mako cotton duvets with hypoallergenic 90 percent down filling, plasma TV with in-room movies, minibar, radio, private safe, a hair dryer, terry cloth bathrobes and slippers, and Moulton Brown bath amenities.

The ship offers open-seating dining in its main restaurant as well as bistro dining featuring lighter fare, coffees, espresso, cappuccino, and snacks at the Lido Bar. Wine is served gratis at dinner, and beer and soft drinks at lunch and dinner. Some meals take place ashore. Snack baskets are available between 2:00 p.m. and midnight.

Public facilities include a small fitness center with treadmills and exercycles, a sundeck with a Jacuzzi, an e-mail station (Wi-Fi is available throughout the ship), a lounge, a library, a boutique, and several bicycles. Entertainment includes nightly piano music for listening and dancing, destination lectures, wine tastings, folkloric performances, movies, cooking demonstrations, and game nights. All gratuities, shore excursions, and many extras are included in the cruise price.

Itineraries of varying lengths have the vessels traversing the rivers of Europe to visit such cities as Amsterdam, Strasbourg, Prague, Budapest, Vienna, Cologne, and dozens of smaller towns along the way. Select itineraries include pre- and postcruise stays at top hotels in major cities, together with guided sightseeing. Cruise-only versions of these itineraries, without the included pre- or post-stays, can also be purchased for a reduced price. Cruises are offered from April through October, plus Christmas market cruises. Per diem prices start at $374 to $421 for the thirty-eight staterooms and top off from $667 to $754 for one of the fourteen suites (depending upon itinerary and time of year).

## Strong Points

Tauck is an experienced and highly regarded tour operator. Its river-cruising division operates four very new, modern vessels with desired itineraries on the rivers of Europe. The quality of the dining and service, the excellent guided tours, the information and assistance provided aboard ship, the numerous special experiences and meals ashore, the all-inclusive pricing, and the overall service and attention to passengers' needs by the staff set this riverboat experience above most of the competition.

Swiss Emerald, *courtesy Tauck River Cruising*

Swiss Sapphire *suite, courtesy Tauck River Cruising*

Swiss Sapphire *lobby, courtesy Tauck River Cruising*

*White tomato aspic served with grilled sea scallop and mango salsa*

\*\*\*\*\*

*Cappuccino of curry and lemongrass*
*Served with shrimps*

\*\*\*\*\*

### Sautéed Anglerfish
*Escalope served on a pumpkin rusty and ratatouille sauce*
*marinated with virgin olive oil and lime dressing*
Accompanied with a crispy salad bouquet

\*\*\*\*\*

*Strawberry - Banana Shooters with Vodka*

\*\*\*\*\*

### Roasted Beef Tenderloin
*Medium roasted beef tenderloin marinated in red wine and fresh herbs,*
*served with a black truffle Madeira sauce*
Accompanied by potato au gratin and …

*or*

### Asparagus Risotto
*Sautéed in olive oil, shallots and white wine, cooked with fresh asparagus,*
*topped with fresh parmesan cheese*
Accompanied by roasted Cherry tomato Raspe

\*\*\*\*\*

*Grand Dessert Plate*

\*\*\*\*\*

*Coffee, Chocolates and Brandy*

6:00am – 10:00am  Early breakfast in the Lido Bar,  Deck 3 aft.

**6:15am  M.S. Swiss Sapphire Arrives in Plittersdorf**

7:30am – 9:00am   Full breakfast in the Dining Room.

9:00am  Depart by coach for Baden-Baden. We will be using the "Quietvoxes" so please be in the Main Lounge ready for a sound check, at least 10 minutes before the departure time.

9:30am  Arrive in Baden-Baden. Meet our local guides for a walking tour of the old town.

10:00am  Movie: "Gangs of New York" (160 mins). Channel 19 in your cabin.

11:30am  Visit the world famous Baden-Baden casino.

12:00pm  Return to the ship for lunch or stay in town, on your own. Please <u>sign the list on the Reception Desk if you plan to return to the ship for lunch.</u>

1:00pm  Lunch in the Lido Bar. Today's feature: Hot dogs.

1:00pm  Asian lunch in the Dining Room.

Enjoy a free afternoon. We will have a shuttle service between the town center and the ship throughout the afternoon. See the schedule below... Baden-Baden is world famous for its spas. Ask your Tauck Directors for details.

Take some time to pack... If you do not intend to make any purchases this evening, please settle your ship account at the Reception Desk. If you plan on having drinks or visit the boutique after dinner you may settle your account later this evening.

2:00pm  Movie: "Pirates of the Caribbean" (137mins). Channel 19 in your cabin.

4:00pm  Exercise you brain!!! Test your memory, perception, logic and yes, some math skills, with a fun, yet challenging variety of puzzles and tests. Main Lounge.

4:30pm   Movie: "Mama Mia" (104mins). Channel 19 in your cabin.

5:15pm   **ALL ABOARD!!!**

5:30pm   **The MS Swiss Sapphire departs Plitterdorf**

6:30pm   Captain Josef's Farewell Reception, Main Lounge. All drinks are complimentary during the reception. You may choose to dress up a little for tonight's festivities.

7:15pm   Farewell Dinner in the Dining Room.

9:30pm   Azmi, on piano, in the Main Lounge.

9:30pm   Movie: "Oh Brother Where Art Thou" (100mins). Channel 19.

11:30pm  Movie: "Indiana Jones – The Last Crusade" (122mins). Channel 19 in your cabin.

---

### Shuttle Service

| Ship to City Center | City Center to Ship |
|---|---|
| 2:00pm | 3:00pm and 4:00pm |

Our meeting point in Baden-Baden is behind the Evangelical Church; the same spot where we began our tour in the morning.

---

### Before bed on *Wednesday* night please:

- **Be sure you have settled your onboard account and ensure you have removed all items from your cabin safe - PASSPORTS!!!**
- **Return any borrowed items to the Reception Desk: adapters, converters, etc and ensure all reference books and "Quietvoxes" are returned to Steve.**

*Courtesy Tauck River Cruising*

# TUI CRUISES

**Karl-Wiechert-Allee 4**
**30625 Hanover, Germany**
**+49(0)511 566-00**
**+49(0)511 566 1901 Fax**
**www.tui-group.com**

*TUI ALLEGRA*: entered service 2011; 445.5' × 37.6'; 178-passengers; 89 staterooms; German officers and International crew; cruises on European rivers

*TUI MELODIA*: entered service 2010; 445.5' × 37.6'; 178-passengers; 89 staterooms; German officers and International crew; cruises on European rivers

*TUI MAXIMA*: entered service 2003; 418' × 37.6'; 180-passengers; 90 staterooms; German officers and International crew; cruises on European rivers

*TUI SONATA*: entered service 2010; 445.5' × 37.6'; 186-passengers; 93 staterooms; German officers and International crew; cruises on European rivers

*TUI QUEEN* (formerly *Premicon Queen*): entered service 2008; 445' × 37.6'; 102-passenger capacity; 51 staterooms; German officers and International crew; cruises on European rivers

TUI Cruises is a German-based cruise line that is a joint venture between the German tour firm, TUI AG and Royal Caribbean Cruise Line. Operations were started in 2009, when the former *Celebrity Galaxy* was transferred, renamed *Mein Schiff,* and renovated to be more compatible with German tastes. *Celebrity Mercury* followed in 2011 and was renamed *Mein Schiff 2.* These ships are marketed exclusively to a German clientele, and German is the language used on the ships.

Under an exclusive cooperation agreement with Transocean and its owner Premicon, TUI took over operation of the company's eight river cruise ships in 2011. In 2012, TUI will have five ships cruising the European rivers Danube, Rhine, Main and Mosel. Only the German language is used on the ships and almost all passengers are German or Austrian.

The 186-passenger *TUI Sonata* entered service in 2010. Each of the ninety-three cabins has a flat-screen TV, radio, telephone, safe, and bathroom with shower. The 120 square-foot "sofa" cabins have a sofa bed and a wall bed; whereas, the 150 square-foot "double" cabins have two beds that can be converted to a double bed arrangement. Those on the upper and middle decks have French balconies. Public areas in addition to the Sun Deck with parasols, chessboard and shuffleboard include an all-purpose lounge and bar, a dining room, a wellness center with whirlpool, panorama sauna, heated lounges and cardio equipment, a library/wine store/smoking room, a shop and reception lobby.

The 106-passenger *TUI (Premicon) Queen* offers thirty-one 190-square-foot junior suites; sixteen 230-square-foot Deluxe Suites; and four 322-square-foot Queen Suites. The accommodations on the two upper passenger decks have French Balconies, and the four Queen Suites have full balconies, separate living and sleeping areas, three flat-screen TVs, marble bathrooms with shower and tubs. All accommodations have satellite flat-screen TVs, wireless Internet service, safes, and minibars. Public areas include an all-purpose bar and lounge, a restaurant, a Viennese café, a library, a smoking lounge, a theater, a hairdresser and masseuse, a shop, an elevator a wellness area with a whirlpool, and a sundeck with parasols, chessboard, shuffleboard and a putting green.

The 178-passenger *TUI Allegra* and *TUI Melodia* entered service in 2011. Each of the eighty-nine cabins on both ships have flat-screen TVs, radios, telephones, safes, and bathrooms with showers. The 120 square-foot "sofa" cabins have a sofa double bed; whereas the 150 square-foot "double "cabins have two beds that can be converted to a double bed arrangement. Those on the upper and middle decks have French balconies. Public areas in addition to the Sun Deck with parasols, chessboard and shuffleboard include an all-purpose lounge and bar, a dining room, a wellness center with whirlpool, panorama sauna, heated lounge and cardio equipment, a library/wine store/smoking room, a shop and receptions lobby.

The 180-passenger *TUI Maxima* entered service in 2003. Each of the ninety cabins has the same amenities and facilities as on the other ships, as do the common areas.

## Strong Points

These are full-facility riverboats especially designed and operated to please their all German-speaking clientele.

*Courtesy of TUI Cruises*

*TUI Queen stateroom, courtesy of TUI River Cruises*

*TUI Queen dining room, courtesy of TUI River Cruises*

# UNIWORLD BOUTIQUE RIVER CRUISE COLLECTION

**Uniworld Plaza**
**17323 Ventura Boulevard**
**Los Angeles, California 91316**
**(800) 733-7820**
**(818) 382-2709 Fax**
**www.uniworld.com**

*Queen Isabel*: entered service, 2013; 245' × 37'; 59 cabins; 118-passenger capacity; European officers and crew; eleven-day cruises in Portugal and Spain along the Douro River Valley

*River Ambassador*: entered service, 1993; refurbished, 2006; 361' × 37.5'; 128-passenger capacity; 64 cabins; European officers and crew; seven-night cruises along the Rhine, Main, and Danube rivers

SS *Antoinette* and SS *Catherine*: entered service, 2011 and 2014 respectively; 443' × 37.5'; 82 cabins; 164-passenger capacity; European officers and crew; SS *Antoinette* offers seven-night cruises in Netherlands to Germany along the Rhine River; SS *Catherine* will offer seven-night cruises in Southern France

*River Baroness*: entered service, 1994; refurbished, 2005; 361' × 37.5'; 128-passenger capacity; 64 cabins; European officers and crew; seven-night cruises along Seine and Rhône rivers and seven-night cruises in Netherlands, Belgium, Germany, France, Austria, Slovakia, and Hungary along the Rhine, Main, and Danube rivers

*River Beatrice*: entered service, 2009; 410' × 37.5'; 160-passenger capacity; 80 cabins; European officers and crew; cruises on the Danube River

*River Countess*: entered service, 2003; refurbished, 2007; 361' × 37.5'; 134-passenger capacity; 67 cabins; European officers and crew; thirteen days Venice to Venice and on Po River

*River Duchess*: entered service, 2003; refurbished, 2007; 361' × 37.5'; 134-passenger capacity; 67 cabins; European officers and crew; seven- to fourteen-night cruises along the Rhine, Main, and Danube rivers

*River Empress*: entered service, 2001; refurbished, 2005 and 2010; 361' × 37.5'; 134-passenger capacity; 67 cabins; European officers and crew; seven- to fourteen-night cruises along the Rhine, Main, and Danube rivers

*River Princess*: entered service, 2001; refurbished, 2005 and 2010; 361' × 37.5'; 132-passenger capacity; 66 cabins; European officers and crew; seven- to eleven-night cruises in Germany, Austria, Hungary, and Slovakia along the Rhine, Main, and Danube rivers

*River Queen*: entered service, 1999; refurbished, 2003 and 2010; 361' × 37.5'; 132-passenger capacity; 66 cabins; European officers and crew; nine- and twelve-night cruises along the Rhine and Moselle rivers

*River Royale*: entered service, 2006; 360' × 37.5'; 132-passenger capacity; 66 cabins; European officers and crew; seven-night cruises in France on Rhône and Saône rivers

*River Tosca:* entered service 2010; 78-passenger capacity (double occupancy); 39 cabins; Egyptian officers and crew; cruises on the Nile River in Egypt

Uniworld commenced operations in 1976 and has expanded to become one of the largest river cruises and tour companies servicing North American travelers. Its diverse and continually expanding product lineup features deluxe river cruises, escorted land tours, and combined cruise/tours to some of the world's most exciting destinations, including the rivers of Europe, Russia, China, and Egypt. In 2006, a luxury hotel company and Trafalgar Tours purchased Uniworld.

Uniworld programs are designed for a North American audience and include such customized features as all-outside cabins with panoramic windows aboard hotel-style river cruise ships, English-speaking onboard and shoreside staffs, a nonsmoking environment inside the ship, classic cuisine and international specialties, first-class hotel accommodations, round-trip flights aboard major airlines, guided sightseeing opportunities, and the services of an experienced cruise or tour manager throughout the trip. Daily guided shore excursions are included in the pricing. Other additional shore excursions are also available. Selected pre- and postcruise hotel packages are featured as well. For the 2014 cruise season, the riverboat company became "all-inclusive," wherein services and amenities on all ships will be expanded to include unlimited wine, beer and spirits, all gratuities and pre- and postcruise extensions.

On my most recent cruise, I noted that in addition to U.S. and Canadian passengers, there were also passengers from Australia, Spain, Germany, and other parts of the world. The most outstanding features of the cruise experience were the dedication of the staff to varying passenger comforts and needs and the complimentary shore excursions.

The European-based riverboats are designed on the generic European model but are customized to American tastes. Each ship is outfitted as a fine hotel. On the *River Countess, Duchess, Empress, Princess, Queen,* and *Royale,* standard cabins are approximately 151 square feet, whereas suites are 215 square feet. The *River Ambassador*'s cabins are 117 square feet, and the *River Baroness*'s, 128 square feet. On the *River Beatrice,* SS *Antoinette,* and SS *Catherine,* in addition to the standard cabins (163-196 square feet), there are eight 294-square-foot suites and a 391-square-foot owner's suite. Eighty percent of the cabins and suites on these two ships have floor-to-ceiling windows, the top half of which can be opened, a feature that can also be found in Category One staterooms on *River Royale, River Countess,* and *River Duchess.* The suites on the *Antoinette, Catherine,* and *Beatrice* have alcoves with a sitting area and floor-to-ceiling windows that open up, creating the impression of a private indoor/outdoor balcony.

The cruise line's most upscale ships, the SS *Antoinette* has an elegant eighteenth-century French decor. A spectacular ten-foot blue sapphire Baccarat chandelier, which originally hung in New York's Tavern on the Green, adorns the ship's two-story lobby. The lounges and restaurant designs were inspired by the Palace at Versailles. There is marble in the public areas, fine art, and French-period furnishings, resulting in a uniquely different design and style for a riverboat. Other unique features include a movie theater, a glassed-in swimming pool, a small but well-equipped gym, and a fleet of bicycles; and atop ship, on the sundeck, in addition to numerous luxurious lounge chairs, there are two additional venues: the Leopard Lounge, a cocktail lounge with a stunning leopard decor, and an indoor/outdoor additional dining venue. The SS *Catherine* when it comes on line in 2014 will be very similar to the SS *Antoinette* and will sail on rivers in Southern France.

The 118-passenger *Queen Isabel* entered service in 2013, sailing in the Douro Valley. All staterooms and suites are elegantly furnished and sport French balconies. Of the fifty-nine staterooms, thirty-nine measure 161 square feet; eighteen junior suites, 215 square feet; and two full suites, 323 square feet. Those on the upper deck have full balconies, and those on main deck, French balconies. Lower deck cabins have panoramic windows. Public areas include a main lounge, a restaurant, and a sundeck with swimming pool, fitness center, spa, and boutique.

Commencing in 2010, the cruise line offers exclusive services and amenities in all suites, including a bottle of wine upon arrival, a fruit-and-cookie plate, in-room breakfast, morning coffee, shoeshine, and free laundry services. On the *River Beatrice* and SS *Antoinette*, there is butler service for all suite guests and a special evening dinner in the captain's lounge. As noted above, for the 2014 cruise season, services and amenities on all ships will be expanded to include unlimited wine, beer and spirits, all gratuities and pre- and postcruise extensions.

All programs include round-trip air transportation from the United States and Canada (unless the passenger elects to book his or her own air), cruise accommodations, all onboard meals (and complimentary wines, beer, spirits, and soft drinks), all gratuities, all shore excursions, and all transfers. Many of the itineraries offer additional features such as hotel accommodations, select meals on land, and a variety of local entertainment. Theme cruises are offered on select European sailings. Providing a more extensive study of the art, music, and wine defining the regions visited, these theme-cruise voyages include bonus excursions to museums, cathedrals, and vineyards. Special concerts, onboard guest lecturers, and performers are also featured from time to time.

The cruise line also markets riverboats in Egypt, in Vietnam, and in Cambodia along the Mekong River, and in China on the Yangtze in partnership with other companies.

The China/Yangtze River cruises are offered on riverboats owned and operated by Victoria Cruises, the only U.S.-managed operation on that river. Uniworld, however, has offices in China and a full staff to assist customers taking these cruise/tour packages. Victoria Cruises is described later in this chapter.

In March 2010, the *River Tosca* entered service, broadening the cruise line's offerings to Nile cruises in Egypt. This all-suite riverboat features thirty-nine accommodations at 313 to 335 square feet and two presidential suites at 651 square feet. Each accommodation includes French balconies, 100 percent Egyptian cotton sheets and duvets, iPod docking stations, flat-screen TVs, and tiled bathrooms with plush towels, bathrobes, and slippers. Programs ranging from nine to thirteen days include stays at first-class hotels and land excursions to cities in Egypt and Jordan.

All staterooms feature a picture window and beds that can be arranged as one large double or two twins with European-style comforters and duvets with choice of pillows, flat-screen televisions with CNN, hair dryers, direct-dial telephones, and private safes. There are ice buckets in the rooms as well as ice machines in public areas but no refrigerators or minibars. On the newer vessels, magnetic key cards provide added security; Internet stations are available to receive and send e-mails; and each has a fitness center, steam room, and sauna.

Staterooms are located on upper and lower decks. Atop the ships are a sundeck and the bridge. Public areas generally include the main restaurant, four lounges, the reception area, a small shop, a beauty salon, and gymnasium-spa area (on the recent new builds).

Commencing in 2006, a thirteen-day program in Egypt was added with seven-day cruises along the Nile and an optional six-day land extension to Petra in Jordan. The program is offered on the 120-passenger, sixty-cabin *Giselle*. This riverboat features all outside cabins with satellite television, minibars, and music systems; a swimming pool; a gift shop; and international cuisine.

## Strong Points

Comfortable, all-inclusive riverboat cruise experience along some of Europe's most scenic waterways, packaged and geared toward North Americans who prefer a more familiar cruise experience than that offered by the European riverboat lines. Outstanding complimentary shore excursions and attentiveness to passenger comforts and needs. The new SS *Antoinette* and the SS *Catherine* (2014) raise the bar for riverboat elegance.

*SS Antoinette, courtesy of Uniworld Boutique River Cruises*

*Suite, SS Antoinette, courtesy of Uniworld Boutique River Cruises*

*Main lounge, SS Antoinette, courtesy of Uniworld Boutique River Cruises*

*Indoor pool, SS Antoinette, courtesy of Uniworld Boutique River Cruises*

*Lobby, SS Antoinette, courtesy of Uniworld Boutique River Cruises*

**S.S. Antoinette**
Tuesday, September 18th, 2012

# FRENCH DINNER

## Executive Chefs suggestion

Fresh apple cocktail "Normande"(V)
*with raisins and Calvados*

Crème "Crecy" (V)
*Cream of carrot with ginger*

Roasted rack of Aveyron lamb
*served with honey-thyme jus, grilled tomato, ratatouille
and potato gratin*

Bourbon vanilla crème brulée

Traveling *Lite*

## Low fat, carb,- & calorie suggestion

Fresh apple cocktail (V)
*with raisins and Calvados*

Traditional French onion soup (V)

Fried fillet of Halibut "Grenoblaise"
*accompanied by caper-lemon with tender broccoli florets and Savoyard potatoes*

Banana-buttermilk ice cream with fruit skewer

## Daily gourmet chat

„If more of us valued food and cheer and song above hoarded gold,
it would be a merrier world" [J.J.R. Tolkien]

## Wine recommendation

White wine:
Chardonnay, Crocodile's Lair Kaaimansgat, South Africa, 2008
€ 33,00

Red wine:
Promis Ca Marcanda di Gaja, Toscana, Italy, 2008
€ 42,00

In addition, UNIWORLD has carefully selected a choice of complimentary
Red & white wines, assorted beer and soft drinks for you to enjoy with your meal

*Dinner menu, courtesy of Uniworld Boutique River Cruises*

**Boppard, Rüdesheim am Rhein**

**Wednesday, September 26th, 2012**

Docking address
Boppard: Rhein allee, Uniworld portion
Rüdesheim: Hindenburg Allee portion 1

**All aboard time**
Boppard: 7:45 am
Rüdesheim: 6:30 pm

**Expected Weather for Today**
51°/71°C, S'woon

**Expected Weather for Tomorrow**
68°/26°C, Cloudy

**Wellness hours**
Time to relax with our onboard masseur.
Feel free to book a message at the Front Desk.

**Onboard Shop Hours**
9:00 am – 10:00 am

**Cocktail of the Day**
Rosy Nail

**Non-Alcoholic Cocktail of the Day**
Sicily Temple

**Hot Special of the Day**
Rüdesheimer Coffee

**Leopard Lounge opening time**
8:30 pm – closing

**Movies in the Cinema**
Inside Job
at 10:00 am
Shall we dance
at 3:00 pm
Walk the line
at 8:00 pm

---

*Schedule of Activities*

**6:00 am – 7:00 am**
Coffee and pastries for our early risers in the Salon du Grand Trianon

**7:00 am – 8:00 am**
Enjoy our sumptuous breakfast in the Restaurant de Versailles

**7:15 am**
Morning exercise with Ionela in the Swimming pool area

**8:00 am**
All onboard please

**8:30 am**
S.S. Antoinette sets sail for Rüdesheim am Rhein

**9:00 am – 10:00 am**
Late risers light breakfast in the L'Orangerie

**All morning**
Scenic sailing through the "Romantic Rhine Gorge", with commentable by Markus on the top deck and in the Salon Du Grand Trianon

**10:00 am – 10:45 am**
Traditional German Frühschoppen in the L'Orangerie

**12:00 noon – 1:30 pm**
Our sumptuous lunch in the Restaurant de Versailles

**Approx. 1:30 pm**
S.S. Antoinette arrives in Rüdesheim am Rhein

**2:00 pm**
Departure by mini train into the center of Rüdesheim for your time at leisure

---

**3:45 pm**
Departure by bus for our included wine tasting at Castle Vollrads.

Note: The tour departs from the slant resport, not number 1 on your city map. Guests who did not take the mini train into town or leave it at their hotel can meet the wine tasting will be presented on a wander tour. The ship at 3:30 pm.

**3:30 pm – 4:30 pm**
Tea time in the Salon du Grand Trianon, accompanied by music with your onboard musician Greg

**6:15 pm**
Port Talk with Markus in the Salon du Grand Trianon

**6:30 pm**
All onboard please

**6:30 pm – 7:00 pm**
Epicurean cocktail in the Salon du Grand Trianon

**7:00 pm**
S.S. Antoinette sets sail for Germersheim

**7:00 pm**
Epicurean dinner is served in the Restaurant de Versailles

**After dinner**
Classical concert by La Strade in the Salon du Grand Trianon

**Followed by**
Dance music in the Salon du Grand Trianon with our onboard musicians Greg & Margaret

**10:00 pm**
Late night snack available in Leopard Bar

UNIWORLD

*Daily program, courtesy of Uniworld Boutique River Cruises*

# VANTAGE TRAVEL

**90 Canal Street**
**Boston, Massachusetts 02114**
**(800) 322-6677**
**www.vantagetravel.com**

MS *River Discovery II;* MS *River Splendor;* MS *River Venture:* entered service, 2012, 2013, and 2013 respectively; 442' × 38'; 176-passenger capacity

MS *River Navigator:* entered service, 2000; refurbished, 2013; 360' long; 140-passenger capacity

MS *River Odyssey:* entered service, 2013; refurbished, 2007; 410' long: 170-passenger capacity

These ships offer riverboat cruises on the waterways of Holland and Belgium and on the Rhine, Danube, and Moselle rivers and the Main-Danube Canal. Prices include round-trip air from selected U.S. cities, as well as pre- and post-cruise hotel stays.

The newest ships, *River Discovery II, River Splendor,* and *River Venture,* have French balconies on the top two passenger decks, representing 78 percent of the staterooms. All cabins are outside, have twin beds that can convert to doubles, and include flat-screen TVs with in-room movies and CNN, hair dryers, and in-room safes. There are four 225-square-foot junior suites and one 330-square-foot owner's suite. The other staterooms are 165 square feet.

The *River Navigator* and *River Odyssey* were refurbished in 2013 and 2012 respectively and have somewhat similar accommodations. The *Navigator* has four 225-square-foot suites and one 300-square-foot owner's suite, and the *Odyssey* has eight 225-square-foot suites. Other cabins measure 150 square feet. Only cabins and suites on the top passenger deck have French balconies.

All the ships have three passenger decks, a main dining room with free wine at dinner, a multipurpose bar and lounge, a fitness room, ship-wide wireless Internet, a reading room, and a walking/jogging track and lounges on the sundeck. On the three newest ships, an elevator traverses the passenger decks, and a hydraulic chairlift accesses the open-air top deck. A keyboardist entertains nightly, and in selected ports, local entertainers are brought aboard.

*Courtesy Vantage Travel*

*Courtesy Vantage Travel*

# Chefs' Dinner

### Sailing, August 12th, 2013

## Appetizer by our Cold Galley Chef Armando
*"Magret de Canard Fumé sur les Lentilles Marinées et Sauce Moutarde Fig"*
Smoked Duck Breast on marinated Lentils and Fig-Mustard Sauce

## Soup by our Soup Chef Alex
*"Carotte et Orange Soupe au Gingembre et à la Coriander"*
Carrot and Orange Soup with Ginger and Cilantro

## Entrées by our Executive Chef Michal
*"Carré d'Agneau avec Croûte d'Herbes au Ratatouille Provençale"*
Herb crusted Rack of Lamb on Thyme Gravy
served with Rosemary Potato Gratin and Provencal Vegetable
### Or
## by our Chef Agus
*"Filet de Tilapia Grillé sur Feuilles d'Épinards Sautés"*
Broiled Filet of Tilapia on sautéed Leaf Spinach
Potato-Carrot Mousseline and spiced Orange Sauce
### Or
## Vegetarian by our Chef Jane
*"Aubergine Parmigiana"*
Breaded baked Eggplant layered with Tomato and Mozzarella Cheese

## Dessert by our Pastry Chefs Daniel & Mihai
*"Tarte aux Rhubarbe avec Sauce Lait de Poulet"*
Rhubarb Pie with Eggnog Sauce
### Or
Coupe de Glace "St. Tropez"
Strawberry Ice Cream with Melon Salad
### Or
*"Assiette de Fromage"*
Cheese Plate with Crackers and Fruits
### Or
Fresh Fruits of the Season

✿ - Vegetarian

*DAILY PROGRAM*

# CHATEAUNEUF-DU-PAPE/AVIGNON
## Wednesday, August 14th, 2013
*Dress Code for dinner: dressy*
*(no jeans or shorts, please)*

*Partly Cloudy*
*High: 85°*
*Low: 62°*

| | |
|---|---|
| 6:00 am – 7:00 am | Early Riser's Breakfast in the Latitude 52° Lounge and the Captain's Club |
| 7:00 am – 9:30 am | Enjoy your Breakfast in the Compass Rose Restaurant |
| | Color-coded departure by bus to Chateauneuf-du-Pape for a wine and chocolate tasting followed by a scenic drive |
| 9:00 am | green & yellow groups depart |
| 9:15 am | orange & blue groups depart |

**Please take your earphones and receivers**

| | |
|---|---|
| 12:00 noon approx. | The tour returns to the ship |
| **12:15 pm** | **All aboard!** |
| 12:30 pm | The ms River Discovery II departs Chateauneuf-du-Pape |
| 12:30 pm | Enjoy your Lunch in the Compass Rose Restaurant **Or** Light Lunch Buffet in the Captain's Club |
| 2:15 pm | Disembarkation briefing in the Latitude 52° Lounge (We kindly ask at least one member of your party to attend) |
| 2:30 pm approx. | The ms River Discovery II arrives in Avignon |
| 3:00 pm | Color coded departure for the walking tour of Avignon and visit of the Popes Palace |

1st green group departs     3rd orange group departs
2nd yellow group departs    4th blue group departs

**Please take your earphones and receivers**

| | |
|---|---|
| 6:00 pm | **Captain's Farewell Reception** in the Latitude 52° Lounge |
| 6:45 pm | Port talk about the following day in the Latitude 52° Lounge |
| 7:00 pm | **Captain's Farewell Dinner** in the Compass Rose Restaurant |
| After dinner | Enjoy a Gypsy night concert in the Latitude 52° Lounge |
| Afterwards | Music with our onboard musician Rado in the Latitude 52° Lounge |

## *Have a splendid day!*

**Please come and see us at the Hospitality Desk to discuss your future travel plans**

| Smoothie, Cocktails and Hot Drink of the Day: | | Suggested Movie: |
|---|---|---|
| **Carrot - Orange Smoothie** | **€ 5.00** | |
| **Vodka Tonic** | **€ 5.00** | **Les Miserables** |
| **Virgin Mimosa** | **€ 4.00** | |
| **Rüdesheim Coffee** | **€ 4.50** | |

*You will find the daily menu on the reverse side*

# VICTORIA CRUISES INC.

**57-08 39th Avenue**
**Woodside, NY 11377**
**(800) 348-8084; (212) 818-1680**
**Fax: (212) 818-9889**
**www.victoriacruises.com**

*Victoria Anna*: entered service in 2006; renovated in 2010; 6,200 GRT; 268-passenger capacity; 141 cabins; Chinese officers and crew with American, European, or Australian cruise directors; cruises on Yangtze River

*Victoria Grace* (formerly *Victoria Empress*): rebuilt 2012; 3,868 GRT; 198-passenger capacity; ninety-nine cabins; Chinese officers and crew with American, Australian, or European cruise directors; cruises on Yangtze River

*Victoria Jenna*: entered service in 2009; 10,000 GRT; 378-passenger capacity; 189 cabins; Chinese officers and crew with American, Australian, and/or European cruise directors; cruises on Yangtze River

*Victoria Katarina*: entered service in 2004; renovated in 2010; 5,780 GRT; 98 × 15 meters; 264-passenger capacity; 132 cabins; Chinese officers and crew with American, Australian, or European cruise directors; cruises on Yangtze River

*Victoria Lianna* (formerly *Victoria Queen*): rebuilt 2011; 4,587 GRT; 220-passenger capacity; 110 cabins; Chinese officers and crew with American, Australian, or European cruise directors; cruises on Yangtze River

*Victoria Selina* (formerly *Victoria Star*): rebuilt 2011; 4,587 GRT; 218-passenger capacity; 109 cabins; Chinese officers and crew and American, Australian, or European cruise directors; cruises on Yangtze River

*Victoria Sophia* (formerly *Victoria Prince*): rebuilt 2004; renovated in 2012; 4,587 GRT; 200-passenger capacity; 100 cabins; Chinese officers and crew with American, Australian, or European cruise directors; cruises on Yangtze River

(Medical facilities: P-1, EM, MS; OX; WC; L)

Victoria Cruises is an American company that operates downstream and upstream cruises between Chongqing and Yichang on the Yangtze River and Yichang/Chongqing round-trip cruises, with extended cruises to Shanghai, all of which pass by the picturesque Three Gorges region.

The single-seating dining room features Chinese cuisine as well as Western selections. All meals are buffet style. Except for the *Victoria Sophia*, the ships also feature an à la carte dining room with Western and Chinese cuisine at a $45 surcharge per day.

Although passengers are not on shore excursions, onboard activities include lectures and demonstrations relating to Chinese culture. There is also some form of entertainment nightly.

Standard cabins on the *Anna* measure 226 square feet; on the *Jenna*, 224 feet; on the *Sophia*, *Lianna*, and *Selina*, 211 square feet; on the *Katarina*, 206 square feet; and on the *Grace*, 157 square feet. Suites on the various ships range in size from 237 to 646 square feet. Each accommodation has lower twin berths (some of the larger suites have one queen bed), private bathroom with shower and bathtub, and TVs with HBO, CNN, and feature films. Most ships also offer three categories of suites with sitting areas. Ships are smoke free except for the outside observation deck. Facilities on the various vessels include dining halls, cocktail lounges, business centers, gift shops, libraries, fitness rooms, beauty salons, saunas, mah-jongg rooms, and observation decks.

One of the newer and larger ships, *Victoria Anna*, entered service in 2006 carrying 268 passengers. She includes two dining rooms, two elevators, and an entertainment center on the top deck. In 2009, the 8,000-ton, 378-passenger *Victoria Jenna* entered service as the largest cruise/riverboat on the Yangtze with similar facilities as those listed above for the *Victoria Anna*.

Itineraries offered include three-night/four-day downstream and four-night/five-day upstream cruises between Chongqing and Yichang, ranging in price from $880 to $2,560. The seven-day downstream/nine-day upstream cruises that continue to Shanghai range in price from $1,610 to $3,850, and the eight-day Chongqing/Yichang/Chonqing round-trip cruises range in price from $1,610 to $4,370.

Cruises that depart Chongqing at 9:00 p.m. with a shore excursion to Fengdu, or alternatively to Wanzhou, continue through the Qutang Gorge, Wu Gorge, the Xiling Gorge, and the Three Gorges Dam and offer an excursion on a tributary through the Small Three Gorges before disembarking in Yichang. The upstream cruise from Yichang reverses the itinerary. The round-trip cruise includes different shore excursions in each direction and adds tours of Yichang and New Zigui. An optional excursion to White Emperor City at Fengjie may be offered on select sailings. An excursion on upstream sailings called "Tribe of the Three Gorges" is offered, which includes local scenery and cultural performances near Yichang. Cruises that extend to Shanghai include excursions to Wuhan, Mount Huang, and Nanjing.

In 2011, the cruise line introduced the Executive Deck Program, available on all ships. The program includes superior cabin or suite accommodations on Executive Decks, a choice of two dining rooms on all ships, and a host of complimentary amenities, including morning coffee and tea service, Wi-Fi service in the Executive Lounge and lobby, Internet computer usage in the Executive Lounge or Yangtze Bar, laundry service, welcome fruit basket, nightly turn down service with printed daily itinerary, shoe shine service, exclusive shore excursions with groups of six or more, hot and cold drinks all day in the Executive Lounge, happy hour before dinner with wine, beer, soda and snacks in the Executive Lounge, house wine and beer offerings at dinner, and diet soda with dinner.

Pacific Delight, Ritz Tours, Orient Flexi-Pax, and other tour operators use these ships for their cruise/tour packages in China.

## Strong Points

The vessels are geared for a Western clientele yet offer a Chinese environment and a comfortable alternative to explore the Yangtze River.

*Victoria Anna, courtesy Victoria Cruises, Inc.*

Victoria Anna, *courtesy Victoria Cruises, Inc.*

Victoria Anna, *courtesy Victoria Cruises, Inc.*

Victoria Anna, *courtesy Victoria Cruises, Inc.*

# Dinner Menu 晚宴

**冷 菜 Cold Dishes**
泡菜　Yangtze Pickles
闵豆腐　Flavored Bean Curd
蒜泥黄瓜　Cucumber in Garlic Sauce
芝麻肉丝　Shredded Pork With Sesame
夫妻肺片　Chicken & Beef Slices With Hot Sauce

**汤 Soup**
维多利亚西湖汤 Victoria Beef Soup

**热菜 Hot Dishes**
宫保鸡丁　Diced Chicken with Peanuts
蒜香仔排　Garlic Spare Ribs
西芹炒牛肉　Stir-Fried Beef With Celery
菊花鱼　Sweet & Sour Fish
清炒菠菜　Stir-Fried Chinese Spinach
炸土豆饼　Deep-Fried Potato Cakes
什菜拌饭　Fried Rice & Vegetables

**甜点 Dessert**
南瓜饼　Pumpkin Cake
法式煎饼　French Puff-Crepes
新鲜水果　Seasonal Fruit Plate

---

# 欢迎宴会

**冷菜 Cold Dishes**
叉烧肉　Barbecued Pork
开心牛肉　Beef Slices
香油西芹　Celery With Sesame Oil
珊瑚雪莲　Lotus Roots
翠翅黄瓜　Cucumber

**汤 Soup**
什锦海鲜汤　Sea Food Soup

**热菜 Hot Dishes**
干烧武昌鱼　Dry Fried Wuchang Fish
芝士鸡排　Cheese Chicken with Eggplant
百花燕窝　Chicken, Beef & Shrimp in Bird's Nest
八宝石榴鲜　Egg Rolls with Pork & Vegetable
富贵肘子　Roast Pork Knuckle
香菇菜心　Mushrooms With Bok Choy
菜花烩香菇　Country Style Broccoli
菠萝炒饭　Fried Rice With Pineapple
刺猬金瓜　Pumpkin & Sticky Rice Buns

**甜点 Dessert**
苹果派　Apple Pie
冰淇淋　Ice Cream
新鲜水果　Seasonal Fruit Plate

*Courtesy Victoria Cruises, Inc.*

**VICTORIA CRUISES**

# Fengdu 丰都

| Saturday, Oct. 13, 2007 | | Day / Night | Prec. % |
|---|---|---|---|
| Day 4 | Rainy Periods | (°C) 25°/20° (°F) 77°/68° | 70% |

| | | |
|---|---|---|
| 6:00 AM | Early Bird coffee & tea service. | Yangtze Club, Deck 4 |
| 7:15 AM | Dr. Liu teaches the art of Tai Chi – shadow boxing. | Yangtze Club, Deck 4 |
| 7:45 AM | Buffet breakfast service begins. | Dynasty Dining Room, Deck 1 |

**8:45 AM** *Shore Excursion: The* ship is docked at Fengdu. Passengers go ashore to visit the "City of Ghosts", the #1 tourist attraction on the upper reaches of the Yangtze. The temple area on top of Ming Mountain pays tribute to the "King of the Underworld". A local guide introduces the legends surrounding Fengdu, as well as the many displays portraying interpretations of the Afterlife.

**Please Note:** There is a chair lift that can take you to near the top of the hill. (There are close to 100 stairs in stages after that). Return trip fare is 20 Yuan for the chair lift. If you prefer to walk, there over 400 stairs in total, just let your local guide know. Wear good walking shoes, and beware of ghosts!

| | | |
|---|---|---|
| 11:30 PM | Passengers return to the ship. | |
| 12:00 PM | Chinese Tea Culture Display. | Yangtze Club, Deck 4 |

---
### "BLOODY MARY TIME!!!"
☺ 30% off this popular cocktail any time before lunch ☺ YANGTZE BAR, Deck 4 ☺
**Special Drinks of the Day "Black Russian" and "Screwdriver" only 25 Yuan all day!**

---

| | | |
|---|---|---|
| 12:15 PM | Buffet lunch is served. | Dynasty Dining Room, Deck 1 |
| 1:30 PM | **MAHJONG LESSON** Learn the basics of China's favorite pastime in the deck 3 meeting room. | |
| 2:45 PM | *DUMPLING MAKING CLASS* – Learn the basics and watch live vegetable carving demonstrations with our chef in the Yangtze Club. | |
| 3:15 PM | *Afternoon Tea Time* – Tea & biscuits are served for one hour in the Yangtze Club. | |
| 3:45 PM | **"ARTISTS BAZAAR"** – Live demonstrations of traditional Chinese arts together in the Yangtze Club. | |
| 5:00 PM | *"China Through the Eyes of a Resident Foreigner"* – Join Kevin for an informal Q&A session regarding life in a changing society. | Yangtze Club, deck 4 |
| 6:00 PM | DVD SCREENING – Videographer Vincent plays the voyage DVD in the Yangtze Club. | |

---
### 6:00 PM – 7:00 PM
☺ "HAPPY HOUR" in the Yangtze Club ☺ All Drinks 30% off!!! ☺

---

**7:00 PM** Victoria Cruises Farewell Banquet is Served in the Dynasty Dining Room

(formal attire requested but not required)

**9 to 10 PM, its....** Open Floor Dance Nite!
*Choose your favorite dance music with our DJ and dance to your heart's content!*

---
Also, don the attire of the EMPRESS & EMPEROR of the Qing Dynasty and take home a photo souvenir!
We bring the costumes, you bring the camera! (8:30 – 9:30 PM, deck 3 meeting room)

---

(9:30 PM): In-house Movie – "Curse of the Yellow Flower" (Channel 13)

*Courtesy Victoria Cruises, Inc.*

# VIKING RIVER CRUISES, INC.

5700 Canoga Avenue, Suite 200
Woodland Hills, California 91367
(877) 66VIKING; (877) 668-4546
(818) 227-1237 Fax
www.vikingrivercruises.com
info@vikingrivercruises.com

*Viking Aeger, Viking Freya, Viking Idun, Viking Njord, Viking Odin, Viking Tor,* and *Viking Var*: entered service 2012; passenger capacity-190; 95 staterooms; International officers and crew; cruises on the rivers of Europe

*Viking Bragi, Viking Embla, Viking Forseti, Viking Rinda, Viking Skadi*: entered service 2013; passenger capacity 190; 95 staterooms; International officers and crew, cruises on the rivers of Europe

*Viking Alsvin, Viking Atla, VIking Baldur, Viking Buri, Viking Delling, Viking Eistla, Viking Gullvieg, Viking Idi, Viking Ingvi, Viking Heimdal, Viking Hermod, Viking Kvasir, Viking Lif*: entered service 2014; passenger capacity-190; 95 staterooms; International officers and crew; cruises on rivers of Europe.

*Viking Douro*: entered service in 2011; 261' long; 124-passenger capacity; 62 cabins; international officers and crew; cruises on Portugal's Douro River

*Viking Legend* and *Viking Prestige*: entered service 2009 and 2010 respectively; 189/188-passenger capacity; 98/97 staterooms; international officers and crew; cruises on the rivers of Europe

*Viking Sun* and *Viking Helvetia II*: entered service 2005 and 2006 respectively; 198-passenger capacity; 99 staterooms; International officers and crew; cruises on the rivers of Europe

*Viking Europe, Viking Neptune, Viking Pride,* and *Viking Spirit*: entered service in 2001, 2001, 2001, and 2001 respectively; 150-passenger capacity; 75 cabins; International officers and crew; cruises on rivers of Europe

*Viking Sky* and *Viking Danube*: entered service 1999; 150-passenger capacity; 75 cabins; international officers and crew; cruises rivers of Europe

### Ships Cruising in Russia and Ukraine:

*Viking Helgi*: entered service 1984, refurb. 2008; 210-passenger capacity
*Viking Ingvar*: entered service 1989, refurb. 2011; 210-passenger capacity
*Viking Lomonosov*: entered service 1975, refurb. 2003; 202-pasenger capacity

*Viking Peterhof:* entered service 1990, refurb. 2007; 212-passenger capacity
*Viking Truvor:* entered service 1989, refurb. 2009; 210-passenger capacity

### Ships Cruising in China:

*Viking Emerald:* entered service 2011; 256-passenger capacity; 128 staterooms; Chinese and European officers and crew; cruises on Yangtze River

Viking River Cruises was formed in 1997 by a Scandinavian and Dutch consortium. At that time, it purchased four Russian ships. Purchases continued, and by the end of 1999, the fleet had grown to fourteen ships. In March 2000, the company announced the purchase of KD River Cruises of Europe, adding an additional nine river vessels. At the same time, the company established U.S. headquarters in Los Angeles to meet the growing demand of U.S. travelers wishing to experience a cruise on one of Europe's colorful waterways. Subsequently, the company introduced eight all-new, modern river vessels, each accommodating about 150 passengers, and sold off some of the older ships. Commencing in 2012, Viking introduced its new fleet of "Longships." Over two years, fourteen of these vessels were constructed and entered service for the company. By the end of 2013, the line will operate twenty-three European river-cruise vessels, in addition to its ships on other rivers. Thirteen additional Longships entered service in 2014.

The cruise line offers passengers a variety of all-inclusive eight- to seventeen-night cruise and cruise/land packages on many of Europe's, Russia's, Ukraine's, and China's scenic rivers, including the Rhine, Danube, Elbe, Main, Moselle, Rhone and Saone, Seine, Holland's waterways, Russia's waterways, Ukraine's Dnieper, and the Yangtze. There is a land-based Egypt itinerary that includes a Nile cruise. Also available are land-based extensions to major cities. English is the onboard language and is spoken by the staff. Dining is always in an open, single-seating dining room with panoramic river views.

The *Viking Neptune, Viking Pride, Viking Spirit,* and *Viking Europe* entered service in 2001 and feature 170-square-foot outside cabins (standard cabins on bottom deck are 120 square feet) attractively appointed with a generous wardrobe and storage space, writing desks, televisions with CNN and BBC news, hair dryers, 115- and 220-watt electrical outlets, twin beds convertible to queens with European duvets, and small bathrooms with shower, toilet, and vanity. Sixty-three of the seventy-five cabins on each ship have large picture windows that open. There are no refrigerators or filled ice buckets; however, there are ice machines down the hall available to the guests. *Viking Sky* and *Viking Danube,* which entered service in 1999, are similar to these four ships, except four double cabins have bathtubs. Cabin size is from 145 to 151 square feet. There is a small indoor whirlpool and sauna and an elevator between the middle and upper decks.

All three meals are served open-seating in the main dining room with buffet options at breakfast. Lunch features a salad and sandwich bar, or you can order from a menu with at least two options for each course. Dinner is a multicourse meal, sometimes with a fixed menu and other times with two choices for a starter, main course, and dessert. Always offered are grilled steak, chicken, and Caesar salad. The wine list is quite limited and passengers are allowed to bring their own bottles into the dining room. Although a variety coffees and ice tea are available around the clock near the reception area, there is a significant charge for soft drinks, wines, alcoholic beverages, and espresso. Viking offers a Silver Spirits beverage package that covers soft drinks and alcoholic beverages for a rather steep fixed price, which varies by length of the itinerary.

Public areas are limited and include the main lounge and bar; a venue for all port lectures, socializing, and nightly piano music; a small not-very-well-stocked library; and an extensive sundeck with lounges, a covered area, and a few tables. There is a partial promenade deck around the ship and some e-mail facilities. Commencing in 2009, all European, Russian, and Ukrainian ships offer free Wi-Fi service on board. On most of the riverboats, there is no pool, Jacuzzi, sauna, or gym and no deck towels or bicycles.

The highlight of Viking River Cruises is the numerous well-organized, daily shore excursions that are included in the cruise fare. They sometimes include wine tastings and visits to world-renowned museums and historical sites.

In 2005 and 2006, Viking launched two sister ships, *Viking Sun* and *Viking Helvetia*. Each carries 198 guests; and staterooms on the upper deck have panoramic windows that have floor-to-ceiling sliding glass doors.

In 2009 and 2011 respectively, the cruise line's new, state-of-the-art river vessels, *Viking Legend*, and *Viking Prestige* entered service sailing the Rhine, Main, and Danube rivers. They carry 189/188 passengers in 98/97 staterooms, cabins, and suites, respectively. All have hotel-style beds, private panoramic windows with sliding glass doors (on the top two passenger decks only), twenty-six-inch flat-screen TVs, safes, hair dryers, and refrigerators. There are two 340-square-foot suites on each ship. We cruised on the *Viking Legend* during the summer of 2011 and were impressed with the service and the fact that she was more modern and attractively furnished than the other vessels. Dining is the same on all of the Viking riverboats.

In 2012, Viking launched six 190-passenger sister ships: *Viking Aeger, Viking Embla, Viking Freya, Viking Idun, Viking Njord,* and *Viking Odin.* These are the first of Viking's Longships, a new class of vessel within the fleet that has a sophisticated and revolutionary design coupled with high-tech and patent-pending features. In 2013 and 2014, eighteen additional long ships were launched. Each ship has two 445-square-foot Explorer Suites which include a bedroom with a French balcony and a separate living room that leads out to a wraparound veranda with 270-degree views.

Seven Veranda Suites measure 275 square feet with a veranda in the living room and a French balcony in the bedroom. Thirty-nine 205-square-foot Veranda Staterooms have full-size verandas; twenty-two French Balcony Staterooms measure 135 square feet and sport French balconies; and twenty-five standard staterooms on the lowest passenger deck have half-height windows and measure 150 square feet. Three-quarters of the staterooms on these ships have a full veranda, French balcony, or both. (Technically, these are not French balconies since passengers cannot step out onto them.)

The ships feature state-of-the-art additions such as solar panels, an organic herb garden, and an Aquavit Terrace at the bow of the ships where floor-to-ceiling glass windows slide open to provide an indoor-outdoor experience where guests can relax, enjoy the scenery, and dine alfresco. The nomenclature "long ships" does not refer to the length of the ship, but is a reference to ships in the days of the Nordic Vikings. Actually, the ships are the same length as Viking's other vessels.

Viking has a big presence on the waterways in Russia. *Viking Helgi* (formerly *Surkov*), *Viking Truvor* (formerly *Kirov*), and *Viking Ingvar* (formerly *Pakhomov*) were part of the twenty-seven-ship "302" series, designed to offer visitors the very best Russia cruise ship experience. *Viking Helgi* was built in 1984 and was fully refurbished in 2008; *Viking Truvor* was built in 1987 and fully refurbished in 2009; *Viking Ingvar* was built in 1990 and fully refurbished in 2011. These ships now carry 210 guests in two 290-square-foot suites and 104 140- to 160-square-foot staterooms, all of which meet the latest European standards of comfort and elegance, with all hotel-style beds (except for the two single staterooms) and amenities like twenty-six-inch flat-panel TVs with CNN and other English-language programs, in-room refrigerators, telephones, safes, hairdryers, and both 110 and 220 volt outlets. Public areas include three walk-around, open-air promenade decks, a sundeck with shaded sitting areas, and observation lounge, two bars, a library, boutique, an elevator, a restaurant with panoramic views, and a doctor on board.

The *Viking Duoro* entered service in 2011 featuring cruises on Portugal's Douro River. Of the sixty-two staterooms, three are considered junior suites at 226 to 237 square feet, and fifty-nine others vary in size between 140 and 161 square feet. Each accommodation has hotel-style beds with optional twin-bed configurations, a French balcony, telephone, safe, hair dryer, bottled water (replenished daily), flat-panel satellite TV, and bathrobe and slippers upon request. Voltage is 220.

In 2004, the cruise line began offering cruises on China's Yangtze River and now offers three Chinese itineraries that combine exceptional land tours with six- to ten-night Yangtze River cruises. The two original vessels that offered cruises on that river, the *Viking Century Star*, and the *Viking Century Sky* are no longer with the fleet.

In 2011, the cruise line introduced a new ship on the Yangtze, the 256-passenger *Viking Emerald*, featuring five decks with two elevators; 2 605-square-foot Presidential suites; 14 suites; 4 junior suites; 108 deluxe staterooms; an observation lounge and bar; a site for entertainment, lectures, and cocktail hour; a large open-seating dining room serving Western and Chinese cuisine (the ship carries both a European and a Chinese head chef); a lobby/information area; a fitness center; a sauna; a massage room; a doctor's office (with a Chinese doctor); four computers, as well as Internet connections; a small boutique; a tailor; a hairdresser; and a partially covered sundeck and bar, an excellent location from which to view the scenery.

Each of the 128 all-balcony, air-conditioned staterooms and suites, has a private bathroom with a shower, toilet, and sink, hotel-style beds, TV with CNN and movies, a phone, a hair dryer, small complimentary bottles of water and a tea and coffee maker. All accommodations open up through glass doors to balconies with two chairs. The 108 deluxe staterooms measure 250 square feet; the four junior suites 260 square feet and the 14 full suites 305 square feet.

The cruise line offers Yangtze River land and cruise packages from twelve to seventeen days and visits Beijing, Xian, Shanghai, and the Yangtze. An alternative itinerary features three nights in Lhasa, Tibet. In addition, on any Chinese cruise tour, travelers can add a four-night shoppers' paradise extension to Hong Kong and Guilin.

On my cruise in 2006, I found the preparation, presentation, and imagination of the kitchen exceptional. Service throughout the ship is very attentive and friendly; however, passengers must make allowances for the staff's somewhat limited familiarity with English and requests of Western passengers. The Chinese tour escorts are also exceptional and stay with their group of passengers from the moment they disembark the plane until they return home, assisting with baggage, tours, and all special requests. The ships are very modern, spotlessly clean, and far more comfortable than those of the other riverboats that cruise the Yangtze.

The cruise line has ordered two oceangoing ships for delivery in 2014 and 2015 which will be the first ships in the new Viking Ocean Cruise brand. In addition, Viking is considering operating a riverboat on United States rivers.

## Strong Points

Scenic riverboat experience on some of Europe's, Russia's, Ukraine's, and China's most desired rivers and waterways on modern, comfortable vessels. The more recently built river ships offer larger accommodations, a more modern décor and many innovations previously not available on non-oceangoing vessels. Viking's aggressive advertising campaigns have enabled the company to build and fill more ships than any other riverboat company.

*Viking longship, courtesy of Viking River Cruises*

*Veranda suite on longships, courtesy of Viking River Cruises*

*Sundeck on longships, courtesy of Viking River Cruises*

*Lounge on longships, courtesy of Viking River Cruises*

*Aquavit Terrace on longships, courtesy of Viking River Cruises*

*Author with officers of Viking Panorama*

# DINNER MENU

*Monday, September 10, 2012*

**FIRST COURSE**

Salmon Caviar Potato Cake
classic remoulade, micro greens salad, citrus dressing

Parma Ham & Ricotta Flan
white asparagus, balsamic syrup, extra virgin olive oil

Champagne Risotto & Grilled Shrimp
fresh chanterelles, lobster nage

Roasted Forest Mushroom Veloute
crisp bacon lardoons, truffle sabayon

**MAIN COURSE**

Tournedo Rossini Sauteed Foie Gras
glaced fresh vegetables, rissole potatoes, madeira sauce

Baked Lobster Thermidor
sauteed young spinach, wild rice pilaf

Crisp Polenta with Eggplant & Olive Relish
braised fennel and oven dried tomatoes

**DESSERTS**

Espresso & Orange Panna Cotta
warm chocolate soufflé cake, bitter sweet chocolate sauce

Warm Blackberry Tart
pistachio crème brulee, blackberry cabernet sorbet

Fresh Fruits strawberries

Ice Cream coconut, strawberry

Sorbets pineapple

Sauces hot chocolate, butterscotch, mixed berry

 Regional Specialty

**CHEESE PLATE** *The following cheese plate is accompanied by caramelized walnuts, date cake, roasted almonds, dried fruit and breads*

## Roquefort
French; sheep's milk, soft, blue creamy,
salty and strong aroma – honey apple syrup

## Langres
French; cow's milk, wonderful flavor,
washed with champagne brandy – quince jam

## Drunken Goat
Spain; goat's milk, semi-hard, sweet and smooth,
has been soaked in double wine – watermelon marmalade

**ALWAYS AVAILABLE** *The following classic fare entrees are accompanied by fresh sautéed vegetables and baked potato*

## Caesar's Salad
parmesan shavings, garlic croutons

## Grilled Filet of Salmon
dill butter

## Pan Roasted Chicken Breast
rosemary gravy

## Charbroiled New York Cut Sirloin Steak
herb butter

**SUGGESTED WINES** Duckhorn Sauvignon Blanc
Napa Valley, USA 2010  $78

Berlinger Merlot
Napa Valley, USA 2001  $124

*Menu, courtesy of Viking River Cruises*

# VIKING DAILY

## Thursday, May 3rd, 2012

Today's Weather: Overcast
8 – 16 °C / 46 – 61 °F

**Café Breakfast:** Coffee, juice and pastries are offered in front of the Viking Lounge.

**Morning Exercise:** Join your Program Manager Renata for light Qui Gong exercise.

**Anchors Aweigh!** *Viking Sun* leaves Rüdesheim for Braubach.

**Breakfast:** Start your day with a generous breakfast buffet served in the Viking Restaurant.

Enjoy sailing the Rhine River with a commentary by your Program Director Claudia.

*Viking Sun* arrives in Braubach, as soon as all excursion guests have departed **Anchors Aweigh!** as *Viking Sun* leaves Braubach for Koblenz

**Shore Excursion:** Bus ride to Marksburg Castle and guided visit inside. This tour includes walks over cobblestones, steps and uneven ground; for passenger safety and enjoyment, we recommend you be in a very good physical condition to participate fully in this castle visit.

*Viking Sun* arrives in Koblenz

**Lunch:** Our service team welcomes you for lunch in the Viking Restaurant. Enjoy!

**Café Lunch:** We are serving a buffet-style lunch for you in the Viking Lounge.

**Koblenz Walk:** Join your Program Manager for a stroll.

**Galley Visit:** Meet at the reception and enjoy the galley tour. Please sign up at the reception desk.

**Lecture:** Join our external lecturer Dr. Markus Urban for a lecture about the European Union today in the Viking Lounge.

**Cocktail Hour:** Try one of our special cocktails and listen to live music by our musician Dimo in the Viking Lounge.

**Daily Briefing:** Join fellow passengers in the Viking Lounge for an information briefing by your Program Director Claudia.

**International Dinner:** Chef de Cuisine Christiaan and Maître d'Hotel Enio invite you for the Dinner in the Viking Restaurant. Bon appétit!

**Evening Entertainment:** Mingle with fellow passengers for an after dinner drink while enjoying music from the 50& 60's. We have a special cocktail created for tonight called "Red River Rock".

## TODAY'S MOVIES

09:00 AM, 11:00 AM, 01:00 PM,03:00 PM, 05:00 PM, 07:00 PM, 09:00 PM and 11:00 PM

*Hindenburg*  Length: 89 min  Channel: 8

09:00 AM, 11:00 AM, 01:00 PM,03:00 PM, 05:00 PM, 07:00 PM, 09:00 PM and 11:00 PM

*Shelter*  Length: 120 min  Channel: 9

*Daily program, courtesy of Viking River Cruises*

# Chapter Eleven

# Star Awards and Ship Ratings
# in Specific Categories

Because the quality of food, service, and entertainment as well as the general physical condition of ships is constantly changing, it is risky to attempt to compare or rate cruise ships. Any such attempt must reflect a great deal of personal preference and may be somewhat undependable inasmuch as quality can vary from cruise to cruise on the same ship due to a change in chefs, staff, or company policy. In fact, the quality can even change between the date of this writing and the time you are reading this book.

However, travel agents, potential cruisers, and the cruise industry in general have come to rely on travel writers' ratings and opinions. Having a profound desire to make this guide the most helpful and most valuable cruise guide available, I have succumbed to peer pressure and attempted to rate the ships as definitively as possible.

A system of "Star Awards" (overall ratings) will be found below and after each ship listed previously in chapter 11. In addition, ratings in eleven specific categories will be found for at least one ship from each major cruise line. Again, I must emphasize that these are my personal, subjective opinions, and you may disagree with them after you have cruised on the ships being rated. An intelligent traveler should not take the ratings of any guide as gospel. Obviously, every reviewer has his personal preferences and prejudices that may or may not coincide with your own.

## Explanation of Star Awards

Since all ships are not competing for the same potential passengers, it would be unfair to make overall comparisons of ships with vastly different price structures. Obviously, a ship charging $600 to $1,000 per day per person for an average cabin can afford to give its affluent customers more than one charging $150. Therefore, the various vessels have been divided into four major market categories. As was pointed out in chapter 2, pricing policies of cruise lines are confusing, if not deceptive. Therefore, my division into major market categories is based on not only published fares but also onboard costs, included the amenities, the air-sea packages, the economic passenger market the line seeks to attract, and the market it actually does attract.

## Category A—Deluxe

"Black star awards" are given to ships competing for business at the top of the market for the affluent, mature traveler whose prime consideration is not cost: minimum cabin in excess of $400 per person per day, average cabin approximately $500 to $700 per person per day, and top suites may go from $750 to $1,500 per person per day.

## Category B—Premium

"Crisscrossed star awards" are given to ships competing for business between the middle- and top-priced cruise markets for the upper-middle-class segment: minimum cabin in excess of $300 per person per day, average cabin approximately $350 to $450 per person per day, and suites may go from $450 to $750 per person per day.

## Category C—Standard/Mass Market

"Diagonal star awards" are given to ships competing for business in the middle-priced cruise markets for travelers looking for bargains without sacrificing the total cruise experience: minimum cabin in excess of $100 per person per day, average cabin approximately $175 to $275 per person per day, and suites may go from $350 to $600 per person per day.

## Category D—Economy

"White star awards" are given to ships competing for business in the economy cruise market for singles, younger cruisers, and bargain hunters wishing to experience a good time on a cruise but willing to sacrifice comfort, food, and service for price savings: minimum cabin approximately $90 per person per day and average cabin approximately $100 to $150 per person per day.

*Note:* The rates referred are based on published prices. In reality, almost every cruise line offers an array of discounted fares that may average considerably less than the official published fare.

Some ships and cruise lines overlap categories and therefore have been assigned "split designations." An "A/B" (black star/crisscross star) category reflects a ship that provides a product geared to travelers who prefer a luxury vessel at a lower price without some of the amenities or bells and whistles as are included on the pure luxury vessels.

A "B/C" (crisscross star/diagonal star) category is reserved for ships that cannot quite be described as premium because of condition, age, décor, or facilities yet provides passengers a higher-level cruise experience than those in the mass-market division.

An award of six stars in any given market category—A, B, C, or D—represents overall excellence in dining, service, accommodations, entertainment, facilities, amenities, itineraries, condition of the ship, and creature comfort relative to the particular market category. We have given a rating of six-plus stars to a limited number of luxury ships where the attention to passenger comfort and satisfaction is so extraordinary as to entitle these vessels to special recognition. Five stars represent that the vessel is very good in most areas, although it may be excellent or average in some. Three to four stars denote a ship that is average to mediocre in most areas. Two stars are reserved for those ships that are well below average in most areas, and one star suggests readers should have second thoughts before booking passage.

Because the ships have first been divided into market categories based on price, amenities, and clientele, it would not be accurate to compare ratings for ships in different market categories. A five-star award given a ship in Category A does not necessarily mean that the ship offers less overall than a six-star award given vessels in Categories B, C, or D. Be certain you compare apples with apples.

A deluxe-category ship is expected to perform at a higher level than a premium or mass-market category vessel; therefore, the standard of excellence required to receive high ratings for the latter category is less stringent. Be careful not to compare our ratings with those in other cruise guides. Some authors have chosen to use anywhere from three to ten stars, ribbons, anchors, and so on or opt for a hundred-point evaluation system. The reader must be aware of the range of categories used by each reviewer in order to make a valid comparison. (Be advised that most of the smaller riverboats and barges that do not offer a full cruise program have not been rated in this chapter; some ships that have recently changed ownership or that are not marketed in the United States also have not been rated.)

*Courtesy of Silversea Cruises*

*Note:* "N/A" indicates that the tonnage was not made available by the cruise line. "N/R" indicates that ship was not rated due to changes that have occurred since most recent investigation of ship or author has not recently sailed on ship.

## Alphabetical listing of cruise ships with tonnage, market category, and ratings.

| Name of Ship | Cruise Line | Tonnage (GRT) | Market Category | Ratings |
|---|---|---|---|---|
| Abercrombie | Grand Circle Cruises | 280 | N/R | N/R |
| Absolute 2 | France Cruises | N/A | N/R | N/R |
| Adonia | P&O Cruises | 30,277 | B | 5 |
| Adrienne | French Country Waterways | 250 | A/B | N/R |
| Adventure of the Seas | Royal Caribbean | 138,279 | C | 5+ |
| Aegean Odyssey | Voyages Antiquity | 11,563 | N/R | N/R |
| AIDAAura | AIDA Cruises | 42,289 | C | N/R |
| AIDABella | AIDA Cruises | 69,203 | C | N/R |
| AIDABlu | AIDA Cruises | 71,100 | C | N/R |
| AIDACara | AIDA Cruises | 38,557 | C | N/R |
| AIDADiva | AIDA Cruises | 69,203 | C | N/R |
| AIDALuna | AIDA Cruises | 69,203 | C | N/R |
| AIDAMar | AIDA Cruises | 71,100 | C | N/R |
| AIDASol | AIDA Cruises | 71,100 | C | N/R |
| AIDAVita | AIDA Cruises | 42,289 | C | N/R |
| Akademik Ioffe | Quark Expeditions | N/A | N/R | N/R |
| Akademik Sergey | Quark Expeditions | N/A | N/R | N/R |
| Allegria | France Cruises | N/A | N/R | N/R |
| Allure of the Seas | Royal Caribbean | 225,282 | C | N/R |
| Alouette | European Waterways | N/A | N/R | N/R |
| Amabello | AMAWaterways | N/A | N/R | N/R |
| Amacello | AMAWaterways | N/A | N/R | N/R |
| Amadagio | AMAWaterways | N/A | N/R | N/R |
| Amadante | AMAWaterways | N/A | N/R | N/R |
| Amadeus Brilliant | Luftner River Cruises | 1,566 | N/R | N/A |
| Amadeus Classic | Luftner River Cruises | 1,560 | N/R | N/R |
| Amadeus Danubia | Luftner River Cruises | N/A | N/R | N/R |
| Amadeus Diamond | Luftner River Cruises | 2,000 | N/R | N/R |
| Amadeus I | Luftner River Cruises | 1,560 | N/R | N/R |
| Amadeus Elegant | Luftner River Cruises | 1,566 | N/R | N/R |
| Amadeus Princess | Luftner River Cruises | 1,560 | N/R | N/R |
| Amadeus Rhapsody | Luftner River Cruises | 1,566 | N/R | N/R |
| Amadeus Royal | Luftner River Cruises | 1,566 | N/R | N/R |
| Amadeus Symphony | Luftner River Cruises | N/A | N/R | N/R |
| Amadolce | AMAWaterways | N/A | N/R | N/R |
| Amalegro | AMAWaterways | N/A | N/R | N/R |
| AmaLotus | AMA Waterways | N/A | N/R | N/R |
| Amalyra | AMAWaterways | N/A | N/R | N/R |

| | | | | |
|---|---|---|---|---|
| *Amaryllis* | European Waterways | N/A | N/R | N/R |
| *Amaverde* | AMA Waterways | N/A | N/R | N/R |
| *American Glory* | American Cruise Line | N/A | B/C | N/R |
| *American Spirit* | American Cruise Line | 2,000 | B/C | N/R |
| *American Star* | American Cruise Line | 2,000 | B/C | N/R |
| *Amsterdam* | Holland America Line | 62,735 | B | 5+ |
| *Anjodi* | European Waterways | N/A | N/R | N/R |
| *Antoinette* | Uniworld | N/A | A/B | 6 |
| *Aqua Aria* | Aqua Expeditions | N/A | N/R | N/R |
| *Aqua Expedition* | Aqua Expeditions | N/A | N/R | N/R |
| *Aqua Marina* | Louis Cruise Line | 23,149 | N/R | N/R |
| *Arcadia* | P&O Cruises | 83,000 | B | N/R |
| *Arion* | Classical Int'l Cruises | 6,000 | D | N/R |
| *Arkona* | Arkona Touristik | 18,519 | N/R | N/R |
| *A'Rosa* | Arosa River Cruises | 3,500 | N/R | N/R |
| *A'Rosa Bella* | Arosa River Cruises | 3,500 | N/R | N/R |
| *A'Rosa Brava* | Arosa River Cruises | 3,500 | N/R | N/R |
| *A'Rosa Donna* | Arosa River Cruises | 3,500 | N/R | N/R |
| *A'Rosa Lana* | Arosa River Cruises | 3,500 | N/R | N/R |
| *A'Rosa Mia* | Arosa River Cruises | 3,500 | N/R | N/R |
| *A'Rosa Riva* | Arosa River Cruises | 3,500 | N/R | N/R |
| *A'Rosa Stella* | Arosa River Cruises | 3,500 | N/R | N/R |
| *A'Rosa Viva* | Arosa River Cruises | 3,500 | N/R | N/R |
| *Artemis* | P&O Cruises | 44,248 | B | N/R |
| *Asuka II* | NYK Cruises | 49,400 | A | N/R |
| *Asuka* | NYK Cruises | 28,717 | B | N/R |
| *Athena* | Classical Int'l and Page and Moy | 16,000 | D | N/R |
| *Athos* | European Waterways | N/A | N/R | N/R |
| *Aurora* | P&O Cruises | 76,000 | B | N/R |
| *Ausonia* | Louis Cruise Line | 12,609 | D | N/R |
| *Avalon Affinity* | Avalon Waterways | 2,150 | N/R | N/R |
| *Avalon Angkor* | Avalon Waterways | 2,150 | N/R | N/R |
| *Avalon Creativity* | Avalon Waterways | 2,150 | N/R | N/R |
| *Avalon Felicity* | Avalon Waterways | 2,150 | N/R | N/R |
| *Avalon Imagery* | Avalon Waterways | 2,150 | N/R | N/R |
| *Avalon Luminary* | Avalon Waterways | 2,150 | N/R | N/R |
| *Avalon Panorama* | Avalon Waterways | 2,150 | N/R | N/R |
| *Avalon Scenery* | Avalon Waterways | 2,150 | N/R | N/R |
| *Avalon Tapestry* | Avalon Waterways | 2,150 | N/R | N/R |
| *Avalon Tranquility* | Avalon Waterways | 2,150 | N/R | N/R |
| *Avalon Visionary* | Avalon Waterways | 2,150 | N/R | N/R |
| *Avalon Vista* | Avalon Waterways | 2,150 | N/R | N/R |
| *Awani Dream 2* | Awani Cruises | 17,593 | D | N/R |

| | | | | |
|---|---|---|---|---|
| *Azamara Journey* | Azamara | 30,277 | A/B | 6 |
| *Azamara Quest* | Azamara | 30,277 | A/B | 6 |
| *Azura* | P&O Cruises | 116,000 | B | N/R |
| *Bahamas Celebration* | Celebration Cruises | 35,855 | D | 4+ |
| *Bali Sea Dancer* | Classical Cruises | 4,000 | N/R | N/R |
| *Balmoral* | Fred. Olsen Cruise Line | 34,242 | C | N/R |
| *Black Prince* | Page and Moy | 11,209 | C/D | N/R |
| *Black Watch* | Fred. Olsen Cruise Line | 28,492 | C/D | N/R |
| *Bonheur* | France Cruises | N/A | N/R | N/R |
| *Boudicca* | Fred. Olsen Cruise Line | 25,000 | C | N/R |
| *Braemar* | Fred. Olsen Cruise Line | 19,089 | C | N/R |
| *Bremen* | Hapag-Lloyd | 6,752 | B/C | N/R |
| *Brilliance of the Seas* | Royal Caribbean | 90,090 | C | 5 |
| *Caledonian Star* | Special Expeditions | 3,095 | N/R | N/R |
| *Calypso* | Louis Cruise Line/Thomson | 11,162 | D | N/R |
| *Captain Cook's Explorer* | Captain Cook Cruise | 1,160 | N/R | N/R |
| *Caribbean Princess* | Princess Cruises | 113,000 | B | 5+ |
| *Carnival Breeze* | Carnival Cruise Lines | 130,000 | C | 5+ |
| *Carnival Conquest* | Carnival Cruise Lines | 110,000 | C | 5 |
| *Carnival Dream* | Carnival Cruise Lines | 130,000 | C | 5+ |
| *Carnival Ecstasy* | Carnival Cruise Lines | 70,367 | C | 4 |
| *Carnival Elation* | Carnival Cruise Lines | 70,367 | C | 4+ |
| *Carnival Fantasy* | Carnival Cruise Lines | 70,367 | C | 4 |
| *Carnival Fascination* | Carnival Cruise Lines | 70,367 | C | 4+ |
| *Carnival Freedom* | Carnival Cruise Lines | 110,000 | C | 5 |
| *Carnival Glory* | Carnival Cruise Lines | 110,000 | C | 5 |
| *Carnival Imagination* | Carnival Cruise Lines | 70,367 | C | 4+ |
| *Carnival Inspiration* | Carnival Cruise Lines | 70,367 | C | 4+ |
| *Carnival Legend* | Carnival Cruise Lines | 88,500 | C | 5 |
| *Carnival Liberty* | Carnival Cruise Lines | 110,000 | C | 5 |
| *Carnival Magic* | Carnival Cruise Lines | 130,000 | C | 5+ |
| *Carnival Miracle* | Carnival Cruise Lines | 88,500 | C | 5 |
| *Carnival Paradise* | Carnival Cruise Lines | 70,367 | C | 4+ |
| *Carnival Pride* | Carnival Cruise Lines | 88,500 | C | 5 |
| *Carnival Sensation* | Carnival Cruise Lines | 70,367 | C | 4+ |
| *Carnival Spirit* | Carnival Cruise Lines | 88,500 | C | 5 |
| *Carnival Splendor* | Carnival Cruise Lines | 113,300 | C | 5 |
| *Carnival Sunshine* | Carnival Cruise Lines | 101,353 | C | 5 |
| *Carnival Triumph* | Carnival Cruise Lines | 102,000 | C | 5 |
| *Carnival Valor* | Carnival Cruise Lines | 110,000 | C | 5 |
| *Carnival Victory* | Carnival Cruise Lines | 102,000 | C | 5 |
| *Caroline* | France Cruises | N/A | N/R | N/R |
| *Celebrity Century* | Celebrity Cruises | 71,545 | B | 5 |

| | | | | |
|---|---|---|---|---|
| *Celebrity Constellation* | Celebrity Cruises | 91,000 | B | 5+ |
| *Celebrity Eclipse* | Celebrity Cruises | 122,000 | B | 5++ |
| *Celebrity Equinox* | Celebrity Cruises | 122,000 | B | 5++ |
| *Celebrity Infinity* | Celebrity Cruises | 91,000 | B | 5+ |
| *Celebrity Millennium* | Celebrity Cruises | 91,000 | B | 5+ |
| *Celebrity Reflection* | Celebrity Cruises | 126,000 | B | 5++ |
| *Celebrity Silhouette* | Celebrity Cruises | 126,000 | B | 5++ |
| *Celebrity Solstice* | Celebrity Cruises | 122,000 | B | 5++ |
| *Celebrity Summit* | Celebrity Cruises | 91,000 | B | 5+ |
| *Celebrity Xpedition* | Celebrity Cruises | 2,329 | B | N/R |
| *C'est la Vie* | France Cruises | N/A | N/R | N/R |
| *Clair de Lune* | France Cruises | N/A | N/R | N/R |
| *Clelia II* | Classical Cruises | 4,077 | B | N/R |
| *Clipper Adventurer* | Quark Expeditions | 4,364 | N/R | N/R |
| *Club Med II* | Club Med Cruises | 14,000 | B | 4+ |
| *Columbus 2* | Hapag-Lloyd | 30,277 | B | N/R |
| *Coral Princess* | Princess Cruises | 92,000 | B | 5 |
| *Coral Princess* | Captain Cook Cruises | N/A | N/R | N/R |
| *Coral Princess II* | Captain Cook Cruises | N/A | N/R | N/R |
| *Coral* | Louis Cruises Line | 14,000 | D | N/R |
| *Costa Allegra* | Costa Cruise Lines | 28,500 | C/D | N/R |
| *Costa Atlantica* | Costa Cruise Lines | 86,000 | C | 5 |
| *Costa Classica* | Costa Cruise Lines | 53,000 | C | 4 |
| *Costa Deliziosa* | Costa Cruise Lines | 92,650 | C | 5 |
| *Costa Fascinosa* | Costa Cruise Lines | 114,500 | C | 5 |
| *Costa Favolosa* | Costa Cruise Lines | 114,500 | C | 5 |
| *Costa Fortuna* | Costa Cruise Lines | 103,000 | C | 5 |
| *Costa Luminosa* | Costa Cruise Lines | 92,600 | C | 5 |
| *Costa Magica* | Costa Cruise Lines | 103,000 | C | 5 |
| *Costa Marina* | Costa Cruise Lines | 26,600 | C/D | 3+ |
| *Costa Mediterranea* | Costa Cruise Lines | 86,000 | C | 5 |
| *Costa Pacifica* | Costa Cruise Lines | 114,500 | C | 5 |
| *Costa NeoRomantica* | Costa Cruise Lines | 56,000 | C | 4+ |
| *Costa Serena* | Costa Cruise Lines | 114,500 | C | N/R |
| *Costa Victoria* | Costa Cruise Lines | 75,000 | C | 4 |
| *Costa Voyager* | Costa Cruise Lines | 25,000 | C | 5 |
| *Crown Princess* | Princess Cruises | 113,000 | B | 5+ |
| *Crystal Serenity* | Crystal Cruises | 68,870 | A | 6+ |
| *Crystal Symphony* | Crystal Cruises | 51,044 | A | 6+ |
| *Crystal* | Louis Cruise Line | 25,611 | D | N/R |
| *Danubia* | Luftner River Cruises | N/A | N/R | N/R |
| *Dawn Princess* | Princess Cruises | 77,000 | B | 5 |
| *Deutschland* | Peter Deilmann Cruises | 22,400 | B | 5+ |

| | | | | |
|---|---|---|---|---|
| Diamond Princess | Princess Cruises | 116,000 | B | 5+ |
| Discovery | Voyages of Discovery | 20,186 | C | N/R |
| Disney Dream | Disney Cruise Line | 130,000 | B | N/R |
| Disney Fantasy | Disney Cruise Line | 130,000 | B | N/R |
| Disney Magic | Disney Cruise Line | 83,000 | B | 5+ |
| Disney Wonder | Disney Cruise Line | 83,000 | B | 5+ |
| Donaustar | Luftner River Cruises | 1,550 | N/R | N/R |
| Douro Spirit | Uniworld | N/A | N/R | N/R |
| Elizabeth | France Cruises | N/A | N/R | N/R |
| Emerald Princess | Princess Cruises | 113,000 | B | 5+ |
| Emerald | Thomson Cruises | 26,431 | D | N/R |
| Emma | France Cruises | N/A | N/R | N/R |
| Empress | Pullmantur | 48,563 | C | N/R |
| Enchante | European Waterways | N/A | N/R | N/R |
| Enchantment of the Seas | Royal Caribbean | 82,910 | C | 5 |
| Esperance | France Cruises | N/A | N/R | N/R |
| Estella | France Cruises | N/A | N/R | N/R |
| Etoile | France Cruises | N/A | N/R | N/R |
| Eurodam | Holland America Line | | | |
| Europa | Hapag-Lloyd | 28,890 | A | |
| German-speaking guests 6; others 5+ | | | | |
| Europa 2 | Hapag-Lloyd | 40,000 | A | |
| German-speaking guests 6+; others 5+ | | | | |
| Explorer of the Seas | Royal Caribbean | 138,279 | C | 5+ |
| Fifty Years of Victory | Quark Expeditions | N/A | N/R | N/R |
| Fiji Princess | Blue Lagoon Cruises | N/A | N/R | N/R |
| Finnmarken | Hurtigruten | 15,000 | N/R | N/R |
| Fleur de Lys | European Waterways | N/A | N/R | N/R |
| Fram | Hurtigruten | 12,700 | A/B | N/R |
| Freedom of the Seas | Royal Caribbean | 154,407 | C | 5+ |
| FTI Berlin | FTI Cruises | 9,570 | N/R | N/R |
| Fuji Maru | Mitsui OSK | 23,340 | N/R | N/R |
| Funchal | Classical Int'l Cruises | 9,562 | D | N/R |
| Giselle | Uniworld | N/A | N/R | N/R |
| Golden Odyssey | France Cruises | N/A | N/R | N/R |
| Golden Princess | Princess Cruises | 109,000 | B | 5 |
| Grand American Queen | Great American | 3,707 | B | N/R |
| Grand Celebration | Ibero Cruceros | 47,262 | C/D | N/R |
| Grand Holiday | Ibero Cruceros | 46,053 | C/D | N/R |
| Grand Mistral | Ibero Cruceros | 47,900 | N/R | N/R |
| Grand Princess | Princess Cruises | 107,500 | B | 5 |
| Grand Voyager | Ibero Cruceros | 25,000 | C/D | N/R |

| | | | | |
|---|---|---|---|---|
| *Grande Caribe* | American Canadian Caribbean Line | 98 | C/D | N/R |
| *Grande Mariner* | American Canadian Caribbean Line | 98 | C/D | N/R |
| *Grandeur of the Seas* | Royal Caribbean | 73,817 | C | 5 |
| *Hanseatic* | Hapag-Lloyd | 8,378 | A/B | N/R |
| *Hebridean Princess* | Hebridean Island | 2,112 | N/R | N/R |
| *Hirondelle* | European Waterways | N/A | N/R | N/R |
| *Horizon II* | French Country Waterways | 190 | A/B | N/R |
| *Imagine* | France Cruises | N/A | N/R | N/R |
| *Independence of the Seas* | Royal Caribbean | 154,407 | C | 5+ |
| *Independence* | American Cruise Line | 3,000 | B | 3 |
| *Insignia* | Oceania Cruises | 30,277 | B | 6 |
| *Island Princess* | Princess Cruises | 92,000 | B | 5 |
| *Islander* | Linblad Expeditions | N/A | N/R | N/R |
| *Jewel of the Seas* | Royal Caribbean | 90,090 | C | 5 |
| *Kapitan Dranitsyn* | Quark Expeditions | N/A | N/R | N/R |
| *Kong Harald* | Hurtigruten | 11,200 | N/R | N/R |
| *La Bella Vita* | European Waterways | N/A | N/R | N/R |
| *La Belle Epoque* | European Waterways | N/A | B | N/R |
| *La Bonne Amie* | Independently Owned | N/A | A | N/R |
| *La Dolce Vita* | European Waterways | N/A | N/R | N/R |
| *La Marguerite* | AMA Waterways | N/A | B | N/R |
| *La Nouvelle Etoile* | European Waterways | N/A | N/R | N/R |
| *La Reine Pedaque* | European Waterways | N/A | N/R | N/R |
| *L'Arte de Vivre* | European Waterways | N/A | N/R | N/R |
| *L'Austral* | Ponant Cruises | 10,700 | B | 5 |
| *L'Horizon* | CDF Croisieres de France | 47,000 | C | N/R |
| *Le Bon Vivant* | Independently Owned | N/A | N/R | N/R |
| *Le Boreal* | Ponant Cruises | 10,700 | B | 5 |
| *Legend of the Seas* | Royal Caribbean | 63,100 | C | 5 |
| *Liberty of the Seas* | Royal Caribbean | 154,407 | C | 5+ |
| *L'Impressionniste* | European Waterways | N/A | N/R | N/R |
| *Litvinov* | Uniworld | N/A | B | N/R |
| *Lofoten* | Hurtigruten | 2,661 | N/R | N/R |
| *Louis Majesty* | Louis Cruise Line | 40,876 | D | N/R |
| *Luciole* | France Cruises | N/A | N/R | N/R |
| *Lycianda* | Blue Lagoon Cruises | N/A | N/R | N/R |
| *Lyubov Orlova* | Quark Expeditions | 4,251 | N/R | N/R |
| *Maasdam* | Holland America Line | 55,575 | B | 5+ |
| *Magna Carta* | European Waterways | N/A | N/R | N/R |
| *Majesty of the Seas* | Royal Caribbean | 74,077 | C | 4 |
| *Mare Australis* | Cruceros Australis | 2,664 | N/R | N/R |
| *Marina* | Oceania Cruise Line | 66,084 | A/B | 6 |
| *Mariner of the Seas* | Royal Caribbean | 138,279 | C | 5+ |

| | | | | |
|---|---|---|---|---|
| *Marjorie II* | Abercrombie & Kent | N/A | N/R | N/R |
| *Maxim Gorki* | Black Sea Shipping | 25,000 | D | N/R |
| *Meanderer* | Abercrombie & Kent | N/A | N/R | N/R |
| *MegaStar Aries* | Genting Hong Kong | 3,300 | C | N/R |
| *Mein Schiff* | TUI | 77,713 | B | N/R |
| *Mein Schiff 2* | TUI | 77,713 | B | N/R |
| *Midnatsol* | Hurtigruten | 15,000 | N/R | N/R |
| *Minerva* | Swan Hellenic | 12,500 | N/R | N/R |
| *Mirabelle* | France Cruises | N/A | N/R | N/R |
| *Monarch* | Pullmantur | 73,397 | C | 4 |
| *Moon Goddess* | Sonesta Nile | N/A | N/R | N/R |
| MSC *Armonia* | MSC Cruises | 58,625 | C | 4+ |
| MSC *Divinia* | MSC Cruises | 139,400 | C | 5 |
| | (Yacht Club) | | A | 6 |
| MSC *Fantasia* | MSC Cruises | 137,93 | C | 5 |
| | (Yacht Club) | | A | 6 |
| MSC *Lirica* | MSC Cruises | 59,058 | C | 4+ |
| MSC *Magnifica* | MSC Cruises | 95,128 | C | 5 |
| MSC *Melody* | MSC Cruises | 35,140 | C/D | N/R |
| MSC *Musica* | MSC Cruises | 92,400 | C | 5 |
| MSC *Opera* | MSC Cruises | 59,058 | C | 4+ |
| MSC *Orchestra* | MSC Cruises | 92,400 | C | 5 |
| MSC *Poesia* | MSC Cruises | 92,677 | C | 5 |
| MSC *Preziosa* | MSC Cruises | 139,400 | C | 5 |
| | (Yacht Club) | | A | 6 |
| MSC *Sinfonia* | MSC Cruises | 58,625 | C | 4+ |
| MSC *Splendida* | MSC Cruises | 137,936 | C | 5 |
| | (Yacht Club) | | A | 6 |
| *Murray Princess* | Captain Cook Cruises | 1,500 | N/R | N/R |
| *Mystique Princess* | Blue Lagoon Cruises | N/A | N/R | N/R |
| *Nanuya Princess* | Blue Lagoon Cruises | N/A | N/R | N/R |
| *Napoleon* | European Waterways | N/A | N/R | N/R |
| *National Geographic Endeavor* | Linblad Expeditions | 3,132 | N/R | N/R |
| *National Geographic Explorer* | Linblad Expeditions | N/A | N/R | N/R |
| *Nautica* | Oceania Cruise Line | 30,277 | B | 6 |
| *Navigator of the Seas* | Royal Caribbean | 138,279 | C | 5+ |
| *Nenuphar* | French Country Waterways | 280 | A/B | N/R |
| *Niagara* | France Cruises | N/A | N/R | N/R |
| *Niagara Prince* | American Canadian Caribbean Line | 99 | D | N/R |
| *Nieuw Amsterdam* | Holland America | 86,273 | B | 5+ |
| *Nile Goddess* | Sonesta Nile Cruises | N/A | N/R | N/R |

| | | | | |
|---|---|---|---|---|
| *Noordam* | Holland America Line | 82,305 | B | 5+ |
| *Nordkapp* | Hurtigruten | 11,386 | N/R | N/R |
| *Nordlys* | Hurtigruten | 11,200 | N/R | N/R |
| *Nordnorge* | Hurtigruten | 11,386 | N/R | N/R |
| *Nordstjernen* | Hurtigruten | 2,568 | N/R | N/R |
| *Norwegian Breakaway* | Norwegian Cruise Line | 144,017 | C | N/R |
| *Norwegian Dawn* | Norwegian Cruise Line | 92,250 | C | 4 |
| *Norwegian Epic* | Norwegian Cruise Line | 155,873 | C | 5+ |
| | (Courtyard suites) | | A | 6 |
| *Norwegian Gem* | Norwegian Cruise Line | 93,502 | C | 5 |
| *Norwegian Jade* | Norwegian Cruise Line | 93,502 | C | 4+ |
| *Norwegian Jewel* | Norwegian Cruise Line | 93,502 | C | 5 |
| *Norwegian Pearl* | Norwegian Cruise Line | 93,502 | C | 5 |
| *Norwegian Sky* | Norwegian Cruise Line | 77,104 | C | N/R |
| *Norwegian Spirit* | Norwegian Cruise Line | 75,338 | C | N/R |
| *Norwegian Star* | Norwegian Cruise Line | 91,000 | C | 4+ |
| *Norwegian Sun* | Norwegian Cruise Line | 78,309 | C | 4+ |
| *Nymphea* | European Waterways | N/A | N/R | N/R |
| *Oasis of the Seas* | Royal Caribbean | 225,282 | C | N/R |
| *Ocean Diamond* | Quark Expeditions | N/A | N/R | N/R |
| *Ocean Dream* | Pullmantur | 35,000 | D | N/R |
| *Ocean Majesty* | Page and Moy | 10,417 | D | N/R |
| *Ocean Monarch* | Page and Moy | 15,739 | D | N/R |
| *Ocean Nova* | Quark Expeditions | N/A | N/R | N/R |
| *Ocean Princess* | Princess Cruises | 30,270 | B | 5 |
| *Oceana* | P&O Cruises | 77,000 | B | N/R |
| *Oceanic Odyssey* | Spice Island Cruises | 5,218 | N/R | N/R |
| *Oosterdam* | Holland America Line | 82,305 | B | 5+ |
| *Oriana* | P&O Cruises | 69,153 | B | N/R |
| *Orient Queen* | Louis Cruise Line | 15,781 | D | N/R |
| *Orient Venus* | Venus Cruises | 21,884 | N/R | N/R |
| *Orion* | Orion Expedition Cruises | 4,000 | B | 5 |
| *Orion II* | Orion Expedition Cruises | 4,077 | B | 5 |
| *Pacific Dawn* | P&O Cruises Australia | 70,000 | C | N/R |
| *Pacific Dream* | CDF Croisieres de France | 47,000 | C | N/R |
| *Pacific Explorer* | Cruise West | N/A | N/R | N/R |
| *Pacific Jewel* | P&O Cruises Australia | 70,000 | C | N/R |
| *Pacific Pearl* | P&O Cruises Australia | 64,000 | C | N/R |
| *Pacific Princess* | Princess Cruises | 30,277 | B | 5 |
| *Pacific Sun* | P&O Cruises Australia | 47,262 | C | N/R |
| *Pacific Venus* | Venus Cruises | 26,518 | N/R | N/R |
| *Panache* | European Waterways | N/A | N/R | N/R |
| *Panorama I* | Classical Cruises | 599 | N/R | N/R |

| | | | | |
|---|---|---|---|---|
| *Papillon* | France Cruises | N/A | N/R | N/R |
| *Paul Gauguin* | Paul Gauguin Cruises | 19,200 | B | 6 |
| *Pearl Mist* | Pearl Cruises | 8,700 | N/R | N/R |
| *Perla* | Louis Cruise Line | 16,710 | D | N/R |
| *Poesia* | MSC Cruises | 89,600 | C | N/R |
| *Polar Star* | Hurtigruten | 3,500 | N/R | N/R |
| *Polaris* | Linblad Expeditions | 2,214 | N/R | N/R |
| *Polarlys* | Hurtigruten | 12,000 | N/R | N/R |
| *Pride of America* | Norwegian Cruise Line | 80,843 | C | N/R |
| *Princesa Cypria* | Louis Cruise Line | 9,984 | D | N/R |
| *Princess* | French Country Waterways | 280 | A/B | N/R |
| *Princess Danae* | Classic International Cruises | 16,335 | D | N/R |
| *Princess Daphne* | Classic International Cruises | 15,833 | D | N/R |
| *Prinsendam* | Holland America Line | 37,848 | B | 5+ |
| *Prosperite* | France Cruises | N/A | N/R | N/R |
| *Queen of the Mississippi* | American Cruise Line | 3,500 | N/R | N/R |
| *Queen of the West* | American Cruise Line | N/A | N/R | N/R |
| *Queen Mary 2* | Cunard Line | 151,400 | | |
| | (*Queens Grill* class) | | A | 6+ |
| | (*Princess Grill* class) | | A | 6 |
| | (*Britannia*) | | B/C | 5 |
| *Queen Victoria* | Cunard Line | 90,000 | | |
| *Queen Elizabeth* | Cunard Line | 90,400 | | |
| | (*Grill* class, both ships) | | A | 6+ |
| | (*Britannia*, both ships) | | B/C | 5 |
| *Radiance of the Seas* | Royal Caribbean | 90,090 | C | 5 |
| *Reef Endeavor* | Captain Cook Cruises | 3,125 | N/R | N/R |
| *Reef Escape* | Captain Cook Cruises | 1,850 | N/R | N/R |
| *Regatta* | Oceania Cruises | 30,277 | B | 6 |
| *Renaissance* | European Waterways | N/A | A | 6 |
| *Rhapsody of the Seas* | Royal Caribbean | 78,491 | C | 5 |
| *Richard With* | Hurtigruten | 11,205 | N/R | N/R |
| *River Adagio* | Grand Circle Cruises | 1,935 | N/R | N/R |
| *River Allegro* | Grand Circle Cruises | 1,219 | N/R | N/R |
| *River Ambassador* | Uniworld | N/A | N/R | N/R |
| *River Anuket* | Grand Circle Cruises | 2,350 | N/R | N/R |
| *River Arethusa* | Grand Circle Cruises | 1,219 | N/R | N/R |
| *River Aria* | Grand Circle Cruises | 1,935 | N/R | N/R |
| *River Artemis* | Grand Circle Cruises | 1,219 | N/R | N/R |
| *River Athena* | Grand Circle Cruises | 1,219 | N/R | N/R |
| *River Baroness* | Uniworld | N/A | N/R | N/R |
| *River Beatrice* | Uniworld | N/A | N/R | N/R |
| *River Bizet* | Grand Circle Cruises | 1,950 | N/R | N/R |

| River Chardonnay | Grand Circle Cruises | 822 | N/R | N/R |
|---|---|---|---|---|
| River Cloud II | Sea Cloud Cruises | N/A | N/R | N/R |
| River Concerto | Grand Circle Cruises | 1,935 | N/R | N/R |
| River Countess | Uniworld | N/A | N/R | N/R |
| River Discovery | Vantage Travel | N/A | N/R | N/R |
| River Duchess | Uniworld | N/A | N/R | N/R |
| River Empress | Uniworld | N/A | N/R | N/R |
| River Explorer | Vantage Travel | N/A | N/R | N/R |
| River Harmony | Grand Circle Cruises | 1,949 | N/R | N/R |
| River Hathor | Grand Circle Cruises | 630 | N/R | N/R |
| River Melody | Grand Circle Cruises | 1,949 | N/R | N/R |
| River Navigator | Vantage Travel | N/A | N/R | N/R |
| River Odyssey | Vantage Travel | N/A | N/R | N/R |
| River Princess | Uniworld | N/A | N/R | N/R |
| River Queen | Uniworld | N/A | N/R | N/R |
| River Rhapsody | Grand Circle Cruises | 1,949 | N/R | N/R |
| River Royale | Uniworld | N/A | N/R | N/R |
| River Symphony | Grand Circle Cruises | 1,935 | N/R | N/R |
| River Tosca | Uniworld | N/A | N/R | N/R |
| Riviera | Oceania Cruises | 66,084 | A/B | 6 |
| Roi Soleil | France Cruises | N/A | N/R | N/R |
| Rosa | European Waterways | N/A | N/A | N/A |
| Rossia | Grand Circle Cruises | 3,570 | N/A | N/A |
| Rotterdam | Holland America Line | 61,854 | B | 5+ |
| Royal Clipper | Star Clippers | 5,000 | B | 4+ |
| Royal Crown | Hebridean Island Cruises | N/A | N/R | N/R |
| Royal Star | Star Lines/Sea Air Holidays | 5,360 | D | N/R |
| Royal Princess | Princess Cruises | 141,000 | B | 5+ |
| Ruby Princess | Princess Cruises | 113,500 | B | 5+ |
| Ryndam | Holland America Line | 55,819 | B | 5+ |
| Saga Pearl II | Saga Cruises | 18,591 | C | N/R |
| Saga Ruby | Saga Cruises | 23,492 | C | N/R |
| Saga Sapphire | Saga Cruises | 37,301 | C | N/R |
| Sanctuary Nile Adv | Abercrombie & Kent | N/A | N/R | N/R |
| Sapphire Princess | Princess Cruises | 116,000 | B | 5+ |
| Sapphire Thomson | Cruises/Louis Cruises | 12,183 | D | N/R |
| Saroche | Abercrombie & Kent | N/A | N/R | N/R |
| Savoir Faire | European Waterways | N/A | N/R | N/R |
| Scottish Highlander | European Waterways | N/A | N/R | N/R |
| Scenic Crystal | Scenic River Cruises | 2,721 | N/R | N/R |
| Scenic Diamond | Scenic River Cruises | 2,721 | N/R | N/R |
| Scenic Emerald | Scenic River Cruises | 2,721 | N/R | N/R |
| Scenic Pearl | Scenic River Cruises | 2,721 | N/R | N/R |

| | | | | |
|---|---|---|---|---|
| Scenic Ruby | Scenic River Cruises | 2,721 | B | N/R |
| Scenic Sapphire | Scenic River Cruises | 2,721 | B | N/R |
| Sea Bird | Linblad Expeditions | 100 | N/R | N/R |
| Sea Cloud | Sea Cloud Cruises | N/A | A/B | N/R |
| Sea Cloud II | Sea Cloud Cruises | N/A | A/B | N/R |
| Sea Lion | Linblad Expeditions | 100 | N/R | N/R |
| Sea Princess | Princess Cruises | 77,000 | B | 5 |
| Sea Spirit | Quark Expeditions | 4,500 | N/R | N/R |
| Sea Voyager | Linblad Expeditions | 354 | N/R | N/R |
| Seabourn Legend | Seabourn Cruise Line | 10,000 | A | 6+ |
| Seabourn Odyssey | Seabourn Cruise Line | 32,000 | A | 6+ |
| Seabourn Pride | Seabourn Cruise Line | 10,000 | A | 6+ |
| Seabourn Quest | Seabourn Cruise Line | 32,000 | A | 6+ |
| Seabourn Sojourn | Seabourn Cruise Line | 32,000 | A | 6+ |
| Seabourn Spirit | Seabourn Cruise Line | 10,000 | A | 6+ |
| SeaDream I | SeaDream Yacht Club | 4,250 | A | 5+ |
| SeaDream II | SeaDream Yacht Club | 4,250 | A | 5+ |
| Sea Spirit | Quark Expeditions | 4,500 | N/R | N/R |
| Serenade of the Seas | Royal Caribbean | 90,090 | C | 5 |
| Serenade | Louis Cruise Line | 37,584 | N/R | N/R |
| Seven Seas Mariner | Regent Seven Seas | 48,075 | A | 6+ |
| Seven Seas Navigator | Regent Seven Seas | 28,803 | A | 6 |
| Seven Seas Voyager | Regent Seven Seas | 42,363 | A | 6+ |
| Shannon Princess II | European Waterways | N/A | N/R | N/R |
| Silja Europa | Silja Line | 59,914 | D | N/R |
| Silja Festival | Silja Line | 34,419 | D | N/R |
| Silja Serenade | Silja Line | 58,376 | D | N/R |
| Silja Symphony | Silja Line | 58,376 | D | N/R |
| Silver Cloud | Silversea Cruise | 16,800 | A | 6 |
| Silver Explorer | Silversea Cruises | 6,072 | A | N/R |
| Silver Shadow | Silversea Cruises | 28,258 | A | 6+ |
| Silver Spirit | Silversea Cruises | 36,000 | A | 6+ |
| Silver Whisper | Silversea Cruises | 28,258 | A | 6+ |
| Silver Wind | Silversea Cruises | 16,800 | A | 6 |
| Sky Wonder | Pullmantur | 46,314 | D | N/R |
| Sovereign | Pullmantur | 73,192 | C | N/R |
| Spirit of Adventure | Saga Cruises | 9,570 | C | N/R |
| Splendour of the Seas | Royal Caribbean | 69,130 | C | 5 |
| SS Antoinette | Uniworld | N/A | A/B | 6 |
| St. George I | Sonesta Nile Cruise | N/A | N/R | N/R |
| Star Clipper | Star Clippers | 2,298 | C | 4+ |
| Star Flyer | Star Clippers | 2,298 | C | 4+ |
| Star Goddess | Sonesta Nile Cruise | N/A | N/R | N/R |

| | | | | |
|---|---|---|---|---|
| *Star Pisces* | Genting Hong Kong | 40,000 | D | N/R |
| *Star Princess* | Princess Cruises | 109,000 | B | 5 |
| *Statendam* | Holland America Line | 55,819 | B | 5+ |
| *Stella Australis* | Cruceros Australis | 4,500 | N/R | N/R |
| *Sun Bird* | Louis Cruise Line | 37,584 | D | N/R |
| *Sun Boat III* | Abercrombie & Kent | N/A | N/R | N/R |
| *Sun Boat IV* | Abercrombie & Kent | N/A | N/R | N/R |
| *Sun Goddess* | Sonesta Nile Cruise | N/A | N/R | N/R |
| *Sun Princess* | Princess Cruises | 77,000 | B | 5 |
| *SuperStar Aquarius* | Genting Hong Kong | 50,760 | C | N/R |
| *SuperStar Libra* | Genting Hong Kong | 42,276 | C | N/R |
| *SuperStar Virgo* | Genting Hong Kong | 76,800 | B/C | N/R |
| *Swiss Emerald* | Tauck River Cruises | N/A | N/R | N/R |
| *Swiss Jewel* | Tauck River Cruises | N/A | N/R | N/R |
| *Swiss Pearl* | AMAWaterways | N/A | N/R | N/R |
| *Swiss Sapphire* | Tauck River Cruises | N/A | N/R | N/R |
| *Swiss Treasure* | Tauck River Cruises | N/A | N/R | N/R |
| *Terra Australis* | Odessa America | 1,899 | N/R | N/R |
| *Terra Moana* | Paul Gauguin Cruises | 3,504 | B | N/R |
| *Thomson Celebration* | Thomson Cruises | 33,900 | N/R | N/R |
| *Thomson Destiny* | Thomson Cruises | 37,000 | D | N/R |
| *Thomson Dream* | Thomson Cruises | 55,000 | D | N/R |
| *Thomson Spirit* | Thomson Cruises | 33,900 | N/R | N/R |
| *Tikhi Don* | Grand Circle Cruises | 3,570 | N/R | N/R |
| *Trollfjord* | Hurtigruten | 15,000 | N/R | N/R |
| *TUI Allegra* | TUI Cruises | N/A | N/R | N/R |
| *TUI Melodia* | TUI Cruises | N/A | N/R | N/R |
| *TUI Maxima* | TUI Cruises | N/A | N/R | N/R |
| *TUI Mozart* | TUI Cruises | N/A | N/R | N/R |
| *TUI Queen* | TUI Cruises | N/A | N/R | N/R |
| *TUI Sonata* | TUI Cruises | N/A | N/R | N/R |
| *Veendam* | Holland America | 57,092 | B | 5+ |
| *Ventura* | P&O Cruises | 115,000 | B | N/R |
| *Vesteralen* | Hurtigruten | 6,261 | N/R | N/R |
| *Via Australis* | Cruceros Australis | 2,664 | N/R | N/R |
| *Victoria Anna* | Victoria Cruises | 6,200 | N/R | N/R |
| *Victoria Grace* | Victoria Cruises | 3,868 | N/R | N/R |
| *Victoria Jenna* | Victoria Cruises | 10,000 | N/R | N/R |
| *Victoria Katarina* | Victoria Cruises | 5,780 | N/R | N/R |
| *Victoria Sophia* | Victoria Cruises Inc. | 4,587 | N/R | N/R |
| *Victoria Liana* | Victoria Cruises Inc. | 4,587 | N/R | N/R |
| *Victoria Selina* | Victoria Cruises Inc. | 4,587 | N/R | N/R |
| *Viking Aeger* | VikingRiver Cruises | N/A | N/R | N/R |

| | | | | |
|---|---|---|---|---|
| *Viking Embla* | Viking River Cruises | N/A | N/R | N/R |
| *Viking Emerald* | Viking River Cruises | N/A | N/R | N/R |
| *Viking Europe* | Viking River Cruises | N/A | N/R | N/R |
| *Viking Freya* | Viking River Cruises | N/A | N/R | N/R |
| *Viking Fontaine* | Viking River Cruises | N/A | N/R | N/R |
| *Viking Helgi* | Viking River Cruises | N/A | N/R | N/R |
| *Viking Helvetia II* | Viking River Cruises | N/A | N/R | N/R |
| *Viking Idun* | Viking River Cruises | N/A | N/R | N/R |
| *Viking Ingvar* | Viking River Cruises | N/A | N/R | N/R |
| *Viking Legend* | Viking River Cruises | N/A | N/R | N/R |
| *Viking Lomonosov* | Viking River Cruises | N/A | N/R | N/R |
| *Viking Neptune* | Viking River Cruises | N/A | N/R | N/R |
| *Viking Njord* | Viking River Cruises | N/A | N/R | N/R |
| *Viking Odin* | Viking River Cruises | N/A | N/R | N/R |
| *Viking Pakhomov* | Viking River Cruises | N/A | N/R | N/R |
| *Viking Peterhoff* | Viking River Cruises | N/A | N/R | N/R |
| *Viking Prestige* | Viking River Cruises | N/A | N/R | N/R |
| *Viking Pride* | Viking River Cruises | N/A | N/R | N/R |
| *Viking Primadonna* | Viking River Cruises | N/A | N/R | N/R |
| *Viking Schumann* | Viking River Cruises | N/A | N/R | N/R |
| *Viking Sky* | Viking River Cruises | N/A | N/R | N/R |
| *Viking Spirit* | Viking River Cruise | N/A | N/R | N/R |
| *Viking Sun* | Viking River Cruises | N/A | N/R | N/R |
| *Viking Surkov* | Viking River Cruises | N/A | N/R | N/R |
| *Viking Truvor* | Viking River Cruises | N/A | N/R | N/R |
| *Vision of the Seas* | Royal Caribbean | 78,340 | C | 5 |
| *Volendam* | Holland America Line | 61,396 | B | 5+ |
| *Voyager* | Voyages of Discovery | N/A | N/R | N/R |
| *Voyager of the Seas* | Royal Caribbean | 138,279 | C | 5+ |
| *Westerdam* | Holland America Line | 82,305 | B | 5+ |
| *Who Knows* | France Cruises | N/A | N/R | N/R |
| *Wind Spirit* | Windstar Cruises | 5,703 | B | 5+ |
| *Wind Star* | Windstar Cruises | 5,703 | B | 5+ |
| *Wind Surf* | Windstar Cruises | 14,745 | B | 5+ |
| *World* | ResidenSea Management Ltd. | 43,524 | A | N/R |
| *Zaandam* | Holland America Line | 61,396 | B | 5+ |
| *Zamba Queen* | AMA Waterways | N/A | N/R | N/R |
| *Zenith* | Pullmantur | 47,255 | C | N/R |
| *Zuiderdam* | Holland America Line | 82,305 | B | 5+ |

# Explanation of Ship Ratings

All ships are not excellent, good, or bad across the board, and some excel in one area and fall short in others. For example, there are several Category A—Deluxe ships that are known for impeccable food and service and fine accommodations yet offer little entertainment and activities and could be poor choices for younger singles or children. On the other hand, some Category D—Economy ships have only passable food and service and numerous small or inadequate cabins yet provide so much fun and entertainment that less demanding, budget-minded, younger cruisers would have a more rewarding experience.

I have used a simple five-point system:

| | | |
|---|---|---|
| Five stars | excellent | the best available at sea |
| Four stars | very good | one notch below the best, but better than most |
| Three stars | good | average |
| Two stars | fair | below average |
| One star | poor | a rose by any other name |

# Explanation of Categories

The ships are ranked according to how they measure up in the following eleven categories:

1) Casual/buffet facility: quality of food presentation and preparation
2) Dining rooms and specialty restaurants: gourmet quality of food, preparation, presentation, caliber of wines, tableside preparations, and availability of special orders
3) Service in dining rooms
4) Service in cabins
5) Activities and entertainment: quantity and quality
6) Average cabin: spaciousness, decor, and facilities included
7) Outside deck area: spaciousness for passenger capacity, condition, decor, and facilities available
8) Inside public area: spaciousness for passenger capacity, condition, decor, and facilities available
9) Physical condition of ship, public areas, and cabins
10) Special activities and facilities for children
11) Good ship for singles

| | *Casual/Buffet Facility* | *Dining Rooms & Specialty Restaurants* | *Service in Dining Rooms* | *Service in Cabins* |
|---|---|---|---|---|
| **American Cruise Line** *Independence* | N/A | ***+ | ****+ | **** |
| **Azamara Club Cruises** *Journey* *Quest* | ***** | ***** | ****+ | ***** |
| **Celebration Cruise Line** *Bahamas Celebration* | ***+ | **** | ****+ | **** |
| **Carnival Cruise Lines** *Breeze* *Conquest* *Destiny* *Dream* *Freedom* *Glory* *Legend* *Liberty* *Miracle* *Pride* *Spirit* *Triumph* *Valor* *Victory* | **** (lunch & dinner) *** (breakfast) | **** (dining room) ***** (specialty restaurant) | ***+ | ****+ |
| **Carnival Cruise Lines** *Elation* *Imagination* *Inspiration* *Fascination* *Paradise* *Sensation* | **** (lunch & dinner) *** (breakfast) | **** | ***+ | ****+ |

| Activities and Entertainment | Average Cabin | Outside Deck Area | Inside Public Area | Physical Condition of Ship, Public Areas, and Cabins | Special Activities and Facilities for Children | Good Ship for Singles |
|---|---|---|---|---|---|---|
| ** | *** | N/A | ** | *** | * | * |
| ****+ | **** | ***** | ***** | ***** | * | * |
| **** | * (some) ** (some) | ** | *** | ** | **** | *** |
| ****+ | ****+ | ***** | ***** | ***** | ***** | ***** (young)<br><br>*** (mature, over 60) |
| ****+ | ****+ | **** | **** | ***** | ***** | ***** (young) *** (mature, over 60) |

| | *Casual/Buffet Facility* | *Dining Rooms & Specialty Restaurants* | *Service in Dining Rooms* | *Service in Cabins* |
|---|---|---|---|---|
| **Celebrity Cruises** *Constellation* *Infinity* *Millennium* *Summit* | **** | ****₊ (dining rooms) *****₊ (alternative specialty restaurant) | **** (dining rooms) *****₊ (alternative specialty restaurant) | ***** |
| **Celebrity Cruises** *Century* | **** | ****₊ (dining rooms) *****₊ (Murano) | **** (dining rooms) *****₊ (Murano) | ***** |
| **Celebrity Cruises** *Equinox* *Sojourn* *Eclipse* *Silhoutte* *Reflection* | **** | ***** (dining rooms) *****₊ (Murano) | **** (dining rooms) *****₊ (specialty restaurants) | ****₊ |
| **Costa Cruise Lines** *CostaVictoria* *CostaRomantica* | *** | ***₊ | *** | ***₊ |
| **Costa Cruise lines** *CostaAtlantica* *Costa Deliziosa* *Costa Fortuna* *Costa Luminosa* *Costa Magica* *CostaMediterranea* *Costa Pacifica* *Costa Serena* | *** | ***₊ (dining rooms) ***₊ (specialty restaurant) | ***₊ | ***₊ |

| *Activities and Entertainment* | *Average Cabin* | *Outside Deck Area* | *Inside Public Area* | *Physical Condition of Ship, Public Areas, and Cabins* | *Special Activities and Facilities for Children* | *Good Ship for Singles* |
|---|---|---|---|---|---|---|
| ****+ | ***** | ***** | ***** | ***** | **** | *** |
| **** | ***** | ***** | ****+ | ***** | **** | *** |
| ***** | ****+ | ***** | ***** | ***** | ** | *** |
| **** | **** | ***** | **** | ***** | **** | **** |
| ***** | ****+ | ***** | ***** | ***** | ****+ | **** |

| | Casual/Buffet Facility | Dining Rooms & Specialty Restaurants | Service in Dining Rooms | Service in Cabins |
|---|---|---|---|---|
| Crystal Cruises<br>*Crystal Symphony*<br>*Crystal Serenity* | ***** | *****<br>(dining room)<br>*****<br>(specialty restaurants) | ***** | ***** |
| Cunard Line<br>*Queen Victoria*<br>*Queen Elizabeth* | **** | *****+<br>(grill rooms)<br>****<br>(other rooms) | *****+<br>(grill rooms)<br>****<br>(other rooms) | **** |
| Cunard Line<br>*Queen Mary 2* | **** | *****+<br>(grill rooms)<br>****<br>(other rooms)<br>*****<br>(specialty restaurant) | *****+<br>(grill rooms)<br>****+<br>(other rooms)<br>*****<br>(specialty restaurant) | ***** |
| Disney Cruise Line<br>*Disney Magic*<br>*Disney Wonder*<br>*Disney Dream* | **** | ****<br>(dining rooms)<br>*****+<br>(specialty restaurant) | **** | **** |
| Hapag-Lloyd<br>*Europa* | ***** | ***** | ***** | ***** |
| Hapag-Lloyd<br>*Europa 2* | ***** | ****+ | ***** | ***** |

| Activities and Entertainment | Average Cabin | Outside Deck Area | Inside Public Area | Physical Condition of Ship, Public Areas, and Cabins | Special Activities and Facilities for Children | Good Ship for Singles |
|---|---|---|---|---|---|---|
| *****₊ | ****₊ | ***** | ***** | ***** | ** | ** (young) **** (mature, over 60) |
| ****₊ | **** | ***** | ***** | ***** | * | *** (mature, over 60) * (young) |
| ****₊ | ****₊ | ***** | ***** | ***** | **** | **** |
| **** | ***** | ***** | ***** | ***** | *****₊ | ** |
| ** | *****₊ | **** | **** | ***** | ** | ** |
| *** | *****₊ | ***** | ***** | ***** | **** | **** |

| | Casual/Buffet Facility | Dining Rooms & Specialty Restaurants | Service in Dining Rooms | Service in Cabins |
|---|---|---|---|---|
| **Holland America Line** *Amsterdam* *Maasdam* *Rotterdam VI* *Ryndam* *Statendam* *Veendam* *Volendam* *Zaandam* | **** | **** (dining rooms) ****+ (specialty restaurant) | **** | **** |
| **Holland America Line** *Eurodam* *Nieuw Amsterdam* *Noordam* *Oosterdam* *Westerdam* *Zuiderdam* | ****+ | **** (dining rooms) ***** (specialty restaurants) | **** (specialty restaurants) | ****+ |
| **MSC Cruises** *Fantasia* *Divina* *Preziosa* *Splendida* | *** | ***+ (dining rooms) **** (specialty restaurants) | ***+ (dining rooms) ****+ (specialty restaurants) | **** *****+ (Yacht Club) |
| **MSC Cruises** *Lirica* *Opera* | *** | **** | **** | **** |
| **MSC Cruises** *Orchestra* *Musica* *Poesia* | *** | **** (dining rooms) *** (specialty restaurant) | **** | **** |
| **Norwegian Cruise Line** *Norwegian Sun* | ***** (food) *** (service) | ****+ (dining rooms) ****+ (specialty restaurants) | ****+ | ****+ |

| Activities and Entertainment | Average Cabin | Outside Deck Area | Inside Public Area | Physical Condition of Ship, Public Areas, and Cabins | Special Activities and Facilities for Children | Good Ship for Singles |
|---|---|---|---|---|---|---|
| **** | **** | ***** | ***** | ***** | ****+ | *** (young) ***** (mature, over 60) |
| **** | ****+ | ***** | ***** | ***** | ****+ | *** (young) ***** (mature) |
| ***** | ***+ ****+ (Yacht Club) | ***** | ***** | ***** | *** | **** |
| ***** | ***+ | **** | **** | ***** | ***+ | *** |
| ***** | ***+ | ***** | ***** | ***** | *** | **** |
| ****+ | **** | **** | **** | ***** | ****+ | ****+ |

| | *Casual/Buffet Facility* | *Dining Rooms & Specialty Restaurants* | *Service in Dining Rooms* | *Service in Cabins* |
|---|---|---|---|---|
| Norwegian Cruise Line<br>*Norwegian Epic* | ****₊ | ****<br>****₊<br>(some of each) | **** | **** |
| Norwegian Cruise Line<br>*Norwegian Star*<br>*Norwegian Dawn*<br>*Norwegian Jewel*<br>*Norwegian Gem*<br>*Norwegian Pearl* | *****<br>(food)<br>***<br>(service) | ****<br>(dining rooms)<br>****₊<br>(specialty restaurants) | **** | *** |
| Oceania<br>*Insignia*<br>*Regatta*<br>*Nautica* | ***** | *****<br>(dining rooms)<br>*****<br>(specialty restaurants) | ***** | ***** |
| Oceania<br>*Marina*<br>*Riviera* | ***** | ***** | ****₊ | **** |
| Paul Gauguin Cruises<br>*Paul Gauguin* | ***** | ***** | ****₊ | ***** |
| Princess Cruises<br>*Caribbean Princess*<br>*Crown Princess*<br>*Emerald Princess*<br>*Ruby Princess*<br>*Royal Princess* | **** | ****<br>(dining room)<br>*****<br>(steakhouse) | ****₊ | **** |
| Princess Cruises<br>*Diamond Princess*<br>*Sapphire Princess* | **** | **** | ****₊ | **** |

| | *Activities and Entertainment* | *Average Cabin* | *Outside Deck Area* | *Inside Public Area* | *Physical Condition of Ship, Public Areas, and Cabins* | *Special Activities and Facilities for Children* | *Good Ship for Singles* |
|---|---|---|---|---|---|---|---|
| | *****+ | *** <br> ****+ <br> (some of each) | ***** | ***** | ***** | ***** | **** |
| | ****+ | **** | ***** | ***** | ***** | ***** | ***+ |
| | ****+ | **** | ***** | ***** | ***** | * | ** |
| | ****+ | ***** | ***** | ***** | ***** | * | ** |
| | ** | **** | **** | **** | **** | * | * |
| | ***** | **** | ***** | ***** | ***** | ***** | **** |
| | ***** | **** | ***** | ***** | ***** | ***** | **** |

| | Casual/Buffet Facility | Dining Rooms & Specialty Restaurants | Service in Dining Rooms | Service in Cabins |
|---|---|---|---|---|
| **Princess Cruises**<br>*Dawn Princess*<br>*Sun Princess*<br>*Golden Princess*<br>*Grand Princess*<br>*Sea Princess*<br>*Star Princess* | ★★★★ | ★★★★<br>(dining rooms)<br>★★★★₊<br>(specialty restaurants) | ★★★★₊ | ★★★★ |
| **Princess Cruises**<br>*Ocean Princess*<br>*Pacific Princess* | ★★★★ | ★★★★ | ★★★★₊ | ★★★ |
| **Regent Seven Seas**<br>*Seven Seas Mariner*<br>*Seven Seas Voyager* | ★★★★★₊ | ★★★★★₊<br>★★★★★₊<br>(Signatures) | ★★★★★ | ★★★★★ |
| **Regent Seven Seas**<br>*Seven Seas Navigator* | ★★★★★₊ | ★★★★★ | ★★★★★ | ★★★★★ |
| **Royal Caribbean**<br>*Adventure of the Seas*<br>*Enchantment of the Seas*<br>*Explorer of the Seas*<br>*Freedom of the Seas*<br>*Grandeur of the Seas*<br>*Independence of the Seas*<br>*Legend of the Seas*<br>*Liberty of the Seas*<br>*Mariner of the Seas*<br>*Navigator of the Seas*<br>*Rhapsody of the Seas*<br>*Splendour of the Seas*<br>*Vision of the Seas*<br>*Voyager of the Seas* | ★★★★₊ | ★★★₊<br>(dining rooms)<br>★★★★<br>(specialty restaurants) | ★★★★ | ★★★★ |
| **Royal Caribbean**<br>*Brilliance of the Seas*<br>*Jewel of the Seas*<br>*Radiance of the Seas*<br>*Serenade of the Seas* | ★★★★₊ | ★★★₊<br>(dining room)<br>★★★★<br>(specialty restaurants) | ★★★★ | ★★★★ |

| Activities and Entertainment | Average Cabin | Outside Deck Area | Inside Public Area | Physical Condition of Ship, Public Areas, and Cabins | Special Activities and Facilities for Children | Good Ship for Singles |
|---|---|---|---|---|---|---|
| ****+ | **** | ***** | ***** | ***** | ***** | **** |
| **** | **** | **** | **** | *** | * | * |
| **** | *****+ | ****+ | ***** | ***** | ** | ** |
| **** | *****+ | **** | ****+ | ***** | ** | ** |
| ***** | **** | ***** | ***** | ***** | *****+ | ****+ |
| ***** | **** | ***** | ***** | ***** | *****+ | ****+ |

| | Casual/Buffet Facility | Dining Rooms & Specialty Restaurants | Service in Dining Rooms | Service in Cabins |
|---|---|---|---|---|
| Royal Caribbean<br>*Oasis of the Seas*<br>*Allure of the Seas* | ***** | **** | **** | **** |
| Seabourn Line<br>*Seabourn Legend*<br>*Seabourn Pride*<br>*Seabourn Spirit* | *****+ | *****+<br>(dining room)<br>*****+<br>(specialty restaurant) | *****+ | ***** |
| Seabourn Line<br>*Seabourn Odyssey*<br>*Seabourn Sojourn*<br>*Seabourn Quest* | *****+ | *****+<br>(dining room)<br>*****+<br>(specialty restaurant) | *****+ | *****+ |
| SeaDream Yacht Club<br>*SeaDream I*<br>*SeaDream II* | ***** | *****+ | *****+ | ***** |
| Silversea Cruises, Ltd.<br>*Silver Cloud*<br>*Silver Wind* | ***** | ***** | ***** | ***** |
| Silversea Cruises, Ltd.<br>*Silver Shadow*<br>*Silver Spirit*<br>*Silver Whisper* | ***** | ***** | ***** | ***** |
| Star Clippers, Inc.<br>*Star Clipper*<br>*Star Flyer* | ****+ | ****+ | **** | *** |
| Star Clippers, Inc.<br>*Royal Clipper* | **** | **** | *** | *** |

| | *Activities and Entertainment* | *Average Cabin* | *Outside Deck Area* | *Inside Public Area* | *Physical Condition of Ship, Public Areas, and Cabins* | *Special Activities and Facilities for Children* | *Good Ship for Singles* |
|---|---|---|---|---|---|---|---|
| | ***** | **** | *****+ | *****+ | ***** | *****+ | ***** |
| | **** | *****+ | **** | ***** | ***** | * | ** |
| | **** | *****+ | ***** | ***** | ***** | * | ** |
| | * | **** | **** | **** | **** | * | * |
| | *** | *****+ | **** | ***** | ***** | * | * |
| | **** | *****+ | ***** | ***** | ***** | * | * |
| | * | *** | ** | *** | *** | * | ** |
| | * | *** | *** | *** | **** | * | ** |

| | *Casual/Buffet Facility* | *Dining Rooms & Specialty Restaurants* | *Service in Dining Rooms* | *Service in Cabins* |
|---|---|---|---|---|
| Windstar Cruises *Wind Spirit* *Wind Star* | ***** | ***** | **** | ****+ |
| Windstar Cruises *Wind Surf* | ***** | ***** (dining room) | **** | ****+ |

| *Activities and Entertainment* | *Average Cabin* | *Outside Deck Area* | *Inside Public Area* | *Physical Condition of Ship, Public Areas, and Cabins* | *Special Activities and Facilities for Children* | *Good Ship for Singles* |
|---|---|---|---|---|---|---|
| ** | **** | **** | ***+ | ***** | * | * |
| ** | ****+ | **** | ****+ | ***** | * | * |

# Index

# Index of Cruise Liners

# Index of Cruise Ships

# Index of Ports of Call

*A resident of Florida, Steven B. Stern has sailed on over 790 cruise ships, riverboats and hotel barges, visited every major port of call in the world, and personally inspected virtually every ship currently in operation. He is also the author of "Stern's Guide to European Riverboats and Hotel Barges", "Stern's Guide to the Greatest Resorts of the World", and "The Indispensable Guide to Foreign Words and Phrases."*